English Manuscript Studies 1100–1700

English Manuscript Studies 1100–1700

VOLUME 13

New Texts and Discoveries in Early Modern English Manuscripts

Edited by
Peter Beal

THE BRITISH LIBRARY

First published in 2007 by
The British Library
96 Euston Road
London NW1 2DB

British Library Cataloging in Publication Data

A cataloguing record for this publication is
available from The British Library

ISBN 978-0-7123-4977-2

Typeset in Monotype Baskerville by
Hope Services (Abingdon) Ltd
Printed in England by
Biddles Ltd, King s Lynn, Norfolk

Contents

How to Become an Elizabethan Statesman: Lord Henry Howard, the Earl of Essex and the Politics of Friendship

Paul E. J. Hammer

In December 1992, Durham University Library sought to augment its very large holdings of papers of the Howard family of Naworth in Cumberland by purchasing a parcel of books and manuscripts that were the residue of the library of Lord William Howard of Naworth (1563-1640), great-grandfather of the first Earl of Carlisle.[1] The six manuscript items in the purchase included an eighteenth century precedent book and five notebooks that turned out to be written by Lord William Howard's uncle, Lord Henry Howard (1540–1614).[2] Four of the notebooks are quarto sized, while one is a larger folio. How and when these notebooks became part of the collection at Naworth is unknown, although Lord William was an antiquary and noted collector of manuscripts and it seems likely that he acquired the volumes after his uncle's death.[3] Now catalogued as Howard Library MSS 1–5, these manuscripts provide invaluable information on the intellectual interests and writings of Lord Henry Howard. One of these notebooks—Howard Library MS 2—also offers important insights into the nature and working of high politics during the final years of the reign of Elizabeth I, and Howard's part in them.

Lord Henry Howard was the younger son of Henry Howard, Earl of Surrey, the eldest son and heir of Thomas Howard, third Duke of Norfolk. The Howards were more than just illustrious noblemen and territorial magnates in East Anglia. Having risen to ducal status as partisans of Richard III, the family survived the first Duke's death at Bosworth (and his posthumous attainder by Henry VII) to recover the dukedom of Norfolk in 1513 and repeatedly inter-married with the royal line under Henry VIII.[4] However, Surrey and Norfolk were losers in the bitter power struggle that accompanied Henry VIII's physical decline during 1546 and suffered the consequences of the dying king's determination to remove those who might imperil his young son's hold on the throne. Despite Norfolk's long and distinguished record of service to Henry, the very intimacy of their family connection with the Tudors weighed against the two Howards. Both were condemned to death for treason. Norfolk was saved at the last minute by the king's death and spent the whole of Edward VI's reign in the Tower, but Surrey was beheaded on 19 January 1547.[5] Henry Howard's childhood lesson in the terrible price that could be exacted on those who gambled and lost in Tudor politics was given further grim reinforcement by the fall of his older brother, Thomas, who succeeded as fourth Duke of Norfolk in 1554. Already suspect over his attempt to become Mary Queen of Scots's fourth husband in 1569–70, Norfolk was convicted of complicity in a Catholic plot against Queen Elizabeth and beheaded in 1572.[6] To complete the tale of woe, Norfolk's oldest son Philip—who was allowed to succeed as Earl of Arundel in 1580, but not to recover the family dukedom—was himself convicted of treason and sentenced to death in 1589. Although Elizabeth chose not to sanction the beheading of yet another generation of the Howard family, Arundel died in the Tower in 1595.[7] Henry Howard himself repeatedly came under suspicion of intriguing with partisans of Mary Queen of Scots or Catholic conspirators during the 1570s and '80s, being arrested at least five times. Although he was a conspicuous figure at Elizabeth's Court during the projected Anjou Match of 1579–81, Howard's barely concealed Catholicism and the collapse of the pro-Catholic group who had pinned their hopes on Anjou saw him thrust out of Court in the 1580s.[8] Howard found life in the political wilderness a bitter experience, especially during his harsh treatment after the exposure of the Throckmorton Plot in 1583. In October 1589, not long after his final spell in confinement, he complained that the annuity which he had been granted by the Queen had been stalled for over thirteen months and that pressure from a creditor threatened to deny him 'anie other habite then a beggeres cloke'.[9] Even as late as 1593, he wrote 'from my littell celle of Grenwich whear, by the honorable fauor of my L*ord* Admirall, I haue a roufe to couer my heade from the rayne which ells I haue not any whear'.[10]

Despite such indignities, Lord Henry Howard ultimately proved to be one of the great survivors of Elizabethan high politics. Howard's strenuous efforts to recover favour drew heavily upon another aspect of his family heritage. His father, Surrey, is known as the 'Poet Earl' because he pioneered the writing of blank verse and sonnets in English.[11] As a younger son and either temperamentally unsuited to military service or denied the opportunity to serve because of lingering doubts about his loyalty, Henry Howard sought to make his way in the world by wielding the pen more systematically and frequently than his father had done. In addition to a stream of letters written in elevated style, Howard wrote a series of occasional tracts that sought to profess his loyalty to the Elizabethan regime and showcase his intellectual and rhetorical skills. These writings included: a public contribution to the 'Admonition Controversy' of the 1570s, championing the ecclesiastical authorities and attacking the presbyterianism espoused by the puritan Thomas Cartwright, which was printed in 1574;[12] a Latin panegyric of Queen Elizabeth ('Regina Fortunata') in the mid-1570s;[13] a riposte in manuscript form to *The Gaping Gulf*, John Stubbes's inflammatory tract challenging Elizabeth's intended marriage to the French Catholic Duke of Anjou in 1579;[14] a lengthy polemic against 'expositions of dreames, oracles, reuelations, inuocations of damned spirites, iudicialles of astrologie, or any other kinde of pretended knowledge whatsoeuer, de futuris contingentibus', which was printed in 1583;[15] a response to John Knox's notorious polemic against rule by female sovereigns *The First Blast of the Trumpet Against the Monstruous Regiment of Women* (1558), written belatedly in the late 1580s;[16] and a translation of Charles V's supposed political testament for his son, Philip II of Spain, which circulated widely in manuscript form.[17]

Although he made forays into print in 1574 and 1583, Howard normally disseminated his works in the more gentlemanly form of manuscript circulation. Indeed, he made a practice of using special presentation copies of his writings as highly personalised gifts to courtiers whose good will he sought to win, or hold.[18] Other than the Queen, the chief focus of Howard's literary output was William Cecil, first Baron Burghley, the Lord Treasurer and Elizabeth's leading councillor in the 1590s. Howard's brother Norfolk had cultivated friendly relations with Burghley in the 1560s and Howard recognised the paramount importance of continuing this relationship and extending it in the 1590s to embrace Sir Robert Cecil, Burghley's younger son and political heir apparent.[19] Howard repeatedly sent both Cecils small books of prayers, seemingly to reassure them that his own religion was a matter of private devotion rather than politics.[20] Howard's writings were also characterised by the conspicuous display of learning and the full panoply of humanist scholarship. This did not simply represent an attempt to flatter the intellectual pretensions of men such as Burghley, whose many offices included that of Chancellor of the University of Cambridge. Although many of Elizabeth's courtiers were genuinely men of deep scholarly learning, Lord Henry Howard actually taught at Cambridge in the late 1560s—the only nobleman to teach at an English university in the sixteenth or seventeenth centuries. Educated at King's College, Cambridge, at Elizabeth's expense, he subsequently became Reader in Rhetoric and Civil Law at Trinity Hall.[21] Howard's earliest surviving work was written while at Trinity Hall and dedicated as a gift to his sister, Lady Katherine Berkeley. This was a treatise on natural philosophy and systematically explored such questions as 'What is nature', 'Of the principles of thinges', 'Del mundo. Of the worlde', 'Of heauen', 'Of the elements in speciall and first of fyre'.[22] After he moved to Court a few months later, Howard's academic training and outlook encouraged him to combine his scholarly tendencies with more political objectives. His *Defensatiue* against 'pretended knowledge' published in 1583, for example, can be seen as partly deriving from academic politics, embodying a direct attack on astrological predictions by the Harvey brothers, who were well-known and controversial figures in Cambridge.[23] It was no coincidence, however, that the Harveys also had links with the Earl of Leicester and Sir Philip Sidney, opponents of Howard at Court during the Anjou Match affair. Howard's scholarly inclinations and ability to deploy a wide variety of reading material as political ammunition was even more evident in his response to accusations by his first cousin and former close friend, Edward De Vere, seventeenth Earl of Oxford, in 1581.[24] According to Howard's report, one of their quarrels concerned the dangerous question of whether 'armes might be iustlie taken against princis'. When Oxford (allegedly) affirmed this proposition, Howard set himself 'against him, and withall declared that I was in redinesse, and had made my collection, wantinge but leysure onlie to write against that cause. He said I could not iustifie the contrary, I told him yes, both by the scriptures, by the stories [*i.e.* histories], by the lawes, and by the wisest, and best deuines, eyther protestant ore Catholicks, that liued at this daye in Europe'.[25]

The five notebooks now held at Durham University Library demonstrate how Howard created the sort of 'collection' which he apparently assembled in preparation for rebutting Oxford's claim. In good humanist fashion, points are extracted from a wide variety of sources—largely in Latin, but also including some materials in Greek, Spanish and English—and gathered under specific topical headings.[26] Howard Library MSS 1 and 3, for example, mainly contain material relating to alchemy and may have some connection to the writing of his *Defensative* of 1583, or perhaps another treatise that was not completed. MS 4 contains detailed notes on topics relating to women and may constitute raw materials for the 'Dutifull Defense of the Lawful Regiment of Women' which Howard wrote in 1589–90. MS 5, a larger folio-sized volume, contains notes of religious devotion but, like the other manuscripts, also features a range of additional material, including a draft of a letter to Sir Philip Sidney requesting his intercession to help secure Howard's release from house-arrest in 1584.[27] MS 2 consists of notes relating to the general theme of nobility. As a member of the senior line of the Howard family and a kinsman of many of the most illustrious aristocrats in the realm (and a cousin of the Queen herself), Howard had a profound personal investment in matters relating to honour and aristocracy, which was made all the more intense by his sense of unjust exclusion from courtly life during much of the 1570s and the 1580s. Howard was always conscious that he was not only the brother and grandson of dukes—at a time when England no longer had a single duke—but also that his brother had been Earl Marshal, the realm's chief overseer of matters of honour and supervisor of the heralds who verified, awarded and created coats of arms for gentlemen and would-be gentlemen. Howard's notes on nobility and related topics are arranged under headings such as 'Definitio Nobilitatis et Etimologia' (fol. 10r), 'Origo Nobilitatis' (fol. 12r), 'Fortuna et diuitia an nobilem efficiant' (fol. 17r), 'An nobilitas amittatur paupertate' (fol. 58r), 'Feciales' (fol. 77r), 'Artes moechanica*e* an nobilitati derogent' (fol. 79r) and 'Nobilitatis inimici qui?' (fol. 81r).[28] An example of these notes can be seen in PLATE 1, which shows a page with two headings, 'Nobilis an ignobilis possit fieri' and 'An perdatur per infamia*m*'.[29] The headings are in the more Italic hand which Howard routinely used in his letters, while the actual notes which he abstracted from his reading are written in a rather tighter, neater hand. Like many of the pages in Howard MS 2, most of the notes here are struck through with diagonal lines, presumably indicating that these materials had been used in the (unknown) treatise for which Howard originally gathered them. Howard's note at the top left-hand of the page, which characteristically ignores the line-ending in the formation of words, reads: 'nobility maie be religata by attainder but not extincte: suspendid but not endid'.

Howard Library MS 2 now contains approximately 120 pages, with at least fourteen of the original pages having been removed at some point.[30] In addition to the materials relating to the theme of nobility, a number of pages contain lengthy notes in Howard's hand of a rather different nature. These are gathered under headings such as 'Consideration of his person', 'The necessarie use of suche a person in this time for the seruice and reasons whie all sortes of me*n* are satisfied', 'Inconueniencis of wrestlinge', and 'Meanes of aduancement'. As the headings suggest, these notes alternate between comments in the third person ('he', 'his') and those in the second person ('you', 'your Lordship'). In contrast to the gatherings of material for some form of

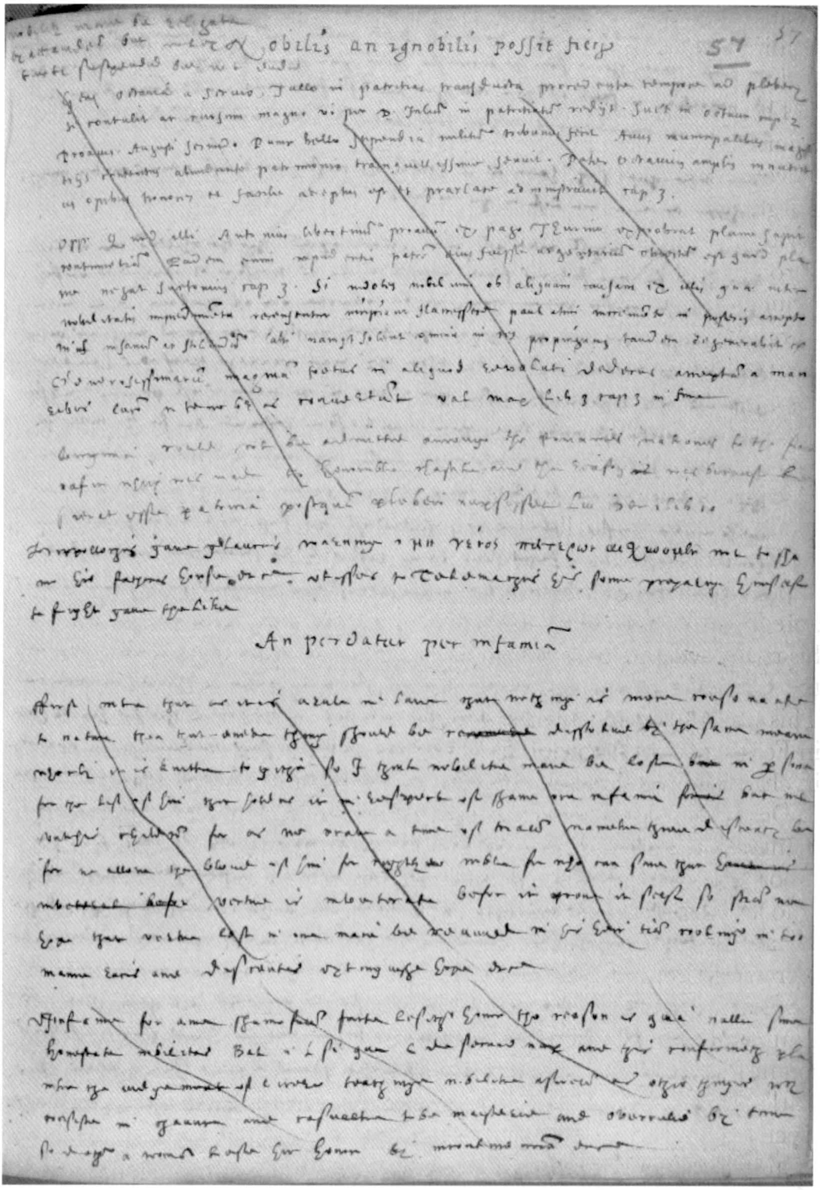

57

obilis an ignobilis possit fieri

An perdatur per infamiam

PLATE 1. *A page of Howard's commonplace book, notes showing extracts from his reading gathered under specific headings: Durham University Library, Howard Library, MS 2, fol. 57r. (Original page size 232 × 174mm.) Reproduced by permission of Durham University Library.*

treatise on nobility, these notes therefore constitute comments on the qualities of a particular nobleman and political advice directly addressed to him.

The peer upon whose personal qualities Howard ruminated, and to whom he offered political guidance, can be readily identified as Robert Devereux, second Earl of Essex (1565–1601).[31] A former ward of Lord Burghley and the step-son of Leicester, Essex established himself as a royal favourite in the late 1580s. He repeatedly led military expeditions abroad and became a member of the Privy Council in 1593. Essex's subsequent efforts to promote himself as the natural candidate to succeed Burghley as the Queen's leading councillor caused tensions with the ageing Lord Treasurer and his son, Sir Robert Cecil. Disagreements over the direction of the war and what constituted appropriate behaviour towards the Queen helped to escalate matters by the mid-1590s and pro- and anti-Essex groupings emerged at Court, and beyond. Essex's refusal to be deflected from pursuing what he regarded as necessary policies gradually eroded his hold on Elizabeth's favour, but his military reputation, charismatic personality and illustrious lineage (especially in comparison with the Cecils) were widely believed to guarantee his success. After Burghley's death in 1598, however, Essex and his rivals became locked in an increasingly open struggle over access to the Queen's person and influence over the looming royal succession. This was a struggle which Essex ultimately lost and it cost him his head in February 1601, clearing the way for Cecil to take over the Earl's role in championing James VI of Scotland as Elizabeth's successor.

Despite his long and frequent contacts with the Cecil family, Lord Henry Howard enjoyed an even closer friendship with Essex during the 1590s. The two peers were distant cousins and Essex was one of those who received a presentation copy of Howard's tract in defence of female rule in 1589–90.[32] Sir Henry Wotton, who served as one Essex's secretaries in the 1590s, later wrote that Howard 'was commonly *primae admissionis* by his [*i.e.* Essex's] bed side in the morning'.[33] During the summer of 1596, when Essex was leading an expedition against the Spanish port of Cadiz, Howard was specifically noted as one of the Earl's supporters at Court.[34] At the same time, Howard and Sir Robert Cecil exchanged conspicuously friendly letters about Essex's success in Spain and other matters, demonstrating that neither man wanted Howard's special friendship with the Earl to become a cause of division between them.[35] Howard maintained this approach even as the relationship between Essex and Cecil crumbled into bitter recrimination in the closing years of the decade. Although he joined the glittering array of aristocrats who dined with Essex after his surprise return from

Ireland in September 1599—and hence spurned the rival group of courtiers who dined with Cecil—Howard was reported by one astute observer of the Court as being 'held a newter' for his desire to remain on good terms with both sides, which made him suspect in the eyes of die-hard Essexians.[36] Nevertheless, Howard's unwillingness to allow his friendship with Essex to make himself an enemy of Cecil, in particular, masked a passionate commitment to the Earl which was demonstrated in more private ways. Howard regularly signed his letters to Essex 'Your L*ordship's* most affectionately humbly & eternally'. On learning that Essex's wife had suffered a miscarriage in December 1596, Howard wrote that 'I would loose of mine owne bloude to saue yo*u*rs & hould all those giuen ou*e*r utterly *in sensum reprobissimum* whose mallice can distinguish at this day betwene the savegarde of yo*u*r worthy p*er*son and the life of yo*u*r Cuntry'.[37] As will be seen below, such extreme sentiments about the public worth of Essex were not merely an extravagant means of ingratiating himself with the Earl.

There is abundant evidence that Howard was deeply involved in Essex's political affairs in the 1590s, especially during 1596–7. A number of Howard's letters survive as copies among the papers of Anthony Bacon, who oversaw much of the Earl's intelligence gathering and other politically delicate matters involving foreign states.[38] Howard and Bacon shared similar antiquarian and literary interests and regularly passed papers to each other in the course of their work for Essex. This explains why Bacon made copies of Howard's letters and why a volume of Howard's own papers now held by the British Library contains copies of Essexian materials which he clearly obtained from Bacon.[39] In September 1597, when Bacon's hands were too gout-ridden to write a letter of news for Essex (who was then away on campaign), Howard stepped into the breach and reported to the Earl in Bacon's place.[40] Further evidence suggests something of Howard's own work for Essex: 'the occasions of my attendinge his L*ordsh*ip are full of trewe loue and speciall use'.[41] When Essex was created Earl Marshal in December 1597, Howard reminded him of 'the delight w*hi*che I take in all studies that tende to yo*u*r seruice' and reported that, 'since my laste beinge w*i*th yow, I haue laboured aboue my strengthe, not onlie in ryflinge all corners of my dustie Cabinet about notes belonginge to an honor that dothe nowe concerne yo*u*r self, but besides in swepinge downe the coppwebes euerie other where that I maie rightly iudge, and yow maie truly und*er*stande, what is due to yo*u*r aucthoritie'.[42] One product of such 'ryflinge' and 'swepinge downe' was a treatise which Howard completed for Essex before the latter's departure for Ireland in early 1599. Here Howard again demonstrated his deep concern for matters of honour, and for the maintenance of proper respect for aristocratic distinction, by penning an 'Audite' of the abuses by heralds in granting coats of arms since the time when his brother Norfolk had been Earl Marshal. Howard concluded by urging Essex to use his authority 'to make one *feu de ioy* of all the Patentes that haue [been] bestowed w*i*thin thirtie yeeres by p*er*sons that were insufficient to graunt [them] and for suche unworthy causes as are not uouchable before an upright examiner'.[43]

The notes in Howard MS 2 shed further light on the close relationship between Howard and Essex and suggest the extent to which Howard offered political advice to the Earl—and the extent to which the Earl was willing to seek this advice.[44] Howard wrote his notes for Essex on pages which remained unused in his notebook of gatherings on topics relating to nobility. The choice of pages and Howard's own cross-referencing make it clear that most (and probably all) of these gatherings had already been entered into the notebook before he started making his notes for Essex. Given his consistent emphasis upon the Earl's status as the embodiment of aristocratic virtue, it seems likely that Howard deliberately chose this notebook as a suitable location for notes about Essex, rather than simply because it had an adequate number of blank pages. The notes themselves are characterised by frequent interlineations and additions in the left-hand margin and occasional cross-references, suggesting that at least some sections were subject to repeated development or expansion. The rough, worked-over nature of the notes also suggests that Howard probably did not show them to Essex in this state. Although many of them are explicitly addressed to 'your Lordship', the immediate audience for these notes was Howard himself. Presumably, Howard either produced fair copies of specific sections for presentation to Essex or briefed him on their contents verbally. If Howard did produce fair copies for Essex, the sensitive nature of this material—and the potential for Howard's position at Court to be compromised by exposure of it—made them a natural candidate for burning. Then, as now, such destruction of confidential documents seems to have been a regular practice.[45]

Although the connections among the various sets of notes are often confusing, Howard seems to have developed his ideas for Essex under the following headings:

'Consideration of his person' [fols. 37r–8r]
'Consideration of causis of corruptio*n*' [fols. 81v–82r, follows on at fols. 8r–9r]
'Unpossible to doe goode any oth*er* way' [fols. 97r–98v]

'Electio Amicoru*m*' [fols. 115v–116v]
'The reuolution of his particular fortuna. Bona animi corporis fortuna*e*. The meane of his aduancemente' [fol. 117r–v, follows on at fol. 36r-v]
'His cariage and encomberance in the place euer since his cominge thither' [fol. 118r–v]
'The necessarie use of suche a person in this time for the seruice and reasons whie all sortes of me*n* are satisfied' [fol. 119r–v, follows on at fols. 79v–80r]
[Section with heading obliterated] [fol. 120r–v]
'Awnseres to the difficulties. Patience worketh miracles' and 'Inpossible to doe good any other waye' [fols. 121r–122v, follows on at 97r–98v]
'Certaintie to doo good this waye. tempore prudentia patientia' [fol. 123r–v, follows on at 128r–130r]
'Inconueniencis of wrestlinge' [fol. 124r–v, follows on at fol. 4r]
'Meanes of aduancement' [fols 125r–127v, follows on at fols. 63r–68v, follows on at 13r–14v]

In light of the clustering of these notes towards the latter part of the notebook and frequent tendency for sections to spill towards the front, it seems likely that the notes towards the end may constitute Howard's earlier entries in the book. Howard also clearly added to some sections on more than one occasion. The notes on 'The reuolution of his particular fortuna' at folio 117, for example, were apparently written after those that appear in later folios. This is suggested by a cross-reference that Howard added at the top of folio 117r ('Prouidence brought him in uerte 119'), but also, more strongly, by the way in which pages are used. When he needed extra space to complete (or expand) 'The reuolution of his particular fortuna', for example, Howard apparently turned to folio 36 because the following folios had already been filled with other (and hence earlier) notes, beginning with 'His cariage and encomberance' on folio 118. Although notes on 'Certaintie to doo good this waye' were expanded after those on 'Inconueniencis of wrestlinge' had been at least begun on folio 124 and after 'Meanes of aduancement' had covered folios 125–8, the continuation of 'Certaintie to doo good this waye' to include folios 128–30 seems to suggest that these notes were expanded before the completion of those on 'The reuolution of his particular fortuna', 'The necessarie use of suche a person', 'Awnseres to the difficulties', 'Inconueniencis of wrestlinge' or 'Meanes of aduancement', all of which could only be extended by turning to earlier folios because this section had already taken the pages which they might otherwise have occupied.

A typical example of Howard's notes for Essex can be seen in PLATE 2, which illustrates one page from the series of notes on 'Meanes

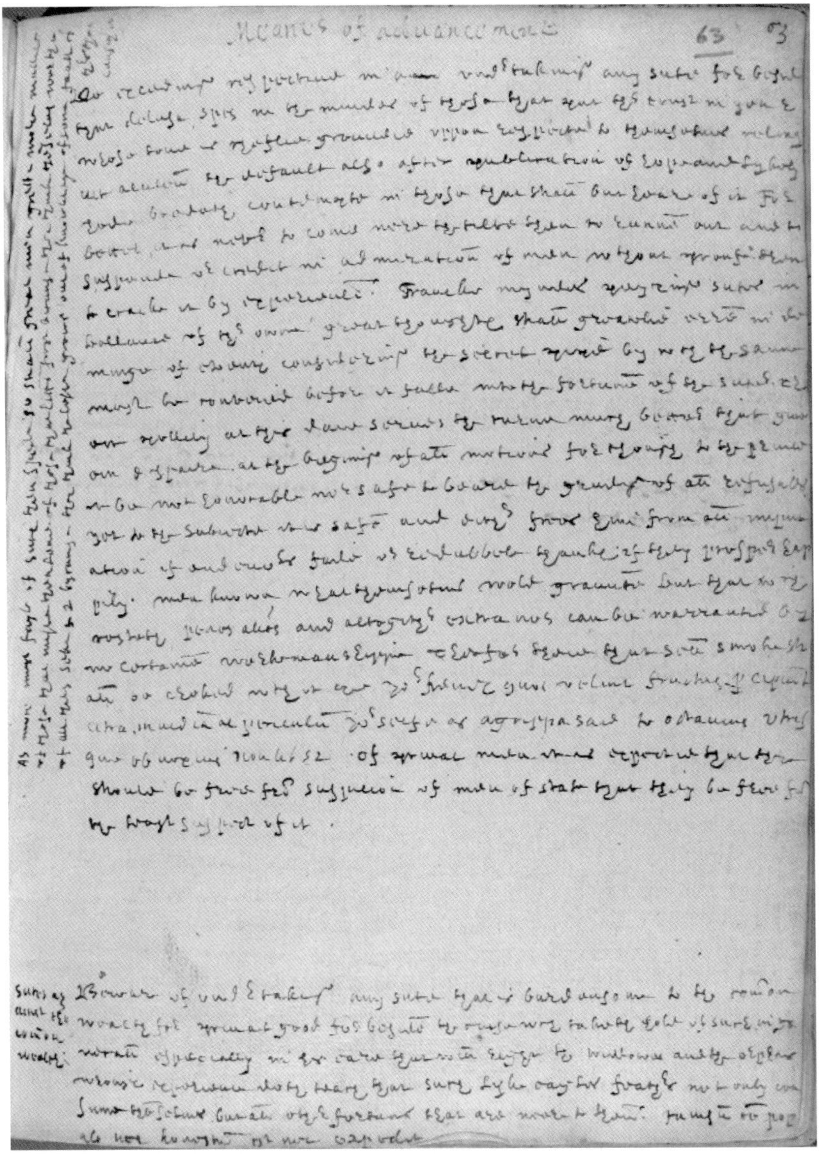

PLATE 2. *A page of Howard's commonplace book, notes of political advice for the Earl of Essex: Durham University Library, Howard Library,* MS 2, *fol. 63r. (Original page size 232 × 174mm.) Reproduced by permission of Durham University Library.*

of aduancement'. As the plate shows, these notes are largely written in English and often have additional material inserted in the left-hand margin. The marginal comment at the bottom of this page simply notes the subject matter of the adjacent material ('Sutes against the co*m*mon wealth'), while the longer marginal comment above effectively summarises the whole top paragraph (beginning 'Be exceeding respectiue in ~~a..~~ und*er*taking any sute . . .'): 'As more must fayle of sutes then spede so shall great men gette more mallice of those that misse then loue of those that hitte, first, bicause they think the*m*selus worthie of all they seke &, 2, bycause they think the losse growes out of knowledge of some fault of th*er*s that causith it'. As might be expected of a sixteenth-century scholar, Howard's notes are studded with frequent Latin quotations. Phrases in Greek, by contrast, are small in number and rarely amount to more than a few words. The page shown in PLATE 2 is unusual in featuring only one short quotation: 'yo*ur* frendes quos uelint fructus p*er*cipiu*n*t citra inuidia*m* ac periculu*m* yo*ur*selfe as Agrippa said to Octauius utrisque obnoxius Dion lib 52. Of priuat men it is expectid that theye should be free fro*m* suspicion; of men of stat that they be free fro*m* the least suspect of it'.[46] The work cited here, Cassius Dio's *Roman History*, the extant books of which recount the fall of the Republic and the early years of the Empire, is the most frequent source of quotations in Howard's notes for Essex. As was the norm in this period, Howard quotes from a Latin version of this text, rather than the original Greek. Howard does likewise with Thucydides' *History of the Peloponnesian War*, from which he quotes occasionally. After Cassius Dio, Howard's heaviest debt is to Livy, whose *Histories* of Rome (*Ab Urbe Condita*) are repeatedly cited from Books 32–42. Although the surrounding notes on nobility include a variety of materials, including some in Spanish, Howard's notes for Essex are bolstered exclusively with classical references.

Such quotations from classical histories reflect the instinctive tendency of educated men such as Howard and Essex to cast the politics of their own day in terms of Roman and Greek paradigms. The humanist education of sixteenth-century Europe made it seem natural to seek understanding and intellectual authority mainly (although not exclusively) from the classical past. This encouraged a relentless classicization of the interpretation of politics in Renaissance England which, among other things, emphasised a concern with aristocratic 'virtue' and how the actions of individuals reflected their moral (or immoral) qualities. Although some work has been done on the Elizabethan 'reading' of Livy (ironically, involving Gabriel Harvey and Philip Sidney, both targets of Howard's sniping in the early 1580s), most modern scholarship has emphasised the classicization of political interpretation through the growing popularity of studying Tacitus.[47] Essex, in particular, was strongly linked with the spread of Tacitism, both as a patron of Tacitist intellectuals and as a practitioner himself.[48] Although Howard's notes for Essex in Howard MS 2 show no overt reliance upon the works of Tacitus, the Earl's reception of Howard's arguments may well have been influenced by his own study of the latter historian. More generally, Essex's interest in studying politics helps to provide an intellectual context for the political advice contained in Howard's notes.

Essex's desire for self-improvement and determination to fulfill the highest aspirations of his rank and lineage made him eager for expert guidance. In various writings which were copied and disseminated in his name (some of which he seems to have written himself), Essex repeatedly emphasised the importance of diligent study for would-be statesmen. In a letter addressed to his friend Fulke Greville, Essex discussed at length the employment of university scholars as 'gatherers' to compile information under specific headings in precisely the same manner that Howard filled his notebooks.[49] Essex also repeatedly emphasised the necessity of improving one's judgement by consultations or 'conferences' with those who were specialists in their own field. As he instructed one of his academic clients in 1596: 'as yow were wonte to do in every new studye, seeke out some experte man to conferr withall . . . with whome yow must use some arte to applye yourselfe to their nature, and yealde them that kinde of respecte which they themselves would have, ffor when yow honor them muche, thoughe yow hurte them you profuite your selfe'.[50] Essex's willingness to 'apply' himself to the natures of those whom he consulted meant that he was willing to grant them greater lattitude than the dictates of social etiquette would normally allow. Francis Bacon, the brother of Anthony and one of the Earl's most conspicuous and highly-favoured dependents during the 1590s, claimed 'the more playnely and frankely yow shall deal w*i*th my L*ord*, not onely in disclosing particulars but in gyuing him caueats and admonishing him of any erro*ur* w*hi*ch in this action he may comytt (such is his nature), the better he will take it'.[51] In the case of Howard (as with Francis Bacon), Essex clearly found the private study of politics both instructive and highly congenial. If scholars such as the Oxford classicists Henry Savile and Henry Cuffe helped him to explore the lessons of Tacitus, Howard was a fellow Cambridge man (indeed, a former don there), a friend, kinsman and social near-equal who had direct personal experience of courtly politics at its most volatile. This practical dimension to Howard's advice—and his ability to observe events at Court for himself, following his readmission there in the 1590s—was perhaps especially important. For all his diligence, Essex struggled to put into practice the political insights which he gleaned from academic study, partly because he often found it hard to conceal his frustration when events went awry and partly because his rivals had read a similar range of classical history and drawn their own conclusions. In this light, it is perhaps significant that many of the classical references in Howard's notes seem to reflect later additions to illustrate or reinforce specific points, often in the form of inter-lining. This tendency emphasises that these notes are the product of Howard's own cogitation, rather than the result of systematically interrogating particular texts. The later addition of many Latin quotations could also support the idea that Howard subsequently produced fair copies of his notes for presentation to Essex, although it might also simply reflect a humanist scholar's instinct to buttress his own ideas with relevant classical materials.

An alternative interpretation of the notes in Howard Library MS 2 is that they may embody Howard's own jottings in preparation for—or arising from—specific 'conferences' with Essex. As already noted, Essex seems to have had a particular fondness for this means of intellectual self-improvment, presumably deriving from his days as a student at Trinity College, Cambridge.[52] More importantly, Howard's notes look strikingly similar to those which are known to have been made for (or from) 'conferences'. Notes of this sort survive, for example, for the series of consultations in which Francis Bacon (by then Viscount St Alban) offered detailed political advice to George Villiers, recently created Duke of Buckingham, in late 1623 and early 1624.[53] If Howard's notes similarly reflect the contents of conferences held with Essex, they would reinforce this volume's status as a kind of intellectual and political arsenal for Howard and underline his active involvement in trying to shape the direction of Elizabethan politics through his relationship with Essex.

Howard's notes in Howard Library MS 2 spell out both the political analyses which he offered to Essex and his own views about the Earl and his qualities. For Howard, Essex's combination of high aristocratic birth and manifold virtues marked him out as a vehicle for divine intervention in England's affairs. Howard's notes on 'The reuolution of his particular fortuna' begin with the proposition that 'The uerie time and manner of his aduancement proue ane argument of prouidence pro bono publico. His rising to the ou*er*throwe of one that opened his mouth and utterid blasphemies against heauene &c. The same god that made Hester graciouse in the sight of Ashuerus and adorned hir w*ith* giftes to please the king pro bono publico gaue the lyke grace to him. Bona animi corporis fortuna*e* &c' (fol. 117r).[54] Essex was therefore not only a special recipient of God's grace, but his meteoric rise to royal favour also shattered the hopes of Sir Walter Ralegh, who was regularly accused of blasphemy and atheism—and despised by Howard himself.[55] Howard also saw God's hand in the irony 'That his fathers greatest enemy should be his inducer' (fol. 117r), referring to Essex's late step-father, the Earl of Leicester, whom Howard blamed for the misfortune of his own brother Norfolk.[56] Essex's providential arrival transformed both the Queen and the Court: 'the uerie face of the courte at yo*ur* approche putting one the uesture of ane aft*er* spring made proufe of the good happe that followes you. Beside it was observid that the Quenes owne youth and gallant spirite was renewid and reuiued, as the psalme speakes of ane eagele' (fol. 117v).[57] Howard repeatedly emphasises this contrast between Essex's youthful energy and a Queen, Court and Privy Council that were old and in urgent need of renewal. In explaining 'The necessarie use of suche a person in this time for the seruice and reasons whie all sortes of me*n* are satisfied', he repeats the observation that 'Prouidence brought him in' and argues 'The Councell of the state waxing olde w*i*th the time it selfe, w*hi*ch dulleth and abateth oftentimes the edge of the most pregnant wittes, it was necessarie that one should be brought in to quicken spirites and to giue encouragement to oth*er*s that should followe him. Nature hauing infusid this spark onlie wantid a fresh gale of winde to kindele it' (fol. 119r).[58] Indeed, Essex's qualities were such that he was able to overcome the usual rules of politics: 'Though he wear enuied at the first, as young mens fauo*ur*s ar not compatible w*i*th olde menns declynacion, yet he so farre ou*er*came it w*i*th patience and curtesie as euen Cato himself, though a Stoicke and a ma*n* carelesse of the worlde that was wont out of enuie Scipionis allastare magnitudine*m*, wolde not haue enuied his intereste' (fol. 117v).[59]

Essex's qualities were remarkable for their completeness, especially 'in this barren age wherin natur is so scant in hir proportions to honorable [*i.e.* aristocratic] howsis': 'One reason of proportion drawen out of Plato moues me most of all, for euerie man is to be usid and employed in that quality for w*hi*ch natur made him most fitte, as one that is apte to riding, leaping, uaulting, writing &c. Nowe when I see that this lord is apte to euerie thing that tendeth eith*er* to the grace of a ientilman, to the quality of a soldier and the p*er*sone of a councello*ur* &c, I conclude that he was borne to publick hono*ur*, not to priuat officis' (fol. 117r). Such logic not only reinforced Howard's desire to assist Essex, but also implied a role of importance for himself, as the friend and adviser to a man of destiny: 'no ma*n* is borne for satisfaction of priuat humo*ur*s but for his cuntries good' (fol. 123r). This view of the nature of politics echoed Essex's sense of his own political significance, which Howard's praise and urgings undoubtedly helped to strengthen. Time and again, Essex emphasised that his actions were driven, not by selfish ambition, but by his duty to fulfill 'the publike use for which wee are all borne'.[60]

Virtue lay at the heart of Howard's appreciation of Essex and of the advice which he offered to the Earl. Qualities such as those possessed by Essex naturally drew lesser men to him ('as flies doo fro*m* ane olde baie leafe in the spring to a swete uiolette': fol. 117v), but they also excited the jealousy of those at Court who feared the exposure of their own shortcomings by comparison with him—and the consequent loss of their power. Such men sought to defend themselves by traducing Essex and trying to convince the Queen that the very qualities for which he was admired actually marked him out as dangerous: 'All his uirtewes drawne into the nature of uices: fortitude, temeritie; mariage, estrangement; affabilitie and swetnesse of disposition, popularitie. Possunt quide*m* o*mn*ia audere qui hoc ausi sunt. His uerie pollitick insinuation into the good will of forain states that in the *Queen's* seruice haue had occasion to deale w*i*th him hath bene made suspiciouse' (fol. 120v).[61] Nevertheless, Howard was convinced that Essex's combination of breeding, youth and virtue would inevitably triumph in the end: 'Among o*ur* councell so*me* are eith*er* so farre worne or so base in humor or so drownid in delight or so carelesse of the publike as yo*u* are not lyke to haue any competitor but the littell one, whose fearfull nature can not contend against yo*ur* strong spirite then a foxe w*i*th a lione' (fol. 123r). Howard's disparaging reference here to 'the littell one' is especially significant because the councillor in question is Sir Robert Cecil, with whom Howard exchanged so many friendly courtesies. To a degree, it would seem, Howard shared the disdain for Cecil which many of those around Essex expressed far more forcibly and cruelly.[62] However, while some of the Earl's partisans regarded Cecil as an enemy and a councillor whose significance would evaporate entirely upon the death of his formidable father, Howard's comment here offers a different analysis.[63] The reference to the fox and the lion is an obvious allusion to Machiavelli's famous discussion of these animals, in which Machiavelli argues that a successful prince must combine the qualities of both creatures.[64] Howard therefore implies that the Queen's service will be best served by a continued partnership on the Privy Council in which the fox-like Cecil acknowledges the superiority of the lion-like Essex and shapes his actions accordingly. As Howard continues, 'Beside the enuie w*hi*ch he [*i.e.* Cecil] must drawe, by discent, fro*m* his frendes, the long draught of the time, and a thousand oth*er* accidentes, will make him rath*er* carefull to deserue yo*ur* protection then to impugne yo*ur* proceedings' (fol. 123r).

Given the signs that apparently pointed towards Essex's ultimate dominance among the Queen's councillors, how should he respond to the slurs cast upon him by his detractors? The key themes of Howard's advice to the Earl are that he must be patient ('Patience worketh miracles'), that he must deny his critics opportunities to do him harm and, above all, that he must tend to his relationship with Elizabeth. Howard warns Essex at length about the 'Inconueniencis of wrestlinge' if this involves conflict with the Queen. Royal indignation with Essex would make Elizabeth more prone to delight in the illusion of 'harmonie' offered by his rivals, while the Earl himself would incur 'The odiouse report of putting the *Queen* into discontentment and by consequent of ouerthrowing the state of hir health, w*hi*ch, considering o*ur* state, is co*m*mune malu*m*, beside all sutes &c' (fol. 124r).[65] By failing to ground his actions upon the contentment of the sovereign who symbolically embodied the whole realm, Essex would lay himself and all who sought to do virtuous deeds open to attack by their jealous critics: 'It seteth tounges at libertie to depraue good desert. Rememb*er* w*i*th yo*ur* self. Rememb*er* in the iourney to Portingale, fortitude was temerity. In y*our* going twice into fraunce to assist a feble king against a tirantes force, Loue to yo*ur* cuntrie was ambition. In the detention of Lopez, witte and loyalty wear idele curiositie and oppression. Expencis for the seruice of yo*ur* princess and hono*ur* of the courte wear waste of humo*ur*. Actiuitie want of staie, magnanimitie intemperance, playness in proceding ignorance of state, care to reduce aduisis to the grounde of hono*ur* popularitie' (fol. 124v). Here Howard makes his point by directing Essex to recall how he was unfairly criticised during each of his major undertakings between early 1589 and early 1594, every one of which prompted furious rebukes from the Queen before subsequently becoming a cause of praise.[66] As Howard well knew, the consistent misinterpretation of his intentions rankled deeply with the Earl.

Howard also offered Essex a whole range of detailed advice about how to advance his interests in more active ways. Essex needed 'to settell his estate from raueling into any furd*er* wante', thereby denying his enemies potential leverage and removing the need to 'wearie' the Queen with repeated requests for reward (fol. 125r). He should 'worke so as all great intelligence w*i*th states and princes maie rest in your hande and the best wittes abroad maie liue at yo*ur* deuotion' (fol. 125r). Essex should also use his patronage to hold 'eu*er* in yo*ur* protection and care a Seminary of forward mindes and spirites to be recomended to placis of importance and of speciall trust when occasion doth serue and, in the meane time, drawe them into such peculiar actions of merite to the state as, being settelid in graciouse opinion pendente spe, they maie be found more capable of benefit and honor accedente opportunitate' (fol. 126r).[67] Howard suggests that Essex's nature is too forgiving ('from whose nature it is furder to doo hurt to any ma*n* and in whose minde the best phisicia*n* could hardly tell what humor he might purge') and that he should endeavour 'To kepe men in a greater awe of offering y*o*u wronges then y*o*u have don hith*er*to' (fols. 122r, 126r). Essex should 'take dayly notes' on the 'false iugglers' at Court, storing up evidence to use against them 'or at the least you maie reteyne them in yo*ur* danger w*hi*ch will make them conformable' (fol. 125r).[68] As the Queen's favourite, he must 'kepe of all aspirers to ~~prefer~~ the place of favo*ur* while you maie'. If the Queen showed herself determined to take up a fresh protégé, Essex should protect his interests by firstly seeking 'if it be possible to diuert [the] streame of hir affection to some person that is at yo*ur* beck; if this succede not then to make him yo*ur*s that is electid by the p*ar*tie [*i.e.* the Queen] but be sure that his estate be meane and rath*er* nede yo*ur* helpe then check yo*ur* height' (fol. 125r–v). Nevertheless, the necessity for such stratagems could be reduced, or avoided altogether, if Essex attended to pleasing the Queen: 'Since the *Queen* is most affectid to yo*ur* self and most delightid w*i*th yo*ur* praise, to giue hir full allowance in this kinde . . . The glasse of hir time being nowe farr ron*n* will giue hir occasion of sollace in delightes and pleasurs of the time. Herin y*o*u ~~be~~ must profess yo*ur* selfe a workma*n* if you meane to receiue any good' (fols 125v–6r).

Although the precise dating of Howard's notes of advice for Essex remains uncertain, it seems likely that they were written over a period of months or even several years. Some of Howard's notes, such as a series of basic 'how to' instructions about acting as a Privy Councillor, seem to reflect Essex's need for expert guidance around the time of his appointment to the Council in February 1593.[69] Howard's support might well help to explain Essex's sudden transformation after taking his Councillor's oath: 'hys Lo*rdshi*p is become a newe man, cleare forsakinge all hys former youthfull trickes, carriinge hym sealf w*i*th uery honorable grauyty and singulerly lyked of boath in p*ar*liam*en*t and at [the] Counsayle table both for hys speeches & iudgm*ent*'.[70] Many of the specific suggestions offered by Howard also seem to reflect policies which Essex actively pursued in the years following his appointment to the Council. Essex, for example, established himself as Elizabeth's leading employer of spies and intelligencers in the first half of the 1590s. Although the Earl had apparently been introduced to 'matters of intelligence' by Francis Bacon in early 1591 and although much of his success in this field after 1592 could be attributed to the work of Anthony Bacon, the scale of his investment in foreign intelligence and cultivating foreign dignitaries during the middle years of the decade may well owe something to Howard's encouragement.[71] A more striking example of Howard's influence on Essex seems to be his advice about fostering 'a Seminary of forward mindes and spirites'. By 1595, Essex was making a point of recruiting university men to perform services for the Queen abroad, emphasising to them that 'the cheife ende of my employinge yow be rather your inablynge hereafter then your present service'—exactly as Howard suggested.[72] The contents of Howard's notes therefore seem to reflect Essex's interests during the years 1593–5, which fits with their mention of the Earl's accusations of treason against Dr Roderigo Lopez (who was arrested in January 1594 and executed five months later) and the conspicuous absence of any reference to the Earl's famous victory at Cadiz in June 1596 or to Sir Robert Cecil's appointment as Secretary of State a month later.

If this date of 1593–5 is correct, Howard's notes were written during the period when Essex was busily transforming himself from the Queen's young favourite into a genuine international statesman. Howard was concerned at the political consequences of this transformation, which fundamentally challenged the basis on which the Queen had originally made Essex her favourite. Howard believed that Essex's ambition was a suitable use for his manifold talents and, indeed, necessary for the good of both the Queen and the realm—and accordingly assisted the Earl's designs with his advice and support. Nevertheless, he worried that Essex's dogged pursuit of larger political goals was blinding him to the very personal basis of his relationship with Elizabeth. Howard warned him that those who 'will make th*er* building sure must resorte to th*er* module; they that will make th*er* fortune stedfast to the first groundes of th*er* eleuation'. According to this 'principle', 'If that w*hi*ch pleasid at the first be sodainly w*i*thdrawen, adieu to favo*ur*' (fol. 123v). A similar 'deduction' proved 'that the waie to make uppe yo*ur* haruest is to plie this plotte of grounde. The waie to wepe in winter is to sleepe in the time of seede and folding uppe yo*ur* armes to referre all to destinie. The pleasing of the Quens humor is, and daily will be more and more, the helme of authoritie. The waie to please hir is to wond*er* at hir excellent p*er*fection and to content hir thoughtes. Hir thoughtes are not contentid w*i*thout simpathie w*i*th those in whom she takes delight. This simpathie requirs accorde not discrepancie, affection not opposition, hunger not satietie' (fol. 128v).

As Howard's sharp warning about 'accorde not discrepancie' suggests, Essex's determination to promote policies which he considered essential for the national good during the mid-1590s increasingly entangled him in the very sort of 'wrestlinge' which Howard warned would be dangerous. Essex's advocacy of a more aggressive military strategy in the war against Spain, and of the necessity of fuller cooperation with England's French and Dutch allies (whom the Queen mistrusted), repeatedly put him at logger-heads with Elizabeth. Essex's belief that only his own presence could guarantee the success of major new military expeditions abroad, and his repeated efforts to take command of them, was even more at odds with the constant attentiveness to the personal desires of the Queen which Howard enjoined upon him.[73] Howard therefore sought to convince Essex to cease pursuing commands abroad: 'The cariage of martiall forcis, if it could stand w*ith* yo*ur* hono*ur*, wear better lefte in anoth*er* hande', especially as 'princes in th*er* later times are fearfull and suspiciouse' and further military activity would only become 'burdensom' to him. As a student of politics and history, Howard was perhaps inherently wary of relying too much upon military success ('The carrier of a martiall course may be smooth but wise men fear the ende of it', fol. 130r). However, the specific conjunction of an elderly sovereign and a Court and Privy Council packed with men who envied Essex and who hoped to profit if he suffered a setback alarmed Howard profoundly: 'I could thinke that no ma*n* liuing wear so fitte to ioyne action, to aduise and to prosequ*u*te a course of life wherunto nature hath so manie wais enabelid y*o*u, but, as it standeth at this instant oth*er*wise, unlesse you fitte theas measurs by yo*ur* pollicy and w*i*thall ca*n* leaue a councell more enclyned to excuse yo*ur* ou*er*sightes then to detract fro*m* yo*ur* desertes, w*hi*ch I will see befor I will beleue oth*er*wise, you shall by forraine action giue fuele to the flame, set fier to the pier and arme yo*ur* enemies against yo*ur* selfe' (fol. 127r). Although Essex might feel an issue was worth the risk of clashing with the Queen and be willing to gamble on continued military success, Howard was determined to remind him of how much was at stake: 'If yo*ur* L*ordship's* humor might be thought of only, the case wear more tollerable but, assur yo*ur*selfe, yo*ur* iudgement will be callid into question that, hauing thus long liuid in that place w*hi*ch many me*n* affect w*i*th most ambitiouse desirs, you haue let it slippe out of yo*ur* handes lyke that dreame of treasure, as the prophet saies, and at his waking findeth but his handes emptie' (fol. 129r). The extreme bluntness of this advice surely reflects Howard's recognition that his own best hope of future advancement also trembled in the balance whenever Essex calculated that the pursuit of some immediate political goal should take priority over 'the pleasing of the Quens humor': 'Yo*ur* pollicy must be to stande uppon the strength of the Q*ueen's* affectione least y*o*u be thought not to neclect it' (fol. 129v).[74]

These impassioned urgings by Howard are remarkable for their similarity to the advice which Francis Bacon apparently gave Essex during the same period. Bacon's counsel is best-known from a letter to Essex which was written in October 1596, but its contents clearly reflect a prolonged series of earlier discussions between its author and the Earl.[75] Like Howard, Bacon was alarmed by the Queen's growing 'cold malignant humour' towards Essex and saw the urgent necessity of the Earl soothing her anxieties: 'win the Queen: if this be not the beginning, of any other course I see no end'. Echoing Howard's analysis of the impression given by Essex's militarism and the dangers to which this might subject him at the Court of an ageing Queen, Bacon asks 'whether there can be a more dangerous image than this represented to any monarch living, much more to a lady, and of her Majesty's apprehension?'. For Bacon, like Howard, it was this 'militar dependence' that offered 'the impression of greatest prejudice' and it demanded the same response: an end to the pursuit of military command 'to cure the Queen's mind in that point'. Like Howard, Bacon also suggested that Essex consider pleasing the Queen by building up a new favourite ('so as the subject hath no ill nor dangerous aspect towards yourself') and tending to his own estate: 'the inequality between your estate of means and your greatness of respects, is not to be neglected. For believe it (my Lord) that till her Majesty find you careful of your estate, she will not only think you more like to continue chargeable to her, but also have a conceit that you have higher imaginations'. Bacon's constant emphasis is upon the need for Essex to change the appearance given by his actions, rather than the aim of those actions: 'keep it in substance, but abolish it in shows to the Queen'. For all his emphasis upon virtue and keeping Essex's 'handes unspottid actions untaintid and thoughtes uncorruptid' (fol. 119v), Howard recognised the same point as Bacon: 'Let bonu*m* publicu*m* uel salte*m* specie*m* publici be the ground of all yo*ur* procedinges' (fol. 67r).[76]

Although there is no evidence that Bacon ever saw Howard's private notes for and about Essex, there can be little doubt that these two frequent companions of the Earl discussed the fortunes of their patron at length and in detail. In addition to the close correspondence between the notes in Howard MS 2 and Bacon's letter of October 1596, there are some interesting parallels with other near-contemporary writings by Bacon. Although Bacon pointedly dedicated the volume of *Essayes* which he published at the beginning of 1597 to his brother rather than to Essex, the essay 'Of Followers and Friends' is commonly interpreted as a form of advice to the Earl.[77] The essay opens: 'Costly followers are not to be liked, least while a man maketh his traine longer, hee maketh his wings shorter'. In his notes, Howard makes precisely the same point to Essex, albeit using a rather more dramatic avian image which underscores the depth of his own social conservatism: 'Couet not to many followers for it rather encreaseth enuie then honour. The world accountes it but an effect of present reputation bicause men ar apte lyke carrion crowes to followe glorie and to forsake ther frendes again as lise flie from a deade carcase' (fol. 68v). Bacon famously closes his essay with the pungent assertion that 'There is little friendship in the worlde, and least of all betweene equals . . . That that is, is betweene superiour and inferiour'. Bacon prefaces these final comments with words marked out from the rest of the text by the use of italic font: '*For lookers on many times see more then gamesters, And the uale best discouereth the hill*'. Intriguingly, Howard uses the same phrase in his advice that Essex should 'Take councell': 'Take councell of any faythfull and wise frende. Lookers one see mor often tims then gamsters, as reasone with a clowde is more bright then when she is obscurid or dazelid' (fol. 66v)[78]. Such shared use of metaphors in similar contexts certainly does not 'prove' Howard's influence on Bacon (or vice versa), especially as these ideas and phrases were hardly original. Nevertheless, the parallels are suggestive and reinforce the impression of ideas aired and shared between Howard and Bacon during their close association with Essex in the mid-1590s.

If Howard and Bacon agreed on both the general diagnosis and many of the specific remedies for Essex's increasingly queasy political fortunes in the mid-1590s, they also shared the frustration of seeing Essex reject, or ignore, their advice. Unfortunately for them, the lesson which seems to have impressed itself most forcibly upon Essex's mind after repeatedly enduring royal fulminations over his various acts of service was not that he should reframe his actions for 'the pleasing of the Quens humor' and avoid giving political ammunition to his enemies, but that Elizabeth would always come to appreciate the rightness of his actions once he could counter the insinuations of his adversaries by speaking to her directly. As both Howard and Bacon realised, this strategy depended entirely upon the Queen remaining open to his persuasion and the continuance of his access to her. After Essex's unauthorised return from Ireland in September 1599, he was denied this access, which left him prey to the words of his enemies and the profound anxieties which this prospect aroused in him. The result was political disaster, culminating in Essex's insurrection in London, consequent charges of treason and execution in early 1601.

The responses of Howard and Bacon to this slowly unfolding political tragedy were subtly, but significantly, divergent. Bacon seemed to distance himself openly from Essex, making conspicuous display of his 'superior duty' to the Queen and repeatedly assisting in the crown's prosecution of Essex.[79] As with his printing of his *Essayes*, Bacon sought to over-write his earlier private association with Essex with a new and notably public image, in this case as the Queen's devoted servant. Although he offered support to Essex in secret, the common impression was of a man who had abandoned his patron—even though his own brother, Anthony, remained a staunch partisan of the Earl.[80] By contrast, Howard balanced his continued cultivation of Cecil with a pointed unwillingness publicly to disavow Essex, as his attendance at the Essexian dinner party at Court in September 1599 demonstrated.[81] When Bacon sought Howard's support in clearing himself from the rumours that he had turned against Essex, Howard responded with a letter that judiciously, but unmistakably, reproved Bacon's behaviour: 'a gent. so well born, a wise gent. so well levelled, and a gent. so highly valued by a person of his [*i.e.* Essex's] virtue, worth and quality, would rather have sought all occasions of expressing thankfulness (so far as duty doth permit) than either omit opportunity or increase indignation'.[82] For his part, Howard sought to play the role of conciliator at Court, 'infinitely' travailing in his efforts to fashion a *rapprochement* between Essex and Cecil over the summer of 1600.[83]

Despite the doubts which he caused die-hard Essexians (although apparently not the Earl himself) by being a political 'neuter', Howard's efforts to reconcile Essex and Cecil enabled him to maintain open and honourable relationships with both men. More importantly, Howard's endeavours demonstrated his value to James VI of Scotland, whose interests were directly affected by the factional struggle at Elizabeth's Court. Whether this connection to James sprang from his partisanship for Mary Queen of Scots in the 1580s or arose from his intimate association with Essex and Anthony Bacon (who seems to have orchestrated the creation of an alliance between Essex and James during 1593–4), Howard was a man whom James believed he could trust and seemed to be one of the few intimates of Essex who remained politically unhampered by the Earl's eclipse in the closing months of 1599.[84] Howard's long cultivation of Cecil made him ideally equipped to urge the secretary to support James's claim to the succession, which became a critical task once Essex's political decline eroded his ability to champion the King's claim from a position of strength. Howard's crypto-Catholicism also made him a figure who could urge his fellow religionists to support James's cause.[85] For his part, Cecil would have been well aware of Howard's ties to James. Indeed, Cecil's recognition that Howard's friendship offered a potential means to loosen Essex's hold on the King's favour undoubtedly helped to encourage his displays of good will towards Howard. Anxious to save Essex and to mollify Cecil, James directed Howard to 'deale betuixt essex and 10 [Cecil] for a conformitie betuixt thaime'.[86] Although Howard's frantic efforts could not prevent the final destruction of Essex, he confirmed himself in the King's opinion as 'my deare and faithfull 3'.[87] In the wake of Essex's death, James firmly informed Cecil that Howard would henceforth act as the chief intermediary between them.

Although Howard clearly lamented the fall of his friend, Essex's failure created a political opportunity for Howard which he exploited for all he was worth in the last months of Elizabeth's reign.[88] In his secret correspondence with Scotland, Howard made sure that the king was warned against those whom he viewed as enemies, especially 'the diabolical triplicity, that is, Cobham, Raleigh and Northumberland', whom he claimed held a daily 'conventicle' at Durham House, Ralegh's London residence, to plan how they could win James to their purposes.[89] Howard also suggested more active measures against them to Cecil. In private notes which both reflect the insights gained by bitter personal experience and recall his earlier politic urgings to Essex, he advised Cecil that 'as my L*ord* of Lest*er* dellt w*i*th my broth*er* . . . so must you embark the gallant Cobham, by yo*ur* witte and interest, in some cours the Spanish waie as eith*er* may reueale his weakeness or snare his ambition'.[90] At one point, these notes even touch upon the fate of Essex, which Howard cites as a cautionary tale of failing to control one's passions in politics when confronted with unexpected difficulties: 'It did my L*ord* of Essex no great good, as I conceiue, that furie thrust out strong*er* passionis uppon a sodan thwart then repentance aft*er*ward could coole, for men growe more wise yet princies growe not less sensitiue'.[91] However, Cecil was a master at veiling his true feelings and had little need to be warned of such dangers.[92] Cobham and Ralegh were duly condemned for conspiring with Spain in the opening months of the new reign, while Northumberland was later caught up in the Gunpowder Plot of 1605.[93]

James's accession in March 1603 finally brought Howard his long-awaited reward: 'Patience worketh miracles' indeed. Upon his arrival in England, the new king informed Howard and two of his nephews that 'I love the whole house of them', opening the way for the revival of the senior Howard line.[94] Howard himself was created a Privy Councillor and subsequently Warden of the Cinque Ports (Cobham's old office) and Earl of Northampton. No longer starved of money, he built an extravagant London mansion, Northampton House, and filled it with jewels, plate, art and books. After the death of Cecil (by then Earl of Salisbury) in 1612, Howard succeeded to his place as Chancellor of the University of Cambridge and the dominant member of the Privy Council, which he retained until his own death in 1614. As Privy

Councillor for James VI and I, the ideas and words with which Howard had filled his private notebooks during Elizabeth's reign now flowed into a torrent of speeches and documents intended for public consumption.[95] Although his words and analyses had ultimately been unable to steer Essex to political success under Elizabeth, Howard's own career in the new reign proved him to be the consummate Jacobean statesman.[96]

NOTES

I would like to register special thanks to Prof. Linda Levy Peck for alerting me to the existence of the Howard Library MSS soon after their sale in 1992 and to Dr Peter Beal for his indulgence over my tardiness in completing this article. I also wish to acknowledge my gratitude to Durham University Library for permission to cite and reproduce material from Howard Library MS 2. Note that abbreviations in quotations from manuscript sources are indicated by the use of italics and light punctuation has been added to aid comprehension.

1 The volumes were purchased at Sotheby's sale of 14 December 1992 (lot 171). The Howard of Naworth family, which Lord William established, was headed by the Earls of Carlisle from 1661. According to the current handlist, the Howard of Naworth Papers (HNP) at Durham University Library (hereafter DUL) were acquired in several tranches (the last in 1999) and amount to no less than 230 metres of shelving. Although manorial documents extend back to the twelfth century, most of the papers date from the eighteenth and nineteenth centuries. For Lord William Howard, see *Selections from the Household Books of the Lord William Howard of Naworth Castle*, ed. G. Ormsby (Surtees Society, 68, 1878) and R. Ovenden and S. Handley, 'Lord William Howard (1563–1640)' in *Oxford Dictionary of National Biography* (hereafter *ODNB*).

2 For Lord Henry Howard, who was created Earl of Northampton by James I in 1604, see L. L. Peck, *Northampton: Patronage and Policy at the Court of James I* (London, 1982); L. L. Peck, 'The Mentality of a Jacobean Grandee' in *The Mental World of the Jacobean Court*, ed. L. L. Peck (Cambridge, 1991), pp. 148–68; and P. Croft, 'Howard, Henry, Earl of Northampton (1540–1614)' in *ODNB*.

3 The will of Lord Henry Howard contains a bequest of £2,000 to his nephew and appointed him one of his overseers, but does not mention a bequest of books or papers: E. P. Shirley, 'An Inventory of the Effects of Henry Howard, KG, Earl of Northampton, Taken on his Death in 1614, together with a Transcript of his Will', *Archaeologia*, 42, pt. ii (1869), 375–8. Northampton's library was apparently sold to his great-nephew, Thomas Howard fourteenth Earl of Arundel, in 1615 (Peck, Mentality', pp. 151, where 'nephew' should read 'great-nephew'). The nature and disposal of Arundel's library, including many of Howard's books, is discussed in L. L. Peck, 'Uncovering the Arundel Library at the Royal Society: Changing Meanings of Science and the Fate of the Norfolk Donation', *Notes and Records of the Royal Society*, 52 (1998), 3–24.

4 Thomas Howard, Earl of Surrey was created second Duke of Norfolk in 1513 as a reward for his victory over James IV of Scotland at Flodden. Two of Henry VIII's wives—Anne Boleyn and Katherine Howard—were members of the Howard

family, while Mary Howard, daughter of the third Duke and sister of Surrey, married the king's illegitimate son, Henry Fitzroy, Duke of Richmond and Somerset (d.1536). Mary Howard, dowager Duchess of Richmond and Somerset acted as guardian for Henry Howard and his brother after their father's execution. Henry VIII's marriage to Anne Boleyn made the Howard family cousins (at varying degrees of remove) to Elizabeth I.

5 For Surrey, see especially S. Brigden, 'Howard, Henry, Earl of Surrey (1516/17–1547)' in *ODNB* and W. A. Sessions, *Henry Howard, the Poet Earl of Surrey: a Life* (Oxford, 1999). For Norfolk, see M. A. R. Graves, 'Howard, Thomas (1473–1554), third Duke of Norfolk' in *ODNB* and D. M. Head, *The Ebbs and Flows of Fortune: the Life of Thomas Howard, third Duke of Norfolk* (Athens, GA, 1995). The fall of the Howards in 1546-7 is further discussed in S. Brigden, 'Henry Howard, Earl of Surrey, and the "Conjured League"', *Historical Journal*, 37 (1994), 507–37 and P. R. Moore, 'The Heraldic Charge against the Earl of Surrey, 1546–47', *English Historical Review*, 116 (2001), 557–583.

6 M. A. R. Graves, 'Howard, Thomas (1538–1572), fourth Duke of Norfolk' in *ODNB;* N. Williams, *Thomas Howard, fourth Duke of Norfolk* (London, 1964); F. Edwards, *The Marvellous Chance: Thomas Howard, fourth Duke of Norfolk and the Ridolphi Plot, 1570–1572* (London, 1968); G. Parker, 'The Place of Tudor England in the Messianic Vision of Philip II of Spain', *Transactions of the Royal Historical Society*, 6th series, 12 (2002), 185–207. Note that, unlike his brother Henry or his son Arundel, Norfolk was not a Catholic.

7 J. G. Elzinga, 'Howard, Philip [St Philip Howard], thirteenth Earl of Arundel, (1557–1595)' in *ODNB.* Arundel was deemed one of the Thirty-Nine Catholic Martyrs of Tudor England in the nineteenth century and was finally canonised in 1970.

8 Howard's religion was the subject of comment even after his restoration to royal favour in the 1590s. In the final months of Elizabeth's reign, 'L[ord] H[enry] Howard would come and continue in prayer when the Q[ueene] came, but otherwise would not endure them, seeming to performe the duty of a subject in attending on his prince at the one tyme, and at the other using his conscience. He would runne out of the Q[ueenes] chamber in hir sicknes when the chaplein went to prayer. Their prayer, for him, [was] like a conjuracion for a spirit': *The Diary of John Manningham of the Middle Temple, 1602–1603,* ed. R. P. Sorlien (Hanover, NH, 1976), p. 246. For discussion of Howard's religion, see Peck, *Northampton*, pp. 8–9, 12.

9 London, British Library, Cotton MS Titus C VI, fol. 41v, Howard to Lord Treasurer Burghley, 29 October 1589.

10 ibid., fol. 52r, Howard to [Burghley?], 25 July 1593. This letter is erroneously labelled as being addressed to Sir Robert Cecil. The Lord Admiral, Charles Howard, second Baron Howard of Effingham, was a cousin of Henry Howard (he was the son of a younger son of Thomas Howard, second Duke of Norfolk). Although the head of a cadet branch, Lord Admiral Howard was the most politically significant member of the extended Howard family during the second half of Elizabeth's reign and was created first Earl of Nottingham in 1597: R. W. Kenny, Elizabeth's *Admiral: the Political Career of Charles Howard, Earl of Nottingham, 1536–1624* (Baltimore, 1970).

11 Sessions, *Surrey*, esp. chap. 10; *Henry Howard, Earl of Surrey: Poems,* ed. E. Jones (Oxford, 1964). Perhaps significantly, in light of Henry Howard's heavy use of Latin sources for his own work, Surrey also translated part of Virgil's *Aeneid*: *The 'Aeneid' of Henry Howard, Earl of Surrey,* ed. F. H. Ridley (Berkeley, CA, 1963).

12 *A Defense of the Ecclesiasticall Regiment in Englande Defaced by T. C. in his Replie agaynst D. Whitgifte* (London, 1574).

13 Howard himself penned the single copy of this work, which was written on vellum and embellished with a colour portrait of Elizabeth for presentation to the Queen: H. R. Woudhuysen, *Sir Philip Sidney and the Circulation of Manuscripts, 1558–1640* (Oxford, 1996), p. 100. The portrait shows Elizabeth clearly represented in the guise of the Virgin: *Elizabeth: the Exhibition at the National Maritime Museum,* ed. D. Starkey and S. Doran (London, 2003), pp. 200–1.

14 *John Stubbs's Gaping Gulf with Letters and Other Relevant Document,* ed. L. E. Berry (Charlottesville, VA, 1968), pp. 153–94.

15 *A Defensatiue against the Poyson of Supposed Prophesies* (London, 1583). Further editions were subsequently published in 1620 and 1622.

16 'A Dutifull Defense of the Lawful Regiment of Women': this work was written at the urging of Lord Burghley during 1589–90. As Amanda Shephard notes, Howard's reference to Elizabeth's Court having already endured for thirty-two years suggests that this tract was completed in 1590: A. Shephard, *Gender and Authority: the Knox Debate* (Keele, 1994), pp. 34–5.

17 In his dedication of this translation to Elizabeth, Howard writes that it was presented to her after 'twelue yeares sequestration from the comforte of your cheerefull lookes' (BL, Lansdowne MS 792, fol. 1r).

18 For example, Woudhuysen (p. 101) lists four presentation copies of Howard's 'Dutifull Defense', bound in purple velvet and customised with verses to each recipient and/or their coat of arms. Peter Beal extends this list, adding a copy later given by Howard to Sir Robert Cotton and the copy presented to Burghley (and bearing the latter's annotations): P. Beal, *In Praise of Scribes: Manuscripts and their Makers in Seventeenth-Century England* (Oxford, 1998), p. 215.

19 It should be noted that the professions of good will between Norfolk and Cecil (Lord Burghley from 1571) were counter-balanced by later repeated accusations by Catholic polemicists that the parvenu Burghley had tricked Norfolk and deliberately sought the Duke's death to demonstrate his power over the realm's 'ancient nobility'. This accusation was most conspicuously aired in [Anon.], *A Treatise of Treasons against Q. Elizabeth, and the Croune of England diuided into two partes* ([Louvain], 1572) and in the 'Cecil's commonwealth' tracts of 1592, such as [Anon.], *An Aduertisement Written to a Secretarie of my L. Treasurers of Ingland* ([Antwerp], 1592). Howard, however, seems to have blamed Robert Dudley, Earl of Leicester (d.1588) for his brother's troubles, rather than Burghley (Peck, *Northampton*, p. 20). This is significant because Howard's circle of crypto-Catholic courtiers during the Anjou Match affair seem to be the source for information contained in the notorious 'Leicester's commonwealth' libels of the mid-1580s: *Leicester's Commonwealth: The Copy of a Letter Written by a Master of Art of Cambridge (1584) and Related Documents,* ed. D. C. Peck (Athens, OH, 1985).

20 Peck, *Northampton*, p. 220 n. 26. When sending Burghley a 'littell booke', Howard wrote that he had feared the loss of his work when his papers were roughly searched. He also apologised for 'the badde writing of the booke, for that it is myne owne, beinge forcid to take this extraordinary labore by the ignorance of the scrieueneres of this towne, who in a Latine coppye for the moste parte make as many faultes as pointes'. He hoped Burghley would accept it as 'witnesse of my plaine deuotion . . . when your Lo*rd* shall consider that the matter out of which this treatise is compilid is the word of god itselfe' (BL, Cotton MS Titus C VI, fol. 39r–v, Howard to Burghley, 27 March 1589).

21 Peck, 'Mentality', p. 150.

22 Oxford, Bodleian Library, Bodleian MS 616. Howard's dedication is dated from Trinity Hall on 6 August 1569 (fol. 12v). An annuity from Lady Berkeley subsequently became a linchpin of Howard's finances.

23 V. F. Stern, *Gabriel Harvey: His Life, Marginalia and Library* (Oxford, 1979), p. 70 *et seq.* Richard Harvey was the chief target of Howard's book.

24 A. H. Nelson, *Monstrous Adversary: The Life of Edward De Vere, 17th Earl of Oxford* (Liverpool, 2003), esp. p. 249 *et seq.*

25 BL, Cotton MS Titus C VI, fol. 5v, Howard to Queen Elizabeth [early 1581?].

26 Howard also heavily annotated his books, another standard feature of Renaissance scholarship: N. Barker, 'The Books of Henry Howard, Earl of Northampton', *Bodleian Library Record*, 13 (1988–1991), 378; M. Peltonen, 'Francis Bacon, the Earl of Northampton and the Jacobean Anti-Duelling Campaign', *Historical Journal*, 41 (2001), 12. For an illustration of Howard's copious annotations, see the image of his copy of Alessandro Piccolomini, *Sfera del Mondo* (1579), reproduced in Peck, 'Uncovering the Arundel Library', 17.

27 The draft is dated 27 August [1584]: Howard Library MS 5, fol. 40r.

28 Respectively, 'The definition and derivation of "nobility"', 'The origin of nobility', 'Whether fortune and wealth may create a nobleman', 'Whether it may be lost by impoverishment', 'Heralds', 'Whether the mechanical arts may debase nobility', and 'Enemies of nobility—who?'.

29 'Whether an ignoble man may be able to become noble' and 'Whether it may be lost by infamy'.

30 The foliation, which is marked in Howard's hand and is used by him for cross referencing (eg. 'uerte fol. 36', '97 p 2' [meaning the verso of folio 97], runs 1–4, 7–38, 49–102, 105–135. Stubs are visible after folios 38 and 102. The notebook itself measures 232 × 174mm.

31 Essex is actually mentioned by name at folio 122r. For Essex, see P. E. J. Hammer, *The Polarisation of Elizabethan Politics: The Political Career of Robert Devereux, 2nd Earl of Essex, 1585–1597* (Cambridge, 1999). By a curious quirk of fate, an important batch of Essex's letters, including many to Queen Elizabeth, were the most expensive lot offered in the same sale in December 1992 in which the Howard Library MSS were bought by Durham: 'Elizabeth and Essex: The Hulton Papers', sale catalogue (Sotheby's, 1992). The Essex letters failed to sell in 1992 and it was not until several years later that they were finally purchased by the British Library, where they are now Additional MSS 74286–7.

32 Cambridge, Mass., Harvard University, Houghton Library, fMS Eng 826: 'A dutifull defence of the Lawfull Regiment of Weomen devided into three bookes'. This copy bears Essex's arms and Latin verse in Howard's hand praising him as 'Pieridum decus es, equitum flos, gloria campi,/Artibus instruxit te tua Diva suis' (You are worthy of the children of Pierus [*i.e.* the Muses], the flower of knights, the glory of the field,/Your Goddess [*i.e.* the Queen?] has instructed you in her arts'.

33 Sir Henry Wotton, *A Parallel betweene Robert late Earle of Essex, and George late Duke of Buckingham* (London, 1641), p. 6.

34 Hammer, *Polarisation*, p. 290.

35 Historical Manuscripts Commission (hereafter HMC), *A Calendar of the Manuscripts of the Most Hon. the Marquis of Salisbury, KG, &c, preserved at Hatfield House, Hertfordshire*, 24 vols (London, 1883–1976), VI, 193–4, 271, 497; London, Lambeth Palace Library, MS 658, fols 97r–8r, 141r, copies of Cecil to Howard, 28 July and [month of July] 1596.

36 HMC, *Report on the Manuscripts of the Lord De L'Isle and Dudley preserved at Penshurst Place*, 6 vols (London, 1925-66), II, 397. There is no sign that the Earl himself shared this view.

37 Lambeth MS 660, fol. 275r, copy of Howard to Essex 'this Tuesday Morning at 7' [December 1596].

38 For Bacon, the older brother of Francis, see Hammer, *Polarisation, passim*; D. Du Maurier, *Golden Lads: Sir Francis Bacon, Anthony Bacon and their Friends* (New York, 1975); A. Stewart, 'Bacon, Anthony (1558–1601)' in *ODNB*. Most of Anthony Bacon's papers are now held at Lambeth (MSS 647–662), although some important materials also survive in the BL (eg. Add. MS 4125) and the University of Edinburgh Library (Laing MSS, III, No. 193). Virtually all of this material relates to the period before 1598, which suggests that this inveterate hoarder and copier of documents deliberately destroyed much of the material he had accumulated in order to limit the fall-out from Essex's defeat. This culling of papers makes it difficult to make firm pronouncements about the extent of Howard's dealings with Bacon after 1597.

39 These materials include copies in Howard's own hand of several letters by Essex to the Queen (BL, Cotton MS Titus C VI, fols. 172r–v, 173r, 173r–v, 173v), excerpts taken from several of Essex's letters (in Latin) to Antonio Perez in 1595-7 (fols 297r–8r) and one original letter from Essex to Howard, which is dated '6 of Iuly att Midnighte' [1597?] (fol. 174r). The letters from Essex to Perez from which Howard took his excerpts seem to include some not printed in G. Ungerer, *A Spaniard in Elizabethan England: the Correspondence of Antonio Perez's Exile,* 2 vols (London, 1974–6), I, 298 *et seq.*

40 Lambeth MS 661, fol. 237r–v, Howard to Essex, endorsed by Bacon as 14 September 1597. As with a number of Howard's writings, the ink in this letter has faded and it is now difficult to read. Howard also wrote a short letter on his own behalf to Essex on the same date, thanking the Earl for his kindness to his nephew Lord Thomas Howard (ibid., fol. 238r).

41 Lambeth MS 656, fol. 125r, Anthony Bacon to Essex, [30 March 1596/7]. Although 'yow will not seeme to know yt from me', Bacon reports Howard's fury when he was twice mistakenly denied access to Essex.

42 BL, Harley MS 286, fol. 268r, Howard to Essex [after 25 December 1597]. For the circumstances of Essex's creation as Earl Marshal, see Hammer, *Polarisation*, p. 386 *et seq.*, and BL, Cotton MS Titus C VI, fols 176r–7r, Cecil to Howard [December 1597].

43 Folger Shakespeare Library, MS V.b.7, pp. 97–8. This manuscript is an early seventeenth century scribal copy of 'A briefe discourse of the right use of gevinge armes, w*ith* the late abusis about that matter, and the beste meane by w*hich* they may be reformid orderly. Written by Henry Howard Earl of Northampton'. The terminal date for the work's completion is suggested by Howard's reference to Essex's 'dep*ar*ture hence' (p. 98). Peck (*Northampton*, p. 221 n. 39) suggests that this treatise may have been started as early as 1597. Part of Howard's original draft apparently survives in BL, Cotton MS Faustina E I.

44 A very similar set of holograph notes by Howard for Essex survives as Cotton MS Titus C VI. fol. 393 *et seq.* under the general heading of 'CONCILIA SALUTARIA' ('Advantageous Counsels'). Repeated mention of Essex's victory at Cadiz (fol. 395r–v) suggests that these notes—unlike those contained in Howard MS 2—were written during 1597–8. I hope to do detailed work on these materials in the future and will not discuss them further here.

45 For example, a letter from Anthony Bacon to James VI of Scotland in early 1596 disappeared 'in a fume' after the King had read it. Essex also ordered a 'great burning of his bookes and writings' before his final arrest in 1601 (Hammer, *Polarisation*, pp. 171, 308).

46 'Your friends may receive those rewards for which they wish without jealousy and danger but yourself, as Agrippa said to Octavius, are exposed to both. Dio book 52'.

47 L. Jardine and A. Grafton, '"Studied For Action": How Gabriel Harvey Read his Livy', *Past & Present*, 129 (1990), 32–78.

48 Hammer, *Polarisation*, p. 307 *et seq.*

49 '. . . they should like labourers bring stone, timber, mortar and other necessaries to your building. But you should put them together and be the master-workman yourself' (*The Letters and Life of Francis Bacon*, ed. J. Spedding (7 vols, London, 1861–74), II, 26). At least in Howard Library MSS 1–5, it seems that Howard served as both his own 'labourer' and 'master-workman'. Like a number of documents associated with Essex, this letter is usually ascribed to Francis Bacon, although its true authorship probably cannot be determined with certainty. A miscatalogued fair copy of the letter written in the hand of Edward Reynoldes, Essex's personal secretary, survives as London, National Archives, SP 14/59/4 (fols 4r–5v). For discussion of this document and its connection with Greville's recruitment of John Coke from Trinity College, Cambridge, in 1589-90, see P. E. J. Hammer, 'The Earl of Essex, Fulke Greville and the Employment of Scholars', *Studies in Philology*, 91 (1994), 167–80.

50 P. E. J. Hammer, 'Essex and Europe: Evidence from Confidential Instructions by the Earl of Essex, 1595–6', *English Historical Review*, 111 (1996), 380. The recipient was Robert Naunton, Public Orator of the University of Cambridge, who was granted leave to serve the Earl abroad. In the same instructions, Essex reminded Naunton that 'rules and patternes of pollecy are aswell learned out of olde Greeke and Romayne storyes, as out of states which are at this daye' (ibid., p. 378).

51 NA, SP 12/238/138 (fol. 206r), Francis Bacon to Thomas Phelippes, [April 1591?].

52 Conferencing was a standard technique, along with reading, for gathering specialist knowledge in the early modern period. Richard Mulcaster, for example, specifically urges the value of conferences in his manual on education, especially for the aspiring 'politike counsellour': *Positions Wherin those Primitiue Circumstances be Examined which are Necessarie for the Training up of Children* (London, 1581), pp. 203–4. Mulcaster's *Positions* was among the books bought for Essex's education during 1581: Hammer, *Polarisation*, p. 29.

53 Bacon's notes for conferences with Buckingham on 23 December 1623 and 2 January 1624 are printed in Spedding, *Letters and Life of Francis Bacon*, VII, 442–7.

54 'Pro bono publico': 'for the common good'; 'Bona animi corporis fortunae': 'gifts of the mind, the body and of fortune'.

55 For Ralegh's widespread reputation for 'atheism', see, for example, [Anon.], *An Aduertisement Written to a Secretarie of my L. Treasurers*, p. 18. On the early rivalry of Essex and Ralegh, see P. E. J. Hammer, '"Absolute and Sovereign Mistress of her Grace"? Queen Elizabeth and her Favourites, 1581–1592', in *The World of the Favourite*, ed. J. H. Elliott and L. W. B. Brockliss (New Haven, CT, 1999), pp. 38–53. Howard's personal antipathy towards Ralegh presumably had its origin in the latter's association with the same group of crypto-Catholic courtiers as Howard during 1579. Ralegh subsequently abandoned them and turned to their enemy Leicester: D. C. Peck, 'Ralegh, Sidney, Oxford and the Catholics, 1579', *Notes and Queries*, 223 (1978), 427–31.

56 The wild claim that Leicester had arranged the poisoning of Essex's father in order to marry his widow (Essex's mother) was most famously aired in the 'Leicester's commonwealth' pamphlets. The supposedly shared suffering at Leicester's hands presumably reinforced Howard's feelings towards Essex.

57 The allusion is to Psalm 103, verse 5: '. . . thy youth is renewed like the eagle's'.

58 A Latin quotation, seemingly from Thucydides, is interlined here. Cf. fol. 80r: 'at y*our* calling to councell, all hartes and handes being aduancid to hope of y*our* hon-

o*ur* as if, euen at the uerie instant, the state it selfe, ~~h~~ after many daies of [*unclear word*] had begon to breath after a long wasting maladie. That he maie be in the state as the sinnowes are in a naturall body'.

59 'Scipionis allastare [*i.e.* allatrare] magnitudine*m*': 'to rail against the greatness of Scipio'.

60 Hammer, *Polarisation*, p. 399.

61 'Possunt quide*m* o*mn*ia audere qui hoc ausi sunt': 'the men who dared to do this can dare to do anything'. This quotation is from Livy, Book 40, section 9. Further quotations from this passage (the speech of Perseus of Macedonia against his brother, Demetrius) are interspersed throughout this block of notes. 'Mariage' refers to the revelation in late 1590 of Essex's secret marriage to the widow of Sir Philip Sidney, which angered the Queen. The countess remained unwelcome at Court even after Essex recovered royal favour (Hammer, *Polarisation*, pp. 89–90, 202, 284).

62 The closest Howard seems to come to echoing the criticisms made of Burghley's (and later Cecil's) domination of government—expressed in most outrageous form in the 'Cecil's Commonwealth' tracts of 1592—are his comments under 'Causis of corruption', which lament the rampant flattery at Court and its corrosive effect on virtue, the vacancy of many high offices of state, and the hold on power which was exercised by an unnamed few: 'Som ar mountid so high in place as no hand ca*n* come nere them. To touch them w*i*th suspicion is capitall, to examin th*er* procedinges business [*i.e.* busy-ness], to censur th*er* procedinges faction; no prouf is acceptid, be it as bright as the son, and though thinges doo appere yet the one warrant maie suffice for all frater noster est &c ['he is our brother'—*i.e.* 'he is one of us'] to conceal all outrage and knauerie' (fol. 8r).

63 Before Cecil's formal appointment as Secretary of State in July 1596, some Essexians still treated him as totally dependent upon his father's status ('the father and the son'). Anthony Bacon, a cousin of Cecil, privately mocked him as 'like a little pot soon hott', while the Spanish exile Antonio Perez nicknamed him 'microgibbus' (little hunchback) and 'Robertus diabolus' (Robert the devil) (Hammer, *Polarisation*, pp. 290–1, 346, 357).

64 *The Prince*, chapter 18 ('Concerning the Way in which Princes should Keep Faith').

65 'co*mm*une malu*m*': 'an injury done to all'. 'Beside all sutes &c' presumably means that the Queen would also become resistant to his requests for suits.

66 The events mentioned are: Essex's involvement in the Portugal expedition of 1589; Essex's command of an English army in Normandy during 1591–2; Essex's accusations of treason against Roderigo Lopez, a physician in the royal household, at the end of 1593 and start of 1594; and Essex's heavy expenditure as the Queen's chief host for foreign dignitaries visiting the Court.

67 'pendente spe': 'while hope remains unfulfilled'; 'accedente opportunitate': 'when opportunity arrives'. Howard's reference to a 'Seminary of forward mindes and spirites' is an interesting choice of phrase, especially as Catholic priests trained in new English seminaries on the Continent ('seminary priests') were regularly being executed as traitors by the Elizabethan regime. As a crypto-Catholic, Howard is presumably also making a little joke about his own faith, secure in the knowledge that Essex (if he ever read or heard this phrase) favoured toleration for English Catholics who opposed Spain.

68 'Hunterers gain mor by stalking then w*i*th howndes' is interlined here.

69 For example: 'Bewar of dealing in any hatefull cause and rath*er* seke that it maie be referrid into the handes of oth*er* me*n* . . . Neuer make dispatche w*i*thout good warrant and direction from the Queene and let yo*ur* secretary kepe a note of the time

and enstructions that maie be y*our* warrant when ther ariseth any question . . . In all y*our* councells referre the resolution to the *Queen's* owne wisdom, having made the case so cleere by debating pro and contra as in hir owne discresion she must preferre that y*o*u lyke . . . Eschewe as much as lies in y*o*u to speak y*our* opinion first, for beside that time and lesire giues advantage in the dealing &c, the ambition of speaking first draweth from some enuie, from others ielousie . . . Let y*our* motions *euer* be propoundid by sollicitors of a seconde forme and of a worse account for by this meane, if they be reiectid, you shall auoide enuie, censure and myslyke; if acceptid, yet in respecte you haue a higher interest in fauor and opinion, it is an easie matter to deriue all praise and comendacion to y*our* selfe onlye' (fol. 13r–v).

70 Folger MS L.a.45, Anthony Bagot to Richard Bagot, 1 March 1592/3.

71 For Essex and intelligence, see Hammer, *Polarisation*, chap. 5.

72 Hammer, 'Essex and Europe', p. 374.

73 The conflict between Essex's desire to campaign abroad and Elizabeth's desire to enjoy his company is most clearly described in a letter by Sir Robert Cecil to Sir Christopher Hatton of September 1591: 'hee [Essex] contrarily to her Majestie writeth peremptorily for leave for 6 weekes att the least (though the troupes retourne), wherof her Majestie collecteth his small desire to see her as shee doth requite him accordingly with crossing him in his most earnest desire, wherin (as one that wisheth him all honorable fortune) I pray God to put in his minde to make her Majestie's absolute will his perfectest reasone and to frame his actions to her Majestie's likeinge' (P. E. J. Hammer, 'Letters from Sir Robert Cecil to Sir Christopher Hatton, 1590–1591', in *Religion, Politics and Society in Sixteenth-Century England*, ed. I. W. Archer *et al.*, Camden Society, 5th series, 22 (2003), p. 260).

74 As Howard notes in another part of his notes: 'Y*our* L*ordship* hath alreadie settelid a notable impression of y*our* own sufficiency in all mens myndes and many men haue settelid th*er* loue to th*er* hope and expectation uppon y*our* selfe. To leaue this place wear to abandon y*our* flocke to the wolfe and giue them that enuied y*our* hono*ur* the same advantage that Alcibiades wold not to som in Athens: to plaie uppon him w*i*th all th*er* shott both great and small' (fol. 98r).

75 *Letters and Life of Francis Bacon*, II, 40–5. This letter survives only as scribal copies (eg. BL, Additional MS 72407, fols 10r–11v), but it was printed in the 1650s by Bacon's literary executor and former chaplain, who ascribed its authorship to him. The contents and tone of the letter seem to support this attribution: William Rawley, *Resuscitatio, Or Bringing into Publick light Severall Pieces of the Works . . . of . . . Francis Bacon* (London, 1657), sig. Ooo3v–Ppp1v (paginated as 'Seueral Letters Written by this Honourable Authour to Queen Elizabeth, King Iames Diuers Lords and Others', pp. 106–10).

76 'bonu*m* publicu*m* uel salte*m* specie*m* publici': 'the public good, or rather the appearance of the public [good]'.

77 Francis Bacon, *Essayes* (London, 1597), pp. 4–6. Anthony Bacon immediately sent a copy to Essex with the offer—perhaps reflecting some embarrassment at his brother's action—to 'transferre my interest [in the book] unto y*our* L*ordshi*p' (Anthony Bacon to Essex, 8 February 1596/7: Lambeth MS 655, fol. 120r).

78 The same phrase also opens a letter to Essex from Lord Keeper Egerton, which formed a very widely copied pairing with Essex's reply: 'It is often seen that a stander-by seeth more than he that playeth the game . . .'. This may be a coincidence, reflecting a commonplace phrase, or it may perhaps be an intentional allusion to the end of Bacon's essay (which was re-published during 1598). Egerton's letter was written in an attempt to defuse Essex's 'great quarrel' with Elizabeth during the summer and autumn of 1598, which would make reference to friendship

between 'superiour and inferiour' highly apposite. Egerton was a some-time patron of Bacon and a 'neuter' in the factional politics of the late 1590s who (like Howard) hoped to see Essex reconciled with the Queen and his fellow Councillors.

79 HMC, *Salisbury*, IX, 406.

80 Francis Bacon's attempt to aid Essex in secret was most notoriously demonstrated by his writing of letters in mid-1600 that purported to be from his brother Anthony to Essex and Essex's reply. The intention was that they would be shown to the Queen as evidence of the Earl's good behaviour: *Letters and Life of Francis Bacon*, II, 191 *et seq*. Although the letters did circulate at Court, their chief effect was to cause Bacon intense embarrassment during Essex's trial in February 1601.

81 Peck, *Northampton*, pp. 16–18.

82 HMC, *Salisbury*, IX, 406–7. Numerous scribal copies of Bacon's letter and Howard's reply survive, suggesting that the letters were circulated.

83 HMC, *De L'Isle and Dudley*, II, 481. Howard may have been working for this goal from the time since the autumn of 1599 (ibid., p. 404).

84 For the forging of the alliance between Essex and James VI, see Hammer, *Polarisation*, p. 167 *et seq*.

85 Hence Cecil later joked about Howard to James: 'whom thogh I can not make either puritane or protestant, yet must I protest him to all men to be *et virum et ciuem bonum* [both a good man and a good subject], and towards your Majesty my lyfe shold be pledg, if it were needfull to you, that he hath ever ready his gantlet of defiance against Pope and Cardinalls in generall' (*Correspondence of King James VI of Scotland with Sir Robert Cecil and Others in England During the Reign of Queen Elizabeth* (Camden Society, 1861), p. 36).

86 ibid., p. 2. Note that James VI and his English correspondents used a system of numerical ciphers to reduce the risk of exposure: Lord Henry Howard was '2', Cecil was '10', James VI was '30'. For a fuller list of the ciphers, see ibid., pp. xxxv–vi.

87 ibid., 25.

88 Howard's continuing connection with the lingering Essexian interest was reflected in his patronage of the late Earl's servants, such as his secretary Edward Reynoldes. Howard's goods in 1614 also included 'a Tablett of Gold with a picture of my lord of Essex', 'A picture of the Earle of Essex' and 'A picture of the two children of the late Earle of Essex' (Shirley, 'Inventory', pp. 349, 356, 357).

89 *The Secret Correspondence of Sir Robert Cecil with James VI of Scotland*, [ed. Sir David Dalrymple] (Edinburgh, 1766), pp. 29–30. Henry Brooke, eighth Lord Cobham, was Cecil's former brother-in-law. Cobham and Ralegh were Essex's most bitter enemies and the Earl believed that they actually intended to murder him in early 1601. Henry Percy, ninth Earl of Northumberland, was Essex's brother-in-law. With Essex gone, Northumberland clumsily aspired to dominate James's future government at the expense of Cecil.

90 BL, Cotton MS Titus C VI, fol. 383r. Howard's mention of 'the gallant Cobham' here is, of course, sarcastic.

91 ibid., fol. 388r. There is an inaccurate and incomplete transcription of this passage in *The life and letters of Sir Walter Ralegh*, ed. E. Edwards, 2 vols (London, 1868), II, 440.

92 Assuming that these notes reflect what he actually told Cecil, Howard may perhaps have raised the issue of Essex's fall to indicate indirectly that he did not blame Cecil for the Earl's demise.

93 M. Nicholls, 'Two Winchester Trials: The Prosecution of Henry, Lord Cobham, and Thomas, Lord Grey of Wilton, 1603'. *Historical Research*, 68 (1995), 26–48, and idem, *Investigating Gunpowder Plot* (Manchester, 1991), *passim*.

94 HMC, *Report on the Manuscripts of the Family of Gawdy, formerly of Norfolk* (London, 1885), p. 88. One of the nephews whom Howard presented to the King on this occasion was Lord William Howard, from whose library Howard's notebooks ultimately came to the University of Durham in 1992. Another nephew of Howard's nephews, Thomas Lord Howard of Walden, was promptly created Lord Chamberlain and Earl of Suffolk.

95 For example, Howard's concern for noble virtue and to prevent the depraving of 'good desert' was strongly reflected in his 1613 treatise against duelling. Ironically, this tract made him a target for public criticism by Francis Bacon: Peltonen, 'Francis Bacon, the Earl of Northampton and the Jacobean Anti-Duelling Campaign', pp. 1–28.

96 Peck, 'Mentality', *passim.*

Lancelot Andrewes's 'Orphan Lectures': The Exeter Manuscript

P. G. Stanwood

There has recently come to light an early seventeenth-century manuscript of Lancelot Andrewes's *Apospasmatia SACRA:* or *A Collection of posthumous and orphan lectures.*[1] For the first and only time published in 1657—some thirty years after Andrewes's death in 1626—their authorial integrity has ever since been in doubt. In a hastily contrived preface, the notable Laudian Thomas Pierce declared '*that this* Volumne *of* Notes *was only taken by the* Eare *from the* voluble Tongue *of the* Dictator, *as he deliver'd them out of the* Pulpit; *and so are infinitely* short *of their* original perfection'. Pierce continues painstakingly to discredit these 'Notes', which, had he been consulted, would not have appeared. In reflecting and extending this judgement, James Bliss rejects the 'Orphan Lectures' for inclusion in the eleven volume edition of Andrewes's *Works* in The Library of Anglo-Catholic Theology, noting that 'there does not appear to be sufficient evidence to justify one in ascribing these sermons, at least in their present form, to Bishop Andrewes'.[2] Thus this substantial body of work, comprising over 700 octavo pages, has remained marginal to most students of Andrewes.[3]

In recounting the early years of Andrewes's life, Henry Isaacson, his amanuensis and biographer, declares 'that in S. Paul's Church . . . he read the lecture thrice a-week in the term time' besides often preaching at St Giles'.[4] The only record that we have had until now of these lectures and sermons is provided by the 'Orphan Lectures', a systematic study and exegesis of the first four chapters of Genesis, verse by verse, as well as a number of homilies on various other texts from both Old and New Testaments. Most of these exegetical or homiletic sections are extensive, carefully wrought, fully coherent, and entirely characteristic of Andrewes's unmistakable style. The notion that any of them might have been the notes of an auditor is most improbable, though one might accept the possibility that Andrewes considered expanding or revising them.[5]

The manuscript of the 'Orphan Lectures' that I have examined gives unique testimony to the authenticity of this work and firmly corroborates its authorial integrity. Now privately held in Exeter, its present owner took possession of the manuscript at the closure of the Presbyterian College in Carmarthen in the early 1960s, and it has remained with him since that time. How it came to be in Carmarthen is unclear; but two loose leaves, evidently preliminary, offer some glimpse of provenance. On the first, an endorsement, almost illegible, in an early seventeenth-century hand identifies the manuscript: 'The most lerned [. . . two indecipherable words] / Docter Andrewes Sermons in Paules 1591 / when he was appointed to Preach the / Divinitye lecture for 3 yeares together in the 4 Termes // [the numeral '4' was inserted by a different hand, probably much later]. And in St Gyles [parish?] 1597. 1598. 1599./ ' Below is a later inscription, signed by one 'Daniel Hollingworth': 'This booke I giue unto my Grand Nephew Mr John Cholmeley for ever.' Below Hollingworth's signature is yet a further and much later assignment of the book, which begins with the date 'August 8. 1754. Given by Nicolas Styleman (of Snetsham in Norf.) Esqr. to John Jones'[6]. This leaf was at some time pasted to the inside of the (now loose) front cover, and its verso has a pencilled date, 'Jan. 22. 1598[?99]'.

The second of these loose leaves gives a fuller statement by Daniel Hollingworth, in his hand: 'To my Deare beloued Mr John / Chomely the younger my young Nephew / Sir Paule Pinder that was Ambassader / Near xx yeares in Turkey famose in the / Turkish History had and [Bouand?] this book And / Docter Hacket of St Andrewes in Holborne hath / Tould mee, *Neuer a Devine in England / Could Capp: Sir Paule Pinder in purest Christianitie / And he with his owne hands gaue to the / poure & to Hospitalls & to Churches & / Bulding of Paules in his owne dayes with his owne hands / Fortie Thousand Pounds And had noe / Pictshure in his house But the Pictshure / of Docter Andrewes And hath oft sayd / To mee, That since St Pauls dayes / The Church of God had Neuer / his Fellow. //* soe say I think.' Hollingworth's name appears below this inscription, but in the hand perhaps of the recipient, who glosses the proper names 'Hacket', 'Andrews', and 'Pindar', quoting from *Treatise of Temples*, 1638, chap. 25.[7]

One may reasonably presume that 'this book' refers to the manuscript that Hollingworth was giving to his nephew. This single loose leaf might once have been part, not of the present manuscript, but of one that now survives only in four pages (or the two leaves of one folio sheet) of prefatory matter which must have been copied much later—perhaps mid-century—from the principal manuscript under discussion, or else another like it (see PLATE 1). The reference to Pindar's having been already in Turkey would place the Exeter Manuscript sometime between 1609 and 1623 (somewhat short of twenty years), the time when Pindar was engaged in his various foreign missions. But of course we do not know that Pindar had 'this book' with him when he was abroad, or whether he acquired it after he returned and retained it for years afterward (he died in 1650)—nor do we know how Pindar came to have the manuscript in the first place or exactly how he disposed of it. Yet to judge only from the scribal and orthographic appearance of the manuscript itself, one concludes that it was written within the first quarter of the century, possibly as early as 1600. It would be pleasing to think that Pindar carried it with him on his travels, an unprovable but perfectly credible possibility.

The Exeter Manuscript begins with folio 2r, the first folio sheet in fact being the one that contains the earliest inscription, 'Doctor Andrewes Sermons . . . ' that forms the paste-down on the inside of the front cover, that is, folio 1r, and with the pencilled date '1598[?99]' on the verso. The leaf in Hollingworth's hand that describes Sir Paul Pindar's ownership of the Exeter Manuscript might have become detached and offered as a preliminary leaf to a second manuscript, now lost, that includes only four prefatory pages. The surviving pages (of this one folio sheet) still retain fragments in the gutter of the binding thread. Certainly we do have what seems to be the beginning of a second manuscript; the hand is obviously much later than that of Exeter (see PLATE 2).

Measurements of the Exeter Manuscript (and also of the single loose leaf) are 290 × 195 mm. (pot folio). There are 276 folios; the final one, folio 276r is a paste-down on the end cover. Five leaves have been cut out at 243v–244r. The gatherings are bound up variously, in six, seven, or often nine folio sheets. At the beginning of the manuscript are the lectures at St Paul's, from f. 2r to 228r; 228v is blank; a different scribe begins at f. 229r, with the earlier lectures at St Giles', and with some repetition of material that has appeared earlier in the manuscript. Compared with the printed text of 1657, the Exeter Manuscript employs throughout orthography and scribal forms of the earlier seventeenth century. There are numerous variants, chiefly of an accidental rather than a substantive kind; but several sections are unique to this manuscript, or else greatly altered in the printing. Notable amongst these sections is Andrewes's sermon on the Apocalypse, misplaced in 1657, but remarkable for its author's discussion of eucharistic doctrine (see PLATE 3).

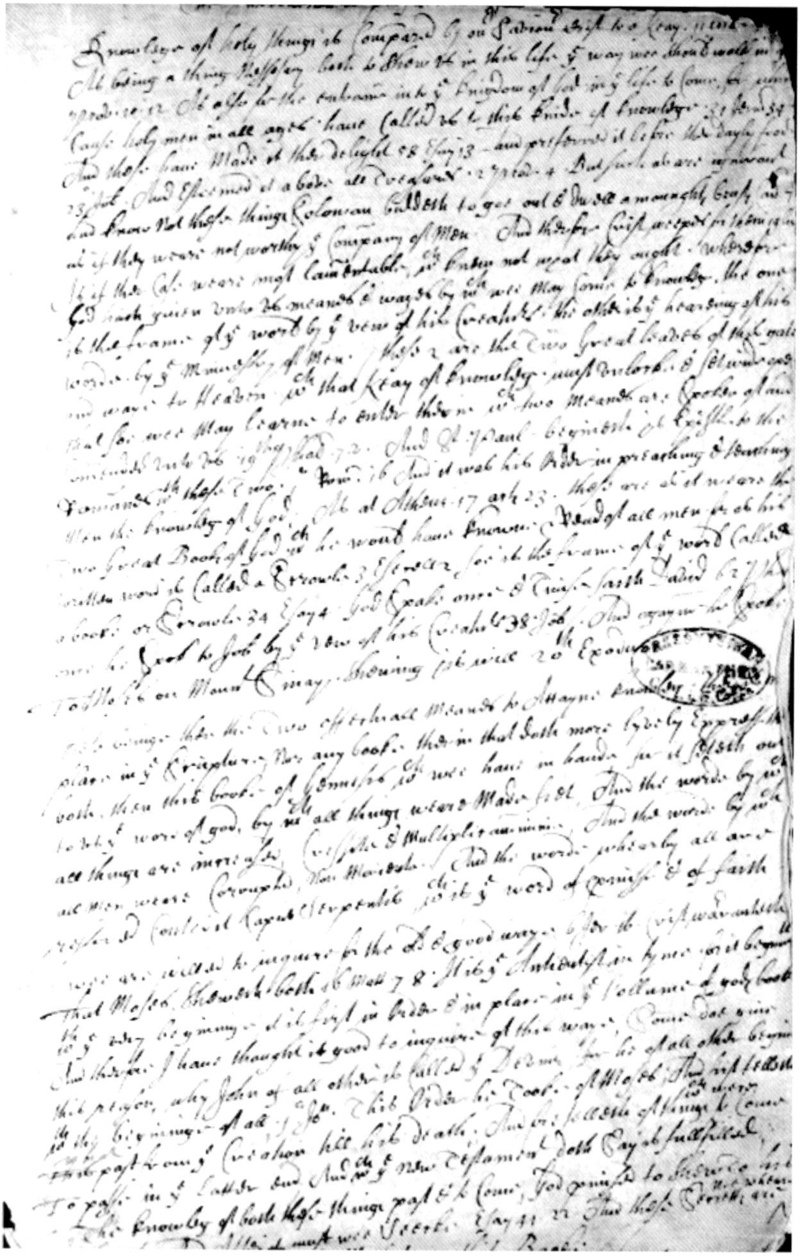

PLATE I. *The opening page of the loose leaf accompanying the Exeter Manuscript (Original page size 290 × 195mm.) Reproduced by permission of Professor Ivan Roots.*

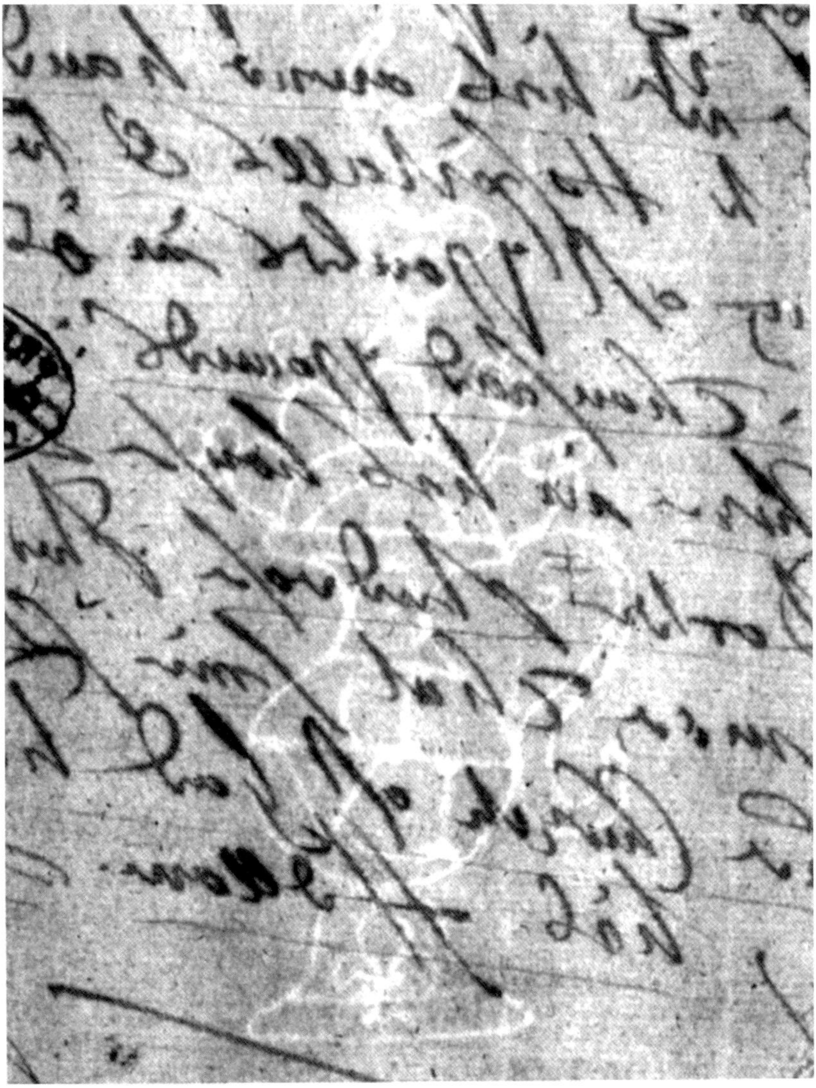

PLATE 2. *Watermark of the loose leaf accompanying the Exeter Manuscript (similar to Heawood 3616, c.1644–6), the same watermark appearing also in the preliminary, detached page (Original page size 290 × 195mm.) Reproduced by permission of Professor Ivan Roots.*

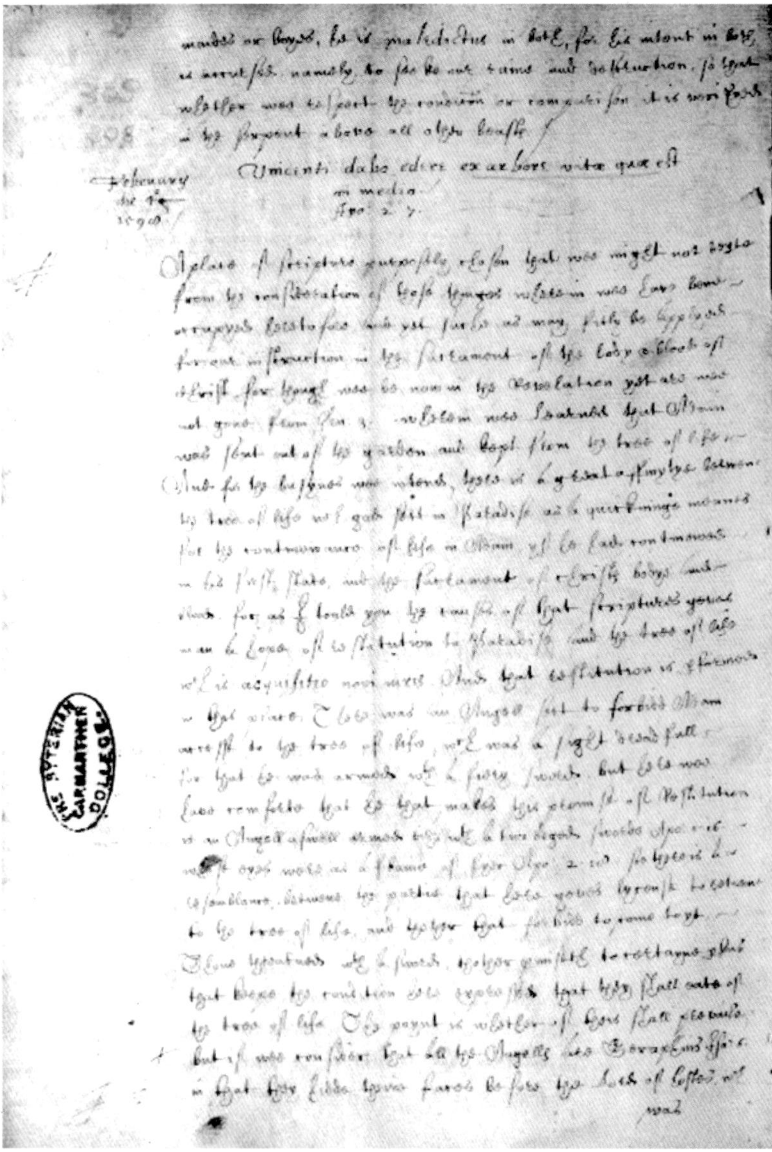
Vincenti dabo edere ex arbore vitae quae est
in medio
Apo: 2. 7.

PLATE 3. *Folio 146v of the Exeter Manuscript, with the beginning of the sermon on Revelation, in the hand of the principal scribe, whose work appears on ff. 2r–228r, the hatchmarks that appear randomly in the margin being a curious feature of this part of the manuscript (Original page size 290 × 195mm.) Reproduced by permission of Professor Ivan Roots.*

COMPARISON WITH THE PRINTED VERSION

The relationship of manuscript to printed text is complicated, but the following comparison of the two indicates principal differences.

The manuscript opens with 'Knowledge of holy things is Compared by our Saviour Christ to a Keay', which appears in the Addenda of 1657 (pp. 657 ff.), ff. 2r–v. Then follow the lectures on Genesis, preached at St Paul's:

Gen. 1.1–11	3r–37r
12	37r–v
14	37v–38v
16–30	38v–48r

Manuscript and printed text are very different from verse 12 on. There is no manuscript text for verses 13, 15, or 31; but 1657 continues the sequence from verses 12–31 without interruption.

Gen. 2 begins at 48r.

1–19	48r–107r
21–24	107r–114v

Gen.2.20 is missing from the manuscript, which continues with Gen. 2.21 through 2.24, where this section ends; but 1657 continues through verse 25, that is, the end of chap. 2.

Gen. 3.1–5	114v–125v
6	Omitted from the MS
7	125v–128r
8–14	128r–146v

Apoc. 2.7 146v–150v

The date '9.Aug:1620./' appears in the margin of 128r, at the beginning of the lecture on Gen.3.8, in a hand different from that of the scribe, but contemporary with it. At this point, the manuscript ends Gen. 3 with verse 14 (ff.. 141r–146v); however, it then gives Andrewes's lecture on Revelation 2.7 (ff. 146v–150v), which 1657 removes to the concluding section of homilies 'preached upon severall choice Texts' (pp. 572–8). Now 1657 continues to the end of Gen.3 (that is, verse 24). And ff. 229r–276r, in the hand of a different but contemporary scribe, complete these verses of Gen.3, beginning with (and repeating the discussion of) verse 14.

Gen. 4.1–26 150v–228r The lower half of 228r is blank; 228v is also blank.

This section of the manuscript is very carefully copied, and the printed text follows it closely, but with many accidental variants. Also, the verse headings are all from the Vulgate; earlier sections are inconsistent in this usage.

The manuscript continues with 229r, in a different but similar hand, and concludes at 276r.

Folio 229r is headed: 'Mr. Doctor Andrewes Sermons at S^t^. Giles without Criplegate.' (see PLATES 4 and 5)

Gen. 3.14[1] 229r–234r [in margin: 'Junij die 18 1598']
The copy is identical with ff. 141r–146v, the first part of Gen. 3.4: 'Then the Lord god saide to the serpent because thou hast done this thou art cursed above all Cattaile and every beast of the feild.'

Gen. 3.14[2] 234v–239r [in margin: 'Junij die 25 1598']
The second part of the verse, appearing also in 1657: 'Uppon thy belly shalt thou goe and dust shalt thou eate all the dayes of thy life.'

Gen. 3.15[1] 239r–243v [in margin: 'Julij die 2°. 1598'] 'I will alsoe putt enmitye betwene thee and the woeman and betwene her seede and thy seede.' [In 1657]

Gen. 3.15[2] 243v–246v [in margin: 'Aug. 20. 1598']
The second part of the verse, appearing also in 1657: 'He shall breake thyne head, and thou shalt bruise his heele.' [The lectures for Gen. 3.14 and 15 have been detached from the regular sequence in 1657, and misplaced at the end of the volume. Five leaves have been cut out from the manuscript between 243v and 244r; only a few lines on Gen.3.15 remain at the bottom of 243v, but a substantial portion of what may belong to the lecture on Gen.3.16 remains as 244r–246v.

Gen. 3.16 *'Unto the woman he said, I will greatly multiply thy sorrow and thy conception; in sorrow thou shalt bring forth children; and thy desire shall be to thy husband, and he shall rule over thee' (KJV).*
What remains of this lecture, which is decidedly about the scriptural text, is quite different from what occurs in 1657. Andrewes writes with expansive vigour, in a fashion reminiscent of his lecture on Gen. 2.18, about the creation of Eve.

Gen. 3.17–24 246v–276r
Apart from conventions of orthography and punctuation, the printed text follows the manuscript closely. Yet 1657 would seem to have been set from a different manuscript (or several manuscripts?).

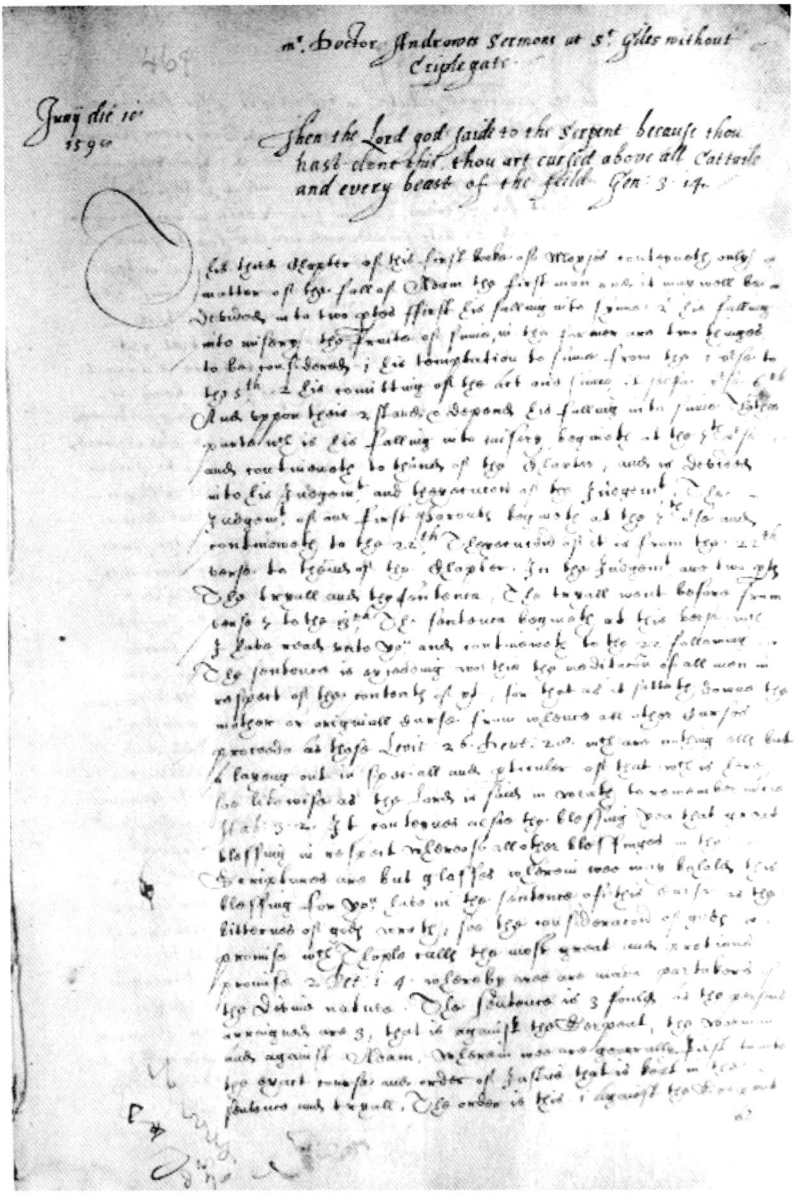
mr. Doctor Andrewes Sermons at St. Giles without Criplegate.

Junij die 10 1590

Then the Lord god saide to the Serpent because thou hast done this, thou art cursed above all Cattaile and every beast of the feilde Gen: 3. 14.

PLATE 4. *Folio 229r of the Exeter Manuscript, where a different scribe takes over and continues to the end of the volume (f. 276r), this page beginning the repetition of ff. 141r–146v with numerous minor differences (Original page size 290 × 195 mm.) Reproduced by permission of Professor Ivan Roots.*

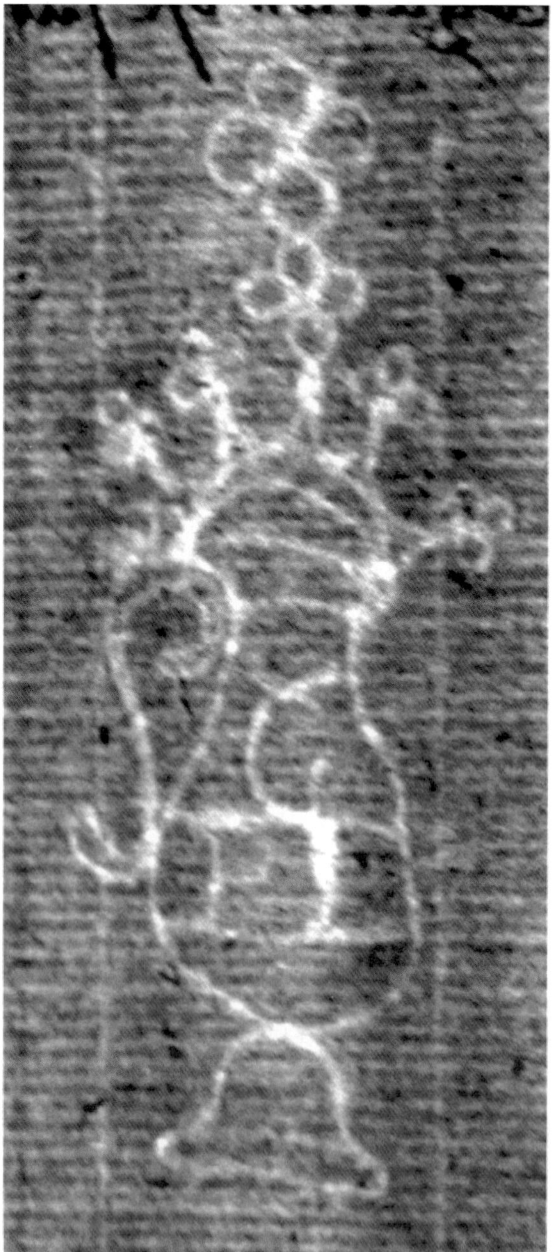

PLATE 5. *Watermark of fol. 228r, the paper stock common to the entire bound volume (Original page size 290 × 195 mm.) Reproduced by permission of Professor Ivan Roots.*

CONCLUSION

The existence of the Exeter Manuscript, a volume, which, as we have seen, contains two different though contemporaneous versions of the 'Orphan Lectures', as well as the fragment of still another manuscript in yet a further and third hand, suggests that more manuscripts may yet come to light; for Andrewes's lectures and sermons of his early career must have enjoyed some circulation— how widely we cannot, of course, know. Of interest also is the fact that 1657 is incomplete, obviously hastily compiled from a manuscript (or manuscripts) that were conveniently at hand, or readily available to Thomas Pierce and such loyal printers as Moseley and Royston. Yet in missing or confusing the sections that do appear in the Exeter Manuscript, the printers cause one to query how else they might have been misled. The sermon on Revelation 2.7, for example, is especially significant; for in it Andrewes is developing his 'high' view of the eucharist with considerations 'suche as may fitly be applied for instruction in the sacrament of the body & blood of Christ'[8] , yet the sermon is relegated to the miscellaneous section following the discourses on Genesis (beginning at p. 515). Clearly, a new edition of the 'Orphan Lectures' is needed that will bring together all the material that we now possess. Such an edition should allow full comparison of manuscript to printed text and thus help also to illuminate Andrewes's own practises of composition and doctrinal belief.[9]

NOTES

1 'Delivered at St. Pauls and St. Giles his Church'... Never before extant... London, Printed by *R. Hodgkinsonne*, for *H. Moseley, A. Crooke, D. Pakeman, L. Fawne, R. Royston,* and *N. Ekins*. 1657.

2 See Andrewes, *Works,* vol. 11: *Two Answers to Cardinal Perron, and Other Miscellaneous Works* (Oxford, 1854), p. lxxvii. But see Arthur T. Russell, *Memoirs of the Life and Works of . . . Lancelot Andrewes* (Cambridge, 1860): 'A careful perusal of the ["Orphan Lectures"] would have led the editor [i.e. Thomas Pierce] . . . into the full conviction that the substance of the volume was attributable only to Andrewes' (pp. 382–3).

3 But see Peter McCullough's recent edition, *Lancelot Andrewes: Selected Sermons and Lectures* (Oxford, 2005), which includes two complete items from 1657: 'A Lecture on Genesis 2.18 delivered at St Paul's, 18 October 1591'; and 'A Sermon on Isaiah 6.6–7, Preached at St Giles Cripplegate, 1 October 1598'. The sermon on Isaiah is one of several on various texts—but not from Genesis—given from 1598–1600. See McCullough's introduction, pp. xvii–xx, and especially his commentary on these two sermons, pp. 353–65, 378–90.

4 See *Works,* cited in n. 2, p. viii.

5 See P. J. Klemp, '"Betwixt the Hammer and the Anvill": Lancelot Andrewes's Revision Techniques in the Manuscript of His 1620 Easter Sermon', *Papers of the Bibliographical Society of America* 89 (1995): 149–82, on Cambridge, Trinity College MS B.14.22. This miscellany contains a copy of the Easter sermon in the hand of Andrewes's secretary Samuel Wright, much annotated and corrected by Andrewes.

6 An additional, but misleading note likely in John Jones's hand, appears at the bottom of this leaf, probably for his own information: 'N.B. These Lectures upon the beginning of Genesis do not appear amongst the printed works of Bp. Andrews, nor are they mentioned in the Biographia Britannica, in the account of his Life & Writings there set down, unless they are the Apospasmatia mentioned in Not[e]. H. art[icle]. 16.' Indeed, there is a mention of the 'Orphan Lectures' in the several editions of *Biographia Britannica* (London, 1747–66, 1778–93, etc.), correctly cited here.

7 *De Templis, A Treatise of Temples* (London, 1638), by 'R. T.' Chapter 25, near the end of the book, treats 'Of the rewards which such receive, who build and adorn Churches'. The quotation from Pindar appears on pp. 230–1.

8 In this sermon (or 'lecture'), Andrewes carefully develops the typology of the Tree of Life as a restorative means of grace. See MS f. 146r: 'though wee be now in the Revelation yet are wee not gone from Gen: 3: wherein wee learned that Adam was sent out of the garden and kept from the tree of life. . . . [T]here is a great affinytye betwene the tree of life wch god sett in Paradise as a quickininge meanes for the continewance of life in Adam . . . [for] restitution to Paradise and the tree of life . . . is performed in this place [Rev. 2.7]'.

9 A list and description of Andrewes's known manuscripts appears in Peter Beal, *Index of English Literary Manuscripts,* vol. I, part 1 (London, 1980), pp. 3–11, currently being revised for the database *CELM.* See also H.R. Woodhuysen, 'Manuscripts at Auction: January 1993 to December 1994', in *English Manuscript Studies 1100–1700* 6 (1997), p. 253, items 3 and 4 (19 July 1994). A careful comparison of the many and different scribes of all Andrewes's known manuscripts (not only of the Exeter Manuscript) would probably be helpful in establishing a genealogy of manuscripts and their transmission. But identification of scribal hands is very difficult. My observations are presently limited; but I am quite sure that the examples provided by the Exeter Manuscript do not reveal the hand of such familiar figures as Henry Isaacson, Samuel Wright, or the scribe or scribes of the several sermons in Cambridge, Emmanuel College MS 3.1.13.

Cecil and the Soul: Donne's *Metempsychosis* in its Context in Folger Manuscript V.a.241

Lara M. Crowley

Readers have debated the identity of 'he whose life yow shall find in the end of this booke', the final inhabitant of the 'Deathles Soule' in John Donne's *Metempsychosis*, since the seventeenth century.[1] Ben Jonson held that the soul rested in Calvin, and Edmund Gosse, owner of one of the few extant seventeenth-century manuscript copies of *Metempsychosis*, later claimed that Elizabeth hosted the soul. Few critics have challenged Gosse's interpretation, but Brian Mark Blackley convincingly argues, in agreement with M. van Wyk Smith and Dennis Flynn, that the 'he' (not 'she') whom Donne discusses cannot possibly be Elizabeth but is, in fact, 'the manipulator behind the throne, Robert Cecil'.[2] Donne, not surprisingly, never names the conniving Cecil; as of August 1601 Donne still maintained promise of political advancement. Due to disagreements about this unnamed object of ridicule and other contested elements of *Metempsychosis*, Blackley proposes, 'the work has tested its readers and the readers have been inadequate, possibly through misreading symbols or ignorance of some coding of his language that has been lost since Elizabethan times. But Donne has disguised his meaning so well that even his contemporaries might not have perceived all of the work's potential'.[3]

But can we determine how contemporary readers interpreted a Renaissance poem? We have extant letters by poets and readers of verse that throw light on their understanding of certain poems, but Donne reminds us that letters, like other forms of written material, are 'permanent' and therefore potentially dangerous; he tells Henry Goodyer, 'in them I may speak to you in your chamber a year hence before I know not whom, and not hear my self'.[4] The self-censoring required of Renaissance letter-writers challenges our capacity to use epistolary remarks as interpretive tools for verse, especially verse with possible political implications. We are further challenged in having so few

Renaissance interpretations available. Even though examples of specific literary criticism in letters, marginalia, and similar forms of evidence in the period are comparatively rare and frequently ambiguous due to their personal cryptic and encoded nature, we fortunately have another means to access contemporary literary interpretations: the manuscript contexts of the works.

Gosse's copy of *Metempsychosis*, found in Folger Manuscript V.a.241, can provide evidence, even if indirect, that at least one of Donne's contemporaries read *Metempsychosis* as a political satire. Clues exist within the accompanying manuscript contents, which, it seems, were carefully and purposefully grouped. That the collector found connections between *Metempsychosis* and the other works in the manuscript is evident from what Neil Fraistat has called 'contexture'—the arrangement of the book itself and each poem's relationship to its surrounding verse.[5] Though scholars have demonstrated the value of 'contexture' study for many published books, 'contexture' of Renaissance manuscript collections has not been thoroughly considered, mainly because authors often had little, if anything, to do with their preparation. However, the process of analyzing manuscript 'contexture' may allow for valuable insights into Renaissance verse, as the case of *Metempsychosis* in V.a.241 demonstrates.

THE MANUSCRIPT

Folger MS V.a.241[6] is a quarto of 69 leaves, pp. [*34*] 1–100, 110–111 [*2*] with the collation $[a]^{12}[b]^{4}[c]^{6}(+[c]_{7})[d–o]^{4}(+[o]_{5})[p]^{4}$.[7] Folios 23 and 68 seem to be singletons, and folio 69 is tipped in.[8] The contents of this composite manuscript consist of three primary sections: *Metempsychosis* (3r–16v); English translations of six dialogues attributed to the Greek satirist Lucian (17v–67v); and a potentially unfinished fable entitled 'The Tale of the Fauorite' (67v–68v).[9] 2r and 17r are title-pages written in a hybrid secretary display script (possibly in the same hand): 2r reads 'Dr: Donnes Μετεμφύχωοις. with. Certaine select Dialogues, of Lucian. and The Tale of The Fauorite' (PLATE 1), and 17r announces only the first of the six dialogues: 'I. The Dialogue of Truth:' (PLATE 2). There is evidence in the manuscript of pricking and ruling,[10] and margins are ruled in a sepia ink in folios containing *Metempsychosis* but not in those containing the first dialogue; another form of sepia ink frames the remainder of the manuscript.[11] No catchwords are found in folios 1–17, but folios 18–68 contain catchwords and contemporary pagination in brown ink.

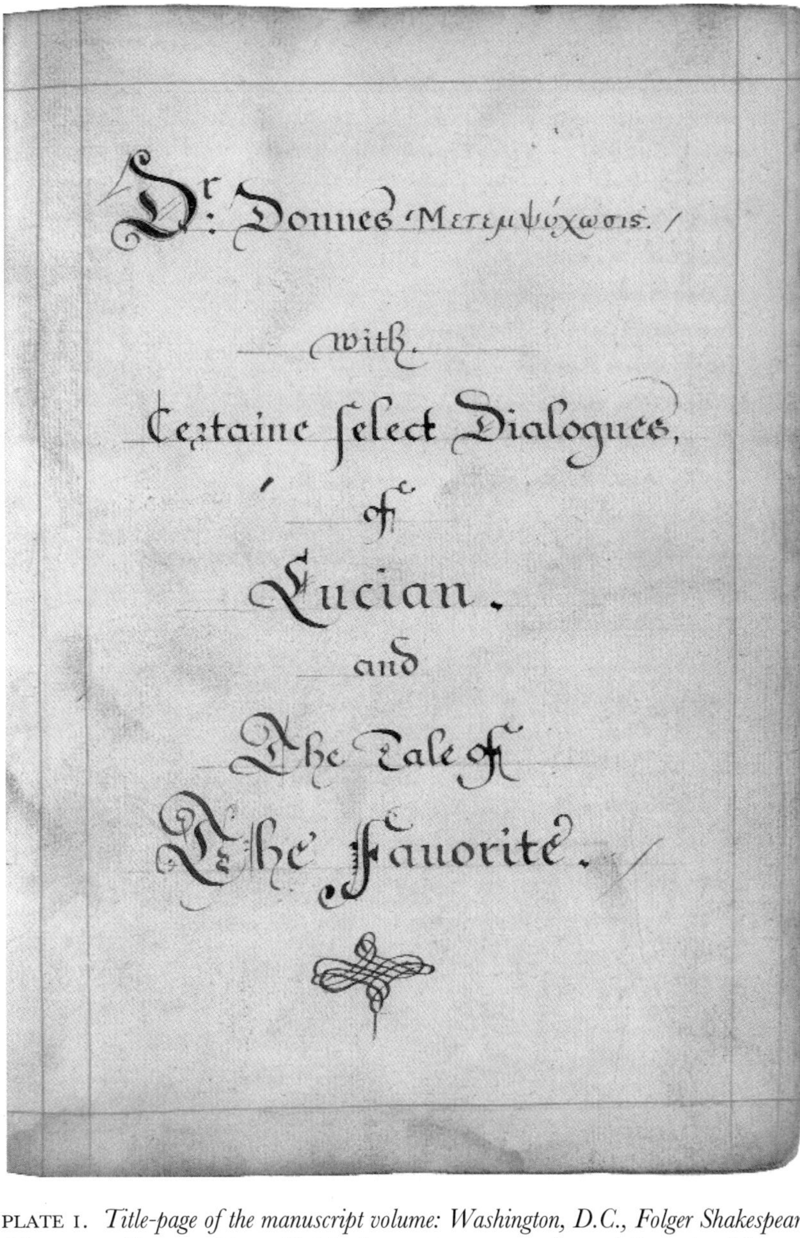

Dr: Donnes Μετεμψύχωσις.

with

Certaine select Dialogues,

of

Lucian.

and

The Tale of

The Fauorite.

PLATE 1. *Title-page of the manuscript volume: Washington, D.C., Folger Shakespeare Library,* MS *V.a.241, fol. 2r (Original page size 225 × 160mm.) Reproduced by permission of the Folger Shakespeare Library.*

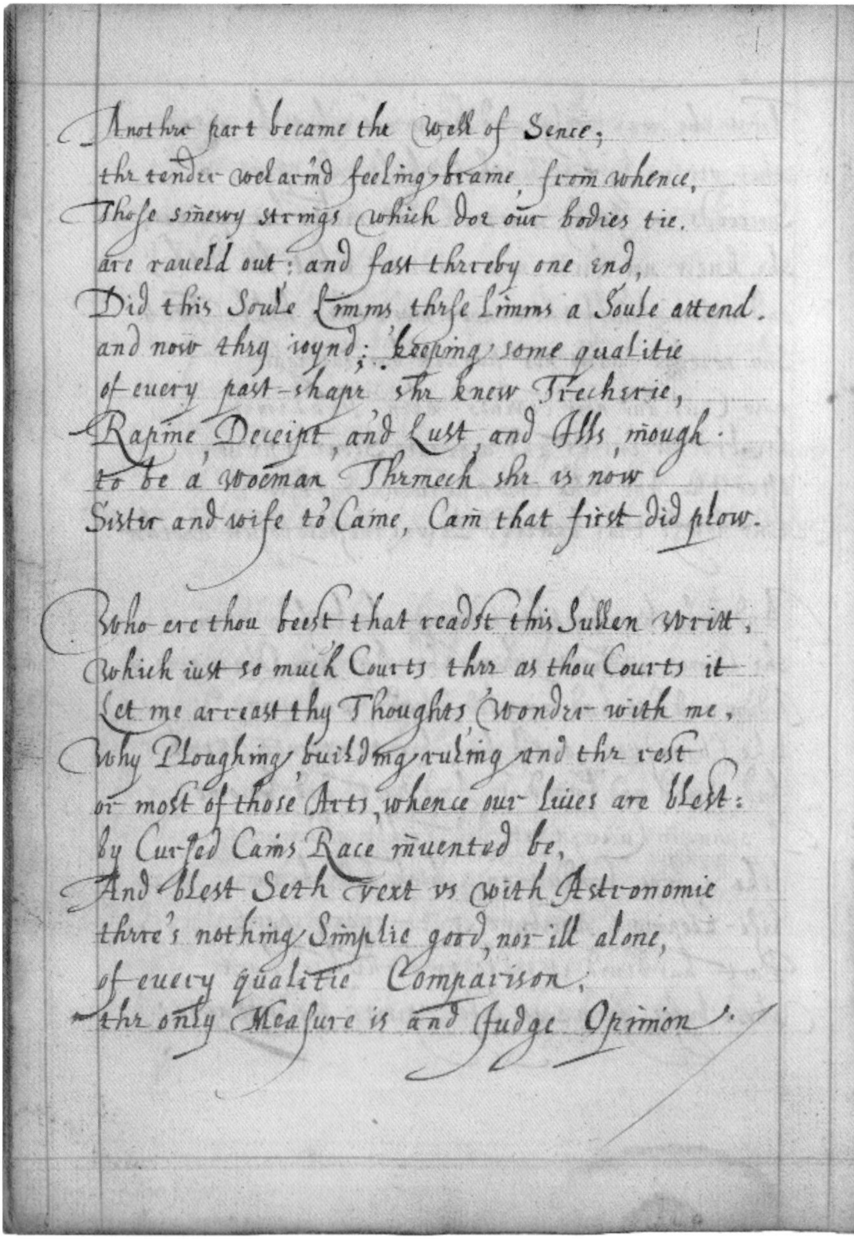

Another part became the Well of Sence,
the tender well arm'd feeling braine, from whence,
Those sinewy strings which doe our bodies tie.
are raueld out; and fast thereby one end,
Did this Soule limms, these limms a Soule attend.
and now they ioynd; keeping some qualitie
of euery past shape she knew Trecherie,
Rapine, Deceipt, and Lust, and Ills enough
to be a woeman Themech she is now
Sister and wife to Caine, Cain that first did plow.

Who ere thou beest that readst this Sullen writt,
which iust so much Courts thee as thou Courts it
Let me arrest thy Thoughts, wonder with me,
Why Ploughing, building, ruling and the rest
or most of those Arts, whence our liues are blest:
by Cursed Cains Race invented be,
And blest Seth vext vs with Astronomie
there's nothing Simplie good, nor ill alone,
of euery qualitie Comparison,
the only Measure is and Judge Opinion.

PLATE 2. *Final stanzas of* Metempsychosis *and title-page for the first dialogue: Washington, D.C., Folger Shakespeare Library,* MS *V.a.241, fols 16v–17r (Original page size 225 × 160mm.) Reproduced by permission of the Folger Shakespeare Library.*

1. /

The Dialogue of Truth :- /

There are at least three scripts present in the primary sections of the manuscript. *Metempsychosis* is written in an elegant italic script and consistently appears as two stanzas per page, ten lines per stanza. Folios 18r–23v contain the first dialogue in a traditional secretary script with approximately 29–32 lines per page, while folios 24r–67v present the remaining five Lucian dialogues in another secretary script with approximately 32 lines per page; the concluding 'Tale of the Fauorite' (67v–68v) is also written in this second secretary script. All six dialogues are provided with prefatory arguments written in an italic script, probably by the person who also employed the second secretary script.[12]

There appear to be two different papers present in the manuscript, those of folios 1–23 and 24–68. There are horizontal chain lines on all leaves: the chain lines are approximately 30mm apart in folios 1–23 and approximately 26mm apart in folios 24–68 and the three endleaves.[13] Although watermarks are difficult to discern in some sections, the watermark present in folios 1–23 is a circle, while the watermark in folios 24–68 is a large coat of arms.[14] In addition to differences in watermarks and chain lines, the variations in marginal borders, ruling, and pricking in these sections indicate that two separate papers were brought together to form this composite book. But unused sewing holes in folios 17–23 suggest that the first dialogue and its title-page were bound together previously as a separate booklet.

In addition to the primary sections, the manuscript contains two other works. The text filling both sides of folio 69 is a two-page essay entitled 'Concerning Tragedy' in a late italic hand suggesting eighteenth-century composition. The leaf appears to have been accidentally inverted when it was tipped in so that the verso page should be recto.[15] There is also a small leaf tipped in between folios 43 and 44 that contains a six-line satiric poem about lawyers written in an italic script.[16]

Regarding the binding, the book was rebacked, probably during the nineteenth century: its original brown calfskin boards have a simple blind tooling of triple-lined fillet around the border made by an egg/oval head roll. The later spine reads 'D^R. DONNE'S METEMSYCHOSIS.— M. S.' tooled in gold letters within a dotted tooling around the border made by a gilt pinhead rope and an anthemion-crowned floret stamp at the top, with evidence of one at the bottom.[17]

As for provenance of the manuscript, Gosse dates it to the first quarter of the seventeenth century from the evidence of the scripts and stocks of papers. The manuscript's Latin inscription 'Liber Rogeri Bradon. / Queritur Ægestas quapropter factus Adulter / in promptu. causa est, desidiosus erat' (1r) indicates the earliest known owner of this manuscript: Roger Bradon circa 1620. The manuscript was later in the collection of Sir Thomas Phillipps (1792–1872), being Phillipps MS 18640, and was acquired in one of the subsequent Phillipps sales by Gosse.[18] The manuscript was included in the Gosse estate sale of 1929, and the Folger Shakespeare Library purchased it from Stevens and Brown in 1941.

METEMPSYCHOSIS IN MANUSCRIPTS

V.a.241 contains one of the eight extant manuscript copies of *Metempsychosis* and a reasonably dependable reading text of the poem. Although editors once discredited this version as unreliable,[19] Herbert J. C. Grierson chose to incorporate readings from V.a.241 into his edition of *Metempsychosis* and was followed by John T. Shawcross and W. Milgate.[20] Milgate suggests that this version of the poem, which he calls 'G', and another version of the poem 'H' (British Library, Harley Manuscript 3998) descend from a common original manuscript source with peculiar readings not contained in the source of the other manuscript copies.[21] He argues that the other six manuscript versions ultimately derive from a 'common source, a copy of the poem that was in some ways defective and that could not have been the source of either *G* or *H*'.[22] The V.a.241 version, Milgate suggests, was 'made with only reasonable care' and is therefore more appropriate to consult for 'correction of the deficiencies in the large collections'. However, he believes that 'G' preserves the only right reading of line 137 ('to see the Prince, and haue soe fild the way' [7r]) and that there are 'Twenty other readings G shares only with H, of which most are certainly right, and none can be proved wrong'.[23]

But, 'right' readings aside, this version of *Metempsychosis* compels our interest on other grounds: its manuscript context. At first the contents appear totally unrelated, works copied in several scripts on distinct papers that were grouped and bound by chance. Unrelated materials were often gathered in manuscript books in this way, as seen in Harley MS 3998. An incomplete version of *Metempsychosis* written in a neat italic hand is found on folios 154–67, between a series of short essays in another hand on various matters, such as bowling, and a letter in yet another hand regarding the Oath of Conformity.[24] No other poetic pieces are included in the manuscript, and there is no apparent reason for the grouping of its contents.

Folger MS V.a.241 is different: material details suggest that a collector assembled its particular pieces for a purpose. First, the arguments introducing each dialogue standardize the format.[25] As mentioned previously, folios 17–23 seem to have comprised a separate booklet, as demonstrated by unused sewing holes. The scribe who copied dialogues 2–6 and their arguments also added an introductory argument for the first dialogue on 17v; the addition of the argument causes this dialogue to appear to be the first of a unified group. The first dialogue begins at the top of a recto page (18r), while all subsequent dialogues begin just below their arguments (PLATES 3 and 4). Also, 'I.' has been written faintly above the title 'The Dialogue of Truth' (17r), most likely to make this dialogue seem to be only the first of others.

In addition to this attempt to unify the dialogues, a scribe constructed an elaborate title-page (2r) that calls attention to all of the contents of the book. The title-page, inscribed 'Dr: Donnes Μετεμφύχωοις. with. Certaine select Dialogues, of Lucian. and The Tale of The Fauorite', effectively transforms the piecemeal sections of the manuscript into a coherent whole. Such a title-page—created by a scribe in order to draw attention to the book as a deliberately constructed unit—is by no means common among manuscripts. In addition, its language calls attention to the purposeful choice of 'Certaine select' Lucian dialogues for this book; the compiler chose these specific works for a reason.[26]

If these works were purposefully combined, as the title-page and arguments suggest, someone must have seen a connection among these seemingly unrelated works. There are at least three potential links: connections of genre, motif, and theme.

SATIRE

First, the contents chosen for this manuscript clarify this Renaissance reader's understanding of the hotly contested issue of genre in *Metempsychosis*. While the poem has been categorized as 'epic, allegory, mock- or anti-epic, Bartasian parody, formal paradox, and essay', Blackley's argument that the work is a satire is supported by its context in V.a.241: 'the work's true genre is that of satire, and the other prominent characteristics which relate to epic (and mock-epic) are not distinctions of genre, but of mode'.[27] The dialogues that follow *Metempsychosis* in V.a.241 are satirical as well.[28] Lucian of Samosata (*circa* 120–180 C.E.) created a new genre, the satiric dialogue—an invention with elements of the Socratic philosophical dialogue, Old Comedy, and Menippean satire that 'combines the philosophical inquiry of dialogue with the humorous mockery of comedy'.[29] Many of this Second Sophistic period rhetorician's approximately eighty extant works are satiric dialogues, which present an ironic portrait of human degradation in the same vein as *Metempsychosis*, although often through a more light, comedic approach 'to play upon the gap between a concept of normality which writer and audience share, and what passes for normality within the text'.[30] Lucian's views on both philosophy and religion are difficult to pinpoint, but he addresses contemporary issues of morality, spirituality, and social obligations through satire and irony by placing historical type figures into fantastical situations. Lucian, like Donne in *Metempsychosis*, makes no direct reference to historical and cultural politics, but scholars claim that Lucian's contemporaries often would have recognized the inspirations for his stock characters. Although V.a.241 contains six dialogues identified as 'Lucian', the first dialogue[31] is in fact Maffeo Vegio's *Dialogue between Truth and Philalethes*, written in Florence in 1444 but long believed to be Lucian's.[32] The five true Lucian dialogues lack titles in the manuscript but are commonly referred to in modern editions as *Timon the Misanthrope*, *The Cock*, *Charon*, *The Ship*, and *Icaromenippus*.

Through their Latin translations of these and other Lucian dialogues, Thomas More and Erasmus recognized the importance of Lucian's dialogues and helped to promote his reputation in sixteenth-century England;[33] yet, Lucian's influence on Donne has been relatively ignored.[34] Lucian gained popularity in fifteenth-century Italy when Latin translations of the relatively unknown author began to flourish, but Donne's ancestor was the first Englishman to print Latin translations of Lucian (1506).[35] R. Bracht Branham suggests that, at least in More's lifetime, 'he was probably more widely read as the translator of Lucian than the author of *Utopia*'.[36] More's dedicatory letter to Thomas Ruthall and Erasmus's preface to *The Cock* imply their admiration for Lucian's rhetorical abilities and aptitude as a moral philosopher capable of instruction and delight in the Horatian vein, unlike previous Latin translators like Vegio, who 'merely imitated the outward trappings of Lucianic dialogue, such as the mythological settings and interlocutors'.[37] One unpublished study argues that More's and Erasmus's satirical works demonstrate Lucianic influence and that satires by all three authors inspired Donne's verse satires: 'while Donne's direct references to Erasmus and More are infrequent (to Lucian there are none at all), the similarity of Donne's satiric methods to his predecessors' shows his debt to them'.[38] It is possible that a contemporary reader of Donne's verse satires would connect them with Lucian and, specifically, with More's translations because of the family connection and the similar satirical methods. The coupling of *Metempsychosis* with Lucian's satirical dialogues in V.a.241 suggests that its compiler classified the poem as satire.

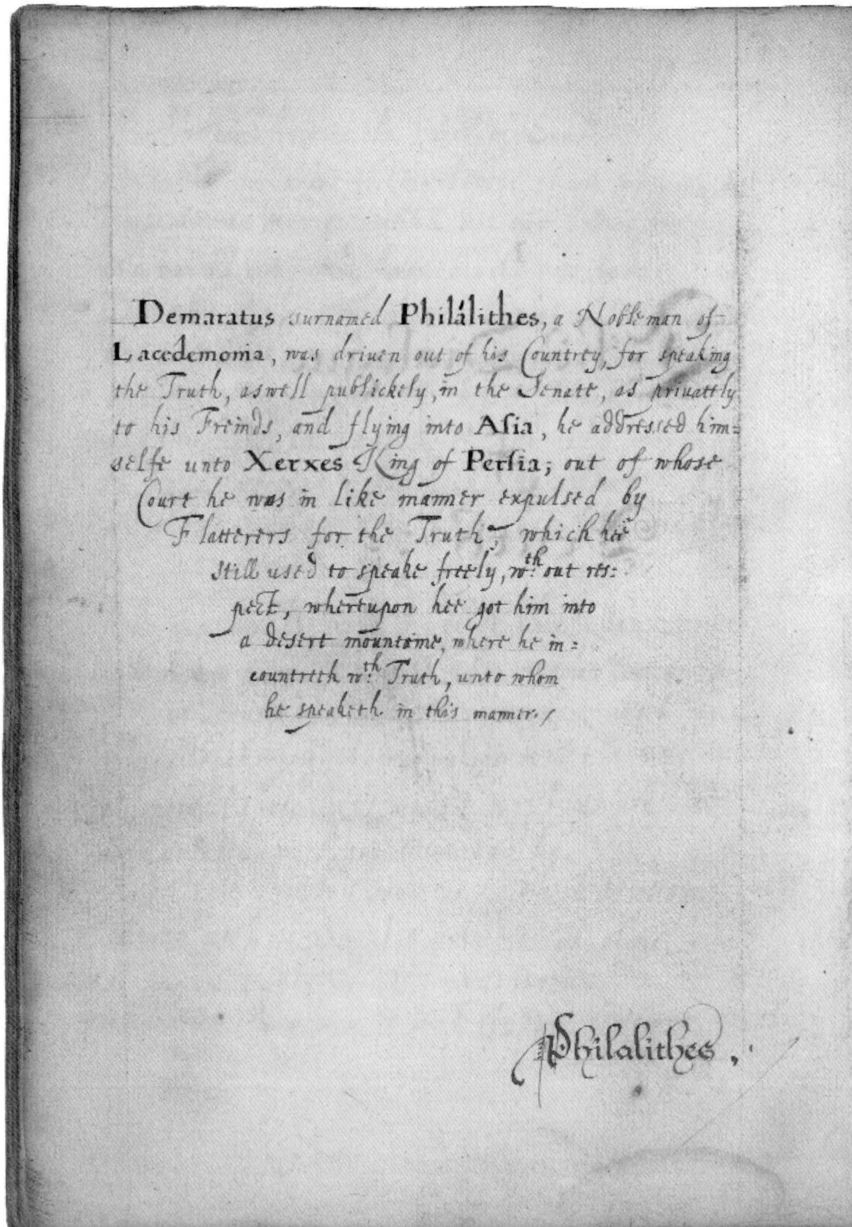
Demaratus surnamed Philálithes, a Nobleman of
Lacedemonia, was driuen out of his Countrey, for speaking
the Truth, aswell publicktly, in the Senatt, as priuattly
to his Friends, and flying into Asia, he addressed him=
selfe unto Xerxes King of Persia; out of whose
Court he was in like manner expulsed by
Flatterers for the Truth, which hee
still used to speake freely, wth out res=
peet, whereupon hee got him into
a desert mountaine, where he in=
countreth wth Truth, unto whom
he speaketh in this manner./

Philalithes,

PLATE 3. *Argument and initial page of the first dialogue, the argument set out on a separate page, unlike subsequent arguments which are each written on the initial page of the dialogue: Washington, D.C., Folger Shakespeare Library, MS V.a.241, fols 17v–18r*

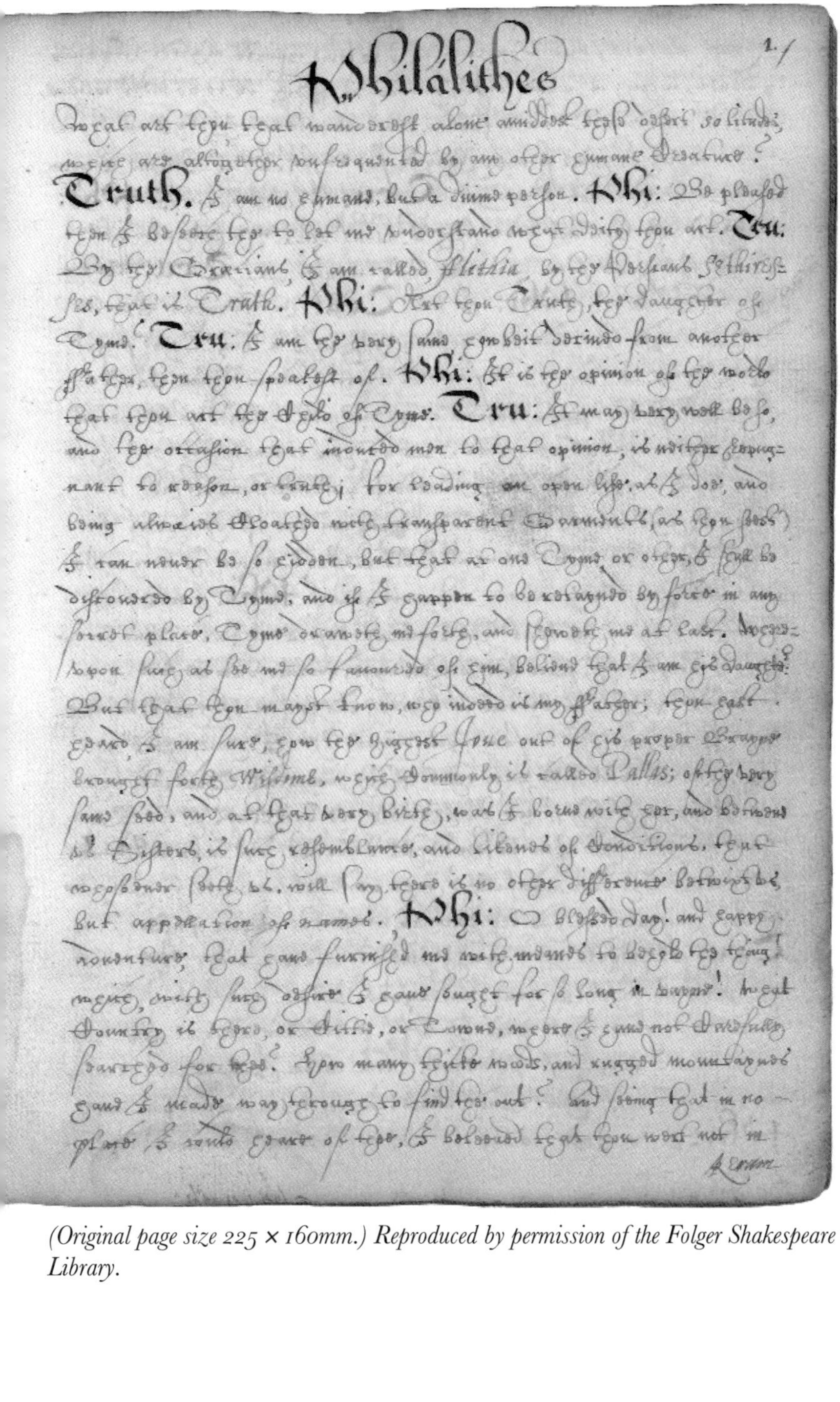

Philalithes

What art thou that wanderest alone amiddest these desert solitudes,
where are altogether unfrequented by any other humane Creature?
Truth. I am no humane, but a divine person. Phi: Be pleased
then I beseech thee to let me understand what deity thou art. Tru:
By the Grecians I am called Aletheia, by the [illegible]
ses, that is Truth. Phi: Art thou Truth, the daughter of
Tyme? Tru. I am the very same, howbeit derived from another
ffather, then thou speakest of. Phi: It is the opinion of the world
that thou art the child of Tyme. Tru: It may very well be so,
and the occasion that moved men to that opinion, is neither repugnant to reason, or verity; for seeing me upon like as I doe, and
being alwaies cloathed with transparent Garmentes, (as thou seest)
I can never be so hidden, but that at one tyme or other, I shall be
discovered by Tyme, and if I happen to be restrayned by force in any
secret place, Tyme draweth me forth, and sheweth me at last. whereupon such as see me so favoured of him, believe that I am his daughter.
But that thou mayst know, who indeed is my ffather; thou hast
heard, I am sure, how the biggest Jove out of his proper Braynes
brought forth Wisdome, which commonly is called Pallas; of the very
same seed, and at that very birth, was I borne with her, and betweene
us Sisters, is such resemblance, and likenes of conditions, that
whosoever seeth us, will say there is no other difference betwixt us,
but appellation of names. Phi: O blessed day! and happy
adventure, that have furnished me with meanes to beholde the thing!
which, with such desire I have sought for so long in vayne! what
Country is there, or Cities, or Townes, where I have not carefully
searched for thee? How many thick woods, and rugged mountaynes
have I made way through to find thee out? and seeing that in no
place I could heare of thee, I beleeved that thou wert not in
Rerum

(Original page size 225 × 160mm.) Reproduced by permission of the Folger Shakespeare Library.

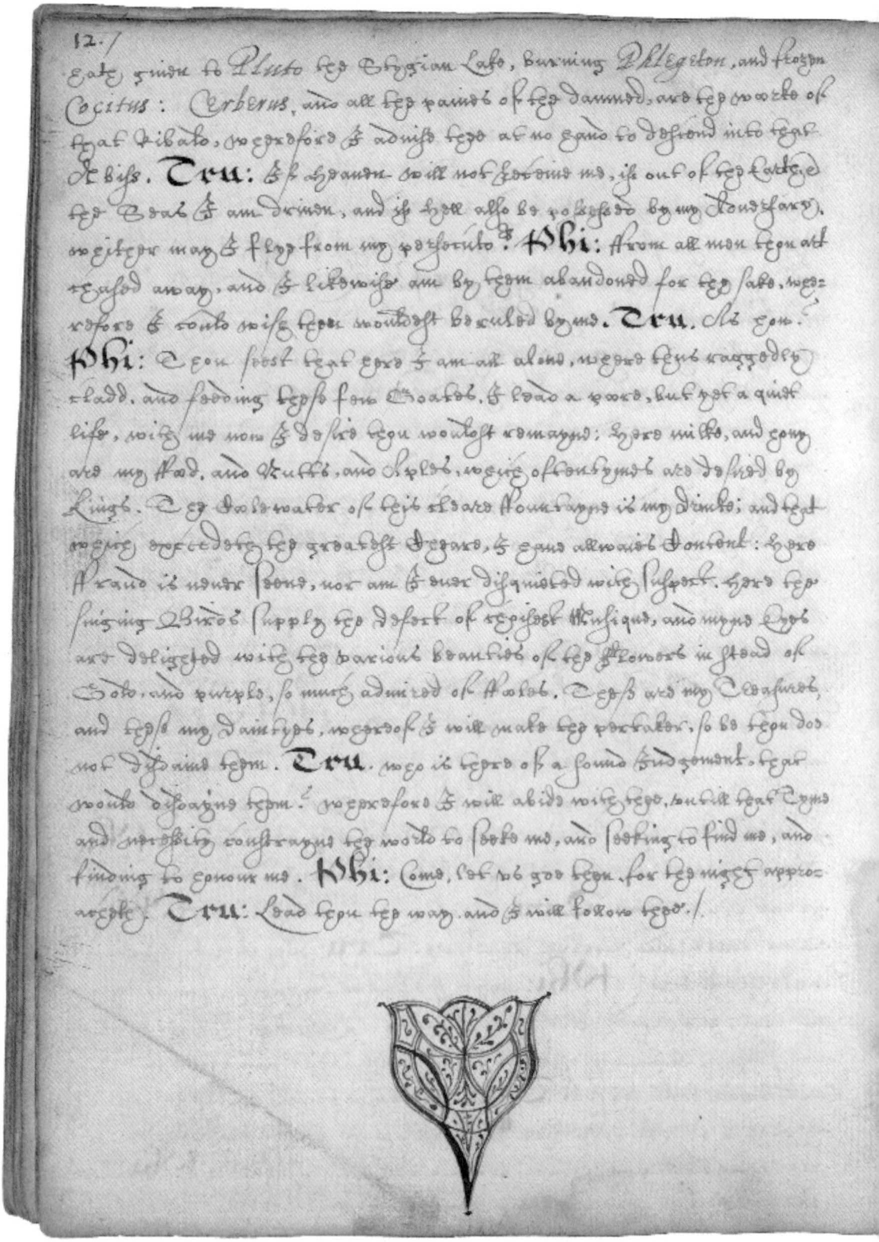

12./
hate, given to Pluto the Stygian Lake, burning Phlegeton, and frozen Cocitus: Cerberus, and all the paines of the damned, are the worke of that tirant, wherefore I advise thee at no hand to descend into that Abiss. Tru: the heaven will not receive me, if out of the Earth the Seas I am driven, and if hell also be possessed by my Adversary, neither may I flye from my persecutor. Phi: From all men thou art chased away, and I likewise am by them abandoned for thy sake, wherefore I could wish thou wouldest be ruled by me. Tru. As how. Phi: Thou first seest that here I am all alone, where thus raggedly cladd, and feeding these few Goates, I leade a poore, but yet a quiet life, with me now I desire thou wouldst remayne: here milke, and hony are my food, and Curds, and Whey, which oftentymes are desired by Kings. The Colde water of this cleare fountayne is my drinke; and that which exceedeth the greatest degree, I have allwaies content: here fraud is never seene, nor am I ever disquieted with suspect. here the singing Birds supply the defect of costlie Musique, and myne eyes are delighted with the various beauties of the flowers in stead of Gold, and purple, so much admired of Fooles. These are my Treasures, and these my dainties, whereof I will make thee partaker, so be thou doe not disdaine them. Tru. who is there of a sound Judgement that would disdaine them? wherefore I will abide with thee, untill that Tyme and necessity constrayne the world to seeke me, and seeking to find me, and finding to honour me. Phi: Come, let us goe then, for the night approacheth. Tru: Leade thou the way, and I will follow thee./

PLATE 4. *Final page of the first dialogue and initial page of the second dialogue: Washington, D.C., Folger Shakespeare Library, MS V.a.241, fols 23v–24r (Original page size 225 × 160mm.) Reproduced by permission of the Folger Shakespeare Library.*

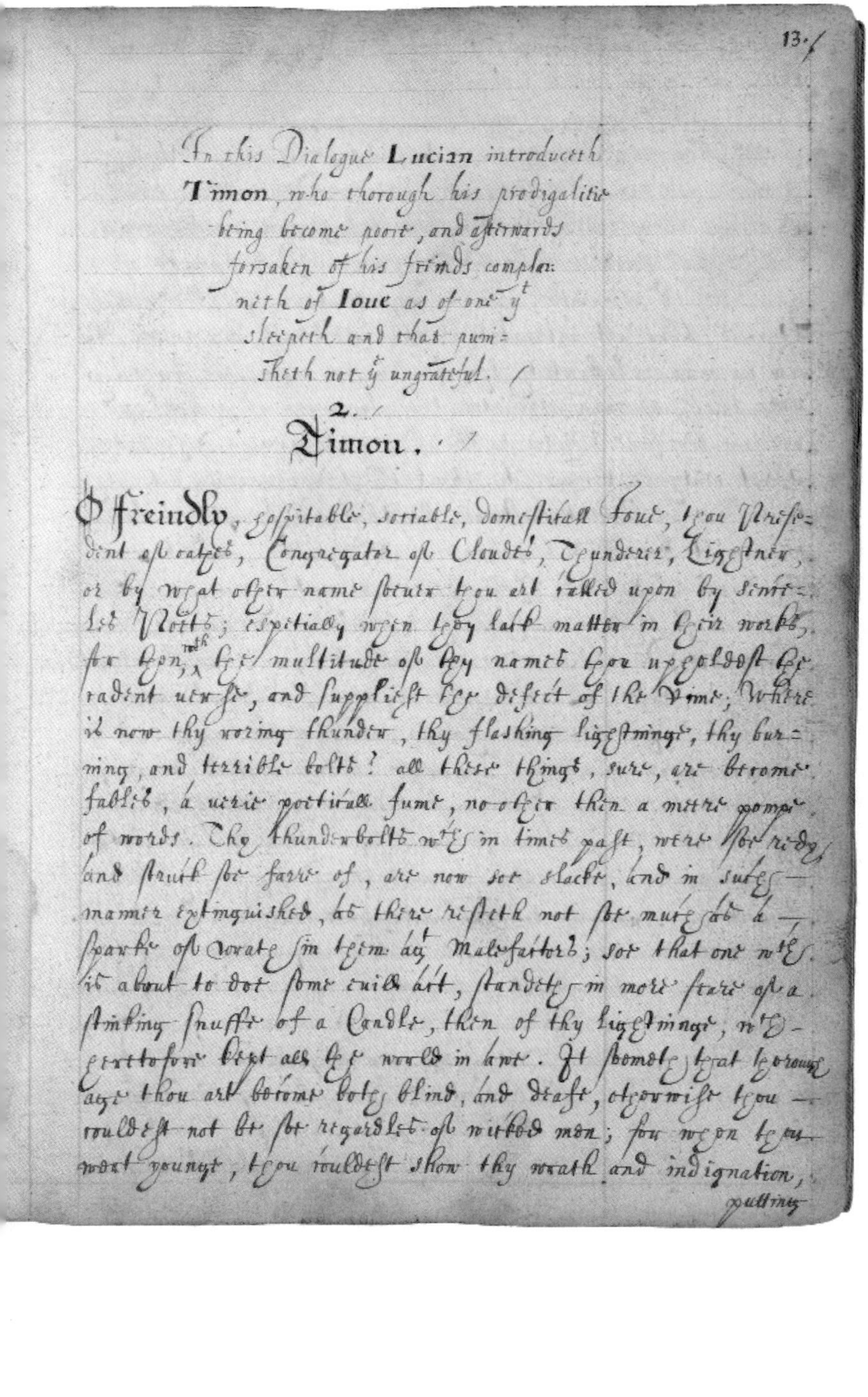

13.

In this Dialogue **Lucian** introduceth **Timon**, who thorough his prodigalitie being become poore, and afterwards forsaken of his friends complai-neth of **Ioue** as of one yt sleepeth and that puni-sheth not ye ungratefull.

2.

Timon.

O freindly, hospitable, sociable, domesticall Ioue, thou Presi-dent of oathes, Congregator of Cloudes, Thunderer, Lightner, or by what other name soeuer thou art called upon by sence-les Poetts; especially when they lack matter in their workes, for then, with the multitude of thy names thou upholdest the cadent verse, and supplyest the defect of the Ryme; Where is now thy roring thunder, thy flashing lightninge, thy bur-ning, and terrible bolts? all these thinges, sure, are become fables, a verie poeticall fume, no other then a meere pompe of words. Thy thunderbolts wch in times past, were soe ready, and strucke soe farre of, are now soe slacke, and in such manner extinguished, as there resteth not soe much as a sparke of wrath in them agt Malefactors; soe that one wch is about to doe some euill act, standeth in more feare of a stinking snuffe of a Candle, then of thy lightninge, wch heretofore kept all the world in awe. It seemeth that through age thou art become both blind, and deafe, otherwise thou couldest not be soe regardles of wicked men; for when thou wert younge, thou couldest show thy wrath and indignation, putting

MIGRATING SOUL

In addition to genre, the motif of a soul migrating through various bodies links these Lucian dialogues to *Metempsychosis* and to the concluding fable. Pythagoras's theory of the transmigration of souls was known during the Renaissance, most conspicuously through Book 15 of Ovid's *Metamorphoses*, and alluded to in such works as *Twelfth Night*, *The Merchant of Venice*, and *Doctor Faustus*.[39] Donne's progress follows the soul through vegetable, animal, and human forms, and one host is a lusty male sparrow, a bird found elsewhere in this manuscript. In 'The Tale of the Fauorite' a king tells his most intimate courtier his deepest secret: through killing himself, the king can transfer his 'first spiritts' into a dead bird, thereby bringing that animal to life for a time (68v). Then the king returns to life when the bird, a sparrow, passes the 'borrow'd Soule' back into the king (68v). Additionally, in the manuscript's third Lucian dialogue Micyllus the shoemaker harasses his rooster for waking him from a pleasant dream of riches, only to be shocked when the cock answers him and explains that his soul has inhabited many bodies, including the philosopher Pythagorus, Aspasia the courtesan, many other animals, and even a king.

FALSE FLATTERERS

Yet, the central connection among these 'Certaine select' dialogues, *Metempsychosis*, the fable, and even the inserted satirical poem is topical and thematic: the dangers posed by false flatterers.[40] First in the manuscript is *Metempsychosis*, dated 16 August 1601, a significant year in English history and in Donne's life for many reasons, not least of which is the Essex rebellion. The poem describes the transmigration of a soul from Eve's apple to Cain's wife and sister, Themech. The soul appears to adopt the evils it encounters or enacts in each incarnation, sinking further into degradation with each inhabitant. Donne's speaker in the introductory epistle recalls Sidney's models of virtue and vice: 'None writes soe ill that he giues not something Exemplarie to follow, or flie' (3r)—certainly 'flie' in the case of *Metempsychosis*. After Themech's death, this 'model' soul supposedly passes through humans until the time of composition when the text suggests that the soul resides in an English man: 'he' of the epistle, 'this great Soule which here amongst vs now / Doth dwell, and moues that hand and Tongue and Brow, / Which as the Moone the Sea, moues vs' (5v).[41] The man most empowered to move Elizabeth at the time of composition was Robert Cecil.[42]

Donne's speaker seems to attack Cecil in several episodes of *Metempsychosis*, including the sections devoted to the elephant and the ape. The soul, housed in a mouse, enters the head of 'Natures great Masterpece an Eliphant' (13v), gradually eating the elephant's brain until its death. This 'iust and thankfull' elephant who 'on himself relies' (13v) resembles the much-admired Essex, whose fall from favor often was attributed primarily to Cecil.[43] Like Essex, the elephant has faults. Blackley recalls that the elephant's 'nature hath giuen him noe knees to bend' (13v); even after the Ireland debacle, Essex refused to kneel in supplication, prompting Elizabeth's anger and rejection.[44] Also, 'His Sinewy Proboscies' which 'did remishly Lie' (13v) could recall Essex's alleged relationship with the much older queen. While Blackley perceptively questions the reading of Cecil as mouse because its death along with its prey hardly resembles Cecil's hasty advance after Essex's demise, Smith argues that the mouse's death serves as a threat: Essex's downfall would cause Cecil's fall as well.

What seems to be mockery of Cecil also appears in the 'toilefull Ape' (15r) episode. Like the ape—called 'toyfull' in other versions of the poem—the exceedingly ambitious Cecil 'reacht at things too high; but open way / there was' (15v).[45] Comparisons of the deformed Cecil to an ape abound in contemporary epitaphs and, according to Blackley and Smith, in contemporary beast fables. Smith argues that as of 1601 most allegorical beast fables were political satires, and he claims that Cecil is satirized as an ape in Spenser's *Mother Hubberd's Tale* and Richard Niccols's *The Beggar's Ape*, which includes both an elephant and a wolf, as does *Metempsychosis*. However, like *Metempsychosis* these satires are 'heavily camouflaged in order to protect their authors from the wrath of the powerful persons they attack'.[46]

While these episodes of *Metempsychosis* seem to target Cecil specifically, not all sections satirize Elizabeth's little ape, but general disgust with a court where one always fears sabotage and conspiracy appears to be peppered throughout the poem.[47] For example, the 'whelp' (14r) of the wolf and watchdog is a double agent who plays Abel's loyal servant while selfishly preying on sheep, demonstrating the speaker's image of a court favorite, 'a spy (to both Sides false)' (15r) who appears concerned with others while advancing himself, not the state. In another episode, when the 'Sea-Pye' takes 'the Silly fish, where it disputing lay / And so ends her doubts, and her, beares her away', the speaker claims, 'Exalted she is but to the Exalters good, / As are by great Ones. Men which lowly stood / It rais'd to be the Raysers Instrument and food' (10v). Certainly all sea creatures appear to be 'Instrument and food' to the whale, challenged by no one while voraciously consuming all it needs to survive as king of the ocean. The speaker laments this 'hero's' unparalleled power: 'O might not States of more Equality, / consist, and is it of necessitie, / That thousand guiltles Smals to make one Great must die' (12r). Without warning, the whale suddenly is attacked by a 'haile-find Thresher and Steelebeak'd Swordfish' who 'onlie attempt to doe what all doe wish' (12v). Smith argues that the whale is Essex, undermined by Anthony and Francis Bacon, although one could argue that the attacking fish are Cecil and Ralegh. Or perhaps the whale is not Essex at all but Elizabeth:

> He hunts not Fish, but as an officer,
> stayes in his Court, as his owne Nett, and there,
> All Sutors of all Sorts themselues inthrall,
> So on his back lies this whale wantoning
> and in his Gulf-like throat sucks euery thing; (12r)

If the 'wantoning' whale is Elizabeth, toying with her 'Sutors of all Sorts', this successful rebellion against the 'Tirant' could represent Donne's wishful thinking. In their hasty, ill-planned rebellion, Essex and his followers were like the fish: 'not throughly arm'd, / with hope, that they could kill him, nor could doe / good to themselues by his Death' (12v). However, unlike the whale who 'neuer harm'd' its attackers (12v), Elizabeth gave Essex cause to strike, and, if the whale represents Elizabeth, there is no obvious choice for Essex's accomplice fish except possibly the third Earl of Southampton. As in many episodes, arguments weaken when the poem is taken too literally. In fact, attempting to match each poetic player with a political counterpart seems unnecessary. Blackley calls attention instead to Donne's general satire of uneven authority relationships and condemnation of the abuse of power by people in high political positions, intimates who hold sway over both the monarch and the masses and advance or destroy careers while hiding safely behind curtains. Regardless of living counterparts, if specific people were intended, these characters demonstrate the perils of conspiracy and false flattery.

This fear of a dangerous, conniving counselor is prevalent throughout the Lucian dialogues. *Timon the Misanthrope*,[48] better known for its influence on Shakespeare, addresses the gods' mercy toward the once wealthy and influential Timon. He has lost fortune and status by being undermined by flatterers disguised as friends who left him penniless and shunned from society, digging outside of the city to sustain himself. When Zeus takes pity on Timon and sends Mercury to earth to restore his wealth, Timon rejects the money, for riches have 'beene the cause of much mischeife vnto mee, giuing mee up into the hands of flatterers, betraying mee to the hatred, and enuie of others' (29r). When Timon finally accepts his fortune, former friends including a lawyer and a philosopher reappear, only to be assaulted by Timon. Ingratitude, insincerity, and hypocrisy permeate the story.

Hazards of authority and power, especially regarding one's nearest and dearest friends, constitute a focus for the other Lucian tales as well. In the third dialogue of the manuscript (*The Cock*),[49] Micyllus's rooster explains that when his soul inhabited a king he was miserable, even in times of seeming peace and prosperity, because kings constantly face 'feares and suspitions, or the treacherey, and conspiracies of their seruants' (39v). According to the cock, destitution is better than wealth, for rich leaders live in fear of 'that wch is worst then all the rest', being undermined by intimate friends: 'they must stand in feare, to be betraied by those that are most inward' (39v). Mercury echoes condemnation of a wealthy lifestyle in the fourth dialogue, *Charon*,[50] when discussing a tyrant who refuses to die, not wanting to leave his riches behind to an untrustworthy heir. Micyllus reappears and, convinced of the cock's wisdom, laughs at the vanity of the paranoid tyrant whom Micyllus so admired on earth.

In *The Ship*,[51] three men discuss their greatest wishes: Adimantes for unsurpassed riches and adoration, Samippes for elected positions as military leader and monarch, and Timolaus for magic rings that give god-like status on earth. Licinius criticizes his friends' wishes throughout their pilgrimage, expressing no such desires and pointing out the dangers of these lifestyle choices. He especially ridicules Samippes. Such a leader, Licinius says, must worry not just about the public dangers of battle but the private dangers of conspiracy. Licinius describes Samippes's imagined reign: 'thou stoodest not onlie in doubt of thine enemies, but of a thousand plotts and treacheries, from those that were neerest about thee, besides the dissimulation, and flatteries of such, as seemed thy freinds, for none were truly soe unto thee, but made a shew of it' (56r). While this 'shew' of false flattery is not discussed specifically in the final dialogue, *Icaromenippus*,[52] Jove does lament the fickle nature of mankind, calling men inconstant and selfish, ready to flatter whichever god suits their purpose.[53]

Ridicule of the conniving and selfish does not end with the dialogues, but can be traced in the playful poem tipped in between folios 43 and 44:

> for fees to any form he moulds a cause
> the worst has merits and best has flaws
> fiue guineas make a criminal to day

And ten to morrow wipe the stain away
who must like lawyer either starve or plead
& follow right or wrong where guineas lead.

While at first the poem merely seems to be a lawyer joke, the verse clearly echoes another seventeenth-century poem:

For fees, to any form he moulds a cause,
The worst has merits, and the best has flaws.
Five guineas make a criminal to-day;
And ten to morrow wipe the stain away. (lines 159–62)

These lines appear in 'Canto IV' of 'The Dispensary', a poem by English poet and physician Samuel Garth published in 1699.[54] 'The Dispensary' praises benevolence and mocks those who do not support the poor. Even these brief lines revisit mockery of the selfish through (not surprisingly) satire. And, if any profession has been coupled with 'favorites' of the wealthy, lawyers have taken the brunt of such criticism.

Disgust with court flatterers is most explicitly demonstrated in folios 67v–68v, the fable called on the title-page 'The Tale of the Favourite' but on 67v called 'The Fable of San 'Foy' (PLATE 5)—an especially interesting title when considering the argument that Donne satirizes Spenser in *Metempsychosis*.[55] A segment of the tale's introductory argument examines the dangers of leaders maintaining 'Fauorites':

> In this Tale, or Discourse following, the Author endeuors to delineate the impotent loue, that some Princes (though otherwise uertuous men,) beare to their undeseruing Fauorites, and sometimes to the hazard of their owne estat's . . . For, Subiects ouer-hastilie raised by their masters Loue, do often abuse that fauour, & either are taken by their fortunes, or do take. (67v)

This fable, which depicts 'a man of a faire p*ro*mising outside, but who had nothing left within to make it good, but a fine flattery, and courtlie falsehood' appears unique to this collection. (For a full transcription of the argument and fable, see the Appendix below.) The story ends abruptly with the crafty courtier using his knowledge regarding the king's mysterious powers to ingratiate himself with the king of Mercia further so that San Foy later can steal the king's wife and wealth.

While the introductory argument outlines the tale's promised examination of consequences for a monarch who prizes his favorite subject too much, the tale concludes before the king discovers San Foy's treachery. In fact, the fable seems incomplete, introducing the malicious courtier but then providing little elaboration regarding the participants' fates. Several features of this section of the manuscript suggest revision or deleted material. First, there is a discrepancy between this lengthy argument and the brevity of the tale, which constitutes only two pages (68r–68v). Second, there are two hanging catchwords, an anomaly in the manuscript because catchwords are accurate throughout the other sections containing them. The catchword on 67r is 'wee', but 'hither' begins the next page (67v). In addition, the catchword 'It' graces the final page (68v), but the prose ends abruptly on that page, indicating that at some point there might have been additional material.[56]

Finally, there appear to be missing leaves from the book. Folio 67r is numbered '99', but 67v appears to be labeled '109', not the expected page '100'. A stray mark on the second 'o' in what appears once to have been '100' causes the 'o' to look like a '9', and page '109' is followed by page '110' (68r). Upon close inspection this stray mark seems to be the curve of the *h* in 'hither'. However, the two most likely explanations for this scenario seem improbable: if the scribe paginating the manuscript was also the scribe writing the text, he must have written '100' at the top of this page, written the text on the page, and then misread his own handwriting before paginating '110'; if a separate scribe paginated the manuscript, he labeled page '100' and then failed to provide a page number for 68r until the second scribe copied his text onto 67v. Another complication is that the scribe's representation of 'h' is not consistently curved throughout the manuscript.[57] One might suggest that this stray mark was made accidentally during the original pagination, causing mis-numbering of the remaining pages. But there appears to be evidence of cancellanda in the form of stubs between folios 67 and 68 (pages '109' and '110'), suggesting purposeful tampering.[58] Because 68r has an even page number ('110') instead of the expected odd number, the scenario becomes more complex than the potential excision of four leaves, doctoring of page numbers, and writing of a condensed version of the tale. If only one of these three circumstances were present, one might assume a scribe merely made a mistake, but the combination of the unusually brief tale, hanging catchwords, and mis-numbering suggests intentional alteration of the manuscript.

These strange material details indicate a real possibility that an original longer fable could have been removed from this manuscript for some reason that we cannot know with certainty but can surmise. If a scribe had transcribed a longer version of the tale which required excision, that scribe could have thought the method least likely to attract attention would be simply to change the second 'o' to a '9', (or perhaps to benefit from the coincidence that the loop of the 'h' causes the 'o' to look like a '9'), label the next leaf '110', and begin the extremely short version of the

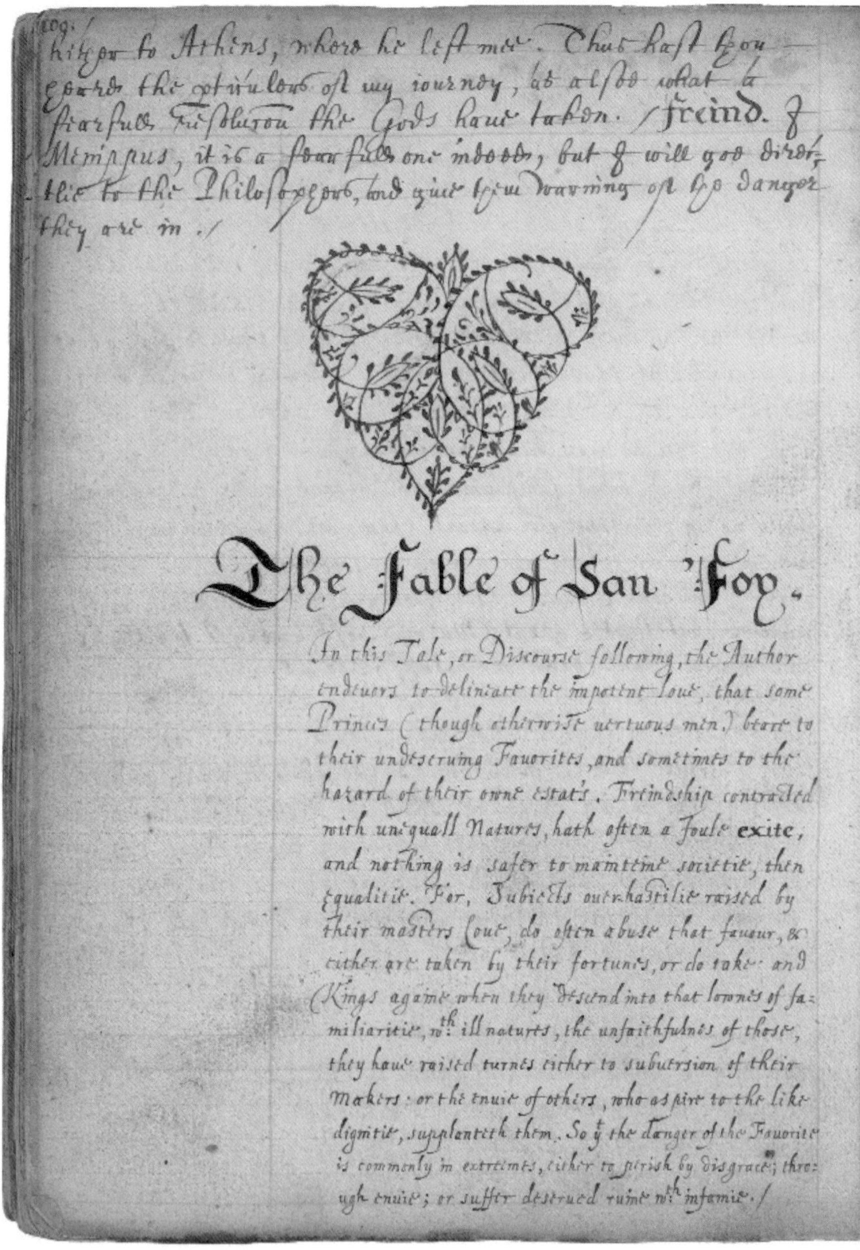

109.
hither to Athens, where he left me. Thus hast thou
heard the particulars of my iourney, as also what a
fearfull resolution the Gods haue taken. / Freind. I
Menippus, it is a fearfull one indeed, but I will goe direct-
lie to the Philosophers, and giue them warning of the danger
they are in. /

The Fable of San Foy.

In this Tale, or Discourse following, the Author
endeuors to deliniate the impotent loue, that some
Princes (though otherwise vertuous men) beare to
their undeseruing Fauorites, and sometimes to the
hazard of their owne estat's. Freindship contracted
with unequall Natures, hath often a foule exite,
and nothing is safer to maintaine societie, then
equalitie. For, Subiects ouerhastilie raised by
their masters loue, do often abuse that fauour, &
either are taken by their fortunes, or do take: and
Kings againe when they descend into that lownes of fa=
miliaritie, wth ill natures, the unfaithfulnes of those,
they haue raised turnes either to subuersion of their
Makers: or the enuie of others, who aspire to the like
dignitie, supplanteth them. So yt the danger of the Fauorite
is commonly in extremes, either to perish by disgrace; thro=
ugh enuie; or suffer deserued ruine wth infamie. /

PLATE 5. *Conclusion of the Lucian dialogues, the argument of the fable and the first page of the fable (erroneously paginated 109–10 instead of 100–1): Washington, D.C., Folger*

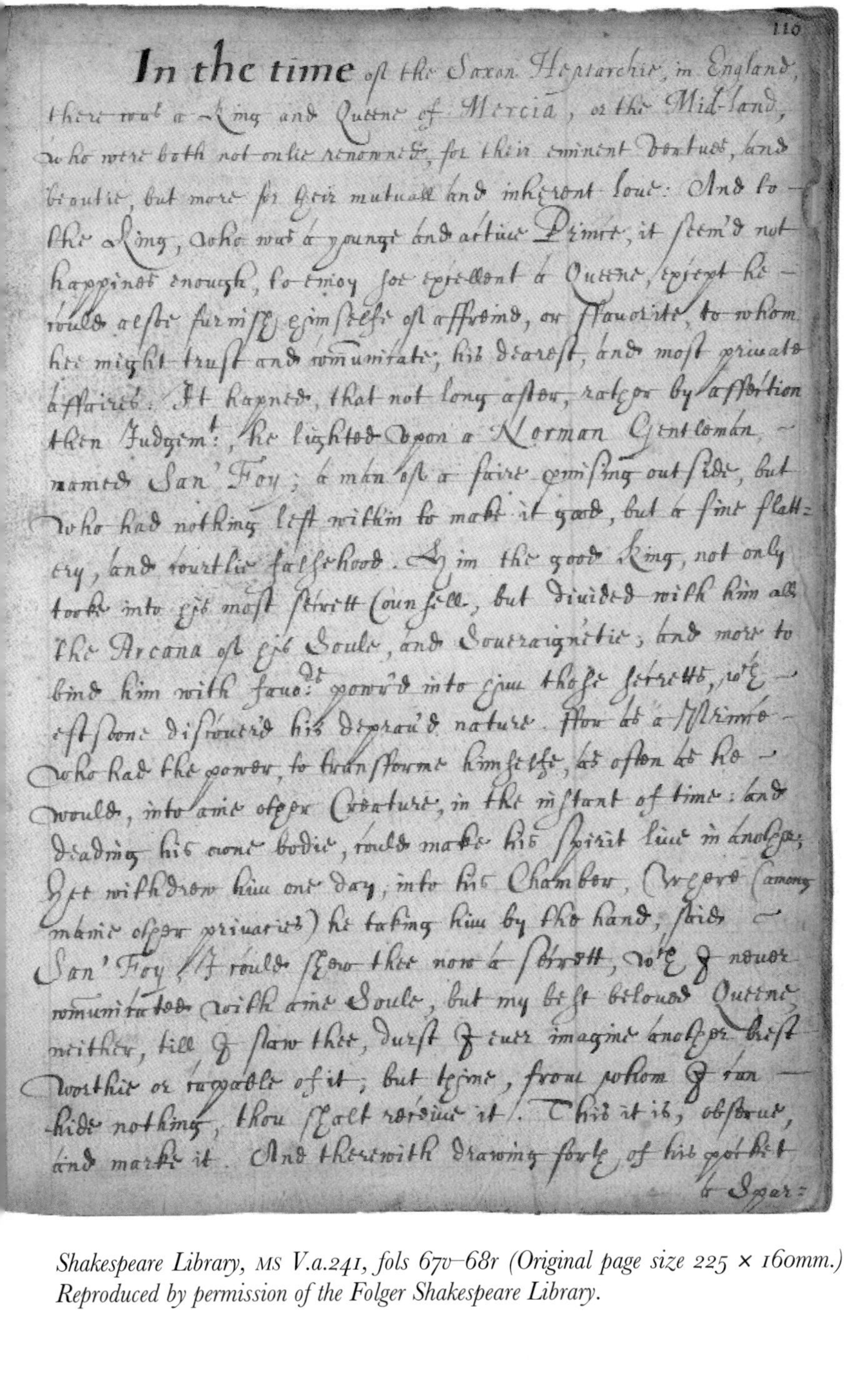

110

In the time of the Saxon Heptarchie, in England, there was a King and Queene of Mercia, or the Mid-land, who were both not onlie renowned, for their eminent vertues, and beautie, but more for their mutuall and inherent love: And to the King, who was a younge and active Prince, it seem'd not happiness enough, to enjoy soe excellent a Queene, except he could also furnish himselfe of a friend, or Favourite, to whom he might trust and communicate, his dearest, and most private affaires. It happned, that not long after, rather by affection then Judgmt:, he lighted upon a Norman Gentleman, named San'Foy; a man of a faire seeming outside, but who had nothing left within to make it good, but a fine flattery, and courtlie falshood. Him the good King, not only tooke into his most secrett Counsell, but divided with him all the Arcana of his Soule, and Soveraignitie; and more to bind him with favors: powr'd into him those secretts, wch eftsoone discovered his deprav'd nature. For as a Chimæra who had the power, to transforme himselfe, as often as he would, into anie other Creature, in the instant of time: and deading his owne bodie, could make his spirit live in another; Hee withdrew him one day, into his Chamber, (where (among manie other privacies) he taking him by the hand, said San'Foy, I could shew thee now a secrett, wch I never communicated with anie Soule, but my best beloved Queene, neither, till I saw thee, durst I ever imagine another brest worthie or capable of it; but thine, from whom I can hide nothing, thou shalt receive it. This it is, observe, and marke it. And therewith drawing forth of his pocket a paper:

Shakespeare Library, MS V.a.241, fols 67v–68r (Original page size 225 × 160mm.) Reproduced by permission of the Folger Shakespeare Library.

fable, hoping that a reader would not notice the discrepancy. Given the previously discussed historical context and the fates to befall future 'favorites', including Ralegh, a reader easily could understand the danger that would surround the owner of a book containing such a scandalous tale, potentially one that did not bury its topical references as deeply as *Metempsychosis*. The poem's veil is so thick that modern readers still cannot decipher the exact political references, if any exist, with certainty. As Ernest W. Sullivan, II argues, 'Textual scholars need to ponder why as well as how a text and its versions were created', for manuscript and print miscellanies are often 'monoscripts—each having its specific, private, experiences informed by a single vision'.[59] Through considering the works that the compiler of V.a.241 deliberately brought together in this manuscript book, works linked by genre, motif, and theme, we are given a window into the 'single vision' of a contemporary reader who interprets Donne's complex poem as political satire.

CONCLUSIONS

This contemporary reader's interpretation of *Metempsychosis* only becomes apparent when we read Folger MS V.a.241 as a complete unit. Not all Renaissance manuscripts were haphazardly constructed. Many manuscript miscellanies were designed with great care; their compilers provided indices, summaries of contents, and in this case even a carefully constructed title-page that draws attention to the contents as a cohesive group. Scholars now recognize the value of considering the manuscript context of Renaissance poetry.[60] Sullivan suggests that the discoveries possible when one closely analyzes such manuscript miscellanies have 'profound implications not only for the study of the authorship, dating, manuscript circulation, and texts of Renaissance verse generally but also for our understanding of the function of verse in the aesthetic, social, political, and economic life of the Renaissance'.[61] Considering manuscripts like V.a.241 as complete units enhances, even alters our knowledge of Renaissance authors and their works. When we approach such manuscripts as entities whose structure, material details, and contents merit investigation, we enrich our understanding of the malleable and conversational nature of much Renaissance manuscript poetry, of authorial canons and 'ownership' of poetic creations, of political circles of poets such as Donne, and of contemporary readers and their interpretations of poems.

This composite manuscript seems to have been compiled by a contemporary reader interested in satire of the court and its manipulative flatterers. Smith concludes his case for Cecil as the soul by admitting, 'Whether any of Donne's contemporaries caught on to the poem's "conceit" we cannot say for certain'.[62] Yet, 'evidence' for a contemporary interpretation *does* exist in this collector's choice of texts for this manuscript. Renaissance readers may not have left critical essays expounding their poetic interpretations, but clues remain in marginal comments, poetic sequence, and other elements of 'contexture'. Through analyzing Folger Manuscript V.a.241, we provide support for a political interpretation of *Metempsychosis*, with its thrasher sharks and swordfish vying to control the crown.

APPENDIX

The prefatory argument (fol. 67v) and tale (fols 68r–v) in MS V.a.241 are printed with the permission of the Folger Shakespeare Library. The transcription from the secretary script is mine.

The Fable of San 'Foy

In this Tale, or Discourse following, the Author endeuors to delineate the impotent loue, that some Princes (though otherwise uertuous men,) beare to their undeseruing Fauorites, and sometimes to the hazard of their owne estat's. Freindship contracted with unequall Natures, hath often a foule exite, and nothing is safer to mainteine societie, then equalitie. For, Subiects ouer-hastilie raised by their masters Loue, do often abuse that fauour, & either are taken by their fortunes, or do take: and Kings againe when they descend into that lownes of familiaritie, w:th ill natures, the unfaithfulnes of those, they haue raised turnes either to subuersion of their Makers: or the enuie of others, who aspire to the like dignitie, supplanteth them. So y^{t} the danger of the Fauorite is commonly in extreemes, either to perish by disgrace; through enuie; or suffer deserued ruine w:th infamie.

In the time of the Saxon Heptarchie, in England, there was a King and Queene of Mercia, or the Mid-land, who were both not onlie renowned, for their eminent vertues, and beautie, but more for their mutuall and inherent loue: And to the King, who was a younge and actiue Prince, it seem'd not happines enough, to enioy soe excellent a Queene, except he could alsoe furnish him selfe of a ffreind, or ffauorite, to whom hee might trust and com*m*unicate, his dearest, and most priuate affaires. It hapned, that not long after, rather by affection then Iudgem:^{t}, he lighted vpon a Norman Gentleman, named San 'Foy; a man of a faire p*ro*mising outside, but who had nothing left within to make it good, but a fine flattery, and courtlie falsehood. Him the good King, not only tooke into his most secrett Counsell, but diuided with him all the Arcana of his Soule, and Soueraign'etie; and more to bind him with fauo:^{rs} powr'd into him those secretts, wch eft soone discouer'd his deprau'd nature. ffor as a Prince who had the power, to transforme himselfe, as often as he would, into anie other Creature, in the instant of time: and deading his owne bodie, could make his spirit liue in another; hee withdrew him one day, into his Chamber, where (among manie other priuacies) he taking him by the hand, said San 'Foy, I could shew thee now a secrett, wch I neuer com*m*unicated with anie Soule, but my best beloued Queene, neither, till I saw thee, durst I euer imagine another brest worthie or capable of it; but thine, from whom I can hide nothing, thou shalt receiue it. This it is, obserue, and marke it. And therewith drawing forth of his pocket a Sparrow, hauing shutt all the doores, the king laid himselfe vpon the floore, on his back, his face upwardes, and bad him feare nothing. Then stifling the bird, he putt the dead bill into his mouth, and breath'd upon it. Instantlie the Kings bodie became cold, and a Carkasse, whilst the sparrow begun to pipp, and hopp about the Roome, and San 'Foy amazed with the suddaine Reuiuall of the bird, now sitting on his head, then on his shoulder, then flying about the chamber chirping, then hoppng upon his hand, at length, returning to the dead King, and inserting his bill, in his cold lipps, restor'd his borrow'd Soule, and fill'd the emptie veines, with the first spiritts. San 'Foy, astonish'd at the Sight, humbly begg'd of the King the knowledge, and key of the Secrett. Hee as willing to grant, as the other was to aske it, bad him lie downe in the same manner as he saw him to doe before, and giuing him an herbe to chaw in his mouth, and laying another within his brest, held the dead Sparrow to his Mouth, and will'd him to breath thereon. San 'Foy, fearlessly did it; when the bird began to take ioy in his bold flight, fiue or six times about the roome, and at last returning to the Carkasse of San 'Foy, animated it againe. That by daily participating, and practising this Secrett, hee grew more and more into the kings bosome, and vnder concealement of his owne to-be-abhorred Mischeife, he putt on the Maske, or vizor of a most obsequious seruant. ffor within hee was soe possessed with the thirst of soueraigntie, and the lust of enioying the Queene, his mistresse, as the onlie hope of his safetie, was to make good his trecherie, in the highest degree; and by a new varietie of Manners, and a confus'd temper of vices to come forth in one, and the same person, an appearing freind, and a most cruell enemie. See now, I pray yow, whether the furious lusts, or the frantick desires of the Ambitious, will transport the guiltie?

NOTES

I am indebted to William H. Sherman for alerting me to the existence of this manuscript and for providing extensive feedback and advice during its investigation. I thank Brian Mark Blackley, Donna B. Hamilton, M. Thomas Hester, Ernest W. Sullivan, II, and particularly Peter Beal for their helpful ideas and kind advice. This study also benefited from suggestions by Hugh Adlington, Dennis Flynn, Annabel Patterson, Gary A. Stringer, and other members of the John Donne Society present at the 2005 conference and from assistance by Folger Library staff members. For reading versions with patience and a careful eye, I am obliged to Timothy D. Crowley.

1 3v, 4r. All quotations from *Metempsychosis* are taken from Folger MS V.a.241.

2 Brian Mark Blackley, 'The Generic Play and Spenserian Parody of John Donne's "Metempsychosis"', Dissertation (University of Kentucky, 1994), p. 159. Also see M. van Wyk Smith, 'John Donne's *Metempsychosis*', *Review of English Studies*, NS 24 (1973), 17–25, 141–52, and Dennis Flynn, 'Donne's *Ignatius His Conclave* and Other Libels on Robert Cecil', *John Donne Journal*, 6.2 (1987), 163–83. The 1635 printed edition changes 'hee' to 'shee', and subsequent seventeenth-century printed editions maintain this reading. But the 1633 'hee' echoes all but one extant manuscript (Harvard College Library MS Eng 966.5): manuscript evidence supports the choice of 1633 editors.

3 Blackley, p. 38.

4 John Donne, *Letters to Severall Persons of Honour (1651)*, Introduction by M. Thomas Hester (Delmar, New York, 1977), pp. 114–5.

5 Neil Fraistat, 'Introduction: The Place of the Book and the Book as Place', *Poems in Their Place: The Intertextuality and Order of Poetic Collections*, Edited by Neil Fraistat (Chapel Hill, North Carolina; London, 1986), p. 3.

6 I am greatly indebted to Heather Wolfe of the Folger Library for her generous assistance with this manuscript description; she directly contributed many elements of the description.

7 Absolute certainty regarding collation of the manuscript is complicated by its delicate nature and its tight binding, but the formula provides the likely collation.

8 The stub for folio 23 appears between folios 27 and 28.

9 The manuscript also contains three endleaves, as well as preliminary and final binder's leaves. Folios 1–68 measure 223 × 166mm. The leaves appear to contain a slightly red tint at the edges due to cutting and to the addition of a speckled red edge decoration. Portions of words at the edges of leaves, such as 8r, substantiate the notion that larger pages were cut after the writing occurred.

10 There is evidence of pricking in folios 24–47. There is lead or graphite ruling in folios 3–17 and blind ruling with faint pricks in folios 18r, 20r, 21v, and 22r.

11 Folios 1–16 contain one upper margin 13mm from the paper edge, one lower margin 14mm from the paper edge, and two marginal indicators on each side: 12mm and 22mm from the binding and 6mm and 15mm from the paper edge. Folios 24–68 contain one upper margin 22mm from the paper edge, one lower margin 10mm from the paper edge, two marginal indicators on the inner side 12mm and 22mm from the binding, and one marginal indicator on the outer side 46mm from the page edge. There is also a quite faint marginal indicator of darker ink 8mm from the paper edge.

12 The prefatory argument for the first dialogue is written on 17v (the back of the title-page), a page presumably left blank when the dialogue was originally created. The

scribe who composed the remaining arguments and dialogues probably added this argument to the first dialogue to keep the format consistent.

13 Chain lines are not distinguishable in folio 69.

14 This coat of arms contains an eagle, crown or castle, and lion rampart. C. M. Briquet labels the watermark 2291 (*Les Filigranes Dictionnaire Historique des Marques du Papier*, Vol. I [New York, 1966; Reprint]). Edward Heawood lists it among "Coat of Arms" as 481 (*Watermarks Mainly of the 17th and 18th Centuries* [Holland, 1950]).

15 'Concerning Tragedy' contains striking verbal echoes of an article by Joseph Addison in the *Spectator*, Volume 39, dated Saturday, April 14, 1711.

16 The poem appears on the recto side of the inserted leaf, and some notes on 'motion' and 'velocity' are written on the verso side.

17 J. Franklin Mowery of the Folger Library kindly provided this description of the manuscript binding.

18 'Phillipps MS 18640' appears inside of the front pastedown, as do 'Donne', 'Opened 5 Ap 67', and an illegible note, all in faint pencil. Written on the rear pastedown is 'Folger ac# 410819', and on the lower right appears 'Mr E. Spencer'.

19 Gosse claims, 'This is a copy, not very intelligently made, either from the poet's handwriting or from an early transcript of the same. It presents some fifty or sixty slight variants, many of them obvious misreadings, but several which are distinct improvements upon the printed text, and one or two which actually clear up difficulties in the latter' (*The Life and Letters of John Donne, Dean of St. Paul's*, Vol. I [Gloucester, Massachusetts, 1959; Reprint of 1899], pp. 140–1).

20 *The Poems of John Donne*, ed. Herbert J. C. Grierson (London, 1912); *The Complete Poetry of John Donne*, ed. John T. Shawcross (Garden City, New York, 1967); *John Donne: The Satires, Epigrams, and Verse Letters*, ed. W. Milgate (Oxford, 1967).

21 The poem also appears in the following six manuscripts: Trinity College Library, Dublin, MS 887; Norton MS 4503 (Harvard College Library MS Eng 966.3); the Puckering MS (Trinity College Library, Cambridge, MS R.3.12); the Denbigh MS (British Library Add. MS 18647); the Cambridge Balam MS (Cambridge University Library MS Add. 5778c); and the O'Flahertie MS (Harvard College Library MS Eng 966.5).

22 Milgate, p. lxii.

23 Milgate, p. lxiii.

24 *Metempsychosis* is written on a stock of paper different from that in the rest of the manuscript. Though unlikely, it is possible that a second hand begins on 159r. Beneath the last line is the signature of 'Edward Smith' (167r), and Edward Smith also seems to have signed the top right corner of the first page of body (155r). The signature appears quite different from the scribe's hand. The poem is not complete: the epistle ends with 'None wrights so ill' (154r), and the body of the poem ends with 'Sister and wife to Cain yt first did plow' (167r). Generally there seems to be no connection between the manuscript contents or even a reason for their order. They range from notes on 'D^{r}. Conant. his lectures at Alhallowes on fridayes' of 1657 (112r–141r) to a 1597 report on 'The ecclesiasticall Discipline, as it hath been pra[cticed] since ye refomac[i]on of ye Church by ye Ministers, Elders and Deacons of ye Churches of Guernsey, Iersey, Sarck, and Orkeny' since 1576 (203r–214v).

25 Because the dialogues lack titles in this manuscript and the arguments appear to be original works, I have included each argument when discussing the accompanying dialogue. All transcriptions from the manuscript are mine. In cases in which the scribe has relegated part of a line-ending word to the following line (usually with a colon, not a hyphen), I have combined the two word segments.

26 Because this title-page is found on the second leaf of the twelve-leaf quire containing *Metempsychosis*, it seems likely that the poem's scribe left some initial leaves blank with the intention of adding other materials, perhaps a title-page and/or dedication. Potentially, this scribe served as compiler of the manuscript and actually created the existing title-page.

27 Blackley, pp. 24–5.

28 I will refer to the dialogues by their modern titles. For more on modern translations, refer to H. W. Fowler and F. G. Fowler's translations of Lucian in *The Works of Lucian of Samosata*, 4 vols. (Oxford, 1905).

29 David Marsh, *Lucian and the Latins: Humor and Humanism in the Early Renaissance* (Ann Arbor, Michigan, 1998), p. 42. For further study of Lucian and his influence during the Renaissance, also see Christopher Robinson, *Lucian and His Influence in Europe* (Chapel Hill, 1979) and Craig R. Thompson, *Translations of Lucian: The Yale Edition of the Complete Works of St. Thomas More* (New Haven; London, 1974).

30 Robinson, p. 20.

31 The argument of the first dialogue reads, 'Demaratus surnamed Philalithes, a Noble man of Lacedemonia, was driven out of his Countrey, for speaking the Truth, as well publickely, in the Senatt, as priuately to his Freinds, and flying into Asia, he addressed himselfe unto Xerxes King of Persia; out of whose Court he was in like manner expulsed by Flatterers for the Truth, which hee still used to speake freely, w[th]:out respect, whereupon hee got him into a desert mountaine, where he incountreth w[th]: Truth, unto whom he speaketh in this manner' (17v).

32 This dialogue depicts the difficulties of the goddess Truth, who is attacked by false flatterers who throw Truth out of court, leaving her forced to retreat to the care of animals. Generally, Maffeo Vegio (1407–58) is best known for his 1428 supplement to the *Aeneid*, but he also composed three Latin dialogues that demonstrate the inspiration of Lucian in external trappings if not spirit and color. Being misinterpreted as an original Lucian dialogue during the sixteenth and seventeenth centuries, *Dialogue between Truth and Philalethes* survives in at least fifteen manuscripts and six incunabula and was translated into Dutch, French, German, and Italian. For more on Vegio and other early Lucian translators and imitators, consult Marsh, especially pp. 67–71 and pp. 110–4.

33 Although More did not translate any of the dialogues present in this manuscript, Erasmus translated *Timon*, *The Cock*, and *Charon*, and later added *Icaromenippus* to their second edition (1514). More did translate *Menippus*, a counterpart to *Icaromenippus*. Both dialogues depict Menippus's search for knowledge of the gods and the universe through voyages to other worlds, to hell in *Menippus* and to heaven in *Icaromenippus*.

34 In 1506, Erasmus and More completed the first edition of their Latin translations of Lucian. This edition includes twenty-eight dialogues translated by Erasmus and three dialogues and a declamation translated by More, as well as More's response to Lucian's declamation. Subsequent editions with additional dialogues soon followed. Various scholars have analyzed Lucianic influence on Erasmus's *Praise of Folly* and *Colloquies* and Sir Thomas More's *Utopia*. Howard B. Norland claims that More's method of blending theater with traditional forms of dialogue proves that *Utopia* was modeled more closely on Lucian dialogues than any other source ('The Role of Drama in More's Literary Career', *The Sixteenth Century Journal: Journal of Early Modern Studies* 13:4 [Winter 1982], 59–75). Warren W. Wooden suggests that the central character of *Utopia* is a Lucianic satiric persona and that other Lucianic elements are present in the work ('Thomas More and Lucian: A Study of Satiric

Influence and Technique', *Studies in English* 13 [1972], 43–57). And R. Bracht Branham compares the satiric structure, ironic stance, and moral message of *Utopia* to the Lucian dialogues that More translated ('Utopian Laughter: *Lucian* and Thomas *More', Moreana* [July 1985], 23–43).

35 There are few extant printed English translations prior to the mid-seventeenth century. According to Henrietta R. Palmer, only three separately printed Lucian dialogues—*Necromantia, Toxaris*, and *Cynicus*—are extant in sixteenth-century English translations, and none of these works is included in this manuscript (*List of English Editions and Translations of Greek and Latin Classics Printed Before 1641* [London, 1911]). The first collection of Lucian dialogues in English was translated by Francis Hickes and printed in 1634. This edition, in which Hickes claims to translate directly from the Greek, contains four of the five Lucian dialogues in this manuscript (*Icaromenippus*, *The Cock*, *Timon*, and *Charon*). After Thomas Heywood's 1637 edition, Jasper Mayne adds his own translations to Hickes's work in 1638; *The Ship* is among his additions. Because the dialogues in this manuscript appear to have been written prior to 1620, the English versions in V.a.241 could have been original translations, although they might have been copies of other versions circulating in manuscript.

36 Branham, p. 23.

37 Marsh, p. 67.

38 Patrick Joseph Quinlan, 'John Donne's Satires in Light of the Lucianic Tradition', Dissertation (University of Colorado at Boulder, 1980), p. 30.

39 See Faustus's final soliloquy, *The Merchant of Venice* 4.1, and *Twelfth Night* 4.2, in which Malvolio and the clown discuss the possibility of a human soul being housed in a bird.

40 It should be noted that several elements that may or may not be related to *Metempsychosis* also recur in these dialogues. First, Lucian's metaphor of the world as stage, often borrowed by Donne, Shakespeare, Ralegh, and others, occurs frequently. Also, Lucian's well-known mockery of hypocritical philosophers, who live extravagant lifestyles while ridiculing pleasure and extolling whatever quality each considers virtuous, surfaces in each dialogue. In addition, *Timon*, *The Cock*, and *The Ship* depict a parvenu: 'A figure of dubious origins, the parvenu rises by dishonest means, is notorious for his immorality, and positively profits by his ignorance' (Robinson, p. 19). Interestingly, many contemporaries held such a view of Robert Cecil's father, Lord Burghley, who was not born into the aristocracy but rose to power.

41 Smith argues, 'it is surely inconceivable that the Lord Keeper's ambitious young secretary would have either dared or wanted to attack the Queen, quite apart from the fact that the Epistle promises us a male protagonist. It is much more likely that while "the Moone" here is, indeed, the Queen, the "great soule" who moves her is not her own animating soul, but the protagonist, the powerful contemporary who is allegorized throughout the poem as the soul of havoc exerting its baleful influence on the world around it. The "great soule", in other words, is a power behind the throne: sinister, influential, but nevertheless rather ridiculous. This, exactly, was the contemporary view of Robert Cecil, Secretary of State' (p. 143).

42 John Guy characterizes England in the 1590s as 'a hydra, constantly sprouting new heads' because of little constancy among members of the court: 'councillors and office-holders oscillated in the queen's favour'. Courtiers and laypeople wondered about 'the whirlpool of relationships in which the queen and her favourites lay at the vortex' ('Introduction: The 1590s: The Second Reign of Elizabeth I?' *The Reign of Elizabeth I: Court and Culture in the Last Decade* [Cambridge, 1995], p. 2). Though the

cult of Elizabeth remained intact until her death, some flux subsided in 1596 when Elizabeth finally filled the position of Secretary of State (vacant since the death of Sir Francis Walsingham in 1590) with Robert Cecil, solidifying his position as her most prominent counselor.

43 In 'Donne's *Ignatius His Conclave* and Other Libels on Robert Cecil', Dennis Flynn argues that the elephant recalls Essex and that this episode is one of several Donne libels on Cecil and his politics.

44 See Blackley for a thorough analysis of Donne's possible reactions towards Essex's rebellion and Cecil's potential role in Essex's fall.

45 Kenneth James Hughes offers another reading of this episode in which Tethlemite represents Cecil, 'the leader of the anti-Essex party', who becomes the ape—or Essex—killer. Hughes argues that the entire poem is a political satire of British monarchs, beginning with Henry IV as the mandrake root and tracing the soul through Elizabeth I as Themech ('Donne's 'Metempsychosis' and the Objective Idea of Unreason', *Central Institute of English and Foreign Languages Bulletin* 18 [1982], 15–39).

46 Smith, p. 141. Blackley builds on Smith's suggestion to provide an extensive comparison of *Metempsychosis* and *Mother Hubberd's Tale* in 'The Generic Play and Spenserian Parody of John Donne's "Metempsychosis"'. On Satires of Cecil, see also Pauline Croft, 'The Reputation of Robert Cecil: Libels, Political Opinion, and Popular Awareness in the Early Seventeenth Century', *Transactions of the Royal Historical Society*, 6 (1991), 43–69.

47 Searching for Cecil in every tale is fruitless because the sequence of tales is insignificant; as Smith points out, 'the incidents of the poem do not outline a linear biography of Cecil but rather present a series of more or less topical anecdotes that illustrate the growing corruptions of the political world of which Cecil is the prime avatar' (p. 150).

48 This argument reads, 'In this Dialogue Lucian introduceth Timon, who thorough his prodigalitie being become poore, and afterwards forsaken of his freinds complaineth of Ioue as of one y[t] sleepeth and that punisheth not y[e] ungrateful' (24r).

49 The introductory argument states, 'In this Dialogue Lucian introduceth a certaine Shoemaker, named Micyllus, who dreamed he was become heire vnto a great estate, and whilst he is entertained by this Dreame, his Cocke with crowing awaketh him, wherewith being uerie angrie, he beginneth to speake to the Cocke, and the Cocke answeareth him' (32r).

50 This argument reads, 'In this Dialogue Lucian introdueth [*sic.*] Charon reasoning with Clotho, one of the three fatall Sisters, about Mercuries delay in conducting the Sowles of such as were dead, to his boat, in the meane while Mercury arriuing, deliuers the occasions of his stay, which was a certaine dead Tyranne whose Soule by no meanes would come along, but sought all the wais it could to escape and returne in the world againe' (42r).

51 The argument for the fifth dialogue says, 'In this Dialogue Lucian introduceth certaine Persons making Castles in the aire, and first he faineth y[t] they went to the hauen to see a great ship, that was newly arriued, by occasion whereof they enter in to these fant'sies. The interlocut:[ers] are. Licinius. Timoläus, Adimãtes, Samippes' (49r).

52 This argument reads, 'In this Dialogue Lucian introduceth a certaine Man called Menippus, who being not satisfied by the Philosophers about matters of the heauens determineth to flie thither himselfe, and so be resolued. First then he faigneth Menippus to be newlie descended from heauen, and talking to himself of the measure, and distance of the way, he had made, a freind of his demaundeth of him what is that he talketh so of, whereupon Menippes discourseth his Voyage unto him' (58v).

53 Also, after his 'freind' says that surely Menippus 'becamest an hauke, or a Crowe' to fly to heaven (59r), Menippus explains that he 'tooke mee a great Eagle, and a verie strong Vulture, and cutt of both their wings' to essentially transform into a bird for his quest (59v).

54 *The Works of the English Poets, from Chaucer to Cowper; including the Series Edited, with Prefaces, Biographical and Critical, by Dr. Samuel Johnson: and the Most Approved Translations. The Additional Lives by Alexander Chalmers, F.S.A.*, 21 Vols. Vol 9 (London, 1810), p. 438. The verses in this manuscript might be a satiric poem Garth later appropriates, an early Garth verse circulating amongst a coterie, or a memorial reconstruction of someone's favorite portion of Garth's poem, among other options.

55 Perhaps this character name inspired a reader to add 'Mr E. Spencer' to the rear pastedown. Blackley examines the relationship between Donne's poem and *Mother Hubberds Tale* and *The Faerie Queene*, specifically comparing Spenser's dedicatory letter to Sir Walter Ralegh with Donne's prefatory epistle in *Metempsychosis*.

56 Catchwords appear on folios 18–68 with the one exception of 67v (p. 100/109), which contains no catchword.

57 For example, 'h' in 'Rhadamanth' on 48r, line 4 has a straight line, while the 'h' in the same word in line 15 is curved.

58 There appear to be stubs, which probably remain because folios once present in this section were cut out of the manuscript. Although unlikely, it is also possible that the apparent cancellanda between folios 67 and 68 is actually the stub of folio 69.

59 Ernest W. Sullivan, II, 'The Renaissance Manuscript Verse Miscellany: Private Party, Private Text', *New Ways of Looking at Old Texts: Papers of the Renaissance English Text Society, 1985–1991*, Edited by W. Speed Hill (Binghamton, New York, 1993), pp. 289–97, quotations on p. 297 and p. 290.

60 For example, Sullivan has edited both Dalhousie manuscripts, an effort which led him to suggest that traditional Group II Donne poems may not descend from Donne's collection efforts (*The First and Second Dalhousie Manuscripts: Poems and Prose by John Donne and Others, A Facsimile Edition*, Edited by Ernest W. Sullivan, II [Columbia, Missouri, 1988]). According to Sullivan, the poems derive from an Essex family collection and were given to family members for patronage and preferment. Sullivan proposes that 'the monoscript ancestor' of the Dalhousies and Lansdowne 740 is Trinity College, Dublin, MS. 877. Material details and scribal choices support the argument that the Dalhousies were copied from Essex family documents; this discovery provides valuable potential insights into the Group II tradition and the circulation of manuscript verse generally. Sullivan argues, for example, that the presence of 'Elegie: The Expostulation' in this manuscript informs our knowledge of authorship: Donne (who served on a military campaign with Essex) and not Jonson (who was not closely connected with Essex or otherwise represented in the manuscript) is the rightful author of the debated poem ('The Renaissance Manuscript Verse Miscellany: Private Party, Private Text', pp. 293–4).

61 *The First and Second Dalhousie Manuscripts: Poems and Prose by John Donne and Others, A Facsimile Edition*, p. 12.

62 Smith, p. 152.

New Manuscript Texts of Sermons by John Donne

Jeanne Shami

When Evelyn Simpson and George Potter were preparing their edition of Donne's sermons in the 1950s and 1960s, they proposed to establish their text by examining all extant manuscripts and early printed editions. At the time, they identified and described six manuscript sources containing versions of sixteen Donne sermons.[1] During the course of their investigations, they were made aware of a seventh manuscript source, the Ellesmere MS, described in Appendix A of Volume 2, although never incorporated into their stemma.[2] This seventh source did not expand the number of Donne sermons in manuscript, but provided additional witnesses to seven sermons, and exploded the notion of a finite number of sermon witnesses.

In 1992, while reading unattributed sermon manuscripts in the British Library, I identified three additional manuscripts containing Donne sermons. The most important of these was a scribal presentation copy of Donne's 1622 Gunpowder Plot sermon, corrected in Donne's own hand.[3] This essay takes as its subject the two remaining manuscript sources, both from the Harley collection.[4]

HARLEY MS 6946 (H1): PHYSICAL DESCRIPTION

Harley 6946 is a quarto collection of five sermons—all by John Donne—dating from the 1620s. From the physical evidence, it is not clear how long the five sermons have traveled together or how they came to be bound by the British Museum as a single volume. Near the top of folio 1*r, in black ink, is written 'IV. Excellent Sermons'. Near the bottom of the leaf is written 'Preachd & wrote in ye 17. Cent. / The Title to John 11: 35'.[5] The volume also bears the shelfmarks '161. A. 47 / 6946', '19 B / 1', and '42. g / XLII. G'.

The manuscript, not including later endpapers and inserted blanks, comprises sixty leaves, each measuring approximately 198 × 155mm.

and unruled. The entire volume was foliated by the British Library in pencil in the upper right-hand corner. The last two gatherings have page numbers on the recto side of the leaves (in the same hand): f. 35r = p. 1; f. 39r = p. 2; f. 43r = p. 3; f. 47r = p. 4; f. 49r = p. 1; f. 53r = p. 2; f. 57r = p. 3. Collation by watermarks is as follows: 1^{12} fols. 1–11 + 1 blank; 2^{12} fols 12–22 + blank; 3^{12} fols 23–34; 4^{16} fols 35–48; 5^{12} fols 49–60.[6] The composition of the volume leaves no doubt that these five sermons were bound together as a coherent set of separates.

Each of the sermons is in a different secretary hand (see PLATES 1–4). Sermon one is written on a single paper stock bearing a watermark similar to Heawood 1768 (a fleur-de-lis, dated England 1616). Sermons two and three are on a single paper stock bearing a watermark similar to Heawood 479 or 480 (a coat of arms, dated England, early seventeenth century, or Amsterdam, *c.*1620). Sermons four and five are on a single paper stock bearing a watermark similar to Heawood 840 (a cockatrice, dated Holland 1619). The two concluding blank leaves bear a watermark similar to Heawood 140 (a shield bend, dated Rochester 1625).

TEXTUAL SIGNIFICANCE OF HARLEY MS 6946 (H1)

Proverbs 8:17

The first sermon in the volume (fols 1r–11r: PLATE 1), on Proverbs 8:17, was preached to Queen Anne of Denmark, 14 December 1617, at Denmark House.[7] Potter and Simpson thought very highly of the sermon: 'Donne has found himself in the pulpit; he is mastering the literary medium he adopted so late in life; and a great artist in prose has emerged from his two-year period of experimentation and uncertainty' (I, 138). Seventeenth-century readers and collectors of sermons agree. It exists in one printed version (F26) and in three manuscript versions (M, E, and H1). Collation of these extant witnesses supports the following conclusions: (1) H1 provides the best extant manuscript witness, closely related to M, even more closely related to E (both of which are relatively good manuscript sources), but, in the end, derived from a source that is closest to that which served as copy-text for F26; (2) moreover, substantive variants between H1 and F26, as well as a scribal hand that clearly antedates that edition, indicate that H1 is not copied from F26.

The evidence to support these conclusions falls into three parts: (1) evidence that H1, M, and E share a common source, but that H1 is more closely related to E than to M; (2) evidence that, despite these findings, H1 is more closely related to the manuscript that was the source for F26, although it is not itself that source; and (3) evidence that, where

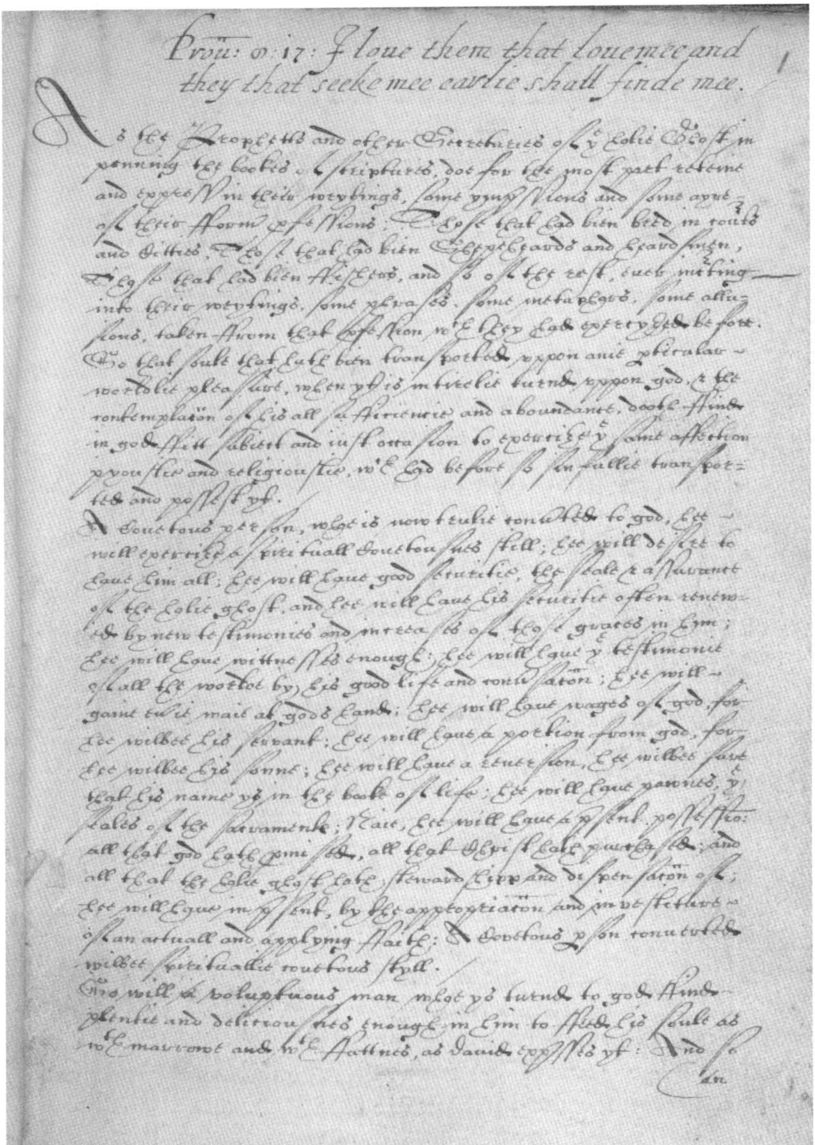
Prov: 8:17: I loue them that loue mee and
they that seeke mee earlie shall finde mee.

PLATE 1. *The first page of Donne's sermon on Proverbs 8:17 in manuscript H1: London, British Library, Harley MS 6946, fol. 1r (Original page size 198 × 155mm.) Reproduced by permission of the Board of the British Library.*

H1 stands alone, there is not a single case in which it offers a superior reading that *requires* emendation of F26.

In the body of the sermon itself, H1 sides with the manuscripts against F26 roughly half as often as it sides with F26 against the manuscripts. Many times all three manuscripts agree in wording that differs in a minor way from that in F26. This includes occasions where the two groups differ in using singular and plural, in prepositions, in spelling, and in word order from one another. Frequently, the manuscripts agree more substantively in omitting words and phrases found in F26.[8] Additionally, several readings adopted by M and E, and used by Potter and Simpson to emend F26, are supported by H1.[9] Most, but not all, of these are listed correctly by Potter and Simpson in their notes, but these notes ought not to be relied on for accuracy in accidentals. Additionally, in almost every case in which E provides the correct reading (a reading which Potter and Simpson have used to emend F26), H1 supports that reading, suggesting that H1 and E are more reliable and more closely related than H1 and M.[10] On only three occasions does H1 side with E in incorrect readings (lines 313, 343, 441), none of them substantive. These examples do not include the two cases in which H1 sides with E regarding marginalia. In one important case, Potter and Simpson do *not* note a variant in E, now supported by H1, which is clearly correct. On line 56, F26 and M read 'we are not for that' instead of the more sensible 'we care not for that' of both E and H1.

The pattern of variants demonstrates that H1 is closely related to the manuscript that was the source for F26. This is most clearly illustrated by comparing marginalia, which suggest that H1 derives directly from the lost original holograph that served as the source for the copy-text for F26, although it could not be that copy-text itself.[11] On nine occasions, H1 sides clearly with F26 against the other manuscripts, including readings that are incorrect.[12] These are the most important proofs that H1 is more closely aligned with F26 than with the manuscripts, and that H1 is aligned with the manuscripts, either singly or together, primarily when they agree with F26 (on seven occasions all four sources agree; on six others H1 agrees with F26 and one other manuscript). On three occasions only, H1 sides with both of the manuscripts against F26 (omission of 'Ambrose' (although M has a floral device in the margin at that point); omission of 'Early' (although M has 'Marie', in a different hand, inserted there); 'Mutual' (where all three manuscripts have 'Mutuus'); and omission of 'First Part. The Person'.

In addition to the evidence from marginalia, some key variants link H1 closely with F26 although in most cases Potter and Simpson emend the text to agree with readings in M and E.[13] Furthermore, H1 supports

F26 in including the phrases 'and not *amavit*' (163) and 'saies the apostle' (205) omitted in M and E. These substantives, along with the numerous accidentals, minor variants, and marginal variants support the claim that F26 is derived from the same source as H1.

Where H1 stands alone, the variants can be grouped into several categories. The majority are scribal errors or minor variants that do not substantially alter the text of the sermon. These include additions or deletions of single words (articles or prepositions for the most part), variations in singular or plural, and differences in punctuation, especially terminal (question marks, periods, semi-colons, parentheses). There are three cases, excluding marginalia, in which H1 incorrectly copies a Latin word or phrase, and one instance where it misreads the word 'enjoying' (line 74) as '*Eniogenie*'. Occasionally the scribe of H1 omits phrases that are included in all other sources. These can be attributed to eye-skip or inattention.[14] On several occasions H1 offers an alternative, but not necessarily better, reading of passages that are textually corrupt.[15] Several cases where H1 stands alone are clearly scribal errors, as on line 74, mentioned above, and probably on line 266, where the manuscripts and F26 read 'in whom Princes and Subjects, Angels and men, and wormes are fellow servants', and where H1 reads 'in whom Princes and Subjects, Angels and men, men and wormes are fellow servants'. However, it can be argued that this reading is rhetorically more satisfying than that in the other sources, and that it positions men equivocally with Angels and with worms, a paradoxical identification Donne might have intended. A reading at lines 381–2 shows H1 alone among the manuscripts in missing the sense of F26. F26 reads 'Thou must not so think him in heaven, as that thou canst not have'. H1, however, misreads 'so think' as 'seeke' and then copies its source to read 'Thou must not seeke him in heaven as thinkinge thou thou canst not have'. This reading is clearly in error.

Genesis 2:18

The second sermon in H1 (fols 12r–22v: PLATE 2) was preached at the marriage of Sir Francis Nethersole and Lucy Goodyer.[16] Until the discovery of H1, there were only two witnesses for this sermon: F50 and M. Although I will be discussing each sermon separately, it is important to remember that this sermon and the following one on Hosea 2:19 were copied on the same paper stock, although written in different hands.

This manuscript witness supports the following conclusions: (1) H1 is so close to F50 that it might have been copied from the lost original holograph posited by Potter and Simpson; (2) however, certain substantive variants (not attributable to scribal error) between H1 and F50

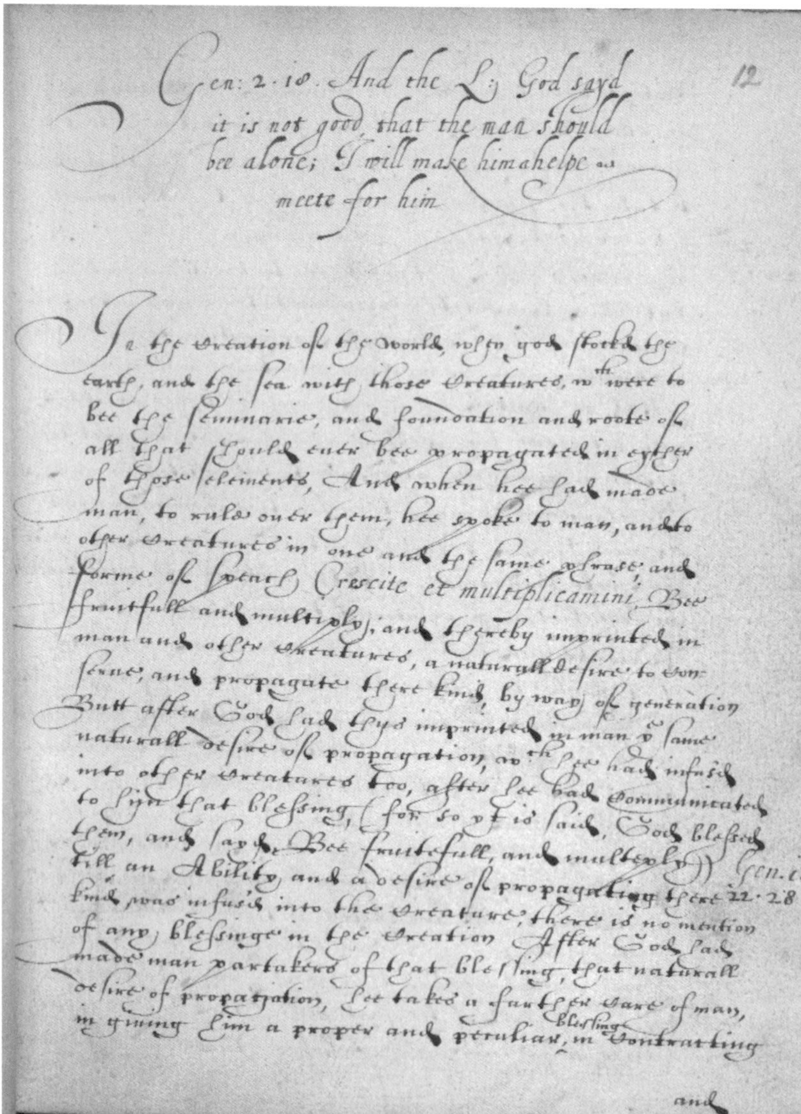

PLATE 2. *The first page of Donne's sermon on Genesis 2:18 in manuscript H1: London, British Library, Harley MS 6946, fol. 12r (Original page size 198 × 155mm.) Reproduced by permission of the Board of the British Library.*

prove that—however close they are—they were derived from separate sources; (3) furthermore, H1 differs from M in several substantive variants and almost certainly derives from a better manuscript source than that which produced M.

My analysis indicates that H1 almost always supports F50 against M. There are six places where H1 agrees with M against F50, but all but one of these are inconsequential.[17] This occurs at line 437, where the manuscript reading ('divers') is preferable to F50's 'repugnant,' although Potter and Simpson have not emended F50. However, since it is inconceivable that 'repugnant' is a scribal error for 'divers,' one must conclude that, however close H1 is to F50, they do not derive from an identical source.

H1's direct connection to F50 is further reinforced by a consideration of the marginalia, which correspond closely to F50 and are more accurate than those of either F50 or M. Of twenty-eight marginal references (the number in F50), H1 differs from F50 in seven cases. Six of these differences are omissions, while the seventh agrees with M in giving 'Rom.12.1' (the more precise reading) as opposed to F50's 'Rom.12' at line 244. Furthermore, H1's superiority to M is evident in that H1 supports F50 in six instances where there is no marginal reference in M (marginal lines 80, 130, 262, 328, 352, 368), and in two other cases supports F50's marginal reference where M is in error (marginal lines 39, 364). The marginal references suggest, then, that F50 derives from a manuscript source connected to H1 more closely than to M.

In the thirty-five cases where H1 stands alone for this sermon, the variants can be grouped into several categories. The first of these comprises readings for which H1 is clearly wrong;[18] the second group includes readings where both make sense and neither reading is preferable;[19] the third group includes readings where F50 is preferable to H1, although both are possible.[20] The most significant variants in the final group comprise those five readings which are preferable in H1: H1's clearer 'in yor body' for 'in it' (105); 'inventory' instead of 'inventories' (135); 'sonne, to' instead of 'sonne' (139); H1's 'untangle' where F50 reads 'un-entangle' and M reads 'entangle' (159); and 'understanding' instead of 'understandings' (344). Taken together, these variants indicate that H1 provides the best available text for this sermon, and that it is almost certainly derived from the lost original holograph posited by Potter and Simpson. It is an accurate copy of a manuscript source that is superior to M and very closely related to the manuscript that was the copy-text for F50.

Discussion of this manuscript cannot end without an introduction to the 'corrector,' who, in this sermon, makes two important interventions to correct the manuscript. The first is at line 59, where H1 has omitted 'not,' thus completely changing the meaning of the line which in F50 reads 'it is not good for man to be alone'. The second correction occurs at line 396 where the correct word 'peace' is inserted above the scribal 'praise' in order to produce the phrase that appears in F50 ('all such conversation as may violate his peace'). The non-scribal correcting hand uses dark ink and an italic hand, but is not the same correcting hand observed by Potter and Simpson in E. It is not clear when these corrections were made, and it is even possible that the owner of the manuscript corrected these words from a copy of F50. This is possible since these are two of the most important deviations from F50 in the entire sermon.

Hosea 2:19

Of the five sermons contained in H1, more witnesses survive for this sermon than for any of the others: F50, Q6, M, P, E, and H1 (fols 23r–34v: PLATE 3).[21] Potter and Simpson note that the sermon is found in two forms: an earlier form represented in M and P and a slightly revised form found in F50, Q6, and E, very close to but not identical with the copy-text for F50. The textual evidence substantiates several conclusions: (1) H1 belongs to the revised stream found in F50, E, and sometimes Q6; (2) while copied from a common source, these witnesses are not copied from each other; (3) both E and H1 are excellent copies deriving from a common source that is very close to but not identical with F50; (4) H1 is closest to F50 of all existing witnesses, both print and manuscript, and is probably a more accurate copy of the manuscript from which E derives; (5) this source is different from that for either of the other two streams which Potter and Simpson posit as descending from Donne's lost original holograph for this sermon.[22]

Evidence for the first conclusion is clearest when one examines the variants cited by Potter and Simpson (II, 368–9) that indicate a revised state of the manuscript. Most often when H1, E, and F50 combine—but not always—they combine to produce the correct reading. A few examples of such substantive differences leading to a 'revised' or correct reading include the following: 'later' instead of 'latter' (3); 'moderate' instead of 'modest' (57); 'first use' instead of 'ayme' (115, 188); 'birth' for 'beauty' (213); and 'professes' for 'protests' (274). Even weak or incorrect readings support this family relationship between H1, E, and F50.[23] The weak reading 'transportation' instead of 'transplantation' at line 144 is perhaps the clearest example of this connection. On several occasions, H1, E, and F50 omit lines that are included in the other manuscripts: for example, they omit 'though there were foure rivers in Paradise' at lines

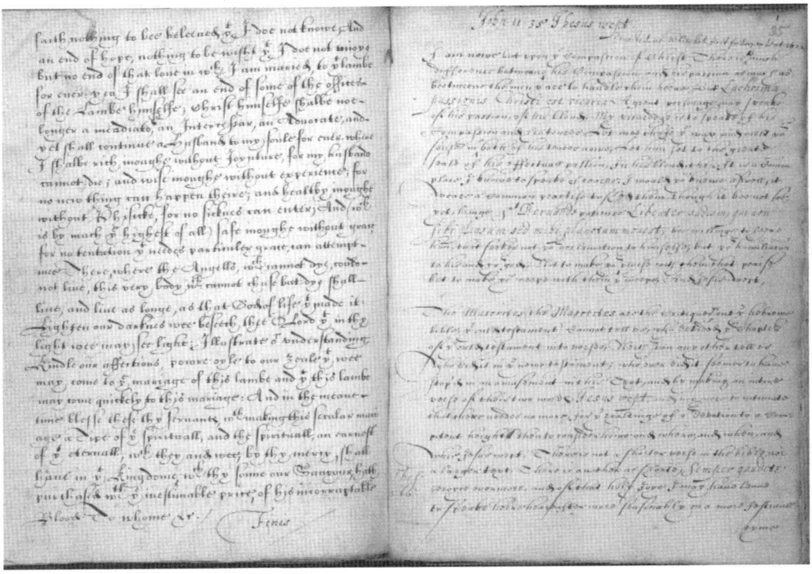

PLATE 3. *Opening in manuscript H1 showing the last page of Donne's sermon on Hosea 2:19 and the first page of his sermon on John 11:35: London, British Library, Harley MS 6946, fols 34v–35r (Original page size 198 × 155mm.) Reproduced by permission of the Board of the British Library.*

40–1. They also include lines omitted in M, P, and sometimes Q6, such as 'when they dissolve marriage upon legal kindred, because my Grandfather adopted that womans Father' at lines 64–5. These substantive variants are only a fraction of the minor variants from M, P, and sometimes Q6 represented in H1, E, and F50.[24]

Evidence that H1, E, and F50, though closely related, were not copied from the same source is provided in instances where H1 combines with either source to differ substantially from F50 or E, and, particularly, where H1 combines with other sources to disagree with both E and F50. H1 and F50 side against the other sources, including E, in several circumstances. Several of these involve omissions of words and phrases, such as E's omission of 'the service of' (70), 'dwell there, and' (126), and 'to heighten them; it is a shadowing of them' (325). On the very next line (325), E differs from both H1 and F50, this time by an addition, reading 'yet perchance' where the other sources read 'yet'. On line 345, E omits 'and many,' where H1 and F50 include it. Where H1 sides with F50 against all other sources, Potter and Simpson have emended the text against these readings.[25]

There are several places, however, where H1 sides with E *against* F50. Some of these are small verbal differences: a plural at line 111 or 'that's' for 'that is' at line 113–14. Nevertheless, some show that the scribe for H1 was able to interpret words that eluded the scribe and corrector of E. At line 258, for example, the correct Latin word is '*zelotopiae*.' F50 reads '*velotypiae*,' M reads 'zelotipia,' while P reads 'zelotipie.' Only Q6 and E agree with H1 in this instance. H1 combines with E (and sometimes other sources) in several other important cases as well, improving F50's 'there are' to 'there be' (268) or 'that is' to 'this is' at line 302. All of these examples confirm the very close relationship between H1, E, and F50 while at the same time confirming that the three, while copied from a common source, are not copied from each other. This is particularly evident in the places where H1 combines with other sources to disagree with both E and F50. The most interesting example occurs at line 484 where Q6, M, and P read correctly 'soe,' F50 and H1 read 'to,' and E reads both: that is, the scribe probably copied 'to' from its source (the source connected with H1 and F50), but the corrector has written above it the correct word 'soe.' It seems unlikely that he corrected it from M or P, although it is possible that he had a copy of Q6 and recognized it as a better reading. On the basis of this evidence, we can conclude that, E, H1, and F50, while very close, have not been copied or corrected from one another.

The patterns of marginal reference support these conclusions. Of the thirty-six marginal references found in F50, fully eight are references supported in both E and H1, and not supported by Q6, M, and P. Potter and Simpson have argued on the basis of variants that F50 and Q6 did not derive from the same manuscript; so, if we take out Q6 and identify those marginal references in which H1 and E support F50 while M and P do not, the number rises to sixteen. If we add to these references those in which all witnesses agree, the number rises to eighteen. Then if we add those references for which all the manuscripts support F50, though not Q6, the number rises to twenty-four. If we add those references which are supported by both H1 and E and one other manuscript (either M or P), the tally is thirty-one. If we then consider one peculiar example in which F50 has 'Jer.22.30' in the margin, while both E and H1 have simply '22.30' beside Jeremy in the text, this leaves only four marginal references in which H1 and E do not support F50. Of these four, H1 has the correct reference twice ('Ambros.', '2. Cor. 11.2'), where E has 'Ambick.' and '2. Cor. 2.1'. In one instance, H1 and F50 agree—erroneously—('Esay 53.4') while E has no marginal reference. In only one instance does H1 not support F50—at line 478 where F50 has '*In aeternum*,' a reading supported only by E. The evidence of the marginalia, confirms, then, that H1 is closest to F50 of all existing witnesses, both print and manuscript, and that it is probably a more accurate copy of the manuscript from which E derives. This suggests a common source for both E and H1 that is different from that for either of the other two streams which Potter and Simpson posit as descending from Donne's lost original holograph.

Where H1 stands alone, the variants can be grouped into several categories, almost all of them attributable to scribal error. Some are alterations in word order (as with line 19, where H1 has 'are wee carried' while F50 reads 'we are carried); variations between singular and plural forms where either might be correct (as with H1's 'consideration' versus F50's 'considerations' at line 22); and minor verbal variations (as when H1 reads 'a place' while F50 reads 'the place' at line 35). The scribe of H1 had occasional difficulties with Latin; he writes 'Pepentian' for 'Peputian' at line 56, 'Viri' for 'V[U]ri' at line 112. And in six cases, H1 stands alone in a reading that is incorrect but that can be attributed to scribal error.[26] There are also two places (at lines 29–30, 291–2), in which H1 stands alone against all other witnesses, but these are not significant for understanding the textual transmission of this sermon. On the whole H1 and E are excellent copies of the manuscript from which the copy-text for F50 was derived, and are closely related to one another and to the Folio version.

The non-scribal corrector made only one correction to this manuscript, but it is significant. At line 178, where the text clearly should read as it does in F50 ('not break promise'), the corrector adds the 'not'. As with the previous sermon, this one comes closer to the Folio reading with the non-scribal correction.

John 11:35

This sermon exists in only two witnesses: H1 (fols 35r–48v: PLATE 3) and F50.[27] Comparison of the two leads to the following conclusions: (1) H1 is not the direct source for F50; (2) H1 and F50 nonetheless derive from a common source; (3) F50 is a rhetorically and grammatically superior version, and perhaps represents a revised version of the sermon; and (4) the non-scribal corrector has made a number of significant changes to H1, but is not correcting from F50. We should also be reminded that both this sermon and the one that follows were written by different scribes, but on identical paper stock.

The first conclusion is based on several types of evidence: that provided by differences in marginalia, that provided by the non-scribal corrector, and that provided by variant readings, whether correct or erroneous. Differences between the marginalia of H1 and F50 indicate that, for this sermon, H1 is not the source for F50. It is much more lightly annotated than F50 (marginal references at lines 3, 136–7, 329–30, 368–70, and 683 are not found in H1, for example). With one exception (at line 25) H1 lacks information that F50 includes (at lines 39, 139, 487, and 738), and in three instances, although the scribe is close to F50, his readings are incorrect. Comparing the marginalia of H1 and F50 supports the argument that H1 and F50 derive from a common source.

Other evidence that supports this conclusion is provided by the very fact that the non-scribal corrector produces several key readings that conflict with F50. These are analyzed in detail below. However, the bulk of the evidence to prove that H1 is not the direct source for F50 occurs by examining variants between the two witnesses.

The second conclusion is supported by a crucial common error in the marginalia, and by considering the five incorrect readings specifically emended by Potter and Simpson. At line 651, both H1 and F50 incorrectly cite 'Exo: 22.19' (F50 has 'Exod. 22. 19'), where the correct reading, provided by Potter and Simpson, is 'Exod.22.29'. Of the five places where Potter and Simpson emend F50 (without benefit of H1), H1 and F50 agree in four (at lines 200, 206–7, 219, and 236). In one case, however, H1 supports an emendation by Potter and Simpson.[28] On the whole, however, H1 is an admirable copy of the sermon, even if it did not serve directly as copy-text for F50, a conclusion supported by examining the variants where H1 stands alone.[29]

The third conclusion is supported by variants where H1 stands alone. These number fewer than ninety, and the majority are minor, involving omissions of words which do not alter the text substantially and which can be attributed to scribal differences or errors.[30] Others are differences between singular and plural where either form might be acceptable (as at lines 108, 162, 378–9, 685), differences between contracted and full forms, or differences between archaic and modern forms (as at lines 692, 463, 571, 572, 628). Several variants between H1 and F50 indicate that the manuscript from which F50 derives directly was produced by a scribe who understood Latin better than the scribe of H1 (as at line 433 where H1 has the incorrect 'Mommentum' while F50 correctly prints 'monumentum', or line 554 where H1 incorrectly has '*Illachrimabilius*' while F50 correctly prints '*Illachrymabilis*'). At line 336, the H1 scribe even 'corrects' the word 'manus' to the (nonsensical) 'manas'. Some variants are explicable as miscopying of contracted forms, as at line 428 where H1 has 'y^{e}' while F50 has 'that' where either might be acceptable, or line 598, where H1 has the somewhat redundant 'y^{t} it is,' while F50 has the cleaner 'that is'. Some minor variants are simply the result of errors in H1, as in line 496 where H1 incorrectly has 'in in' instead of F50's correct 'it in,' or line 71 where H1 incorrectly has 'spleent' for F50's 'spleene.'

Major variants between H1 and F50 can be grouped into several categories. Some are simply small rhetorical differences, usually with F50 producing a superior version that provides greater emphasis, clarity, or variety. This suggests that F50 might represent a revised form of H1. For example, H1's redundant rendering 'how shall wee raise this Salamander and this Serpent, when this Salamander and this Serpent is all one person' becomes 'how shall we raise this Salamander and this Serpent, when this Serpent and this Salamander is all one person' (110–11). The reversal of the terms 'Salamander' and 'Serpent' makes the resulting passage an example of antimetabole, a figure of speech which minimizes the repetition and emphasizes the literal identification between the two animals that the text intends. Not all of the stylistic turns of F50 involve complex figures of speech, however; two of the most effective are the simplest. At lines 254–5, F50 takes indirect speech (H1 urges listeners to 'Behould and see if euer there weare any sorrowe, any teares like his [Christ's],' while F50 replaces 'his' with 'mine' and places the passage in italics to represent Christ's direct speech, rendering the exhortation more compelling as a result). The simple addition of 'and' (at line 318) changes H1's 'true Orthodoxall' to 'true and Orthodoxall,' a reading that is rhetorically more balanced and clear. Another example of F50's rhetorical superiority to H1 occurs at line 394. H1 says that the son should 'ratefie and rectifie' his father's memory, an inelegant phrase that rhymes awkwardly and contains two words that are to function as synonyms without being so. The phrase in F50 is 'rectifie and redeeme,' one which is both logically and rhetorically more apt in this context. Several variants reveal differences in word choice that lead to substantially different readings, although in these cases the reading in F50 is preferable. For example, at line 114, H1 has 'imployed', a word which could refer literally to the miraculous means by which Christ raised Lazarus from the dead. F50 prints 'implied,' a reading which interprets the 'that' which follows not literally ('that' union of scattered pieces that occurred when Lazarus was raised from the dead), but more largely as 'that' miracle of miracles implied by Christ's raising of a man 'scattered' into several sins. And at line 729, F50's 'then he was before' is only marginally preferable to 'then before he had,' although the differences are sufficient to indicate that the scribes were not working from the same exemplar. One small difference nonetheless changes the emphasis of a line considerably. At line 646, H1 reads that David wept for Absolon, but in doing so wept not for the Child by Bathsheba; 'he could not suspect so much danger in him'.

In F50, the last clause reads 'he could not suspect so much danger in that', changing the pronoun reference from a direct and literal reference to the Child by Bathsheba ('him') to 'that', which suggests that David was not weeping for the danger to his soul caused by 'that' act of adultery, but for 'that' entire situation. The change makes David's sinning and not the human consequence of his sin, his son Absolon, the cause of his weeping.

Some differences are omissions attributable to eye-skip, and F50 includes these. The most important of these occurs at line 475 where the rhetorically emphatic phrase 'even that temporal prosperity' is omitted in H1. At line 169 and again at line 176, H1 has readings no doubt caused by scribal error, in both cases harking back to previous words ('person' rather than the correct 'party' and 'some man may' rather than 'and some man will') rather than recording the variation that F50 includes.

The largest numbers are readings in which F50's text improves on the clearly incorrect H1 reading. I have identified at least twenty-eight cases in which F50 has superior readings to H1 that go beyond improvements in spelling, Latin, and the minor errors listed above. Some of these are simply cases where F50 supplies a more precise or complete wording. At line 184, for example, F50 correctly supplies '*into the wildernesse*' where H1 has 'in'; similarly, F50 has the more precise 'others interpretations' where H1 has 'other'. At line 115, F50 includes the missing word 'it' in the phrase 'calls it,' thus clarifying the grammatical antecedent of the pronoun, and at line 550, F50 correctly prints 'be impenitent' where H1 has 'the impenitent,' a reading that makes no sense in the sentence. Later, the missing words 'a thing' before 'indifferent' are supplied by F50 where H1 prints the ungrammatical 'an indifferent' at line 589.

A whole group of differences is more substantive, removing errors and ambiguities. At line 243, F50 correctly prints that the men for whom Jesus wept were 'none of' his kindred, while H1 says they were 'out of' that group; at line 304–5, F50 reads 'humane and pious officiousnesse,' a phrase that makes sense of the ungrammatical 'pious and officiousnesse' found in H1. The scribal error in H1 which results in a prelate's having 'rested' rather than 'resisted' heretics is not reproduced in F50; nor is the statement that Christ wept amid the 'Callamities' rather than the 'acclamations' of the people at line 462. While 'Callamities' might make sense, it is clearly not the intended word, as indicated by the Latin 'acclamationes' that it translates. At line 387 H1's incorrect 'lack my selfe' is correctly produced as 'lack my help' in F50. And at line 435, H1's clearly incorrect 'writinge' correctly reads 'rising' in F50. And, significantly, H1's ungrammatical 'to the first' is printed in F50 at line 737 as 'to thee, first'. One of the most important of these substantive corrections occurs at line 552. There, F50 correctly prints the phrase 'that doe not afford them' while H1 omits the 'not,' thus reversing the idea of the sentence. In one case, F50 fills in what in H1 is a large blank space with the phrase 'of feare of' (lines 470–1).

Among the variants where H1 stands alone, these are generally inferior to F50, grammatically and rhetorically. At most, six examples of superior readings in H1 can be identified.[31] One verbal difference (275) is difficult to interpret. F50 has 'We stride over many steps at once; waive many such considerable circumstances as these.' The word 'waive' is puzzling in this context, but suggests that these circumstances are not going to be material to the main circumstance that might have provoked weeping, that Lazarus was dead. H1 has the same sentence, but supplies the word 'ioyn' instead of 'waive,' thus suggesting that we will not simply ignore these reasons, but join them together to give weight to the final and most important circumstance, that Lazarus was dead. In fact, each word produces a substantially different means of arriving at the same end, and it is not likely that F50 mistook 'ioyn' for 'waive,' so we could conclude (though this is unnecessary) that they derive from different manuscript sources on the basis of this variant. Perhaps the most interesting variant, however, occurs at line 207. There, F50 reads 'it is not always good to go too far, as some good men have gone before.' This is a perfectly acceptable reading, but H1 substitutes 'donne' for 'gone,' suggesting that the scribe was either copying from a document that punned on Donne's name, or, on his own, inserted it at that point. Such a suggestion is mere speculation, but corresponds to our knowledge that Donne frequently punned on his name.

The fourth conclusion is supported by analysis of the changes made by the non-scribal corrector. His several changes to this manuscript are significant. In some cases, they correct the sermon to agree with F50, but it is clear that he is not correcting from the Folio, given the number of changes that are not consistent with F50's readings. The most significant of these occurs at line 285 where the second hand 'corrects' the reading 'carcasse' by crossing it out and writing 'dead body'. This reading is difficult to justify. F50 has 'Carcasse', and the connotations of that word are appropriate to the sermon's emphasis on a moment when Christ is 'disunited, dead, hee is none of us, hee is noe Man' (20–21). Similarly, where F50 describes the lowly nature of humanity as 'like stones, like dirt' (213) the corrector has written over 'dirt' to create the word 'dust.' 'Dust,' with its connotations of death or impermanence, is appropriate to the context, but not as apt as the word 'dirt' which communicates the baseness of humanity that is the focus in the sermon at this point. At other points in the manuscript, the corrector underlines a word and then writes his preferred version above it. This occurs, for example, where the H1 scribe has written 'remaynes' (669) and the non-scribal corrector has written above it 'reseaues,' a reading that coincides with F50's 'receives'. It also occurs where the H1 scribe has written 'propheticall' (529), but the corrector has written above it (without crossing out the incorrect word) 'pontificall'. Most (but not all) of the corrections coincide with readings in F50, although they could have been arrived at without access to F50 or to its manuscript source. At line 64, for example, the H1 scribe has clearly misunderstood the source and written 'a welbeelonging' where the correct reading is 'a Well, belonging'. The corrector has crossed out 'welbe,' which occurs at the end of the line, and written 'well' above it. At the beginning of the next line, in the margin, the corrector has placed 'bee' alongside 'longing' to create one word. Other specific corrections that bring H1 into conformity with F50 occur at lines 120, 161, 375, and 321. At line 379, the corrector has crossed over 'death' and written 'faiths,' the correct word although not found in plural form in F50. Several changes made by the corrector at lines 1, 349, 646, and 725 are neutral. They do not improve the text, necessarily, but they are possible readings. However, it is clear that the corrector took great pains with this manuscript, altering words, phrases, and perhaps even letters to achieve the best readings. We see this especially at line 64, where the words 'the' and 'this' modifying 'text' are alternately crossed through, with the corrector eventually opting for 'this' (which is inserted before 'text'). The reading in F50 is 'the,' but the number of revisions, even over such minute changes, suggests that the corrector was particularly painstaking. Finally, while it is impossible to determine whether corrections that strike through letters are scribal or non-scribal, several such corrections or changes to Latin words suggest that the corrector had small knowledge of Latin. For example, at lines 345 and 346, he correctly strikes through the final *a* of 'Quia,' but fails to insert the *s* that would produce the correct form 'Quis' in both cases. Perversely, 'manus' (the correct word) is changed to 'manas' at line 336. However, at line 565, someone correctly crossed through the *a* in 'asani' to produce the correct reading 'sani.' Similarly, it is uncertain whether the H1 scribe or the corrector changed 'waters' at line 108 to the correct 'water', or changed 'heighth' (which is also the reading in F50) to 'height' at line 22 by blotting out the final *h*. The corrector was much more active in this manuscript than in previous ones in the collection.

1 Thessalonians 5:16

As with the previous sermon, H1 (fols 49r–60r: PLATE 4) provides the only extant manuscript source for this text. Potter and Simpson relied

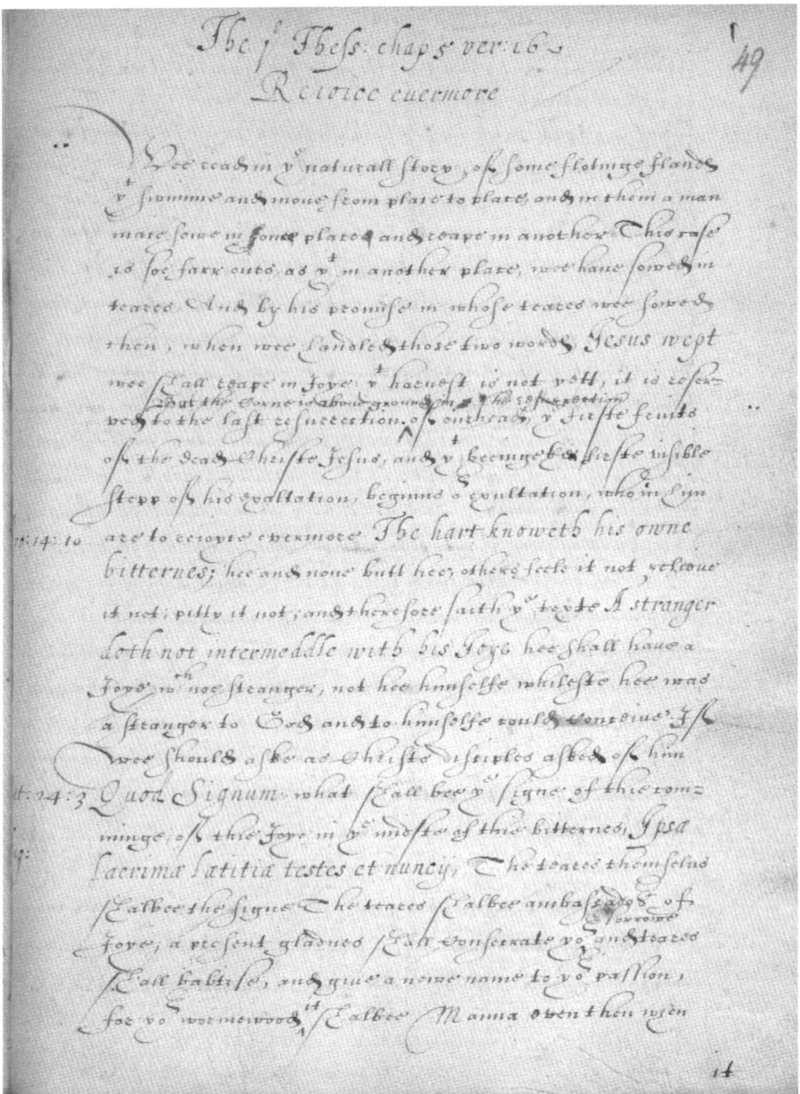

PLATE 4. *The first page of Donne's sermon on 1 Thessalonians 5:16 in manuscript H1: London, British Library, Harley MS 6946, fol. 49r (Original page size 198 × 155mm.) Reproduced by permission of the Board of the British Library.*

on F50 as their copy-text and emended slightly.[32] Therefore, H1 is valuable for what it can tell us about the manuscript tradition supporting this sermon. Evidence from this examination supports the following conclusions: (1) F50 appears to be a slightly revised version of the sermon as found in H1; (2) in the case of marginalia, however, H1 is superior to F50; (3) most variants can be attributed to scribal error, and suggest that H1 and F50 are closely related; (4) however, H1 was not the copy-text for F50; and (5) more than one non-scribal corrector has handled this manuscript, but it was not corrected from F50.

The evidence supporting the first conclusion includes a number of variants, several of which are substantive. These variants indicate that F50 is a better version of the sermon, eliminating verbal errors found in H1, offering readings that are rhetorically more effective, that show careful reading of the text, and that appear to be deliberate changes unlikely to be the work of a compositor. The nature of these changes also supports the third and fourth conclusions above. F50 appears to be a slightly revised version of the sermon, deriving from a source that is similar to, but not identical with, H1.

There are numerous examples where F50 eliminates verbal errors in H1. Some variants occur, usually when H1 has misconstrued the Latin word, as at line 81 where H1 reads '*Gebenna*' instead of F50's correct '*Gehenna*'.[33] Some minor variants occur at places where H1 is clearly in error but where the correct reading appears in F50.[34] Some of the most significant changes, however, include the following: H1 incorrectly reads 'inwardly,' which F50 restores to the correct reading 'outwardly' (118); H1 incorrectly cites '*Peter*' (124) when the correct citation is '*Paul*'; H1 incorrectly has us laughing 'at' God's deliverances, whereas F50 correctly reads that wisdom and gravity allow us to laugh 'in' these deliverances; at line 197, H1 miswrites 'hard' for 'heard'; at line 325, H1 incorrectly reads 'thou' (a singular) for the correct word 'they' (a plural) necessary for sense; and, H1 uses the incorrect pronoun 'w^{ch}' (494) which F50 corrects to 'who.' At line 413, F50 correctly supplies the subjunctive 'finde' where H1 reads 'finds.' At line 392 H1 has the incorrect nominal form 'sedition' where F50 reads 'seditious,' and, finally, at line 580, H1 reads 'wch the God' for the grammatical 'of which, God' supplied by F50. One substantive variant cannot be explained by any of the common causes of scribal error. At line 401, H1 reads 'iust, and not cruell' where F50 reads 'not unjust, nor cruell'. There are subtle rhetorical differences between these two readings, but both are acceptable, as is the reversal between 'must we' (H1) and 'we must' (F50) at line 418 or 'iustly maie' (H1) and 'may justly' at line 420.

F50 offers a better reading that alters the text substantively in a number of other circumstances as well. For example, H1 omits the word 'life'

(29–30), a reading that appears in F50. Other places where F50 includes words omitted in H1 occur at line 77 where H1 omits 'in' creating the ungrammatical 'at peace and favour with God'; at line 89 where H1 omits '*thy God*'; at line 101 where H1 omits the subject of the clause, 'Christ'; at line 523 where F50 restores 'exceeding'.

Some readings in F50 are rhetorically more effective. Only a few examples must suffice here. At line 71, for instance, H1 reads, awkwardly, 'is y[t] noe rest' whereas F50 reads 'that is not Rest'. At line 182, the insertion of the word 'then' omitted in H1 supplies a more effective transition, while at line 192, the insertion of 'first' before 'faintnesse' contrasts rhetorically with the 'last' verse; at line 237 the addition of 'even' stresses the contrast between joy and labour in Eden more than H1's simple 'in'; and at line 327, F50's 'here' is much more dramatic, bringing the audience directly into the text's application, than H1's 'there'. At line 421, H1 reads 'trially', a fairly nonsensical adverb, while in F50 this is expanded for clarity to read 'that is, trialls'; and at line 460, F50 has the more rhetorically emphatic 'a fountaine, the fountaine of joy' while H1 reads simply 'a fountayne of joy'.

The evidence supporting the second conclusion is also substantive. Comparison of the marginal references in H1 and F50 suggests that they do derive from a related (though not identical) source. In fully seventy instances, H1 and F50 coincide, differing in small matters of spelling or punctuation (sixty-nine of these provide the correct annotation, but in one case, both H1 and F50 agree on an incorrect reading); on four occasions, H1 differs from F50 and is incorrect; on eight occasions, H1 differs from F50 and improves upon the reading or adds a marginal notation not in F50 (three of these appear as additions or emendations in Potter and Simpson); and on one occasion H1 and F50 differ from each other, but both are incorrect. This degree of similarity suggests a high correlation between the two versions of the sermon, but the high degree of variance in accidentals (though changing nothing in the content) makes it almost certain that H1 did not serve as copy-text for F50. Significantly, though, both H1 and F50 use 'Luc' to refer to the evangelist in most cases (as at lines 102 and 567), 'Bern.' to refer to Bernard (as at lines 467, 484), and 'Esai' to refer to the prophet Isaiah (as in lines 106–7 and 568). In two cases, H1 and F50 coincide exactly. At line 46, both have only 'Part,' which Potter and Simpson have emended to '[I] Part.' However, the most important case is at lines 106–7 where both H1 and F50 have the incorrect marginal reference 'Esai 62.1,' which Potter and Simpson have corrected to 'Esai 62.5.'

The eight occasions on which H1 improves on F50 fall into several categories. At lines 57, 60, 187, 190, 201, and 204, H1 has annotations which do not appear in F50. Potter and Simpson have, in fact, added those to their edition at lines 57, 60, and 204. The final two readings in which H1 corrects F50 occur at lines 75 and 127, and, in both cases, Potter and Simpson have emended F50 to correspond to the correct reading found in H1. So, whereas F50 reads 'Banner' at line 75, H1 and Potter and Simpson read 'Bannez,' and whereas F50 reads 'Amo.' at line 127, H1 and Potter and Simpson read 'Amb.'. This comparison of marginalia suggests that at least in this aspect, H1 is superior to the manuscript that served as a copy-text for F50.

Nonetheless, H1 does not always offer the better reading, and some substantive differences from F50 suggest that at least in some matters, F50 provides a superior text. On the four occasions where H1 differs from F50 and is incorrect, for example, the difference is attributable to the H1 scribe's unfamiliarity with Latin or with the details of the Biblical text (see lines 48–9, 92–3, 185, and 496). The one occasion on which both H1 and F50 differ from themselves and from the correct reading occurs at line 566. Potter and Simpson have there emended F50's incorrect 'Mat. 9.15' to the correct 'Matt.19.17'. H1 reads 'Matth: 7: 15,' a reading which is incorrect, but which is closer to F50 than to the correct reference. In other words, these differences, while substantive, are explicable as scribal errors in H1.

The evidence supporting the third conclusion includes minor variants that can be grouped into a number of categories and can be attributed to scribal error, common copying errors, inability to construe Latin words and proper names, reversals of word order, and omissions. Several minor variants occur between H1, which uses the more archaic verbs ending in 'th,' and F50, which uses the *s* ending (for example, at line 12, H1 has 'saith' while F50 has 'saies').[35] Variation between singular and plural forms where these do not alter the meaning of the text and where grammar is retained occur in a number of places. For example, at line 156, H1 has 'calamitie' while F50 has '*calamities*'.[36] Some minor variants involve omission of a word, such as an article, as at line 93 where H1 has 'reste' while F50 has 'a rest'.[37] Some variants involve a minor difference in preposition, word form, or pronoun, as at line 95 where H1 has 'unto Men' while F50 has 'to Men'.[38] A related form of variant occurs where superscribed words are transcribed in full (sometimes creating error) as in line 25 where H1 incorrectly reads 'y^{t} that' while F50 reads 'that'. Some variants involve contractions as at line 404 where H1 has 'that's' while F50 has 'that is'.[39] All of these variants are minor and can be attributed to scribal error. The sum of them indicates that F50 derives from a manuscript that is superior to H1 in correcting obvious copying errors and errors in Latin, or in making fewer of them.

Some of the substantive evidence supporting the fourth conclusion has been noted above, but is further supported by the high degree of variance in accidentals, particularly in the marginalia. One notes that, in general, H1 is fuller than F50, having '1 Pet chap: 4: ver 13' where F50 has 'I Pet.4.13' at line 518–19, or 'Psa: 2 ver: 2' where F50 has 'Psal.2.2.' at line 161. It is also supported by a number of 'neutral' variants, some of which must be attributed to scribal error, but which clearly indicate that H1 and F50, while closely related, clearly belong to different manuscript traditions. Typical of these variants is one at line 16, where H1 has 'thie Joye' while F50 has 'this Joy', or at line 20–1 where H1 reads 'wormewood it shalbe' for F50's 'Wormwood shall be'. H1's 'to have donne' at line 58–9 fits as grammatically as F50's 'done', and it makes sense to say that the joy of the text 'is' (F50) or 'is in' the rest and testimony of a good conscience. Whether H1's 'Allmightie God' is preferable to F50's '*God*' is debatable, as is the variant at line 207 which says that despairing of others 'may' (F50) or 'will' (H1) lead to despair in oneself. Whether their secret sins are the 'cause' (H1) or the 'causes' (F50) of God's judgments at line 398 is debatable, as is the question of whether God is the place where all 'men' are (as in H1) or where all 'good men' are (as in F50, line 449), although the adjective provides rhetorical parallelism with adjectives used to describe kings and priests. Nor is it significant that men are described at line 451 as 'sick' in H1 or 'sickly' in F50.[40]

Despite the many cases in which F50 differs from and/or improves upon H1, the manuscript could be used to emend several places in F50. This is certainly the case with the marginalia, in which H1 shows itself to be superior to F50, but is true in other readings as well. I have identified fourteen places where H1 has a marginally or substantially superior reading to F50. The following are typical of the most significant improvements:[41] line 181 (where H1's 'this *Gaudete*' adds rhetorical emphasis to F50's '*Gaudete*'), 266 (where H1's 'may reioice' is superior to F50's 'may joy'), and 305 (where H1's 'soe' continues the rhetorical parallelism broken by F50's 'and'). More significant improvements occur at line 12 (where H1's 'releaue,' a word that makes more sense in the context, has probably been miscopied in F50 to read 'retaine'); 59 (where H1's 'occasions not,' in which 'occasions' is correctly the verb, becomes in F50, 'occasions, is not,' a reading that leads to the strange phrase 'to have lyen still, and done no wrong occasions, is not this Joy' instead of the more sensible 'to have lyen still, and done no wrong occasions not this joy'); 300 (where F50 has the incorrect 'When in a' which has been emended by Potter and Simpson to 'when a,' a reading supported by H1); 329 (where H1's 'another kind of service weare in this' is better than

F50's 'another kind of service then in this,' though both are grammatically correct); and 370 (where H1's rhetorical question 'will hee not bee angry too' is preferable to F50's direct question 'will he be angry too').

The evidence for the fifth conclusion is a pattern of non-scribal corrections, not in the 'corrector' hand observed in previous sermons, which suggests that this witness was corrected by more than one hand, or corrected before being bound. For example, at line 131 the text in F50, quoting Ambrose, reads 'Risus non irrisio diffidentis, sed exultatio gratulantis.' In H1, the word 'sed' has been omitted from the quotation and inserted in a hand unlike that of the scribal corrections or that of the 'corrector' of previous sermons. Moreover, there is a pattern, similar to that recorded in the Gunpowder Plot sermon (see note 3 below), at lines 619, 922, and particularly 1346, where someone has corrected a proper name or Latin term. In H1, this kind of correction occurs regarding the spelling of a name (*Deboragh*, corrected twice to 'Debora' at line 173). The corrections at line 179 from '*Superredere*' to '*Superidere*' and at line 274 where the scribe's '*Noagh's*' is corrected to '*Noah's*' by blotting out the *g*, and at line 476 from '*Currut*' to '*Currus*' indicate a similar pattern of correction of terms that would not have been understood by the scribe, but would be by the corrector. The unique status of this volume as entirely comprising sermons by Donne, the special knowledge of the compiler who has grouped the sermons according to weddings (the first three) and sermons on the two shortest Scriptural texts (the last two), the excellent quality of the marginalia, and the relatively few differences between this text and F50 all combine to support the conjecture that this sermon was possibly a scribal copy of Donne's lost original holograph from which the text that produced F50 was derived. However, despite similarities in handwriting between the added word 'sed' and Donne's handwriting (particularly the *s* and curled back *d*) the Latin errors *not* corrected in H1 make the conjecture that this correction was by Donne improbable, as does the *e* of 'sed', which is not Donne's typical italic *e*. In the end, then, it is imprudent to conclude that this is a copy corrected by the author, and we must attribute the corrections to a corrector more knowledgeable than the original scribe.

HARLEY MS 6356 (H2): PHYSICAL DESCRIPTION

Harley 6356 is a large composite volume of miscellaneous historical and theological tracts, some printed and annotated, but for the most part written in a variety of scribal hands. The table of contents at the end of the volume is in the hand of Abraham Pryme (1671–1704), a Yorkshire antiquary of Huguenot descent, who apparently gathered and ordered the materials.[42] Many of his manuscripts passed to John Warburton (1682–1759), then herald to Lord Shelburne, and are part of the British Library's Lansdowne manuscripts. As an antiquary and collector of historical manuscripts, Pryme had access to many rarities, and the volume has already proven of interest to scholars of early-modern Cyrillic manuscripts.[43]

The volume is foliated in pencil by the British Library and also paginated in ink on recto leaves by Pryme. The two sermons by Donne—on Matthew 21:44 and Ecclesiastes 12:1—occupy folios 118r–143v (Pryme's pages 232–[283]). A preliminary leaf, folio 117r (p. 230), bears the inscription 'Donum honoratissimæ & amicissimæ fœminæ Annæ Sadlier'. Because the leaves are now mounted on guards it is impossible to tell whether this inscribed leaf belongs to the subsequent gathering.

The leaves each measure approximately 195 x 145mm. They are not ruled uniformly. The sermon on Matthew 21:44 (fols 118r–31v) is ruled on the right and left-hand margins on fols 118r–127r; 127v–128r are not ruled; 128v–129r are ruled; 129v–130r are not ruled; 130v–131r are ruled; 131v is unruled. The sermon on Ecclesiastes 12:1 (fols 132r–143v) is not ruled. The rulings seem contemporaneous with the manuscript, and the pages were trimmed after ruling.

The sermons are copied in two scribal secretary hands. The first occupies fols 118r–133v and then the first five lines on fol. 134r before the second hand takes over (see PLATE 5). The second scribe also appears to have proofread the copy for both sermons and to have made several corrections, insertions, and deletions on the leaves copied by the first scribe. Both sermons are copied on a single paper stock bearing a pot watermark very similar to Heawood 3582 or 3583 (both of which are dated 1621 from blank sheets in *Bacon's Letters*).[44] Examination of watermarks indicates that the sermons are on two gatherings. The first comprises thirteen leaves, with the first leaf (folio 116a) missing. The second gathering, beginning at folio 130, comprises fourteen leaves, with folios 143a and 143b missing. That the sermons themselves are complete, are copied on a single paper stock, and contain no blank sheets supports this hypothesis.[45]

TEXTUAL SIGNIFICANCE OF HARLEY MS 6356 (H2)

The two sermons on Matthew 21:44 and Ecclesiastes 12:1 exist in more manuscript copies than any other of Donne's sermons.[46] They almost always travel together (E and A are the exceptions), and Potter and

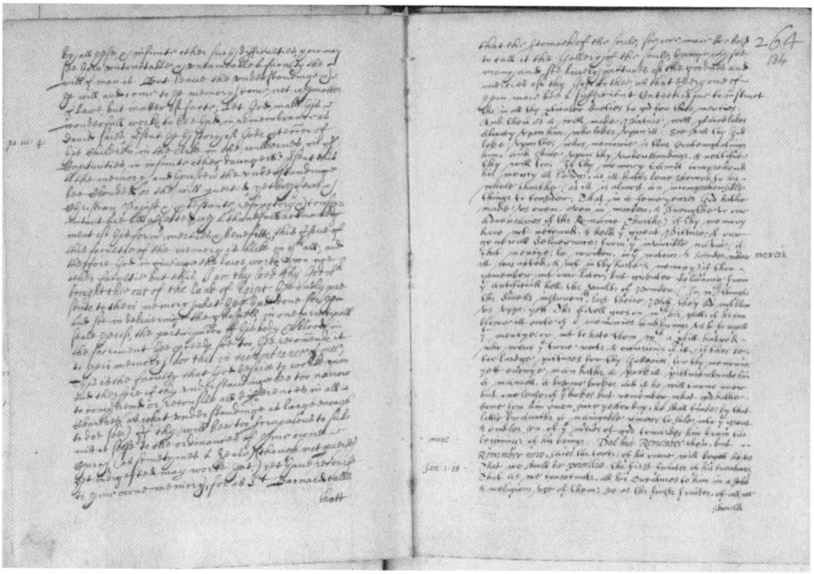

PLATE 5. *Opening in manuscript H2 showing the change of hand on the right-hand page in the copy of Donne's sermon on Ecclesiastes 12:1: London, British Library, Harley* MS *6356, fols 133v–134r (Original page size 195 × 145mm.) Reproduced by permission of the Board of the British Library.*

Simpson relied heavily on their collation of these manuscript witnesses to derive the textual conclusions they outline in their edition (I, 66). In most important cases, H2 supports their conclusions. For our purposes, the two sermons will be considered together, since in H2 they were clearly copied at the same time, were corrected by the same scribe (who took over copying in the second sermon), and circulated together rather than as separates. As a consequence, their textual history is linked.[47]

The sermon on Matthew 21:44 occurs in Q6, F50, M, D, L, Dob, and H2. The sermon on Ecclesiastes 12:1 occurs in F26, S, M, D, L, Dob, A, E, and H2. This analysis of the two will focus particularly, but not exclusively, on those examples used by Potter and Simpson to support their textual conclusions.

Matthew 21:44

Several points of particular emphasis derived from this new textual witness include the following for the sermon on Matthew 21:44: (1) H2 shares important similarities with the manuscripts (rather than F50), particularly Q6, M, and Dob, although the number of substantive variants from Q6 and Dob makes it clear that H2 does not derive directly from the copy that was the common source for these two witnesses; (2) of these three witnesses, H2 is most closely related to M, although it is superior to M in its understanding of Latin; (3) H2 is definitely not related closely to D and L, which, Potter and Simpson argue, derive from a different source (less accurate and now lost) than that used for Q6, Dob, and M; (4) H2 is not copied or corrected from F50 or Q6; in fact, corrections by a second scribal hand indicate that H2 has been corrected from a common source for M; (5) variants where H2 stands alone are, for the most part, minor. Conclusions that supplement these and alter Potter and Simpson's stemma follow analysis of the sermon on Ecclesiastes 12:1.

Evidence supporting the conclusion that H2 shares similarities with the stream represented by Q6, M, and Dob (rather than F50) is significant. In the particular examples selected by Potter and Simpson from the eighty-eight places where F50 stands alone, for example, H2 supports the manuscript versions. At lines 165, 268–9, 270, 272, and 283, H2 omits the clarificatory 'that is' of F50. Neither does H2 add the single, clarifying words of F50 at lines 164 ('false'), 188 ('sinful'), 494 ('that'), 494 ('to')—although H2 does not follow the manuscripts here either—and 589 ('own' twice). In none of the sixteen places identified by Potter and Simpson as additions of clarifying phrases does H2 conform to F50.

However, the evidence indicating that H2 does not derive from the manuscript that was the common source for Q6 and Dob is substantial, leaving M as a primary link between H2 and the manuscript traditions. Potter and Simpson observe that 'Q6 and Dob vary far more widely from F50 than does any other text or combination of texts, Q standing alone against all the other texts 203 times, and Q and Dob together against the others 183 times' (I, 58). Although they give limited credence to John Hayward's theory that 'there are variants in Q which represent an earlier version of this sermon', they conclude that the earlier version is represented only in the thirty or so places where Q agrees with all the manuscripts, and not in the nearly 400 places in which Q6, Q6/Dob, or M/Q/Dob differ from the others (I, 62).[48] They think it unlikely that any Q6/Dob variant is anything but a scribal error. The specific examples which Potter and Simpson use to illustrate the kinds of errors common to these two sources indicate that, with one exception, the text of H2 does not conform to these sources.[49] Of those more serious errors, those that Potter and Simpson say 'make a sort of half-sense, but not good sense, and certainly not a sense intended by Donne' (I, 58–9), H2 differs from Q6 and Dob in all four cases cited (lines 130, 195, 270, and

250–2). The most important variant of the four is the one at lines 250–2 where Q6 and Dob 'make nonsense out of what is in the other texts a perfectly clear sentence' (I, 59). F50 reads, correctly, 'his sheets every night, as though his neighbours next day were to shrowd and wind him in those sheets; he shuts up his eyes every night, as though his Executors had closed them'. Q6 and Dob garble this phrase so that it reads 'sheets every night as thugh his executors had closed him, as thouh his neighbours next day were to shrowd and wind him in those sheets'. H2 reads with F50 in this important case. Where Q6 stands alone, Potter and Simpson characterize the errors as 'glaring and gratuitous' variants. In all three cases (at lines 109, 206, and 382), H2 reads with F50 and the other texts. Moreover, H2 does not follow Dob (where it stands alone) in adding or changing unimportant words in the examples Potter and Simpson cite at lines 19 and 329.

Their textual analysis allows Potter and Simpson to admit the possibility that, as Hayward had suggested, three passages show an earlier version of the sermon in Q6 that have been revised in F50, thus agreeing that there are variants in Q6 that represent an earlier version of the sermon, although only those places where Q6 agrees with all the manuscripts. In these three passages, the evidence regarding H2 is not clear. At lines 523–35, H2 agrees with Dob ('saieth the Prophet farther' rather than Q6's 'the Prophet saith further'). In this variant, H2 is closer to M, D, and L ('saith the Prophet further') than to Q6. In the second passage, lines 600–1, however, H2 agrees with Q6, M, Dob ('our enemies') rather than D and L ('our sinnes') or F50's 'other mens infirmities'. Finally, in the third passage, H2 stands alone (line 293), although its 'that the rock was' is closer to Q6, M, Dob, D, L's 'that Rock was' than to F50's 'the same Rock was'. The conclusion appears to be that H2 represents an intermediate position between the earlier manuscripts and F50 (and very little relation to the stream represented by D and L).

H2's relation to M is closer than that between H2 and Q6/Dob. When Potter and Simpson examine variants in which M stands alone, they conclude that these variants comprise egregious errors copying Latin or skips of the eye or mind common to all manuscripts. They describe M's scribe as 'trying to set down what he actually saw, not what he thought he ought to see or what he thought Donne ought to have written' (I, 63). H2 does not include the Latin blunder at line 287 ('Judaciam' instead of 'audaciam') or at line 531 ('instancari' instead of 'instaurari'). But at line 519 (although H2 does not read with M's 'Comuniam') it does not provide the correct form, 'Comminuam,' found in F50. It reads, instead, 'Communuam', a reading that can be explained as a slight copying error or misreading (*u* for *i*) rather than an egregious blunder. At lines 311 and 384, H2 does not conform to M's erroneous readings. One can conclude that while the scribe for H2 may have been copying from a source similar to that for M, he was a more careful copyist, perhaps more familiar with Latin than the M scribe.

One can conclude with certainty, however, that H2 does not belong to the same manuscript family as D and L. This conclusion is based on the fact that in the nineteen places Potter and Simpson identify where Q6, M, and Dob agree against all other sources, H2 sides with M, Q6, and Dob rather than with F50, D, and L. So, H2 reads 'confident' rather than 'perfect' at line 445, 'unexpressible' rather than 'unspeakable' at line 102 (although Q6 has 'inexpressible'), and 'courage and confidence' rather than 'knowledge and confidence' at lines 111–12 (although Q6 reverses the order to 'confidence and courage'). Two places cited by Potter and Simpson to confirm the close relationship between D and L also place H2 clearly with Q6, M, Dob. In the first (446–8) F50's version is clearly revised, Q6's is nonsense (although clearly deriving from this manuscript stream [I, 65]), while the version in D and L contains two errors. A phrase ("if they fall upon this stone, sinne') is omitted, and 'stoppe' is misread as 'stoope'. In the second example (601–2), H2 sides with Q6, M, and Dob in reading 'our enemies'; D and L have the clearly incorrect 'our sinnes'; and F50 reads 'other mens infirmities'. These examples suggest that H2 should be filiated in the same stream as M and Dob.

The sermon on Matthew 21:44 in H2 is not copied or corrected from F50 or Q6. For one thing, there are too many substantive cases where H2 sides with the manuscripts. Moreover, where the sermon is corrected by the second scribe, virtually all the corrections are made to conform to F50, Q6, and all the manuscripts.

The marginalia for the sermon on Matthew 21:44 are inconclusive, and do not assist in identifying H2 more closely with any of the printed or manuscript witnesses of this sermon. However, variants in marginalia place this sermon in a stream more closely resembling Q and Dob than any of the other sources. This appears to contradict the findings resulting from collation of the texts of the sermon itself, but can be explained, in part, by the fact that the marginalia seem to be in the hand of the second scribe who reviewed both sermons in the manuscript and who may have corrected the text of the sermons from a manuscript source close to M. However, the number of places where H2 omits a marginal reference where it is present in all of the other manuscripts—though not necessarily Q—suggests that H2 was not copying marginalia from any of these sources.[50]

Scribal corrections by the second scribe (excluding marginalia) occur throughout the two sermons. In the sermon on Matthew 21:44, there are twenty such cases. In seventeen instances, the correction brings H2 in conformity with all extant witnesses. In one instance, at lines 422–3, the addition of 'at ye entrance . . . a while y^e^' brings H2 into conformity with F50, but uses the verb form 'discernes' rather than 'discerneth,' the form that appears in Q6 and in all of the manuscripts. In only two instances do corrections to H2 disagree with Q6, F50, and the manuscripts. At line 416, where F50 has 'and' (supported by Q6, Dob, and L), H2 has 'or', a reading supported by M and D. At line 209 of H2, the scribe has made a deliberate correction to the phrase 'if in all controversies, booke controversies, and sword controversies' by striking through the first 'controversies', apparently finding the repetition unnecessary or rhetorically infelicitous. In this one instance, H2 stands apart from all extant witnesses of the sermon.

Where H2 stands alone—in some sixty-one places—the variants are mostly minor. They include minor additions (at lines 255 and 520), minor omissions,[51] variations from singular to plural where either could be correct,[52] minor variations in word form,[53] careless repetition (at line 102), minor reversals in word order,[54] and minor errors causing minor grammatical problems.[55]

Several variants, however, require more detailed discussion. At least four places offer readings that are clearly superior to those provided by F50 and that could be used to emend it. At line 122, for example, F50 says that God does not 'expose them to be subjects, and exercises of the malice of others', while H2 reads 'exercisers', a word that parallels 'subjects' and makes sense of what is otherwise an odd phrase. Again at lines 362–3, H2's 'look' is preferable to F50's 'to look', and at line 466, H2's 'who' is preferable to F50's 'which'. Finally, H2's reading 'breaking us in our estates' is preferable to F50's 'in our states', as the more precise word for the action that we might impute to 'falsehood in servants, to oppression of great adversaries, to iniquity of Judges' (508–9). In two places, the text of H2 has been corrected, once to produce the reading 'undertake' that agrees with F50 (171) and once to produce an incorrect reading (209) by striking through the necessary word 'controversies' (discussed above). Some readings expose points that show how the variant streams emerged. H2's singular reading at line 293, discussed above, for example, shows how H2 (which reads 'that the rock was') is closer to the manuscripts and Q6 (which reads 'that rock was') than to F50's 'the same rock was'. And at line 494, F50's 'to a broken, and a contrite heart' is midway between 'a broken, and a contrite heart' of Q6, M, Dob, D, and L and H2's '& broken & contrite heart'. In the end, however, variants where H2 stands alone are minor, and do not suggest that H2 was copied from a substantially different source from that which produced the other witnesses in the Q6/Dob/M stream.

Ecclesiastes 12:1

Potter and Simpson's textual conclusions based on manuscripts extant when they devised their original stemma were never altered when they discovered E, and need to shift slightly to accommodate this manuscript as well as H1 and H2. Based on the collation of witnesses for the sermons on Proverbs 8:17 and Hosea 2:19 in H1, and the two sermons in H2, the relationship between M and E (posited in Potter and Simpson's discussion of E) has been confirmed, and some of its particulars examined. Placing H1 as a whole is difficult because only two sermons can be usefully compared with enough existing sources. The texts of all five sermons appear most closely related to the folio versions. Placing H2 is also difficult. However, examination of the manuscript as a whole—and particularly the sermon on Ecclesiastes 12:1—suggests that Dob, M, E, A and H2 derive from a common source, while L and D clearly derive from a separate stream. The slight evidence cited by Potter and Simpson for aligning A more closely with L and D particularly in light of A's relation to Dob and H2, suggests that it derives from the common source that produced these manuscripts rather than with L and D, which are clearly separate. I would tentatively alter their stemma by placing Dob, H2, and A in one stream as poor copies of a common source for all the manuscripts but L and D; M, P, and E in another (in which P is a poor copy, M is a good copy, and E is an even better copy of the common source); and L and D in a third stream descending from a less good common source from which the sermons in the other main stream derived.

As Potter and Simpson noted in their textual introduction, the sermon on Ecclesiastes 12:1 exists in two distinct forms: one represented by the pirated *Sapientia Clamitans* and by all extant manuscripts (including E and H2, which were not available for consideration at the time of the Potter and Simpson edition), and the other by F26.

The evidence that L and D derive from a source clearly different from that which produced the other manuscript witnesses is compelling, and the least subject to misinterpretation. Some of it, on its own, could only *suggest* this conclusion. For example, at line 67, while H2 and Dob, M, E, and A differ over whether the line should read 'ye Jesuitts & dominicans (H2) or 'the Jesuites and the Dominicans' (Dob, M, E, A), the phrase is omitted entirely from L and D. Other examples of phrases and words omitted, or of differences that cannot be ascribed to scribal error or misreading, support this conclusion.[56] However, the following variants prove conclusively that H2, Dob, M, E, and A derive from a manuscript source that is separate from that which produced L and D. At line 66, for example, the first group reads, correctly, 'bitternesses' where the second reads, nonsensically, 'bitter nurses'. Again, at line 59, the larger group reads 'yeares' for the second group's 'daies'. At line 124, it reads 'a manuell, a bosome booke' while the second reads only 'a bosome booke'. At line 208, the larger group contains the phrase 'The Judgm^{t} takes houlde of us,' a phrase omitted from the smaller group. At line 216, the larger group reads 'irrevocable,' while the smaller group 'irrecoverable'. And at line 297, the larger group reads 'profession' whereas the smaller reads 'possession'.[57]

The position of A within Potter and Simpson's stemma also requires revision based on additional information provided by H2. Their treatment of A, a manuscript which contains an error-ridden version of the sermon, is puzzling. They are quite right to observe that 'A is a poor manuscript, which contains about two hundred variants, almost all of which can be rejected' (I, 57). And it is also certain that L and D derive from a common source. However, the connection that they posit between that stream and A is not borne out—either by the examples they cite, or by a collation of all extant manuscripts. Potter and Simpson cite only two 'substantive' variants to support their conjecture. One example that supports their claim occurs at line 36, where H2, L, D, and A offer 'first remember' for 'remember,' the reading of M, Dob, and E. However, their second example does not. At line 316, Dob, M, [and E] offer 'consummated and perfected', A offers 'perfected and consummated', and L, D offer 'praefixed and consummated'. On the basis of this evidence, Potter and Simpson conclude that A aligns more closely with L and D than with M and Dob. I would argue, however, that the simple reversal of words 'consummate' and 'perfected' is less substantive than the variance between 'perfected' and 'praefixed'. It is much more plausible that the careless scribe of A reversed the word order, and arguable that the manuscripts that keep the same words 'perfected' and 'consummated', though not in the same order, are more closely connected than the manuscripts that keep the same word order ('consummated' at the end of the phrase) but with completely different words 'perfected' and 'praefixed' in the initial position.[58]

H2's relation to the other extant manuscripts is complex. Looking more closely at all of the evidence, there are many instances in which M, Dob, E, and A agree against L and D; and in most of these cases, H2 sides with Dob, M, E, and A. A large number of these variants can easily be explained as copyists' errors.[59] In some instances, one of the groups omits a minor word present in the other group; some variants involve reversals in word order, as at line 57 where Dob, M, E, A, and H2 read 'of the revelation concerning Antichriste' rather than 'concerning AntiX of the Revelation' of L and D.[60]

In a small number of instances, however, H2 sides with L, D against Dob, M, E, and A, although all of these variants could be attributed to scribal error.[61] On another seventeen occasions, H2 reads with L, D, and A against the other manuscripts.[62] On seven occasions this pattern is reversed so that H2 reads with Dob, M, and E against L, D, and A.[63] These examples make placing A problematic, but their relative scarcity (compared to the many examples where A reads *with* Dob, M, and E, and the even greater number where Dob and A read together in combination with some or all of the other manuscripts) does not support Potter and Simpson's conclusion that A belongs to the stream that produced L and D.

Moreover, there are clear instances in which M and E form a recognizable stream which, for the most part, differs from H2. Of the twenty-nine occasions in which M and E combine alone against the other manuscripts, H2 reads against both manuscripts in all but three cases. Most of these instances are minor, involving minor slips, omissions, miscopyings, and differences in spelling that provide no substantive evidence for filiating H2 with either of the streams.[64] Of the three occasions on which H2 reads with M and E, line 22 is the most significant. There, H2, M, and E read 'doe it now, nunc', while Dob reads 'do that now and', A reads 'do it now let', and L, D read 'do it now and'. Of the twenty-six places where H2 reads against M and E, the most substantive variants are in line 56 (where H2 and the others read 'Christ Jesus' while M and E read 'Jesus Christ'), line 116 (where H2 and the others read 'harte & memory' while M and E read 'memorye'), lines 148–9 (where M and E omit the phrase 'to god in an'), line 234 (where H2 and the others read 'lightening' while M and E read 'lighting'), and line 397 (where M and E omit 'thinges').

Given the patterns already described, placing H2 is more difficult than for any of the other manuscripts. My sense is that H2 is closest to Dob and A. Including the instances in which Dob, M, E, and A read with H2 against L and D, H2/Dob/A read together one hundred and sixty-three times with or without support from other manuscript sources. H2 reads with these latter in all but twenty-seven places. In addition, there are thirty-two cases in which H2 reads only with A. Some of these are substantive, as when H2 and A omit 'by this light . . . all our creatures and actions' (254), found in all other manuscripts. Similarly, H2 and A read, incorrectly, 'yt is professed advisedlie' (286) where Dob, M, and E read, correctly, 'that is, professe it advisedly'. Both H2 and A also omit the rhetorical repetition of 'all the waters' at line 318. And both read 'sought' instead of 'taught' at line 326. Finally H2 and A read 'disproportionable' instead of 'disproportion'd' at line 406. All of these findings suggest that H2 is closest to Dob, particularly when Dob sides with A, and, secondarily, with the M, E stream. Given the carelessness of A, there are numerous instances (one hundred and twenty-three) in which A differs from all of the other manuscripts, including H2. The vast majority of these are explicable as copyists' errors, scribal misreadings, omissions, and slips common to such a careless job. Some of them, however, are substantive.[65] In addition, there are twenty-three instances in which H2 sides with all the other manuscripts against Dob. These differences, like those when the manuscripts side against A, are not substantive, but include word reversals, variations between singular and plural forms, omissions or additions of relatively unimportant words (such as articles), miscopyings and clear slips or errors. However on the two occasions (lines 116–17, 343) where H2 reads with Dob against all the other manuscripts, they are clearly correct. Lines 116–17 caused the scribes a great deal of trouble. H2 and Dob read 'if thou remember not our later, but greater deliverance from y^{t} artificiall hell'. M and E read substantially the same as H2 and Dob, except that they have 'latter' instead of 'later'. L reads 'if noe. remember y^{t} artificiall Hell, or later but g^{t}er deliverance'. D has yet another version, adding the sentence 'yet the Devill goes forward wth his plot', before continuing 'If not remember that artificiall Hell our later but greater deliverance'. The manuscript that comes closest to H2 and Dob is A which reads our 'late' instead of 'later' deliverance.

H2 reads against all the other manuscripts in several places. Many of these are minor, recording variations in word order, in verb forms and tenses, in singular and plural, and in pronouns, as well as minor omissions, additions, and slight verbal variants.[66] Of the variations in word order, none creates grammatical, syntactical, or rhetorical problems, and can be explained as cases where the H2 scribe simply turned the words of the phrase around but did not consider the 'error' sufficiently egregious to cross out what he had written and to insert the other wording.[67] All of these differences are explicable as scribal errors caused by inattention, misreading, or miscopying. None should be read as deliberate attempts to correct errors, or as evidence of revision. Nor does it seem likely that H2 was copied from a source that differed substantively from those known to Potter and Simpson, particularly Dob.

Several major variants exist between H2 and the other manuscript sources. Many of these substantive differences are explicable as errors, or as attempts by the scribe to 'improve' on the text before him. Taken together, they reveal typical patterns of scribal miscopying and error, but several substantive variations are inexplicable except by positing a source for H2 that was different from those that produced the other manuscripts. For example, H2 reads 'daie' (23) where all the other manuscripts read 'light,' the scribe apparently copying from a source or himself translating literally the Latin word 'die'. Again at line 49, H2 translates 'stomachus animae', 'the stomack of the soul', an addition that Potter and Simpson ascribed to William Milbourne's editorship, but which may very well have come from a common source for H2 (since H2 does not support S in all of the other cases discussed by Potter and Simpson as examples of Milbourne's editorial intervention).[68] Again at line 227, H2 adds the translation after '*in diebus*', 'not in the day, but in the daies, &c.' This is a wording that resembles that added in F26, suggesting that H2 might be derived from the common source for both versions. H2 also omits the clarifying phrase 'by this light' at line 254. Some variants are clearly errors, as at line 250, where H2 reads 'cernerentur' instead of the correct '*viderentur*', possibly repeating that word from the previous line. The same is true at line 120 where H2 wrongly reads 'occasions' when the correct word is 'occasioners', referring to those who perpetrated the Gunpowder Plot. And, in all but one case, omissions that result from eye-skip can be attributed to careless copying.[69]

While many variants are just that—variations with neutral impact on the text—it is hard to see how H2 substituted 'on' for 'forward' at line 120 unless copying from a source that contained the more forceful word. The same is true for H2's 'shines' (348) instead of 'burnes,' and H2's 'so mangled soe torne' (417) instead of 'soe defaced and soe mangled'. While either makes sense, the variant is not likely to be the result of scribal miscopying.[70] In some cases, these variants where H2 stands alone clarify the text and provide a potentially superior reading. Take, for example, lines 105–6 where Potter and Simpson have used the reading of M and L ('as a well made and a well-placed picture lookes always upon him, that lookes upon it'). Dob and E omit the second 'a,' but H2 expresses precisely what the text intends: 'as a well made picture well placed . . .'. In this wording the picture is at the centre of the two modifiers, the second of which gains greater emphasis and thereby reinforces the sense that it is the placing of the picture as much as its quality as a picture that is important.

For this sermon, the scribe/corrector takes over from the first scribe on folio 264, six lines from the top. All but one of the thirty scribal corrections bring this manuscript witness into conformity with all other witnesses, and show the second scribe, the corrector, to be a careful copyist. The exception to this principle occurs at line 179 where the scribe inserts 'et' where all other copies have 'and,' although even this correction could be interpreted as a version of the word required.

H2's marginalia offer no clear pattern that would help to place H2 within the existing scheme of manuscript relationships offered by Potter and Simpson. If one ignores those eleven places where all of the manuscripts have some version of the marginal reference found in H2,[71] and those seven places where all manuscripts but A agree substantively with H2,[72] the one place (at line 35) where only E has a reference, and the one place (line 62) where L has a marginal reference, we see that H2 agrees with all but one of the manuscripts a total of twenty times. It differs from M and E together on five occasions (at lines 43, 45–6, 101, 129, 130), and when M and E combine with one or more of the other manuscripts on seven occasions (at lines 48, 248, 346, 488, 505, 513, 514). This pattern suggests that H2 is not derived from the manuscript sources for M and E. Nor does it derive from the L, D stream. H2 sides with L, D (and S) only once against all the other manuscripts, although this is a substantive case.[73] Twice (at lines 198 and 485) H2 sides with the other manuscripts against L, D, and twice (at lines 249 and 538) against L, D, and A. From these observations, one can conclude that H2 derives from the common source for Dob, M, and E, but one that is closer to Dob than to M or E.

In those four places where H2 stands alone (at lines 115, 291, 401, and 428), the marginalia do not support any definite conclusions. At line 115, H2 adds the marginal note 'mercie'; at line 291, H2 reads 'levit.23.29' where the other manuscripts omit the verse; at line 401, H2 reads (incorrectly) 'Iam:3.27'; and at line 428, H2 reads 'Electionum' (where the other manuscripts omit the reference, and E reads 'Elect.'). In three of these cases, however, H2 is closer to F26 than any of the other witnesses. At line 291, the fuller reference is that offered in F26; at line 401, F26 correctly reads 'Thren. 3.27' (at line 336 of that revised text); and at line 428, H2 (and to some extent E) includes the marginal reference to 'Electionum' that occurs at line 357 of the revised text. From these examples one could conclude that H2, while not derived directly from any of the existing manuscripts sources, derives from a source that was a common source for the revised text in F26.

TRANSMISSION OF HARLEY MS 6946 (H1)

This manuscript contains copies of five sermons. The first three sermons, all preached by Donne at marriages, exist in other manuscript copies.[74] However, it is significant that in this manuscript, the only known collection of sermons entirely by Donne, they have been collected as a thematic gathering. The last two sermons in H1 are also a thematic pair: the first is on the shortest sorrowful biblical text (John 11: 35, 'Jesus Wept', preached at Whitehall on the First Friday of Lent, 1622); the other is on the shortest joyous biblical text (1 Thessalonians 5:16, 'Rejoyce Evermore'). This sermon is one of three described in F50 as preached at St Dunstan's, a statement challenged by Potter and Simpson, who question both the date and the location. They find it odd that Donne would have fulfilled his 1622 promise to preach on the second text of the pair 'at a little parish church like St. Dunstan's'. They also express the expectation in this sermon that some of his auditors would have heard the first sermon, although the wording of the sermon also supports the view that these sermons are like 'floating Islands, that swim and move from place to place; and in them a Man may sowe in one place and reape in another: This case is so farre ours, as that in another place we have sowed in teares, and by his promise, in whose teares we sowed then, when we handled those two words, *Jesus wept*, we shall reape in Joy' (X, 213). The more compelling argument put forward by Potter and Simpson for believing that this sermon was preached at St Paul's is that Donne's rebuke of the irreverence of some of his listeners was more appropriate at St Paul's where that fault was 'particularly noticeable'. At St Paul's, they argue, divine service was held in the chancel or choir. The third reason for assigning the sermon to St Paul's is that if the sermon on 'Jesus Wept' was preached in 1622, it seems unlikely that Donne would have referred to it more than a year later, in another congregation, and have expected his hearers to understand the reference. Potter and Simpson do not, in the end, decide whether the sermon should be assigned to St Dunstan's or St Paul's, but on the basis of their conjectures and this additional manuscript evidence that at least one listener thought of them as a pair, and had them copied as such, it seems likely that the sermon was preached at St Paul's (see the reference to 'this Quire'[X, 223]), probably in 1622 or 1623, rather than at St Dunstan's sometime after April 1624.

The possible links to Holland suggested by the dating of the paper stock are also intriguing. In 1622 and 1623, a date approximately contemporaneous with the contents of this manuscript, a Dutch embassy to London that included Constantijn Huygens brought this young secretary into contact with Donne at the home of Sir Robert Killigrew (briefly ambassador to The Hague). Huygens's enthusiasm for Donne's sermons is expressed in a poem written in 1678, cited in Bald, and put into context by Paul Sellin.[75]

The fact that this manuscript contains only sermons by Donne, that they are intelligently rather than randomly grouped, and that they are closely related to the printed sources (which generally represent revised or later copies of these texts), makes H1 an important manuscript for further analysis of Donne's sermon texts, as well as of habits of collection and transmission of his sermons.

TRANSMISSION OF HARLEY MS 6356 (H2)

The manuscript appears to be a gift from Anne Sadleir (1585–1671/2), as the inscription indicates. The *ODNB* identifies her as the second of Sir Edward Coke's ten children and a literary patron. Her religious conformity to the Church of England is evident in her surviving correspondence which chronicles her disputes with her Roman Catholic nephew Herbert Aston and the New England Puritan divine Roger Williams, but most decidedly by her use of the *Book of Common Prayer*, even during its proscription in the 1650s.[76] Her personal papers include religious and autobiographical meditations and a sermon dedicated to her by Andrew Marvell the elder. On the basis of her collection of modern manuscripts, Arnold Hunt observes that 'she was regarded as a cultivated patron with strong literary interests.'[77] He adds that her correspondence confirms that she actively solicited gifts of this sort, and circulated them to others.[78] In his catalogue of manuscripts in the Inner Temple Library, J.C. Davies notes further that in addition to her books from her father's library, many of the manuscripts donated by Lady Sadleir and housed in the Petyt Collection were 'devotional manuscripts or manuscripts of sermons'.[79] He adds that a printed commentary on Psalms 68–82, also donated to the Library, is 'the kind of work one would expect to be in the library of Mrs. Anne Sadleir'.[80] Hunt concludes that she was 'extremely well read in contemporary English Protestant divinity, and clearly read her books very thoroughly and attentively, as many of them are heavily annotated, underlined, or pointed, with quote-marks running down the margin, in the manner commonly used by Renaissance readers to highlight passages suitable for transcription into a commonplace book.'[81]

CONCLUSION

These two additional manuscripts of Donne's most widely copied and distributed sermons can tell us a great deal about the transmission of

Donne's sermons, gradually adding to the picture thought complete in the 1960s, and modified only slightly since then. The manuscripts also tell us something about the place of women, such as Anne Sadleir, as patrons and distributors of sermons. The attachment of her name to a manuscript of sermons (H2), readily available and commonly circulated, suggests that she was in the mainstream of sermon patronage. H1 demonstrates, however, both the circulation of high-profile occasional sermons (of which other manuscript copies exist), and of two sermons connected to Donne in particular. Its importance as the only manuscript devoted exclusively to sermons by Donne, and in texts that are close to the revised texts represented in the printed folios, is undeniable. Further archival research in libraries, record offices and other collections may well turn up additional Donne manuscripts in due course. This is the kind of complication that Donne's textual editors welcome.

NOTES

1 These sources are described in *The Sermons of John Donne*, ed. George R. Potter and Evelyn M. Simpson, 10 vols (Berkeley, 1953–62), I, 33–45.

2 *Sermons*, II, 365–71.

3 This discovery was first announced in *English Manuscript Studies*, 5 (1995), 63–86. A parallel-text edition, including an introduction and diplomatic transcription of the sermon, was published as *John Donne's 1622 Gunpowder Plot Sermon: A Parallel-Text Edition*, ed. Jeanne Shami (Pittsburgh, 1996).

4 Manuscript sigla throughout are from Potter and Simpson except for H1 and H2 (the subject of this essay) and R (BL, Royal MS 17. B. XX), namely: M = Merton MS (Oxford, Bodleian MS Eng. th. c. 71); Dob = Dobell MS (Cambridge, Mass., Harvard MS Eng 966.4); D =Dowden MS (Bodleian MS Eng. th. e. 102); L = Lothian (Edinburgh, National Library of Scotland MS 5767); P = St Paul's MS (London, St Paul's Cathedral MS 52. D. 14); E = Ellesmere MS (now Cambridge University Library MS Add. 8469); and A = Ashmole MS (Bodleian MS Ashmole 781). Print sigla are also taken from Potter and Simpson, namely: F80 = *LXXX Sermons* (1640); F50 = *Fifty Sermons* (1649); F26 = *XXVI Sermons* (1660); Q6 = *Six Sermons* (1634); S = *Sapientia Clamitans.*

5 On the first folio of the sermon on John 11:35 (fourth sermon in the collection) is the date 1622.

6 It is unclear why fol. 44v is blank, but the sermon is complete as it stands.

7 This sermon occurs in Potter and Simpson, I, 236–51.

8 See omissions at lines 59 ('to love and to enjoy'), 145 ('I have said you are Gods'), 179 ('in the Text'), 258 ('that is'), 264 ('all men make up but one mankind'), 272–3 ('If thou hast hated as thou shouldst hate'), 279–80 ('to anything else, so doth it also principally another way, that is, rather then': H1 = E only in this example), 343 ('and lost him in the holy City'), 371 ('we have found the Messias'), 432 ('First seek the Kingdom of God'), 437–8 ('Seek me and ye shall live'), and 442–3 ('of any action').

9 These include 'where' (line 375); 'stations' instead of 'Nations' (398); 'marring' instead of 'marriag' (463); and 'condemned' rather than 'condemnable' (493). Other

notable places where the three manuscripts read against F26 include lines 118, 130, 134, 275, 276, 284, 378, 386, 408, 496, 510. However some of the key substantives that indicate clearly that H1, M, and E share a common source include the following substantive variants between manuscripts and printed folio: 'orderlye' instead of 'now in our order' (202); 'an acte' instead of 'a manifold act' (274–75); ' actions, yea, and' instead of 'actions, and' (285); 'wither towards us' instead of 'wither in us' (301); 'him, was' instead of 'him; this was' (317); 'or forward' instead of 'or to look forward' (351–52): 'to' instead of 'that we should' (433); and 'them' instead of 'the Chaldeans' (519).

10 Emendations to F26 by Potter and Simpson at lines 61 ('tooke'), 63 ('far,'), 65–6 (the unitalicized 'I had all I desir'd'), 82 (the italicized '*I love them that love me*'), 133 ('writes'), 144 ('*dixi*'), 150 ('mine'), 193 ('heathen)'), 194 ('therein;'), 210 ('inhumanity'), 246 ('happy?'), 253 ('definition'), 272 ('*bene*'), and 405 ('also') indicate the closeness in both substantives and accidentals between H1 and E.

11 This conclusion is based on the fact that H1 has no marginal reference that matches the following in F26: Jer.31.3; The Affection (Amor M, E); Cant.5.8; and Jo: i.3.4 (which should be John 1:34).

12 Num.11.15; Ose 2.14 (which should be Hosea 2:19; M has Osea 2:14); Rom. 1.30 (which should be Rom. 1:31); two marginal references to Augustine; Deut. 30.11; omission of Esay 65.1; Grego: (where M has Gregorie and E has Gre: and then *Ibid beneath that); and Psalm 32.6 (where M and E have Ose 32.6).

13 Significant emendations of H1/F26 to M/E include the following: 'To conclude this' becomes 'To contract this, the' (151); 'any affection' to 'to any thing' (279); 'can object nothing' to 'cannot object anythinge'(286); 'may easily be' to 'easye to be' (400); 'religious Princes' to 'Religion' (406); omission of 'afterward by the preaching of the Gospell' included in M and E and by Potter and Simpson as an emendation (425); and 'vacuity' to 'vacancye' (502).

14 These include omission of 'all discourses,' an appositive phrase, on line 172; omission of 'Tentations to sin are all but whisperings' on lines 413–14, although this is the second time the clause is used, and may constitute an error of repetition in F26, M, and E; omission of 'early had he sought thee in the Church amongst' from lines 499–500, creating a nonsensical reading 'Thus hypocrites' instead of 'Thus early had he sought thee in the Church amongst hypocrites'; and omission of an entire explanatory phrase as well as part of the ensuing quotation at lines 109–10: 'as it is often expressed in this Chapter; *She crieth,*'.

15 On line 57, for example, Potter and Simpson use M's reading 'we are as good as if we were without it' instead of F26's 'we were as good as we were' or E's 'we were as good we were without it.' H1 reads 'we were as good bee without it,' a reading that is *possibly* superior to the others, both grammatically and rhetorically, and may possibly explain E's version. On lines 276–7, F26 reads 'that man whom thy virtue and thy example hath declined, and kept from offending his, and thy God'. M reads 'that man whom virtue hath declined from that which kept him from his and thy God', a reading which makes little sense, while E reads 'that man whom virtue hath declined and kept from his and thy God', a reading which is also faulty. H1 reads 'that man whom virtue hath declined and kept from offending his and thy God', a reading which restores one crucial word (also found in F26), but which, by omitting 'and thy example', renders the sense less clearly than F26. The fact that all of the manuscripts are garbled at these points, suggests a common source for all three.

16 This sermon is printed in Potter and Simpson, II, 335–47.

17 Four of these occur at lines 393, 394, 395, and 397 where both M and H1 have 'that's' instead of F's 'that is'. At line 50, both H1 and M have the correct word 'God', incorrectly printed as 'good' in F50. H1 also supports M's 'divers' at line 437 as opposed to F50's 'repugnant'.

18 These include 'Adducit' instead of 'Adduxit' (21); 'friends' instead of 'friend' (140); the omission of '*quemvis*' (192); the omission of 'but not that he shall not mary' (221); 'priests' instead of 'priest' (219); proferenda' instead of 'praeferenda' (236); 'pruaricationem' instead of 'in praevaricationem' (361–2); 'consequenda' instead of' consequendae' (379–80); 'simili' instead of 'similis' (420); and 'Berseba' instead of 'Bathsheba' (431).

19 'executed' instead of 'exercised' (25); 'societie' instead of 'societies' (41), although I prefer H1; 'does' instead of 'doth' (47); 'y^{t}' instead of 'it' (67); 'selfe' instead of 'selves' (103); 'God' instead of 'our God' (141); 'they expresse' instead of 'they can expresse'(164); 'what's' (twice) instead of 'what is' (294); 'of all the whole' instead of 'of the whole' (334); 'those' instead of 'these' (424); and 'together,' omitted by F50 and M (439).

20 lines 48–9 where H1 reads 'make a helper' and F50 reads 'make him a helper'; line 72, where H1 reads 'that, then that' and F50 reads 'then, that that'; line 115, where H1 reads 'bee' and F50 reads 'shall be'; line 117, where H1 reads 'ordinarily how' while F50 reads 'how ordinarily'; line 171, where H1 reads 'affection' and F50 reads 'affections'; line 207, where H1 reads 'then' and F50 reads 'there'; and line 332, where H1 reads 'provided' and F50 reads 'proceeded'.

21 This sermon is printed in Potter and Simpson, III, 241–55.

22 See their stemma, I, 73.

23 These occur at lines 31, 40, 43, 60, 64, 124, 144, 325, 383, 386, and 391–2.

24 At line 77, H1 appears to be the only manuscript supporting F50's incorrect reading of 'cause' for 'case,' until we see that the corrector for E has inked out the 'u' in 'cause' to produce the correct word. This suggests E's close relation to H1 and F50, but also suggests that E's corrector was able to correct errors by reading carefully for sense rather than simply copying what was in front of him. However, it may simply mean that E's corrector was working from another manuscript.

25 For example, at line 127 H1 and F50 have 'one to' while Q6, E, M, and P have the correct 'to one'. The same thing occurs at line 138, where H1 and F50 have 'to' while Q6, M, and P have 'to one'. In this case, however, while E originally had the same reading as F50 and H1, it has been corrected by the second hand with the insertion of 'one'. On line 305, H1 and F50 read 'this she', but Potter and Simpson use the evidence of Q6, E, M, and P to emend to 'that she'.

26 At line 139, the scribe repeats a phrase 'or any, or any other' while F50 correctly has 'or any other'. At line 158, F50 correctly has the 'Ancients' where H1 reads 'the ancient'. On the next line (159), H1 reads 'yor' where the correct word is 'the'. Then at lines 281–2, H1 incorrectly reads 'as if', where F50 has the correct form 'as that if'. On line 327, H1 reads 'Action' where F50's 'Actions' is more obviously correct. On line 402, H1 omits a word necessary for sense: reading 'this his' instead of F50's correct 'this is his'. And finally, at line 516, H1 reads 'understanding' when the plural form is required for sense. F50 correctly has 'understandings'.

27 The sermon is printed in Potter and Simpson, IV, 324–44.

28 At line 287, where the sense clearly requires a comma rather than a full stop after 'Victor,' Potter and Simpson insert it and delete the period. H1 supports this emendation.

29 I would like to thank graduate student Stephen King (now graduated from University of Alberta with his Ph.D.) for thinking through with me some of the textual variants between H1 and F50 in his paper for English 830, 13 March 1995 entitled 'And How Shall They Hear Without a Preacher?': The Printed Sermon as Compensation for an Absent Priest'. Many of his observations relating to rhetorical and stylistic variants have been incorporated into the present more detailed and technical discussion. I would also like to thank Stephen King, Dave Gray, and Cindy Mackenzie for assistance in transcribing manuscripts for this study.

30 Examples of this occur at lines 76, 77, 327, 380, 426–7, 526, 531, 668, 675, and 683.

31 One is slight, but H1 is clearer; at line 454, F50 prints 'humane too' (where H1's 'humane teares too' is grammatically implied). Similarly, H1's inclusion of 'that' before 'there' at line 551 adds clarity to the text. And at line 679, H1's 'tells us' is marginally preferable to F50's 'tells' in that it provides an object for the verb. H1 also has the grammatically correct agreement ('shall not his looking . . . make us weep') at line 540 where F50 has the ungrammatical 'makes'.

32 This sermon is printed in Potter and Simpson, X, 213–28.

33 Similar errors occur at line 108 where H1 has '*Gautete*' while F50 has the correct form '*Gaudete*', and at line 116 where H1 reads 'somnum' while F50 has the correct '*Sonum*'. At line 412, H1 incorrectly reads '*Gaudete*' while F50 reads '*Gaudere*'. At line 533, H1 reads '*Sin in nominae*' for the correct '*Si in nomine*' in F50; at line 548, H1 reads '*subilationem*' (a non-word) where F50 correctly reads '*jubilationem*'; and at line 570, H1 reads '*sacietas gaudiorum*' whereas F50 correctly reads '*Satietas gaudiorum*'.

34 These errors occur at lines 24 , 49, 74, 109, 119, 130, 175, 349, 363, 388, 460, 486, 564, and 575.

35 Although occasionally the pattern is reversed, similar variants occur at lines 23 (twice), 28, 42, 89, 113, 114, 131, 142, 165, 211 (twice), 212, 213 (twice), 217, 267, 271, 287, 378, 411, 438, 445, 460–1, 468, 476, 478, 481 (where there is also a minor reversal in word order), 484, 499, 552, 556, and 571 (twice).

36 Similar variants occur at lines 413, 417, 423, 424, 426, 458, and 501.

37 Similar variants occur at line 15, 34, 72, 120, 129, 190, 295, and 346.

38 Similar variants occur at lines 56, 100, 348, 394, 416, 440, 468, 507, and 537.

39 Similar variants occur at line 73, 443, 501, 523, and 558.

40 In one substantive case, H1 and F50 both agree—incorrectly—and are emended by Potter and Simpson. This occurs at line 320, where H1 and F50 both read 'which are' (an ungrammatical reading that turns the main clause into a subordinate clause). Potter and Simpson emend to 'are'.

41 Others occur at lines 312 (where H1's 'to minister to' is more explicit than F50's 'to'); 429 (where H1's English 'tentations', referred to metaphorically as '*custodes*', is preferable to the translation of one Latin word '*tentationes*' by another '*custodes*' in F50); 488 (where H1's 'but better hereafter then that' is more direct than 'but not better then that hereafter' in F50); and 496–7 where H1's clear 'saies yt father' and 'saies hee againe' becomes, simply, 'sayes that Father'.

42 I would like to thank Hilton Kelliher for his assistance in identifying Pryme's hand. Information on this antiquary is available in the *ODNB*.

43 See Vladimir Burtsev, *Russian Documents in the British Museum* (London, 1926).

44 The following website provides illustrations of watermarks from Bacon's papers: http://www.geocities.com/Athens/Acropolis/2216/clsctexts/bacon_watermarks.htm

45 I concur with Dennis Flynn, whose discovery of a copy of the letter thought by Potter and Simpson to 'prefix' the sermon on Matthew 21:44 makes it virtually certain that the letter refers to the Ecclesiastes sermon instead. The fact that the two

often traveled together supports Flynn's reading. See 'Donne Manuscripts in Cheshire,' *English Manuscript Studies*, 8 (2000), 280–92.

46 They are printed in Potter and Simpson, in II, 179–96 and II, 235–49 respectively.

47 At the same time, I would like to distinguish this comment from the dodgy assumption proffered by Potter and Simpson that the textual character of manuscripts written in a single hand 'could be described as a whole' (II, 367), and that manuscripts containing sermons by different scribes must be discussed separately. As discussion of H1 has indicated, these five sermons, although transmitted in the hands of five different scribes, have many points of common textual contact, including paper, watermarks, and the provenance of the collection as a whole. Although Potter and Simpson speak of the 'source' for M (and for other manuscripts transcribed in one hand), it is equally possible to speak of 'sources' for the sermons in these collections (especially L, which contains other sermons, as well as possible sermons by Donne whose authorship is still disputed). In other words, it is unwise to assume that the character of the Merton manuscript is more homogeneous than, say, the character of H1 (or of H2, for that matter), based solely on the number of hands used. See Ernest W. Sullivan, II, 'The Renaissance Manuscript Verse Miscellany: Private Party, Private Text' in W. Speed Hill, ed., *New Ways of Looking at Old Texts: Papers of the Renaissance English Text Society, 1985–1991* (Binghamton, NY, 1993), pp. 289–97, for a discussion of the error of 'monoscript' assumptions.

48 Hayward's arguments were made in his 'A Note on Donne the Preacher' in *A Garland for John Donne*, ed. Theodore Spencer (Cambridge, Mass., 1931), pp. 75–97.

49 These examples (cited by Potter and Simpson to support their view of Q6 and Dob) occur at 206 (where the other sources omit 'and his peace'), and 49 (where Q6 and Dob reverse the word order). The exception—where H2 does support Q6 and Dob—occurs at line 105, where H2 also omits 'Almighty'.

50 These occur at lines 55, 62–3, 108–09, 138, 175, 258–59, 287, 289–90, 298, 451, 473, 519, 531, 540, and 551.

51 These occur at lines 79, 214, 221, 254, 363, 422, 494, 523, 527, and 601–2.

52 These occur at lines 65, 164, 304, 323, 332, 515, 570, and 604.

53 These occur at lines 70, 105, 112, 115, 130, 135, 138, 139, 281, 282, 302, 332, 336, 360, 366, 372, 527, 572, and 597.

54 These occur at lines 141, 330, and 384–5.

55 These occur at lines 132, 154, 168, 226, 253, 272, 494, 519, and 570.

56 At line 286, where only H2 and A read 'yt it is professed advisdedlie', and Dob, M, E read 'that is, professe it advisedly', L and D read 'that is, preferred it advisedly'. Again at 318, where H and A read 'God hath gathered all the waters of life into one place' and Dob, M, and E read 'God hath gathered all the waters, all the waters of life into one place', L and D omit the phrase entirely. At line 372, H2, Dob, M, and E read 'perfitt', A omits the word entirely, and L, D read 'forfeit'. At line 440 H2, L, and D read 'into ye balance and Compaire itt', while Dob reads 'into balance and comparison', M reads 'into the balaunce', and E and A read 'into the ballaunce and comparison'. At line 477, H2 reads 'began' with M, while Dob, E, and A read 'begunne' and L, D read 'did'.

57 Other substantive verbal variants occur at line 311 ('above' instead of 'about'); 381 ('deiectinge' instead of 'deiection'); 398 ('nowe' instead of 'too'); 418–19 (where 'non est temperantia' is omitted from L, D); 423 ('frowardness' instead of 'froward courses'); and line 563 ('quorum ego' instead of 'ego').

58 In this particular case, E sides with M, Dob, (and, I would argue, A), while H2 sides with L and D.

59 These occur at lines 26, 32, 43, 63, 67, 89, 113, 122, 144, 146, 252, 266, 267, 271, 274, 289, 317, 331, 346, 362, 378, 379, 428, 453, 474, 515, 526, 544, 580, and 600.

60 Similarly, at line 585, the larger group reads 'have I' while the smaller reads 'I have', and at 599 the larger group's 'Christ Jesus' reads 'Jesus Christ' in the smaller.

61 So, H2, L, and D omit 'to' which is present in the other group (166); H2 reads 'Jesus Christe' with L, D against 'Christ Jesus' in the larger group (246); H2 includes 'of' (288), whereas it is omitted from the larger group; H2 joins with L, D to read 'which were' instead of 'as were' (331), 'the' instead of 'that' (347), 'late' instead of 'a late' (394), and 'thy' instead of 'the' (432).

62 These variants occur at lines 4, 23, 31, 36, 42, 49, 152, 189, 190, 212, 217, 248, 282, 291, 295, 529, and 550.

63 These variants occur at lines 2, 157, 186, 284, 354, 440, and 554.

64 H2 reads with M and E at lines 22, 281, and 287 and against M and E at lines 3, 5, 7, 18, 24, 27, 55, 56, 81, 82, 86, 116, 117, 142 (twice), 148–9, 152, 156, 220, 334, 379, 397, 459 (twice), 529, and 593.

65 A reads 'now' for 'then' (at line 14); 'divers' for 'lively' (103); 'mercies and goodness' for 'goodnes and mercies' (103); 'it' for 'that fire' (205–6); 'Lord' for 'end' (330); 'undervaluing' for 'overvaluinge' (363); 'continuance' for 'continence' (420); 'conceit' for 'conceave' (470); and 'happiness' for 'supplement' (485). On several occasions, A omits words and entire phrases found in the other manuscript sources ('God in the second … betweene' at 299–300, 'or a fift day … hast' at 380; 'undelibly' at 539; 'That soule' at 540; and 'I know' at 565–6). At line 463, where the other sources have 'Creatorem' in the margin, A has the word 'Creatorum' in the text itself and no marginal reference.

66 In five cases, H2 offers verb forms or tenses that differ from those in the other manuscripts ('directeth' and 'requireth' at lines 11 and 15 instead of 'directs' and 'requires'; 'said' for 'saies' at 248; and 'here is' and 'there is' for 'here's' and 'there's' at 439 and 531). Variations between singular and plural occur at lines 16, 106, 269, 446, and 580. Variations in pronouns occur at lines 77, 88, 89, 120, 160, 249, 317, 397, 428, 446, 542, 578, and 584. Minor additions or omissions occur at lines 38, 59, 61–2, 67, 77, 87, 171, 176, 214, 283, 314, 342, 352, 375, and 421. A large number of variants offer incorrect or slightly different wordings, but are not considered substantive. These occur at lines 66, 84, 100, 125, 142, 163, 185, 203, 229, 230, 244, 274, 276, 278, 298–99, 338, 341 (twice), 350, 357, 385, 403, 406 (twice), 452, 460, 465, 466, 484, 485, 489, 500, 528, 559, 560, 588 (twice), 600, and 607.

67 These occur at line 9–10, 123, 236, 239, 339–40, 571, and 578.

68 Potter and Simpson consider variants where M agrees with S, and in all of these examples, H2 sides with the other manuscripts, rather than with M and S. As for those places where S stands alone (and which Potter and Simpson attribute to the editorship of William Milbourne), H2 sides with the other manuscripts against S. In only this one case, H2 supports S against all the other manuscripts. This change cannot be attributed to Milbourne, then, but to the manuscript that was the common source for S (and M).

69 Some of the most apparently significant variants are the result of eye-skip, as at lines 179–80 where H2 omits 'and nunc in die, now whilst it is day; the Lord will heare thee'. At line 180, H2 includes an extra '*nunc in die*', leaving readers to speculate which of the phrases was omitted by H2. Nonetheless, this variant confirms that eye-skip was the cause of the omission, rather than a deliberate choice on the part of author or scribe. Only two lines later, H2 omits another phrase ('what day soever thou callest upon him, and *in quacunque die*'). The amount of material omitted in these

three lines suggests more than eye-skip as the cause; however, the text in H2, despite these omissions, makes sense. A particularly egregious example of eye-skip in H2 occurs between lines 358–61 (from 'even they humility' to 'and he ca suffer'). Clearly, the scribe or the copyist of his source omitted everything between the two instances of 'suffer'. Once more, at lines 447–8, H2 reads 'ringe out', thus omitting the rhetorical pointing of the phrase 'ringe, till thy last bell ringe, and ringe out'. H2 omits another phrase, at lines 499–500 ('not only not separate thee' as in Dob, M, E, L, and D, or 'not only separate' as in A).

70 See further examples of variants that possibly suggest separate streams at lines 451, 471, and 606.

71 These occur at lines 42, 167, 170, 176, 180, 181, 193–96, 392, 402, 411, and 435.

72 These occur at lines 179, 182, 213, 228, 237, 465, and 498.

73 All of these sources have the marginal reference to Psalm 111:4 at line 80, a reference that is omitted in the other sources.

74 These are the sermons on Hosea 2:1, Proverbs 8:17, and Genesis 2:18. See the table in Potter and Simpson, I, 52.

75 R.C. Bald, *John Donne: A Life* (Oxford, 1970), pp. 441–2. See also Paul R. Sellin, '*So Doth, So Is Religion': John Donne and Diplomatic Contexts in the Reformed Netherlands, 1619–1620* (Columbia, 1988), and Koos Daley, '"And Like a Widdow Thus": Donne, Huygens, and the Fall of Heidelberg,' *John Donne Journal*, 10.1–2 (1991), 57–69.

76 On the basis of his extensive study of Mrs Sadleir's papers and annotations in books, Arnold Hunt, 'The Books, Library, and Literary Patronage of Mrs. Anne Sadleir (1585–1670),' in *Early Modern Women's Manuscript Writing: Selected Papers from the Trinity/Trent Colloquium*, ed. Victoria E. Burke and Jonathan Gibson (Aldershot: Ashgate, 2004), pp. 205–36, determines (p. 216) that 'she belonged to a moderate conformist tradition with marked affinities to puritanism'.

77 Hunt, p. 211

78 Hunt, p. 211. Mrs Sadleir's correspondence with Donne's friend and executor, Bishop Henry King, is discussed in this article (pp. 212–13), lending further support to the association of the inscription with H2.

79 J. C. Davies, ed., *Catalogue of manuscripts in the library of the Honourable Society of the Inner Temple*, 3 vols (Oxford, 1972), I, 87.

80 Davies, I, 88.

81 Hunt, p. 209.

Shakespeare and other 'Tragicall Discourses' in an Early-Seventeenth-Century Commonplace Book from Oriel College, Oxford

Guillaume Coatalen

In a letter to E. W. B. Nicholson, the then librarian of the Bodleian, attached to the inside cover of MS Latin misc. b. 6, dated April 28 1898, C. B. Heberden writes 'I do not like to destroy them [the manuscripts] without asking whether by any chance you might care to have them at the Bodleian.' Obviously, the principal of Brasenose College thought they had as little worth as the person who scratched 'Little Worth' in crude letters into its calfskin cover. The hand looks like a seventeenth-century one, and might belong to someone tidying up the compiler's papers after his death.

Heberden states that Lat. misc. b. 6 ('Libor C') and MS Eng. misc. d. 28 ('Libor A') were handed down from principal to principal, which led the authors of the *Summary Catalogue of Western Manuscripts in the Bodleian Library* to infer that they may be the work of Samuel Radcliffe, the principal of Brasenose from 1614 to 1647/8—safely adding that 'the writer was certainly an Oxford man'[1]—but a comparison between Radcliffe's earlier and squarer hand and the one found in both manuscripts proves this attribution to be a myth.[2] It is by no means certain that the manuscripts were bequeathed from principal to principal and it cannot be established which principal of Brasenose got hold of the manuscripts first. Students tended to move freely from one college to the other in the early seventeenth century, so it is hardly surprising that Oriel manuscripts should find their way to Brasenose College.

Though the allusion to *Romeo and Juliet* in a sermon preached twice at the University Church in 1620 and 1621 is recorded in the first volume of the *Shakespere Allusion-Book* (1932), originally compiled in 1909,[3] and in Chambers' *Facts and Problems* (1930), who mentions 'several passages from Shakespeare',[4] the contents of MS Eng. misc.d.28 have not been discussed since. The dramatic material exceeds sixty extracts altogether. In addition to the lines from *Romeo and Juliet*, the manuscript offers three extracts from *Richard II*, five from *Hamlet* and two from *Othello*. The amount of material taken from Chapman's plays is quite remarkable, namely fifteen extracts from *Bussy D'Ambois*, three from *All Fools*, sixteen from *Byron's Conspiracy*, seven from *Byron's Tragedy*, and two from *Sir Giles Goosecap*. Finally, extracts from a variety of plays occur: two from *Volpone*, four from Fletcher's *Thierry and Theodoret*, and one from Beaumont's *Scornful Lady* and Dekker's *If It Be Not Good*.

The number of lines taken from play-books does not make MS Eng. misc. d. 28 unique. Drummond's *circa* 1606–1614 (National Library of Scotland, MS 2059), Edward Pudsey's[5] *circa* 1600–1615 (Bodleian MS Eng. poet. d. 3) miscellanies and the mid-late seventeenth-century anthology by John Evans '*Hesperides*, or the Muses Garden'[6] contain a wealth of dramatic quotations. However, what is unique about MS Eng. misc. d. 28, is that they should be kept in such a serious university commonplace book close to classics and theological works. Dramatic extracts usually occur in verse miscellanies of a lighter nature, such as Archbishop Sancroft's late seventeenth-century manuscript book of jests (Bodleian, MS Sancroft 97).

No extracts are copied from manuscript sources apart from, perhaps, Robert Devereux's *Apology of the Earl of Essex*, which circulated widely,[7] thus the interest of the manuscripts does not lie in any alternative variants for the passages quoted. MS Eng. misc. d. 28 is significant for at least three reasons. One is that, in some cases, very few manuscript versions of the plays are extant. Secondly, evidence concerning the first readers of playbooks in general, and of Shakespeare in particular, is relatively rare.[8] Thirdly, the manuscript offers a unique insight into the reading practice and literary tastes of an Oxford man in the early seventeenth century.

Only the discovery of sermons in the scribe's hand incorporating the extracts would be conclusive. It is nevertheless my contention that the dramatic extracts were compiled in MS Eng. misc. d. 28 to be used in sermons. I discuss the authorship and date of both manuscripts before describing them. I then transcribe the dramatic extracts recorded in MS Eng. misc. d. 28 and proceed to assess the compiler's treatment of them.

AUTHORSHIP AND DATE

Who compiled the dramatic extracts ? Unfortunately, MS Eng. misc. d. 28 bears no name. A closer inspection of MS Lat. misc. b. 6 reveals the presence of charges against an unidentified leading member of the college (p. 463) in a hand distinct from all the other hands in both manuscripts. The transcription is diplomatic: no attempt has been made to supply letters for abbreviated words, apart from 'in pr*imum*'; 'pnal' is most probably an abbreviated form of 'p*erso*nal' even though it might be construed as 'p*e*nal'.[9] Square brackets [ ] indicate illegible letters.

The list runs as follows:

in pr*imum* yt he bought his place of L.
witnesse old merick and Price

2. that he took of Bird for a fr[ ]
20^{l}.
3. yt he took in the felling of 500 marks
of trees to M^{r}. Purefy 50.^{l}
4. yt he is altogether pnal in his
government
5. yt he hath made a false register
in the book
6 that he is defamed for an old=with
black Besse and principal Bradhil
his maid witnesse Saloway and
gil jones and Bradshawes wife
7 that he hath taken out certaine
writings which he hath not restored
8 yt he keeps the Colledge mony in
his hands contrary to statute
9 that he denyes his fellowes a copy
of the statutes m ^{r}
10 yt he threatned to register Charles
Tooker and Mr Horne for not lending
the manciplemony which himself
had said, it was on their choice whether
they would or no.

Bribery is alleged in the first charge, although it is difficult to tell what the place, most likely in college, could be. One Francis Price was admitted at Oriel College in 1638 and one Thomas Price in 1642.[10] One John Bird (a citizen in 1612) occurs in 'Lists of Citizens Taking the Oath to Observe the Privileges of the University',[11] and on 3 October 1615 the oath was taken by John Bird, Mayor, presumably the same man.[12] The witnesses are probably college servants like 'black Besse' and 'gil jones'. Ralph Bradhil was principal of St Mary Hall from 1591 to 1632 and

Clerk of the market in 1611.[13] The fourth charge supplies an important clue as to a hypothetical identity of the writer of the commonplace books for 'M^{r}. Puresy' is Purefoy, the Parliamentary Commandant of Farringdon, spellt 'Purefy' in the Dean's register of Oriel College.[14] The charge tallies with a piece of information mentioned in the college registers, dated 21 February 1645/6, according to which 'It was agreed at [John Saunders's] suggestion to allow . . . Purefoy, 40 loads of timber from the Wadley estate at half price'.[15] Hence, the list of charges at the end of 'Libor C' was probably written shortly afterwards. A comparison with Saunders's hand in the College Register proves beyond doubt that the manuscripts do not belong to him[16] but rather to someone reporting the charges against him or maybe even to the person who made the charges.

A rough estimate of the contents of MS Eng. misc. d. 28 ('Libor A') indicates that it is indeed the labour of an Oxford man, as noted by the catalogue entry. The compiler, who was proud of the achievements of the university, drew a list of 'Writers of the most famous uniuersity of Oxford since ye beginning of Queene Elizabeths raigne' at the end of the manuscript. Oxford men wrote most of the contemporary works from which extracts occur in 'Libor A'. One is explicitely about the university, that of the antiquary Brian Twyne entitled *Antiquitatis Academiæ Oxoniensis Apologia* (1608) which occurs in MS Lat. misc. b. 6 as well. Even more significantly, perhaps, a great number of sermons included in MS Eng. misc. d. 28 were delivered at St Mary's, the University Church.

MS Lat. misc. b. 6 reads 'Quæstiones Com. Oxon: 1618 habitæ' (p. 158) and 'Gratulatoria cu*m* primûm in Coll. Oriell admissus fui. 11' (p. 159) in a hand identical to one of the Latin hands in MS Eng. misc. d. 28. This might suggest that the compiler was awarded a B.A. degree,[17] presumably in 1618, but the information could mean anything from another degree[18] to a fellowship.[19] The number '11' is not a date, it belongs to a pagination, as shown by the top of the following page which has '12'. Beneath, the compiler picked out three questions, from a printed source of academic questions now lost, for which 'D° Tookero seniore' was respondent (pp. 154, 156, 157). 'D°' may be short for 'Doctor'. One question, 'An ingenia feliciora fuit ad studioru*m* patientiam ineptiora? Aff.', was answered for the M.A. in 1618.[20] The compiler may have read for the M.A. when he copied these disputations.

The scanty evidence is not conclusive and identifying the compiler with any certainty is impossible at this stage. The Tookers of Maddington came from a prominent gentry Wiltshire family.[21] Most of its members were educated at Oxford and there were at least four Tookers at Oriel in the early seventeenth century: two fellows—Charles

Tooker born in 1609 and his elder brother Robert[22] born in 1597—and two John Tookers. According to the college registers, the fellows were of gentle birth but not the students. In fact, since the name was fairly common, the Tookers may have belonged to distinct families.

'D° Tookero seniore' may be Robert Tooker, admitted probationer on 27 September (Touker), and perpetual scholar on 28 September 1618.[23] But a John Tooker, who was 22 years old in 1615, was admitted Commoner at Oriel in 1617–18.[24] This John may be the other John's elder brother, aged 19 in 1619.[25] Thus 'senior' would apply to both Robert and John Tooker, who were admitted in 1618. John Horne is another possible candidate.[26] He too was admitted in 1618. Moreover, he is associated with Charles Tooker in the list of charges transcribed above. Given the insufficient evidence, the compiler may be Robert Tooker, John Tooker or John Horne but he may well be any other member admitted in 1618, assuming the year is 1618.[27] However, manuscripts belonging to a fellow would have had more chances to survive at Oxford. Because of the sermons and religious pamphlets contained in both manuscripts, John Cowling[28] and Hugh Yale,[29] two divines and treasurers at Oriel College, are two more possible candidates.

The extracts themselves offer routes to establishing a partial prosopography of the Oriel man, but caution must be exercised, for it is difficult to avoid reading erroneous information into them. Inevitably, such thinking tends to be circular and most parts of the picture will necessarily remain blurred, unless another source confirms the reasons for choosing the passages entered in the manuscript.

The amount of religious literature in the manuscript suggests the compiler read theology. It is clear that he has no liking for Catholics,[30] nor is he in favour of reforming the Church. He writes 'reforming—like them that quench the fire by / pulling downe the house' below a passage taken from Chapman's *All Fools* on 'extreame Loue' (23: the numbers within parentheses refer to the numbering of the extracts in my transcript)—which makes him a man of the *via media*. The personal comments in black ink, 'sub di*uinum* erga regi fidelitas' (below 25) and 'fidelitas erga ‹re›gem' (below 45), suggest he believed in the divine right of kings, a Laudian tenet.

Many student commonplace books written at Cambridge, Oxford and the Inns of Court in the 1620s and 30s display misogynistic verse.[31] So does MS Eng. misc. d. 28 which contains Overbury's 'with clothes and tires our iudgements bribed be / And woman is least part of what we see' ([col.] 899). Yet the manuscript does not quite belong to the type in that it contains quite a number of passages dealing with celibacy and the long robe, a distinct if somewhat related issue.

The compiler was probably wondering whether it was suitable or not to be married and have children.[32] The thirty-second article of religion, 'Of the Marriage of Priests', states that 'it is lawful for them, as for all other Christian men, to marry at their own discretion, as they shall judge the same to serve better to godliness'. A priest had the right to marry, and the three extracts in the manuscript which consider the topic could help to make up one's mind. Was 'the comfort of two hearts / In one delicious harmony united' (22) at all possible? He concludes 'haue wife and children' after Montaigne's advice taken from Book I, chap. 38 ([col.] 633). But he also records Bacon's opposite view in the fifth essay 'Of Marriage and Single Life' of the 1612 edition, 'A single life is prop*er* to Church men' ([col.] 914), a view held by Herbert in his *Country Parson*, 'The Country Parson considering that virginity is a higher state then Matrimony, and that the Ministry requires the best and highest things, is rather unmarryed, then marryed'.[33] Marriage was lawful for a priest but it watered down the love of God. In the words of the Swiss theologian Gualter, quoted in Burton's *Anatomy of Melancholy*, it is 'a thing in itselfe laudable, good, and necessary, but many, deceived and carried away with the blind love of it, have quite laid aside the love of God, and desire of his glory'.[34] Leantio's speech against marriage in Middleton's *Women Beware Women* (III, i), written *c.*1614–5, which does not occur in the manuscript, would have been most apposite in such a context.

Whether the owner of the manuscripts was wary of women because of his unloving mother is impossible to prove. What does seem clear, however, is that the compiler was fascinated by the Senecan figure of the 'cruel Tigresse' seeking revenge on her own children in John Fletcher's *Thierry and Theodoret* (48–50). A passage copied from Bacon's 'Of Parents and Children' from the *Essays* on the 'middest' children who 'neverthelesse, prove ye best' ([col.] 914) may have to do with the compiler's identity. Similarly, the occurrence on the same column of 'Nobility of birth commonly abateth industry' and 'Besides Noble p*er*sons cannot go much higher', taken from 'Of Nobility' in the *Essays*, may be linked to the family's uncertain social status. The Tookers of Madington had arms in the first visitation,[35] but the second visitation noted that there was 'no proofe of his Armes' for '[Charles] Tucker of Abingdon'.[36] One particular passage from Bacon's *Essays*, 'Integrity is ye Judges portion . . . Lands and prop*er*ty. Essay 36 of judicature pag 122' may be linked to land cases which involved the compiler ([col.] 920). Was he a 'deformed person' ([col.] 918), to quote Bacon's phrase copied in his commonplace book? At this stage the question bears no answer, if the figurative sense of the word is meant, that of 'perverted, distorted, morally ugly, offensive, or hateful',[37] a timely reminder of how slippery it is to work out the meaning ascribed to the extracts. The risk of becoming as reckless an interpreter as Sir Politic Would-be in *Volpone* is difficult to avoid.[38]

The material quoted in MS Eng. misc. d. 28 ranges in date from 1579, 'The discouery of a gaping gulfe etc. John Stubbes who therefore lost his hand 8° pag 96'[39] ([col.] 949), to 1623, 'Pilgrim of Castile. Transl into English 1623. 4° pagina. 150'[40] ([col.] 1194). 1616, the date of a 'translation printed in Latine letters by Henrie Barker' [p.] 3, a likely reference to Robert Barker's 1616 Bible, provides a safe *terminus post quem* for the beginning of the compiling. Presumably, about half the material was copied after 1616 and the *terminus ante quem* for the whole manuscript may even be 1620, the date of the second edition of Twyne's work, whose title is quoted with no date. Since the dramatic extracts occur on few consecutive pages, they must have been copied shortly after 1622, the date of the *Othello* quarto quoted in the manuscript. The last item of the manuscript, *The pilgrime of Casteele*, a translation of Lope de Vega's romance, *El peregrino en su patria* (Barcelona, 1604), was transcribed after 1623. Thus, the material between [cols.] 738 and 1179 dates from either between 1622 and 1623 or from after 1623. Given the dates and order of the editions recorded in MS Eng misc. d. 28, the manuscript ('Libor A') seems to have been written between 1616 and 1625.

The vernacular material in MS Lat. misc. b. 6 ('Libor C') must have been written shortly after 1626, the date of Christopher Potter's translation of Fr. Paulo's *Quarrels of the Pope Paul V with the State of Venice*[41] (pp. 143–4, 188–9, 229, 303–9), whereas the Latin extracts may have been compiled earlier, but presumably not before 1611, the date of Donne's *Ignatius* (pp. 276–81).

It is unlikely that the manuscripts were completed much later than 1626, since no works dating after then occur. That Middleton's hugely popular *Game at Chess*, performed in 1624 and published the following year, is not quoted from might indicate that MS Eng misc. d. 28 was completed before 1625. An alternative explanation would be that the compiler simply chose not to copy from the play.

DESCRIPTION OF THE MANUSCRIPTS

Neither manuscript is, strictly speaking, a commonplace book. There are traces of an older scriptural miscellany in MS Eng misc. d. 28, but the leaves that bear the headings are few. A method for compiling a scriptural commonplace book is copied on the third page but it does not seem to have been applied. The alphabetical index of topics applies to the Latin material only, which covers about a quarter of the manuscript. [Col.] 1196 supplies a list of extracts, 'according to the page and letter' which 'are not referd to any head and so not crost, as others be' or 'any text certainly found'. The list contains most of the literary material and an analysis of all the references in the index reveals that not a single literary extract occurs in it. MS Lat. misc. b. 6 contains neither index nor headings.

MS ENG MISC. D. 28 ('LIBOR A')

'Libor A' [*sic*] is a folio volume in a contemporary vellum cover which contains 649 leaves measuring approximately 295mm in height by 190mm in breadth, bearing an 'A' on its fore-edge, to signal its title, which was common in the 1630s.[42] A stub precedes what is left of the first leaf and bears fragments of an alphabetical index reading 'D . . . Da . . . Dea . . . John'. On the last folio, traces of a table of contents remain in which some page numbers are visible. The present collation runs 1 stub, 1 torn leaf, 1^3, $2–3^8$, 4^2, $5–19^8$, 20^6, 21^{10} (minus one leaf), $22–30^8$, 31^6(stub in ii), $32–39^8$ (stub in 33.i, 36.ii–iii, 38.viii), $40–41^2$, $42–44^8$, 45^4, 46^2 (two slivers), 47^8. A thin 15mm-wide strip of Medieval parchment in Latin was pasted onto the first endpaper for reinforcement. The paper bears two watermarks: a left-handled pot with a crescent and band inscribed PD/O and a pillar with a band inscribed GVAR.[43] The leaves are divided into 1,195 numbered columns lettered vertically with some red crosses. Trefoils are drawn before the commonplace headings, which are repeated in the index. A pagination beginning '1' (above [col.] 911) runs to '94' (above [col.] 1000).

The hand of the vernacular extracts is a mixture of cursive late secretary and italic. Characteristic secretary forms include the initial *v* with its long descender, the long-tailed *h* and the *g* with its cross-stroke. The hand uses the italic *a* and *l*. It is sometimes tiny and difficult to read because it was written so rapidly but is otherwise neat. The ascending loop of the *r* is remarkable. The *q* is identical to a *g* and the minims in *m*, *n*, *u*, *v*, *w* are often similar. The *es* are often difficult to distinguish from *s*. The compiler uses a few contractions, the common y^e and y^t and *per pro*. The tiny Latin notes in black ink are often almost illegible as are the faded notes in pencil. Even though italic letters are not used consistently, their presence follows the scribal and printed conventions of the time: for quotations, more often for Latin than for English, and for proper names and titles. The compiler had some Hebrew ([col.] 477), which was expected from a divine. A distinct and perhaps earlier secretary hand occurs at the top of pp. 1–6, 458, 462–506, for Latin, Scripture and

Greek (for example above [col.] 956). At the top of pp. 530–40, a tiny round italic hand was crammed in for lack of space. The pages contain answers to academic questions written above in a larger hand, which is the one used for Latin headings in the manuscript. The top of pp. 532–5 combines two hands, a mixed hand and an italic. The mixed hand exhibits the same letter forms as the main hand for vernacular literature. At first sight, the English hand used on pp. 571–94 seems to be distinct from the hand used on pp. 244–570, 595–603 but it is not, it is simply smaller. It is similar to the hand used before [col.] 476 and smaller than the hand used for Harington's *Orlando* (pp. 246–59). The English hand used on pp. 7–8 ([cols.] 1–3) could belong to another person. The Latin hand used [cols.] 3–17 is written with a larger nib but otherwise exhibits similar letter forms as the main vernacular hand. The compiler uses two hands for Latin: a neat italic for verse, for instance Horace's (pp. 119–26), and a mixed hand. He often switches from one to the other as shown by columns 419–20, when he copied extracts from Seneca's tragedies. The index is a mixture of all the hands to be found in the manuscript. Surprisingly enough, all the hands used for the extracts copied in the columns proper seem to belong to the same person. Depending on speed and care, the hand is more or less slanted, large or minute. From [col.] 326, '11 Psalm: 2.3.4. vers: by doctor King' onwards, the compiler uses his main hand except for [cols.] 462–476, where he uses his neat pre-[col.] 326 Latin hand again. The older long straight *s* occurs in [cols.] 4–22, rarely later on, and never in the literary extracts.

MS LAT. MISC. B. 6 ('LIBOR C')

This long ledger-size volume, which measures approximately 385 mm in height by 165 mm in breadth, is made out of what was originally two distinct manuscripts. Each of the 466 leaves comprises two quarto leaves joined head to foot, the upper margin of the bottom leaf being pasted on to the lower margin of the top leaf. In view of the 'Libor C' and 'Libor A' inscriptions on the covers (written thus, instead of the correct Latin 'Liber'), it is likely that another similar commonplace book, now lost, was designated 'Libor B'. The compiler wrote on the pages before they were bound in ordinary vellum. The manuscript is in a sorry state. The first gathering of eight leaves, which is followed by a stub, is torn, including a table of contents. Several paginations are crossed out. The present collation runs $1–8^8$, 9 (a stub), 10^8, 11^4 (minus one leaf), $12–23^8$, 24^{10}, 25^8, 26^6, $27–32^8$ (32.ii–iv are torn). The paper was probably taken from other written leaves and used again. The paper of the top part bears a pot watermark similar to the one in 'Libor A', that of the bottom bears one similar to the pillar watermark.

The same brown ink is used as in 'Libor 'A', for annotations in particular. An identical Latin hand occurs on the top and bottom of pp. 9–88. From the top of p. 89 italic forms are preferred, but the other hand is used at times. The marginal annotations are written in the same hand in both parts of the manuscript. From the bottom of p. 122, the italic hand is to be found. On pp. 419–50, the hand of the top is more careful than the hand of the bottom, it exhibits more italic forms as well. The same hand as that used for vernacular extracts in 'Libor A' is used at the bottom of pp. 140–4 and from the bottom of p. 430 to the end of the manuscript. 'Gratulatoria cu*m* primû*m* in Coll. Oriell: admissus fui 11' is written in the same hand as 'Libor A' (p. 1). The Latin headings are written in an identical hand in both manuscripts: see, for example, 'Ex T Liuii decad:4a:lib:1°:' (top of p. 435), and the dotted line at the bottom of p. 451 drawn between the excerpts from Hawkins and Boccaccio is identical to the ones in the other manuscript.

Not the least interesting aspect of 'Libor C' is its composite nature, which is not common, and makes it possible to read it in two ways: as two distinct volumes or as a single one. The compiler filled in the leaves of both parts and went to great pains to glue them together, perhaps to read, in some cases at least, one half as some sort of commentary on the other. That early modern readers were interested in multiple reading is well-known. 'Libor C' offers a modest version of a 'book wheel', the spectacular machine which enabled scholars to read several books simultaneously.[44] Thanks to this peculiar montage, to take a single example, Erasmus's *Colloquia* might yield a suitable commentary on Plautus, one of the humanist's favorite playwrights (pp. 387–407).

TRANSCRIPTION OF THE DRAMATIC EXTRACTS IN MS ENG. MISC. D. 28 ('LIBOR A')

In the following transcriptions these editorial conventions have been observed: (1) The v/u and i/j graphs are retained. (2) Letters supplied are italicized in the transcript. (3) Square brackets enclose editorial interpretation. (4) Pointed brackets enclose scribal deletions. (5) [col.] stands for column. The author and title of the extracts are added. The extracts are numbered and line-references given.[45] Only significant variants are reported. The compiler's coded titles and authors are deciphered in brackets. For the coding system used by the compiler to identify each play, see p. 154 below.

SHAKESPEARE, *RICHARD II* (1598), STC 22309

[col.] 697

~.

1. the tongues of dying men Inforce attention
like deep harmony where words are scarce
they are seldome spent in vaine for they
breath truth that breath their words in
paine. He y^{t} no more must say, is listned more
Then they whom youth and ease hath taught
to gloze, more are mens ends markt then
their liues before. The setting sunne and musick
at the close, As the last tast of sweets is
sweetest last Writ in remembrance more
then things long past. UIf, Usbhfekz,
pg Skdibse Uif tfdpoe. cz Tiblftqf [THe, Tragediy, of
Richard The second. by Shakespeare]
bsf. 4°. pag: 68

II.i.5–14

morientis hominis loquela verissima

2. —supplant the Irish Rebells those roughheaded
kernes, Which liue like venome where no
venome else But only they haue priviledge
to liue.

II.i.156–158

[col.] 698

3. each substance of a greife hath twenty
shadowes, Which shew like greife it self, but
are not so: For sorrowes eyes glazed, with
blinding teares Deuide one thing entire to
many obiects.

~.

II.ii.14–17:
3 are] are Q3 is Q1–2 Q4–5

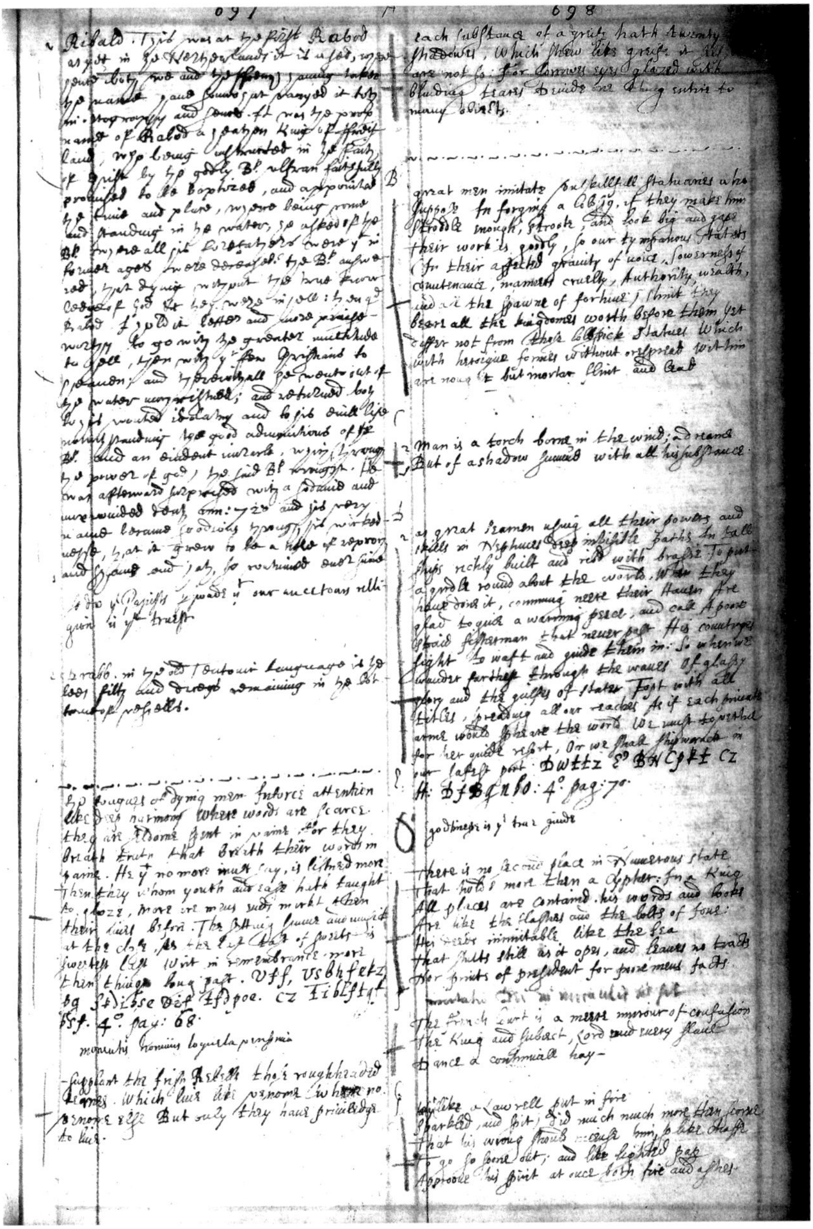

PLATE I. *Columns 697 and 698 of 'Libor A': Oxford, Bodleian Library,* MS *Eng. misc. d. 28, p. 355 (Original page size 295 × 190mm.) Reproduced by permission of the Bodleian Library, University of Oxford.*

GEORGE CHAPMAN, BUSSY *D'AMBOIS* (1607), STC 4966

4. great men imitate vnskillfull statuaries who
suppose In forging a Colossq. if they make him
Stroddle enough; stroote, and look big and gape
Their work is goodly, so our ty mpanous statists
(In their affected grauity of uoice, Sowerness of
countenance, manners cruelty, Authority, wealth,
and all the spawne of fortune) think they
beare all the kingdomes worth before them Yet
differ not from those Col<o>ssick Statues Which
with heroique formes without orespread Within
are nought but mortar flint and lead

1607 edition, Sig. [A2], I.i.6–17:
1 men imitate] men flourish; and doe imitate

5. ~ Man is a torch borne in the wind; a dreame
But of a shadow summ'd with all his substance.

Sig. [A2], I.i.18–9

6. ~ as great Seamen using all their powers and
skills in Neptunes deep invisible paths In tall
ships richly built and ribd with brasse To put
a girdle round about the world, When they
haue done it, comming neere their Hauen Are
glad to giue a warning peece, and call A poore
staid fisherman that neuer past His countryes
sight to waft and guide them in: So when we
wander farthest through the waues Of glassy
glory and the gulfes of stater Topt with all
titles, spreading all our reaches As if each priuate
arme would spheare the world We must to vertue
for her guide resort, Or we shall shipwrack in
our safest port. Dwttz E'BNCpktCz
H: DIBqnbo: 4°. pag: 7° [Cussy D'AMBoisBy G: CHApman]

Sig. [A2^{r-v}], I.i.20–33

godlinesse is y^{r} true guide

7. There is no second place in Numerous state
That holds more then a Cypher: In a King
All places are containd. his words and looks
Are like the flashes and the bolts of Joue:

His deeds inimitable like the Sea
That shuts still as it opes, and leaues no tracts
Nor prints of president for poore mens facts.

Sig. [A2^{v}], I.i.34–40

imitatio Dei in miraculis ad sit [in pencil]
The French Court is a meere mirrour of confusion 8.
The King and subiect, Lord and euery slaue
Dance a continuall hay—

Sig. [B1^{v}], I.ii.24–7:
1 The] Our 1 confusion]confusion to it

9. <>(y^{t}(like a Lawrell put in fire
Sparkled, and spit) did much much more than scorne
That his wrong should misuse him, so like chaffe
To go so soone out; and like lighted pap*er*
Approoue his spirit at once both fire and ashes.

Sig. [C1], II.i.69–73

[col.] 699

10. —wheres law?
See how it runnes much like a turbulent sea
Heere high and glorious as it did contend
pure
To wash the heauens, and make the Starres more
And here so low, it leaues the mud of hell
To euery common vew. this pardond?—

Sig. [C3^{v}], II.ii.24–9:
6 'this pardond?'] added by the compiler

11. —he is a Prince and their prerogatiues
Are to their lawes as to their p*ar*dons are
Their reseruations after Parliaments
One guits another: forme giues all their essence

Sig. [D1], II.ii.120–3:
1—he is a Prince] I and a Prince:

12. I now am subiect to the heartlesse feare
Of euery shadow, and of euery breath
And would change firmnesse with an aspen leafe
So weak a guilty conscience.

Sig. [D3^{v}], III.i.5–9:
1 I] But 4 So weak a guilty conscience.] So confident a spotlesse conscience is; / So weake a guilty:

13. he<>l turne his outward loue to inward hate
A princes loue is like the lightnings fume
Which no man can embrace but must consume.

Sig. [O1^{v}], III.i.111–3

anti ca vita periculosa.
dei amor non nisi in altera vita p*er*fectus

14. You that (like a murthering peece making lanes
in Armies The first man of a rank the whole
rank falling) If you haue once wrongd one
man, y'are so farre From making him amends
that all his race Freinds and associates fall
into their chace.

Sig. [F2], III.ii.380–4:
1 You that] That 6 their chace.] your chace:

15. Heres nought but whispring with us: like a calme
Before a tempest, when the silent aire
Layes her soft eare close to the earth to hearken
for y^{t} shee feares. is comming to afflict her;
Some fate doth ioyne our eares to heare it comming.

Sig. [F4], IV.i.103–7

16. A worthy man should imitate the weather
That sings in tempests, and being cleere is silent

Sig. [G3^{v}], IV.ii.99–100

17. —he must appeare
Like calme security before a ruine
A politician must like lightning melt
The very marrow and not print the skin.

Sig. [G4^{v}], IV.ii.166–9:
1—he must appeare] yet will I appeare

18. a valiant vertuous young faire —
Yet as the winds sing through a hollow tree,
And (since it lets the*m* passe through) let it stand:
But a tree solid, since it giues no way,
To their wild rages, they rend up by th'roote
So this full creature now shall reele and fall
Before the frantique puffs of purblind chaunce
That pipes through emp ty men and makes the*m*
daunce.

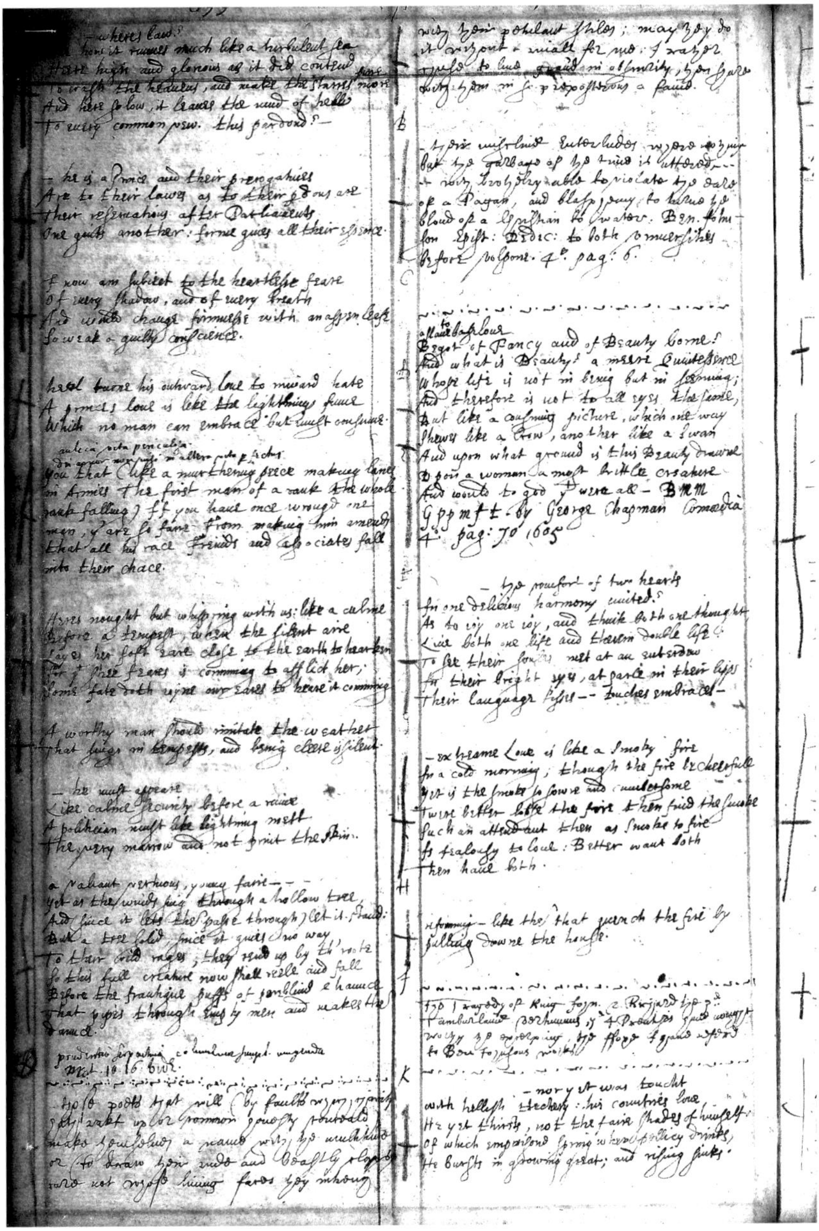

PLATE 2. *Columns 699 and 700 of 'Libor A': Bodleian Library, MS Eng. misc. d. 28, p. 356 (Original page size 295 × 190mm.) Reproduced by permission of the Bodleian Library, University of Oxford.*

Sig. [I1^{r-v}], V.iii.45–8:
1 a valiant vertuous young faire —] Yoong, learned, valiant, vertuous, and full mand;

prudentia serpentia co lumbæ semp*er* ingenda
mat.10.16.vide

~.

[cols.] 699–700

BEN JONSON, *VOLPONE IN WORKES* (1616), STC 14751

19. those poets that will (by faults which charity
hath rakt up or common honesty conceald)
make themselues a name with the multitude
or (to draw their rude and beastly claps)
care not whose liuing faces they intrench
with their petulant stiles: may they do
it without a riuall for me: I rather
chuse to liue grau'd in obscurity, then share
with them in so preposterous a fame.

1616 edition, pp. 444–5:
1 those poets that] those, that 7–8 I rather chuse] I choose rather

[col.] 700

20. —their miscline Enterludes where no thing
but the garbage of the time is uttered—
—with brothelry able to uiolate the eare
of a Pagan, and blasphemy to turne the
bloud of a Christian to water. Ben John—
son Epist: Dedic: to both vniversities
before volpone. 4°. pag: 6.
~.

p. 445

GEORGE CHAPMAN, *AL FOOLES* (1605), STC 4963

21. to
a slaue baseloue
Begot of Fancy and of Beauty borne?
And what is Beauty? a meere Quintessence

Whose life is not in being, but in seeming;
And therefore is not to all eyes the same,
But like a cousning picture, which one way
Shewes like a Crowe, another like a Swan
And upon what ground in this Beauty drawne
Vpon a woman a most brittle creature
And would to god y^t were all—Bmm
Gppmft . by George Chapman Comædia [All Fooles]
4.° pag: 70 1605

1605 edition, Sig. [A1^v], I.i.42–51:
1–2 a slaue /to/ baseloue]
11 y^t] (for my part) that

22. —the comfort of two hearts
In one delicious harmony united?

As to ioy one ioy, and think both one thought,
Live both one life and therein double life:
To see their soules met at an entervew
In their bright eyes, at parle in their lipps
Their language kisses—touches embraces—

Sig. [B1^v], I.i.112–19:
7 Their language kisses] kisses: and t'obserue the rest

23. —extreame Loue is like a smoky fire
In a cold morning; though the fire be cheerefull
Yet is the smoke so sowre and cumbersome
Twere better loose the fire then find the smoke
Such an attendant then as Smoke to fire
Is Jealousy to loue: Better want both
Then haue both.

Sig. [C3], I.ii.59–64:
1—extreame] In deede such

reforming—like the*m* that quench the fire by
pulling downe the house.

~.

The tragedy of King John. & Richard the 3d:
Tamburlaine, vertumnus, ye 4 Prentises haue nought
worthy the excerping, the ffoxe I haue referd
to Ben Johnsons works.

~.

GEORGE CHAPMAN, *THE CONSPIRACIE OF BYRON* (1608), STC 4968

24. —nor yet was toucht
with hellish trechery: his countries loue
He yet thirsts, not the faire shades of himself:
Of which empoisond spring when pollicy drinks,
He bursts in growing great, and rising sinks.

1608 edition, Prologus, ll. 17–21

[col.] 701

25. O tis a dangerous and a dreadfull thing
To steale prey from a Lyon; or to hide
A head distrustfull in his opened iawes;
To trust our bloud in others vaines, and hang
Twixt heauen and earth in vapors of their brea<th>
To leaue a sure pace on continued earth
And force a gate in iumps fro' towre to towre
As they that do aspire; from height to height.
The bounds of loyalty are made of glasse.
Soone broke but can in no date be repaird
Byrons Conspiracy. by George Chapman 4.°
pag. 90: 1608

Sig. [C2], I.ii.137–46:
8 that do] doe that

subdi*uinum* erga regī fidelitas
therfore will men make good former breach with new plots.

26. To values hard to draw, we use retreates
And, to pull shafts home (with a good bow arme)
We thrust hard fro' us—

Sig. [C3^{v}], II.i.25–7

27. I haue wonderd that y^{r} wit and spirit
And profit in th' experience of slaueries
Imposd on us; in those meere pollitigue tearmes
Of loue fame loyalty can be carried up
To such an height of ignorant conscience;
of cowardise and dissolutions
In all the freeborne spirits of royall man —

—We must (in passing to our wished ends
Through things calld good and bad) be like ye aire
That euenly intepposed betwixt the seas
And the opposed Element of fire;
At either toucheth but p*er*takes with neither
Is neither hot nor cold but with a slight
And harmlesse temp*er* mixt of both extreames.

Sig. [E1^{v}], III.i.25–30, 40–8:
1 I haue] Both heard and 2 th'] in 2 of] of the

28. Laffin: you p*er*swade as if
you could create: what man can shunne
The searches and compressions of y^{r} graces.
Byr: We must haue these lures whe*n* we hawke
for freinds
And wind about the*m* like a subtle riuer
That (seeming only to runne on his course)
Doth search yet as he runnes; and still finds out
The easiest paths of entry on the shore;
Gliding so slily by as scarce it toucht
Yet still <e>ates something in it; so must those
That haue large feilds and currents to dispose.

Sig. [E2], III.i.64–74:
1 you p*er*swade as if] You perswade,

reprehensio quō

29. —he will obtaine:
He draweth with his weight, and like a plummet
That swaies a dore, with falling of, pulls after.

Sig. [E2^{v}], II.ii.1–3:
1—he will obtaine:] *La Fin*, is in the right; and will obtaine;

30. —we will admire Byron, praise him—
we will take his picture
Such, tricks the Archduke usd t'extol his greatnesse
Which comp lements though great men hold absurd
And a meere remedy for desire of greatnesse.
Yet great men use the*m*; as their state potatoes
High cullises, and potions to excite
The lust of mans ambitions—

Sig. [E2^{v}], III.ii.13–18:
1—we will admire Byron, praise him—— / we will take his picture] added by the compiler
5 their state] they eate 7 mans ambitions] their ambition

[col.] 702

There are so oft attempts made against his p*er*son 31.
That sometimes they may speed, for they are plants
That spring the more for cutting, and at last
Will cast their wished shadow

Sig. [F1], III.ii.191–4

proditio non semp*er* tame[n]

32. —treason to a credulous eye
He comes inuisible vailed with flattery
And flatterers looke like freinds, as wolues like Dogs.

Sig. [F2], III.ii.244–6:
1—treason] Be circumspect, for

33. —De Laffin and such corrupted Heralds
Hird to encourage and to glorify cheeks
May force what breath they will into their
Fitter to blow up bladders then full men:
Yet may puff men to, with p*er*swasions
That they are gods in worth, and may rise Kings
With treading on their noises.—

Sig. [F2], III.ii.263–9

34. —prosperity is at highest degree
The founte and handle of calamity
Like dust before a whirlewind those men fly
That prostrate on the grounds of fortune ly
But being great (like trees that broadestsproute)
Their owne top-heauy state grubs vp their roote:

Sig. [F3], III.iii.25–30:
5 But] And

35. —for a subiect to affect a kingdome
Is like the Cammel y^{t} of Joue begd hornes:
As such madhungry men, as well may eate
Hoat coles of fire to feede their naturall heate

Sig. [G2 v], IV.i.138–141:
1—for] But for

36. He that wines Empire with the losse of faith
Outbyes it; and will bankrupt; you haue layd
A braue foundation by the hand of vertue:
Put not the roofe to fortune: foolish statuaries,
That under little Saints suppose great bases,
Make lesse to sence the saints, and so where fortune
Aduanceth vile minds to states great and noble,
She much the more exposeth the*m* to shame,
Not able to make good, and fill their bases
With a conformed structure.—

Sig. [G3], IV.i.176–185

37. —counsailes
Held to the line of iustice still produce
The surest states, and greatest being sure
Without which fit assurance in the greatest,
As you may see a mighty promontory
More digd and undereaten, then may warrant
A safe supportance to his hanging browes,
All passengers auoid him, shunne all ground
That lyes within his shadow, and beare still
A flying eye upon him: so great men
buylding
Corrupted in their grounds and ~~buyding~~ out
Too swelling fronts for their foundations;
When they most should be propt are most forsaken,
And men will rather thrust into the stormes
Of better grounded States, then take a shelter
Beneath their ruinous and fearefull weight
Yet they so oversee their faulty bases
That they remaine securer in conceipt
And
[col.] 703
And that security doth worse presage
Their neere destructions, then their eaten grounds;
And therefore heauen it self is made to us
pe*r*fect Hieroglyphick to expresse
The idlenesse of such security
And the graue labour of a wise distrust

In both sorts of the all enclyning starres
Where all men note this difference in their
shining
As plaine as they distinguish either hand:
The fixt starres wauer and the erring stand.

Sigs. [G3$^{r\text{-}v}$], IV.i.186–203–13

38\. Those as the aire containd within our eares
If it be not in guiet; nor refraines
Troubling our hearing with offensiue sounds;
But our affected instrument of hearing
Repleat with noise and singings in it self
It faithfully receiues no other voices:
So of all iudgments if within themselues
They can not equall differences without the*m*
s And this wind that doth so sing in y^{r} eares.

Sig. [H3], V.ii.58–67:
1 Those] For 'They suffer spleene, and are tumultuous;' a skipped line after line 6

39\. s I know is no desease bred in y^{r} self
But whisperd in by others; who in swelling
Your vaines with empty hope of much, ye~~t~~t able
To p*er*forme no thing; are like shallow streames
That make themselues so many heauens to sight;
Since you may see in them the moone, the stars
The blew space of the aire; as far fro' us
(To our weak sences) in those shallow streames
As if they were as deep as heauen is high
Yet with your middle finger only sound the*m*
And you shall peirce them to the very earth
And therefore leaue them and be true to me.

Sig. [H3], V.ii.68–79

40\. self
Innocence that make a man in tune still with him—
No thought gainst thought, nor as it were
In the confines, Of wishing and repenting doth
possesse, Only a way ward and tumultuous peace

But (all p*ar*ts in him freindly and secure
Fruitfull of best things in all worst seasons.

Sigs. [H3^{r-v}], V.ii.85, 88, 94–97:
1 Innocence] O Inocence, the sacred amulet, / Gainst all the poisons of infirmitie: /
Of all misfortune, iniurie, and death, / That makes a man, in tune still in himselfe; /
Free from the hell to be his owne accuser, / Euer in quiet, endles ioy enioying; /
No strife, nor no sedition in his powres: / No motion in his will, against his reason,
6 of best] of all best

GEORGE CHAPMAN, *THE TRAGEDIE OF BYRON* (1608), STC 4968

41. In him as by a christall that is char'md
I shall discerne by whom and what designes
My rule is threatned—Byrons Tragedy.
pag: 100: by George Chapman 1608

1608 edition, Sig. [I4], I.i.97–9

42. Enough of these eruptions ; our graue Councellour
Well knowes that great affaires will not be
fo rged
But upon Anvills that are lin'd with woll;
We must ascend to our intentions top
Like clouds that must not be seene till they be up
—you must giue temperate aire to your wind
Else will our plots be frostbit in the floure.

Sig. [K1^{v}], I.ii.52–55:
5 must not be seene] be not seene

Sig. [K1^{v}], I.ii.44–5:
6 wind] vnmatcht, and more then humaine winde;

[col.] 704

43. My head is none of those ~~vnde~~ neighbour nobles
That euery pursiuant brings beneaththe Axe
If they bring me out, they shall see Ile hatch
Like to the black thorne, that puts forth his leafe,
Not with the golden fawnings of the sunne
But sharpest showers of haile and blackest frosts
Blowes batteries breaches, showers of steele and bloud
Must be his downright messengers for me
And not the misling breath of policy
Ile not to'th King—

Sig. [L3^{v}], III.i.124–132:
1 is none] rules none 10 Ile not to'th King—] added by the compiler

44. Nor wisht I that my Treasury should flow
With gold that swom in, in my subiects teares.

Sig. [M2], III.ii.51–52

45. Think you it not as strong a point of faith
To rectify y^{r} loyalties to me
As to be trusty in each ohers wrong?
Trust that deceiues our selues is treachery
And Truth that truth conceales an open ly:

Sig. [N4^{v}], IV.ii.180–184

fidelitas erga <re>gem
po[t]estate quatenus dissimulare licet
uitam inuiū illicitu

46. —now is ambition quite oue[rt]hrowne by ~~its owne~~
treason; so haue I discernd An exhalation
that would be a Star ffall when [t]he Sunne
forsook it, in a sinck. Shoes euer ouerhrow
y^{t} are to large; And hugest Canons burst
with ouercharge.

Sig. [O2], IV.ii. 291–95:
1—now is ambition quite oue[rt]hrowne by ~~its owne~~ / treason;] added by the compiler

~.~.~.~.~.~.~.~.~.~.~.~.~.~.~.~.

JOHN FLETCHER, *THIERRY AND THEODORET* (1621), STC 11074

47. —you think
The name of greatnesse glorifies y^r actions
And strong power like a penthouse, promises
To shade you fro' opinion—no
The sinnes we do people behold through optiques
which shewes vm ten times more then common
vices And often multiplies vm: Tragedy
of Thierry and Theodoret: 4°: pag: 80:
1621.

1621 edition, Sig. [B1 ^{v}], I.i.19–25:
1—you think] added by the compiler
4–5 between 'no' and 'The', the compiler skips '; take heede mother, / And let vs all take heede, these most abuse vs'

48. —I know her temper
And in discouering her I haue let loose
A Tigresse whose rage being shut up in darknesse
Was greuious only to her self; which brought
Into the vew of light, her cruelty
Prouokt by her owne shame will turne on him
That foolishly presumd to let her see,
The lothd shape of her owne deformity.
I would I had not told of this her leudnesse.

Sig. [B4^v], II.i.38–46:
2 in] feare (if such a word become a king,) / That
9 I would I had not told of this her leudnesse.] added by the compiler

49. O let her meet my blow doate on her death
And as a wanton vine bowes to the pruner
That by his cutting of more may encrease
So let her fall to raise me fruite
If I the King of heires I must kill her
I meet first comming out of the temple so the
wiser man sayes –

Sigs. [G3^v]–[G4], IV.i.58–61:
4 skips 'haile woman, / The happiest, and the best (if thy dull wil / Do not abuse thy fortune) *France* ere found yet.' after 'fruite'
5–7 If I the King of heires I must kill her
I meet first comming out of the temple so the
wiser man sayes—] added by the compiler

[col.] 705

50. Forget not mother what are children
Nor how you haue gron'd for the*m*, to what loue
They are borne inheritours, with w^{t} care kept
And as they rise to ripenesse, still remember
How they imp out y^{r} age, and when time calls y^{n}
That as an Autumne flower you fall, forget not
How round about y^{r} hearse they hang like penons:

Sig. [K3^{v}], V.ii.105–111:
1 mother] I beseech you

SHAKESPEARE, *ROMEO AND JULIET* (1609), STC 22324

51. Tis almost morning I would haue thee gone
And yet no farther then a wantons bird,
That lets it hop a little from his hand,
Like a poore prisoner, in his twisted gyues,
Then with a silken thread plucks it back againe
So iealous louing of his Liborty. Tragedy of
Romeo and Juliet. 4°: pag: 84:

II.ii.149–154:
2 And] But Q1–2; And Q3   3 That] Who Q1; That Q2–3   3 his] her Q1; his Q2–3
5 Then] And Q1–3   5 plucks] puls Q1; plucks Q2–3   6 So iealous louing] Too louing iealous Q1; So louing Iealous Q2–3

eadem p*er*uenit pro*ĭnde* cadere.

This Mr Richard/^{son} Coll. Magd: inserted hence
into his Sermon, preached it twice at St Maries
1620. 1621. applying it ~~the~~ to gods loue to
his Saints either hurt with sinne, or aduersity
neuer forsaking the*m*.

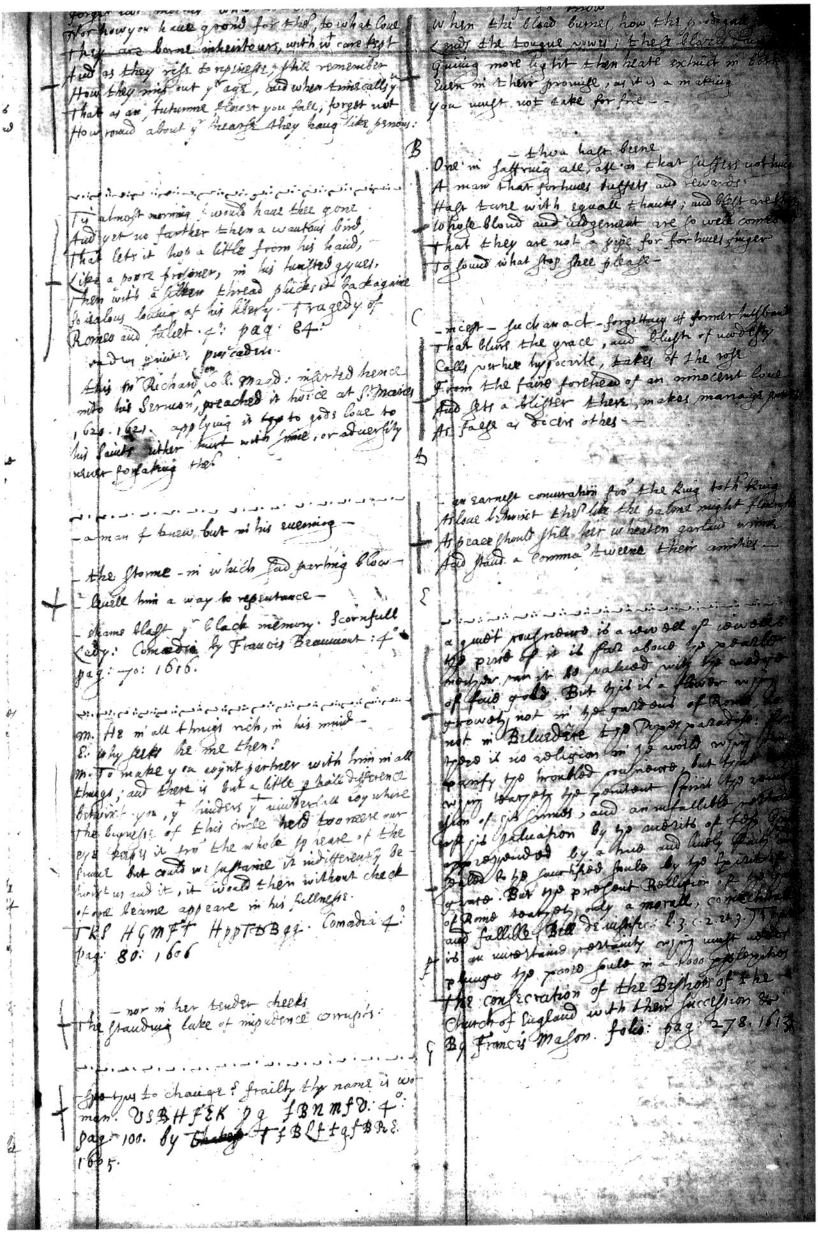

PLATE 3. *Columns 705 and 706 of 'Libor A': Bodleian Library,* MS *Eng. misc. d. 28, p. 359 (Original page size 295 × 190mm.) Reproduced by permission of the Bodleian Library, University of Oxford.*

BEAUMONT AND FLETCHER, *THE SCORNFUL LADIE* (1616), STC 1686

52. —a man I knew but in his evening—
—the storme—in which sad parting blow—
—leuell him a way to repentance—
—shame blast y^{r} black memory. Scornful
Lady: Comædia by Francis Beaumont : 4°
pag: 70: 1616.

1616 edition, Sig. [E4^{v}], III.i.182–3, III.i.184–5:
2—the storme—in] a tyrant storme our beaten barke /
Bulg'd vndervs; in
Sig. [E4], III.i.147, III.i.166–7:
3 to] to his

~.~.~.~.~.~.~.~.~.~.~.~.~.~.~.~.~.~.~.

GEORGE CHAPMAN, *SIR GYLES GOOSECAPPE* (1606), STC 12050

53. M. He in all things rich, in his mind—
E: Why seeks he me then?
M: To make you ioynt partner with him in all
things; and there is but a little p*ar*tiall difference
betwixt you, y^{t} hinders y^{t} universall ioy where
The bignesse of this circle held too neere our
eye keepes it fro' the whole spheare of the
sunne but could we sustaine it indifferently be—
twixt us and it, it would then without check
of one beame appeare in his fullnesse.
TKS HGMFT HppTDBqq. Comædia 4°: [SIR GILES GooSECpp]
pag: 80: 1606

1606 edition, Sig. [D1^{v}], II.i. 190–4, 200–7:
1 M. He in all things rich, in his mind –] he is a gentleman / he is noble; as he is welthilie furnished with true know- / ledge, he is rich and therein adorn'd with the exa- / ctest complements belonging to euerlastinge noblenesse
5 ioy where] ioynture: The

54. —nor in her tender cheeks
The standing lake of impudence corrupts:

Sig. [H4],V.i. 157–8:
1 her] his

SHAKESPEARE, *HAMLET* (1605), STC 22276A

55. shee thus to change? frailty thy name is wo—
man. USBHFEK pg JBNMfU: 4°: [TRAGEDI of HAMLeT
by SHAKespeAQD]
pag 100. by ~~Thakes~~ TIBLftqfBRE.
1605:

1605 edition, Sig. [C1^{v}], I.ii.146:
1 shee thus to change] added by the compiler
[col.] 706

56. I doe knowe
When the blood burnes, how the prodigall soule
Lends the tongue vowes; these blazes daughter
Giuing more light then heate extinct in both
Euen in their promise, as it is a making
You must not take for fire—

Sig. [C4^{v}], I.iii.115–20

57. —thou hast been
One in saffring all, all as that suffers nothing
A man that fortunes buffets and rewards
Hast tane with equall thanks; and blest are those
Whose bloud and iudgement are so well comedled,
That they are not a pipe for fortunes finger
To sound what stop she please –

Sig. [G4^{v}] , III.ii.70–76:
2 as that] that

58. —incest—such an act—forgetting of former husband
That blurs the grace, and blush of modesty,
Calls vertue hippocrite, takes of the rose
From the faire forehead of an innocent loue
And sets a blister there, makes marriage vowes
As false as dicers oathes—

Sig. [I2^{v}], III.iv.40–45

59. —an earnest coniuration fro' the King toth' King,
As loue betwixt them like the palme might flourish,
As peace should still her wheaten garland winne
And stand a Comma' tweene their amities—

Sig. [N.v], V.ii.38–42:
1 'As England was his faithfull tributary,' skipped by the compiler
3 winne] weare

~.~.~.~.~.~.~.~.~.~.~.~.~.~.~.~.~.~.

THOMAS DEKKER, *IF IT BE NOT GOOD* (1612), STC 6507

[col.] 738

60. Lawier—that wretch for's coate dos sue
But his coat's gone, and his skin flead of too
If his purse be orematchd KG. KU. Cf. opu.
hppe. uif. EKWfM. KT. KO. KU. by Thomas
Dekkar. p. 60. 4°: 1612. [IF. IT. BE. not. good. the. DIVEL.
IS. IN. IT.]

1612 edition, Sig. [H1], III.iii.85–87

judiciis iniquitas [in pencil]

~.~.~.~.~.~.~.~.~.~.~.~.~.~.~.~.

SHAKESPEARE, *OTHELLO* (1622), STC 22305

61. I will with jealousy blind him—So will I
turne her vertue into pitch And out of her
owne goodnesse make the net That shall
enmesh them all. URBHfEX:pg:PUff
mmp:&t by w. shakespeare. pag: 100. 4°. 1622.
=eta typia [in pencil] [TQAGedy:of:OTeello]

1622 edition, Sig. [F3v], II.iii.324–326:
1 I will with jealousy blind him] not in Q22

—did he liue now 62.
This sight would make him do a desperate turne,
Yea curse his better Angell fro' his side
And fall to reprobation.
desperatio ab afflictionis [in pencil]
Sig. [M4], V.ii.220–222

~.~.~.~.~.~.~.~.~.~.~.~.~.~.~.~.~.~.

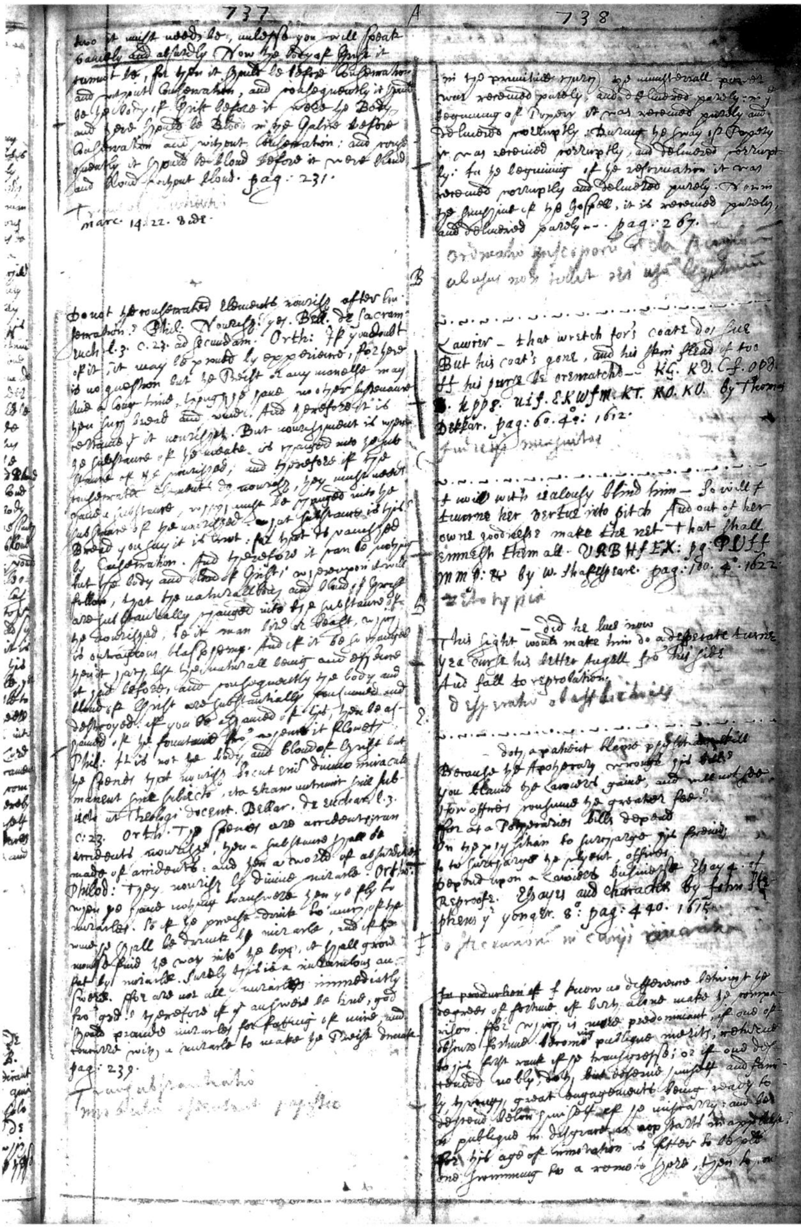

PLATE 4. *Columns 737 and 738 of 'Libor A': Bodleian Library,* MS *Eng. misc. d. 28, p. 375 (Original page size 295 × 190mm.) Reproduced by permission of the Bodleian Library, University of Oxford.*

A COMMENT ON THE COMPILATION OF THE DRAMATIC EXTRACTS

A comparison with variants in extant quartos of the plays suggests the compiler used the third quarto (1598) of *Richard II* (1–3) and that the third quarto of *Romeo and Juliet* (1609) is his ultimate source when he quotes an extract from the play 'inserted' into a sermon (51). He makes typical scribal mistakes such as inversions, and all but very few variants are substantive. The beginning and the end of a given passage may be adapted and lines skipped as in extract 60. Words are sometimes added to the original printed text, as for example when the compiler defines 'Such an act' as 'incest' in extract 58. Extracts are quoted out of context and '[made to] stand, as it were, on [their] own feet',[46] a typical feature of commonplacing. On one occasion only (58), the writer retains the names of characters 'Laffin' and 'Byr', for what reason it is impossible to establish with any certainty.

How significant is his choice of extracts? All in all, the earliest reception of Renaissance plays is difficult to assess. Contemporary drama tends to be under-represented in inventories, either because it was considered frivolous or simply because much of it was in small, cheap formats.[47] Everyone is familiar with the marking of plays,[48] but, oddly enough, since marking often precedes copying, few commonplace books containing dramatic extracts survive, the richest being those cited earlier. Relatively few extracts from, or allusions to, Shakespeare's plays survive in manuscripts dated before 1650.[49]

The compiler's choice of plays, *Hamlet*, *Romeo and Juliet*, *Othello*, *Richard II* is in accordance with the revealing 'List of Shakspere's Works. Arranged According to the Number of Allusions to Each' before 1649 in *The Shakespere-Allusion Book*,[50] in which *Hamlet* comes first, *Romeo and Juliet* third, *Othello* eighth and *Richard II* ninth, not entirely the verdict of the printed editions. Although contemporary allusions to Shakespeare's plays have been noticed since,[51] and the ranking according to the frequency of allusions may have changed, it is clearly plays which were among the most popular ones at the time that figure in MS Eng. misc. d. 28. Perhaps Shakespeare's comedies were not serious enough to be excerpted in a manuscript full of sermons and classics. Still, other comedies by Chapman, Jonson, Beaumont and Dekker are quoted. All the passages taken from Shakespeare were commented upon by the reader of the Meisei Shakespeare folio around 1630.[52] *Richard II* was John Bodenham's favourite play: it is quoted forty-seven times in his *Belvedere*.[53]

There is far more Chapman than any other playwright in MS Eng. misc. d. 28, probably because he discusses serious matters, such as tyranny and the arbitrary power of courtiers. Even though *Bussy D'Ambois* and its sequel were popular plays in their time, very few extracts survive in manuscript.[54] *Thierry and Theodoret* was published anonymously and is now ascribed to Fletcher in collaboration with Massinger and Beaumont.[55] Since the extract copied from it comes at the end of a series of plays by Chapman, it is conceivable the play was ascribed to him. The placing of this quotation is not conclusive evidence, however, and should not encourage us to add *Thierry and Theodoret* to Chapman's canon. What it does imply, at the very least, is that the compiler thought the play sounded like Chapman's or shared the same concerns.

Many university verse miscellanies in manuscript from the 1620s and 1630s contain pieces by Jonson, but extracts from his plays occur in very few.[56] The compiler may have seen *Volpone* when it was acted at Oxford, perhaps in 1606. According to Jonson's epistle, *Volpone* was successful at Cambridge and Oxford. Only one other manuscript contains excerpts from *The Scornful Lady*. It is Abraham Wright's (1611–90), an Anglican divine's miscellany which also contains some *Hamlet*.[57]

Certain plays were not to be excerpted: 'The tragedy of King John & Richard the 3d: Tamburlaine, vertumnus,[58] ye 4 Prentises haue nought worthy the excerping' (above 24). The list is a heterogeneous one which comprises two history plays, a tragedy, a Latin comedy and a city comedy. 'The tragedy of King John', presumably *The Troublesome Reign* (1591,1611, 1621), is best known as Shakespeare's source for his *King John*. It is now thought to be quite a subtle play and it is not easy to know why the compiler discards it. *The Tragedy of King John*, printed 1591, *Richard III*, written and performed *c.*1591, *Tamburlaine*, written *c.*1587, *The Four Prentices of London c.*1600, may have sounded old-fashioned by the time the compiler chose his extracts. Thus, the contents of the list would be partly determined by a shift in taste. The prologue to Part I of *The Troublesome Reign* alludes to the success of *Tamburlaine*, 'You that . . . / Have entertained the Scythian Tamburlaine, / And given applause unto an Infidel',[59] which may account for the presence of both plays in the black list. Robert Greene attacks Marlowe 'daring God out of heauen with that Atheist *Tamburlan*'.[60] A theologian would have agreed with him. Moreover, the compiler might have been suspicious of *Tamburlaine* because of a theatrical style associated with Marlowe's play, notably by Ben Jonson who rebukes 'the *scenicall* strutting, and furious vociferation'.[61] *Richard III* was probably not included for the same reason. An educated man might well have despised Thomas Heywood's popular play *The Four Prentices of London,* which was ridiculed in Beaumont's *Knight of the Burning Pestle* (1607). The lines taken from Jonson's epistle to *Volpone* prove that he did not condemn drama as such, but only the most popular sort, the 'miscline [maslin] Enterludes' which were blasphemous (20). One gets the impression that all the plays that occur in the commonplace book belong to the highest and purest type of drama in the canon. Chapman, Shakespeare, Jonson, Beaumont, Dekker and Fletcher are treated as classics. It seems that the compiler could quote from *Volpone*, but only from Jonson's 1616 folio, 'the ffoxe I haue referd to Ben Johnsons works', above (24), which presented the dramatist as a classic. Matthew Gwinne's Latin comedy, *Vertumnus*, was performed at Christ Church before the King who fell asleep, during his progress at Oxford on 29 August 1605.[62] Apparently, the play was thought to be too dull to be quoted from.

Three features are particularly noteworthy in the handling of the dramatic extracts—the unusual coded forms of the names of the plays and their authors, the numbering of the pages in the quartos, and the mottoes which precede some of the extracts.

The cipher is the simplest to devise. It is a variant of the so-called rotate-one Cæsar cipher, named after Julius Cæsar who used it in his correspondance.[63] In the compiler's cipher B becomes A, C becomes B, and so on up to Z which becomes Y. Aulus Gellius (*Attic Nights* 17.9.1–5) and Suetonius (*Life of Julius Cæsar* 56), whose works feature respectively in MS Eng. misc. d. 28 (pp. 220–44) and in MS Lat. misc. b. 6 (pp. 55–69, 172), give details on Cæsar's cipher. Although cryptology was increasingly popular in the sixteenth and seventeenth century,[64] MS Eng. misc. d. 28 seems to be a unique instance of a university commonplace book displaying a cipher for authors and titles of plays only. Ironically enough, the word 'Cypher' occurs in Chapman's extract 7 and writing in cipher illustrates the compiler's interest in 'Hieroglyphick[s]' (38). The cipher is so easy to break that it was probably meant to ward off someone peeping over his shoulder for the briefest instant. If someone walked into his room and had a glimpse of the manuscript lying on a desk, he would not be able to read the sources of the extracts, whereas the compiler himself could decipher them almost immediately. The use of a code for titles and authors suggests only that coding the extracts might attract unnecessary attention to them, but that a careless reader would not readily identify them. Perhaps, the quotations were not sufficiently well-known to be instantly ascribed to the true authors. The compiler generally chose to keep his sources to himself, but was not entirely consistent.

As noted by Chambers, the pagination of the extract from *Romeo and Juliet*, as in other extracts from Shakespeare in the manuscript, does not belong to any early quarto. Greg suggested to Chambers 'that the compiler probably had before him a bound collection of quartos, paginated by hand',[65] but his solution does not seem to work. Although the absence of a pagination in most extant editions of the plays makes it almost impossible to check the pagination given in MS Eng. misc. d. 28 and counting the number of pages is further complicated by dedicatory epistles, indexes and other ancillary material, even the fattest quarto collection of plays could not have been numbered to produce the relevant figures, which I set out below:

column	play	page given by the compiler	quarto signature	use of a cipher
697	*Richard II*	68	?	yes
698	*Bussy D'Ambois*	70	A2r-v	yes
700	*Volpone*	6	?	no
700	*All Fools*	70	A1v	yes
701	*Byron's Conspiracy*	90	C2r	no
703	*Byron's Tragedy*	100	I4r	no
704	*Thierry and Theodoret*	80	B1v	no
705	*Romeo and Juliet*	84	?	no
705	*The Scornful Lady*	70	E4v	no
705	*Sir Giles Goosecap*	80	D1v	yes
705	*Hamlet*	100	C1v	yes
738	*If It Be Not Good*	60	H1r	yes
738	*Othello*	100	F3v	yes

If you take out the Jonson (where p. 6 is correct for the quarto) and change the first Bussy from '70' to '70', then the range of figures is 60–100. This seems to indicate that the compiler is in fact taking his extracts not from the plays themselves but from somebody else's manuscript collection of extracts.[66]

The mottoes scribbled between the extracts in black ink or in pencil belong to two distinct types: personal glosses and allusions to classical or scriptural sources. Quite a few seem to be personal glosses which may be partly based on sources but more often than not elude identification.

The compiler glosses 'The bounds of loyalty are made of glasse. / Soone broke but can in no date be repaird' (*Byron's Conspiracy*, I.ii.145–6) with 'therfore will men make good former breach with new plots' (below 25). Below (31) from the same play, he notes that treason is not always that bad, 'proditio non semp*er* tame[n]'. The personal note which reads 'imitatio Dei in miraculis ad sit' placed below (7) takes up Chapman's comparison between the King and God, which is common in metaphysical verse. When Herbert writes 'Think the king sees thee still; for his King does'[67] ('The Church-Porch', l. 122), he alludes to the all-seeing eyes of both God and King, a line whose moral sense is comparable with the compiler's 'po[t]estate quatenus dissimulare licet / uitam inuiū illicitu' below (45). Similarly, when he adds 'dei amor non nisi in altera vita p*er*fectus' before (14), the 'princes loue' becomes divine love. Apart from the traditional image of God as King, the equation was probably further enhanced by the belief in the divine right of kings, central to James's reign. The Anglican divine Abraham Wright (1611–90), who 'was using plays [. . .] as rhetorical primers for his own sermons',[68] and the reader who copied the annotations in the Meisei copy of the Shakespeare folio were both fascinated by Othello's jealousy and Iago's villainy.[69] So was our compiler who was stirred by Desdemona's pathetic death, as shown by his note, 'desperatio ab afflictionis' below (62). The cryptic comment in pencil beneath Iago's lines (61) seems to read '=eta typia', which might be understood as the 'seventh type' or 'phase' of jealousy, presumably in a medical classification. Chapman is cited as another authority on jealousy (23), when he compares the effect of jealousy on love with that of smoke on fire.

Extract 1 occurs in *England's Parnassus* (1600),[70] and the compiler may have remembered it from the anthology. Another early modern annotator, that of the Meisei Shakespeare folio, wrote 'The words of dieing men of weght to persuade' in the margin.[71] The extract is comparable to Chapman's 'a good man dying utters oracles', an idea taken up in his *Gentleman Usher*, IV.iii.61, which may be traced back to Plato's *Apology*, XXX, and which is most likely a translation of a passage from Erasmus's *Encomium Moriæ*, *sub fine*, 'Idem arbitror esse in causa cur laborantibus vicina morte, simile quiddam soleat accidere ut tamquam afflati prodigiosa quædam loquantur'.[72] The compiler may have had Erasmus in mind when he wrote the gloss 'morientis hominis loquela verissima' in black ink beneath (1). It seems he felt he had the right to copy the lines from *Richard II* because they echoed Erasmus's Latin. Furthermore, the close proximity of the extracts from Shakespeare and Chapman in the commonplace book owes something to their relying on Plutarch, via Erasmus.[73]

The compiler's favourite scriptural verse is Math 10: 16: 'ecce ego mitto vos sicut oves in medio luporum estote ergo prudentes sicut serpentes et simplices sicut columbæ' in the Vulgate, 'bee yee therefore wise as serpents, and innocent as doues' in the Geneva 1592 version. The marginal note in the Geneva version reads 'Christ shiweth how the ministers must behaue themselues vnder the crosse', which a student in divinity could meditate upon. The verse is alluded to at least three times, and cross-references to the occurrences in the manuscript are given [cols.] 625, 674 and below (18). It is commented upon by St Augustine *Sermo* 44. 1–2 and by Bacon in a meditation, 'There are neither teeth, nor stings, nor venom, nor wreaths and folds of serpents which ought not to be all known, and as far as examination does lead, tried.'[74] After Tyndale in *The Obedience of a Christian Man*,[75] the compiler draws a link between the wisdom of serpents and betrayal, one of his chief interests, illustrated by Chapman for example (31). The motto below (60), 'judiciis iniquitas', is comparable to Daniel 13:5: 'egressa est iniquitas de Babylone a senibus iudicibus' in the Vulgate, 'iniquity came out from Babylon, from the ancient judges' in the Douai-Rheims version, Challoner revision. The rule 'godlinesse is y^{r} true guide', below (6), may be based on 1 Timothy 4:8 'godlinesse is profitable unto all things'; 1 Timothy 6:6 'godlines is great gain', or 1 Timothy 6:11 'follow after righteousnes, godlines' in the Geneva 1592 version. The scriptural allusions tend to prove that the dramatic extracts were read in the light of the Bible, a habit alien to the modern reader.

Why did the scribe copy the extracts? The note on Mr Richardson's insertion of the *Romeo and Juliet* extract (II.i.221–6) in a sermon shows that the compiler had in mind similar exegetical readings. Incidentally, the application is not too dissimilar from Herbert's 'silk twist let down from heav'n'[76] in 'The Pearl. Matth. 13. 45' (l.38). However, the compiler was also interested in Juliet's tragic death at the end of the play for he remarked 'eadem p*er*uenit pro*inde* cadere', below (51). Richardson's sermon may have been heard first hand at St Mary's, the University Church, which is so close to Oriel College.[77] Usually it is patristic literature and classics that occur in sermons, not vernacular literature, which was not considered serious enough to be printed as marginal references or in indexes of authors.[78] The marginalia of sermons are composed almost exclusively of scripture. The presence of some Shakespeare in a sermon seems, at first sight, to be an intriguing exception, but Bishop King's sermons contain echoes of *Hamlet*, *Lear*, *Macbeth*, *Volpone* and *The Alchemist*. Like our anthologist, King knew Overbury and Montaigne's *Essais*.[79] Thomas Adams quoted *The White Devil* (III.ii.204–6) in his *Diseases of the Soul* (licensed 29 November 1614) 'for his description of a man consumed by lust'[80] and borrowed lines from *The Duchess of Malfi* (V.ii.337–338) in his *Meditations Upon the Creed* (1629).[81] Prynne has a significant passage on the frequency of borrowings from 'poeticall Play-house phrases, Clinches, and strong lines' in sermons:

> consisting either of wanton flashes of luxurious wits,or meere quotations of humane Authors,Poets, Orators, Histories, Philosophers, and Popish Schoole-men; or *sesquipedalia verba*, great empty swelling words of vanity and estimation more fitter for the Stage, from whence they are ofttimes borrowed, (then the Pulpet,) unsutable for Ministers . . .[82]

The passage is related to the heated correspondance on the subject of drama between the Italian jurist Alberico Gentili and John Rainolds—author of *Th' ouerthrow of stage-playes* (1599) and president of Corpus Christi College—which discusses the dramatic aspects of oratory, as set out by Theophrastus, Quintilian, Macrobius, Tertullian, Tacitus and other authorities.[83] This may be the rantings of antitheatrical prejudice, but the anger derives from quite a number of real sermons which must have been heard at church. Ultimately, it seems that the dramatic extracts in MS Eng. misc. d. 28 were meant to provide material for sermons. In another part of the manuscript, 'advice to preaching' is jotted down in black ink ([col.] 685) between extracts taken from Verstegan's *Restitution of Decayed Intelligence* (1605). The literary passages would feed the compiler's invention and furnish him with numerous topics in the form of comparisons.

CONCLUSION

True, the compiler's handling of playwrights is ambiguous. His use of a cipher, which hardly camouflages names and titles, is not consistent. He appears to hesitate as to whether they are worthy to be excerpted or not. Yet, for all his qualms, the playbooks are seen as classics in the literal sense of the term, since the extracts are often direct translations of classical authorities, in their original versions, or, as in Chapman's case, glossed by Erasmus in one of his handy collections of similes and *sententiæ*.

One of the most interesting features of the codex is the allusion to Nicholas Richardson's sermon quoting *Romeo and Juliet*. Although Richardson's practice seems to be unique, his case shows how inadequate modern classifications of genres may be. Sermons may owe more to drama than was previously thought. The dramatic dimension of the spiritual wrestling staged by metaphysical poets, notably George Herbert, has long been noticed, but that a preacher resorted to the language of what was often thought to be frivolous entertainment throws new light on the complex interplay between two competing genres.

NOTES

This article is dedicated to my son, Arthur, who is already very much interested in book spines. I am grateful to Steven May for encouragement and comments, to Peter Beal and *EMS* readers for reading unwieldy drafts and for invaluable corrections. I wish to thank Rob Petre, the archivist at Oriel College, Oxford, for his help and patience in answering numerous requests, and Corinne Blanchaud for trying to make sense of my Latin transcriptions.

1 Madan, F., H. E. Craster, N. Denholm-Young et al. (eds.), *Summary Catalogue of Western Manuscripts in the Bodleian Library, Oxford*, 7 vols. (Oxford, 1895–1953), VI, 163 (32547). 'Tragicall discourses' occurs in MS Eng. misc. d. 28, column 1193.

2 I am grateful to Elizabeth Boardman, the archivist of Brasenose College and former archivist of Oriel College, for information on both colleges in the period and for showing me samples of Radcliffe's hand and various documents related to him—MSS Edmonton 11, Harowden 33, Principal 4. Given the circumstances of Radcliffe's death—no laywer attended the drafting of his will—it is extremely unlikely that he passed on his personal books to his successor.

3 C. M. Ingleby, *The Shakespere Allusion-Book*, 2 vols. (Oxford, 1932), I, 279. First noted in *The Periodical*, N° XVI (1 Dec 1901), 14, 'in a MS. commonplace book of the time of Charles I in the Bodleian Library we find the anecdote, with reference to the passage in *Romeo and Juliet*, A ii, scene 2'.

4 E. K. Chambers, *William Shakespeare, A Study of Facts and Problems*, 2 vols. (Oxford, 1988), II, 227.

5 See J. M. Gowan, ed., *An Edition of Edward Pudsey's Commonplace Book* (c. *1600–1615*) *from the Manuscript in the Bodleian Library* (unpub. M. Phil., University of London, 1967).

6 See G. Sorelius, 'An Unknown Shakespearian Commonplace Book', *Library*, 5th ser. 28 (1973), 294–308, and Beal, *IELM*, I/i, 149–50.

7 H. R. Woudhuysen, *Sir Philip Sidney and the Circulation of Manuscripts, 1558–1640* (Oxford, 1996), 147–8. The scribe may well have used STC 6787.7 or 6788 as an exemplar, even though he writes 'manuscriptum' ([col.] 605) since the word is followed by '1596' or '1598', which pre-date the earliest known edition.

8 See K. Duncan-Jones, 'Much Ado with Red and White: The Earliest Readers of Shakespeare's *Venus and Adonis*', *Review of English Studies*, 44 (1993), 479–501; S. Roberts, 'Reading Shakespeare's Tragedies of Love: *Romeo and Juliet, Othello*, and *Antony and Cleopatra* in Early Modern England', 108–33, in J. Howard and R. Dutton, ed., *The Blackwell Companion to Shakespeare's Tragedies* (Oxford, 2003); and J. Siemon, '"The power of hope?" An Early Modern Reader of *Richard III*', 361–78, in J. Howard and R. Dutton, ed., *The Blackwell Companion to Shakespeare's Histories* (Oxford, 2003). For information on marginalia in Shakespeare's First Folio and quartos, I am indebted to Heidi Brayman Hackel, Jill Whitelock, John Jowett, Jill Cogen, Stephen Tabor, Liz Osman, Georgianna Ziegler, Noriko Sumimoto and Julie Gardham.

9 I owe this reading to Mordechai Feingold.

10 C. L. Shadwell, *Registrum Orielense: An Account of the Members of Oriel College, Oxford*, 2 vols. (London, 1893), I.

11 A. Clark, ed., *Register of the University of Oxford. vol 2: 1571–1622. Pt I: Introductions* (Oxford Historical Society, vol. 10; Oxford, 1887), 307 *bis*, 308, 309, 310, 311, 312, 313.

12 One of the 'Assistentes' (ibid, 309).

13 *Brasenose College Register: 1509–1909* (Oxford Historical Society, vol. 55, 1909), 56.

14 Rev. G. C. Richards and Rev. H. E. Salter, ed., *The Dean's Register of Oriel, 1446–1661*

(Oxford Historical Society, vol. 84, 1926), 309 (21 February 1645/6), hereafter *DRO*.

15 *DRO*, 309 (21 February 1645/6).

16 I am indebted to Rob Petre who kindly supplied two examples of Saunders' hand from the Dean's Register (ref GOV 4 A1).

17 "admissio' and 'admissus' are used most frequently of the B.A. degree, and the Bachelors of Law, Medicine, and Theology' (Clark Vol II, Part I, 48).

18 'admissus est' is used for Thomas Wyatt's licence for M.A. in 1602/3 (*DRO*, 218).

19 I am grateful to Mordechai Feingold for a discussion on 'admissus' and information on the university curriculum in the seventeenth century.

20 'In Comitiis, MA Quæstiones Philosophicæ' (Clark II/I, 178).

21 For their pedigree see R. Colt Hoare, *The Modern History of South Wiltshire*, 6 vols. (London, 1822–44), II, 37.

22 Charles and Robert's grandfather, William Tooker was a fellow of New College, Oxford in 1577, Dean of Lichfield in 1602, and chaplain to Queen Elizabeth (A. Wood, *Athenæ Oxoniensis*, 2 vols. (London, 1692), II, 288; W. H. Jones, *Fasti Ecclesiæ Sarisberiensis*, 2 vols. (London, 1879–81), II, 403). Their father was Charles Tooker of Wiltshire, of plebeian stock. He took his B.A. at Gloucester Hall on 28 November 1586 and went on to Lincoln's Inn (J. Foster, *Alumni Oxonienses, 1500–1714*, 2 vols. (Oxford, 1891), II). Their uncle was Giles Tooker, educated at Balliol College, admitted to Lincoln's Inn on 18 June 1581. It was while Giles held the office of Master of the Library, in 1622, that Dr. Donne made his present of 'six volumes of the Bible, with the comment of Lyra, etc., and the Glosses, etc.' to the Society on resigning the preachership (M. S. and C. Thorpe, illust. by M. S. Thorpe, *Biographical Sketches of Lincoln's Inn Men* (London, s.d.), 63. See too G. Keynes, *A Bibliography of Dr. John Donne* (Oxford, 1973), 261–2. I am grateful to Guy Holborn, the librarian of Lincoln's Inn, for sending information on the Tookers).

23 Robert Tooker was the son of a gentleman from Berkshire. He entered Balliol on 6 July 1613 aged 15 (*OCR*).

24 'ds Tooker' of plebeian stock, was admitted Commoner in 1617–8. He matriculated at Exeter College, on 5 May 1615, aged 22 (*Registrum Orielense*, I).

25 John Tooker was from London and of plebeian stock, he matriculated at St John's College on 18 June 1619, aged 19 (ibid).

26 John Horne was the son of a gentleman from Hertshire. He entered Oriel College on 27 October 1615, aged 16 (*OCR*).

27 Eleven commoners were admitted 1617–8, viz.: Branker, ds Tooker, Higford, Duncombe, Purrefye, Broune, ds Hunt, ds Twitty, Peate, Heron, Burleigh (*Registrum Orielense*, I). Seventeen Commoners were admitted, 1618–9, viz: Hubbocke, Rutter, Allen, Bloacksome, Taylor, Wauker, Harrise, Morgans, Swaine, Ridutt, Freeman, Lloyd, Plimpton, Jones, Topping, Racster, sen. Racster (ibid).

28 John Cowling took his B.A. at Exeter College on 26 May 1615 (*OCR*).

29 Hugh Yale took his B.A. at BNC on 21 June 1615 (*OCR*).

30 See his note in black ink ([col.] 634) 'so do the papists in their cloisters'.

31 Chetham's Library, Manchester MS Mun. A. 4. 150: see *The Dr. Farmer Chetham MS*, ed. A. B. Grosart, Chetham Society Publications, vol. 89 (Manchester, 1873).

32 On the issue see H. L. Parish, *Precedent, Policy, and Practice: Clerical Marriage and the English Reformation* (Aldershot, 2000).

33 George Herbert, *Works*, ed. F. E. Hutchinson (Oxford, 1941), 236–7.

34 R. Burton, *The Anatomy of Melancholy*, eds. T. C. Faulkner, N. K. Kiessling, R. L. Blair, comment J. B. Bamborough, M. Dodsworth, 3 vols. (Oxford, 1989–2000), III, Part. 3. Sect. 4. Memb. 1 Subst., 335, ll. 3–5.

35 *Visitations of Berkshire*, I, 135.
36 Ibid I, 1.
37 *OED*.
38 The character was a by-word for foolish readers as in John Marriot's lines prefixed to George Wither's *Faire-virtue* (1622), 'I entreated him [Wither] to explain his meaning in certain obscure passages; but he told me how that were to take away the employment of his interpreters. Whereas, he would purposely leave somewhat remaining doubtful, to see what Sir Politic Would-be and his companions could pick out of it' (J. F. Bradley, ed., *The Jonson Allusion-Book, A Collection of Allusions to Ben Jonson from 1597 to 1700* (New Haven, 1922), 126–7).
39 John Stubbs, *The discouerie of the gaping gulf* (1579), STC 23400.
40 Lope Felix de Vega Carpio, *The pilgrime of Casteele* (1623), STC 24630.
41 Paolo Sarpi, *The history of the quarrels of Pope Paul V. with the state of Venice* (1626), STC 21766.
42 See the frontispiece of the comedy *Pedantius*, 1631, reproduced in Sir Walter Raleigh, *Shakespeare's England: An Account of the Life & Manners of his Age* (Oxford, 1916), I, 227.
43 Heawood 3499 (blank paper, 1617).
44 See the often reproduced print from A. Ramelli, *La Diverse et Artificiose Machine* (1588), pl. 188.
45 Line-references are to *King Richard II*, ed. A. Gurr (The New Cambridge Shakespeare, Cambridge, 2003); Chapman, *Plays, The Tragedies with 'Sir Gyles Goosecape'*, gen. ed. A. Holaday (Cambridge, 1987); Chapman, *Plays, The Comedies, Critical Edition*, gen. ed. A. Holaday (Urbana, 1970); *The Dramatic Works in the Beaumont and Fletcher Canon*, gen. ed. F. Bowers, 10 vols (Cambridge, 1966–96), II and III; *The First Quarto of Shakespeare's Romeo and Juliet*, ed. F. G. Hubbard, University of Wisconsin Studies in Language and Literature, No. 19 (Maddison, 1924); *Hamlet: Second Quarto 1604–5*, ed. W. W. Greg (Oxford, 1964); Dekker, *Dramatic Works*, ed. F. Bowers, 4 vols (Cambridge, 1953–61), III; and *The First Quarto of Othello*, ed. S. McMillin (Cambridge, 2001).
46 Hilton Kelliher, 'Contemporary Manuscript Extracts from Shakespeare's *Henry IV, Part I*', *English Manuscript Studies*, 1 (1989), 144–81 (p.161).
47 There are some interesting exceptions. The library of Scipio le Squyer (d.1659) contained plays by Jonson, Middleton and, apparently, *Romeo and Juliet* (F. Taylor, 'The Books and Manuscripts of S. Le Squyer, Deputy Chamberlain of the Exchequer, 1620–59', *Bulletin of the John Rylands Library*, 25 (1941), 137–64). The library of Sir Edward Dering (d.1644) had Beaumont and Fletcher (three copies of the *Woman Hater*), Jonson, Band, Cuffe and Ruffe (six copies), George Ruggle and Shakespeare and exasperating items like '27 playbookes' and 'ten playbookes' totalling approximately an extraordinary 217 (R. J. Fehrenbach and E. S. Leedham-Green, *Private Libraries in Renaissance England* (Marlborough, 1992), vol I., PLRE 4, 137–269). That of Sir Roger Townshend (*c.*1625) in the same volume (PLRE 3, 79–135) has Chapman, John Cooke, John Day, Jonson and Seneca in English. I owe this note to Elisabeth Leedham-Green.
48 See H. B. Hackel, 'The "Great Variety" of Readers and Early Modern Reading Practices', 150–2, in D. S. Kastan, ed., *A Companion to Shakespeare* (Oxford, 1999).
49 See British Library Add MS 64078 edited and discussed by Kelliher 'Contemporary Manuscript Extracts', 144–81. See too ShW 44, ShW 74 and ShW 79 in Beal's *IELM*. A few other MSS are known.
50 Ingleby, *Shakespere Allusion-Book* II, 540.
51 Recently discovered allusions to Shakespeare's plays include D. Farley-Hills,

'Another Jonson Allusion to Shakespeare?', *Notes and Queries*, 245 (2000), 473–75 and R. F. Kennedy, 'Some New Shakespeare Allusions', *Notes and Queries*, 245 (2000), 464–67.

52 A. Yamada, ed., *The First Folio of Shakespeare: A Transcript of Contemporary Marginalia in a Copy of the Kodama Memorial Library of Meisei University* (Tokyo, 1998). The edition uses C. Hinman's through-line-numbers, (TLN), first adopted in the Norton facsimile edition of *The First Folio of Shakespeare* (New York, 1968).

53 Ingleby, *Shakespere Allusion-Book* I, 73.

54 According to Peter Beal (*IELM* I/1, 192) extracts from *The Conspiracy and Tragedy of Charles Duke of Byron, Bussy D'Ambois,* and *Eastward Ho* occur in John Evans's miscellany *Hesperides, or the Muses' Garden* (*c.*1655). Extracts from *All Fools*, transcribed from the edition of 1605, occur in a miscellany compiled by William Drummond of Hawthornden; *c.*1606–14. National Library of Scotland, MS 2059 (Hawthornden vol VII), fols. 209r-v (Beal ChG 7). An extract, headed 'Irus', from *The Blind Beggar of Alexandria*, occurs in a miscellany compiled by Edward Pudsey (1573–1613); 1600s. Bodleian, MS Eng. poet. d. 3, fol. 41 (Beal ChG 8). Extracts from *Cæsar and Pompey* occur in a miscellany perhaps partly by one William How; mid-seventeenth century. Folger, MS V. a. 87, fol. 24. All the other manuscripts recorded in Beal's *Index* are exempla of early editions with manuscript corrections (Beal ChG 9).

55 See C. Hoy, 'Francis Beaumont and John Fletcher', 15, in F. Bowers, ed., *Jacobean and Caroline Dramatists* (Dictionary of Literary Biography, vol 58, Detroit, 1987).

56 Bodleian, MS Rawl. poet. 142, f. 19v., 'a verse miscellany probably compiled by an Oxford man and once owned by one William Bloys'; *c.*1630s (Beal JnB 737) is the only other manuscript with an extract from *Volpone*, apart from *Hesperides* (Beal 235), and the songs 'Come my Celia, let vs proue' III.vii.166–83 (Beal JnB 443–50), and 'That the curious may not know' III.vii.236–9 (Beal JnB 542–8).

57 Beal B&F 166, British Library Add. MS 22608, fols. 96v–8.

58 Matthew Gwynne, *Vertumnus sive annus recurrens* (1607).

59 Quoted by G. K. Hunter, *The Oxford History of English Literature, English Drama 1586–1642, The Age of Shakespeare* (Oxford, 1997), 218.

60 Robert Greene, 'To the Gentlemen readers' prefixed to *Perimedes the Blacksmith* (1588), Sig. [A^3r], quoted in R. Levin, 'The Contemporary Perception of Marlowe's *Tamburlaine*', *Medieval and Renaissance Drama in England*, 1 (1984), 52.

61 Ben Jonson, *Discoveries*, ed. G. B. Harrison, Bodley Head Quartos (London, 1923), 33 quoted in C. Marlowe, *Tamburlaine the Great*, ed. J. S. Cunningham (Manchester, 1981), 31.

62 G. B. Harrison, *A Jacobean Journal 1603–1606* (London, 1941), p. 228.

63 See his *Gallic Wars*, v. 48, quoted in D. Kahn, *The Codebreakers: The Story of Secret Writing* (New York, 1968), p. 48.

64 See J. S. Galland, *An Historical and Analytical Bibliography of the Literature of Cryptology* (New York, 1970).

65 Chambers, *Shakespeare* II, 227.

66 I am grateful to the reader of this journal for the remarks and chart on pagination.

67 George Herbert, *Works*, ed. F. E. Hutchinson (Oxford, 1941).

68 Kirsch, 260.

69 'A uery good play both for lines and plot, but especially ye plot. Iago for a rogue and Othello for a iealous husband 2 parts well pend. Act: 3 hye scene beetwixt Iago and Othello, and ye I sce: of ye 4 Act beetween ye same shew admirably ye uillanous humour of Iago when hee p[er]suades Othello to his iealousy' (fol. 84v: Kirsch, p. 237); discussed by Roberts, 'Shakespeare's Tragedies of Love', 121–3. See

'Inclination to goodnesse Counsell friendlie in shew tending to destruction in effect damnable deuice to vndoe thrie friends at ones vnder professed friendship' on [TLN 1432–1494], 268, and 'discouerie of Iagoes most damnable and Incredible villanies' on [TLN 3411–3540].

70 54. Recorded in Ingleby, *Shakespere Allusion-Book* II, 470.

71 Yamada, *First Folio*, 107.

72 F. L. Schoell, 'George Chapman's "Commonplace Book"', *Modern Philology* 17 (1919–20), 202.

73 The passage from *Richard II*, proves, once again, how complex an issue imitation is. It is difficult to know which playwright was inspired by the other or whether each of them was, unconsciously or not, translating Erasmus, or one of Erasmus's sources.

74 Francis Bacon, *Major Works*, ed. B. Vickers (Oxford, 1996), 91.

75 'The serpent's wisdom is to keep his head and those parts wherein his life resteth. Christ is our head and God's word is that where our life resteth. So cleave therefore fast unto Christ and unto those promises which God hath made us for his sake is our wisdom. Beware of men (saith he) for they shall deliver you up unto their councils and shall scourge you. And ye shall be brought before rulers and kings for my sake. The brother shall betray or deliver the brother to death and the father the son. And the children shall rise against father and mother, and put them to death' (W. Tyndale, *The Obedience of a Christian Man*, ed. D. Daniell (London, 2000), 8).

76 ed. Hutchinson.

77 According to J. Bloxam and W. D. Macray, *Register of the Members of St. Mary Magdalen College, Oxford* (London, 1894–1915), vol. III, Nicholas Richardson matriculated from Corpus Christi College on 10 June 1608, aged 13, but moved to Magdalen in 1610 when he was elected a Demy, the college term for a Scholar. He came from Kent—or at least had links with that county—because he was elected to a Fellowship at Magdalen which was only open to candidates from there. In 1614, Richardson was elected a Fellow of Magdalen, and resigned his Demyship. He remained a Fellow until 1631. He took his B.A. in 1611 and his M.A. in 1614. He became a Bachelor of Divinity in 1624. In 1630, he became Rector of Slimbridge, a village in Gloucestershire and died in 1644. According to *The Letters of John Chamberlain to Dudley Carleton*, ed. N. E. McClure (Philadelphia, 1939), Vol. II, 487, a sermon was given by 'one Richardson, a young man of Magdalen College, Oxford' at St Paul's Cross on 24 March 1623. The writer said that Richardson preached 'reasonably well, and the better because he was not long, nor immoderate in commendation of the time, but gave Queen Elizabeth her due'. Bloxam also reports that verses of his were published in two collections of poetry, *Luctus Posthumus* of 1612 and *Jacobi Ara* of 1617. Richardson is interesting precisely because he is so very typical of a Fellow of his day: this progression from Demyship to Fellowship to a College living was what most Fellows of the same background aimed for. I am grateful to Robin Darwall-Smith, the archivist of Magdalen College, who kindly sent me the information, which is quoted verbatim.

78 See Raleigh's *History of the World* (1614) listed as a source in Daniel Featley's *Clavis Mystica* (London, 1636), Sig. [A3^v].

79 Mary Hobbs, ed., *The Sermons of Henry King (1592–1669), Bishop of Chichester* (Aldershot, 1992), 53. I am indebted to Peter McCullough who kindly informed me that, apart from Marlowe's *Faustus*, no allusion to English vernacular literature occurs in Donne's sermons. Compare 'And as those Angels, which came from Heaven hither, bring Heaven with them, and are in Heaven here' (Potter and Simpson, VII, 71) and Mephistopheles, 'Hell hath no limits, nor is circumscrib'd / In one selfe place / And

where hell is, must we ever be' (ed. R. Gill [scene 5] 124–6). Peter McCullough added that in 'Against the worshipping of Imaginations', preached at St Giles' Cripplegate 9 January 1592, in *XCVI Sermons* (1629), pt. 2, 25–38, Lancelot Andrewes defends the use of secular sources in preaching: 'Which they [the Fathers] did the rather, for that, besides divers other places, not so apparant, they find S. Paul, in matter of doctrine alleaging Aratus a heathen Writer, in his Sermon at Athens. And againe, in matter of life, alleadging Menander, a Writer of Comoedies, in his Epistle: And thirdly, in matter of report onely without any urgent necessity, alleaging Epimenides, or as some think Callimachus.' The margin glosses the Menander reference as 1 Cor. 15.33.

80 I am indebted to Richard McCabe, who drew my attention to the connection. See C. R. Forker, *Skull Beneath the Skin, The Achievement of John Webster* (Carbondale, 1986), 461.

81 See R. W. Dent, *John Webster's Borrowings* (Berkeley, 1960), index and 111–12.

82 William Prynne, *Histrio-Matrix* (1633), 935.

83 See Alberico Gentile and John Rainolds, *Latin Correspondence on Academic Drama*, trans. and intro. L. Markowicz (Salzburg, 1977).

'His Acts Transmit to After Days': Two Unpublished Poems by Aurelian Townshend

Gabriel Heaton

The complete corpus of work left by Aurelian Townshend, the Caroline court poet and masque writer, has not been securely established. Most of Townshend's poetry circulated exclusively in manuscript during his lifetime and his work was not collected in print until 1912, when the poems and masques were edited by E. K. Chambers.[1] In 1983, Cedric Brown's edition of Townshend's work included several works not known to Chambers, and Dr Peter Beal has recently made further additions to the canon.[2] This article introduces yet further additions to the canon: two commendatory poems by Townshend found among the Additional Manuscripts in the British Library, London, both of which are here published for the first time.

The first of these two poems, 'To my Lord North, vpon his Pöems', is addressed to Dudley, third Lord North (1582–1666), a melancholic and impoverished nobleman. The second is 'An Ode: Vpon the happy Birth of our sweete yonge Prince', which celebrates the birth of the future Charles II, on 29 may 1630. The first part of this article considers the manuscripts of these poems: the handwriting (both poems are written in the same hand); their provenance; and the connection between Lord North, who owned both manuscripts, and Townshend. The content of the poems is considered in the second part of the article. They are, like much of Townshend's verse, court-oriented works with a firm base in compliment. Poetry itself is a central subject in both poems. 'To my Lord North' is curiously inattentive to the voice and style of North's poems, but it does present a coherent model for poetry. Townshend's ode for Prince Charles's birth is concerned as much with the response of other poets, especially Ben Jonson, to that birth as it is with the event itself. It is primarily the light that these poems shed on Townshend's thinking about poetic practice that makes them a significant addition to the canon.

THE MANUSCRIPTS

'To my Lord North' is found in British Library [BL], Add. MS 27407, fol. 5; 'Vpon the happy Birth' is in BL, Add. MS 27408, fols 112–13. The poems are found in two composite folio volumes of miscellaneous papers dating from the early seventeenth to early eighteenth centuries, originally from a single collection (see below), and bound in the nineteenth century.

Paper

'Vpon the happy Birth' is written on a bifolium of the 'pot'-sized paper common in the seventeenth century, with a sheet size of 403 × 294mm. It bears a number of fold marks that are consistent with the poem having been folded up into a small packet, and this is confirmed by darkened areas on fol. 113v where the outer edges of the packet were exposed to handling. The single leaf containing 'To my Lord North' measures 307 × 203mm. This was not the same paper as 'Vpon the happy Birth' since a full sheet of this paper would have been slightly larger (approximately 406 × 307 mm). It has a similar series of folds but lacks any darkened areas; this is probably because it was also a bifolium, but the original conjugate leaf has been lost.

The bifolium with 'Vpon the happy Birth', which was written in the summer of 1630, has a watermark of a crossbow in a circle surmounted by a trefoil, measuring 55 × 41mm.[3] There is a countermark of initials, perhaps reading 'G P', but the paper is damaged. The single leaf on which 'To my Lord North' is written has no watermark or countermark.

Manuscript separates were folded into packets so they could be more easily carried or enclosed within letters. However, no related letters or other para-texts, which might have revealed the circumstances in which the Townshend poems were originally presented, are now found with the poems. It is therefore difficult to reconstruct the contexts within which the manuscripts were written, and especially to understand the relationship between the sender, Townshend, and the recipient, Lord North.

Handwriting

The two poems are copied out in the same handwriting (see PLATES 1 and 2). This is a formal italic hand, leaning to the right with sweeping descenders such that although a regular and wide white space is consistently left between lines, penstrokes occasionally intersect (e.g. lines

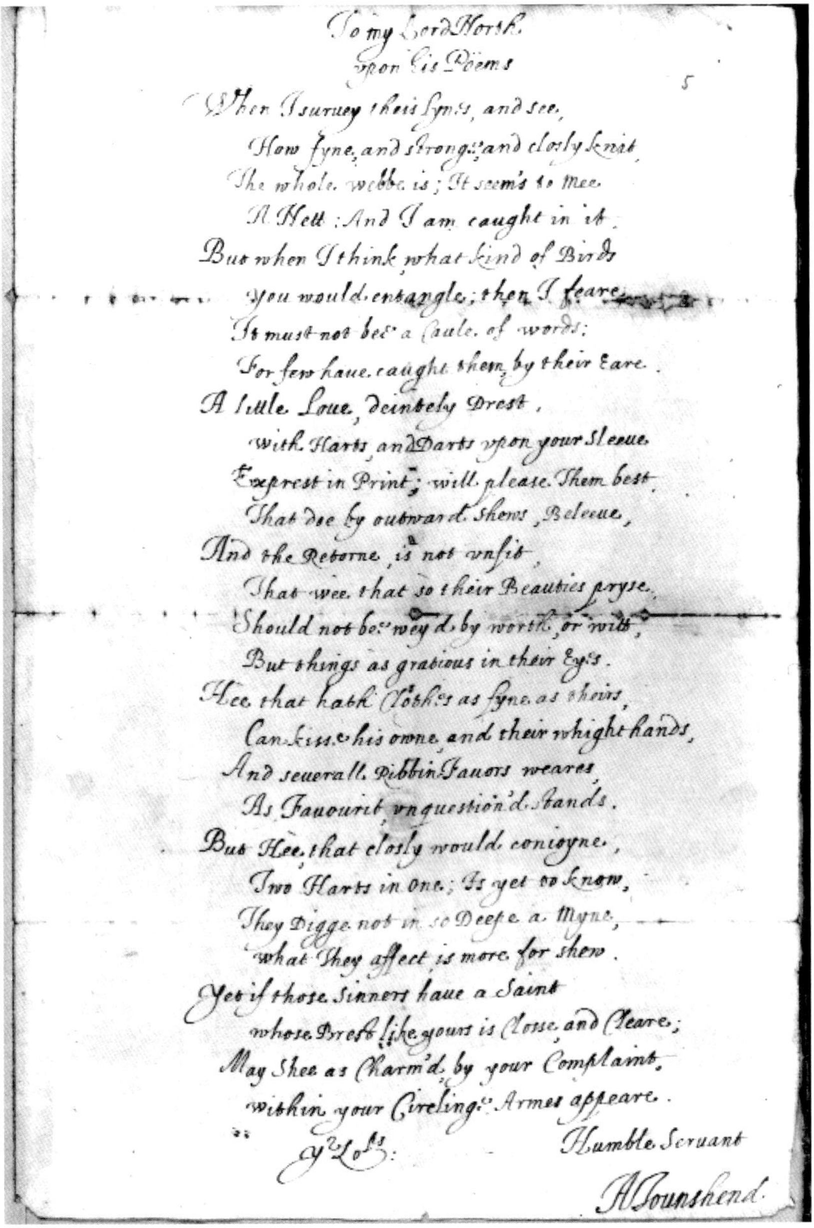

To my Lord North.
vpon his Poems

5

When I suruey theis lynes, and see,
How fyne, and strong, and closly knit,
The whole webbe is; It seem's to mee
A Nett: And I am caught in it.
But when I think what kind of Birds
you would entangle; then I feare
It must not bee a Caule of words:
For few haue caught them by their Eare.
A little Loue, deintely Drest,
with Harts, and Darts vpon your Sleeue,
Exprest in Print; will please Them best,
That doe by outward Shews, Beleeue,
And the Returne, is not vnfit,
That wee that so their Beauties pryse,
Should not bee wey'd by worth, or witt,
But things as gratious in their Eyes.
Hee that hath Clothes as fyne as theirs,
Can kiss his owne, and their whight hands,
And seuerall Ribbin Fauors weares,
As Fauourit vnquestion'd stands.
But Hee, that closly would conioyne,
Two Harts in One; Is yet to know,
They Digge not in so Deepe a Myne,
what They affect is more for show.
Yet if those Sinners haue a Saint
whose Brest like yours is Close, and Cleare;
May Shee as Charm'd by your Complaint,
within your Circling Armes appeare.

Yr Lops: Humble Seruant
A Townshend

PLATE I. *Manuscript of Townshend's poem 'To My Lord North': London, British Library, Additional ms 27407, fol. 5r (Original page size 307 × 203mm.) Reproduced by permission of the British Library Board.*

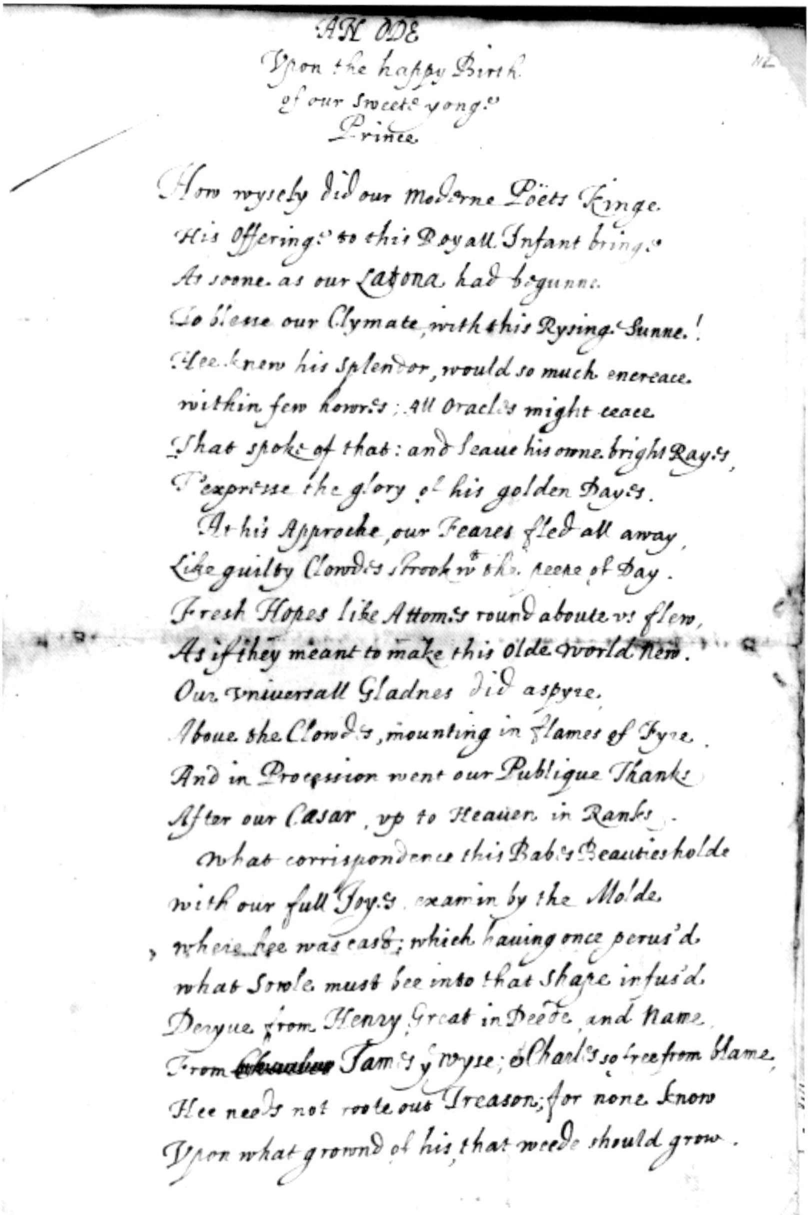

AN ODE
Upon the happy Birth
of our Sweete yonge
Prince

How wysely did our Moderne Poëts Kinge
His Offerings to this Royall Infant bringe
As soone as our Latona had begunne
To blesse our Clymate, with this Rysing Sunne!
Hee knew his Splendor, would so much encreace
within few howres; All Oracles might ceace
That spoke of that: and leave his owne bright Rayes,
T'expresse the glory of his golden Dayes.
At his Approche, our Feares fled all away,
Like guilty Clowdes strook wth the peepe of Day.
Fresh Hopes like Attomes round aboute vs flew,
As if they meant to make this Olde world New.
Our vniversall Gladnes did aspyre,
Above the Clowdes, mounting in flames of Fyre.
And in Procession went our Publique Thanks
After our Caesar, vp to Heauen in Ranks.
What corrispondence this Babes Beauties holde
with our full Joyes, examin by the Molde
where hee was cast; which having once perus'd.
what Sowle must bee into that Shape infus'd.
Deryve from Henry Great in Deede, and Name,
From ~~[illegible]~~ James ye wyse; & Charles so free from blame,
Hee needs not roote out Treason; for none know
Upon what grownd of his, that weede should grow.

PLATE 2. *Manuscript of Townshend's poem 'Upon the happy birth': London, British Library, Additional ms 27408, fol. 112r (Original page size 294 × 201mm.) Reproduced by permission of the British Library Board.*

21–23 of 'Vpon the happy Birth', lines 27–29 of 'To my Lord North'). Distinctive letter forms are common to both samples: the occasional secretary *e*; *p* in which the bowl does not meet the stem and with an angled hook on the descender; consistently short *s*; a short *t* which is only the height of linear letters; the otiose limb on majuscules with a vertical or diagonal stem (e.g. *A*, *F*, *H*, *I*); and the formation of *T* by an upstroke followed by a curving leftward stroke so that the stem meets the crossbar at its right edge.

This consistent and attractive hand cannot positively be identified as the poet's own, but neither can it be discounted as being Townshend's hand. A letter written by Townshend to Sir William Trumbull on 13 March 1621 provides the best document for comparison (PLATE 3).[4] Like the hand responsible for the poems, it is a right-leaning italic hand, neat and consistent, with generous spacing between lines. But where the overall aspect of the writing of the poems is rounded with gentle curves, the letter is in a markedly more angular hand. Descenders in the poems mostly curve to the left, whereas in the letter they tend to be formed with a much straighter line leading to an acute angle at the terminal point, after which the line returns upwards. Ascenders are much more pronounced in the letter, most obviously in the sweeping curve on the stem of *d*. But some differences, at least, may be cosmetic; for example, the much thicker pen-line in the poem hand is the result of a different cut of the nib. Furthermore, the hand in the letter to Trumbull does share many of the distinctive forms of the poem hand: the limb that runs to the left off the top of several letters (such as *A*, *H*, *I*); the distinctive formation of *T*; *t* formed without a pen-lift; and there are examples of *p* with an open bowl in the letter to Trumbull. It is also perhaps notable that all three signatures ('A Townshend'), although not identical, are very similar in form.

Given that the letter was written several years before the poem and is a less formal manuscript, we should expect some variation in the handwriting samples. Nevertheless, the similarities between the poems and the letter are not sufficient to claim the hand in the poems as Townshend's. To make that claim it would be necessary to demonstrate that the features common to the samples are individual characteristics or idiosyncrasies that can safely be used as evidence (*i.e.* that they are not simply generic characteristics common to many contemporary hands), while the differences are less distinctive and can be explained as natural variation. This has not proved possible.

Other possible examples of Townshend's hand are of little assistance. Another presentation manuscript of a Townshend poem, 'Tis but a while, since in a uestall flame', was written to Charles I in the early

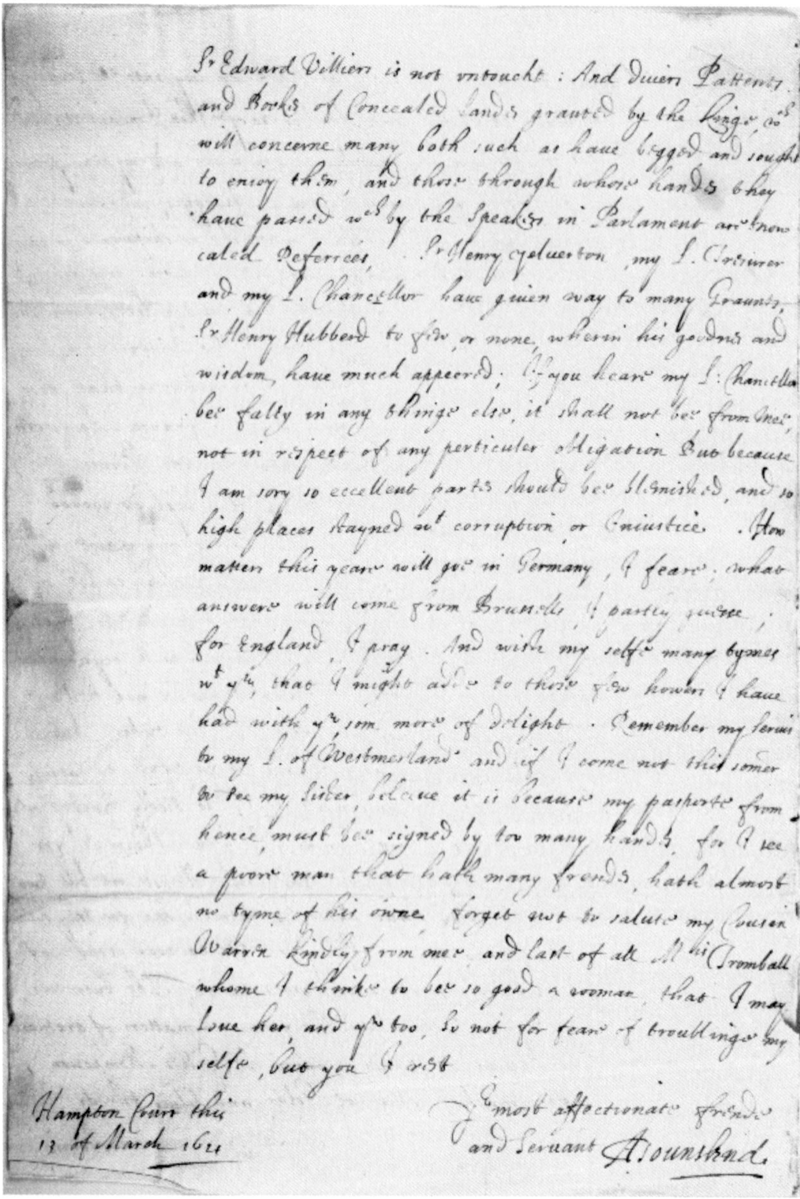

Sr Edward Villiers is not untoucht: And diuers Pattents,
and Books of Concealed lands graunted by the Kinge, &c
will concerne many both such as haue begged and sought
to enioy them, and those through whose hands they
haue passed wch by the Speaker in Parlament are now
called Referrees, Sr Henry Yeluerton, my L. Treasurer
and my L. Chancellor haue giuen way to many Graunts,
Sr Henry Hubberd to few, or none, wherin his goodnes and
wisdom, haue much appeered; If you heare my L: Chancellor
bee faulty in any thinge else, it shall not bee from mee,
not in respect of any perticuler obligation but because
I am sory so excellent parts should bee blemished, and so
high places stayned wt corruption, or iniustice. How
matters this yeare will goe in Germany, I feare; what
answere will come from Brussells I partly suspect;
for England I pray. And wish my selfe many tymes
wt you, that I might adde to those few howers I haue
had with you som more of delight. Remember my seruice
to my L. of Westmerland and if I come not this somer
to see my Sister, beleeue it is because my pasporte from
hence, must bee signed by too many hands; for I see
a poore man that hath many frends, hath almost
no tyme of his owne. Forget not to salute my Cousen
Warren kindly from mee and last of all Mris Trombull
whome I thinke to bee so good a woman, that I may
loue her, and you too, so not for feare of troublinge my
selfe, but you I rest

Hampton Court this
13 of March 1621

Yr most affectionate frende
and Seruant ATounshend.

PLATE 3. *The second page of Townshend's autograph letter signed ('ATounshend') to William Trumbull, 13 March 1620/1: London, British Library, Add. ms 72360, fol. 129v (Original page size 295 × 205mm.) Reproduced by permission of the British Library Board.*

1630's, but this manuscript (PLATE 4) cannot be accepted as being in Townshend's hand.[5] Unlike the examples discussed so far it is mostly in a secretary hand, although proper names and some other words are in italic. There are also a number of features of the italic hand that are not found in the other samples (an elaborate majuscule *P*, a long *s* in *ss*). The 'signature' in this manuscript, although relatively similar to the others, has been written out with much greater care.

The problem is complicated because it is known that Townshend was an accomplished penman capable of writing in a number of different hands. In 1600 Robert Cecil wrote that Townshend 'would be able with a little exercise to write faire hands'.[6] The letters that Townshend wrote to Cecil and others during his European travels between 1601 and 1603 provide ample evidence of his skill. This is easily the largest surviving set of documents in Townshend's hand. A number of the letters are preserved among the Cecil Papers in Hatfield House, while others are among the State Papers in the National Archives.[7] At least four distinct hands, several of them fine examples of calligraphy, are found in these letters. Townshend was, it seems, keen to demonstrate his abilities to his patron. Examples of these hands can be seen in PLATES 5 and 6. Letters written in foreign languages nearly thirty years before the poems would never be an entirely trustworthy guide to Aurelian Townshend's hand in 1630, but they do prove that he was versatile as a penman. This versatility means that he was capable of writing the manuscripts of the poems, although further evidence would be necessary to establish for certain that he was in fact responsible for them.

Date

Aurelian Townshend was born before December 1583, but most of his surviving poetry probably dates from the 1630s. The similarity of the two manuscripts discussed here, and their common provenance, strongly suggest they were written at about the same time, in the 1630s. Since most of North's lyrics referred to in 'To My Lord North' were, however, written in the first decade of the seventeenth century, composition of the poem could pre-date the surviving manuscript by up to twenty years.

Provenance

The ownership of the collection of separates of which BL Adds 27407 and 27408 form part can be traced back to the Norfolk antiquary Peter Le Neve (1661–1729).[8] After Le Neve's death his large collection passed

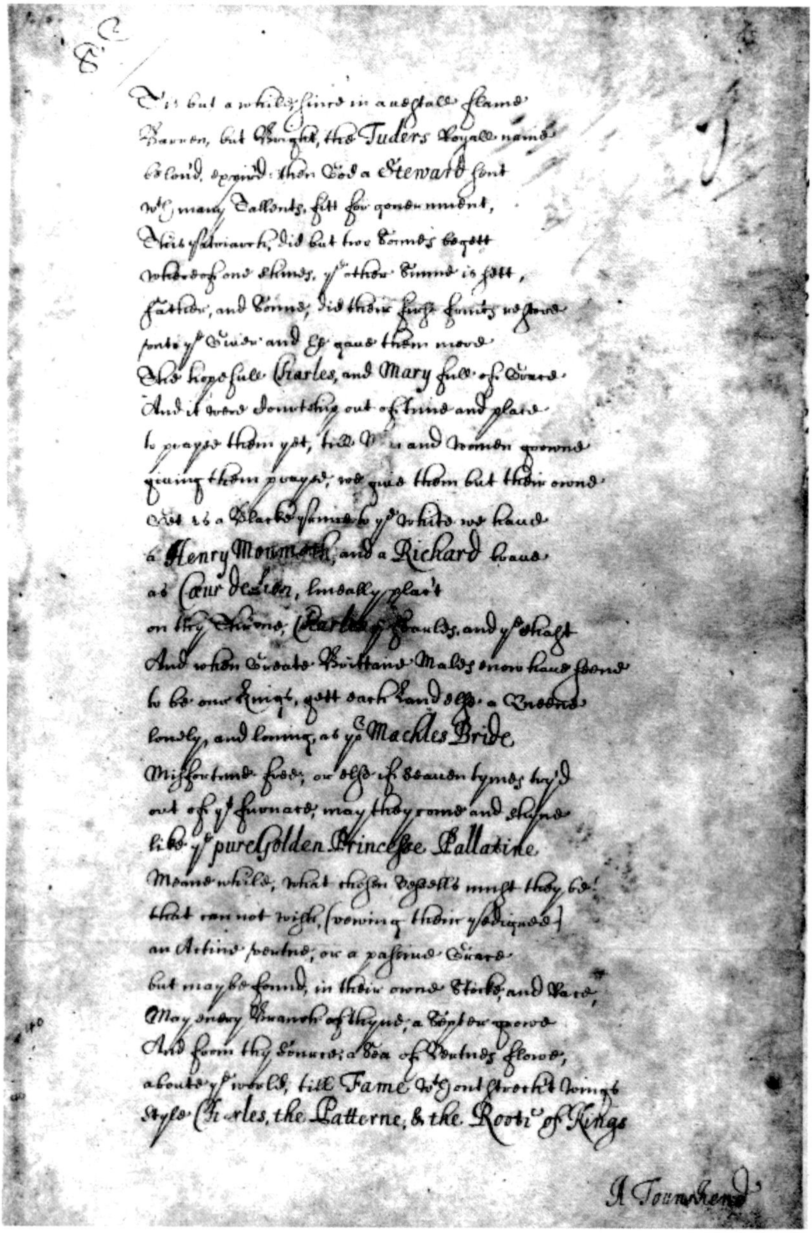

Tis but a while, since in a uestall flame
Barren, but bright, the Tuders Royall name
[illegible] expir'd: then God a Steward sent
wth many Tallents, fitt for gouernment,
This Patriarch, did but two Sonnes begett
whereof one shines, ye other Sunne is sett,
Father, and Sonne, did their first fruits wch were
unto ye Giuer and He gaue them more
The hopefull Charles, and Mary full of Grace.
And it were somthing out of tyme and place
to prayse them yet, till Men and women growne
giuing them prayse, we giue them but their owne
Yet 'tis a blacke [illegible] ye white we haue
a Henry Monmouth, and a Richard braue
as Cœur de Lion, lineally plac't
on thy Throne, Charles ye Bould, and ye Chast
And when Greate Brittans Maids now haue found
to be our Knight, gett each [illegible] a Queene
lonely, and louing, as ye Mackles Bride
Misfortune free; or else if seauen tymes try'd
out of ye furnace, may they come and shine
like ye pure Golden Princesse Pallatine
Meane while, what chosen vessells must they be!
that can not wish, (vewing their pedigree)
an Actiue Fortune, or a passiue Grace
but may be found, in their owne Stocke, and Race,
May euery branch of thyne, a Scepter growe
And from thy Sonnes, a Sea of Subjects flowe,
aboute ye world, till Fame wth out stretcht wings
styles Charles, the Patterne, & the Roote of Kings

A Townshend

PLATE 4. *Manuscript of Townshend's poem ''Tis but a while, since in a uestal flame': London, British Library, Egerton ms 2603, fol. 62r (Original page size 320 × 205mm.)*

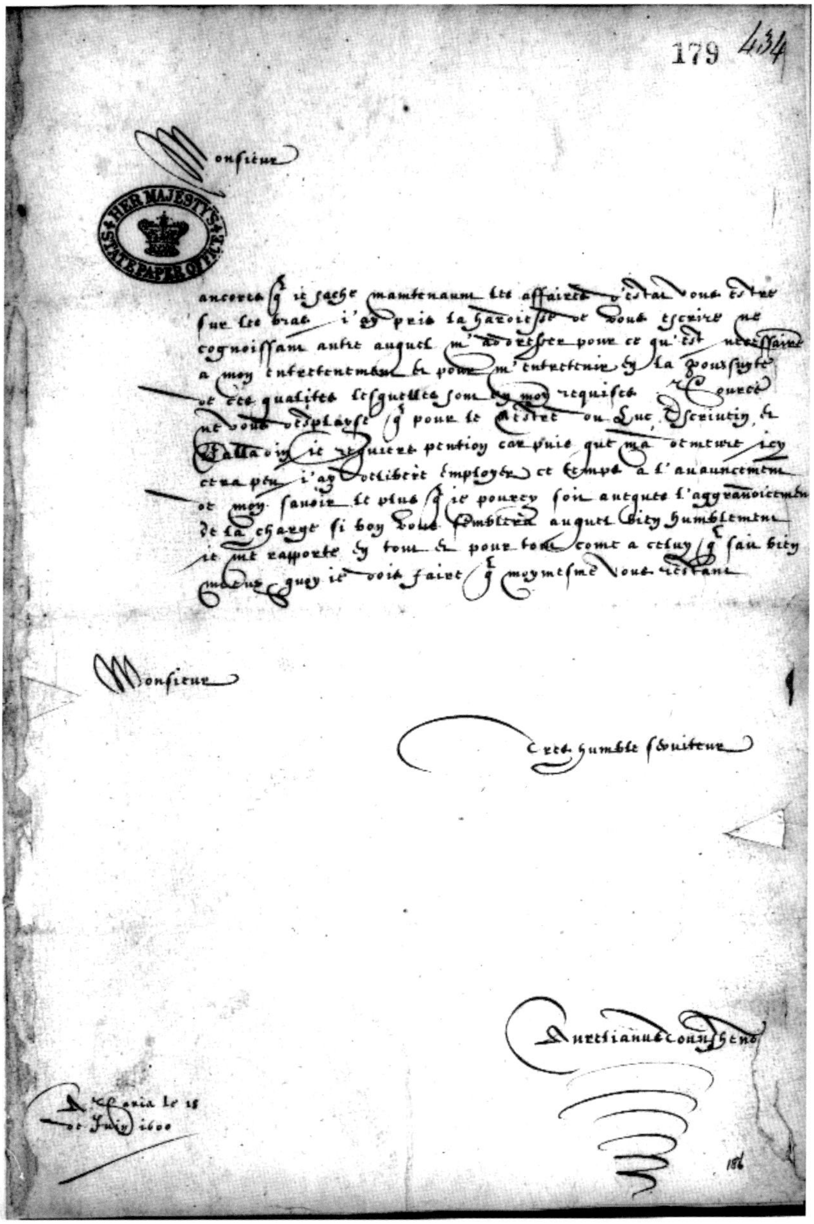
179 434

Monsieur

Monsieur

Vostre humble serviteur

Aurelianus Tounshend

PLATE 5. *Townshend's autograph letter signed ('Aurelianus Tounshend'), in French, to Sir Henry Neville, 18 June 1600: Kew, National Archives, SP 78/44, fol. 179r (Original page size 295 × 195mm.) Reproduced by permission of the National Archives.*

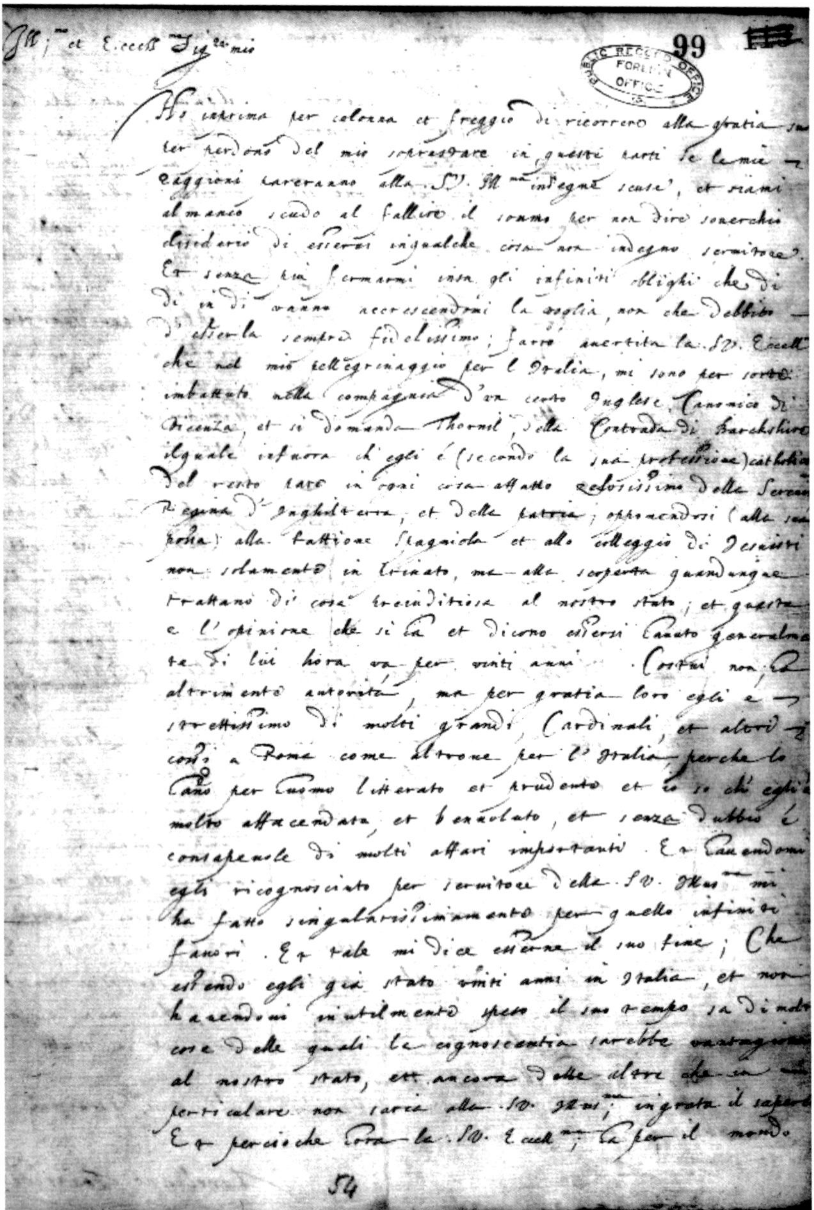
Ill.mo et Eccell.mo Sig.re mio

99

Ho istima per colonna et freggio di ricorrere alla gratia su
per perdono del mio sopraestare in queste parti se le mie
raggioni pareranno alla S.V. Ill.ma indegne scuse, et siami
almanco scudo al fallire il sommo per non dire souerchio
desiderio di esserui in qualche cosa non indegno seruitore.
Et senza piu fermarmi ivi gli infiniti obblighi che di
di in di vanno accrescendomi la voglia, non che debbito
d'esserla sempre fidelissimo; farro auertita la S.V. Eccell.ma
che nel mio pellegrinaggio per l'Italia, mi sono per sorte
imbattuto nella compagnia d'vn certo Inglese Canonico di
Vicenza, et si domanda Thornil, della Contrada di Barckshire
ilquale infuora ch'egli é (secondo la sua professione) catholico
del resto pare in ogni cosa affatto zelosissimo della Serenis
Regina d'Inghilterra, et della patria; opponendosi (alla sua
posta) alla fattione Spagniola et allo collegio di Iesuiti
non solamente in priuato, ma alla scoperta quandunque
trattano di cose pregiuditiose al nostro stato; et questa
e l'opinione che si ha et dicono essersi portato generalmen
te di lui hora va per vinti anni. Costui non ha
altrimente autorità, ma per gratia loro egli é
strettissimo di molti grandi, Cardinali, et altri
così a Roma come altroue per l'Italia, perche lo
hanno per huomo litterato et prudente et io so ch'egli é
molto affacendato, et beneuolato, et senza dubbio é
consapeuole di molti affari importanti. Et hauendomi
egli ricognosciuto per seruitore della S.V. Ill.ma mi
ha fatto singularissimamente per quello infiniti
fauori. Et tale mi dice esserne il suo fine; Che
essendo egli gia stato vinti anni in Italia, et non
hauendoui inutilmente speso il suo tempo sa di molte
cose delle quali la cognoscentia sarebbe vantaggiosa
al nostro stato, et ancora delle altre che in
perticulare non sarà alla S.V. Ill.ma ingrata il sapere
Et perciòche hora la S.V. Eccell.ma ha per il mondo

54

PLATE 6. *First page of Townshend's autograph letter, in Italian, to Sir Robert Cecil, 9 May 1602: Kew, National Archives, SP 99/2, fol. 99r (Original page size 300 × 215mm.) Reproduced by permission of the National Archives.*

to his executor, Thomas Martin, himself an antiquary, who auctioned off a portion at the Bedford Coffee House in a sale running from 22 February to 19 March 1731.[9] These manuscripts were not included in that sale, but Martin is known to have kept back much of the collection. When Martin died in March 1771 his collection was acquired by Thomas Worth, a Diss chemist. Worth sold Martin's collection at a sale on 28–29 April 1773, but the poetry separates were not included in this sale; it is almost certain that they had already passed from Worth to the antiquary Sir John Fenn (1739–94), who was given some manuscripts by Worth and purchased others before the sale—including a substantial portion of the Paston letters, which he later edited.[10] When Fenn died his manuscript collection passed to his nephew, William Frere, who completed Fenn's editorial work on the Paston letters. Finally, in 1866 William Frere's son, Philip Frere of Dungate, Cambridgeshire, sold his father's manuscripts. The Le Neve separates, by this time bound into three volumes, were purchased for the British Museum at the sale of Sir John Fenn's library, Puttick and Simpson, 17 July 1866, lots 420–422.[11]

There is clear internal evidence that a sizeable portion of the earlier material in the Le Neve poetry collection once belonged to Dudley, third Lord North. The manuscript volumes include two poems on the death of Anne of Denmark that were included in North's collected literary works, *The Forest of Varieties* (London, 1645).[12] There are also two poems in North's own hand in the bound volumes.[13] Townshend's commendatory poem on North's verses is only one of several poems in the collection addressed to Lord North.[14] One of these, a copy of a verse epistle addressed to Ben Jonson that was sent to North, reveals that a friend of Jonson's saw North as a potential ally in the poet's plea for patronage from Prince Henry, with whom North was closely associated.[15] Other contemporaneous separates in the collection are also likely to have belonged to North, including Jonson's *Entertainment at Theobalds* and Donne's elegy on Prince Henry's death.[16] No external evidence has so far been uncovered that connects Le Neve to the Norths, but the seat of the Lords North was Kirtling in Cambridgeshire, so the early provenance of these manuscripts was entirely East Anglian.

The probability is very strong that these two Townshend manuscript poems, physically very similar and in the same hand, shared a common origin. Given the presence of so many North manuscripts in the Le Neve collection, we can be fairly certain that both 'To my Lord North' and 'Vpon the happy Birth' belonged to North himself.

Townshend and North

The presence of manuscript poems by Townshend among Lord North's papers suggests that the two men had some form of personal relationship.[17] North was never a significant literary patron and his estate was greatly reduced by the 1620s and 30s. Townshend would have known this, so is unlikely to have sent him verses in an attempt to secure patronage.[18] Furthermore, North's poetry did not engender many responses either during his lifetime or subsequently, so the very existence of this commendation is unusual.[19] On the other hand, Townshend's poem on North's poetry probably post-dates the verses it praises by two decades and commends them for features that North himself did not see in them, which suggests that the two men had not discussed North's verses before that poem was written.

North and Townshend had much in common: they were about the same age, both spent considerable time travelling abroad in the first decade of the 1600s, and both were in Italy at about the same time in 1602. Townshend was certainly not of North's social standing, but he moved in similar circles, initially through his position as a client to members of prominent families such as the Cecils and the Herberts, and later as a peripheral figure around court. Both men wrote poetry and knew poets.[20] Both also had a particular interest in court entertainments: Townshend wrote masques, while North took part in a number of entertainments between about 1610 and 1614, most of which were associated with Prince Henry; in later years he also put on entertainments at Kirtling.[21] At a time when poetry was mostly associated with youth, both men continued to write well into their middle age. It may be that their relationship developed after 1630. It is certainly striking that in or shortly after November 1632 they wrote poems on the same subject: the response of English poets to the death of Gustavus Adolphus, which inspired North's 'An Invective to our Poets upon the death of the victorious King of Swedeland' (*Forest of Varieties*, p. 75) as well as Townshend's 'Elegy on the death of the King of Sweden: sent to Thomas Carew'.

The Texts

The following are semi-diplomatic transcriptions of the poems in BL, Add. MS 27407, fol. 5, and Add. MS 27408, fols 112–13. Superscript letters have been silently lowered and contractions have been expanded, with expansions rendered in italic.

'TO MY LORD NORTH'

To my Lord North
vpon his Pöems

When I suruey theis lynes, and see,
How fyne, and stronge, and closly knit,
The whole webbe is; it seem's to mee
A Nett: And I am caught in it.
But when I think, what kind of Birds
You would entangle; then I feare,
It must not bee a Caule[22] of words:
For few haue caught them, by their Eare.
A little Loue, deintely Drest,
With Harts, and Darts vpon your Sleeue
Exprest in Print;[23] will please Them best,
That doe by outward shews, Beleeue,
And the Retorne, is not vnfit,
That wee that so their Beauties pryse,
Should not bee wey'd by worth, or witt,
But things as gratious in their Eyes.
Hee that hath Clothes as fyne as theirs,
Can kisse his owne and their whight hands,
And seuerall Ribbin Fauors weares,
As Fauourit, vnquestion'd stands.
But Hee that closly would conioyne,
Two Harts in One; Is yet to know,
They digge not in so Deepe a Myne,
what They affect is more for shew.
Yet if those Sinners haue a Saint
whose Brest like yours is Closse, and Cleare;
May Shee as Charm'd, by your Complaint,
Within your Circlinge Armes appeare.
y*our* L*ordshi*ps Humble Seruant
A Tounshend

Commentary

This poem was written on a sequence of love poems that Lord North first printed in *The Forest of Varieties*, under the title 'Aurora'. However, as that title suggests, the sequence was among North's earliest work; these poems were begun as early as 1598 and were substantially complete before 1610.[24] North's love poems are addressed to 'Cœlestia', or in some early versions 'Victoria'.[25] A number of manuscript collections of North's sequence of love poems still survive, and Townshend evidently read the poems in one such manuscript.[26] 'To my Lord North' is not a response to the 1645 *Forest of Varieties*. When North came to print his work he encouraged an ironic reading of the 'Aurora' sequence, emphasising that the author-editor of the *Forest* was no longer the same man as the youthful poet, and suggesting the passion they describe was a failing both physiologically (love is 'ever an Ebullition [agitation] of the liver') and psychologically (love results 'where the violent appetite of one object, no better then the rest, gives relish to that alone'). He also explained that, 'The reason why I retaine and expose them with others, is not so much that I esteem them worthy of view or life, as that they were many yeares since Copied and spread abroad beyond my knowledge then, and are now beyond my powers to recall' (*Forest of Varieties*, p. 8).

Townshend's response to North's poems differs markedly from North's own attitude to his poetry, and these differences reveal much about the different models of poetic practice that Townshend and North followed. One significant difference is in the conceptualisation of North's labour as a poet. In his central image of North's verses as a net, 'fyne, and stronge, and closely knit' (l. 2), Townshend praises North's poems for the care with which they have been produced. North himself, however, tended to see his own writing as a compulsion brought on by his melancholia, and saw its virtue as its easiness and fluidity. He wrote quickly (claiming to produce up to four pieces before breakfast); disdained revision; did not believe it necessary to maintain strict metrical form; aimed for ease of understanding; and argued that poems of love should above all aim to please, 'and to please in love, the smoother fac'd the better' (*Forest of Varieties*, p. 4). In what was perhaps a direct rebuttal of Townshend's closely-knit web of words, North also wrote that:

> some of the stricter sort approve onely of verses so close, usefull, and substantially woven, that there must bee neither list, looseness, nor the least superfluity of words: for my part, I am not of that strict order, nor ever yet saw it observed in any Author. (*Forest of Varieties*, p. 5)

As the word 'usefull' suggests, describing North's poems as a net of words emphasises their functionality, and the rest of 'To my Lord North' considers the likelihood of the poems' success in entangling Cœlestia. The association of poet with hunter may have been inspired by one of North's poems. In 'It's true that my affections lately bent'

(*Forest of Varieties*, pp. 37–39), a poem described in one manuscript as 'An apology for the present worke [*i.e.* the 'Aurora' sequence]',[27] the speaker acknowledges that 'my love hath mist its end', but explains that his love has not been wasted by comparing himself to a hunter who takes pleasure in the chase even if he fails to take any game. Townshend's poem also acknowledges that the poems will not win 'Cœlestia', but the reasons given for this by Townshend are very different from anything found in North's work. Townshend's poems often criticise fashionable women, and he here argues that women like 'Cœlestia' do not have the necessary judgement to be caught in North's 'Caule of words' (l. 7): they look only for 'outward shews' (l. 12) so will prefer the feminised courtier with fine clothes and white hands.[28] Even if there should be a 'Saint' among women who is responsive to North's words, such success would be the result of the poem having acted as a magic charm, conjuring her into his 'Circlinge Armes' (l. 28).[29] It is only the male reader—and specifically Townshend himself—who has the capacity to recognise the closely wrought skill of the poems and is 'caught' as a result. Townshend replaces the female addressee with himself as the ideal reader, and suggests that the fruit of the love lyric is not the love of a woman but another poem.

Townshend's poem depends on a contrast between true poetry such as North's, and the gaudily fashionable world where hearts are literally worn on sleeves (l. 10). But while Townshend contrasts North's poems with the ephemeral world of fashion and external beauty, in the 'Aurora' sequence itself North uses such terms to describe his own poems:

> They are as superfluous banquet stuffe are meant,
> Made but to please the outward sense and tast,
> Which though they yeeld no solid nourishment,
> They are not yet a profitlesse repast (*Forest of Varieties*, p. 38).

Underlying Townshend's contrast between poetry's depth and mere surface beauty is the traditional association of the feminine with the physical, as opposed to the masculine domain of word and mind (a distinction figured by Townshend as a fitting response to the male obsession with female physical beauty). Yet North's poems play out gender roles in a distinctive way, to which Townshend is strikingly unresponsive. Rather than being an active hunter, the male speaker in North's poetry is more commonly an abject onlooker.[30] In 'It was that gracious season of the yeare' (*Forest of Varieties*, p. 29) the speaker identifies himself not with the hunter but with the hunted stag, with which he merges to become an Actæon figure, 'By those my selfe-bred, swift-foote hounds pursu'd'. In another poem, 'To winne her from resolving upon a Cloyster'd life' (pp. 18–19), North compares the object of his desire to a bird. But while in Townshend's poem the bird is to be ensnared, North suggests that, 'Birds that long have lived free,/ Caught and Cag'd but pine and die' (p. 19). Townshend had found in North's poems an attempt to ensnare birds like 'Cœlestia', but when North himself compares his lover to a bird it is to argue for her freedom. In summary, it is not North's poetry that Townshend describes to him in 'To my Lord North', but a representation of Townshend's own conception of love poetry.

'VPON THE HAPPY BIRTH'

The Text

AN ODE
Vpon the happy Birth
of our sweete yonge
Prince

How wysely did our Moderne Pöets Kinge
His offeringe to this Royall Infant bringe
As soone as our Latona[31] had begunne
To blesse our Clymate, with this Rysing Sunne!
Hee knew his splendor, would so much encreace
within few howres; All Oracles might ceace
That spoke of that: and leaue his owne bright Rayes,
T'expresse the glory of his golden Dayes.
At his Approche, our Feares fled all away,
Like guilty Clowdes strook w*ith* the peepe of Day.
Fresh Hopes like Attomes round aboute vs flew,
As if they meant to make this Olde world New.
Our vniuersall Gladnes did aspyre,
Aboue the Clowdes, mounting in flames of Fyre.
And in Procession went our Publique Thanks
After our Casar, vp to Heauen in Ranks.
What corrispondence this Babes Beauties holde
with our full Ioyes, examin by the Molde
where hee was cast: which hauing once perus'd
what Sowle must bee into that Shape infus'd
Deryue from Henry, Great in Deede and Name,[32]
From ~~Charles~~ Iames the wyse; & Charles so free from blame,
Hee needs not roote out Treason; for none know

Vpon what grownd of his, that weede should grow.
[113r] What Floures and Fruits, our yonge Apollos Beames,
Must needs produce, Are sett aparte as Theames
For those High Priests that at his Altar kneele;
who in Brasse sheetes wryting with Pennes of Steele,
Shall all his Acts transmitt to after Dayes,
And make his Reigne Immortall; And their Beyes.

A Tounshend.

Commentary

The birth celebrated in this poem was that of the future Charles II, born in St James's Palace on 29 May 1630. Its subject cannot be the son born to the royal couple the previous year, since he had only lived a few hours, and the claim that with his birth 'our fears all fled away' (l. 9) surely refers to the securing of the succession, so we can discount Prince James (born in 1633) as the subject. The birth of Prince Charles brought forth a stream of congratulatory verses. Jonson, Herrick, King, Corbet, Shirley and Randolph, among others, all produced poems, many of which were widely circulated. Rowland Woodward, writing to Francis Windebanke on 21 July, enclosed some verses of his own, but added apologetically that, 'comming to you after the creame of the best witts, this will proue but sower milke to your tast.'[33] Further contributions came from the universities: a volume of poems by members of the University was printed at the Oxford press, and a similar volume from Cambridge appeared the following year, also including poems on the birth of Charles's sister Mary.[34] Townshend's poem praises the birth, and as a congratulatory poem it is much more successful than 'To my Lord North'; but it is also consciously part of a wider poetic response to the event and, like 'To my Lord North', it is concerned with what constitutes successful poetry.

It was of course expected that major public events such as the birth of a Prince of Wales should be commemorated in verse. Such verses were not necessarily written with the King as intended audience (we have already seen that the only known copy of 'Vpon the happy Birth' belonged to Lord North), but for a wider public who were likely to be less interested in protestations of loyalty than in the poet's exercise of wit in finding an individual and appropriate way to express conventional sentiments. Few of these poems had any sort of quasi-official function and the attitudes they expressed were varied: several poems made light-hearted reference to the King's recent Parliamentary troubles, and one poem was sufficiently nuanced to be read by at least one reader as a puritan satire, although in fact its author was no less a figure than Richard Corbet, Bishop of Oxford.[35]

A number of these poems referred to unusual astronomical events that accompanied Charles's birth: Venus was visible during daylight hours on the day of his birth, and there was an eclipse of the sun two days later. These heavenly occurrences may lie behind the celestial imagery of 'Vpon the happy Birth'. Robert Herrick's 'A Pastorall upon the birth of Prince Charles, Presented to the King' makes full use of the parallels to the biblical Nativity, and describes Venus shining 'Bright as the Wise-mens Torch, which guided them/ To Gods sweet Babe, when borne at *Bethlehem*'.[36] Townshend's poem sets out a similar analogical pattern to Herrick's 'Pastoral', although Townshend sees the child as an Apollo rather than as a Christ: as the beautiful youth, the wise and rational god who heals, is associated with the sun, and is a patron of poets.

Townshend also follows many other poets by placing the newborn in a genealogical line. The infant Charles provides a link between the past (the child's male ancestors, lines 21–22) and the future, which is secured by his birth. Townshend can already vocalise the coming generations' praises of the child's future acts since they can be predicted by looking back at his ancestors' glorious deeds. A second poem by Townshend on Charles I's children similarly fantasises that the future will replay the past. This poem, 'Tis but a while, since in a uestall flame', is a slightly later work, probably dating from 1633, and celebrates the royal couple's fecundity.[37] It begins by reviewing the royal genealogy from the death of Elizabeth, then imagines a future which repeats an earlier past, one in which Charles and Henrietta-Maria beget a Black Prince, a Henry V, and a Richard I (lines 13–15), their descendants ultimately becoming 'a Sea of Vertues' that will rule the world.

The idea that heredity ensures a glorious future is a natural fantasy for a monarchy, but Townshend also considers how such glory should be praised. The poem begins not by praising the infant, but by praising the wisdom of 'our Moderne Pöets Kinge' in presenting his offering so promptly. Townshend initially explains this promptitude as commendable because the young prince will soon surpass all praise, but later in the poem it is made clear that the action was also in harmony with appropriate hierarchy: 'Publique Thanks' for the birth go 'vp to Heauen in Ranks' (lines 15–16), so it is right that the 'Pöets Kinge' was the first to praise the birth. Ben Jonson is undoubtedly the poet referred to here.[38] Jonson had a uniquely close association with the early Stuart monarchs, and his 'Epigram on the Prince's Birth' refers in the future tense to the eclipse of the sun that occurred two days after Charles's birth. Jonson also accompanied his poem with a quotation from Martial on the virtue of prompt praise.[39]

The last six lines of Townshend's poem return to the nature of panegyric. It is inevitable that the child will perform great actions, but in these lines Townshend admits that the praise of Charles's actions is a task for those who will surround him when his promise has begun to be fulfilled, rather than those attendant on his birth. Townshend represents himself as an observer of this developing relationship and makes no explicit place for himself either near the head of those praising the prince's birth or among those who praise his future actions. However, there is a connection between those future 'High Priests that at his Alter kneele' and those who praised his birth: the recent offerings are a first indication of love and duty that, by showing their authors' willingness to kneel at his alter, make them appropriate laureates. The significance of literary genealogy in these lines closely parallels that of royal genealogy elsewhere in the poem. In describing their 'Brasse sheetes wryting with Pennes of Steele' Townshend refers to the engraver's burin, but he also gives these future panegyrics a steel-like quality that he elsewhere associates with the work of Jonson. In 'An Elegie Made by Mr Aurelian Townshend in remembrance of the Ladie Venetia Digby', Townshend refers at length to Jonson's poems on Venetia Digby.[40] He describes how Jonson's style had always been 'perfect steele/ Strong, smooth, and sharp, and so could make us feele/ His love or anger' (lines 21–23), but that it learned to 'attract' (l. 24) when 'He sate and drewe thy beauties by the life' (l. 27). The reference to magnetism draws on Jonson's play *The Magnetic Lady* (1632), but Townshend's characterisation of Jonson's poems as 'steely' is noteworthy. The 'steeliness' of Jonson's lines gives them the supple strength and durability that makes them appropriate for the task of transmitting Prince Charles's acts to posterity.

'Vpon the happy Birth' reveals Jonson as a central, if unnamed, exemplary poet for Townshend, but Jonson is also an unspoken presence in 'To my Lord North'. Townshend's comparison of the poet to a hunter reflects Jonson's comparison in his 'Elegie' for Venetia Digby between the poet and an angler. The latter describes how the newly inspired Jonson 'caught as many heartes/ With every line, as thou with every looke;/ Which we conceive was both his baite and hooke' (lines 18–20). The terms of praise for Jonson's poems—strong, smooth, and sharp—are also comparable to the model of poetry described in 'To my Lord North'. These poems delineate an ideal of poetic practice—strong, intricately wrought, aggressively masculine, and closely engaged with authority—for which Jonson provided the best model. Critics have mostly based their judgement of the relationship between the two poets on Townshend's usurpation of Jonson's position of masque-writer for the court, something over which neither man is likely to have had much control. These poems show a much more positive side to their relationship. Further research, especially into the role of Lord North, who had some connection with both Jonson and Townshend, might shed further light on the currents of influence at work. At the very least these poems reveal Jonson to have been a strong and positive model for Townshend.

NOTES

I am very grateful to Dr Peter Beal for discussing Aurelian Townshend's handwriting with me, Dr Mark Bland for sharing his knowledge of the manuscripts of the third Lord North, Professor Ian Donaldson for conversations about the poetry that marked the birth of Prince Charles, an anonymous reader for *EMS* for additional provenance information, and Dr Harriet Knight for proof-reading and comments.

1 *Aurelian Townshend's Poems and Masks*, ed. E. K. Chambers (Oxford, 1912).

2 *The Poems and Masques of Aurelian Townshend*, ed. Cedric C. Brown (Reading, 1983); Peter Beal, 'Songs by Aurelian Townshend, in the hand of Sir Henry Herbert, for an Unrecorded Masque by the Merchant Adventurers', *Medieval and Renaissance Drama in England*, 15 (2003), 243–59; Peter Beal, 'Townshend, Aurelian, *c*.1583-*c*.1649' *Oxford Dictionary of National Biography* (Oxford, 2004). The most significant additional source for poems by Townshend is University College London, Ogden MS 42, a mid-seventeenth century royalist verse miscellany that includes a number of poems by Townshend, including at least two unpublished poems and the full text of a poem on the death of Charles I, of which only a fragment is otherwise known.

3 This is similar to CRSBW.001.1 recorded in the Gravell Watermark Archive (http://www.gravell.org), in a letter dated January 1601. The 1630s is a late date for such crossbow watermarks, which were much more common in the sixteenth century. For further examples see C. M. Briquet, *Les Filigranes*, 4 vols (Amsterdam, 1968), nos 763, 765–70.

4 This letter (BL, Add. MS 72360, fols 129–30) was first noted in Sotheby's sale catalogue *The Trumbull Papers* (14 December 1989), lot 36, and then in Beal, 'Songs by Townshend', p. 252.

5 BL, Egerton MS 2603, fol. 62. This poem is directly addressed to the King, but it is not known whether the surviving presentation manuscript ever belonged to him. It was later owned by the antiquary Sir Frederic Ouvry (1814–81) prior to its acquisition by the British Museum.

6 Chambers, p. xxxvii.

7 These letters, which are addressed to Robert Cecil unless otherwise noted, are: Cecil Papers [CP], 84/69 (2 January 1601); CP 85/163 (28 April 1601); CP 86/137 (1602); CP 87/23 (27 July 1601); CP, 91/106 (7 February 1603); CP 93/110 (15 June 1602); CP 96/11(24 October 1602); National Archives [NA], SP 78 [France]/44, fol. 99 (April 1600), fol. 179 (to Sir Henry Neville, 18 June 1600), fol. 281 (to Michael Stanhope, 5 September 1600), fol. 282 (5 September 1600), fol. 308 (1 October 1600), and fol. 312 (to Michael Stanhope, 4 October 1600); NA, SP 85 [Italy]/2, fol. 97 (27 September 1601); NA, SP 99 [Venice]/2, [vol. 1] fol. 99 (9 May 1602).

8 The manuscripts include a number of items by Peter Le Neve, his brother Oliver, and Thomas Martin.

9 *A Catalogue of the Valuable Library Collected by . . . Peter Le Neve Esq* (London, 1731); Andrea Turner, 'The Best Laid Plans: Peter le Neve and his Misappropriated Manuscripts', *Genealogists' Magazine*, vol. 27 (2002), 208–213; David Stoker, 'Martin, Thomas (1697–1771)', *Oxford Dictionary of National Biography*.

10 *A Catalogue of the . . . Collection of Manuscripts of Thomas Martin . . . Which will be sold by Auction by S. Baker and G. Leigh . . . On Wednesday, April 28, 1773*; David Stoker, 'Fenn, Sir John (1739–1794)', *Oxford Dictionary of National Biography*.

11 Other manuscripts acquired from Frere in 1866 include Additional MSS 27401–6 and 27443–55, the latter of which includes Paston letters and correspondence of Sir John Fenn. See *Catalogue of Additions to the Manuscripts in the British Museum in the years MDCCCLIV–MDCCCLXXV*, vol. 2 (London, 1877), p. 316.

12 Additional MS 27407, fol. 4, 'Vpon the death of Anne of Denmark' ('Braue soul thou hast prevaild, heauen hath its owne') and 'Epitapth' ('Here lyes Iames his true gemm the eies delight'); *Forest of Varieties*, p. 73.

13 Additional MS 27407, fol. 7 ('When first myne eyes thy hea'nly eyes did see') and fol. 153 ('Fayre heau'nly one whome moste my soule adores'). For North's hand see his commonplace book, Oxford, Bodleian Library, North MS adds. e. 1.

14 There are also: two 'accrostiches sur le nom du tres noble, et tres illustre Seigneur Monseigneur NORTHE, baron' by P: De Verzignoll (Additional MS 27408, fol. 110); 'An Epistle Congratulating the Kings amendment In his Sickness the 28th of March. 1619 originally addressed to my Lord North' (Additional MS 27407, fols 63–4, the epistle beginning 'The Ides of our good Caesars malladies'); a Latin epitaph on Roger North, the third Lord's brother, with an English translation (Additional MS 27407, fol. 6, 'Inferiore nuper Borealis in orbe Coruscans', 'The starr of late that shinde in North in this our sphere belowe'); and a copy of a verse epistle to Ben Jonson dating from 1610 that was sent to North (Add. 27407, fol. 8, 'When I, with busie thoughtes, in house of sleep').

15 This poem is discussed in Gabriel Heaton, 'Performing Gifts: The manuscript circulation of Elizabethan and early Stuart court entertainments' (unpublished doctoral thesis, University of Cambridge, 2003), pp. 116–18.

16 BL, Additional MS 27407, fols 127–28, 154–5.

17 Brief biographies of the two men can be found in the *Oxford Dictionary of National Biography*; for Townshend see also Chambers, pp. ix–xxxv; for North see also Dale B. J. Randell, *Gentle Flame: The Life and Verse of Dudley, Fourth Lord North* (Durham, NC, 1983), pp. 10–27.

18 North was the dedicatee of Nicholas Breton's *An Excellent poeme, vpon the longing of a blessed heart* (London, 1601), and of New Haven, Yale University, Beinecke Library, MS 394, a Breton holograph of three prose dialogues. He was one of the several dedicatees of two translations by A. Darcie: Camden's *Annales* (London, 1625), and Pierre Du Moulin's *A Preparation to suffer for the gospell of Jesus Christ* (London, 1623).

19 The only sustained study of North's poetry remains Robert J. Parsons, 'Autobiographical and Archetypal Elements in the Verse of the Third Lord North' (unpublished doctoral thesis, Duke University, 1980).

20 In addition to the poetic separates noted above, the North papers included two Daniel manuscripts that may have belonged to the third Lord, although John Pitcher suggests that these manuscripts derived from James Montagu, whose sister married the fourth Lord North, see his *Samuel Daniel: the Brotherton Manuscript: A Study*

in Authorship (Leeds, 1981), pp. 11–12. *The Forest of Varieties* includes texts addressed to such figures as Lady Mary Wroth (pp. 1–6) and Sir John Suckling (p. 216).

21 'The Autobiography of the Hon. Roger North', in *The Lives of the Norths*, ed. A. Jessop, 3 vols (London, 1972), vol. 3, p. 68.

22 'Caule': A net.

23 'In print': in a precise manner, exactly according to convention.

24 The earliest date is gained from a note in Philadelphia, Rosenbach Museum and Library, MS 240/1, p. 82 (for this reference I am grateful to Dr Mark Bland). The general period of composition is suggested by the presence of many of these poems in North's notebook *c.*1598–1610 (Bodleian, MS North adds. e. 1, fols 25v–57v (rev.).

25 For instance, Bodleian MS North adds.e.2, p. 28.

26 These manuscripts include: San Marino, Huntington Library, MS HM 198 (Part II); Rosenbach MS 240/1; and Bodleian, MS North adds. e. 2. The last two are collections produced by an amanuensis for presentation. See also Margaret Crum, 'Poetical Manuscripts of Dudley, third Baron North', *Bodleian Library Record*, 10 (1978–82), 98–108.

27 Bodleian MS, North adds. e. 2, p. 47.

28 For an analysis of Townshend's use of fashionable women at court as emblematic of inconstancy and vanity, see Kevin Sharpe, *Criticism and Compliment: The politics of literature in the England of Charles I* (Cambridge, 1987), pp. 160–66.

29 A similar pattern of praise for an individual woman within the context of a wider condemnation of women is found in a number of Townshend's poems: for example 'Your smiles are not' (Brown, p. 23) and 'Come not to me' (Brown, pp. 26–29).

30 See Parsons; pp. 137–46.

31 Leto, the mother of Apollo (see l. 25): thus Henrietta-Maria.

32 *i.e.* Henri IV, Henrietta-Maria's father.

33 NA, SP 16/171/23.

34 *Britanniae Natalis* (Oxford, 1630); *Genethliacum illustrissimorum principum Caroli & Mariae a musis Cantabrigiensibus celebratum* (Cambridge, 1631).

35 *The Diary of John Rous*, ed. M. A. E. Green (London, 1856), p. 54.

36 Robert Herrick, *Hesperides* (London, 1648), p. 96.

37 Brown, p. 50.

38 Townshend is not providing a punning reference to Henry King since King's poem 'By Occasion of the young Prince his happy Birth' reflects upon its own delayed appearance—which it claims was a result of the author's distress, because the birth of a son is an intimation of the father's mortality.

39 Ben Jonson, *Poems*, ed. Ian Donaldson (London, 1975), p. 228. Jonson quotes Martial, *On the Spectacles*, xxxi.

40 'An Elegie' is printed in Brown, pp. 52–3. A presentation volume of elegies for Venetia Digby, BL Additional MS 30259, includes both Townshend's piece (lacking its conclusion) and Jonson's 'The Picture of the body and minde of Mistris Venetia Stanley (since Lady Digby)' (fols 1–4v) and the 'Elegie On my Muse [. . .] Lady Venetia Digby' (fols 4v–10v).

Near Neighbours: Another Early Seventeenth-Century Manuscript of *The Humorous Magistrate*

Margaret Jane Kidnie

The canon of early seventeenth-century manuscript drama was expanded in the 1980s to include five anonymous, undated, and mostly untitled plays. Four of these plays were found at Arbury Hall, the seat of the Newdigate family in Nuneaton, Warwickshire, and they are bound together as part of a miscellany that also contains poems and other pieces of writing in a variety of hands.[1] One of these plays, *The twice-chang'd Friar. A comedie*, is furnished with a title page; T. H. Howard-Hill has assigned to the others the titles of *Ghismonda and Guiscardo*, *The Humorous Magistrate*, and *The Emperor's Favourite*. The fifth play is included among the Newdigate papers housed at the Warwickshire County Record Office. Like *Ghismonda and Guiscardo*, it relates the first tale of the fourth day in Boccaccio's *Decameron*; evidently an early draft of *Ghismonda and Guiscardo*, it has been assigned the title *Glausamond and Fidelia*.[2] No edition of any of these five manuscripts has yet appeared in print.

A third, still later manuscript version of the 'Ghismonda' play was edited by Herbert G. Wright as *Ghismonda: A Seventeenth-Century Tragedy* (Manchester: Manchester University Press, 1944). The manuscript Wright edited, housed at the British Library (Add. MS. 34312), is written in a hand distinct from the two 'Ghismonda' manuscripts discovered in Warwickshire.[3] Although the manuscript is evidently scribal, its fifteen whole or partial watermarks (pillars topped with fleurs-de-lys between which are worked the descending letters 'A R' or perhaps 'A D F') match those found in the copy of the 'Ghismonda' play bound in the Arbury Hall miscellany. The hands found in the five manuscript plays associated most closely with Arbury Hall are themselves not identical, but Howard-Hill argues that certain common characteristics suggest a single scribe 'who was well-schooled in both the secretary and Italian hands but who consciously varied his [*sic*] handwriting during the time the manuscripts were written . . . Despite the doubts that may reasonably arise when two manuscripts are placed together, it is much more difficult—impossible I must say now—to argue that these manuscripts derive from two or more hands than to believe they originate from a single one'.[4] The provenance of the manuscripts suggested a possible starting-place for a search for an author, and on the basis of what he describes as a 'diversity' of hand shared among the playscripts and personal papers comprised of three signed letters and a parliamentary diary, Howard-Hill attributed the plays to John Newdigate III (1600–42).[5]

It now emerges that the 'Ghismonda' play is not the only drama associated with the Arbury Hall collection to survive in multiple manuscript versions. In 2004, a team of researchers at the University of Calgary in Alberta, Canada—Jacqueline Jenkins and Mary Polito, with graduate students Amy Britton and J. Sebastien Windle—began editing an anonymous, untitled, and undated manuscript play housed in the university's Special Collections. According to the document's cover sheet, written and signed by its purchaser, Edgar Osborne, the manuscript was found by the collector in 1947 at the 'Watnall Hall Sale'.[6] The play was bought by the University of Calgary in 1972 as part of a collection, according to the university's Special Collections website, of 'British manuscript documents collected by E. Osborne relating to a variety of topics. Includes ballads, letters, play, parliamentary documents, speeches, petitions and applications for letters patent'.[7] In April, 2005, to coincide with the completion of the transcription, the research team at Calgary organized a one-day symposium to discuss the manuscript and their findings, and the proceedings closed with a performance of the play, staged by the Department of Drama, advertised as *Marriage upon Marriage, or, As I Told You Before . . .*.[8] Invited to speak at the symposium, and so provided in advance with a facsimile of the manuscript and its transcript, I recognized the play (hereafter described as the Osborne manuscript) as another version of the Arbury Hall manuscript known as *The Humorous Magistrate*.

The play in its different manuscript versions is a comedy set in rural England. Master Thrifty, the 'humorous magistrate' whose constant repetition of the tag-line 'as I told you before' suggested a subtitle to the Calgary researchers, has a marriageable daughter, Constance. Constance is in love with the dapper Christopher Spruce, son to Mistress Mumble, a rich widow who is hard of hearing. With the help of Master Wild, a gambler and friend to Spruce, Thrifty's housekeeper, Jennet, is made drunk on confets, and Spruce and Constance elope. Once in the woods, the lovers are set upon by thieves and separated. Constance happens upon some shepherds in the midst of a Lord of Misrule celebration, and the King of Shepherds agrees to lead her to the home of Master Welcome, Spruce's uncle, where she is eventually reunited with her future husband. Thrifty punishes his negligent housekeeper after learning of his daughter's flight by revealing to her husband that Thrifty has cuckolded him, and by forcing Jennet to draw a cart across the stage (deliberately inverting the shaming practice whereby women were forced to ride or follow a cart around the village as the penalty for disruptive behaviour). Shortly thereafter, Mumble effects a reconciliation between her son and Thrifty by agreeing to take the Justice of the Peace as her third husband. A third match is clapped up in the final scene when Wild and Sophia, Mumble's daughter, announce that they, too, have fallen in love and wish to marry.

These two manuscripts are 'near neighbours' in that they offer related, yet distinct, texts of the play. The Osborne manuscript, with stab marks in the left margin that indicate it was once bound (PLATE 1), is written in folio with its leaves numbered 1–26; an additional preliminary leaf, unnumbered and blank on the verso, lists 'The Persons of the play'. Apollonia Steele, Special Collections Librarian at the University of Calgary, discovered in the document two watermark designs. The first of these is of a pot on which is worked in two rows the letters 'C | A B'. The second watermark design found in the Osborne copy is of an anchor with the letters 'I' and 'G' suspended from the crossbar, one letter falling on either side of the anchor's shaft.[9] A pot design is also found in the nine watermarks that survive in the Arbury Hall manuscript, the two sets of watermarks differing in their lettering and placement of the handle ('R H' is worked on the pot in place of 'C | A B').[10] A second watermark figure of two pillars rising to a bunch of grapes appears on the Arbury manuscript's two terminal leaves, one of which includes the epilogue, while the other is blank (ff. 143–4). The centre of the watermark is lost in the gutter, but the design otherwise seems closely to resemble Heawood's figure 3492 (reproduced from a Lancastrian manuscript dated 1640).[11] This anomalous watermark may indicate that this epilogue was a late addition to the manuscript; I shall return to its potential significance in the context of authorship and date.

The Osborne hand, penned in light brown ink, is mixed secretary, with the list of characters, speech prefixes, and stage directions written in italic. Stage directions are either centred, or ranged to the right of the dialogue, and for the most part neatly set apart with a half-bracket or enclosed in a box. Examination of the manuscript reveals only a few

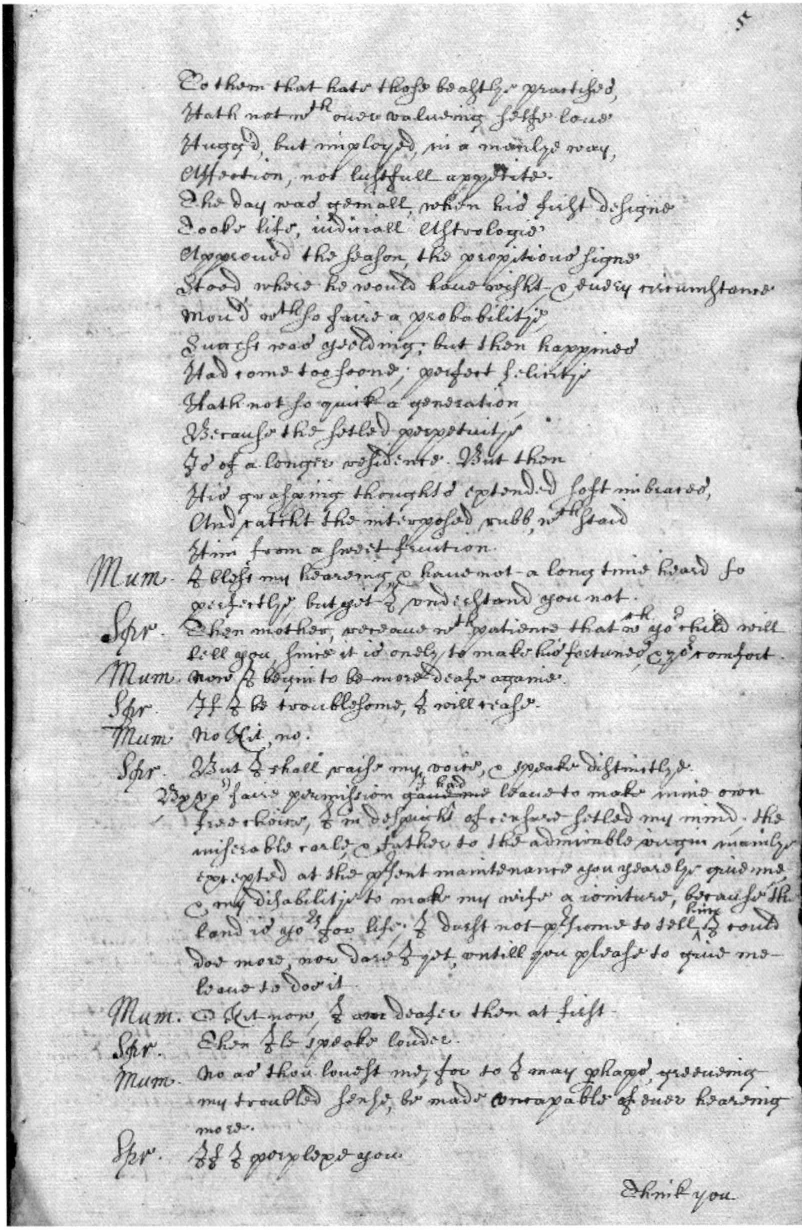

To them that hate those wealthy wretches,
Hath not wth over valuing selfe love
Hugg'd, but imploy'd, in a manlye way,
Affection, not lustfull appetite.
The day was ominall, when his first designe
Tooke life, in ivriall Astrologie
Approved the season, the propitious signe
Stood where he would have wisht, & every circumstance
Mov'd wth so faire a probabilitye,
Sucesse was yeelding; but then happined
Had come too soone; perfect felicitye
Hath not so quick a generation
Because the setled perpetuitye
Is of a longer residence. But then
His grasping thoughts extended soft embraces,
And ratcht the interposed rubb, wch stayd
Him from a sweet fruition.

Mum. I blesse my hearing & have not a long time heard so perfectlye but yet I understand you not.

Spr. Then mother, wch we have wth patience that wth yor child will tell you, since it is onely to make his fortunes, & yor comfort.

Mum. Now I begin to be more deafe againe.

Spr. If I be troublesome, I will cease.

Mum. No Kit, no.

Spr. But I shall raise my voice, & speake distinctlye. By yor faire permission gave me leave to make mine owne free choice, I in despight of richer settled my mind. the miserable earle, & father to the admirable virgin mainly excepted at the present maintenance you yearelye give me & my disabilitye to make my wife a iointure, because the land is yors for life. I durst not presume to sell, ye king could doe more, nor dare I yet, untill you please to give me leave to doe it.

Mum. O Kit now I am deafer then at first.

Spr. Then Ile speake lowder.

Mum. No as thou lovest me, for so I may perhaps preserving my troubled sense, be made uncapable of ever hearing more.

Spr. If I perplexe you.

Thank you

PLATE 1. *A page in the Osborne manuscript of* The Humorous Magistrate*: Calgary, University of Calgary, Osborne Collection, MsC 132, fol. 5r (Original page size 313 × 205mm.) Reproduced by permission of the Edgar Osborne Collection.*

deletions and insertions; on the whole, this is a tidy, carefully presented transcript. There is evidence of corrected eye-skip and in one instance a stage direction subsequently inserted at the top of the page (these can both be seen in PLATE 2); there is also the odd interlined word or short phrase that suggests minor revision. While this manuscript could easily serve as a playbook, it shows little evidence of having been used for performance. In particular, although the late addition of 'aside' to one direction clarifies that the character is to stand apart rather than exit ('Spruce goes one way [aside], they another'; f. 16v), there are neither marks in the left margin nor duplicated stage directions that might suggest the work of a bookkeeper.[12]

The Arbury manuscript, by striking contrast, is heavily worked over. A large chunk of dialogue in the opening scene is cancelled with a series of diagonal and vertical lines (see PLATE 3), and single words throughout the manuscript as well as long passages are scored through and often replaced with densely interlined new material. There is also at least one revised false start. The writer initially brought the penultimate scene to a close with the entrance of the servant, Godfry, to announce the arrival of new guests; this ending is then crossed out in order to continue the action with a long set piece in which a group of characters tries to decide the thing that angers a woman most. The scene in this modified form concludes with the introduction of a slightly revised version of Godfry's earlier entrance. Thus the manuscript, at least in part, shows an author in the process of composition, an inference supported elsewhere in the document by a boxed note that instructs that something (probably a speech or short passage), is 'Hitherto corected in this | Looke from this place | in the other.' (106v: PLATE 4). On the reverse of the same page a marginal note in the left margin running vertically alongside the dialogue reads, 'Dr S. this speech not so cleare & perspicuous'. This note, seeming to invite response from a reader, reinforces the likelihood that this is a draft version. Howard-Hill speculates that this comment—like the first note, in the same hand as the dialogue—is addressed to John III's life-long friend and correspondent, Gilbert Sheldon (future Archbishop of Canterbury), who graduated from Oxford as Doctor of Divinity in 1634.[13]

However, alongside such evidence of original composition in the Arbury manuscript, one also finds copying errors. The phrase 'take her away' near the end of the third act, for example, is wrongly given to Jennet, the housekeeper, who is pleading with her employer for mercy; this misassigned command is crossed out and written out again on the next line as the opening words of Mr Thrifty's concluding speech (f. 124). On the next page, an overlooked short line spoken by Godfry

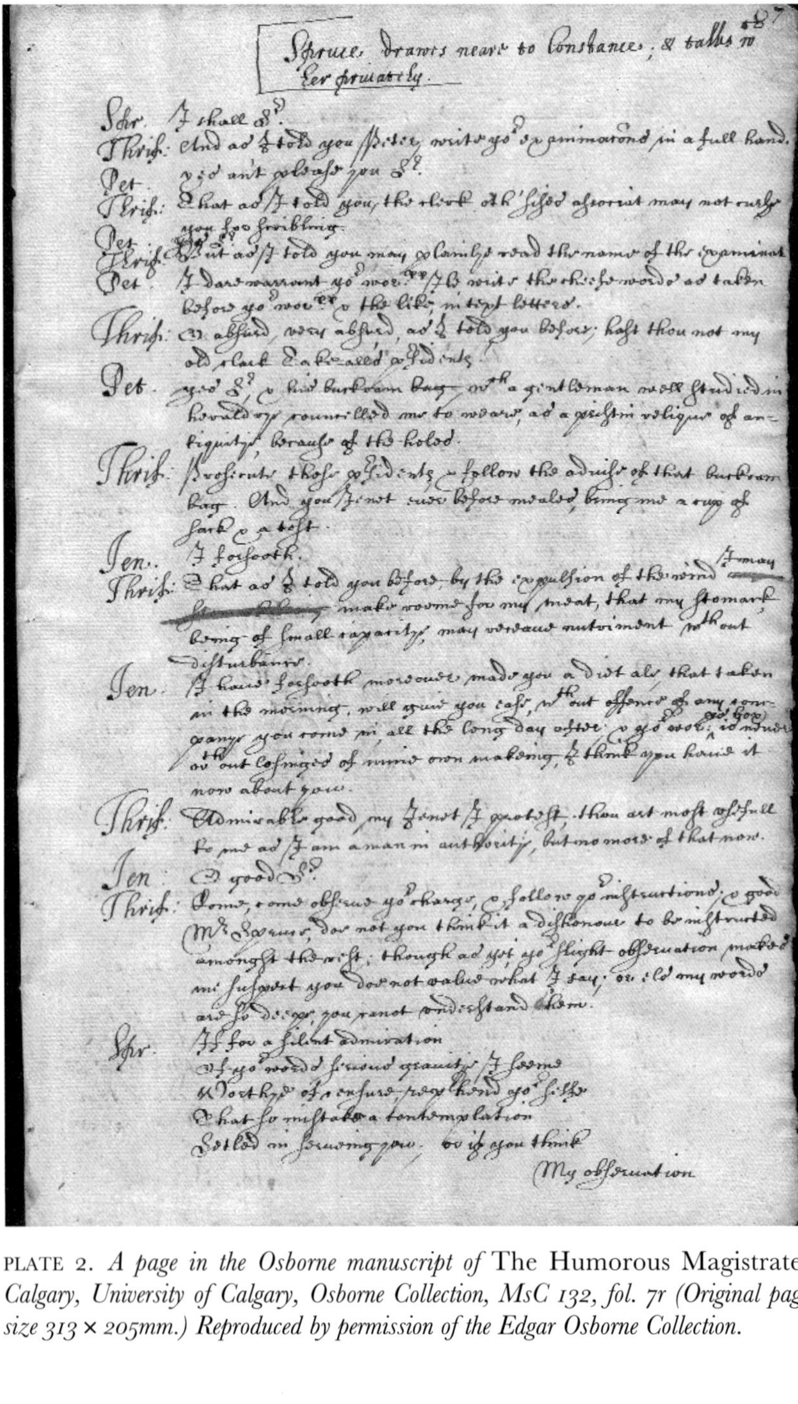

Spruce drawes neare to Constance; & talks wth her privately.

Spr. I shall Sr.

Thrif: And as I told you Peter, write yor examinations in a full hand.

Pet. Yes and't please you Sr.

Thrif: That as I told you, the clerk oth' sessions may not curse you for scribling.

Pet. Yes Sr.

Thrif. But as I told you may plainly read the name of the examinant

Pet. I dare warrant yor worp, Ile write the chiefe words as taken before yor worp & the like, in text letters.

Thrif: O absurd, very absurd, as I told you before; hast thou not my old black Leather'd precedents?

Pet. Yes Sr, & his burckram bag, wch a gentleman well studied in heraldry counselled me to weare, as a speciall relique of antiquity, because of the holes.

Thrif. Prosecute those precedents & follow the advise of that burckram bag. And you Jenet ere before meales, bring me a cup of sack & a tost.

Jen. I forsooth.

Thrif: That as I told you before, by the expulsion of the wind I may make roome for my meat, that my stomack being of small capacity, may receave nutriment wthout disturbance.

Jen. I have forsooth moreover made you a diet ale, that taken in the morning, will give you ease, wthout offence of any company you come in, all the long day after & yor worp, is never wthout Cushions of mine own making, I think you have it now about you.

Thrif. Admirable good, my Jenet I protest, thou art most usefull to me as I am a man in authority, but no more of that now.

Jen: O good Sr.

Thrif: Come, come observe yor charge, & follow yor instructions; & good Mr Spruce, doe not you think it a dishonour to be instructed amongst the rest; though as yet yor slight observation makes me suspect you doe not value what I say; or else my words are so deepe, you canot understand them.

Spr. Its for a silent admiration
Of yor words serious gravity I seeme
Worthy of censure, pray blame yor selfe
That so mistake a contemplation
Setled in serving you. or if you think
(My observation

PLATE 2. *A page in the Osborne manuscript of* The Humorous Magistrate*: Calgary, University of Calgary, Osborne Collection, MsC 132, fol. 7r (Original page size 313 × 205mm.) Reproduced by permission of the Edgar Osborne Collection.*

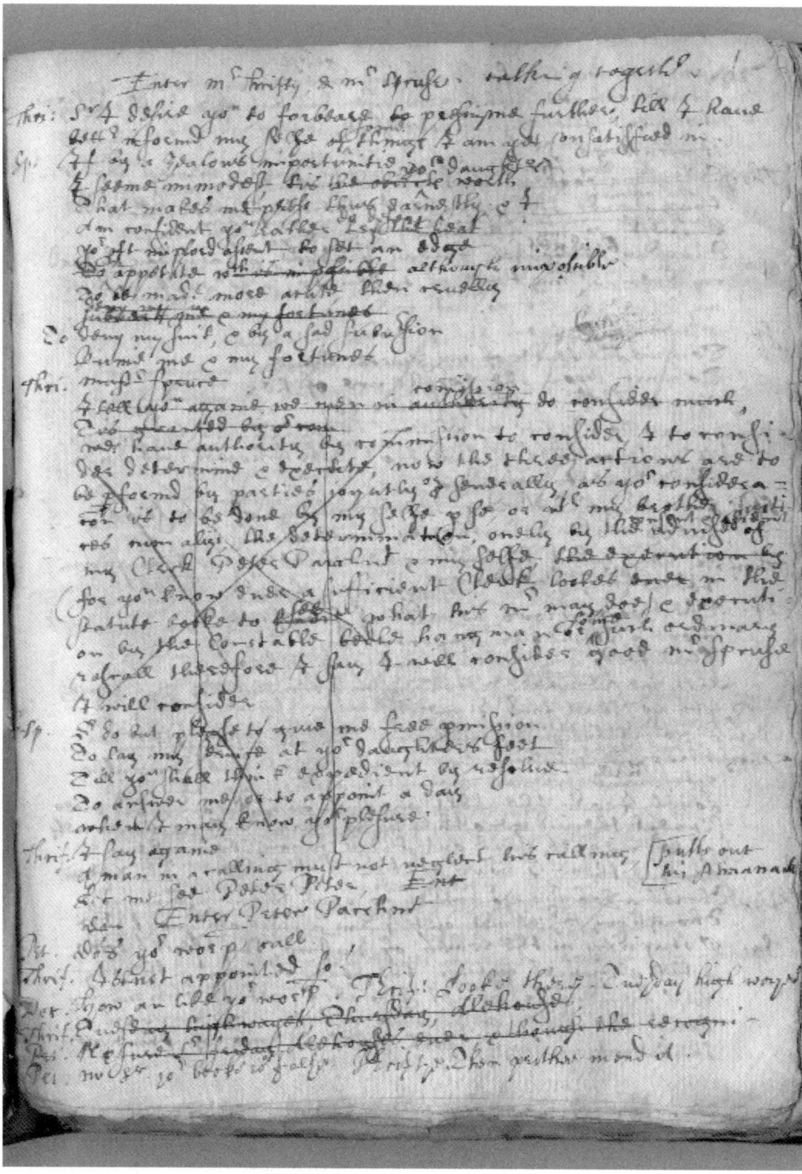

PLATE 3. *A page of the text of* The Humorous Magistrate *in the Arbury Hall miscellany: Warwick, Warwickshire County Record Office,* MS *A414, fol. 105r (Original page size 200 × 150mm.) Reproduced by permission of Lord Daventry.*

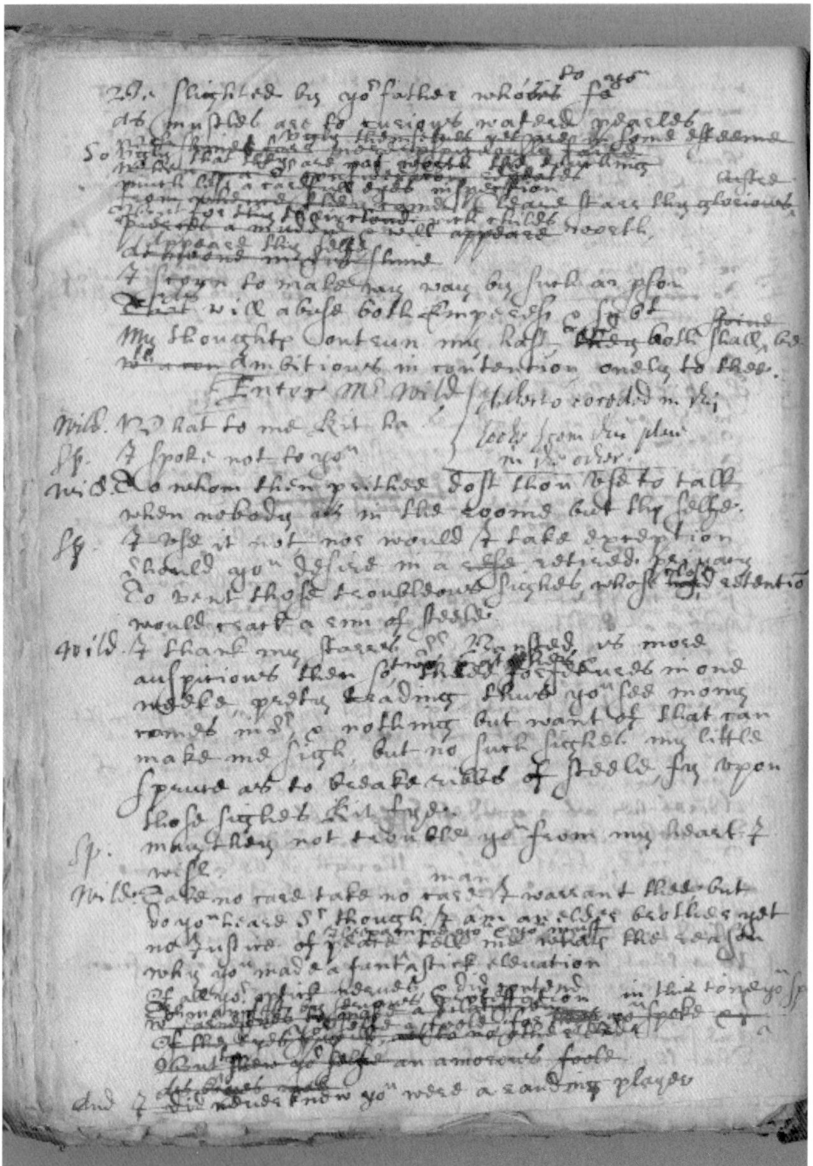

PLATE 4. *An opening of the text of* The Humorous Magistrate *in the Arbury Hall miscellany: Warwick, Warwickshire County Record Office,* MS *A414, fols 106v–7r (Original page size 200 × 150mm.) Reproduced by permission of Lord Daventry.*

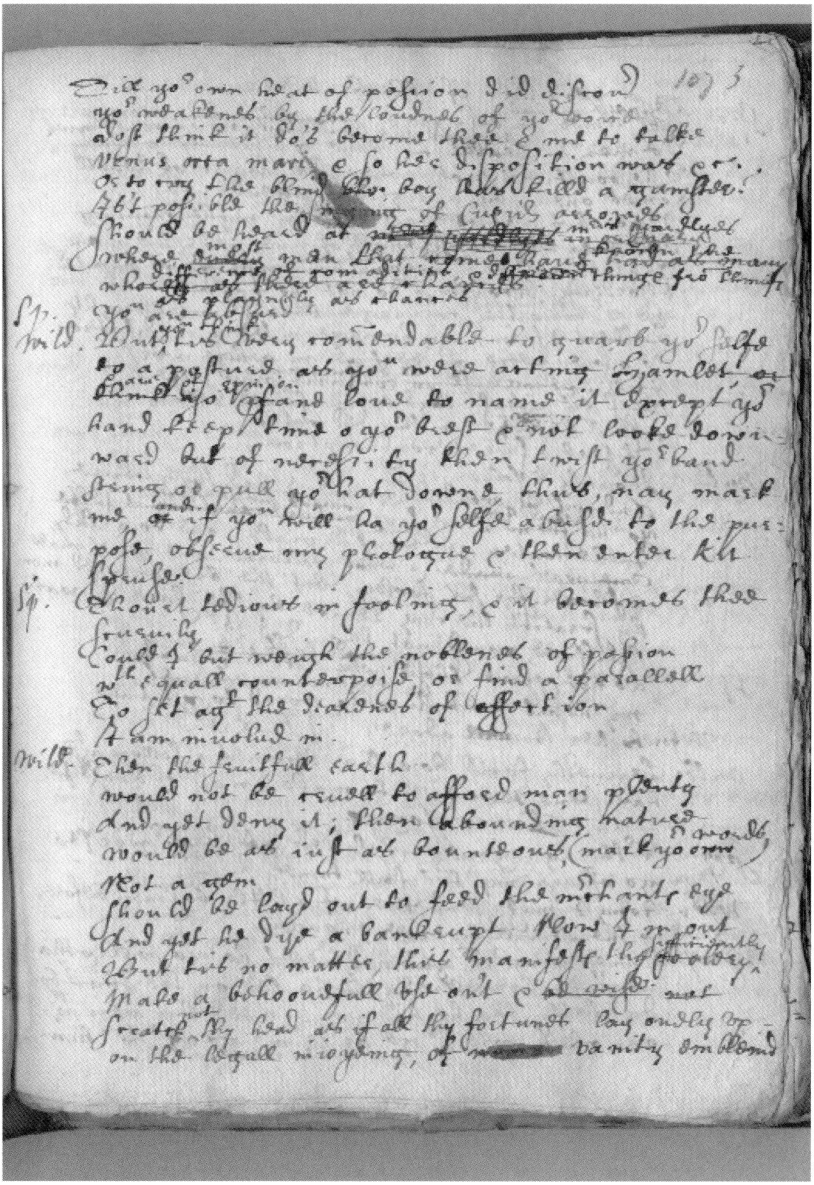

Did yor owne heat of passion did discover
yor weaknes by the loudnes of yor voice
dost think it does become thee & me to talke
Venus orta mari & so her disposition was &c.
Or to say the blind boy cann kill a gamster
Is't possible the singing of Cupids arrowes
should be heard at [illegible]
where [illegible] man that comes [illegible]
[illegible]
[illegible]

Sp.

Wild. Was't not very commendable to guard yor selfe
to a posture as you were acting Hamlet or
[illegible] yor stand loue to name it [illegible] yor
hand kept time o yor brest & not looke down-
ward but of necessity then twist yor band
string or pull yor hat downe thus, nay mark
me and if you will ha yor selfe abusde to the purpose, observe my prologue & then enter kit
Spruse.

Sp. O how't tedious in fooling, & it becomes thee
seriously
Could I but weigh the noblenes of passion
wth equall counterpoise or find a parallell
To set agt the darknes of affection
I am involvd in.

Wild. Then the fruitfull earth
would not be [illegible] to afford man plenty
and yet deny it; then abounding nature
would be as iust as bounteous (mark yor owne words)
Not a gem
should be layd out to feed the merchants eye
And yet he dye a bankrupt. How I run out
But tis no matter, this manifests thy foolery
make a [illegible] out & [illegible] not
scratch not thy head as if all thy fortunes lay onely upon the [illegible] enioying, of [illegible] vanity [illegible]

('you for sooth') during a sequence of dialogue between this servant and Mistress Mumble led to three misassigned speech prefixes. The error was corrected by writing 'you for sooth.' in place of the line wrongly given to Godfry, then squeezing a speech prefix and Mumble's inserted reply to the immediate right of this line, and finally using the space deep in the gutter of the page to reverse the next two speech prefixes from 'Mum' to 'God' and 'Godf' to 'Mum' (f. 125). The Arbury manuscript thus seems to offer a full draft of a play in progress, with the revising author functioning as his or her own copyist; the Osborne version, by contrast, preserves the text in a more polished state.

Certain inconsistencies between the two hands may point to a complex process of transmission—once again, the manuscripts are not identical, but rather, near neighbours. The hands found in the two copies of *The Humorous Magistrate* date to around the second quarter of the seventeenth century, and are similar in their use of a secretary script through which is scattered italic forms; perhaps most noticeably today, the letter *h* in both manuscripts takes its modern shape, not displaying the secretary descender (compare this discussion of hands to PLATES 1–4).[14] They also share a predisposition to add a flourish, resembling a miniscule *u*, to the top right corners of secretary capitals *G*, *S*, and sometimes *F*, and, in what is an unexpected throwback to sixteenth century letter forms, both hands show a marked tendency to place a small dot in the centre of secretary capitals *O*, *B*, *W*, *P*, and *V*. Other traits, however, distinguish the two hands. Terminal *s* in the Arbury Hall manuscript is formed as a loop, the ends of which intersect to form a cross at the top of the letter; the Osborne manuscript, by contrast, prefers a form that looks like an *o* with a hook at the upper right corner. The Osborne hand writes the crossed majuscule secretary *I* using a single continuous pen stroke, whereas the Arbury scribe lifts the pen to form the letter with two separate strokes; majuscule *C* in Osborne, but not in Arbury, looks like an *O* crossed with a horizontal bar; the loop of the miniscule *d* in the Osborne manuscript shows an exaggerated lean to the left, where the same letter in the Arbury manuscript is smaller and more upright; and the final ascender of majuscule *W* flips to the left in the Arbury manuscript and to the right in the Osborne manuscript.

Any comparison of handwriting is complicated by an awareness that writers sometimes alter their hand, consciously or unwittingly, either over time or in different circumstances, a possibility Howard-Hill argues is in fact realized in the five Arbury plays. It should be noted, however, that the diversity of hand Howard-Hill identifies is extremely localised. Specifically, although the hands in the two 'Ghismonda' plays found among the Newdigate papers are quite similar to each other, they are noticeably different from the hands used to write *The Humorous Magistrate*, *The Emperor's Favourite*, and *The twice-chang'd Friar*. For example, the 'Ghismonda' hands strongly favour a secretary *h*, and a long *s* which, when hooked by a ligature to letters *t* and *h*, makes no use of loops on the ascender or descender; in the other plays, secretary *h* is not prevalent, and the slashing long *s* is rarely, if ever, encountered. There are other factors which mark the 'Ghismonda' play within the Arbury miscellany as the odd one out. Dates on items elsewhere in the collection show that it must have been gathered and bound after 1702. The four plays are gathered together at the back of the book, with *Ghismonda and Guiscardo* followed by *The Humorous Magistrate*, *The Emperor's Favourite*, and *The twice-chang'd Friar*, in that order. *Ghismonda and Guiscardo*, however, is separated from the other drama by a leaf, blank on the verso, on which is written the word 'Plays' in the upper right corner; the recto of the next leaf is also blank, with *The Humorous Magistrate* starting on the verso with a list of characters and a prologue. Watermark evidence further links two of the final three plays gathered in the collection, with the pot inscribed with the letters 'R H' found in *The Humorous Magistrate* turning up again in *The Emperor's Favourite*.[15]

Bibliographical analysis would thus suggest that the last three items in the miscellany, with a cover reading 'Plays', already existed as an independent unit prior to the creation of the existing manuscript collection. This is not necessarily inconsistent with the view that the five Newdigate plays (including the 'Ghismonda' play not bound in the miscellany) were written by one author who made use of a variety of hands. Indeed, an interpretation of single authorship is reinforced by the evidence of an unsigned commonplace book housed at the Bodleian, Oxford, attributed by Vivienne Larminie to John Newdigate III, in which one finds two sustained pieces of writing that display precisely the same diversity of hand.[16] But if these hands actually belong to one author, the shift in style happened specifically in the gap of time that fell between the work on 'Ghismonda' and the burst of creative effort that gave us the other three plays.

By contrast, while there is a possibility that the particular and consistent patterns of handwriting one finds in the Osborne and Arbury Hall manuscripts of *The Humorous Magistrate* might belong to a single writer, they seem more likely to suggest two writers whose habits were perhaps shaped by a common exemplar.[17] Although habits of spelling as a potential sign of authorship must be treated with caution since in this period one can find marked inconsistencies even within a single manuscript, it is worth mentioning that there is an exclusive preference in the Osborne manuscript for 'Spruce' as the spelling of the name of the play's romantic lead (it appears forty-two times), as opposed to the Arbury manuscript's strong preference for 'Spruse' (this spelling is used forty-one times, with the other appearing just ten times). The Osborne scribe also avoids writing 'you' with a superscript *u*, a form strongly preferred by the Arbury scribe, and signals an elided *m* or *n* by suspending above the previous letter a shape resembling a large *c*, rather than the lightly hooked bar found in the Arbury manuscript.

There is, in fact, a good match for the Osborne hand to be found in the Arbury miscellany, but not in the drama. A one-page poem that precedes the plays, entitled 'To a Poet whose m^{ris} was painted' (the uncorrected title reads 'Vpon a painted gentlewoman') and dated August, 1637, exhibits the same distinctive scribal characteristics one finds in the Osborne manuscript (see PLATE 5).[18] Moreover, falling into the gutter of this leaf is the bottom half of the same pillars-and-grapes watermark that appears on the two terminal leaves of the Arbury Hall copy of *The Humorous Magistrate*. The realisation that these two writers had shared access to the same stock of paper is useful in terms of suggesting a date for the play. A reference in the fourth act of *The Humorous Magistrate* to a 'Carolus', a coin minted after the accession of Charles I in 1625, suggests the play's earliest possible date of completion. If one assumes that the Arbury epilogue was a late addition to the manuscript, and that the writer of 'To a Poet' likely dated the poem to the month and year it was copied out (rather than to a possible earlier date of composition), the combination of hands and watermarks found in the Arbury miscellany and Osborne copy serves to establish an outer limit for the composition of *The Humorous Magistrate* to near or shortly after 1637.[19]

If the Osborne hand is not authorial, then changes to the manuscript that appear to be revisions rather than corrections become difficult to account for. There are a number of instances of interlined material that might fall into the category of revision. For example, the word 'but' is struck out and 'for' written above it in the clause '~~but~~ [for] sighes are onely vsefull for a woman' (f. 2v), and at the beginning of Act 2, the phrase 'all this time of the yeare' is inserted to clarify the excellence of whey (f. 6).[20] The insertion of 'By' in the left margin, a space usually reserved for speech prefixes, and 'I had' interlined with a caret above 'gave me', which has been crossed out, transforms one of Spruce's sentences to read, '[By] your faire permission ~~gaue me~~ [I had] leaue to make mine own free choice' (f. 5: PLATE 1). This sort of free alteration is not typically associated with copyists, but the sample of inserted words is too small and unsustained to determine conclusively whether the new

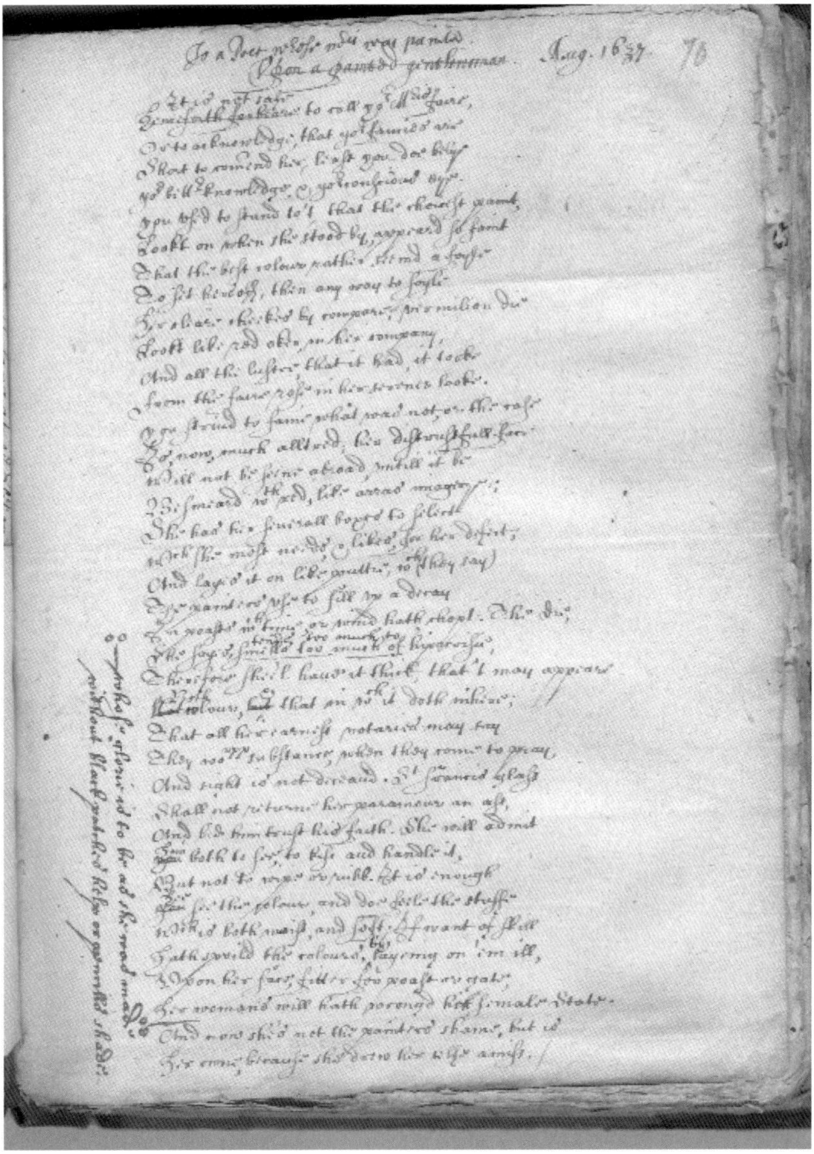

PLATE 5. *A page in the Arbury Hall miscellany with the poem 'To a Poet whose m[ris] was painted . . . Aug. 1637': Warwick, Warwickshire County Record Office,* MS *A414, fol. 70r (Original page size 202 × 152mm.) Reproduced by permission of Lord Daventry.*

material is in the same hand as the rest of the text. The finished transcript might have been read over by the author who introduced in his or her own hand a few corrections and alterations. Alternatively, it seems possible that such revisions might have been contributed by one or more collaborators (one of whom may have copied out the Osborne manuscript) who either worked with the author on the development of the script or altered the script subsequently.[21]

The number of *currente calamo* changes in the Arbury manuscript, especially when compared to the relative cleanness of the Osborne manuscript, suggests a clear direction of revision from the former to the latter. This likelihood is further reinforced by the number of times the Osborne text picks up readings introduced as revisions to the Arbury material. For instance, to return briefly to the penultimate scene, the extended gag about what angers a woman most—introduced to the Arbury manuscript through revision—is not reproduced in the Osborne text. In its place is an enactment by Thrifty of the way a sexually satisfied woman the morning after her marriage will follow after her husband like 'a hen pigeon after . . . her cock' (f. 23v). However, despite returning the scene to a shape that more closely resembles the Arbury text in its first, unrevised, iteration, the Osborne copy closes by following verbatim the Arbury's revised version of Godfry's entrance. The obvious suggestion is that the Osborne scribe was working from copy that derived from the surviving Arbury manuscript.

It seems unlikely, however, that the Arbury manuscript was the immediate source for the Osborne copy. It seems curious, for instance, that neither the prologue nor epilogue with which the Arbury manuscript is furnished survives in the Osborne version. There are also a number of major structural differences between the texts, traces of which are not discerned in the Arbury version: Mr Wild's man—the Scottish horse trainer, Jony—is revised out of the Osborne action; Wild's sudden, fourth-act courtship of Spruce's sister, Sophia, is split over two scenes in the Osborne version; and Mr Strife, a second suitor to Mistress Mumble, is seen off by Thrifty in the Osborne text at the end of Act 2, whereas in the Arbury version the Strife business is concluded as late as the fifth act after Mumble and Thrifty are already married, prompting threats of lawsuits for breach of promise. There are also sets of local verbal changes that point to an intervening version. To take just one example, in the opening scene of the second act Thrifty reproves Spruce for courting Constance, rather than attending him while he gives his servants instruction. Thrifty's speech, as it appears in the Arbury manuscript, is heavily worked over with both deleted and interlined material:

Thrif. ~~Onely to me Iennet onely to me as I told~~
~~yo^{u} Iennet~~ [Come come], obserue your charge & ~~prosecute~~ [follow] your
instructions; & good m^{r} Spruse as I told
yo^{u}, yo^{u} obserue not the lecture I ~~gaue~~ [giue] to
my seruantes but as I told yo^{u} yo^{u} are som=
[yo^{u} truss y^{e} quarry before yo^{u} haue]
what ~~busy~~ [nimble], S^{r}, ~~yo^{u} are yong, & so was I, & the~~
[made a faire stooping, & I assure yo^{u} S^{r} I am the]
~~practick gone I now content my selfe wth~~
[only man that must cry whoo whoop ~~S^{r}~~]
~~repetition of the theorick, I assure yo^{u} S^{r} it~~
~~is I must make or marr yor marketes, & though~~
~~I can tell in what place~~ & if yo^{u} neglect me
S^{r} as I told yo^{u} authority will think it fitt in
discretion to ~~punisth~~ punish yo^{u} pro contemptu (f. 114).

Significantly, while preserving the broad sense of the passage, the Osborne manuscript departs from the Arbury text in its revised state after the first two lines to introduce yet another version of Thrifty's speech:

Thrif. Come, come obserue your charge, & follow your instructions; & good
Mr Spruce, doe not you think it a dishonour to be instructed
amongst the rest; though as yet your slight obseruation makes
me suspect you doe not value what I say; or els my words
are so deepe, you canot vnderstand 'hem (f. 7).

Osborne's obvious partial dependency on the Arbury manuscript, combined with its substantial structural and verbal changes and refinements, strongly indicates that at least one stage of revision, perhaps more, lies between these two extant manuscripts. There is also the possibility that there is not a purely unidirectional transmission of text, the Osborne scribe perhaps instead having access to, and consulting, multiple versions of the play. This is suggested by a surprising copying error that appears in both manuscripts. In the middle of the fourth act, Constance enters with two characters known as Cruch and his wife. Cruch explains, 'I know not the way', and the next speech—'Nor yo^{u} old mother?'—is in both manuscripts wrongly assigned to Cruch's wife. In order to correct the mistake, the Arbury text smudges 'old' and crosses out 'wom:' in order to interline 'Con:' (f. 131v: PLATE 6), while the Osborne text alters 'Cr.' to 'Con' and smudges 'wife.' (f. 19: PLATE 7). Misattributed and misplaced speech prefixes are not uncommon in either of these manuscripts—this is perhaps further evidence of the

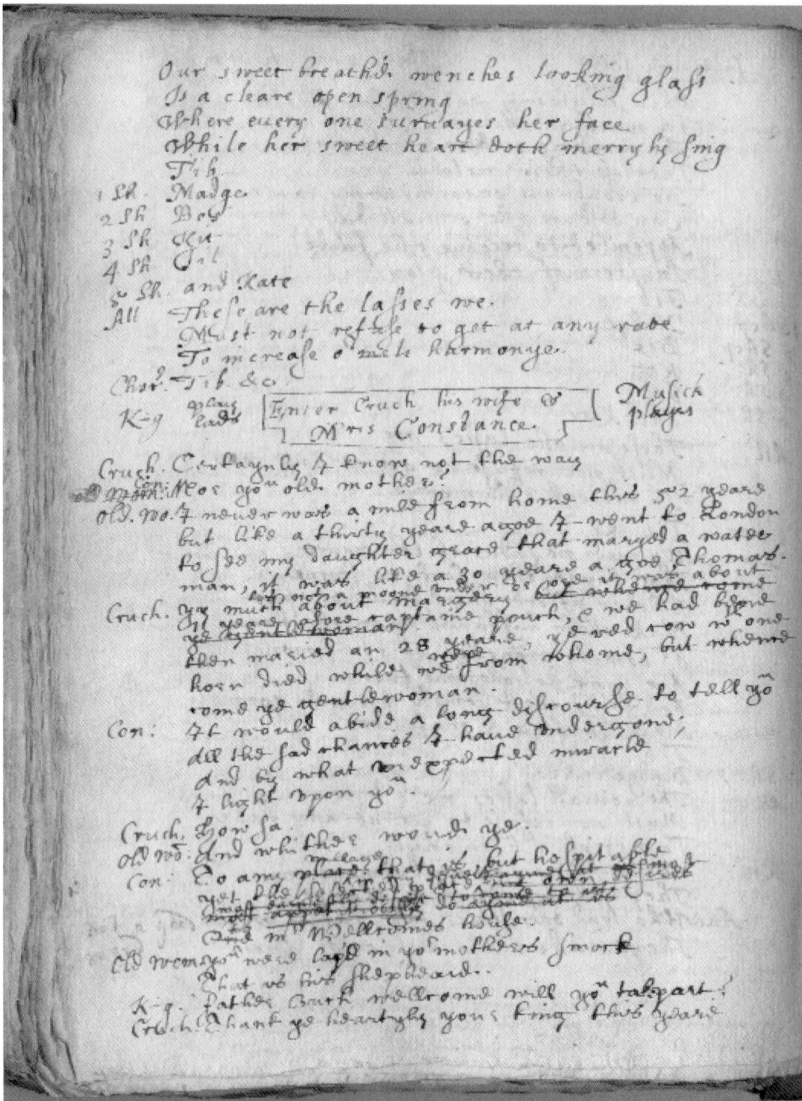

Our sweet breath'd wenches looking glass
Is a cleare open spring
Where every one surveyes her face
While her sweet heart doth merryly sing
Tib.
1 Sh. Madge
2 Sh Bes
3 Sh Kit
4 Sh Gil
5 Sh. and Kate
All These are the lasses we
Must not refuse to get at any rate
To increase our mile harmonye.
Chor. Tib &c.
K-g [Enter Cruch his wife & Mrs Constance.] Musick playes
Cruch. Certaynly I know not the way
Con: Nor yo^u old mother?

PLATE 6. *A page of the text of* The Humorous Magistrate *in the Arbury Hall miscellany: Warwick, Warwickshire County Record Office, MS A414, fol. 131v (Original page size 200 × 150mm.) Reproduced by permission of Lord Daventry.*

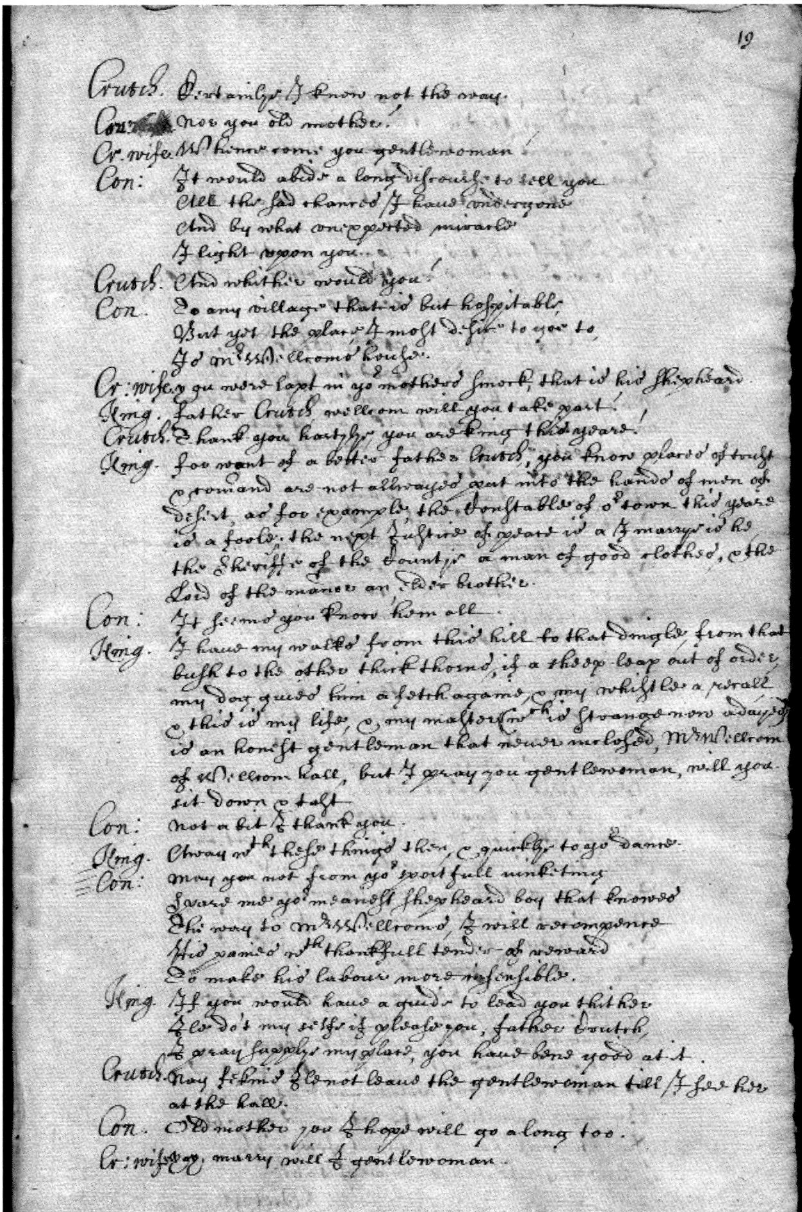
19

Crutch. Certainly I know not the way.
Con: Nor you old mother!
Cr. wife. Whence come you gentlewoman!
Con: It would aske a long discourse to tell you
All the sad chances I have undergone
And by what unexpected miracle
I light upon you.
Crutch. And whither would you!
Con. To any village that is but hospitable;
But yet the place I most desire to goe to,
Is Mr Welcomes house.
Cr: wife. you were kept in yor mothers smock, that is his shepheard.
King. Father Crutch wellcom will you take part!
Crutch. I thank you hartily you are king this yeare!
King. for want of a better father Crutch, you know places of trust
& comand are not allwayes put into the hands of men of
desert, as for example, the Constable of or town this yeare
is a foole, the next Justice of peace is a knave, marry is he
the Sheriffe of the County a man of good clothes, & the
Lord of the manor an elder brother.
Con: It seems you know them all.
King. I have my walks from this hill to that dingle, from that
bush to the other thick thorne, if a sheep leap out of order,
my dog gives him a fetch againe, & my whistle a recall
& this is my life, & my master wch is strange now adays
is an honest gentleman that never meloshed, Mr Welcom
of Welcom hall, but I pray you gentlewoman, will you
sit down & tast
Con: Not a bit I thank you.
King. Away wth these things then, & quickly to yor dance.
Con: May you not from yor sportfull merriting
Spare me yor meanest shepheard boy that knowes
The way to Mr Welcoms, I will recompence
His paines wth thankfull tender of reward
To make his labour more insensible.
King. If you would have a guide to lead you thither
Ile do't my selfe if please you, father Crutch,
I pray supply my place, you have bene good at it.
Crutch. Nay sirs, I'le not leave the gentlewoman till I see her
at the hall.
Con. Old mother you I hope will go along too.
Cr: wife. Ay, marry will I gentlewoman.

PLATE 7. *A page in the Osborne manuscript of* The Humorous Magistrate*: Calgary, University of Calgary, Osborne Collection, MsC 132, fol. 19r (Original page size 313 × 205mm.) Reproduced by permission of the Edgar Osborne Collection.*

existence of a version prior to the Arbury manuscript since it was customary to add speech prefixes after writing out a page of text, a practice which occasionally led to misassignment.[22] What seems significant about this particular instance of confusion, however, is that the same error occurs in both texts at exactly the same place. A possible explanation of the coincidence could be that both manuscripts here look back to a common, no longer extant, version in which the error originally appeared.

Study of these manuscripts thus points to the likely existence at one time of four copies or partial copies of *The Humorous Magistrate* in revised or partially revised states. This is consistent with findings in the rest of the Newdigate collection of drama. In addition to the three surviving 'Ghismonda' plays already documented by Howard-Hill, extensive marginal markings throughout *The twice-chang'd Friar* accompanied by marginal comments such as 'Not this' (repeated nineteen times), 'not transcribed', and 'Hactenus' (Latin for 'no more of this') suggest that a scribal copy of a third play in the collection was likewise undertaken. What emerges from this evidence is the picture of a lively scene of creative production and transmission of dramatic texts.

The plays are probably amateur, so there is no surprise to find the texts lacking clear signs of professional performance such as a licence or playhouse markings (although the crosses and vertical lines in the left margin of *The twice-chang'd Friar*, written in an ink of different colour from that in the body of the play, might perhaps point to preparation for performance). But it seems hard to imagine that this much textual activity, drawing on the labours of multiple writers (the hand(s) in the Arbury and Osborne copies of *The Humorous Magistrate*, plus the hand that wrote the British Library scribal copy of *Ghismonda*), would be generated in the absence of staged production. While it is not inconceivable that drafts of the plays, after the manner of closet drama, were written for pleasure, and copies of the texts then circulated among family and friends, it seems potentially significant that a second miscellany in the Newdigate collection contains a manuscript copy showing alterations and revisions of Thomas Goffe's *The Raging Turk, or Bajazet the Second* (printed 1631). According to the quarto title page, this tragedy was 'vvritten by Thomas Goffe, Master of Arts, and Student of Christ-Church in *Oxford*, and Acted by the Students of the same house'. It thus seems at least feasible that the manuscript drama under discussion here might somehow be linked to a collaboration among gentlemen and students associated with the university. As Howard-Hill notes, the division of the drama into acts, and the tendency to furnish the plays with prologues and epilogues, point to a playwright who 'seems to have written with the prospect of production'.[23] That these plays were written by an author attuned to live performance is further indicated by their theatrical language and imagery, and careful attention to staging. In the Arbury version of *The Humorous Magistrate*, for instance, one finds an allusion to Shakespeare, when Wild likens the melancholy Spruce to a 'randing player' who will 'guarb' himself to a posture as though he 'were acting Hamlet' (ff. 106v–107; see PLATE 4).[24] This allusion is altered in the Osborne version to the more generalized theatrical description of Spruce as a lover 'acting' to his 'glass' (f. 2v). The provision of stage directions in all of the plays is substantial, with the Osborne manuscript's making use of the 'Exiturus' direction ('makes to exit') found in other plays in the Arbury Hall collection (albeit not in its copy of *The Humorous Magistrate*). One also finds a heavily reworked direction in the Arbury manuscript of *The Humorous Magistrate* cuing to enter '2 or 3', then '5 or 6', and finally 'as many country wenches as shepheards wth prouision' (f. 130v). This record of revision is perhaps less likely to signal closet drama than someone, perhaps the playwright, giving careful thought to the practicalities of staging a busy fourth act scene with available resources. The same direction in the Osborne version reads, 'Enter 6 countrye wenches wth prouision' (f. 18).

There is no firm evidence either to support or disprove speculation that these plays were performed in the early seventeenth century.[25] But significantly, if John Newdigate III during his possession of Arbury Hall in the 1620s and 1630s wrote the playtexts, or was somehow otherwise involved with their preparation, perhaps for instance through patronage—merely the provenance of the bulk of the manuscripts implies some kind of close connection during this period to the Newdigate estate—there was a social network in place that could have provided opportunity for performance. The Newdigates were intimates of the Burdett family at Foremark near Repton in the neighbouring county of Derbyshire. Thomas Burdett (1585–1646/7) was a member of the Warwickshire gentry who, as a result of his marriage to Jane Francis in 1602, maintained estates at both Bramcote (situated just east of Arbury Hall) and Foremark. In 1622, their daughter, Bridget, married Thomas Gresley of Drakelowe, Derbyshire (d.1642), a close friend of John and his brother, Richard, from their days at Trinity College, Oxford (1618–20).

This web of personal connections linking the Burdetts and Newdigates is relevant because Lady Jane, according to Larminie's account of her life, was a literary patron who 'gained renown as an unusually learned woman at the hub of a circle of literary-minded gentry'.[26] The sermon delivered after her death in March, 1637 by the family chaplain, Thomas Calvert, along with a selection of elegies and epitaphs written by friends and admirers, including John Newdigate III, was published in 1650 under the title *The wearie Souls wish: or, The Doves wings*. In the volume's dedicatory letter, and as Larminie argues, 'at least in partial reference to the literary circle at Foremark', Calvert describes a time, still preserved in living memory, when 'This Nation was full of feastings, Masks, and Comedies, the unruly Children of wanton peace'. Now, he continues, 'we . . . are come to act nothing but passively in sad and grave Tragedies'.[27] Calvert's reference to pre-war theatrical entertainment, albeit fleeting and imprecise, is suggestive, particularly in light of the wealth of manuscript drama from the same period housed just forty kilometres (twenty-five miles) away in the library of Arbury Hall.

Watnall Hall, located on the outskirts of Nottingham, was the Nottinghamshire seat of the Rolleston family until the estate fell into disrepair and the house was demolished in 1962. If his notes are accurate, this is where Osborne found and bought his copy of *The Humorous Magistrate*. The Osborne copy, as already explained, was probably prepared as early as the third, and as late as the fourth, decade of the seventeenth century. In the absence of a record of transfer, it is impossible to know when exactly, or in what circumstances, the manuscript came into the possession of the Rollestons.[28] There seems to be no record of the Rollestons among the gentry in attendance at Foremark. However, the Rollestons and Newdigates had other mutual acquaintances, not least in the powerful Willoughby family. Middleton, located next door to Arbury Hall at the north-east tip of Warwickshire, was the Willoughby family seat for five hundred years; in the 1580s, Sir Francis Willoughby embarked on the construction of Wollaton Hall in Nottinghamshire, on family property situated next door to Watnall Hall. The Willoughbys thus actively maintained estates in the late sixteenth and early seventeenth centuries that put them into immediate proximity with both the Newdigates and the Rollestons. There was an especially close association, founded in shared literary interests, between the Newdigates and the Derbyshire branch of the Willoughby family.[29] Archival records likewise confirm dealings between the Willoughbys and Rollestons. In order to finance Wollaton Hall, for instance, Sir Francis was forced to sell property in northern Leicestershire, just over the Nottinghamshire county border from his estate at Willoughby-on-the-Wolds. This property, described in the title deeds as the manor of Wymeswold (also known as Wymeswold Crowhole), was bought in 1592 by William Ballard who purchased it as part of a marriage contract negotiated on behalf of his son, Edward, and Valyntyne, daughter of Lancelot Rolleston of Watnall, Nottinghamshire.[30]

The social and legal threads linking the Rollestons and Newdigates in the early seventeenth century offer only circumstantial evidence of their possible interaction. And yet the families shared not only a network of friends and acquaintances, but a geographical proximity that could well have facilitated the passing of manuscript drama between their houses; the distance between the estates of Watnall Hall and Arbury Hall, after all, despite the county border, was approximately sixty kilometres (forty miles). The completion of Newdigate House at the heart of Nottingham in the second half of the seventeenth century would have potentially brought the next generation of Newdigates and Rollestons into even closer contact. These 'near neighbours' of the English Midlands—the Newdigates and Rollestons, and the variant copies of *The Humorous Magistrate* associated with their estates—deserve further research. Such investigation might reveal, in particular, more evidence of the history of the literary production and performance of early seventeenth century manuscript drama.[31]

NOTES

1 MS A414. I am indebted to Lord Daventry for depositing this manuscript collection on extended loan at the Warwickshire County Record Office, and for granting me access to it. I would also like to thank the archivists, assistants, and conservationists at the WCRO for their ready support throughout the preparation of this essay. The Newdigate manuscript plays came to light in 1976 when investigations by Peter Beal into the Newdigate papers, using an early twentieth-century list of them, led to the discovery of shelves of otherwise unrecorded manuscripts, including the plays, at Arbury Hall. Although Beal drafted a letter to the *Times Literary Supplement* about them, the Newdigate family did not at that time want publicity or 'a flood of enquiries' about them. The manuscripts were subsequently microfilmed and catalogued by the Warwickshire County Record Office, leading to T. H. Howard-Hill's independent announcement of them in 1980/88.

2 Warwickshire County Record Office, MS CR136/B.766. Howard-Hill provides for all five plays an account of provenance and hand, and a description of their action in 'Boccaccio, *Ghismonda*, and its Foul Papers, *Glausamond*', *Renaissance Papers* (1980), 19–28, and 'Another Warwickshire Playwright: John Newdigate of Arbury', *Renaissance Papers* (1988), 51–62. The existence of four plays bound together in 'a seventeenth-century MS. volume from a Warwickshire library' was first noted by an anonymous contributor to *The Gentleman's Magazine* ('"The twice chang'd friar. A comedie": (MS. temp. Charles I)', *The Gentleman's Magazine* 300 (1906), 285–90.

3 Howard-Hill, 'Boccaccio, *Ghismonda*, and its Foul Papers, *Glausamond*', p. 24; see also W. W. Greg, *Dramatic Documents from the Elizabethan Playhouses: Stage Plots, Actors' Parts, Prompt Books* (Oxford, 1931), p. 356.

4 'Another Warwickshire Playwright', p. 58.

5 'Another Warwickshire Playwright', p. 59. For the personal papers, see Warwickshire County Record Office, MS CR136/B.330, B.331, B.332, and MS CR136/A.1–3. This attribution has been in part accepted in the revised third edition of the *Annals of English Drama, 975–1700* (Alfred Harbage, rev. S. Schoenbaum, rev. Sylvia Stoler Wagonheim (London, 1989)). All six plays appear in the Anonymous Plays listings; the three plays that rework the story of Ghismonda (but not the other three), are cross-referenced to Newdigate in the Manuscript Author index. Vivienne Larminie, an authority on the sixteenth and seventeenth century Newdigate family, remains unconvinced by the attribution: 'Whilst John's interest in drama is undeniable, and his taste for writing poetry attested, whilst he was probably in the right place at the appropriate period, and whilst the hand in which the plays are written could easily be one of the several variations he adopted, the attribution of the plays seems to this writer to remain unproven' (*Wealth, Kinship and Culture: The Seventeenth Century Newdigates of Arbury and Their World* (Woodbridge, Suffolk: The Royal Historical Society, 1995), p. 160 n. 20).

6 The full inscription on the cover sheet reads, 'Watnall Hall Sale | 1947 | No title. No effort | made to trace authership [*sic*] | Handwriting c Mid or later | 17th Century | Edgar Osborne | More likely 18th Century' (University of Calgary Special Collections, MS C132.27). I have been unable to locate any record of a sale in 1947, and there is a chance that Osborne's memory of the estate sale is inaccurate. The Local Studies Library in Nottingham owns a Catalogue for an auction held by Walker, Walton & Hanson at Watnall Hall 9–10 December, 1954. The catalogue's title-page states that 'THE LIBRARY OF BOOKS' will be sold along with furniture, portraits and paintings, china and porcelain, and objects of art. None of the lot descriptions, however, mentions manuscript drama. I am grateful to Tony Horton of the Woodborough (Nottingham) Local History Group for his help in tracking down this catalogue.

7 Harry Campbell, Chief Librarian of Toronto Public Library, acted as the agent between Osborne and the University of Calgary, and it seems the acquisition was concluded in January 1972. I am grateful to Apollonia Steele for this account of provenance, and to Mary Polito for sharing with me parts of her continuing research into the Osborne manuscript.

8 The production, directed by Barry Yzereef, had three performances 7–9 April 2005.

9 The anchor design is found in the Osborne copy on ff. 21–6 and on the unnumbered leaf that contains the list of characters; the pot design is on all other leaves. Both watermarks are found near the centre of the leaf.

10 All but one of the watermark pots in the Arbury manuscript of *The Humorous Magistrate* range across the gutter of the book; the pot on f. 139 is fully visible, standing upright and parallel to the gutter. The other watermarks are located on ff. 109–10, 113–14, 115–16, 119–20, 125–6, 127–8, 133–4, and 137–8. All references to this miscellany here and throughout follow the continuous folio numbers introduced into the manuscript by the Warwickshire County Record Office archivists.

11 Edward Heawood, *Watermarks: Mainly of the 17th and 18th Centuries* (Hiversum, 1950).

12 W. W. Greg and William B. Long agree that the convention, albeit not invariable practice, was for the bookkeeper to make use of the left margin for annotations (see Greg, *Dramatic Documents*, I, 213, and Long, '*John a Kent and John a Cumber*: An Elizabethan Playbook and Its Implications', in *Shakespeare and Dramatic Tradition: Essays in Honor of S. F. Johnson*, ed. W. R. Elton and William B. Long (Newark, 1989), pp. 125–43). However, textual evidence of performance is difficult to discern with confidence, especially where there is no licence (as one would expect of amateur

drama). Greg tentatively proposed in *The Shakespeare First Folio: Its Bibliographical and Textual History* that one might distinguish foul papers and playbooks by signs such as the consistent removal from the latter type of manuscript of variant speech prefixes and literary or permissive stage directions (Oxford, 1955, pp. 105–42, see especially p. 142). The usefulness of such rules of thumb has since been challenged by Long who points to the occasional nature of bookkeepers' interventions, usually in order to straighten out a specific staging problem; in the absence of such a tangle, the convention seems to have been to do nothing (William B. Long, 'Stage-Directions: A Misinterpreted Factor in Determining Textual Provenance', *Text* 2 (1985), pp. 121–37, especially pp. 123, 135). Elsewhere Greg himself recognises the difficulty in identifying the use to which manuscripts were put, noting that literary directions 'are commonly left unaltered in prompt copies' while 'even manuscripts showing no connexion with the playhouse at all contain at times distinctively theatrical terms and phrases' (*Dramatic Documents*, I, 208).

13 Howard-Hill, 'Another Warwickshire Playwright', p. 60.

14 On dating the five Arbury plays, also see Howard-Hill, 'Another Warwickshire Playwright'.

15 This is the only watermark found in *The Emperor's Favourite*, and it appears thirteen times (ff. 145–6, 149–50, 153–4, 159–60, 161–2, 167–8, 169–70, 175–6, 179–80, 181–2, 187–8, 191–2, and 193–4). The watermark found throughout *The twice-chang'd Friar* resembles a vase.

16 Sir Francis Hubert's *Life of Edward the second* (ff. 1–73v) is written in the older style hand, while forty-eight 'characters' by John Earle (ff. 83–102) is consistent with the hand that wrote *The Humorous Magistrate*. In the *Summary Catalogue of Post-Medieval Western Manuscripts in the Bodleian Library Oxford* (Oxford, 1991), Mary Clapinson and T. D. Rogers likewise express uncertainty about whether these hands should be recognized as distinct (pp. 715–16). A key detail of relevance to the proposed attribution of the plays to Newdigate is that the Earle entry—presumably with an allusion to John III's correspondence with Gilbert Sheldon—concludes with the note, 'The end of so many of Mr Erles caracters as | were bestowed vpon me by Mr G. S. April: 1627. | in Mr Erles own copie.' (Bodleian Library, MS Eng. poet. e. 112, f. 102). Larminie cites this commonplace book as the sole surviving evidence of John III's 'breadth of [literary] taste', attributing to his hand everything in the book except a concluding two-line epitaph by his brother, Richard (*Wealth, Kinship and Culture*, p. 171). Curiously, especially in light of Larminie's attribution, one notes that the book contains a few pieces seemingly copied in yet another hand; see note 18.

17 This view is supported by Steven May; I am indebted to May, Louis Knafla, and Heather Wolfe, Curator of Manuscripts at the Folger Shakespeare Library, for sharing with me their thoughts on these hands, and to Paul Werstine and John Jowett for their helpful suggestions and advice. To pursue further the Newdigate connection, the Osborne hand bears no resemblance to that of John III's brother, Richard, to the hand of his wife, Susanna, or to his father's or mother's hands; unfortunately, there are apparently no surviving letters or papers in the hands of his three sisters.

18 The poem appears on f. 70 of the miscellany. Larminie describes it as 'a poem of [Newdigate's] own composition' because it shows the influence of John Donne's *Paradoxes*, extracts from which are copied into the commonplace book in the Bodleian. The tenth paradox, 'That a wise man is known by much laughing', prompts the acerbic annotation from 'I. N.', 'wch I see nothing here to proue' (MS Eng.poet.e.112, f. 105v). The neat italic hand that inscribed the *Paradoxes* into the commonplace book along with a few other verses is not of a piece with the mixed

hand(s) that copied Earle's 'characters' or Hubert's *Life of Edward the second*, but it resembles Newdigate's signed letters (see especially MS CR136/B.331). Larminie, one should clarify, makes no claim on the evidence of the commonplace book for the miscellany poem's hand, only for its original authorship. See Vivienne Larminie, 'John Newdigate (1600–1642)', *Oxford Dictionary of National Biography*, and Larminie, *Wealth, Kinship and Culture*, p. 173.

19 There is a chance, of course, that the epilogue was written on paper taken from left-over stock that had not been used up promptly; this would seem a distinct possibility if there were only the poem and the Arbury manuscript to consider. However, the coincidence of hand between the poem and the Osborne copy of the play contributes to a weight of evidence in favour of a dating for *The Humorous Magistrate* in the mid-1630s.

20 Material deleted in the manuscript is likewise deleted here, interlined words and phrases are placed in square brackets either immediately after or above the passages they replace, and editorially expanded contractions are underlined.

21 Determining the agency behind alterations to dramatic manuscripts is notoriously difficult. Eric Rasmussen builds on Werstine's skepticism that one can with any confidence identify the source of revisions to playtexts, arguing first, that various types of cuts signal 'different working habits' rather than the presence or absence of an author (446), and second, that non-authorial revisers are as prone as authors not only to add new passages but to 'tinker' with the text (452–3). As Gary Taylor acknowledges in *The Division of the Kingdoms*, 'anyone concerned about success at [the] aesthetic level would be indistinguishable from the author' (450, n. 154; quoted in Rasmussen, 444). See Eric Rasmussen, 'The Revision of Scripts', *A New History of Early English Drama*, ed. John D. Cox and David Scott Kastan (New York, 1997), 441–60, and Paul Werstine, 'The Textual Mystery of Hamlet', *Shakespeare Quarterly* 39 (1988), 1–26.

22 On scribal practices, see W. W. Greg, *The Editorial Problem in Shakespeare: A Survey of the Foundations of the Text*, 3rd ed. (Oxford, 1962), p. 34, and William B. Long, '"Precious Few': English Manuscript Playbooks', in *A Companion to Shakespeare*, ed. David Scott Kastan (Oxford, 1999), pp. 414–33, p. 416.

23 Howard-Hill, 'Another Warwickshire Playwright', pp. 56–7.

24 'Randing' is synonymous with 'raving, ranting' (*OED* rand, v.^{2}). The *Oxford English Dictionary* does not list 'guarb' as a variant spelling of 'garb' (meaning to dress or clothe), but it seems clear from the context that this is the metaphorical sense, as Wild is dismissing Spruce's behaviour as self-conscious posturing. For further discussion of this theatrical allusion, see Margaret Jane Kidnie, '"Suit the Action to the Word': An Early Seventeenth-Century Allusion to Hamlet in Performance', *Theatre Notebook*, 49 (1995), 62–5.

25 Work on the Records of Early English Drama volumes on Nottinghamshire and Derbyshire is still underway. I am grateful to Alan Somerset, editor of the forthcoming REED volume on Warwickshire, for sharing with me his pre-publication research.

26 Vivienne Larminie, 'Jane Burdett (d.1637)', *Oxford Dictionary of National Biography*.

27 T. C. [Thomas Calvert], *The wearie Souls wish: or, The Doves wings* (York, 1650), sig. A2v. The apparently unique extant copy of this pamphlet is pasted into a scrapbook, and so catalogued at the Bodleian Library as a manuscript (MS Eng. hist. b.159, ff. 238–54).

28 William Cavendish, first Duke of Newcastle (1592–1676), maintained houses at Welbeck Abbey in Nottinghamshire and Bolsover Castle in Derbyshire, and kept a

secretary during this period by the name of John Rolleston. It is tempting on the basis of geographical proximity, the shared family name, and Rolleston's known production of dramatic manuscripts to link the Arbury and Osborne manuscripts to the Cavendish circle. However, Hilton Kelliher has analysed the striking variations in and development of Rolleston's hand in the early 1630s, and none of these scripts seems a close match for the hand found in either extant version of *The Humorous Magistrate* ('Donne, Jonson, Richard Andrews and The Newcastle Manuscript', *English Manuscript Studies*, 4 (1993), 134–73). For further discussion of Rolleston's hand(s) and career, see *Dramatic Works by William Cavendish*, ed. Lynn Hulse, Malone Society Reprints, vol. 158 (1996), and *The Country Captain by William Cavendish*, ed. Anthony Johnson, Malone Society Reprints, vol. 162 (1999).

29 See Larminie, *Wealth, Kinship and Culture*, pp. 129, 137. The account books kept on behalf of John and Richard during their time at Oxford show that in the summer of 1620 Sir Henry Willoughby of Risley (1579–1632) visited and had dinner with the brothers (Larminie, *Wealth, Kinship and Culture*, pp. 132–3).

30 Records of the transfer of the title deeds to Wymeswold in 1592 are found among the papers of the Okeover family of Okeover, Derbyshire, at the Derbyshire County Record Office, ref. D231M/T542–546. Summary of the records was consulted 27 June 2005 through Access to Archives (www.a2a.org.uk).

31 An edition of these two manuscripts, generously supported by a Collaborative Research Grant awarded by the Social Sciences and Humanities Research Council of Canada, is currently underway. The project, based at the University of Calgary, will also investigate the social and theatrical networks in which the manuscripts were produced and circulated, with an emphasis on the performance potential of the two versions. This initiative, led by Mary Polito, draws together an international team of scholars including Susan Bennett, Martin Butler, Jacqueline Jenkins, Margaret Jane Kidnie, and Murray McGillivray. The research undertaken for this article was funded by the Social Sciences and Humanities Research Council of Canada and the University of Western Ontario.

A new poem by Waller? Lady Katherine Howard, the Earl of Northumberland, and an Entertainment on board the *Triumph*

Timothy Raylor

In the summer of 1637 (or, possibly, 1636) Katherine Howard, daughter of Theophilus Howard, second Earl of Suffolk and Warden of the Cinque Ports, was entertained by Algernon Percy, tenth earl of Northumberland and then Lord Admiral of the Fleet on board his flagship, the *Triumph*. The occasion was celebrated in a little known and previously unpublished poem which, it seems possible, was at least in part the work of Edmund Waller, a poet who wrote several addresses for Northumberland and members of his family circle in the later 1630s.

Two copies of the poem are known. One is found in a bundle of poetical manuscripts now housed among the papers of Joseph Williamson in the National Archives, Kew (Public Record Office) but which was almost certainly once part of the Conway Papers—papers belonging to the first and second viscounts Conway (SP 9/51/39–40).[1] The other appears in a royalist verse miscellany written in a folio volume, apparently in a single hand, during the 1650s; it was once in the collection of Sir Thomas Phillipps (MS 4001) and is now in the library of University College, London (Ogden MS 42, pp. 12–16).[2]

The Conway version appears on a single bifolium (each page measuring about 285 × 191mm.) without title (see PLATE 1). Folio 40 bears the watermark of a shield containing a thick cross. This bifolium has been folded three times along the vertical. The sheet has been damaged at the upper inside corners, causing the loss of some line endings. The text is incomplete: the poem ends inconclusively at the foot of folio 40v; an additional leaf, containing its final lines, is evidently missing. The text is written in a neat, competent, and not very distinctive italic hand. The obvious inference from its physical and textual characteristics—folded for despatch, and lacking any kind of explanatory title—is that the

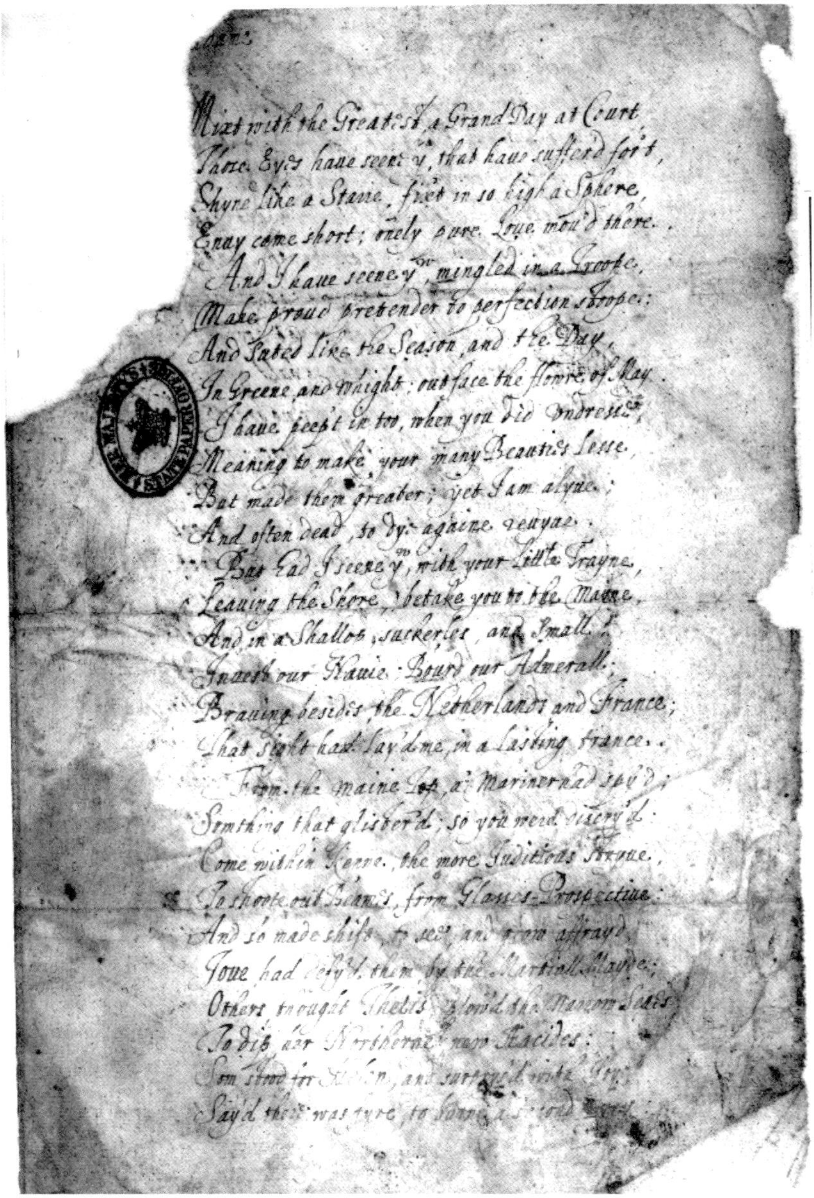

Mixt with the Greatest, a Grand Day at Court
Those Eyes haue seene yu, that haue sufferd for't,
Shyne like a Starre, fixt in so high a Sphere,
Envy came short; onely pure Loue mou'd there.
And I haue seene yu, mingled in a Troope,
Make proud pretender to perfection stoope:
And Suted like the Season, and the Day,
In Greene and Whight: out face the flowre of May.
I haue keept in too, when you did vndresse,
Meaning to make your many Beauties lesse,
But made them greater; yet I am alyue;
And often dead, to dy againe reuyue.
But had I seene yu, with your little Trayne,
Leauing the Shore, betake you to the Maine,
And in a Shallop, suckerles and small,
Inuest our Nauie: Bourd our Admerall;
Braueing besides the Netherlands and France;
That sight had lay'd me in a lasting trance.
From the maine top, a Marriner had spy'd
Somthing that glisterd; so you were discry'd.
Come within Kenne, the more Iuditious striue,
To shoote out Beames, from Glasses Prospectiue:
And so made shift to see, and grow affrayd,
Ioue had defy'd them by the Martiall Mayde;
Others thought Thetis plow'd the Narrow Seas
To dip her Northerne new Aeacides:
Som stood for [illegible], and surpris'd with [illegible]
Say'd there was fyre, to [illegible]

PLATE 1. *First page of the Conway manuscript of 'The Lady Katherine Howards Voyage and Enterteynement, aboard the Triumph': Kew, National Archives, SP 9/51/39–40 (fol. 39r) (Original page size 285 × 191mm.) Reproduced by permission of the National Archives.*

Conway version was sent to someone with full knowledge of the occasion and context of the poem, probably soon after the event. That person was almost certainly Edward, second viscount Conway, a bon viveur and bibliophile,[3] who was present at the entertainment. Conway was a close friend of Northumberland and, in the mid- to late-1630s displayed an active interest in collecting poems by the newly fashionable Waller. Evidence for this interest appears in a postscript to a letter to Conway of 27 July 1637, addressed to him on board the *Triumph* in the Downs, from Sir Kenelm Digby, in which Digby promised to send one of Waller's poems, writing that 'I haue not M^r^. Wallers verses by me, but by the next you shall haue them'.[4] A scribal copy of Waller's poem 'Of His Majesty's receiving the news of the Duke of Buckingham's death', folded for transmission, appears a few leaves before the poem on Lady Katherine's entertainment in the National Archives volume of Conway Papers.[5] For reasons I have explained elsewhere, this is not likely to be the poem promised by Digby. Another possible candidate is 'To the King, on his navy', a Latin translation of which was made by Sir Kenelm's brother, George—perhaps explaining why Sir Kenelm did not have access to his copy in late July.[6]

The Ogden version of the text is not, like the Conway, a contemporary copy. It was, by contrast, entered into a verse miscellany at a later date. It contains the conclusion (ten lines) and a title retrospectively identifying occasion and participants: it is headed 'The Lady Katherine Howards | Voyage and Enterteynement, aboard the Triumph | By the Earle of Northumberland | He being then Lord High Admirall' (see PLATE 2). It also preserves several variant readings, most of which represent minor revisions, and omits two couplets—one, at least, due to scribal eye-skip. The revisions in the Ogden version appear on the whole to reflect an attempt to improve on some of the poem's frequent infelicities by rephrasing pedestrian constructions to generate rhetorical turns (e.g. lines 3–4, 43). Such revisions do not always represent marked changes for the better: Ogden removes the Conway text's repetition of 'hour' in lines 106–7, but only by replacing the banal 'not halfe an howre' with the mere filler 'I cannot say'. Nor am I convinced that Ogden's preference for 'puffs' as opposed to 'breaths' of wind necessarily marks an improvement. It seems possible that each version derives from a draft original, to which improvements were made in the process of copying.

The poem may be dated approximately by pinpointing the date of the entertainment it commemorates. That date may be determined by triangulating internal allusions with external evidence. A *terminus a quo* is furnished by the allusion in line 16 of the poem to Northumberland

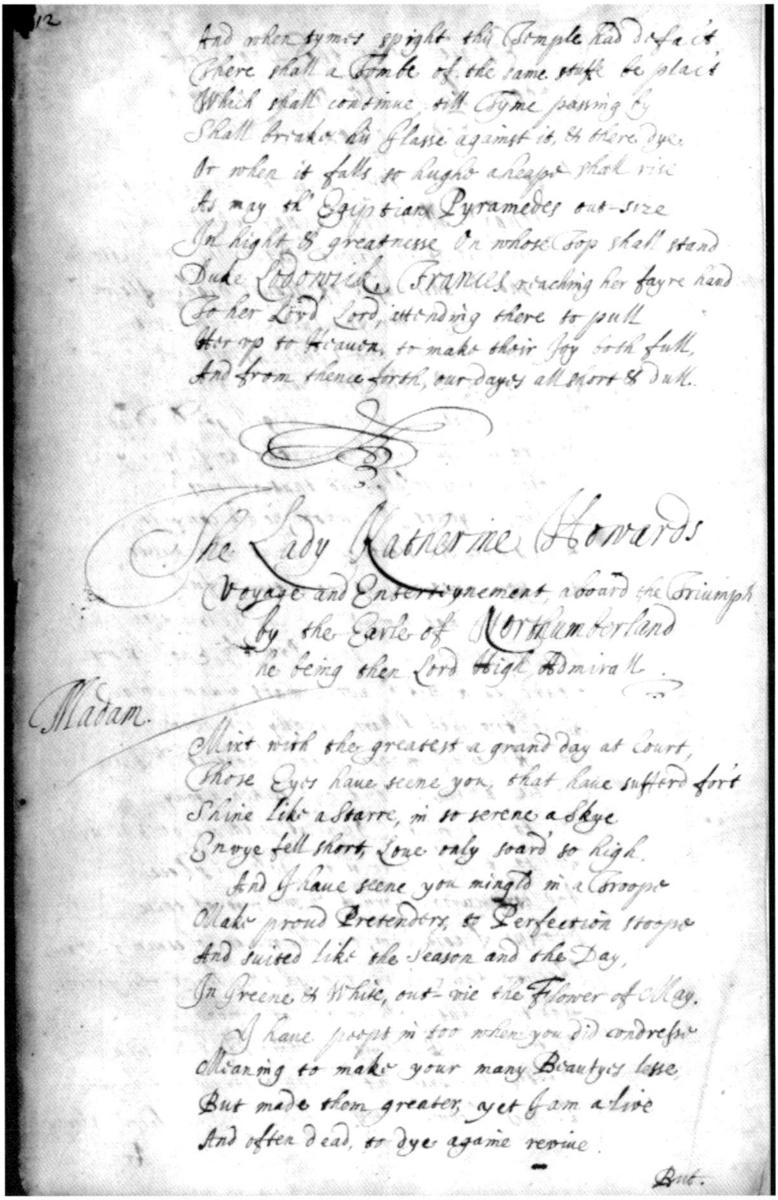
12

And when tymes spight the Temple had defac't
There shall a Tombe of the same stuffe be plac't
Which shall continue till Tyme passing by
Shall breake his Glasse against it, & there dye.
Or when it falls to hughe a heape shall rise
As may th' Egyptian Pyramedes out-size
In hight & greatnesse On whose Top shall stand
Duke Lodowick, Frances reaching her fayre hand
To her Lord Lord, attending there to pull
Her up to Heaven, to make their Joy both full,
And from thence forth, our dayes all short & dull.

The Lady Katherine Howards
Voyage and Enterteynement, aboard the Triumph
by the Earle of Northumberland
he being then Lord High Admirall.

Madam.

Mixt with the greatest a grand day at Court,
Those Eyes haue seene you, that haue sufferd for't
Shine like a Starre, in so serene a Skye
Envye fell short, Loue only soard so high.
And I haue seene you mingld in a Troope
Make proud Pretenders, to Perfection stoope
And suited like the Season and the Day,
In Greene & White, out-vie the Flower of May.
I haue peept in too when you did undresse
Meaning to make your many Beautyes lesse
But made them greater, yet I am alive
And often dead, to dye againe revive.

But.

PLATE 2. *First page of the Ogden manuscript of 'The Lady Katherine Howards Voyage and Enterteynement, aboard the Triumph': UCL Library Services, Special Collections, Ogden* MS *42, p. 12. (Original page size 326 × 217 mm.) Reproduced by permission of UCL Library Services.*

as admiral: a post he first took up in the late spring of 1636.[7] A *terminus ante quem* is provided by Lady Katherine's scandalous secret marriage to George Stuart, Seigneur D'Aubigny, and her concurrent conversion to Catholicism, all of which caused great consternation at court. News about the marriage began to leak out by 10 May 1638.[8] The title of the Ogden version identifies Lady Katherine as 'Howard', and the text itself refers to her as a 'mayde' (line 101), makes no mention of her marriage and presents her in more flirtatious and sexually charged a manner than would be appropriate for a married woman (see, for example, lines 1–12). This affords a window of three possible years during which the poem could have been written: 1636, 1637, and 1638. Since the fleets sailed only during the summer months, putting out in May or June and retiring in September or October, we can discount the possibility of an autumn or winter entertainment.

Internal evidence suggests that the entertainment may have taken place on midsummer's day (24 June): 'The longest Day, was growne the Shortest now', laments the poet, as the entertainment nears its end (line 81).[9] The possibility that the poet is using a degree of poetic license in handling the occasion and its associations cannot, of course, be discounted; but the most obvious interpretation of the longest day is 24 June. The poem is, at any rate, very much a summer poem.[10]

That the entertainment took place in summer allows us to narrow down the possible dates. Lady Katherine's marriage in mid-May 1638 almost certainly rules out that year, leaving 1636 or 1637. Happily, Northumberland's logs for both these years are extant. His log for the 1636 fleet records that he arrived in the Downs on the evening of Friday 24 June after patrolling the south coast for a week.[11] If the entertainment took place on midsummer's day, it cannot have happened in 1636. In 1637, by contrast, Northumberland spent the fortnight of 15–28 June on board the *Triumph* at anchor in the Downs, attending the arrival of the Prince Elector, Charles Louis, and his brother, Rupert, whom he was to carry over to Holland. He dined with them at Deal on 28 June, the weather being too rough for the shipboard entertainment to which he had invited them.[12] Other factors agree to suggest Saturday 24 June 1637 as a likely date for the entertainment. From his letters it is clear that Conway was on board the *Triumph* at this time.[13] The presence of the *Triumph* in the Downs means that it was close to Dover Castle, of which Lady Katherine's father, Theophilus, second Earl of Suffolk, was Constable, thus allowing us to account with ease not only for her visit but also for the anxious attendance, on shore, of her father (lines 101–6).[14] And the expectation of Prince Rupert may have been an added attraction to Lady Katherine, who was then rumoured to be in love with him.[15] As an eligible young lady, she was, moreover, a fashionable figure in the poetry of the moment: writing to her husband in Paris on 5 May 1637, the Countess of Leicester enclosed 'a songe latelie maid of all our younge ladies that are to be maried', and glossed a passage concerning 'K. Hord [Howard?]' by explaining that she had been referred to the previous summer as 'the Queene of Kent'. Lady Leicester was unaware of the poet's identity: 'thaie saie a ge[n]tleman of Graisine [Grays Inn]'.[16]

If the identification of 'The longest Day' as precisely 24 June is not persuasive, then the period 25 June–19 July 1636 affords another possible window for the entertainment. During this period, the *Triumph*, with both Northumberland and Conway on board, was in the Downs.[17] During this period some entertaining was done. In a letter of 8 July Conway describes a visit by 'two or three boates full of gentlewoemen'; but since this was marred by foul weather, which resulted in the ladies getting soaked, it cannot be the occasion celebrated in the poem, which mentions only some mist and gusty wind at dusk (lines 95–9).[18]

The only evidence against dating the poem to the summers of 1636 or 1637 is the title in the Ogden version, which identifies Northumberland as 'then Lord High Admirall'. Northumberland was elevated from Admiral to Lord High Admiral on 18 March 1638 and was ceremonially installed in mid-April.[19] Since this version of the text was copied into the Ogden manuscript some years after the event it is possible that Northumberland's later naval appointment displaced his earlier one in the mind either of the compiler or the copyist of his or her source. It is, moreover, extremely unlikely that Northumberland could have entertained Lady Katherine Howard on board the *Triumph* in the summer of 1638. Not only was she married by mid-May of that year, but Northumberland was, from late April through the summer, incapacitated by illness.[20] He was unable to join the fleet on 10 May but recovered enough to conduct a little business (in London) at the end of the month.[21] He planned in early June to put to sea at the end of the month and seemed, by the middle of the month, to be improving; but he suffered a relapse by the 20th.[22] He recuperated at Sion House, whence he was able to conduct some naval business by the month end.[23] In a letter of 23 July he noted that he was only then well enough to venture abroad again.[24] By the end of August he was reported as being in perfect health, but was sick again in November.[25] The absence of any evidence that Northumberland put to sea during this period squares with the strong evidence against the likelihood of his having done so to suggest that the summer of 1638 was almost certainly not the year of the entertainment on board the *Triumph*.

The knowledge that Northumberland was later to marry Lady Katherine's younger sister, Elizabeth, offers further (negative) evidence for dating the poem prior to 1638. For were it written at a time when both Lady Katherine and the Earl were eligible (that is to say, between the death of Northumberland's wife in December 1637 and Lady Katherine's marriage in May 1638) one would expect the poet to have made more of the romantic potential of the encounter. The absence of any real effort to spin the occasion in this way is quite striking. Little is made of any connection between the couple: it is the ship's crew, rather than the admiral, that drinks Lady Katherine's health (lines 63–9); and it is the poet who has amorous designs upon her (lines 5–12, 125–6). Seen together, Lady Katherine and Lord Algernon are merely praised for their nobility and courtliness (line 76). The only hint of romance on Northumberland's part is his homoerotic attachment to his 'Consort', 'Patroclus' Conway (lines 77–80). In sum, then, the absence from the poem of the kind of romantic rhetoric one would expect to find were it a celebration of an encounter between an eligible and suitable couple furnishes further evidence against its dating from 1638.

The most likely date for the entertainment is, therefore, 24 June 1637, and the poem was almost certainly written shortly afterwards. This dating raises the possibility that this was the very poem Digby promised, on 27 July 1637, to send Conway.

The attribution of the poem to Waller is by no means certain, but there is enough evidence, both internal and external, for it to merit consideration. Let us begin with the external evidence. Waller is a likely candidate for authorship because he was, during the latter half of the 1630s, the unofficial laureate of the Percy interest, addressing Northumberland directly in poems on the death of his first wife in December 1637 and on his recovery from sickness in late 1638, and celebrating him indirectly in several naval poems of the late 1630s. He serenaded Northumberland's sister Lucy in several poems, and his sister Dorothy, her husband and, above all, her daughter and namesake (whom he dubbed 'Sacharissa'), in many others.[26] Of course, Waller was not the only poet to address Northumberland: his friend Sidney Godolphin also furnished a poem on the death of the Earl's first wife, while an unidentified Dr Lewes wrote, like Waller, a poem on the Earl's sickness and recovery.[27] But no poet wrote so regularly for the family as did Waller. He is, *prima facie*, a particularly likely candidate for authorship of the poem on Lady Katherine's entertainment.

Further circumstantial evidence in favour of his authorship may be found in the fact that Waller evidently spent some time at sea during the later 1630s. At the end of the second of his two 'Penshurst' poems, in which the poet laments his failure to win the heart of 'Sacharissa', Apollo appears and orders the poet to abandon his hopeless quest: 'Hang up thy lute, and hie thee to the sea', he exclaims.[28] Jack G. Gilbert has taken this to mark Waller's abandonment of 'the amorous lyric for more serious themes'.[29] But I am not sure that the dating of Waller's poems from this period supports this interpretation; to me it seems more likely that the reference is to be taken a little more literally: after spending some time at Penshurst, the poet took to sea. Waller did spend time on the Kentish coast in the later 1630s. At some point he was at Deal, along with his friend Jerome Weston, second Earl of Portland (later implicated in Waller's 'plot').[30] Perhaps they were among the party of courtiers attending the young Prince Electors, who dined with Northumberland at Deal on 28 June 1637? He also seems to have gone to sea at about this time: one lyric of the period ('Of loving at first sight') is written as from one at sea and (as we shall see below) features a passage strikingly similar to one in the poem on Lady Katherine's entertainment; another, published for the first time in 1789, is entitled 'When he was at sea'.[31]

I know of no evidence to suggest that Waller in 1637 was on the kind of familiar terms with Lady Katherine implied by the poem's tone of jocular intimacy (e.g. lines 9–10). She did, however, appear at court and moved among other ladies of Waller's acquaintance. She is known to have danced in *The Temple of Love* in 1635, and in 1638 she would dance in *Luminalia* along with Lady Dorothy Sidney (Waller's 'Sacharissa') and Lady Anne Rich (on whose death in August of that year Waller would compose an elegy).[32] A few years later, in the spring of 1643, she was heavily involved in the poet's ill-starred 'plot'.[33]

So much for circumstantial evidence. Turning to the internal evidence, we notice that its general stance, style, and manner, furnish reasons for associating the poem with Waller. Its maritime focus is what we might expect from a poet so much concerned with naval affairs as he—a poet who composed at least one other poem involving a voyage and entertainment.[34] The strangely intrusive, self-pitying frame, in which the poet comically laments the desperateness of his own romantic ambitions is typical of the kind of self-regarding, self-deprecating strategy Waller employed in his addresses to the noble ladies he courted (or flattered by pretending to court) in his verses. We might compare it, for example, to the coda of 'Of the marriage of the dwarfs', or with such poems on Sacharissa as 'At Penshurst', in which the poet makes a central feature of his own despair.[35] Finally, its frequently elegant couplets and its graceful (if often slightly vacuous) rhetorical turns—for instance, isocolon: 'Of sortes so various; and of store so great' (line 58); polyptoton: 'Saluting, and saluted, by a Thronge' (line 84)—lend the work an overall flavour that is instantly familiar to those conversant with Waller's work.

Such subjective impressions may be buttressed by more specific parallels between this poem and the known works of Waller. Waller was unusually economical (not to say indolent) in his efforts as a poet, making a habit (much remarked upon by early critics) of plundering his own compositions for rhymes, phrases, lines, and even whole couplets. [36] As we would expect in one of Waller's poems, this poem exhibits many typically Wallerian rhymes.[37] But since these are typical without being unique or even particularly distinctive, they cannot form a basis for attribution.[38] More promising are instances of parallel phrasing. The poem contains two distinctively Wallerian periphrases. Although 'vermilion Dye' for wine does not appear elsewhere in Waller, it is very much in the manner of his 'sable wave' for black ink, for example (*WP*, I, 109). A more distinctive instance of such periphrasis is the term 'Paphian Queene' for Venus (line 29). Waller, uniquely, uses the phrase twice, at very different stages in his career: first in 'Upon the Death of my Lady Rich' (line 21; *WP*, I, 37) in August 1638 (a year or two after the poem on Lady Katherine's entertainment must have been composed) and again, in 1665, in 'Instructions to a Painter' (line 83; *WP*, I, 51). The phrase was not a commonplace; a search of Chadwyck-Healey's *English Poetry* database shows fairly frequent usage during the eighteenth and nineteenth centuries (about 30 hits), following Dryden's employment of it in his *Aeneid* (v. 991), but only two other seventeenth-century examples: in Fanshawe's *Lusiad* (ix. 480) and in Henry King's lyric, 'The Legacy' (line 31). While King's poem might possibly date from the same period as Waller's,[39] Dryden's and Fanshawe's certainly postdate the public appearance of Waller's elegy on Lady Rich in the 1645 editions of his works. Waller, of course, exerted a significant influence on Dryden. While not unique to Waller, the periphrasis is striking both for his unique repetition of it, and for its limited appearance in the work of contemporaries.

In addition to these two periphrases, the poem contains a distinctively Wallerian allusion in the reference to Conway as Patroclus. Outside translations and imitations of Homer and other classical writers, and aside from modern retellings of the Troy story, the figure of Patroclus appears surprisingly rarely in English poetry of this period.[40] Most of the 164 hits in the *English Poetry* database for the period 1500–1660 appear in Chapman's *Homer*, and only three do not fall into the categories just listed. Such references appear in: a short poem of 1611 addressed by John Davies of Hereford to the Earl of Salisbury; Henry King's 1648 'Elegy on Sir Charls Lucas and Sir George Lisle' (line 49);[41] and Waller's poem on the death of Buckingham (line 10; *WP*, I, 11)—a poem which, we noticed above, seems to have been sent to Conway and was written within a year of that on Lady Katherine Howard.

Such parallels are noteworthy but not conclusive. The strongest internal evidence for Waller's authorship comes in the form of three further instances of parallel phrasing. One of these is relatively fleeting. Early in the poem, the poet claims to have seen Lady Katherine depart 'in a Shallop, suckerles, and small' (line 15)—a phrase that echoes Waller's description of Prince Charles off Santander 'In a small shallop' ('Of the Danger His Majesty (being Prince) escaped in the road at St. Andrews', line 94; *WP*, I, 4). The use of the term 'shallop' for a dinghy used in shallow waters (*OED*, 2) occurs rarely in the early modern period, although it becomes a popular poeticism in the nineteenth century. A search of the *English Poetry* database yields only four instances in the period 1500–1660 outside Waller's 'Of the Danger'; in none of these is it modified by the adjective 'small'. And even those four occurrences seem to have a Wallerian pedigree. One occurrence is in Fairfax's *Godfrey of Bulloigne* (xv. 6) and another in the work Fairfax's modern editors presume provided him with the term, Spenser's *Faerie Queene* (III. vii. 27).[42] Its appearance in *Godfrey* provides a connection with Waller because Fairfax's poem was a major—perhaps *the* major—influence on Waller's style and language, from which he borrowed repeatedly, and heavily, over the course of his career.[43] The term appears, moreover, in a canto of *Godfrey* that, due to its concern with maritime matters (it relates the story of a sea voyage), Waller had studied with even more than usual care: from this canto he drew several phrases for his naval poems of the 1630s.[44] The phrase 'shallop' thus seems to have had a distinctly Wallerian line of descent; and the phrase 'small shallop' or 'shallop small' is, in the early modern period, uniquely Wallerian.

There is, however, another, more compelling instance of parallel phrasing in the poem which satisfies the negative test. Reflecting on the unusually calm weather, the poet comments:

> Yet was the Sea, that day so Calme and cleare,
> The Deepes congested Treasures did appeare (lines 31–2)

This couplet is strikingly similar to Waller's apostrophe on 'the smooth bosom of this deep' (line 6; *WP*, I, 100) in his lyric, 'Of loving at first sight'—a poem written (as we have noticed above) as from one at sea:

> No; 'tis so rockless and so clear,
> That the rich bottom does appear (lines 7–8; *WP*, I, 100).

Waller made frequent use of this rhyme; but it is common enough.[45] The overall parallel, however, with its close similarities in content (clear waters revealing riches in the depths), form (rhyme), and diction (deep, clear, appear), seems to me too close for coincidence.[46] I have found nothing quite like it in the *English Poetry* archive. Since Waller's lyric 'Of loving at first sight' did not appear in print until 1645, the passage is unlikely to have been borrowed by another poet in 1637. Nor, in any case, is the couplet so distinctive a 'beauty' as to be a likely source for plagiarists. The most reasonable explanation is that Waller was responsible for both couplets.

Against the evidence for Waller's authorship must be set a serious objection. The poem is not of the quality one expects of Waller. Despite frequent flashes of elegance, it is, as a whole, a slapdash, half-baked affair, all too often displaying undignified phrasing (e.g. 'kenne', line 21; 'Grand Day', line 1), metrical incompetence (e.g. line 1), passages of metrical filler (e.g. line 107), and (occasionally) nonsense—as in the indecipherable paradoxes of lines 11–12. Such shortcomings must count against an attribution of the poem to so competent a versifier as Waller. It has to be admitted, however, that such faults are not untypical of Waller at his worst. He is quite capable of resorting to rhythmic filler and is sometimes guilty of redundant or bathetic phrasing.[47] Unsurprisingly, such shortcomings are especially noticeable in his surviving drafts.[48]

The objection that the poem is insufficiently competent to be Waller's might perhaps be rebutted by reference to the circumstances of its composition. Waller was used to investing much time and effort in cultivating the apparently artless ease of his verse—the well-known story of his spending an entire summer preparing ten lines to inscribe in the Duchess of York's copy of Tasso may be apocryphal, but other evidence confirms the painfully slow pace at which he wrote.[49] Since the celebration of so ephemeral an event as Lady Katherine's entertainment aboard the *Triumph* would have had a very brief window of relevance, a poem on such an occasion would need to be turned out very quickly. Indeed, if it is these lines that Sir Kenelm Digby promised to send Conway on 27 July, the poem must have been in circulation within a month of the occasion it commemorated. Perhaps, therefore, the shortcomings of the poem, and the continued tinkering with it witnessed by the Ogden version, might be the products of hurried composition and premature circulation?

Another possible explanation, which does not exclude the first, is that Waller was not responsible for the whole poem but was merely a 'revisionary author', brought in to tidy up a poem drafted by another hand—an aristocratic member of Lady Katherine's circle, perhaps?[50] This would allow us to dispose of the poem's shortcomings while saving Waller's reputation. This is of course a possibility, and it cannot be ruled out. But the conspicuous presence of that self-referential frame, in which the poet thrusts himself into full view of the reader, seems both too immodest and too distinctively Wallerian to have been appropriate were the poet silently polishing another's rough draft.

We might summarize the case as follows. In favour of Waller's authorship of the poem are: (1) his close literary association with both Northumberland and Lady Katherine (and the absence of any other poet with comparable connections); (2) his interest in maritime matters; (3) the poem's overall texture; (4) its peculiar, self-regarding frame; (5) its employment of (i) a distinctly Wallerian periphrasis, (ii) a uniquely Wallerian combination of technical term and modifier, (iii) numerous rhymes Waller used elsewhere, and, above all, (iv) a couplet strikingly similar in both form and meaning to one of Waller's. Even in the most optimistic light, such evidence is, at best, only moderately persuasive. Against it must be set the evidence of frequent carelessness or incompetence on the poet's part. The available external and internal evidence, then, warrants only the most tentative attribution to Waller of 'The Lady Katherine Howard's Voyage and Entertainment'.

THE TEXT

I have taken as my copy text the Conway version of the poem, in the National Archives ('C'), on the grounds that it is probably closest to the poet's autograph version (the Ogden version having been transcribed into a verse miscellany in the 1650s, presumably from a scribal fair copy). This I have corrected against the Ogden version ('O'), introducing into it such variants as appear to have been authorial revisions, as opposed to scribal errors. All emendations and substantive variants are recorded in the textual notes. In presenting the text, I have silently expanded abbreviations, including ampersands.

The Lady Katherine Howards
Voyage and Enterteynement, aboard the Triumph
by the Earle of Northumberland
he being then Lord High Admirall.

Madame

Mixt with the Greatest, a Grand Day at Court,
Those Eyes haue seene you, that haue suffer'd for't,
Shyne like a Starre, in so serene a Skye
Enuy fell short, Loue only soar'd so high.
And I haue seene you, mingled in a Troope,
Make proud Pretenders to perfection stoope:
And suted like the Season, and the Day,
In Greene, and whight; out-vie the flowre of May.
I haue peep't in too, when you did vndresse,
Meaning to make your many Beauties lesse,
But made them greater; yet I am alyue;
And often dead, to dye againe reuyue.
But had I seene you, with your little Trayne,
(Leauing the Shore,) betake you to the Mayne,
And in a Shallop, suckerles, and small,
Inuest our Nauie; Bourd our Admerall;
Brauing besides, the Netherlands and France;
That sight had lay'd me, in a lasting trance.
From the maine Top, a Mariner had spy'd;
Somthing that glister'd; so you were discry'd:
Come within kenne, the more Iuditious stryue,
To shoote out Beames, from Glasses-Prospectiue:
And so made shift, to see, and grow affrayd,
Ioue, had defy'd them, by the Martiall Mayde;
Others, thought Thetis, plow'd the Narrow Seaes;
To dip, her Northerne, new Æacides:
Som mentioned Helen, and surprys'd with Ioy,
Say'd there was fyre, to burne a second Troy:
The most conclude, it was the Paphian Queene,
Whome they new borne, of the sea foame had seene,
Yet was the Sea, that day so Calme and cleare,
The Deepes congested Treasures did appeare,
And lest the gentlest of them might displease,
The winds were sent, post to th'Antipodes.
Th'Inamour'd Sunne, was seene as he did passe
Tricking him selfe, in that great Looking Glasse.
And the Worlds Godes, who is bald behinde;
Whose Saile still swelling, needs no puffe of wind,
Wafted, and Steer'd you; till you reach't that place,
Where all the Fleete, slept on the Oceans face.

As Distance, Doubt, in many a brest begot,
So your Aproche, hauing dissolu'd the knot,
Shaking of Feare; they sent out such a Showte,
Valleyes, and Hilles, Ecchoed it round abought:
Of went their Bonnets; And then vp, they went,
Pyed, like the Fowle, from th'Easterne India sent;
Som perch't alofte; som swomme vpon the Maine,
Lyting abourd, they kich't them out againe.
This AntiMasque, of Sailers being past,
Commaunders march't; and their Commaunder last;
Who in a Martiall, yet a Courtly wyse,
Fairely saluting, seas'd this Princely Pryse:
Shew'd her the Deckes, Ordenance, and euery place,
The Ship had in her, worthy of that grace
Then raysing her out of this restles Tombe,
For breath he brought her to a spatious Roome
Where Triton-Musick, vsher'd in the Meate;
Of sortes so various; and of store so great,
The Lady Guest, lamented Fowle and Fish,
Should crowde for place, so into euery Dish:
The Table looking, as if Sea, and Land,
Had made a Muster, of their whole Commaund:
Wynes wer not wanting, whose vermilion Dye,
Set in eche Cheeke, a Rubie, passing by;
Which grew the fairer, when she heard her Name,
Infus'd into it, fann'd that frendly flame:
So to conclude, she smyling kiss't the Cup,
Which the whole Crue, as a new Health tooke vp;
Sory to kindle, what she meant to quenche,
She gently rose from her Iuditiall Benche,
And thank't the Maker, of that Mighty Feast;
Then thankes on thanks, as Cups on Cups increac't:
Nor would he owne what his Braue Table bare,
But say'd (, Mistrusting a poore Sea Mans fare,)
She brought her Dyet with her: So admyer'd,
For Courtship both, this Noble Paire retyr'd,
To his owne Cabin; where his Consort laye,
And bosom frend, Patroclus Conaway:
Who with Discourses, hardly to be match't,
Stole Tyme away, though euery Minute watch't.
The Longest Day, was growne the Shortest now,
When theis two Cedars, made a parting Bow,

To one an other; and so pass't alonge
Saluting, and saluted, by a Thronge:
And as She went, her welcome Hand Rain'd Gold;
If not so much, as Poëts fayne of Olde
When Iupiter, did in a Shewre dessend;
Those Drops that fell, were to a Nobler End.
The Braue built Man, downe from the Triumph went
Into her Barge, too short a complement
Had his Commition, giuen him leaue, to part
From that great Charge, which he layd next his Heart,
As She put of (, whether it were the Wind,
The Sea, the SeaMen, or all theis combind)
There came a Puffe (which made the streamers tosse)
Much like a Sighe, vented for som late losse.
The Cannon roar'd; so he that from the shrowdes
Saw her the longest, lost her in those Clowdes;
The Billows rose; The Mist began to fall,
And Night in hast, did for her Mantle call.
The longing Father of this louely Mayde
Season'd with sorrowes, look't abroad, and pray'd,
The Gods vnited, Onely to restore,
His owne againe; and he would aske, no more
Those prayers had wings, And an impulsiue power,
To bringe her safe, into his armes, that hower;
From whence releac't; I cannot say repos'd
She sawe her selfe, in a round Ring inclos'd,
Of frends, so fond, to heare that dayes Euent,
They craued a Iournall; which shee did present,
But skip't her owne Part; meaning to contract,
Her selfe in little; So shee lamed that Act.
But when the Story, that she tooke in hand,
Touch't vpon, Algernoune Northomberland,
Or any way, did of his Actions treat,
Her language flow'd; And she drew him in Great.
Such an Impression her relation wrought
In each ones Fancy, as he sleeping thought,
His Eye as well, inform'd him as his Eare,
So all was seene by those that were not there.
This wonder (Madam) may perhapps be found
The first effected by your Tongues sweet sound
But for your Eyes, the Sands in Saturnes glasse
Can hardly serue for Counters as they passe

And though by Age & many crosses cool'd
He suffers most, who by him selfe is foold.

TEXTUAL NOTES

Emendations of copy-text:

Title O] *C omits*

1 Madame] [[*MS damaged*]adame *C*] Madam *O*

3 in so serene a Skye *O*] fix't in so high a Sphere, *C*

4 fell short, Loue only soar'd so high. *O*] came short; onely pure Loue mou'd there. *C*

6 Pretenders *O*] pretender *C*

8 out-vie *O*] outface *C*

9 *indent O*] *no indent C*

27 mentioned *O*] stood for *C*

29 Queene, *O*] Quee[*MS damaged*] *C*

30 seene, *O*] *MS damaged C*

31 and cleare, *O*] an[*MS damaged*] *C*

32 appeare, *O*] ap[*MS damaged*] *C*

33 displease, *O*] disp[*MS damaged*] *C*

34 Antipodes. *O*] Antip[*MS damaged*] *C*

35 passe *O*] p[*MS damaged*] *C*

36 glasse. *O*] Glasse[. *MS damaged*] *C*

37 who *O*] that *C*

38 puffe *O*] breath *C*

40 all the *O*] the whole *C*

43 sent out such *O*] fell into *C*

51 yet a *O*] yet in *C*

52 this *O*] that *C*

56 For breath he brought her to *O*] He enterteyn'd her, in *C*

57 Triton- *O*] Manly *C*

58 of *O*] in *C*

63 Wynes wer *O*] Wyne was *C*

70 rose *O*] rise *C*

71 that *O*] this *C*

83 so *O*] then *C* alonge, *O*] ~ [*MS damaged*] *C*

85 welcome *O*] Liberall *C*

89 *indent O*] *no indent C* Triumph went] Triumph wen[*MS damaged*] *O*; *MS damaged C*

90 Into her Barge, too short a complement *O*] Came to her Barge; which should haue [*MS damaged*] *C*

91 to part *O*] *MS damaged C*

92 next his Heart, *O*] *MS damaged C*

93 As *O*] When *C* the Wind, *O*] *MS damaged C*

94 combind)] ~, *O*; *MS damaged C*

95 came a Puffe (which made the streamers tosse) *O*] breath'd a Blast, that made th[*MS damaged*] *C*

96 losse. *O*] *MS damaged C*

97 shrowdes] shr[*MS damaged*] *C*

98 Clowdes;] Clowdes[*MS damaged*] *C*

99 Billows rose] B[e *alt. to* i]llow rise *C*
101 *indent O*] *no indent C*
105 Those prayers *O*] This Praier *C*
106 safe *O*] back *C*
107 I cannot say *O*] not halfe an howre *C*
117–26 *O*] *C omits*
120–1 *O shows additional space between lines*
124–5 *O shows additional space between lines; no indent*

Verbal variants:

61–2 *O omits*
65 she *C*] they *O*
97 so he that from the shrowdes *C*] *O omits*
98 *O omits*
99 The Billows rose] *O omits*

NOTES

For their comments on a draft of this article am indebted to John and Nancy Safford, To Professor Michael P. Parker, and to Professor John Burrows, to whom I also owe a large debt for his willingness to subject the poem on Lady Katherine Howard to his rigorous statistical tests. To Professor Harold Love I am grateful both for his critique of an earlier version of this article, for his encouragement of my work on Waller, and for the exemplary scholarship of his *Attributing Authorship: An Introduction* (Cambridge, 2002).

1 Peter Beal, *Index of English Literary Manuscripts*, Vol. I: *1450–1625*, Part 1: *Andrewes—Donne* (London and New York, 1980), pp. 247–8.

2 Peter Beal, *Index of English Literary Manuscripts*, Vol. II: *1625–1700*, Part 2: *Lee—Wycherley* (London and New York, 1993), pp. 135–6; idem, *In Praise of Scribes: Manuscripts and their Makers in Seventeenth Century England* (Oxford, 1998), p. 148. A pencilled note inside the front cover asserts that the manuscript is in the hand of Katherine Philips's friend, Sir Edward Dering; but a comparison with his autograph manuscript of her poems at the University of Texas at Austin (Pre-1700 MS 151) does not support the claim.

3 Timothy Raylor, *Cavaliers, Clubs, and Literary Culture: Sir John Mennes, James Smith, and the Order of the Fancy* (Newark, London, and Toronto, 1994), pp. 47, 92, 95–7.

4 National Archives, SP 16/364/68; printed in E. W. Bligh, *Sir Kenelm Digby and his Venetia* (London, 1932), p. 235.

5 National Archives, SP 9/51/34.

6 See my discussion in 'The Early Poetic Career of Edmund Waller', *Huntington Library Quarterly*, 69 (2006), 239–65 (253–4).

7 It is clear from his log of the voyage that Northumberland boarded the *Triumph* on 15 May: Greenwich, National Maritime Museum, Caird Library, LEC/5.

8 George Garrard wrote to Thomas Wentworth, Earl of Strafford on 10 May 1638 to the effect that the marriage had either already taken or was soon to take place: William Knowler (ed.), *The Earl of Strafforde's Letters and Dispatches*, 2 vols. (Dublin, 1740), II, 165; G. E. C[okayne], *The Complete Peerage*, 13 vols (London, 1910–59); Malcolm Rogers, 'Van Dyck's Portrait of Lord George Stuart, Seigneur d'Aubigny',

in Susan J. Barnes and Arthur K. Wheelock, Jr., *Van Dyck 350*, Studies in the History of Art, 46; Center for Advanced Study in the Visual Arts: Symposium Papers XXVI (Washington, D.C., 1994), pp. 263–80 (270, 274); and see also, CSPD 1638–9, p. 276; Ann Hughes, 'Stuart [née Howard], Katherine, Lady Aubigny', *Oxford Dictionary of National Biography*.

9 A point I owe to Professor Harold Love.

10 There is an apparent allusion to spring in its second and third paragraphs, in which the poet mentions having seen Lady Katherine 'suted like the Season, and the Day, | In Greene, and whight', in which garb she outvies 'the flowre of May', but the grammar of this passage—'I haue seen you'— refers to a past, rather than the present occasion; it does not, therefore, affect our dating of the entertainment. I argue in my forthcoming 'The Masquing Career of Lady Katherine Howard' that it refers to her appearance in the Queen's shrovetide masque of 1631.

11 National Maritime Museum, Caird Library, LEC/5.

12 ibid. The princes arrived at Deal on 28 June. For the entertainment, see *Strafforde's Letters*, II, 84, 85.

13 CSPD 1637, p. 216; Historical Manuscripts Commission [HMC], *Fourteenth Report*, Appendix, Part II (London, 1894), pp. 42–3.

14 We know from his correspondence that her father was at Dover in the summer of 1636 (June-September); CSPD 1636–7, pp. 50, 51, 59, 79, 80, 85, 101, 135, and again in the summer of 1637 (August), CSPD 1637, p. 348.

15 HMC, 77: *Report on the Manuscripts of the Right Honourable Viscount De L'Isle*, Vol. VI: *Sidney Papers, 1626–1698*, ed. G. Dyfnallt Owen (London, 1966), p. 106.

16 HMC, *De L'Isle, VI*, p. 106.

17 National Maritime Museum, Caird Library, LEC/5.

18 HMC, *Fourteenth Report*, Appendix, Part II, p. 36.

19 Northumberland had been appointed Admiral in 1636, the higher title being at that time held in commission; Gerald Brenan, *History of the House of Percy*, 2 vols (London, 1902), II, 220. On his appointment: Brenan, II, 224–6; CSPD 1637–8, p. 321; CSPVen. 1636–9, p. 394; *Strafforde's Letters*, II, 154; on his installation, reported on 16 April: CSPVen. 1636–9, p. 398.

20 *The Poems of Edmund Waller*, ed. George Thorn Drury, 2 vols. (London, 1901), hereafter '*WP*', II, 171; *N&Q*, 4th ser. iii (1869), 222–3 (223). The illness appears to have come upon him suddenly near the end of the month. George Garrard, intelligencer to Northumberland's 'bosom friend' Conway, wrote to Thomas Wentworth, Earl of Strafford on 10 May to the effect that Northumberland had been ill for ten days, followed by two nights during which he appeared to improve: *Strafforde's Letters*, II, 168. By Garrard's count, Northumberland must have fallen ill by 29 April at the latest. Archbishop Laud, by contrast, wrote to Strafford on 14 May and claimed that Northumberland had been sick for three weeks, which would push the date back to 23 April: *Strafforde's Letters*, II, 171. The two claims are not entirely consistent with one another; one writer must be mistaken. Given his proximity to Northumberland, Garrard should probably be counted the more reliable authority.

21 CSPD 1637–8, pp. 428, 474–5.

22 CSPVen. 1636–9, p. 419; HMC, *De L'Isle, VI*, p. 145; CSPD 1637–8, p. 523.

23 *Strafforde's Letters*, II, 179; CSPD 1637–8, p. 578. On 23 July he wrote, for the first time since falling sick, in response to Strafford's letter of 23 April: *Strafforde's Letters*, II, 185.

24 *Strafforde's Letters*, II, 186.

25 CSPD 1637–8, p. 609; HMC, *De L'Isle, VI*, p. 151.

26 Poems to Lucy include, 'The country to my Lady of Carlisle', 'The Countess of Carlisle in mourning', 'In answer to one who writ against a fair lady', and 'Of her chamber'; those to Dorothy and her family include 'To my Lord of Leicester', 'At Penshurst', 'On my Lady Dorothy Sidney's picture', 'To a very young lady', 'To the servant of a fair lady', and other 'Sacharissa' lyrics.

27 On these poems, see David Norbrook, 'An Unpublished Poem by Sidney Godolphin', *RES*, NS 48 (1997), 498–500.

28 *WP*, I, 65 (line 38).

29 *Edmund Waller*, p. 104.

30 CSPD 1636–7, pp. 41–2; National Archives SP 16/342/41—an undated deposition by John Denne, found among items possibly dating from around 1636, mentions that Portland was accompanied to Deal by his brother and a 'Mr Waler'. The identification of this figure as the poet is supported by his known intimacy with Portland: *WP*, I, *xlviii–li*.

31 *WP*, I, 100, 75; II, 181.

32 Stephen Orgel and Roy Strong, *Inigo Jones: The Theatre of the Stuart Court*, 2 vols. (London, Berkeley, and Los Angeles, 1973), II, 705; Lady Anne's name is obscured by an error in Orgel and Strong's list of masquers: for her involvement see Francis Lenton, *Great Britain's Beauties* (1638), quoted in Leota Snider Willis, *Francis Lenton, Queen's Poet* (Philadelphia, 1931), p. 29. For Waller's elegy, see *WP*, I, 37; II, 174.

33 *WP*, II, xlii–xliii.

34 For a good, brief, overview of these poems, see Jack G. Gilbert, *Edmund Waller* (Boston, 1979), pp. 103–8.

35 I owe this observation to John Safford.

36 See, for example, [Philip Neve], *Cursory Remarks on some of the Ancient English Poets, particularly Milton* (London, 1789), p. 65; [Francis Atterbury], 'Preface to the Second Part of Mr. Waller's Poems'; *WP*, I, xxv.

37 The rhyme 'grace/place' (lines 53–4) also appears in 'At Penshurst' (lines 7–8; *WP*, I, 46), and a version of it—'grac'd/plac'd'—in his draft verses towards his *Panegyrick* on Cromwell (see Timothy Raylor, 'Reading Machiavelli; Writing Cromwell: Edmund Waller's copy of "the prince' and its draft verses towards 'A panegyrick to my Lord Protector"', *Turnbull Library Record*, 35 (2002), 9–32 (18)); 'main/again' (lines 47–8) appears in 'The Battle of the Summer Islands' (III, 71–2; *WP*, I, 73); 'found/sound' (lines 121–2) in 'Upon His Majesty's repairing of Paul's' (lines 14–15; *WP*, I, 16); and 'shrouds/clouds' (lines 97–8), found in the plural in 'The apology of Sleep' (lines 27–8; *WP*, I, 81), and in the singular in both 'To my Lady Morton, on New Year's Day, 1650' (lines 21–2; *WP*, II, 7) and 'On St. James's Park, as lately improved by his Majesty' (lines 29–30; *WP*, II, 41). Finally, the internal rhyming of 'Barge' on 'Charge' (lines 90, 92) echoes the use of this rhyme in 'Of the Danger His Majesty (being Prince) escaped in the road at St. Andrews' (lines 39–40; *WP*, I, 2).

38 See Harold Love, *Attributing Authorsh*ip, pp. 90–1.

39 On the dating of this poem, see Margaret Crum (ed.), *The Poems of Henry King* (Oxford, 1965), pp. 247–8.

40 I thank John Burrows for drawing this to my attention.

41 The presence of two close coincidences among this poem and the works of both Waller and Henry King might be explained by biographical and poetic connections between the two men: in 1638 they contributed poems to collections on Ben Jonson, Lady Anne Rich, and George Sandys; Crum (ed.), *Poems of King*, p. 15.

42 *Godfrey of Bulloigne: A Critical Edition of Edward Fairfax's Translation of Tassos Gersalemme Liberata, together with Fairfax's Original Poems*, ed. Kathleen M. Lea and T. M. Gang

(Oxford, 1981), p. 635. The other users of the phrase are Richard Braithwait and Matthew Stevenson. Both were working after Spenser and Fairfax.

43 Warren Chernaik, *The Poetry of Limitation: A Study of Edmund Waller* (New Haven and London, 1968), pp. 219–21.

44 For the borrowings (in 'Of the Danger', 'To the King, on his Navy', and 'The Battle of the Summer Islands') see *Godfrey of Bulloigne*, pp. 635–6; *WP*, II, 154, 161, 180–1.

45 'A la malade' (lines 19–20, 23–4; *WP*, I, 85–6); 'Instructions to a Painter' (lines 105–6: *WP*, II, 52).

46 Two further instances of close but not identical parallelism are perhaps worth noticing: cp. 'surprys'd with Ioy' (line 27) with 'joy surprise', from 'To the King, upon his Majesty's happy return' (line 10; *WP*, II, 36); 'hauing dissolu'd the knot' (lines 42) with 'one link dissolved', from 'Of the Danger' (line 170; *WP*, I, 7).

47 See, for example, the definite article in line 4 of 'In answer to one who writ against a fair lady' (*WP*, I, 24) and the unfortunate combination of syntax, lineation, and rhyme in lines 19–20 of 'At Penshurst' (*WP*, I, 64).

48 See the text and analysis in Raylor, 'Reading Machiavelli', 17–26.

49 Elijah Fenton (ed.), *The Works of Edmund Waller Esqr in Verse and Prose* (London, 1729), p. lxxxiii; cf. Raylor, 'Reading Machiavelli', 22.

50 I take the term from Love, *Attributing Authorship*, pp. 46–9; to Professor Love I also owe this suggestion.

A Computational Approach to the Authorship of 'Lady Katherine Howard's Voyage'

John Burrows

Timothy Raylor has invited me to use the methods of computational stylistics to assess the likely authorship of 'The Lady Katherine Howard's Voyage and Enterteynement'. His own evidence of Edmund Waller's authorship, as set out above, makes a strong case. I offer that opinion immediately to remind the reader of the need to judge whether my own approach remains fair-minded. The text itself and the question of attribution are of particular interest because the putative author is a poet of high standing and because the poem differs from most of his work.

Raylor's contention that the poem is inferior in quality to most of Waller's verse is not one on which the methods of computational stylistics can be brought to bear. But a marked difference in kind from Waller's usual poetic practice does make itself felt when those methods are employed to compare the poem with others on the basis of word-frequencies. Waller is not much given to the retrospective narrative that makes up the main body of this poem. And, though he is more given to the courtly lyric that constitutes the 'frame-poem' here, its combination with narrative yields a curiously shaped hybrid.

A brief paraphrase will show why the shape of the poem makes for an unusual pattern of word-counts among the common words. The first three quatrains address Lady Katherine directly, telling her how the poet-speaker had seen her shining in three different spheres and how powerfully he had been affected. The next six lines treat of the putative effect on him ('had I seene you') of her embarkation, an occasion on which he was not present. The many little deaths of Line 12 would have been transformed, he holds, into 'a lasting trance' (l. 18).

Lines 19–48, still addressed directly to her, are an account of what the ship's crew might be supposed to have seen as she approached and came on board. Lines 49–109, which are couched as third-person narrative, treat of her visit to the ship and her return to shore. Though no speaker is identified, the implied point of view shifts back and forth between Lady Katherine and her host, the Earl of Northumberland. In the remaining twenty-odd lines of the poem, the account she later gives her friends, modestly focussed on Northumberland and not herself, is transmuted into a renewal and heightening of the poet's opening compliment. Thanks to her all-seeing eye and her gift of rhetoric, 'all was seene by those that were not there' (l. 120). The poet, now quite overcome, abandons himself to the despondency proper to late scions of the cult of courtly love.

Much of Waller's early verse consists of love-songs, cousins in miniature of the 'frame-poem' in 'Lady Katherine's Voyage' but unlike its embedded narrative. (The only two notable narratives will be considered in due course.) Most of his later work is on a larger scale, whether that of elegy, of political eulogy, or of the immense divine poems. The narrative-oriented past-tense verbs that predominate in 'Lady Katherine's Voyage' are accordingly less common in almost all his other work. The poem is also marked by its use of pronouns in the first-person singular. In the later work, however, Waller is among the most frequent users of **we/our/us** and the least frequent user of **I/my/me** of the seventeenth-century poets of my main database. The reason is that the later Waller customarily represents himself as speaking for a community—the subjects of Cromwell, of the King, or of the Almighty. In treating chiefly of the attributes of these powerful figures, he turns rather more often to **his** and **their** than to **he/him** or **they/them**. This distinction does not hold in 'Lady Katherine Howard's Voyage', where **she/her** naturally predominates but where the crew figure strongly as **them**. Whereas the early songs often observe convention in preferring **thou/thy/thee** to **you/your**, our poem stands with Waller's later work and also with that of his poetic successors in preferring **you/your**. Among the main relative pronouns, Waller usually prefers **which**. He uses **that** fairly freely but rarely uses **who**. But even at a time when the personally-oriented **that** ('He that died') was still available, the dominance of **who**, in a poem focussed upon particular people, is not implausible. The frequency pattern of most prepositions in 'Lady Katherine Howard's Voyage' also departs from Waller's custom. That may have to do with the energetic physical activity portrayed here. It is nevertheless an unusual kind of difference because prepositional frequencies are generally among the most stable of all authorial habits.

And yet the poem resembles Waller in many other word-counts, including some where the quiet but powerful force of authorial habit might be expected to prevail over the overt effects of a change in genre.

These include a frequent recourse to the demonstratives **this/that/those** and to the conjunction **so**, the latter often showing an unusual though not unique near-fusion of conjunction and adverb of manner (e.g. Lines 97, 112, 120). Waller is among the least frequent users of the main coordinate conjunctions, **and/but/or/nor**: our poem shows low counts for all of them. He is among the more frequent users of **as** and the preposition **like**, the chief markers of English similes: our poem shows high counts for both. By virtue of a strong emphasis upon the things about them, Marvell and Waller outrank all the other seventeenth-century poets I have studied in the rate at which they use the definite article. Our poem uses **the** at an even higher rate.

The methods of computational stylistics make it possible to resolve such conflicts of resemblance and difference. These methods all rely upon setting texts whose authorship is to be tested in a framework of texts whose authorship is known. Since they rest upon processes of comparison, they cannot prove that a given text is certainly the work of a given author. But they can show, on the basis of stated criteria, that a text resembles the work of one author more (or less) closely than it resembles the work of others and, accordingly, that it is likely (or unlikely) to be his or hers.

As a framework of texts whose authorship is known, we shall be using a large database of verse by poets born in the seventeenth century. In its latest form, the corpus of 520,796 words draws upon the work of the twenty-five poets listed below in TABLE 1 (p. 245).[1]

From such a set of texts, the computer enables us to rank all the words used in an overall hierarchy of frequency; to tabulate many different poets' scores for each word in turn; and to identify those common words to which each poet has more or less frequent recourse than his fellows. Such individual divergences from a well-founded norm may reflect habitual choices of subject or of genre or subtler idiosyncrasies of manner. But, provided the chosen sample of a given poet's work is adequate, they are much more likely to reflect the presence of some such propensities than to be the effect of chance. The overall table of frequencies makes a basis for comparing any given poet not merely with any other but with all the others. And, since fresh specimens can be added to the overall table, it is possible to measure their behaviour against the rest. The fact that the words to be studied are allowed, at least at first, to choose themselves on no other basis than their relative frequency avoids the circularity of selecting just such evidence as will favour a preferred outcome.

TABLE 2 (p. **000** below) offers a sketch of the main word-list in descending order of frequency for the first one hundred and fifty words.

It also, for purposes that will emerge, identifies those words where Waller's scores carry him either above or below most of his fellows, locating him in either the top or the bottom six of the twenty-five poets who are included.

In keeping with the practice of most computational stylisticians, all of the texts were modernised to eliminate the discrepancies of spelling that figure in seventeenth-century English texts and affect the word-counts on which analyses like ours rely. Contractions and abbreviations were expanded so that the frequencies of words like **I** and **have**, **do** and **not** are not reduced in texts where forms like **I've** and **don't** are common. A few archaic forms like **ere** were altered so as to standardise the counts of words like **ever** and **before**. A number of homographic forms like **to** and **that** were tagged in such a way as to distinguish infinitives from prepositions, conjunctions from demonstratives and relatives. Those that figure among the most common words are identified in TABLE 2.

For a first trial of the question at issue, I subjected 'Lady Katherine Howard's Voyage' to the 'Delta procedure'.[2] The purpose of this approach is to take a text of doubtful authorship and to establish which of many specimens of known authorship is least unlike it. The other specimens, indeed, can all be ranked according to the degree of their unlikeness. In the investigation just mentioned, where the basis for comparison was the twenty-five-poet database described above, two hundred poems written by members of the database but not themselves included in it, were examined. These poems ranged in length from around one hundred words to almost twenty thousand. It emerged that the Delta procedure has two useful powers. One is positive. For poems of more than two thousand words, Delta ranked the true author first of all—that is, as 'least unlike'—in nineteen cases out of twenty. In the twentieth case, it ranked him second. That high rate of success diminished as the texts grew shorter. With sixty poems ranging from five hundred to fifteen hundred words in length, the true author ranked first in only thirty-one. And yet, with these shorter texts, the procedure displayed a valuable negative power. The true author usually ranked within the first five; not infrequently in the next five; and almost never outside the first ten. The procedure, in fact, was over 90% accurate in indicating which fifteen of twenty-five poets were least likely to have written a given short poem.

The negative function of the procedure is decidedly the more helpful in the case of 'Lady Katherine Howard's Voyage', a poem of just a thousand words. In a number of open trials, Waller ranked between eighth and tenth. He moved up to fifth when a large selection from Waller's *Poems* of 1645, the principal collection of his early work, was put in place of the main set. The only strong positive results emerged when the word-list was modified by excluding all the pronouns and inflected verbs, some of which are the problem-words of my opening comments.[3] From an analysis of the top sixty-nine words of this modified word-list, Waller ranked second (after Swift!). From an analysis of the top forty-nine, he ranked first. On the negative side of the Delta analysis, in short, Waller could not be excluded. And the fact that the poem behaved more like Waller's work when rationally modified word-lists were tested gave some positive colouring to the outcome.

The 'Delta procedure' is still under investigation. The long-established statistical technique known as principal component analysis has now been used in a range of literary studies, including work on Milton, on Rochester, and on documents associated with the American Civil War.[4] According to a major survey of the field, it is to be seen as 'the standard first port-of-call for attributional problems in stylometry.'[5]

The effectiveness of this procedure for work like ours depends upon a fact that needs a little illustration: the frequencies of many common words vary in consonance with each other from text to text. At its most obvious, this consonance can be seen in grammatically driven phenomena like the agreement between subject and verb, or the consistency of number, mood, and tense between one verb and its neighbours. Where **thou** is present, we may certainly expect to find **art** and **wilt**. Where **was** is unusually common, we may reasonably expect to find higher than usual scores for **were** and **had**, lower than usual for **is** and **have**. **Could** is likely to vary in consonance with **would** and **should**, though the last is vanishing from modern use. Above and beyond these simple cases, a wealth of similar consonances makes for subtle but consistent frequency-patterns of many kinds. Although the all-purpose 'like, man' of modern demotic speech carries no obvious grammatical consequences, it does not occur in stylistic isolation and is likely to accompanied by expressions as empty as itself including the ubiquitous 'you know'. Although there is no necessary link between a frequent use of 'so that', 'so . . . that', and '*vb.* + that' in clauses of purpose, result, and noun-object, they usually hive together in the old-fashioned sort of educated writing that commonly carries a higher than usual proportion of embedded relative clauses and a wealth of Latinate polysyllables. A preference for **which** over **that** is not uncommon in such texts and some prepositions are abundant.

Only in extreme cases, like **thou/thy/thee,** are we dealing with phenomena that will either occur frequently or not occur at all in a given text. Almost all will find some place in most ordinary English texts of the last four hundred years or so. We are faced, accordingly, with questions of *concomitant variation* in frequency across a range of texts. They are best approached by establishing a correlation-matrix. Such matrices are tables of correlation-coefficients, showing the respective levels of concomitant variation between all the pairs of variables in a given set of specimens. The coefficients are given as decimal fractions running from 1.000 to −1.000, from a perfect positive correspondence, across a middle ground where little or no correspondence can be observed, down to a perfect negative correspondence.

An analysis of our main set of texts by twenty-five poets yields, for example, correlations of 0.837 between **I** and **me**; of 0.389 between **I** and **you**; and of −0.477 between **I** and **the**. The idea that texts where **I** ranks higher (or lower) than usual are likely to be those where **me** and **you** do so is self-explanatory. The idea that **I** and **the** tend to stand opposed—high when low, and vice-versa—marks a simple contrast between personally and impersonally-oriented texts. But further examples call for more energetic explanation. **I** also correlates at 0.348 with **who**, 0.450 with **since**, 0.434 with **every**, 0.424 with **ever**, and −0.344 with **our**. All of the coefficients cited lie above the accepted levels of 'statistical significance', levels at which there is little ground for dismissing a result as the likely effect of chance. And each of the coefficients cited lies within a vast network in which every member pairs, in turn, with every other member. To examine a large table of this kind, in which (say) the most common ninety-nine words are all correlated with each other is merely to drown in the numbers. To adapt a phrase from quite another context, such a table is a treasure-house of detail but an incomprehensible whole.

The value of principal component analysis is that it picks out the main patterns of such matrices and opens them to explanation. In this procedure, a matrix of correlations for all the individual variables in a given set of specimens is used as the basis for a new compact set of 'components', which distinguish the main lines of patterning in the original matrix and arrange them in descending order of importance. Each component, in turn, shows likenesses and differences among the specimens.[6] When principal component analysis is employed in literary applications, the specimens are texts, parts of texts, or sets of texts. The variables are word-counts, specimen by specimen, for many of the more common English words. The outcome of the analysis can be displayed in simple scatter-plots like those that follow shortly. It is often enough to take the first two principal components as the axes of such a scatter-plot. Sometimes, as in our first, exploratory example, it is worth adding the third principal component to the display.

Whenever texts or sets differing in length are to be compared, the word-counts must be standardised as (say) percentages of the length of each text or set. But even the standardised word-counts for single poems, especially brief ones, tend to diverge more widely from any overall norms than do those of large mixed data-sets. For this reason our opening comparison will include some additional pieces. The most obvious texts to compare with 'Lady Katherine Howard's Voyage' are Waller's only narratives, both early pieces collected in the *Poems* of 1645. 'Of the danger his Majestie (being Prince) escaped at the rode at St. Andere' runs to 1322 words. 'The Battell of the Summer Islands', a mock-epic in three cantos, runs in all to 1777 words. To focus on the narrative element, I have excluded the heavily descriptive opening canto and taken the other two, amounting to 1193 words. For a third specimen of Waller's early verse, I have made a set consisting of 8873 words. This set comprises thirty-one other poems from the 1645 collection. They are the longest of them and they range upward from a threshold of about twenty-two lines (roughly 150 words).

The basis upon which FIGURE 1 rests is a table of standardised word-counts for ninety-nine variables and twenty-nine specimens. The variables, listed in TABLE 2, are the ninety-nine most common words of our main dataset (ninety-nine being the maximum correlation-capacity of our software). The specimens are the twenty-five members of that dataset, as listed in TABLE 1 and the four additional pieces just mentioned. Between the original table of word-counts and the result displayed in FIGURE 1 lie the procedures sketched in the last page or so. But what of the result?

Figure 1. Twenty-five poets and four test-pieces.

Text-plot for the 99 most common words of the main dataset.

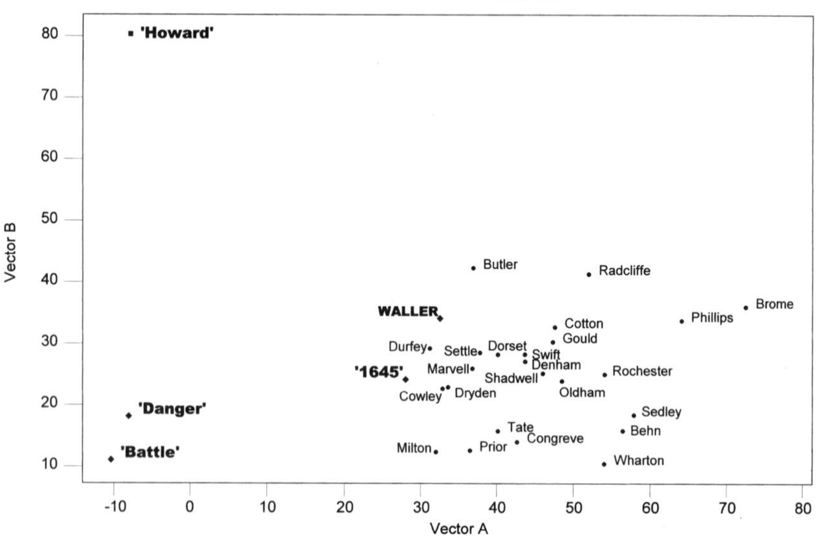

The two axes of Figure 1 are 'vectors' or sequences in which the twenty-nine entries are arranged according to scores deriving from the first two principal components. As a whole, accordingly, such a figure is to be seen as a space in which the entries arrange themselves on the basis of their main resemblances and differences. Quite the most striking feature in the present case is that, on the horizontal axis, the three single-text entries stand far apart from the other twenty-six. Of those three, so close to each other on the horizontal axis, the entry for 'Lady Katherine Howard's Voyage' stands far apart from the two authentic Waller pieces on the vertical axis. Among the other twenty-six entries, there is at first sight an incipient chronological pattern in which most of the poets active before the Restoration lie towards the left (or 'western') side of the main group while their successors lie towards the right. But the locations of Brome, Durfey, and Settle are the most obvious departures from a pattern that does not survive a close inspection. The fact that the entries for the two Waller-sets stand close to each other and among the nearest to the two Waller poems suggests that an authorial factor may be playing some part. But Cowley, Dryden, Durfey, and Milton all lie close enough to them to contest any firm inferences of this kind.

In FIGURE 2, the first principal component still drives the horizontal axis. On the vertical axis, however, the second is replaced by the third. It is as if we had been looking through the lid of a transparent box at the arrangement of its contents. We now add a dimension, look through the side, and see a further perspective. The obvious point of interest in FIGURE 2 is that a marked affinity can now be seen between 'Lady Katherine Howard's Voyage' and 'The Danger . . .' while the latter now stands apart from 'The Battle'. If there is an authorial factor at work in the frequency-patterns that lie behind FIGURES 1 and 2, the flexibility of principal component analysis is enabling it to absorb some real differences between one poem and another.

The proper sequel to an analysis in which the data are allowed to speak for themselves is one in which a direct question is posed and tested. TABLE 2 shows that, of the one hundred and fifty most common words of the main dataset, there are eighty-three for which, in relative frequency of use, Waller ranks in either the first or the last six of our twenty-five poets. A principal component analysis based on this list of eighty-three 'Waller markers' should, by definition, separate our main Waller-set from the other twenty-four. It should also, *ex hypothesi*, show closer affinities among any other Waller-entries than those already seen.

This trial is best managed in two stages. In the first, the existence of a 'Waller signature' is demonstrated. In the second, its effectiveness is brought into question.

Figure 2. Twenty-five poets and four test-pieces.

Second text-plot for the 99 most common words of the main dataset.

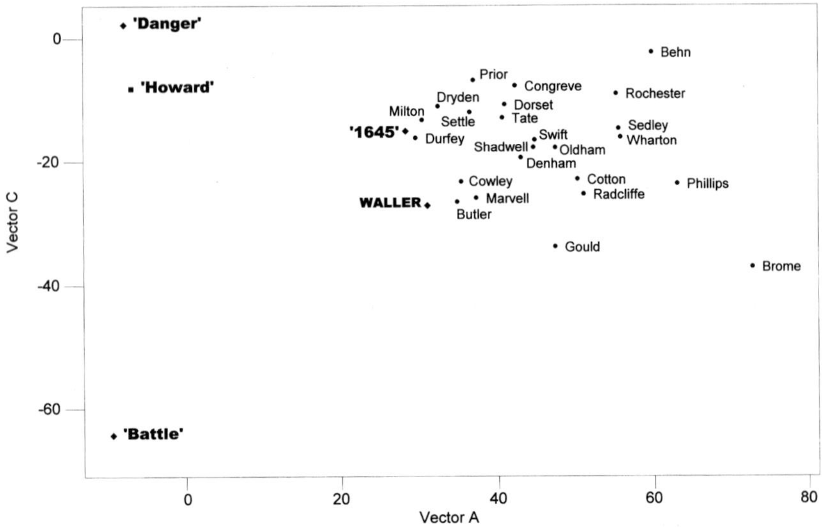

Figure 3a. Twenty-five poets and one test-piece.

Text-plot for the 83 most common 'Waller markers'.

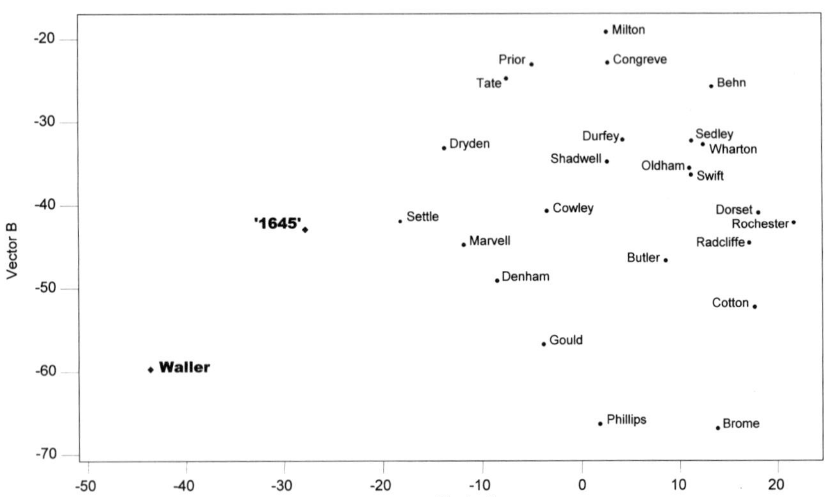

For the first stage, FIGURE 3a represents the outcome of a principal component analysis in which the variables are the eighty-three 'Waller markers' identified above. The twenty-six specimens are the twenty-five members of the main dataset and the small set representing the *Poems* of 1645. As predicted, the two Waller-sets stand close together and they are clearly separated from all the rest.

FIGURE 3b shows why this separation occurs. The eighty-three entries take up their stations according to concomitant frequency-patterns in these twenty-six specimens. In a manner sketched much earlier, the detail of which words align themselves with which others and against which others is rich in suggestions of interest to the student of Waller's verse. These can be pursued by recourse to the texts. But the underlying pattern of FIGURE 3b is simple and unambiguous. The words for which Waller ranks higher than most of his fellows lie towards the 'western' side of the plot, their opposites towards the 'east'. This 'word-plot' is the pattern upon which FIGURE 3a rests and from which it is derived. It amounts, in effect, to a stylistic 'signature' for Waller. If it is well-founded, it should be capable of distinguishing other specimens of his verse from those of other poets.

For the second stage of this new analysis, the same eighty-three variables are employed. 'The Danger', 'The Battle', and 'Lady Katherine

Figure 3b. Twenty-five poets and one test-piece.

Word-plot for the 83 most common 'Waller markers'.

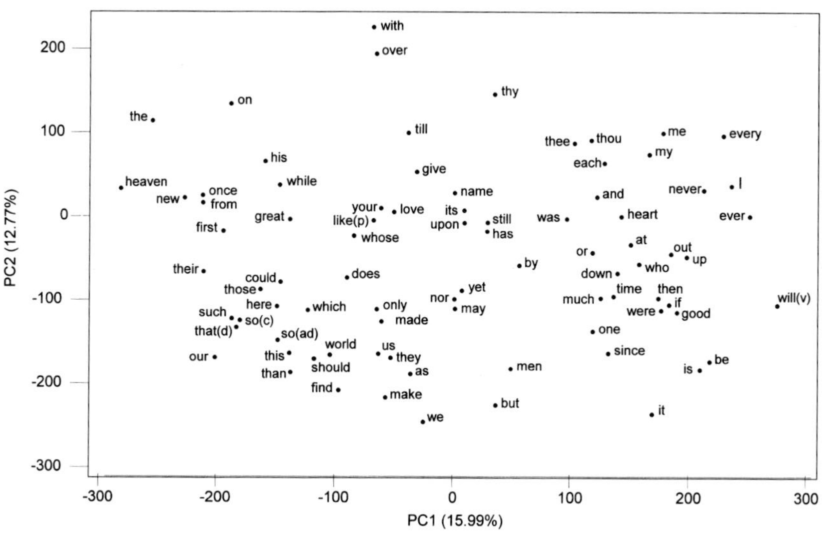

Howard's Voyage' are added to the set of twenty-six specimens. And, to make the test more rigorous, ten further specimens are added. These represent the work of some major poets of the mid-seventeenth century and lie earlier in time than most members of the main dataset. Some are complete but others are samples of about 200 lines from the opening of much longer works. The whole set is listed in TABLE 3 (p. 247 below), with lengths as indicated. Their function, of course, is to test our putative Waller signature. If it were fragile or unreliable, some of the additional entries might be expected to intrude into the ostensible 'Waller-cluster'.

As FIGURE 4 shows, that does not occur. The twenty-four 'non-Waller' entries from the original dataset still make a well-formed central cluster. (This cluster is now so compact that these twenty-four entries are not labelled by their authors' names but are coded alphabetically in the sequence shown in TABLE 1.) The entries for the ten additional specimens are labelled by their authors' names. With one exception, they are widely distributed around the outskirts of the central cluster. The exception, the entry for Vaughan's translation of Juvenal, lies within that cluster. The location of some of the additional entries destroys any suggestion of a chronological patterning. Such a pattern might, for example, have yielded affinities among Vaughan, Davenant, and Fletcher. They are, in fact, among the most widely

Figure 4. Twenty-five poets and fourteen test-pieces.

Text-plot for the 83 most common 'Waller markers'.

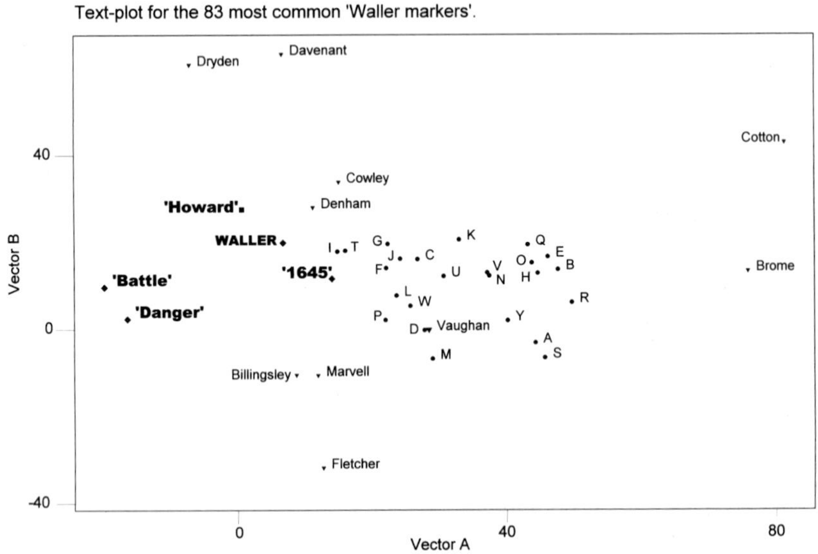

separated entries. Brome and Cotton, on the other hand, are close neighbours from different generations.

As for the authorial factor, FIGURE 4 brings the four Waller-entries into much closer proximity than that seen in FIGURES 1 and 2. The main entry, marked 'WALLER', stands free of the central cluster. The entry for the *Poems* of 1645 is nearby. The entries for 'The Danger' and 'The Battle' still form a pair but lie much closer to the other two. And the entry for 'Lady Katherine Howard's Voyage' rounds out a little group. Whatever its authorship, it is decidedly more like Waller's work than any of the other specimens employed in this comparison.[7]

A further benefit of such comparisons should be observed. The objection that we already know or would confidently suppose that 'Lady Katherine Howard's Voyage' is not the work of Brome, Vaughan, Billingsley, Swift, or any of these others is beside the point. Each of them enhances our representation of the seventeenth-century poetic repertoire and acts as an additional statistical proxy for the unknown and unexaminable writer who may yet be the author of this poem. The wider our sweep across the repertoire, the less space there is for any such interloper. Although we cannot prove that he does not exist, we can show, by a cumulative weight of evidence, that, if he does, he would need to write more like Waller than anybody . . . except Edmund Waller. It should be noted, moreover, that there is no reason at all why an associate of Waller's should actually write like him.[8]

This line of argument can be extended by testing further specimens. The set of thirty texts listed in TABLE 4 (p. 248 below) includes the fourteen of TABLE 3 and adds another sixteen. These others range in length from seven hundred to thirteen hundred words, straddling the thousand words of 'Lady Katherine Howard's Voyage'. They represent most of the genres then fashionable in poems of about this length. Except for John Oldham (born 1653), their authors had all reached adult life before 1660. The two largest authorial sets, four poems apiece, are chosen to represent poets whose stylistic signatures are usually easy (Butler) and much more difficult (Cowley) to identify.

For such a heterogeneous collection of small pieces, cluster analysis is an especially appropriate statistical procedure. It offers rather a harsh test of authorship and the 'family-trees' in which the results are displayed speak plainly for themselves. The procedure is put to excellent use in a recent study of prose-fiction.[9] The principal disadvantage of cluster analysis is that the underlying word-patterns are not made visible; but, as we have seen, these can be approached in other ways.

FIGURE 5 represents the outcome of a cluster analysis in which our thirty texts are compared with each other on the 'non-selective' basis of the 100 most common words. It should be studied from the foot of the page upwards, taking account of the way the clusters form. The texts are identified, along the horizontal axis of the figure, by the numbers attached to them in TABLE 4. The true affinities are not between entries that merely stand beside each other before separating, like Nos. 5 and 6, but between those that form unions, like Nos. 14 and 15. The closest affinities of all are between those pairs that unite soonest, like Nos. 27 and 29.

With some conspicuous exceptions, FIGURE 5 is a picture of failed authorial unions. Four entries (Nos. 1, 2, 4, and 12) stand far from their true partners. In three other cases, two texts by a given author stand in proximity but do not actually unite with each other. Yet Butler's four texts unite as do two of Cowley's four, a level of success that far exceeds the dictates of chance in a game where each authentic union is formed against long odds.

Against this background, the pattern of the Waller entries stands out in high relief. The union between 'The Danger' and '1645' is the very first to form among the thirty texts. They are soon joined by 'The Battle'—but not before 'Lady Katherine Howard's Voyage' has joined them in the first to form of all the trios. And the whole quartet is complete before the Cowley pair or even the first Butler pair has formed. The location of the '1645' entry indicates, moreover, that the quartet rests upon common authorship and not merely upon the (roughly) narrative genre of its other three members.

Figure 5. Cluster analysis for twenty-eight texts.

Analysis based on the 100 most common words of the main dataset.

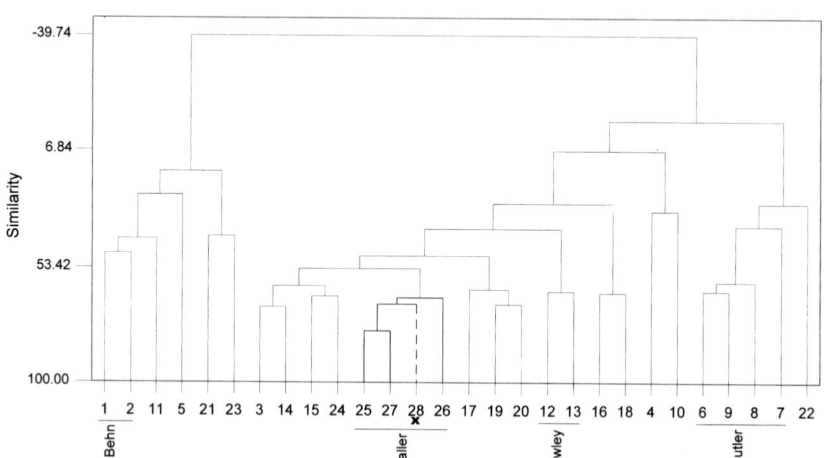

Texts as numbered in Table 4.
x = 'Lady Katherine Howard's Voyage'.

To sum up the computational evidence, the case against Waller's authorship of 'Lady Katherine Howard's Voyage' is that the results of the 'Delta procedure' are mixed; that the poem stands well apart from 'The Danger' and 'The Battle' in FIGURE 1 (though not in FIGURE 2); and that some of my trials suggest that the outcome of the cluster analysis is more than usually sensitive to the length of the word-list employed. The case in favour of Waller's authorship is twofold. In those of our tests where the word-list is self-selecting, the outcome is not predisposed towards any particular author. Yet Waller always makes his presence felt. In those other tests where 'Waller markers' are selected, his claim is brought directly into question. Yet it always holds firm. The strongest feature of the evidence is that the most appropriate word-lists for texts of this length most favour Waller's claim. And, finally, the concurrence of my results with the evidence presented by Timothy Raylor must add weight to both.

TABLE 1. Main set of twenty-five poets

A	Aphra Behn (1640–89) 21,705 words
B	Alexander Brome (1620–66) 29,539
C	Samuel Butler (1612–80) 30,932
D	William Congreve (1670–1729) 30,917
E	Charles Cotton (1630–87) 12,625
F	Abraham Cowley (1618–67) 19,272
G	Sir John Denham (1615–69) 30,092
H	Charles Sackville, Earl of Dorset (1638–1706) 9,586
I	John Dryden (1631–1700) 18,238
J	Thomas D'Urfey (1653–1723), 18,757
K	Robert Gould (1660?–1709?) 29,110
L	Andrew Marvell (1621–78) 23,282
M	John Milton (1608–74) 18,924
N	John Oldham (1653–83) 32,462
O	Katherine Philips (1631–64) 29,004
P	Matthew Prior (1664–1721) 32,000
Q	Alexander Radcliffe (*floruit* 1669–96) 11,889
R	John Wilmot, Earl of Rochester (1648–80) 12,725
S	Sir Charles Sedley (1639?–1701) 10,304
T	Elkanah Settle (1648–1724) 24,080
U	Thomas Shadwell (1642?–92) 14,540
V	Jonathan Swift (1667–1745) 30,974
W	Nahum Tate (1652–1715) 20,333
X	Edmund Waller (1606–87) 16,443
Y	Anne Wharton (1659–85) 12,511.

TABLE 2. The 150 most common words of the main set of texts by 25 poets.

Rank ex 150	W's rank ex 25	Word	Rank ex 150	W's rank ex 25	Word	Rank ex 150	W's rank ex 25	Word
1	1	the	51		did	101	4	men
2	20	and	52		would	102	23	every
3		of	53		now	103		man
4		a	54	25	who(rp)	104	6	whose
5		to(i)	55		that(c)	105	23	out
6		in(p)	56	23	yet	106	1	heaven
7	4	his	57		had	107	25	much
8	6	with	58	25	then	108	24	good
9		to(p)	59	1	such	109	3	while
10	23	is	60		him	110	3	so(c)
11	20	but	61	24	nor	111		well
12		he	62		for(c)	112	24	each
13		all	63	4	like(p)	113	22	only
14	25	I	64	4	love	114		long
15	21	it	65	2	than	115		old
16	3	as	66	6	may	116		day
17	1	their	67		shall	117	5	once
18		her	68	25	me	118		through
19		not	69	23	were	119	21	up(ap)
20	24	be	70	4	great	120		both
21		you	71		there	121	24	heart
22	6	they	72		some	122		art
23		for(p)	73		too	123		wit
24	21	by(p)	74		how	124	2	give
25	25	my	75	5	does	125	23	till
26	4	we	76	23	one	126	2	world
27	2	from	77	25	never	127	25	ever
28		that(rp)	78		them	128		know
29	22	or	79		do	129	2	find
30	1	our	80	1	should	130		fate
31	25	thy	81		though	131	24	its
32	24	was	82		let	132		eyes
33	1	this	83	1	make	133		life
34		when	84	6	could	134		vain
35		are	85	4	those	135		power
36	4	your	86		must	136	20	down
37	24	at	87		an	137		been
38	2	which(rp)	88		where	138		whom

39		no(aj)	89	23	still	139		God
40		what	90	2	us	140		soul
41	5	so(ad)	91	2	here	141	1	new
42	3	that(d)	92		own	142		fair
43	25	will(v)	93	25	thee	143	3	upon(p)
44	2	on(p)	94	2	made	144		whilst
45		can	95	4	has	145	23	since
46		have	96		see	146		come
47		she	97		these	147	24	time
48	25	thou	98		before	148	23	name
49		more	99		thus	149	6	over
50	24	if	100	2	first	150		last

Abbreviations

Rank: Frequency-ranking of each word among the 150 most common words of the main set of texts by 25 poets.

W's rank: Edmund Waller's ranking among the 25 poets (shown only when he lies in the first six or last six places).

Tags: (i) infinitive particle; (p) preposition; c conjunction; (rp) relative pronoun; (aj) adjective; (ad) adverb of degree; (ap) adverbial particle.

TABLE 3. Fourteen texts for analysis.

1	1326*	Billingsley, Nicholas (1633–1709), *The World's Infancy.*
2	1385	Brome, Alexander (1620–66), *The Answer* ('My friend, in troth, I am glad . . .').
3	1537	Cotton, Charles (1630–87), *Epistle to Sir Clifford Clifton.*
4	1315	Cowley, Abraham (1618–67), *To the Royal Society.*
5	1598*	Davenant, Sir William (1606–68), *Gondibert.*
6	1499*	Denham, Sir John (1615–69), *The Fall of Troy.*
7	1170	Dryden, John (1631–1700), *Heroic Stanzas consecrated to the Memory of Oliver.*
8	1748*	Fletcher, Phineas (1582–1650), *The Purple Island.*
9	1536*	Marvell, Andrew (1621–78), *The First Anniversary of the Government under O. C.*
10	1580*	Vaughan, Henry (1622–95), *The Tenth Satire of Juvenal English'd.*
11	1322	Waller, Edmund (1606–87), *Of the Danger his Majesty . . . Escaped.*
12	1193	*do.* *The Battle of the Summer Islands*, Cantos 2–3.
13	8873	*do.* Set of thirty-one poems from the *Poems* of 1645.
14	1000	Anon., *Lady Katherine Howard's Voyage and Entertainment.*

* selection only: first c200 lines.

TABLE 4. Thirty texts.

1	818	Behn, Aphra (1640–89), *On Desire. A Pindarick.*
2	761	*A Pindarick Poem to the Reverend Doctor Burnet.*
3	1326*	Billingsley, Nicholas (1633–1709), *The World's Infancy.*
4	761	Brome, Alexander (1620–66), *The Satyr of Money.*
5	767	*To C. S. Esq.*
6	1385	*The Answer.*
7	705	Butler, Samuel (1612–80), *Satyr upon Drunkenness.*
8	962	*Satyr upon Marriage.*
9	813	*Upon Philip Nye's Thanksgiving Beard.*
10	844	*Upon Modern Critics.*
11	1537	Cotton, Charles (1630–87), *Epistle to Sir Clifford Clifton.*
12	789	*On Tobacco.*
13	816	*Eclogue.*
14	933	Cowley, Abraham (1618–67), *The First Nemaean Ode of Pindar.*
15	816	*Hymn. To Light.*
16	1291	*The Second Olympique Ode of Pindar.*
17	1315	*To the Royal Society.*
18	1598*	Davenant, Sir William (1606–68), *Gondibert.*
19	1499*	Denham, Sir John (1615–69), *The Fall of Troy.*
20	1170	Dryden, John (1631–1700), *Heroic Stanzas consecrated to the Memory of Oliver.*
21	1748*	Fletcher, Phineas (1582–1650), *The Purple Island.*
22	1536*	Marvell, Andrew (1621–78), *The First Anniversary of the Government under O. C.*
23	887	Oldham, John (1653–83), *Upon the Marriage of the Prince of Orange.*
24	1298	*Satyr upon a Woman.*
25	1210	Philips, Katherine (1631–64), *To the Rt. Hon. The Lady E. C.*
26	1580*	Vaughan, Henry (1622–95), *The Tenth Satire of Juvenal English'd.*
27	1322	Waller, Edmund (1606–87), *Of the Danger his Majesty … Escaped.*
28	1193	*The Battle of the Summer Islands*, Cantos 2–3.
29	8873	Set of thirty-one poems from the *Poems* of 1645.
30	1000	Anon., *Lady Katherine Howard's Voyage and Entertainment.*

* selection only: first c200 lines.

NOTES

1 Most of the corpus was prepared by John Burrows and Harold Love, assisted by Alexis Antonia and Meredith Sherlock. The Marvell subset was contributed by Christopher Wortham assisted by Joanna Thompson.

2 This procedure is described and tested in John Burrows, '"Delta": A Measure of Stylistic Difference and a Guide to Likely Authorship,' *Literary and Linguistic Computing*, 17 (2002), 267–87. The results reported are summarised on p. 275.

3 The omission of these eighty-one words is a deliberate intrusion on the free play of the data. Such experiments are best undertaken after the data have first been given free play.

4 Fiona J. Tweedie, David I. Holmes, and Thomas N. Corns, 'The Provenance of *De Doctrina Christiana*, Attributed to John Milton: A Statistical Investigation', *Literary and Linguistic Computing*, 13 (1998) 77–87. John Burrows, 'A Computational Approach to the Rochester Canon', Appendix, Harold Love, ed., *The Complete Works of John Wilmot, Earl of Rochester* (Oxford, 1999), pp. 681–95. David Holmes, 'A Widow and her Soldier; the Case of the Pickett Letters', *Literary and Linguistic Computing*, 16 (2001), 403–20.

5 David I. Holmes, 'The Evolution of Stylometry in Humanities Scholarship,' *Literary and Linguistic Computing*, 13 (1998), 114.

6 The literary use of the procedure is described in more detail in John Burrows and Hugh Craig, 'Lucy Hutchinson and the Authorship of Two Seventeenth-century Poems: a Computational Approach', *The Seventeenth Century*, 16 (2001),259–82. For an account of the statistical analysis itself, see José Nilo G. Binongo and M. W. A. Smith, 'The Application of Principal Component Analysis to Stylometry', *Literary and Linguistic Computing*, 14 (1999), 445–65.

7 If the third principal component is put in place of the second on the vertical axis, the entry for Davenant's *Gondibert* shows a minor-key affinity for 'Lady Katherine Howard's Voyage'. It seems likely that a resemblance in genre between the high-flown tale of old Aribert and the beauteous Rhodalind and that of Northumberland and Lady Katherine is making itself felt.

8 I pass over the possibility of joint-authorship on the ground that the tests I have made show no clear sign of it. On the face of it, the differences in literary form between the frame-poem and the main narrative are quite sharp enough to account for the stylistic differences registered in the word-counts. More rigorous tests might be undertaken and a more definite conclusion might be attainable if a potential second author could be identified and brought into comparison.

9 Hoover, David, 'Frequent word sequences and statistical stylistics', *Literary and Linguistic Computing*, 17 (2002), 157–80. For those who are versed in these matters, I should add that the statistical package I have used for these cluster analyses is MINITAB. For such data as we are examining, Ward's linkages, squared Euclidean distances, and standardized variables seem to yield the most accurate results. This pattern of preferences avoids any undue smoothing of data whose inherent roughness reflects the complexities of the language itself. Like David Hoover, I have benefited from David Holmes's personal recommendation of Ward's method of calculating linkages.

'The hazzard of grosse mistakes in ignorant Transcribers': A New Manuscript Text of Sir Robert Stapylton's *Musaeus on the Loves of Hero and Leander*

Tom Lockwood

Dedicating his *Erotopaignion* in Oxford in 1645, Sir Robert Stapylton explained to his cousin and patron, Henry Pierrepont, Marquess of Dorchester, that this translation of *The Loves of Hero and Leander* was being printed partly at least so as to elevate its text above the vagaries of manuscript transmission.[1] The genesis of the translation, by Stapylton's account, moved it from a world of oral transmission, through manuscript, and unwillingly into print, finding there a stability (if not necessarily an accuracy) that it could not find in any other mode:

> I confesse the report of Poëms borrowed from *Musæus* made so great a noyse, that to mee the Authour had beene lost in the crowd of his Imitatours, if I had not heard his soft lines sweetned by your Lordship's accent; but then, I could not be satisfied till I made triall how the *Greeke* would goe in *English*: my intent being to translate and dedicate it privately to your Lordship. The Translation was forthwith dispatched, the Dedication is now presented, but the intended Privacie lay not in my power; for my acquaintance (who would know what I was doing) had ingaged me for so many Copies, that I held it my safest course, rather to venture upon the Printers pardonable errours, then to runne the hazzard of grosse mistakes in ignorant Transcribers.[2]

Even this apparent acceptance of print, as is clear, has its limits, for Stapylton goes on to assure his patron that in fact the circulation of the printed book will mimic that limited exclusivity achieved by coterie manuscript circulation: 'Yet, as I could not make it altogether private, so I resolved it should not be altogether publique, and have therefore suffered no more to be printed, then the just number promised; which coming into friends hands, I cannot feare any rigid censure.'[3] This is a very limited, circumscribed kind of publication; but, whatever its contemporary effects, Stapylton's dedication, if not his translation, has recently achieved a new kind of public status, having been read as evidence of the ways in which the material circulation of Royalist writing adapted to the changed circumstances in which the Court found itself after its indirect translation from London to Oxford in 1642. As Jerome de Groot has argued, Stapylton in this dedication seems both to recall an earlier mode of exclusive, coterie-based manuscript circulation as well as to indicate the ways in which Royalist writers were coming in the mid-1640s increasingly to regard print as a more controllable, authoritative medium.[4]

In 1647, when a revised version of his translation was printed in London for Humphrey Moseley, Stapylton expanded upon his earlier dedication as he envisaged yet another expansion of his poem's readership. 'But now,' he wrote, two years after first publication, 'finding so many freinds as challeng not a *few copies* but a *whole Impression*[,] I am forced to answer them, as *Pisistratus* did his sons, that I have done my best to convert them to my Opinion, but since I cannot prevaile, I am resolved to be of theirs; and for their sakes, what I writ for my private exercise, shal be exposed to *common censure*'.[5] This second version of Stapylton's translation confronts this anticipated '*common censure*' bolstered by further dedications 'To the Ladies' and 'To the Gentlemen', and a note 'Of Sestos and Abydos', and is followed by a series of long, learned multi-lingual annotations to the poem, together with annotated translations of Ovid's *Heroides* 18 and 19, dedicated, under a separate title-page, to his wife. This work of annotation directs Stapylton's translation at a set of overlapping audiences that might be compared to those reached, first in manuscript in the early to mid–1630s and later in print from 1651 onwards, by James Smith's mock-poem, *The Loves of Hero and Leander*.[6] What is clear, certainly, is that Stapylton's professed relationship to print underwent some change in the two politically changeable years between 1645 and 1647: the earlier edition, printed in Oxford by Henry Hall, makes a slightly different claim to 'royalism' than the later, printed in London by Moseley, as its conception of its own audiences also changes.[7] None the less, the general tendency of Stapylton's translation as it moved from manuscript and through its two printed editions was to address an increasingly large and potentially still-growing readership. Such a trajectory, which changed direction and potential audience still further after the Restoration with the publication of Stapylton's unperformed verse drama, *The Tragedie of Hero and Leander*, has, however, gone some way to obscure the first manuscript origins of

Stapylton's translation so important to the positions adopted in the two printed dedications.[8] Moreoever, since the kind of 'grosse mistakes' likely to be perpetrated by both skilled and 'ignorant Transcribers' are well-known in the study of manuscript verse of the sixteenth and seventeenth centuries,[9] such little attention as Stapylton's English Musaeus has attracted has apparently been content to take his denigration of manuscript transmission without question, if indeed at all.[10]

The recovery of a previously unknown text of Stapylton's translation offers, then, the welcome opportunity to see the poem as it was treated by one such maligned transcriber. Birmingham University Library, MS KWH 56 (bound sequence), contains a scribal text of 338 lines of Stapylton's poem in a version most closely linked to, but not identical with, his second, 352-line translation of 1647, written throughout in a single mixed hand of the mid-seventeenth century; it was bequeathed to the library by the estate of its one-time Librarian, K.W. Humphreys (1916–1994) in 1995.[11] The manuscript text fills each recto and verso of three disjunct folio leaves of handmade laid paper. Now laminated in lightweight Japanese tissue paper, to preserve them from earlier water damage and consequent fragility, each leaf of the manuscript measures approximately 295 × 193mm, and together they are bound between modern endpapers in twentieth-century cloth binding. Folio 1 has a shield watermark in its centre, but the staining that has damaged this leaf (see PLATE 1 together with the two laminating sheets of tissue paper, obscure its detail; fols 2 and 3 show no watermarks, although the regularity of the vertical chainlines in all three leaves, generally between 20—24mm apart, indicate that all the leaves come from a single stock of paper. The original conjugacy of the three extant leaves of the manuscript is impossible now to reconstruct, but it may be that the manuscript once represented two sheets of paper, folded in folio: in this reconstruction, fols 1 and 2 formed the first of these two bifolia, fol. 3 and a (now lost) fol. 4 the second, this lost fol. 4 bearing the watermark of this sheet of paper. The length of Stapylton's translation would have left the possible fol. 4v blank, a format (as Harold Love has argued of material from a slightly later period) that allowed space for an address or description to aid the text's circulation.[12] On the other hand, these three disjunct sheets may always have been so: the transcriber has numbered each page before the first line of transcribed text, 1 to 6, indicating that there once may have been a need to keep the three separate sheets in reading order. Whichever the case, the manuscript was never quired, but rather simply stab-stitched as is indicated by a stab-hole in the gutter approximately 70mm from the head of each leaf; others further down the gutter have been lost to paper damage, and may indeed

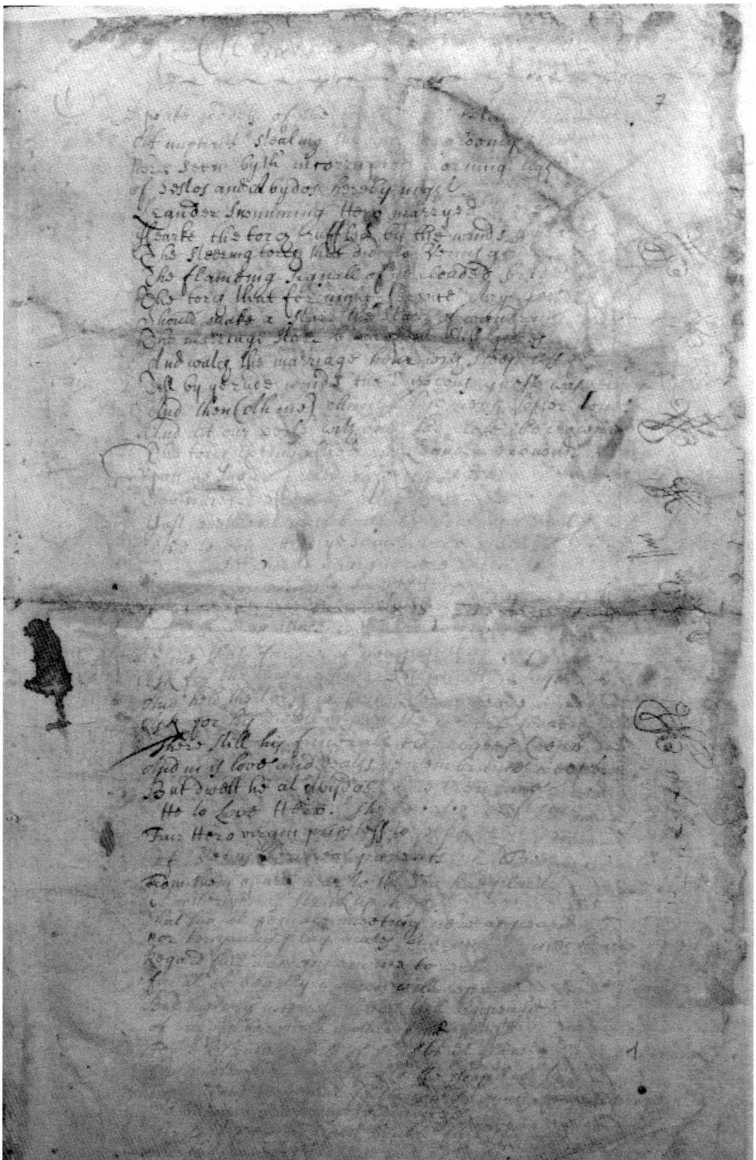

PLATE I. *First page of the scribal manuscript of Stapylton's* Musaeus on the Loves of Hero and Leander*: Birmingham University Library,* MS *KWH 56 (bound sequence), fol. 1r (Original page size 295 × 193mm.) Reproduced by permission of University of Birmingham Information Services, Special Collections Department.*

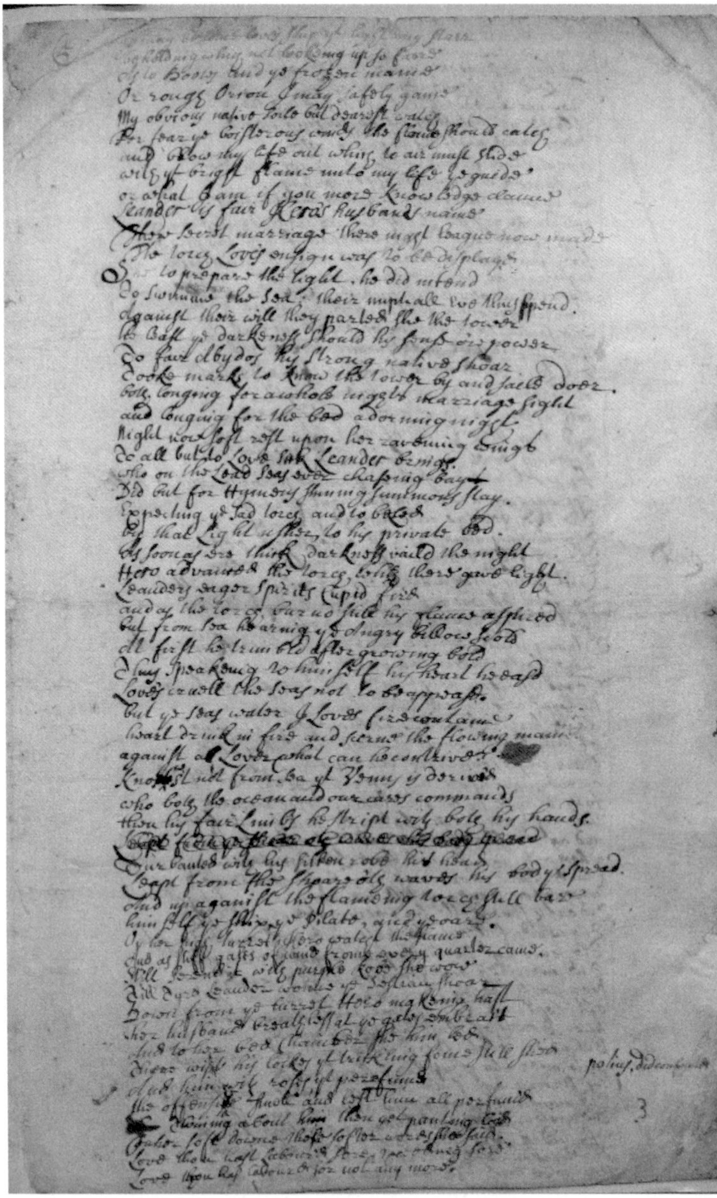

PLATE 2. *Fifth page of the scribal manuscript of Stapylton's* Musaeus on the Loves of Hero and Leander*: Birmingham University Library,* MS *KWH 56 (bound sequence), fol. 3r (Original page size 295 × 193mm.) Reproduced by permission of University of Birmingham Information Services, Special Collections Department.*

have caused it. All three leaves were also at some stage folded horizontally as one unit across their centre, head of leaf to foot of leaf. The fragility of the resulting fold line, as well as the soiling of, and water-damage to, the manuscript, are at their worst on fol. 1r, confirming that it was the outermost leaf in this folded state, a fact that argues for its having taken place after the loss of any possible fol. 4 or else, more radically, for the absence of such a leaf at any stage of the manuscript's existence.

As might be expected, the facile mixed transcribing hand of MS KWH 56 regularly demonstrates both secretary and italic graphs, as can be seen in the illustrations of fols 1r and 3r (PLATES 1 and 2). Sometimes the scribe favours secretary over italic forms—as in the employment of the secretary *h*-graph in terminal digraphs, where the italic *h*-graph more regularly appears initially and medially—but at other times italic and secretary forms are used interchangeably, as in the medial use of the secretary gallows *c*-graph and italic *c*-graph. Miniscule *e*-graph is most often the reversed secretary form, used medially and terminally, although the italic *e*-graph is used in initial position; a variety of *r*-graphs appear, including the modified secretary *z*-graph used at all positions within words. Typical of this hand are a miniscule *t*-graph which rises a little above the *x*-height, and whose shaft is very seldom crossed; and a miniscule *p* in which the lobe of the graph is not closed. That MS KWH 56 is scribal rather than autograph is proved by a comparison with British Library Lansdowne MS 822, fols 23–4, an autograph letter by Stapylton, to Henry Cromwell, of 31 March 1657. Directed to Cromwell, then Commander-in-Chief of the English forces in Dublin, the body of the two-page letter is in a purely italic hand, marked by its very pronounced miniscule *d*-graph, whose ascender rises, swoops off to the left, and then curls counter-clockwise and back across the ascender, forming a loop above the lobe. The contrast between this hand and that of MS KWH 56, in which the ascender of the *d*-graph does tend to the left but never loops back across itself, is marked. Stapylton's letter is subscribed from 'Charing Crosse' and signed, 'Ro: Stapylton;', in a bold spacious round hand. The same signature, with its idiosyncratic punctuation, witnesses British Library Add. Ch. 76952, an indenture between Willi*a*m Michell, William Siddall and Adam Baines, dated 20 June 1652. L.G. Kelly, Stapylton's most recent biographer, mentions neither the letter in Lansdowne MS 822, nor the indenture; moreover, Kelly cautions against a confusion of Sir Robert Stapylton with another contemporary Robert Stapylton, MP and graduate of St Alban Hall, Oxford.[13] Indeed, the contemporary endorsement on Lansdowne MS 822 fol.24r, 'Mr Stapilton | London | 31 March | 1657', would strengthen the supposition that the hand in question belongs to another Robert Stapylton, but for the strong similarities the letter hand bears to that of Stapylton's nephew, Sir Miles Stapylton (1626–1707), as witnessed by two autograph letters by him, British Library Add. MS 27448, fols 293–4 (dated 30 June 1684) and Egerton MS 3336, fols 93–4 (dated 17 December 1688). At the very least, MS KWH 56 is not in the hand of whichever Robert Stapylton wrote BL Lansdowne MS 822, fols 23–4; that the manuscript is scribal is by far the most likely explanation of its palaeographic and textual characteristics.

THE TEXT

What follows is a the text of BUL MS KWH 56 in a diplomatic transcription that draws on an earlier transcription of fols 1–2r in the hand of K.W. Humphreys now loosely slipped into the manuscript's binding. Although my readings on occasion disagree with Humphreys', his transcription preserves, particularly on fol. 1r, some readings that are now, partly because of the poor condition of the manuscript, very difficult to see under either normal or ultraviolet light. Within my transcription, letters inserted by the scribe above the writing line are displayed \thus/, letters inserted on it /thus\; deleted but still legible text is displayed [-thus], illegibly deleted material [-*thus*]. Editorial insertions other than marginal line numbers are indicated by [*italic text within square brackets*]; the line numbers themselves include both the title and the one wholly deleted line (262). Words underlined are either marked thus by the scribe or in one case (line 308) boxed in to key them to the variant readings given in the margin of the transcript; these marginal additions are in the same hand as the rest of the transcript. The punctuation of the manuscript text is very light by comparison with the printed text of 1647, although all four available stops and the question- and exclamation-marks are used by the scribe; a line of inked decorative figures separates the title of the poem from its first line in MS KWH 56, but is not represented in the following transcription.

Musæus on the Love of Hero and Leander

Speake goddess of the torch loves witness made
At nuptials stealing through the gloomy shade
Ne're seen by th' incorrupted morning light
of Sestos and Abydos hereby night
Leander swimming Hero marryed there
Hearke the torch ruffled by the winds I heare

The steering torch that did to Venus guide
The flameing signall of ye clouded bride
The torch that for night service Airy Jove
Should make a starr the starr of wandring love
The marriage starr because it still gives aime
And watch the marriage hour with sleepeless fame,
Till by ye rude winds the Envious guest was blown
And then (Ah me) change hyemens softer tone:
And let our verse with one sad close be crown'd
The torch Extinguished and Leander drownd.
Vpon the shoar parted by ye flood
Too citties Sestos and Abydos stood
Just or'ethwart neighbours his bow Cupid bent
And to both citties ye same Arrow sent
Wherewith a youth a virgin were inflam'd
he Sweet Leander she sweet Hero nam'd.
He at Abydos she at Sestos born
Starr like each other which their Towns Adorne.
Do me that favour if you pass that way
Ask for the tow'r where Sestian Hero lay.
And held the torch wafting Leander o're.
Ask for his dwelling in the adverse shoar
There still his funerall old Abydos keeps
And in is love and deaths remembrance weeps.
But dwelt he at Abydos? how then came
He to Love Hero? she to catch ye flame
Fair Hero virgin priestess to ye power
of Venus her great parents in a Tower
From them apart near to the Sea had plac't
Another Venus strick'ly chast.
That she at female meeting ne're appear'd
nor her young play-mates charming dances hear'd
Regard full womans envie to recline
for at A beauty women will repine.
But she with incense Venus still Appeas'd
of with his heavenly mother Cupid pleas'd
Feare his quiver full of shafts yt glow
But these flameing shafts she escap'd not so.
The Sestians they that feast now so much [-fright] prize
To Venus and Adonis solemnize
Or'e to this holy day in boats full throng
All th'Islanders that to ye sea belong.

[*fol.1v*]
(2) Some from Haemonia from moist Cyprus some
All Phrygia's all Cytherea's women come
non dance on Libanon in perfum'd aire
noe passingers but to this feast repaire,
There wants of neighbouring Abydos none
Of young men y^{t}. love maids not any one
for they to follow will be sure where fame
shall Celebration of a feast proclaime.
nor that the immortall gods their Zeale pursues
but troops of mortall beauty do peruse
Now through the Temple Virgin Hero past
and from her face a lovely splendour Cast
Like the cleare moon when weeping she's beheld
her snowy Cheeks in scarlet Circle swel'd
She lookes as th' blooming damaske-rose you'd swear
Hero a garden full of Roses were.
She blusht all over, in ye polisht stone
beneath ye purple Damask roses shone
From her flow'd many graces then of old
They Ly'd y^{t}. men but 3 graces told
For in each smileing eye of Hero sprung
An hundred Graces this said every tongue
Venus hath now A Preistess worthy her
All men ye maid before her do preferr.
Venuse's preistess anew Venus seem[-'d]/s\
So her ye heart of conquered youth esteems
Nor was there any but he Hero lov'd
and wisht she were his bride where e're she mov'd.
Through the strong fabricke of that sacred place
all eyes, all hearts, all longing went her pace.
One youth admireing of her spoke these words
I've seen what beauty Sparta's Clime affords
And what in Lacedamon so much takes
Where beauty to ye broad world challenge makes
But one so sweet so modest I have not seen
Sure one oth Graces here attends Loves Queen.
I have tyr'd my sight I have sattisfy'd mine eye
Let me but sleep with Hero and then Dye.
I would not wish to be a power divine
If I might live at Home and Hero mine.
But if unto the preistess to pretend

to sacriledge, one like her, Venus send!
this every youth said, there another had
a wound and with concealing it ran mad.
But brave Leander this faire maid when thou
beholds, thou would not of dumb wounds allow
But at ye fiery arrow's very fall
thought with fair hero live or not at all.
Love at her eyebrows did his torches Light
And fir'd Leander's bosome at first sight
for beauty in a mayd whose fame is pure
flies like the feathered shafts and hitts more sure
The eyes are loopehole her eyes fatall dart
That glanced through his eyes and gor'd his heart.
[*fol.2r*]
(3) Amazement feare shame impudence he left
His sence amaz'd on her perfections dwelt
his heart shooke shame, restrain'd him love contrould
that shame, and made him impudently bold
he softly walkt and stood beside ye maid
and slyly too her a by looke conveyed
with silent eyes fording y^{e}. virgins mind
when she Leanders cunning love did find.
She joy'd in her own beauty and even shee,
oft lifted her faire eyes by stealth to see,
Leander's face then look'd away again.
He joy'd that he did love and not disdain.
While now A privat hour Leander watcht
Day to ye west ye light's small stock dispatcht.
And straight the shadowing evening starr appear'd
Then to Approach he no longer fear'd.
But when he saw the skie with Sables hung
he instantly her Rosy fingers wrung.
And fetcht A deep sigh, she did nothing say
But as if Angry snatcht her hand away.
Finding her Discomposure he grew bold
and of her rich flowered garment takeing hold
Pul'd her into the temple secret'st part
as if't were Pilgremige against her heart.
Lingringly followed the sly fooled maid
And threatning thus, A woman's language said
What Stranger art thou mad? why pulls thou so
A maid? away leave let my garment go.

Shunn my rich parents anger to court me
preistess to Venus, it becomes not thee.
'Its hard to come into a virgins bed
Thus lessons men are perfect in thee re\a/d
Leander hearing female fury sound
The symptoms straight of yeilding virgins found
For when with men maids once are furious grown
Their very threatnings promise them the\ir/e [-*illeg.*] own.
Then her sweet smiling and pure necke he kist
And spake these words wherein Loves pang's assist.
Venus next Venus whome I Love
Next Pallas Daughter to Saturnian Jove
Blest he that gott thee she that bare thee blest
For to no mortall forme art thou exprest
The wombe most happy that did thee create
Heare thou my prayer and pitty my loves fate
Preistess to Venus like to Venus do
Come be the Preistess of her pleasures too.
Maids Venus love not; her true Rights if thou
would know: they are ye Nuptiall bed and vow.
Doe you Love Venus? Loves soft laws fullfill
Call me your servant, call me if you will
your husband catcht and caught by Cupids art,
brought to your service by his golden dart.
As Rough Alcides by ye Hermian wand
To Omphale the Lydian maids command
But in ye voyage to your p*re*sence made
my steps sweet Venus not by Hermes stayd
The Corycidian Atalanta fled
You know melanions love and marriage bed.

[*fol.2v*]

(4) But she love single life this virgin mov'd
who made the once despis'd she sole=belov'd
Dear Least ye Goddess frowne be you more kind
Thus he perswaded her against her mind
Softning her soul with Love and passion mixt
Silently on ye ground her eyes she fixt
ashamed the twilight should her blushes meet
repollishing the marble with her feet
and gathering at every little check
given by her heart her robe about her neck

all tokens that a maids consent forerunne
who if she be struck speechless then she's wonne
Loves bitter=sweetness now she working felt
Fair Hero's heart a gentle flame did melt
Leanders lineaments her soule amazd
and while her eyes upon the pavement gaze'd
on her fair necke his never wearyed sight
he fixt untill prevented by ye night.
The dew that on her blushes long had hung
Then dropt, and these words from her sweetest tongue
Stranger thy speech might on a Rock have wrought
who thee the various ways of courtship taught?
Who did (Alas!) thee to my country send?
For all that thou hast spoke is to no end.
For how a stranger wandring as thou art
And faithless can I fix in thee my heart?
nor could we marry publiquely i'ts clear
For of no marriage will my parents heare.
and should my countrey the a stranger shroud
Thy stole love could not long be in a cloud.
News with Advantage slander will unfold
whats don in corners in high ways is told.
yet let me know thy name and natiue coast
My great name Hero I suppose thou knowst.
In this wast tow'r dwell but my nurse and I
And though my native Sestos be so nigh
Such is the doome my cruell parents give
I banisht thence must the seas neighbour live
And with no maids at Dancings I appeare
But day and night from sea winds blustering here
Thus speaking with her voice her face she hid
Again blusht and her self for speaking chid.
Leander on loves highest torture rackt
was soon inspir'd how loves design to Act.
For mans heart pow'rfull Cupid conquers twice
First with his arrows, then with his device.
which ever heals the wounds his arrows made
whil[-es] he that hurts us doth us cure perswade.
he helpt Love post Leander to revolve
who lastly sighing uttert this resolve.
Virgins to come to yee I will not feare, [*in margin* thee]
Billows of fire and water though there were [*in margin* (it) (they)]

Unnavigable to Arrive thy bed
No deep gulf nor no high flowing Tyde I dread
but thy well servant shall ye naves confront, [*in margin* (waves)]
and nightly swim the rageing Hellespont.
For deare I dwell but cross the narrow seas,
your neighbour at Abydos only please
on your high turret to set up a light
which shineing in a Diameter by night

[*fol.3r*]

(5) I may become loves ship yt light my starr
beholding which not lookeing up so farre
As to Bootes and ye frozen maine
Or rough Orion I may safely gaine
My obvious native soile but dearest watch
For fear ye boisterous winds the flame should catch,
and blow my life out which to air must slide
with yt bright flame unto my life ye guide
or what I am if you more knowledge claime
Leander is fair Hero's husbands name
There secret marriage there night league now made
The torch Love's ensign was to be displayd
She to prepare the light, he did intend
To swimme the sea: their nuptiall eve thus spend.
Against their will they parted she the tower
he least ye darkeness should his sense o'repower
To fair Abydos his strong native shoar
Tooke marks to know the tower by and saile doer
both longing for a whole nights marriage sight
and longing for the bed adorning night
Night now soft rest upon her ravening wings
To all but to Love sick Leander brings
who on the Lead seas ever chaseing bay
Did but for Hymens shining summons stay.
Expecting ye sad torch, and to be led
by that Light usher, to his private bed.
As soon as ere thick darkness vaild the night
Hero advanced the torch whi\c/h there gave light.
Leanders eager spirits Cupid fir'd
and as the torch burnd still his flame aspired
but from sea hearing ye Angry billow scold
At first he trimbld after growing bold

Thus speakeing to himself his heart he easd
Love's cruell the seas not to be appeasd.
but ye seas water I Loves fire containe
heart drink in fire and scorne the flowing main
against a Lover what can he contrive?
Kno[-*illeg*]\w/s't not from sea yt Venus is deriv'd
who both the ocean and our cares commands
then his fair Limbs he stript with both his hands
[-Leapt from the shoare o'th waves his body spread]
Turbanted with his silken robe his head
Leapt from the shoare o'th waves his body spread
And up against the flameing torch still bare
himself ye ship, ye Pilate, and ye oare.
On her high turret Hero watcht the flame
And as stiff gales of wind frome every quarter came,
Still screned it with purple Robe she wore
Till Tyrd Leander wonne ye Sestian shoar
Down from ye turret Hero makeing hast
her husband breathless at ye gates embrac't
And to her bed Chamber she him led
There wipt his lockes yt trickling fome still shed
And him with roses, yt per=fum'd [*in margin* potins, did confound]
the offensi\v/e smell and left him all perfum'd
Twining about him then yet panting laid
To her soft downe these softer words she said
Love thou hast Labour'd sore exceeding sore
Love thou has labour'd sor not any more
[*fol.3v*]
Fish, slime, and brine have made thy penance great
Come now into my bosom drop thy sweat
and thus he straight unty'd her Zone and they
The Laws of Gentle venus did obey
They had a wedding but no danceing there
A bride bed but they did no singing heare.
Their secret nuptialls no poet praisd
About their privat bed no torches blaz'd
no dancer in a nimble Capper sprung
no hymens the father or grave mother sung
but darkeness all Loves houres the bride bed made
Drest up the Roome the brides verse was the shade
Far from ye Epithalamions were they matcht
night only at there ceremonies watcht.

Aurora never did Leander veiw
A bride groome in that bed he so well knew
who swam back to Abydos breathing still
those Hymeneall sweats which never fill
But Long vaild Hero mockt her parents sight
A Virgin all they day a wife by night
both often chide ye morning to ye west
and thus the furies of their loves supprest
Enjoying secret but short livd delight
For short time dates their strange stolen marriage Rites.
Approaching winter in a moment formes
The Skies vertigo into horrid stormes
The howling winds as with a beesom sweep
The wett false bottom of ye boyling deep [*in margin* Salt]
Calkt ships which marriners dare not committ
To faithless seas are in ye harbour splitt
But no rogh winter seas can the affright
Strong sould Leander but when the once kind night
now false and cruell gave thy ensigne
Feareless you leapt into feirce Neptunes brine
Unhappy hero should when winter came
have spar'd Leander, no more fed ye flame
of that fraile comett by whose blays they hold
their night commerce but love and fate compeld
an end. now upon the lofty turret rear'd
fates brand. no longer hymens torch appeard
'twas night when most the winds their spirits spent
and ag^{t}. the shoars their rally'd forces sent
when with accustomd hope Leander fed
Clim'd liquid mountains bound for Hero's bed
wave upon wave was pild the main wrought high
The earth shooke the sea was mingled with the skie.
The winds fell out the east and west wind fought
The south ag^{t}. the North great tempests brought
The merciless and foaming surges roard
Poor youth he sea born venus oft implor'd
Oft Neptune king of seas would have enclind
and Boreas of Orythia put in mind
But none helpt, fate by love was not contrould
quite over him ye justling billows rould
his strong legs faile him motionless now stands
The nimble vigour of his active hands

The water down his throat at pleasure flow'd
The Giddy seas their useless drinke bestowed
The torch out as ye sharp wind tost
Her love and life bemoand Leander lost.

COMMENTARY

The standard of this scribal text, as my transcription makes clear, is not universally high; but it is not therefore merely inept. Some marks of possible unfamiliarity, or possible infacility, in the transcriber are evident, though. For one thing, the number of lines transcribed on each page varies between 49 on fol. 1r and 60 on fols 2v and 3v: professional transcriptions tended towards more regularity in their line-count and *mise-en-page* than this. This variance in line-count can partly be attributed to the sometimes variable size of the transcribing hand. So too, line 262 in the manuscript text has been wholly deleted by the scribe: it represents an instance of eye-skip, the scribe's eye leaping over the difficult and unfamiliar word 'Turbanted' to the more commonly encountered 'Leapt', realising and deleting the error, before then beginning again with the omitted line.[14] Comparison with the printed text of 1647 makes clear, too, that two couplets (lines 144–5 and 238–9) have the order of their lines reversed in manuscript, although their sense is preserved. One couplet present in the printed text, 'These ceremonies learn: a maid and be | Preistesse to *Venus, it befits not thee*' (sig. B8r), is entirely absent from the manuscript text following line 149 where it would be expected to occur; the repeated 'Preistess' and 'Maid'/'Maids' in this part of the poem (lines 149–50 in the manuscript text) may have contributed to the omission. One classical name is also garbled by the scribe: the 'Coy *Arcadian, Atalanta*' of the printed text (sig. B8v) becomes the 'Corycidian Atalanta' (line 160). In other respects the manuscript text often varies from the printed text of 1647 simply in the tense of its verbs: 'gives' (line 12) for 'gave' (sig. B5v), and 'spend' (line 235) for 'spent' (sig. B10r) are the first and last such instances. On other occasions, nouns turn from singular to plural. This process is not one-way: 'Starr' in manuscript (line 25) counters 'stars' in print (sig. B5v), as the 'scarlet Circle' in manuscript (line 63) counters 'circles' in print (sig. B6v); but 'shafts' in manuscript (line 101) meet a singular '*shaft*' in print (sig. B7r), and 'eyes' in manuscript (lines 167 and 177) meet with 'eye' in print (sig. B8v).

Yet as well a number of such probable scribally-produced discrepancies, there are a number of other variants between the manuscript and the printed text of 1647 that cumulatively make it clear that MS KWH 56 must represent a separate line of transmission from the printed edition, and certainly cannot be a text derived from a printed exemplum. Some of these variants are single word substitutions; others extend to parts of lines. The first important variant comes at line 62 of the manuscript text: its reading 'Like the cleare moon when weeping she's beheld' varies the printed text of 1647, 'Like the cleare Moon when rising she's beheld' (sig. B6v). The printed reading, 'rising', is more faithful to the Greek original, which is rendered 'rising' by the Loeb translator.[15] The same is true of the manuscript's recolouring of Hero's garments, a change that runs consistently through the scribal text. Where in print (with Musaeus's sanction) Hero is dressed in a '*pure white*' and '*sacred robe*' (sigs B6v, B10v), the manuscript Hero favours a bolder and perhaps less appropriate wardrobe: for her, 'beneath ye purple Damask roses shone' (line 67), and it is 'with purple Robe' that she screens the torch from the winds (line 269). Other variants more properly qualify as indifferent, and are not necessarily unauthorial in origin. The manuscript line 73, 'All men ye maid before her do preferr', compares Hero explicitly with Venus, rather than the mortal comparison of print, 'All men this maide before her Sex preferre' (sig. B6v). The cumulative force of variants such as these is hard to gauge without access to other comparable manuscript texts, but the possibility that they represent a line of transmission for Stapylton's translation more or less independent of its printed editions is strong.

Such paired variants, to which the reader's attention is directed, include the following:

> 'faire' / 'rare' (line 94; sig. B7r), 'gor'd his' / 'graz'd upon' (line 103; sig. B7r), 'by looke' / 'side-looke' (line 109; sig. B7r), 'instantly' / 'silently' (line 121; sig. B7v), 'garment' / 'vesture' (line 125; sig. B7v), 'sly fooled' / 'slow-footed' (line 128; sig. B7v), 'men' / 'maides' (line 135; sig. B7v), 'sweet smiling and pure' / 'sweet-smelling pure-skinn'd' (line 140; sig. B8r), 'catcht' / 'chac'd' (line 154; sig. B8r), 'not by Hermes stayd' / 'not sly Hermes swayd' (line 159; sig. B8v), 'this virgin' / 'this *Venus*' (line 162; sig. B8v), 'wast' / 'vast' (line 196; sig. B9r), 'And with no' / 'Nor with young' (line 200; sig. B9r), 'voice' / 'veyle' (line 202; sig. B9r), 'us cure' / 'our cure' (line 209; sig. B9v), 'Unnavigable' / 'Innavigable' (line 214; sig. B9v), 'well' / 'wet' (line 216; sig. B9v), 'deare' / '*Love*' (line 218; sig. B9v), 'maine' / 'Waine' (line 224; sig. B9v), 'intend' / 'indent' (line 234; sig. B10r), 'ye darknesse should his sense' / 'dark night his sense might' (line 237; sig. B10r), 'and longing' / 'Oft wishing' (line 241; sig. B10r), 'ravening' / 'raven' (line 242; sig. B10r), 'Lead' / lowd' (line 244; sig. B10r),

'Light' / 'Bright' (line 247; sig. B10r), 'husband breathless' / 'breathless husband' (line 272; sig. B10v), 'she him led' / 'in silence led' (line 273; sig. B10v), 'verse' / 'veyle' (line 292; sig. B11r), 'night' / 'Light' (line 312; sig. B11v), 'thy ensigne' / 'thy love the signe' (line 313; sig. B11v), 'The torch' / 'And the false torch' (line 339; sig. B12r), and 'bemoand' / 'bemourn'd' (line 340; sig. B12r).

Not all (or necessarily any) of these manuscript readings would find their way into an edited text; but they represent a valuable addition or supplement to our received text of Stapylton's translation.

One final aspect of the manuscript is worthy of attention: the variant readings and other additions noted in the margin. The four corrections (to lines 212–13, 216 and 275) show the scribe apparently reflecting on the troubling readings taken over from the base text from which MS KWH 56 was copied: the potentially ambigious 'yee' is noted as 'thee' (line 212), the similarly imprecise 'there' is given two alternatives, '(it)' and '(they)' (line 213), and the nonsense 'naves' is corrected to 'waves' (line 216). Less satisfactory is the marginal rewriting of line 275, 'And him with roses, yt per=fum'd'. Clearly the base text duplicated the rhyme-word, *perfumed*, from the following line 276; yet the marginal suggestion, ' poti[*o*]ns, did confound' does not altogether clear the ambiguity. One further piece of marginalia again shows the scribe reflecting on the text in front of him. Lines 61 to 74 are linked together by a left-facing brace in the left-hand margin of fol. 1v; at the centre of the brace is the single word 'beauty'. Here the scribe has clearly drawn attention to one of Stapylton's set-piece descriptions, in a way analagous to the use of italic type to distinguish *sententiae* in the printed text of 1647. To that extent, the manuscript text of *Musæus on the Love of Hero and Leander* is both a re-writing of Stapylton's translation and a contemporary reading of it; in its encounter with the hazard of this scribe's transcript, Stapylton's poem gains rather than loses potential meaning.

That this transcript of *Musæus on the Love of Hero and Leander* does represent what an author might find a potentially hazardous transmission of the poem's text seems, however, clear. It is easiest to account for this manuscript as the product of a line of transmission at some remove from Stapylton's authority, not ignorantly or carelessly done, but demonstrating elements of what might, without prejudice, be called self-consistent corruption. As indicated above, the scribal text of Stapylton's poem in MS KWH 56 appears to be unique: no other copies are recorded in standard first-line indexes.[16] Although this apparent uniqueness is central to the interest of MS KWH 56, it also serves to limit it: without other examples for comparison, it is impossible to say where precisely the manuscript stands in relation to the printed edition of 1647 to which its text is most closely linked, or what might be the source of the speculative emendments noted by the scribe in the margin of the transcript. In conclusion, this transcript of Stapylton's translation seems so regularly in error that it is perhaps tempting simply to take him at his word in his complaint about the 'grosse mistakes' commited by 'ignorant Transcribers'. Such an explanation would allow us to locate the transcript fairly close to the immediate coterie of transcribing readers identified by Stapylton in his printed dedication, and to see in its departures from the poem's printed text confirmation of his exasperation at the scribal deficiencies of his Oxford-based associates. Seen in this light, MS KWH 56 would then be a contemporary, but poor, witness to a poem still close to its author. In the apparent absence of other surviving copies, this seems a likelier explanation than that this transcript represents a late, corrupt and distant stage in the transmission of Stapylton's poem away from, and outside, the privileged network within which it first circulated. Since no other manuscripts apparently survive, it is hard (but not impossible) to see this manuscript as but one of many texts copied and recopied by eager early readers in many gradually degenerating recensions. It would, of course, take the discovery of further transcripts of Stapylton's translation to prove either of these hypotheses. Until such a time as further texts may be recovered, MS KWH 56 may serve as a further reminder—if one were needed—of a mid-seventeenth-century manuscript culture which continues still to offer new discoveries.

NOTES

I am grateful to Robert Cummings, Stuart Gillespie, Marcus Nevitt, Robert Wilcher and Gillian Wright for reading drafts of this article, and to the Special Collections staff of Birmingham University Library, particularly Martin Killeen, for their help in its preparation.

1 The relationship is contextualised by L.G. Kelly, 'Sir Robert Stapylton', *Oxford Dictionary of National Biography*.

2 Sir Robert Stapylton, trans., *Erotopaignion: The Loves of Hero and Leander* (Oxford, 1645), sig.A2v; italic/roman reversed.

3 Stapylton, trans., *Erotopaignion* (1645), sig.A3r; italic/roman reversed.

4 Jerome de Groot, 'Space, Patronage, Procedure: The Court at Oxford, 1642–46', *English Historical Review*, 117 (2002), 1204–27 (p.1212); *Royalist Identities* (Basingstoke, 2004), pp.66–8, there drawing on Sharon Achinstein, *Milton and the Revolutionary Reader* (Princeton, 1994).

5 Sir Robert Stapylton, trans., *Musæus, On The Loves of Hero and Leander* (London, 1647), sigs A4v–5r; italic/roman reversed.

6 Timothy Raylor, *Cavaliers, Clubs, and Literary Culture: Sir John Mennes, James Smith, and the Order of the Fancy* (Newark, 1994), pp.136–42, 229–30.

7 On such claims, see De Groot, *Royalist Identities*, pp.49–50, and Robert Wilcher, *The Writing of Royalism, 1628–1660* (Cambridge, 2001), 255–7; on the politics of this period more largely see Wilcher, *The Writing of Royalism*, pp.221–60, and David Norbrook, who discusses the 'eerie quality' of the cultural life of 1647–49, in *Writing the English Republic: Poetry, Rhetoric and Politics, 1627–1660* (Cambridge, 1999), pp.158–60.

8 Sir Robert Stapylton, *The Tragedie of Hero and Leander* (London, 1669)

9 These are surveyed by Anthony G.Petti, *English Literary Hands from Chaucer to Dryden* (London, 1977), pp.29–32; Harold Love gives a valuable account of their implications for editors in *Scribal Publication in Seventeenth-Century England* (Oxford, 1993), pp.313–56.

10 Douglas Bush, 'Musaeus in English Verse', *Modern Language Notes*, 43 (1928), 101–04; Warren Boutcher, '"Who taught thee Rhetoricke to deceive a maid?": Christopher Marlowe's *Hero and Leander*, Juan Boscán's *Leandro*, and Renaissance Vernacular Humanism', *Comparative Literature*, 52 (2000), 11–52 (p.20); the translation is excluded from the discussion of Musaeus in Gordon Braden, *The Classics and English Renaissance Poetry: Three Case Studies* (New Haven, 1978), pp.55–153.

11 An obituary and a preliminary description of the Humphreys bequest are provided in *BUL Research Libraries Bulletin*, 3 (1995), 2–5.

12 Harold Love, *English Clandestine Satire, 1660–1702* (Oxford, 2004), p. 260.

13 One small canard raised by the *ODNB* entry might here be laid to rest: the promising allusion there to 'BL, translation of Juvenal, Add. MS 9455, fols. 9–116' is in fact a confused reference to BL Add. MS 4455, fols 9–11b, notes on this translation in the late-seventeenth century Oxford commonplace book of John Bennet. The other archival references given in the *ODNB* are all to documents relating to Miles Stapylton, whose life is included in his uncle's entry.

14 *Turbanted* is still not recorded in the *Oxford English Dictionary*, 2nd edition, although its sense is clear.

15 Thomas Gelzer, ed., and Cedric Whitman, trans., *Musaeus: Hero and Leander*, Loeb Classical Library (London, 1975), line 57.

16 eg. those in the Bodleian, in the British Library, at Harvard, or in the Folger Shakespeare library; or in the most up-to-date such resource in print, Stephen Parks, Marc Greitens and Carolyn W. Nelson's majestic *First-Line Index of English Poetry 1500–1800 in Manuscripts of the James M. and Marie-Louise Osborn Collection in the Beinecke Rare Book and Manuscript Library of Yale University* (New Haven, 2006).

Manuscript Miscellanies and the Rochester Canon

Nicholas Fisher

In her elegy *On the Death of the late Earl of Rochester*, Aphra Behn draws attention to the skill of 'the Noble *Strephon*' (Rochester's sobriquet) as a writer of both love poetry and satire (perhaps surprisingly indicating that his work was enjoyed by women as well as men[1]):

> He was but lent this duller World t'improve
> In all the charms of Poetry, and Love;
> Both were his gift, which freely he bestow'd,
> And like a God, dealt to the wond'ring Crowd. . . .
> Satyr has lost its Art, its Sting is gone,
> The Fop and Cully now may be undone;
> That dear instructing Rage is now allay'd,
> And no sharp Pen dares tell 'em how they've stray'd.
>
> (lines 2, 7–10, 27–30)[2]

On occasion, this poetic facility was combined with bawdiness or obscenity. Rochester's friend Samuel Butler, for example, regarded this as a positive feature, complimenting him for being 'so fam'd for writing | Satyrs, so Bawdy and so Biting', while characteristically the hostile Earl of Mulgrave complained that the plaudits awarded to Rochester's songs were 'undeserved' on account of the 'Bawdry barefac'd' and 'obscene words' they contained.[3] Taken together, these comments suggest that despite the absence of a published collection of Rochester's work during his lifetime, there was a common acceptance amongst his contemporaries that his writing fell broadly into the areas of satire, love poetry and libertine writing (this last term including indecent verse).

But is it possible to identify the body of poems that would have been generally known to have been written by Rochester? Vieth's groundbreaking edition of 1968, which resulted from a close examination of manuscript versions of the texts, established the canon to a greater degree of accuracy than had previously been achieved, and it is a tribute to Vieth's scholarship that Harold Love's monumental 1999 edition for Oxford University Press, based on an even more exhaustive study of the manuscript material, made only a few relatively minor adjustments.[4] The present paper, using the *corpus* of 69 poems that Love identifies as being 'probably by Rochester', explores the evidence available in the most important surviving manuscript miscellanies that would indicate the existence during the Restoration period of a common, and accurate, recognition of Rochester's work. An appendix provides a chronology for these poems, as far as can be determined, that indicates when individual poems were in circulation.

By the time of Rochester's death on 26 July 1680, a mere 23 of his poems had reached print. Just five had appeared under his name: three that had been written while he was an undergraduate at Wadham College, Oxford (even if they ever had entered the public consciousness, they would have been long since forgotten[5]) and, more recently, a prologue for Settle's *The Empress of Morocco* in 1673 and the epilogue for Charles D'Avenant's *Circe* in 1677. These two addresses would have been insufficient on their own to support Rochester's reputation as a poet, and in any case it seems that his output of three prologues or epilogues was virtually ignored by his contemporaries because only one in a single copy has survived in manuscript.[6] The remaining eighteen poems, published without ascription, embrace the range of Rochester's poetry in comprising a further work for the theatre (the epilogue to Fane's *Love in the Dark, or The Man of Bus'ness* of 1673) seven satires, nine love poems and one example of libertine writing.[7]

The situation is rendered less straightforward, however, by evidence that while Rochester was still alive, two thirds of these eighteen unattributed poems were circulating in manuscript identifying him as the author (and it is of course possible that some or all of the other six were similarly circulating in manuscripts that have not survived).[8] Chance would appear to have determined whether or not a reader encountered a particular poem actually ascribed to Rochester, but even if it was circulating anonymously, the reader may nonetheless have been aware of its author. This is particularly likely if that person was a courtier, a member of government circles or an associate of Rochester, many of whom, plausibly, might have encountered other poems by Rochester in his autograph or simply have developed an ear for his verse.[9]

Aristocratic convention precluded Rochester from publishing an authorised, printed edition of his poetry, a limitation that similarly applied to his close associates Dorset, Buckingham and, albeit to a lesser extent, Sedley. The private nature of the milieu for which they wrote is well illustrated by Prior's comment in his *Satyr on the Poets* (1707), '*Sidley* indeed and *Rochester* might Write, | For their own Credit, and their

Friends' Delight' (lines 145–46), and in the dedication of a volume of his own poetry, Prior recorded that Dorset had had such little concern for his verses 'that he cared not what became of them, though every body else did'. In not dissimilar vein, the editor of Buckingham's *Works* in 1704 stated that some of the poems had previously 'slipt clandestinely into the Press', a sentiment anticipated by the editor of Sedley's *Works* two years earlier when he had observed, 'if some of these have seen light, without his Knowledge, 'twas by the Perfidiousness of some about him, whom he employ'd to engross [formally copy] what he writ'.[10]

Rather than exercising care to publish his poems, therefore, Rochester distributed them in manuscript, probably singly, amongst his friends in Whitehall. This led to copies being made and the poems being further circulated, often anonymously and frequently through the agency of one or more of the commercial scriptoria. It would be done either in the form of scribal separates or 'in one or both of two kinds of manuscript book, the professionally compiled anthology of libertine and state verse and the privately assembled personal miscellany'[11] put together from separates or small collections of Restoration verse. To a considerable extent, then, even if, as Love suggests, such scribal publishers as Robert Julian 'drew from time to time on each other's separates',[12] the chance availability of particular poems within the scriptorium would have dictated the precise substance of the individual miscellany. The editorial practices of the scribes would also have had an influence, as Michael Brennan and Paul Hammond have explained:

> Restoration scribal miscellanies . . . (as distinct from personal commonplace books) were often assembled by transcribing several small collections of poems, or even items on individual sheets, rather than by the complete transcription of a single exemplar. The scribe therefore acted to some extent as an editor on behalf of the customer or bookseller who commissioned him. The fact that the manuscript miscellanies often include the same poems, but rarely in exactly the same order, indicates that while working to a particular brief (say, to produce a collection of political satires or erotic poems) the scribe would be constrained in his arrangement of the material by the availability of copy texts.[13]

Despite these variables, some consistency in the understanding of the full range of Rochester's work can be perceived in the collections of his poems in the manuscript compilations.

In his *Index of English Literary Manuscripts*, Peter Beal lists seventeen scribal miscellanies that contain 'substantial' numbers of poems believed to be by Rochester.[14] Just eight of these contain twenty or more different poems that Love identifies as 'probably' his: Portland MS

Pw V 40, also known as the Pomfret MS (thirty-one), Yale MS Osborn b 105 (thirty), the Badminton and Gyldenstolpe MSS (twenty-eight), Harvard fMS Eng 636 (twenty-seven), Yale MS Osborn b 334 (the Hartwell MS—twenty-five), the Harbin MS at Longleat House (twenty-two) and the Brotherton MS (twenty-one). The contents of the remaining nine manuscripts range from between four poems (Princeton MS Taylor 3) and fourteen poems (Bodleian MS Eng. misc. e. 536) by Rochester, with the exception of the Edinburgh MS, which contains eighteen within its six distinct collections. Although none of these manuscripts contains as much as half of his *corpus* as currently understood, three of them contain similar numbers of his poems as appeared in the early printed editions: *1680* (thirty-four out of sixty-one poems), *1685* (thirty out of fifty-seven poems) and *1691* (thirty-one out of thirty-three poems, excluding the three stage orations and the three juvenile pieces).[15] A stimulating examination by Love of the ordering of Rochester's songs indicates that groups of the lyrics circulated together in a number of professionally compiled scribal anthologies from different scriptoria; this led him to conclude that these originated from a small manuscript *liber carminum*, or perhaps more than one, 'originally assembled by Rochester himself'.[16] This argument is convincing in terms of supporting the evidence for Rochester's authorship of the songs, but it does not follow that the songs, where scribally published without ascription, would necessarily have been known to be the work of the poet. While readers close to the Court might correctly identify the author, the likelihood is that any such recognition would diminish drastically among readers who were at a further distance. The scribal miscellany comprising Harvard fMS Eng 636, however, provides specific detail of what Rochester's contemporaries would have understood to be his poetic contribution.

Harvard fMS Eng 636, described by Love as 'the second most important contemporary source' for Rochester's poems,[17] appears to be the only surviving scribal miscellany assembled during the author's lifetime to contain a large number of his poems ascribed to him. This valuable manuscript, which Love suggests may have been compiled as early as December 1679, is headed 'A Collection of Poems' and it is written in a single 'pleasingly virtuosic' professional hand. It contains eighty-three poems 'compiled from separates, linked groups and small sub-collections, which were already in general circulation'. A major significance is that, for some eighty per cent of the poems, the author is identified, with thirty-five[18] being ascribed to Rochester ('Quoth the Duchess of Cleveland to Counsellor Knight' is not ascribed, and although supportive of the attribution to Rochester of 'Fucksters you that would be happy', Love does not include it in his grouping of poems 'probably' by Rochester; the seven erroneously ascribed are marked by an asterisk in the two lists that follow below). Twenty-two of the ascriptions to Rochester occur in the first twenty-four poems in the collection (the exceptions are two poems by Sir Carr Scroope that form a satiric group with two of Rochester's poems) and the remainder are spread across the rest of the manuscript singly or in groups of three or four. Of the first fifteen poems, eleven comprise satires and include libertine writing:

The Disabled Debauchee [ascribed to Rochester]
An Epistolary Essay from M.G. to O.B. upon their mutual Poems [ascribed to Rochester]
To a Lady, in a Letter [ascribed to Rochester]
*'In the fields of Lincoln Inn' [ascribed to Rochester, but probably Sedley, to whom attributed in Bodleian MS Don. b. 8]
A Ramble in St. James's Park [ascribed to Rochester]
Artemiza to Chloe [ascribed to Rochester]
*'Deep in an unctuous vale' [Fane, but ascribed to Rochester]
*'Prick Nature's pump cunt's pioneer' [runs on from previous, Rochester attribution implied]
An Allusion to Horace [ascribed to Rochester]
In defence of Satyr [Scroope, no ascription]
On The Suppos'd Author of A late Poem in Defence of SATYR [ascribed to Rochester]
Answer By way of Epigram [ascribed to Scroope]
*'There's no harm in sound cunts nor in arseholes' [poss. John, Lord Vaughan, ascribed to Rochester]
*'When first rebellion struck at the crown' [prob. Dorset, ascribed to Rochester]
Upon Nothinge [ascribed to Rochester].

These are followed by a sequence of nine love poems and libertine verses ascribed to Rochester, and then an assortment of predominantly satirical and libertine verse by him and other authors:

To Love ('Oh! Love how cold and slow to take my part') [ascribed to Rochester]
Upon his leaving his Mistresse [ascribed to Rochester]
Nestor [ascribed to Rochester]
'Phillis, be gentler' [ascribed to Rochester]
Womans Honour [ascribed to Rochester]
The Fall [ascribed to Rochester]

'While on these Lovely Lookes I gaze' [ascribed to Rochester]
On Mrs Willis [ascribed to Rochester]
'By all Loves soft, yet mighty Pow'rs' [ascribed to Rochester]
'Since to restrain our joy' [ascribed to Scroope]
One Writeing Against his Prick [uncertain, no ascription]
'Have you not in a chimney seen' [uncertain, no ascription]
*'O that I could by some new chemic art' (*The Wish*) [ascribed to Rochester]
'Why should so much beauty dread' [ascribed to Fishbourne]
'Fair Cloris in a pigsty lay' [ascribed to Rochester]
Senec Troas. Act. 2. Chor [ascribed to Rochester]
Against Reason and Mankind [ascribed to Rochester]
'An Addition' [ascribed to Rochester]
An Answer to the Satyr against man [Edward Pococke, no ascription]
A Letter from Lord Buckhurst to Mr. George Etherege [ascribed to Dorset]
Mr. Etherege's Answer [ascribed to Etherege]
Another Letter from Lord Buckhurst to Mr. Etherege [Dorset, no ascription]
Mr. Etherege's Answer [ascribed to Etherege]
The Imperfect Enjoyment [ascribed to Rochester]
'One day the amorous Lysander' [ascribed to Aphra Behn]
'Since now my Sylvia is as kind as fair' [ascribed to Mulgrave]
Tunbridge Wells [ascribed to Rochester]
An Epitaph on the Lord Fairfax [Buckingham, no ascription]
The Session of Poets [possibly Settle, no ascription]
'After so many sad mishaps' [uncertain, no ascription]
The Ramble [ascribed to Radcliffe]
Upon the Pyramid [ascribed to Radcliffe]
Mac Flecknoe [Dryden, no ascription]
Prologue to the University of Oxon [ascribed to Dryden]
Epilogue ('No poor Dutch peasant winged') [Dryden, no ascription]
Heroic Stanzas [ascribed to Dryden]
'Tis true great name thou art secure' [ascribed to Sprat]
'We must resign Heaven his great soul' [ascribed to Waller]
Ode ('Now curses on you all you virtuous fools') [Oldham, no ascription]
'My Part is done and you'll I hope excuse' [Oldham, no ascription]
[Satyr] The Argument ('Say Heav'n-born Muse') [ascribed to Rochester]
Satyr. [*Timon*] [ascribed to Sedley]
'Hail happy warrior hail whose arms have won' [ascribed to Lee]
'I sing the praise of a worthy wight' [uncertain, no ascription]
'Fucksters you that would be happy' [ascribed to Rochester]
Love and Life [ascribed to Rochester]
Love to a Woman [ascribed to Rochester]

'Beauty is Nature's quaint disguise' [ascribed to Radcliffe]
'To what intent and purpose' [ascribed to Radcliffe]
'Welcome brave prince unto this land' [Waller, no ascription]
'Thou damned Antipodes to common sense' [Dorset, no ascription]
'Come on you critics find one fault who dares' [Dorset, no ascription]
'From a sensual proud atheistical life' [uncertain, no ascription]
'Disgraced undone forlorn made fortune's sport' [uncertain, no ascription]
*'As in the days of yore was odds' (*The Royal Buss*) [uncertain, ascribed to Rochester]
Dildoides [uncertain, ascribed to Samuel Butler]
'Though ladies of quality's cunts often itch' [uncertain, no ascription]
'Quoth the Dutchess of Cleveland, to Counsellor Knight' [Rochester, no ascription]
''Twas near no purling stream nor shady grove' [uncertain, ascribed to 'Sir C.B.']
'I pass all my hours with a lusty young whore' [uncertain, no ascription]
'The parsons now keep whores' [uncertain, no ascription]
'As Colon drove his sheep along' [Dorset, no ascription]
'In the Isle of Brittain long since famous growne' [ascribed to Rochester]
'Shame of my life disturber of my tomb' [Roscommon, no ascription]
'Tom Jolly's nose I mean to abuse' [uncertain, no ascription]
'Tell me Jack I prithee do' [uncertain, no ascription]
'Sir | That evening Prior came to town' [uncertain, no ascription].

It is remarkable that, in terms of Love's edition of Rochester's poems, the miscellany correctly ascribes so many of them, failing to assign only one minor poem that is nowadays thought to be his. But equally noteworthy is the proportion of poems wrongly ascribed to Rochester: the seven false ascriptions in a total of thirty-five poems amount to an inaccuracy of one in five. This statistic is startling, even though closer examination reveals that the errors centre on just one area of Rochester's output—his simpler libertine verse—and may reflect either a genuine difficulty for readers in identifying an individual stamp in such poems, or what evidently was becoming the common practice of attaching Rochester's name to any libertine verse.[19]

The incorporation of so many accurate ascriptions to Rochester, however, appears to show that the miscellany was based on copy obtained from a source or sources close to Court soon after the date of initial circulation. Although the uneven quality of the texts indicates secondary sources, the assembly may also reflect a more common awareness of authorship that would become lost as the months passed.

Certainly Rochester's contemporary reputation as an important satirist and writer of witty love poetry and libertine verse is amply supported by the work ascribed to him, whether accurately or not. Virtually all his major satires, including 'In the Isle of Brittain long since famous growne', are present, together with Edward Pococke's response to *Against Reason and Mankind.* Arguably the only significant omission is *A very heroical epistle in answer to Ephelia*, which Vieth has described as 'one of the deftest satires in Restoration literature'.[20]

A similar pattern of satires followed by songs, both interwoven with libertine poems, can be identified in Yale MS Osborn b 105. This manuscript, entitled 'Songs & Verses Upon severall occasions', can be dated, along with the Gyldenstolpe MS in Stockholm, to within weeks of Rochester's death. The Yale MS is arguably the most important extant Rochester manuscript, despite the excision of some leaves that contained obscene verses. Vieth identified it as an independent scribal transcript of the copy-text used for the first edition of *1680*, and of the estimated eighty-one poems it originally contained, thirty are by Rochester.[21] Seven of the first eight poems in the manuscript are ascribed to him:

An Epistolary Essay [ascribed to 'Lord R']
Against Reason and Mankind (without the 'Addition') [ascribed to 'E of R']
The Answer [Pococke, no ascription]
A Ramble in St. James's Park [ascribed to 'E of R']
Artemiza to Chloe [ascribed to 'E of R']
The Imperfect Enjoyment [ascribed to 'E of R']
To Love [ascribed to 'E of R']
The Disabled Debauchee [ascribed to 'E of R']
[Satyr] The Argument [Rochester, no ascription]
An Allusion to Horace [Rochester, no ascription]
'When Shakespeare Jonson Fletcher ruled the stage' [Scroope, no ascription]
On The Suppos'd Author of A late Poem in Defence of SATYR [Rochester, no ascription]
Answer By way of Epigram [ascribed to Scroope]
Senec Troas. Act. 2. Chor [Rochester, no ascription]
Upon Nothinge [Rochester, no ascription].

There then follow the songs ''Tis not that I am weary grown' by Rochester (without ascription) and 'In the fields of Lincoln's Inn' (probably by Sedley, but ascribed to Rochester in Harvard fMS Eng 636), and a sequence of songs by Rochester that may be deduced to have originally exceeded two dozen.

Vieth has detailed the authorship of the poems in the Yale MS (only the first few of Rochester's poems are ascribed to him).[22] The fact that most of the thirty-three poems immediately following *The Disabled Debauchee* are by Rochester would seem to evidence a conscious effort by the assembler or scribe to place together all those thought to have been written by him. The presence later in the manuscript of another six poems now thought to be probably by Rochester ('I swive as well as others do', *Tunbridge Wells*, 'When to the King I bid good morrow', *A very heroical epistle in answer to Ephelia*, *On Poet Ninny* and *My Lord All-pride*) might well be accounted for on the basis that either the scribe did not know them to be Rochester's work or that the poems only came to hand after the main group.

It cannot be determined whether the *1680* copy-text actually ascribed to Rochester all the poems by him in that sequence, or whether, if Yale MS Osborn b 105 accurately reflects the ascriptions present in the copy-text, the early owner of the manuscript, the German diplomat Friedrich Augustus Hansen, would have correctly identified their authorship.[23] The balance of probability, however, suggests that only a well-placed reader at Court would have been able to link successfully the individual poems with Rochester, but it is feasible to anticipate that the knowledge would have been passed to the scribal-publisher along with the copy-text, thus enabling that person to appreciate the range of satire, love poetry and libertine writing within Rochester's *opus*. Significantly, the only major absence from the miscellany (but present in Harvard fMS Eng 636) is 'In the Isle of Brittain long since famous growne', a poem generally omitted, too, from the other scribal miscellanies under discussion. It may be deduced that this occurred partly as the result of its politically sensitive content but doubtless also because that content, which resulted in Rochester's banishment from Court, ensured the verses had a quite different pattern of circulation, including oral transmission.[24]

The ordering in the other major scribal miscellanies is broadly replicated. In the Gyldenstolpe MS none of the sixty-five poems has any indication of authorship, and the twenty-eight satiric and amatory verses by Rochester appear compactly within the first forty-six poems in the collection. With the exception of *Tunbridge Wells* and 'In the Isle of Brittain long since famous growne', all the longer satires by Rochester that appear in the Harvard and Yale MSS are reproduced here, albeit in a different order. Next follows a group of fourteen songs, all of which also appear in Yale MS Osborn b 105; two further songs included in the sequence of songs in the Yale MS (*Upon his leaving his Mistresse* and *Nestor*) are positioned in the Gyldenstolpe MS among a group of satiric verses.

The format of satires followed by songs is observable to a greater or lesser extent in the remaining manuscripts (faintly even in the Edinburgh MS), and whereas the Pomfret MS places only two satires (*An Epistolary Essay* and *A Ramble in St. James's Park*) before a group of twelve poems, the Badminton MS intersperses the major works of *Artemiza to Chloe*, *Against Reason and Mankind*, *The Imperfect Enjoyment*, *An Epistolary Essay*, *A Ramble in St. James's Park*, *An Allusion to Horace* and *Upon Nothinge* in a sequence of thirty-four unascribed satiric and libertine poems not exclusively by Rochester that precedes a group of thirteen of his songs.[25] The variation in the choice of satires that precede the collection of songs tends to confirm that there was no authorial collection of Rochester's satires available for scribes as there probably was for his songs.[26] It also indicates the likelihood that, with the exception of the Rochester-Scroope quartet of satires and the accompanying of *Against Reason and Mankind* (including the 'Addition') with Pococke's reply, the satires were mainly assembled as separates rather than in linked groupings.

Common in these manuscripts, too, is the incorporation of libertine verses alongside the satires and love poetry, thus reflecting with accuracy the range of Rochester's writing. Equally, few of Rochester's poems are ascribed to him (usually one or two in each manuscript[27]), rendering it impossible at this distance to deduce the extent to which readers correctly identified Rochester's poems. Two manuscripts, though, hint intriguingly (but probably incorrectly—see below) that there might have been a more widespread awareness of the Rochester canon after the poet's death than has been realised. The Hartwell and Harbin MSS (dated by Beal to '*c.* mid-1680s' and 'late 17th century' respectively) derive from a common source, and both seem to have been prepared by, or for, members of his extended family, that context being emphasised in the Harbin MS by the inclusion of personal letters from Rochester to his wife and son.[28] There can be little doubt that the transcribers of the poems, or the persons commissioning these collections, believed Rochester to be their author.

The Hartwell MS is, uniquely, the only extant scribal miscellany that was clearly intended to consist entirely of Rochester's work, for its title-page has the legend 'Poem's By The Right Honourable John Earle of Rochester'. This is not entirely accurate, for the ensuing contents comprise a text of Rochester's play *Valentinian*, a prose address by William Lovesey, Vicar of Bampton, Devon, twenty-five poems by Rochester (none of them libertine), and Fane's masque for Rochester's play. The presentation of the poems, nonetheless, follows the typical pattern in the scribal miscellanies of commencing with satires and following with love poems. The opening satires are:

Against Reason and Mankind
An Epistolary Essay
On The Suppos'd Author of A late Poem in Defence of SATYR.

There follows a group of 19 love poems:

To Love
The advice
The Discovery
Dialogue
Grecian Kindness
A Dialogue between Strephon and Daphne
Upon his leaving his Mistresse
'Give me leave to raile at you' (second stanza only)
'Phyllis, be gentler, I advise'
To Corinna
Womans Honour Song
'To this moment a rebel, I throw down my arms'
'How happy, Chloris, were they free'
Love and Life
The Fall
'While on those lovely lookes I gaze'
'An age in her embraces passed'
'Absent from thee, I languish still'
Song | A Young Lady to her Antient Lover.

The collection then concludes with two satires, a further love poem and the masque:

Artemiza to Chloe
An Allusion to Horace
A Pastoral Dialogue between Alexis and Strephon
'Haile sacred Cynthia mutable and chast' [Fane].

There is a close congruence between the poems in the Hartwell and Harbin MSS, and while the ordering is generally different, they share a sequence of eight songs, a unique form of *To Love*, and a complete absence of the libertine verse present in the scribal miscellanies described earlier.[29] The order in the Harbin MS is:

Artemiza to Chloe
To Love
Upon his leaving his Mistresse
'Give me leave to raile at you'

'Nothing adds to your fond fire' [Lady Rochester]
'Phyllis be gentler I advise'
To his more than Meritorious Wife
Sequence of 10 prose letters, the last ending with a four-line verse beginning 'Your Husband tight'
To Corinna
Womans Honour Song
'To this moment a rebel I throw down my arms'
'How happy Cloris were they free'
Love and Life
The Fall
'While on those lovely looks I gaze'
'An age in her embraces passed'
The advice
The Discovery
'Absent from thee I languish still'
A Dialogue between Strephon and Daphne
'The freeborn English generous and wise' [included in Love's edition as a 'disputed work']
An Epistolary Essay
Dialogue
Grecian Kindness
Song A Young Lady to her Antient Lover.

The Harbin MS then continues with a poem in Latin by [? George] Shuttleworth and three further poems, Harbin's *Memoirs of Gardening*, a sequence of prose letters and a pedigree chart.

It might be argued that the poems in the Hartwell and Harbin MSS represent, a few years after Rochester's death (and, particularly, after the publication of *1680*), a careful assembly of only those poems that were by then held to be genuine. The two manuscripts, however, in their bowdlerised selection of Rochester's poems, represent stark exceptions to the range of his work that is present in the other important scribal miscellanies. The preparation of a matrix of the poems in these two manuscripts, and the poems correctly ascribed to Rochester in Harvard fMS Eng 636, is instructive.

TABLE

Libertine verses are indicated in **bold**; the presence of a poem in the manuscript is shown by x and its absence by –. For ease of reference, the love verses and satire absent from the Harvard MS are indicated by the use of *italics*.

	Harvard MS	Hartwell MS	Harbin MS
Absent from thee I languish still	–	x	x
After Death nothing is, and nothing Death	x	–	–
Against the Charms our Bollox have	x	–	–
All my past Life is mine no more	x	x	x
All things submit themselves to your command	–	x	x
An Age in her Embraces pas'd	–	x	x
Ancient person for whome I	–	x	x
As some brave Admiral, in former War	x	–	–
Att five this Morn: when Phœbus rais'd	x	–	–
By all Loves soft, yet mighty pow'rs	x	–	–
Cælia, that faithful Servant you disown	–	x	x
Chloe, in Verse by your commande I write	x	x	x
Dear Freind, I hear this Town does so abound	x	x	x
Faire Cloris in a Pigsty lay	x	–	–
Give me leave to raile at you	–	x	x
How blest was the Created state	x	x	x
How perfect Cloris, and how free	–	x	x
I am by Fate slave to your Will	–	–	x
In the Isle of Brittain long since famous	x	–	–
Injurious Charmer of my Vanquish't heart	–	x	x
Love a Woman! Th'rt an Ass	x	–	–
Love bad me hope and I obey'd	x	x	x
Much Wine had past with grave discourse	x	–	–
Naked she lay clasp'd in my longing Armes	x	–	–
Nothinge, thou elder brother, even to shade	x	–	–
Oh! Love how cold and slow to take my part	x	x	x
Phillis, be gentler I advise	x	x	x
Prethy now fond foole give o're	–	x	x
Quoth the Dutchess of Cleveland	x	–	–
Say Heav'n-born Muse, for only thou canst	x	–	–

Strephon, there sighs not on the Plain	–	x	–
Such perfect Blisse faire Cloris, wee	x	–	–
The utmost grace the Greeks could show	–	x	x
Tis not that I am weary growne	x	x	x
To Rack and torture thy unmeaning brain	x	x	–
To this Moment a Rebell, I throw down	–	x	x
Vulcan contrive me such a Cupp	x	–	–
Well Sir, 'tis granted, I said Dryden's Rhymes	x	x	–
Were I (who to my costalready am	x	x	–
What Cruell Paines Corrinna takes	–	x	x
While on these Lovely Lookes I gaze	x	x	x

What the table underlines is the proportion of libertine writing in the Harvard MS, together with the absence to any great extent of a shared understanding of the constitution of Rochester's other verse by the assemblers of the collections. Fifteen of the twenty-seven poems listed in the Harvard MS are decidedly licentious or libertine (and if the eight poems wrongly ascribed to Rochester are also considered, the proportion rises from over half of the collection to almost two-thirds). They include examples both of the licentious satires to which Butler alludes (*A Ramble in St. James's Park*, *The Imperfect Enjoyment* and 'In the Isle of Brittain long since famous growne') and the scurrilous songs criticised by Mulgrave ('Faire Chloris in a Pigsty lay', 'Love a Woman! Th'rt an Ass' and 'Such perfect Blisse faire Cloris, wee') and firmly substantiate Rochester's reputation as the writer of unsavoury verses. Given the rare survival of a manuscript that contains so many ascriptions to Rochester, Harvard fMS Eng 636, it is possible that this association led to the destruction of many similar collections, especially against a background of the moral revolution that gathered pace in the 1680s and resulted in the formation of the Societies for the Reformation of Manners.[30] Some tempering of this image of Rochester, however, is supplied by the presence, in both the Harvard and the Hartwell MSS, of three of his major satires (*Artemiza to Chloe*, *Against Reason and Mankind*, and *An Allusion to Horace*) and several of his love poems (notably 'All my past Life is mine no more', 'How blest was the Created state' and 'Phillis, be gentler I advise'). It is particularly significant in terms of Rochester's amatory poetry that the three manuscripts share only seven poems in this category, for the Hartwell and Harbin MSS contain eleven such poems not in the Harvard MS, and the Hartwell and Harbin MSS each contain one unique poem.

It seems certain that the Hartwell and Harbin MSS represent a deliberate attempt to sanitise and re-define Rochester's poetic *œuvre* (an approach that would be replicated by Jacob Tonson in *1691*). What can be posited confidently is that the 'common source' for the two manuscripts (and also *1691*) comprised a miscellaneous collection, such as the ancestor Vieth identified for *1680*, that also contained libertine poems; feasibly these would have included some, if not all, of those that are present in the Harvard MS, and were ignored in the spirit of removing any potential 'Block of Offence'.[31] The argument that the contents of the Hartwell and Harbin MSS evidence a hidden awareness of the Rochester canon is weakened by the small number of shared ascriptions with Harvard fMS Eng 636, for had it been possible for a scriptorium to assemble a quantity of separates known to be Rochester's (either from his original manuscripts or from an ascribed copy), it is likely that the manuscripts would have shared a far greater proportion of Rochester's songs. Identification of the precise source, and the poems omitted, is impossible on the basis of the current knowledge of the surviving manuscripts, but what can also be posited with reasonable assurance, because of the anonymity which generally clothes Rochester's poems in the nine most extensive manuscript collections of his work, is that both that source, and the ancestor for Yale MS Osborn b 105 (and thus *1680*), were miscellaneous assemblies that contained as numerous ascriptions to Rochester as are present in the Harvard MS.

Ultimately, therefore, the Hartwell and Harbin MSS point to the conclusion that, during Rochester's lifetime, a body of poems that most readers would have known to be by him simply did not exist (this is not to deny a widespread awareness of his authorship of individual poems such as *Against Reason and Mankind* and 'In the Isle of Brittain long since famous growne'). The general absence in the miscellanies of specific ascriptions to Rochester means that it is simply not possible to establish a core of poems that his contemporaries would have correctly identified as his. In addition, Paul Hammond makes the salient point that speculative attribution was all part of the reader's response, and that poems may have been grouped together not on the basis of common authorship, but because they were by, or about, a Rochester-type figure. This would have further weakened any identification of Rochester as the author. Moreover, with most of what is now accepted as Rochester's work circulating in manuscript in a variety of anonymous and ascribed texts, in some instances becoming 'corporate poems' through the modification or the omission of words, lines or verses, or (as with the politically fraught 'In the Isle of Brittain long since famous growne') the mutilation of whole poems, it is apparent that readers in the seventeenth-century would have had wildly differing understandings of the detail of his poetry.[32]

Despite the widespread recognition that Rochester's writing fell within the broad categories of satires, love poems and libertine writing, the evidence of the scribal miscellanies emphasises that contemporary judgments of his work would have been based, at best, on an incomplete and inaccurate assembly of his poems in texts representing, with varying degrees of accuracy, the author's original words. In the face of these considerable limitations, not only is it remarkable that Rochester was saluted as one of the leading poets of his period but it is also richly ironic that, following the publication of Vieth's pioneering edition in 1968, modern readers are more familiar with Rochester's *œuvre* than his contemporaries could ever have been.

APPENDIX

CHRONOLOGY OF ROCHESTER'S POEMS

This list supersedes the table in *English Manuscript Studies 1100–1700*, 8 (2000), pp. 304–308 (and further information on pp. 318–19) which was compiled before the publication of Harold Love's Rochester edition. The poems below comprise the *corpus* of verse 'probably' by the poet, with the addition of the 'stage orations' and three other poems for which a case could be made for inclusion: 'Fucksters you that would bee happy' (Love cannot envisage any other poet 'capable' enough to write it), together with 'What Timon, does old Age, begin t'Approach' and 'God bless our good and gracious King' which traditionally have firm associations with Rochester. The list now takes account of Love's insights and other information that has subsequently come to light, including a contribution by Professor Martin Dzelzainis that arose during the course of his viva examination of the present writer's doctoral dissertation. It will be noted that, generally, Rochester's songs defy dating.

First line & first printing	Date	Evidence
1. Vertues triumphant Shrine! *Britannia Rediviva*, 1660	After 25 May 1660	Charles II landed at Dover on that date
2. Impia blasphemi *Epicedia Academiae Oxoniensis* 1660	After 24 December 1660	Princess Mary died on Christmas Eve

First line & first printing	Date	Evidence
3. Respite great Queen *Epicedia Academiae Oxoniensis*	Probably January 1661 1660	Queen Henrietta returned to France after being delayed by bad weather
4. I am by Fate slave to your Will *The Museum: or the Literary and Historical Register*, vol. 3, 1747	After January 1667	Rochester married on 29 January
5. Chloe, in Verse by your commande I write *Artemisa to Cloe . . .*, 1679	Before 7 May 1669	Date on MS (described *EMS*, 8 (2000))
6. Naked she lay clasp'd *1680*	After December 1670	Contains parody of lines in Dryden's *Conquest of Granada*, first performed December 1670, published 5 February 1672
7. Too longe the Wise *Poems on Affairs of State*, 1704	Possibly spring 1671	May refer to ending of Commons parliamentary session on 22 April 1671
8. All things submit themselves	Before 28 October 1671	Date volume entered in Stationers' Register
9. Cælia, that faithful Servant *A Collection of Poems . . .* 1672		
10. Quoth the Dutchess of Cleveland *1680*	Between 1671 and 1672	Churchill was Cleveland's lover at this time
11. What vaine unnecessary things (Pinto, 1953)	Between March & November 1672	Rochester wrote piece for all-female cast of a play

First line & first printing	Date	Evidence
12. Att five this Morn *Proteus Redivivus*, 1675	Possibly late 1672 or early 1673	References to Marvell's *The Rehearsal Transpros'd* (in print by beginning of December) and Shadwell's *Epsom-Wells* (first acted 2 Dec. 1672). Osborn MS b 52/2 has dating 'An°. 1673'
13. Out of Stark Love *London Drollery*, 1673	1673 or before	Date of first publication
14. As some brave Admiral *1680*	15 February 1673 or before	Date in Tyrrell MS
15. Much Wine had past *1680*	Before March 1673	Letter of 20 March mentions the poem
16. The Gods, by right of Nature *1691*	Before May 1673	Dryden quotes part of poem in Latin in letter to Rochester
17. Wit has of late *Empress of Morocco*, 1673	Before July 1673	Settle's *Empress of Morocco* given Court performance in spring prior to public performance in July 1673
18. Vulcan contrive me *1680*	After summer 1673	Reference to Maastricht, which Anglo-French force stormed on 24 June
19. In the Isle of Brittain *Poems on Affairs of State*, 1697	Late 1673	MS Bod. Rawl. D 924 dated 1673, and Rochester had fled Court by 20 January 1674
20. My Lord These are the Gloves *Letters of Philip, Second Earl of Chesterfield*, 1829	Before December 1673	Mistress Price not a Maid of Honour after this date
21. After Death nothing is *1680*	In or before 1674	Indicated by arrangement of MS Bod. Don. b 8

First line & first printing	Date	Evidence
22. What Timon, does old Age, begin t'Approach *1680*	March–June 1674	Souches and Turenne in position to fight only during these months
23. Say Heav'n-born Muse *1680*	April–June 1674	Mulgrave awarded Order of the Garter on 23 April and Countess of Falmouth married Dorset in June
24. Were I (who to my cost . . .) *A Satyr against Mankind* [1679]	Before June 1674	Dating of King's Coll. Cambridge MS Hayward H 11 13, and alluded to in February 1675
25. Strephon, there sighs not on the Plain *A Pastoral Dialogue between Alexis and Strephon*, 1683	Summer, 1674	Rochester at Bath during the summer; year given on broadside
26. Prethy now fond foole give o're *1691*	About 1674	Imagery, structure and theme close to no. 26
27. As Charms are Nonsence *Love in the Dark*, 1675	February–May 1675	Between first performances of Shadwell's *Psyche* (27 February) and Fane's *Love in the Dark* (10 May)
28. With Equall grace and force (Love, 1999)	After 4 July 1675	Mulgrave wounded in a duel on this date
29. Well Sir 'tis granted *1680*	Winter 1675/1676	Refers to Lee's *Sophonisba* (first performed 30 April 1675); no work later than 1675 mentioned in poem
30. Att Last you'l force mee } }	Before 1676	Date of publication

First line & first printing	Date	Evidence
31. While on these Lovely Lookes } *A New Collection of the Choicest Songs*, 1676		
32. Too late, alas! I must confess *Examen Poeticum*, 1693	Before 1676	Another version of no. 31
33. When to the King I bid (Vieth, 1968)	After January 1676	Arrival of Mazarin in London
34. As Chloris full of harmless *Corydon and Cloris, or The Wanton Sheepherdess* [?1676]	Before April 1676	Licensed 10 April
35. How perfect [/happy] Cloris } Such perfect Blisse }	Before April 1676	Licensed 10 April
36. Tell me noe more of Constancy } *A New Collection of the Choicest Songs*, 1676		
37. Son of a Whore (Vieth, 1968)	June/July 1676 or later	Possible reference to Downs incident (17 June)
38. Madam, If you're deceiv'd *A Very Heroical Epistle from my Lord All-Pride to Dol-Common*, 1679	Possibly summer, 1676	After Mulgrave's duel with Percy Kirke on 4 July 1675, and verbal echo or prefiguration of *Mac Flecknoe* (written July–August 1676)
39. To Rack and torture *1680*	Before end of 1676	Likely to have been written after Scroope's *In Defence of Satyr*, which refers to death of Downs from wounds on 27 June

First line & first printing	Date	Evidence
40. All my past Life }	Before 1677	Date of publication
41. Give me leave to raile at you } *Songs for i ii & iii Voyces* [1677]		
42. I Fuck no more then others do *1680*	Possibly spring /summer 1677	Parodies poem written by Scroope in 1677, who was courting Cary Frazier during winter, 1676–77; also contains echo of Buckingham's *A Familiar Epistle* [1679] written spring/ summer 1677
43. Some few from Wit Davenant, *Circe, a Tragedy*, 1677	Before May 1677	*Circe* was first produced on on 12 May 1677
44. To this moment a Rebell *1680*	Perhaps autumn 1677	Possibly written for festivities surrounding marriage of Princess Mary on 4 November
45. Crusht by that just contempt *1680*	Possibly early 1678	Possible reference in letter dated 25 April
46. Nothinge, thou elder brother *Upon Nothing; A Poem* [1679]	Before 14 May 1678	Note in Osborn MS b 52/2
47. Bursting with pride *A Very Heroical Epistle from my Lord All-Pride to Dol-Common*, 1679	Possibly 1678	Similar style, structure and content as no. 45
48. Dear Freind. I hear this Town *1680*	Autumn 1679	Refers to the Mulgrave / Dryden *Essay on Satyr* circulated in autumn

First line & first printing	Date	Evidence
49. To forme a Plott (Pinto, 1953)	Early 1680	Possible response to slight perceived in Otway's *The Poet's Complaint of his Muse*, published in January
50. What strange Surprise to meet *A Collection of Poems by Several Hands*, 1693	Spring/summer 1680	Letter based on Dryden's *Ovid's Epistles* (advertised 6 February 1680)

UNDATED POEMS

Details of first publication are in brackets—collected editions unless otherwise indicated.

51. Absent from thee I languish still (*1691*)
52. Against the Charms our Ballox have (*1680*)
53. An Age in her Embraces pas'd (*1691*)
54. Ancient person for whome I (*1691*)
55. By all Loves soft, yet mighty Pow'rs (*1680*)
56. Could I but make my wishes insolent (*Welbeck Miscellany No. 2*, ed. Francis Needham, 1934)
57. Faire Cloris in a Pigsty lay (*1680*)
58. Fucksters you that would bee happy (Love, 1999)
59. God bless our good and gracious king (*Miscellaneous Works of Rochester Roscommon*, 1707)
60. Greate Mother of Eneas and of Love (Pinto, 1953)
61. How blest was the Created State (*1680*)
62. I could Love thee till I dye (Hayward, 1926)
63. Injurious Charmer of my Vanquish't Heart (*Valentinian*, 1685)
64. Insulting Beauty, you mispend (*Examen Poeticum*, 1693)
65. Leave this gawdy guilded Stage (Pinto, *Rochester: Portrait of a Restoration Poet*, 1935)
66. Love a Woman! Th'rt an Ass (*1680*)
67. Love bad me hope, and I obey'd (*1680*)
68. My dear Mistris has a heart ([Behn], *Miscellany*, 1685)
69. O Love! how cold, and slow to take my part! (*1680*)
70. Phillis, be gentler I advise (*1680*)
71. Shee yeilds, she yeilds, Pale Envy said Amen (Pinto, 1953)

72. The utmost grace the Greeks could show (*1691*)
73. 'Tis not that I am weary growne (*1680*)
74. 'Twas a dispute 'twixt heaven and earth (*Welbeck Miscellany No. 2*, ed. Francis Needham, 1934)
75. What Cruel Paines Corinna takes (*1680*).

NOTES

1 Rochester's niece Anne Wharton, for example, recognised his skill as a satirist, observing that 'He civiliz'd the rude, and taught the young, | Made fools grow wise' (*Elegy on the Earl of* Rochester', quoted in *Rochester: The Critical Heritage*, ed. David Farley-Hills (London, 1972), pp. 107–08). A few years after the poet's death, Lady Sarah Cowper included *Tunbridge Wells*, *Upon Nothinge*, *On The Suppos'd Author of A Late Poem in Defence of Satyr*, *An Allusion to Horace* and *Against Reason and Mankind* in her manuscript compilation of miscellaneous verse, and Lady Anne Somerset had a copy made of *Against Reason and Mankind* (see Peter Beal, *Index of English Literary Manuscripts. Volume II 1625–1700: Part 2 Lee-Wycherley* (London, 1993), p. 228). See also n. 29 below.

2 *Miscellany, Being A Collection of Poems By several Hands* (London, 1685), pp. 45–9. For an exploration of the impact of Rochester on other contemporary poets, including Anne Wharton and John Oldham, see the present writer's 'Rochester's Contemporary Reception: The Evidence of the Memorial Verses', *Restoration: Studies in English Literary Culture, 1660–1700*, 30 (2006), 1–14.

3 See Butler's 'The Court Burlesqued. Written in the Year 1678' in Samuel Butler, *Posthumous Works In Prose and Verse* (London, 1715), pp. 19–68 (p. 65); Mulgrave's 'An Essay upon Poetry' (1682), lines 81, 82, 86, 88, quoted in *Critical Heritage*, pp. 42–3.

4 *The Complete Poems of John Wilmot, Earl of Rochester*, ed. David M. Vieth (New Haven and London, 1968); *The Works of John Wilmot Earl of Rochester*, ed. Harold Love (Oxford, 1999). Amongst the 73 firm attributions in his edition, Vieth includes *Timon*, *Signior Dildo* and *Written in a Lady's Prayer Book*, whereas Love lists them as 'Disputed works'. Love, unlike Vieth, regards 'Say Heav'n-born Muse, for only thou canst tell', 'Injurious Charmer of my Vanquish't heart', 'Out of Stark Love, and arrant Devotion' and the three juvenile poems (see following note) as genuine work by Rochester (although apart from the first, Vieth regards them as 'possibly' by Rochester). Finally, Vieth includes seven short impromptu poems for which Love does not judge the attribution to be sufficiently strong ('A health to Kate!', 'God bless our good and gracious King', 'Her Father gave her Dildoes six', 'Here's Monmouth the witty', 'I, John Roberts, writ this same', 'Lorraine you stole; by fraud you got Burgundy' and 'Sternhold and Hopkins had great qualms'). Examination of the contemporary reception history of individual poems is, however, beyond the scope of the present paper.

5 'Vertues triumphant Shrine! who do'st engage' (*Britannia Rediviva* (Oxford, 1660), sig. Aa1^{r-v}); 'Impia blasphemi sileant convitia vulgi' and 'Respite great Queen your just and hasty fears' (*Epicedia Academiæ Oxoniensis, in Obitum Serenissimæ Mariæ Principis Arausionensis* (Oxford, 1660), sigs A2^{v}, G1^{r-v}).

6 A copy of the epilogue to Charles D'Avenant's *Circe, A Tragedy* (London, 1677) is located in University of Nottingham Library, MS Portland Pw V 40, f. 225r.

7 The satires comprise: *Tunbridge Wells*, which was published in Richard Head's *Proteus Redivivus: or The Art of Wheedling* (London, 1675); 'Bursting with pride the loath'd

Impostume swel's' and 'Madam, If you're deceived, it is not by my cheat' in the broadside *A Very Heroical Epistle from My Lord All-Pride to Dol-Common* (London, 1679); *Artemiza to Chloe* (London, 1679), *Against Reason and Mankind* ([London], 1679) and *Upon Nothinge* ([London, 1679]) as individual broadsides, and *Senec. Troas. Act. 2. Chor.* in *The Two First Books of Philostratus, Concerning the Life of Apollonius Tynaeus* (London, 1680). The love poems are: 'All things submit themselves to your Command' and '*Cælia*, that faithful Servant you disown' which appeared in *A Collection of Poems Written upon Several Occasions by Several Persons* . . . (London, 1672); 'Out of Stark Love, and arrant Devotion' in *London Drollery* . . . (London, 1673); 'Att last you'l force mee to confess', 'Such perfect Blisse faire Chloris, wee', 'Tell mee noe more of Constancy' and 'While on these Lovely Lookes I gaze' in *A New Collection of the Choicest Songs* ([London], 1676); and 'All my past Life is mine no more' and 'Give me leave to raile at you' in *Songs, for i, ii, and iii Voyces . . . composed by Henry Bowman* (Oxford, 1679). The libertine song is 'As Chloris full of harmless thought', which circulated in the broadside *Corydon and Cloris or, The Wanton Sheepherdess* (London, [?1676]).

8 The six exceptions are the epilogue to Fane's *Love in the Dark*; the love poems 'All things submit themselves to your Command', 'Cælia, that faithful Servant you disown', 'Att Last you'l force mee to confess' and 'Give me leave to raile at you'; and the satire 'Bursting with pride the loath'd Impostume swel's'. Ascriptions to Rochester occur, for example, in Harvard fMS Eng 636 (*Against Reason and Mankind*, *Artemiza to Chloe*, *Tunbridge Wells*, *Upon Nothinge*, *Senec. Troas. Act. 2. Chor.*, 'All my past Life is mine no more', 'Such perfect Blisse faire Chloris, wee' and 'While on these Lovely Lookes I gaze'); Bodleian MS Don. b 8 ('Madam, If you're deceived, it is not by my cheat' and 'Tell mee noe more of Constancy'); Bodleian MS Rawl. poet. 123 ('As Chloris full of harmless thought'); and BL Add. MS 23722 ('Out of Stark Love, and arrant Devotion').

9 Not that Rochester's verse would always be correctly recognised, as the narrator in *Satyr.* [*Timon*] warns:

> He takes me in his Coach, and as wee goe
> Pulls out a Libell, of a Sheete or Two;
> Insipid as the Praise, of Pious Queenes,
> Or Shadwells, unassisted former Scenes;
> Which he admir'd, and prais'd at ev'ry Line,
> At last, it was soe sharpe, it must be mine. . . .
> He knew my Stile (he swore) and twas in vaine
> Thus to deny, the Issue of my Braine.
> Choakt with his flatt'ry I noe answer make,
> But silent leave him to his deare mistake. (ll. 13–18, 25–28)
>
> (*Works of Rochester*, pp. 258–59)

10 For Prior's 'Satyr on the Poets', see *Critical Heritage*, p. 162. See also Prior's *Poems on Several Occasions* (London, 1709), sig. a4^r; *Miscellaneous Works, Written by His Grace, George, Late Duke of Buckingham* (London, 1704), sig. A4^r; *The Miscellaneous Works Of the Honourable Sir Charles Sedley, Bart* (London, 1702), sig. A6^r.

11 Harold Love, 'The Scribal Transmission of Rochester's Songs', *Bibliographical Society of Australia and New Zealand*, 20 (1996), 161–80 (p. 161). But see also the present writer's 'Love in the Ayre' in *That Second Bottle: Essays on John Wilmot, Earl of Rochester*, ed. Nicholas Fisher (Manchester, 2000), pp. 63–80 (pp. 69–70).

12 Harold Love, *Scribal Publication in Seventeenth-Century England* (Oxford, 1993), p. 259.

13 Michael Brennan and Paul Hammond, 'The Badminton Manuscript: A New Miscellany of Restoration Verse', *English Manuscript Studies 1100–1700*, 5 (1995), pp. 171–207 (p. 174).

14 Beal, *IELM*, II/2, pp. 230–4.

15 *Poems On Several Occasions By the Right Honourable, The E. of R*—- (Antwerp, 1680); *Poems On Several Occasions. Written by a late Person of Honour* (London, 1685); *Poems, &c. On Several Occasions. With Valentinian, A Tragedy. Written by the Right Honourable John Late Earl of Rochester* (London, 1691).

16 Harold Love, 'The Scribal Transmission of Rochester's Songs', p. 175.

17 *Scribal Publication*, p. 263.

18 *Against Reason and Mankind*, ll. 1–173 and 174-end (entitled 'An Addition'), are transcribed as two separate poems, each attributed to Rochester, and the poem 'Prick Nature's pump cunt's pioneer' runs straight on from 'Deep in an unctuous vale', implying Rochester's authorship.

19 The only poem falsely ascribed here and also ascribed to Rochester in a further manuscript is 'O that I could by some new chemic art', which Vieth notes is in Taylor MS 3, p. 254 and in an uncatalogued manuscript in the University of Illinois (David M. Vieth, *Attribution in Restoration Poetry: a Study of Rochester's* Poems *of 1680* (London, 1963), p. 490). For the attraction of scurrilous verse to Rochester's name, consider

> Madness and Follys, wch how ere begun
> Were not by *ROCHESTER* sustaynd alone
> Tho He almost alone, the burden bore
> (Beside the monstrous pack, wch was his own)
> Of all that by or Malice, or Illnature late was done.
> Well were it that they would at last give o're—
>   But still as they were wont before
> With Farwells, Droll, and Shredds of Verse
> They vex his Happy Ghost, and miserably disguise his Herse.

(Extract from Samuel Woodford, 'An Ode to the Memory of the Right Honourable John Lord Wilmot Earl of Rochester' (1680), published in *Critical Heritage*, p. 124.)

20 *Attribution in Restoration Poetry*, p.108.

21 See *Attribution in Restoration Poetry*, pp. 56–100, and Beal, *IELM*, II/2, p. 233.

22 See *Attribution in Restoration Poetry*, pp. 93–100.

23 *Scribal Publication*, p. 260.

24 See Harold Love, 'Rochester's "I' th' isle of Britain": decoding a textual tradition', *English Manuscript Studies 1100–1700*, 6 (1997), 175–223.

25 See Brennan and Hammond, 'The Badminton Manuscript', pp. 171–207.

26 See Harold Love, 'The Scribal Transmission of Rochester's Songs', pp. 165, 177.

27 **Pomfret MS**: *On The Suppos'd Author of A late Poem in Defence of SATYR* and possibly *An Epistolary Essay* (described as being 'From E: R: to E: M') and *Epilogue to* Circe (described as 'by the E R—'); **Yale MS Osborn b 105**: *An Epistolary Essay* ('from Y^e^ L^d^: R: to Y^e^ L^d^: M:') and *Against Reason and Mankind, A Ramble in St. James's Park, Artemiza to Chloe, The Imperfect Enjoyment* ['Naked she lay clasp'd'], *To Love, The Disabled Debauchee* (all described as 'By the E of R'); **Badminton MS**: possibly *An Epistolary Essay* (described as being 'From E. R. to E. M.'); **Gyldenstolpe MS**: possibly *An Epistolary Essay* (described as being 'From E: R: to E: M.'), although in only the final poem, entitled 'The chronicle out of Mr Cowley', is the author elsewhere indicated; **Brotherton MS**: 'Injurious Charmer of my Vanquish't heart' and possibly *An*

Epistolary Essay (described as being 'from the E. of R. to my Lord O. B.'); and **Edinburgh MS**: *On The Suppos'd Author of A late Poem in Defence of SATYR*, 'Phillis, be gentler I advise', 'In the Isle of Brittain long since famous growne' and *A Ramble in St. James's Park.* The **Hartwell MS** is uniquely identified as a collection of poetry solely by Rochester, and the **Harbin MS** contains no attributions.

28 Beal, *IELM*, II/2, pp. 232, 234; *Works of Rochester*, ed. Love, p. xxxvii; Harbin MS (Longleat House, Thynne Papers, vol. XXVII), ff. 46^{r}–49^{r}.

29 Love, 'The Scribal Transmission of Rochester's Songs', pp. 171–3. Love posits that the exclusion from the Hartwell and Harbin MSS of Rochester's indecent lyrics indicates that the compilation was prepared for a female readership (*Works of Rochester*, p. 519), but it is interesting that of the twelve poems by Rochester that appeared in *Female Poems On Several Occasions. Written by Ephelia. The Second Edition, with large Additions* (London, 1682), three are indubitably libertine in terms of their subject matter (*The Disabled Debauchee*, *Nestor* and 'As *Chloris* full of harmless thought').

30 See Nicholas Fisher, 'Jacob Tonson and the Earl of Rochester', *The Library*, 6 (2005), 133–60 (pp. 141–3 and nn. 36–42).

31 *Poems, &c. On Several Occasions. With Valentinian, A Tragedy. Written by the Right Honourable John Late Earl of Rochester* (London, 1691), sig. $A6^{v}$. Twenty-one of the twenty-five poems in the Hartwell MS appear here; see *Works of Rochester*, ed. Love, p. xxxvii.

32 'Anonymity in Restoration Poetry', *The Seventeenth Century*, 8 (1993), 123–42 (pp. 132, 138).

Marvell's *The Last Instructions to a Painter*: From Manuscript to Print

Hilton Kelliher

Marvell's *The Last Instructions to a Painter,* the greatest of all the political satires known by the generic name of Advices-to-a-painter, was occasioned by the catastrophic defeat of the English in their home waters during the second Dutch War (1664–1667). Between 10 and 13 June 1667 the Dutch fleet under de Ruyter carried out a daring raid on the coast, firing houses on Canvey Island and then turning south to attack the fleet anchored in the Medway. Having taken Sheerness they sailed up river, skirting the ships that had been sunk to deny them passage, broke the boom at Chatham and in the face of bombardment from Upnor Castle burned three first-rate ships, sailing off and destroying the *Royal Charles.* John Evelyn, himself a commissioner for the sick and wounded in the war, wrote of it as 'a dishonour never to be wiped off: Those who advised his *Majestie* to prepare no fleete this Spring, deserv'd I know not what!'[1] Pepys described the panic that ensued in London at the prospect of a nearer incursion and his own fears, as a naval official, of being attacked by mobs or used as a scapegoat for the failures of the government.[2] Both took the precaution of removing their goods or money to places of safety.

Parliament, prorogued since February, was powerless to respond to the crisis. In the enforced absence from his seat in the Commons Marvell's responded by composing a long and virulent verse-satire. As with his later prose tracts *The Rehearsal transpros'd* (1672) and *Mr. Smirke* (1676), release from daily attendance at the House and the necessity of reporting to his constituents in Hull afforded him ample leisure for literary work. Though in April, 'having nothing of mine own to deserve your acceptance', he had sent his friend Philip, Lord Wharton, Simon Ford's Latin and English verses on the great fire of the previous September, by mid-August, when he wrote a studied letter of consolation to the father of a young man who had just died, he was already working on his satire.[3] The focus of his attack was the political and administrative failures of the ruling court party under Edward Hyde, Earl of Clarendon, Charles II's lord chancellor and principal minister since the Restoration. After summoning his imaginary painter to draw some cruel portraits of leading members of the court he passes to a mock-heroic catalogue of Members of the Commons during the important excise debate of October 1666. This is followed by accounts of the diplomatic attempts made by the English to sue for peace and, in considerable and lively detail, of the Dutch raid. News brought to court of the treaty signed at Breda on 31 July allowed dismissal of the briefly-reconvened parliament and temporarily 'reprieves their guilty lives'.[4] The satire ends with a plea to the King to rid himself of the chancellor, whose removal, initiated on the 25th, was accomplished on the 30th when he finally surrendered the great seal.[5] All the same, the date of 4 September that appears in several contemporary texts of the poem remains credible as that of the poem's completion. Marvell's campaign against the chancellor continued into the following month, when he insisted in the House that some treasonous words allegedly spoken by Clarendon against the King be included in the articles of impeachment.[6]

Though the satire is much more a piece of political activism than a poem about a naval defeat, the course of his life had fitted him supremely well to become the leading anti-poet of the Anglo-Dutch sea campaign. His boyhood had been passed among ships and seamen—or as Samuel Parker sneeringly phrased it 'Boat-Swains and Cabin-Boys'—in Hull, one of the great trading ports of the realm, where his three sisters all married merchants.[7] As a sitting M.P. from the Restoration he looked out for the interests of Hull's Trinity House almost equally with those of his constituents until disabled from a too active role by his election in May 1674 as Elder Brother of the sister house at Deptford, where shortly before his death he was chosen to be younger Warden.[8] These were singular distinctions for one who was neither seaman, naval administrator nor aristocrat, and afford clear testimony to his abilities in maritime matters. At just short of one thousand verses in pentameter couplets his satire is the longest not merely of his own pieces but of any political poem from the reign of Charles II, far exceeding its original in Waller's *Instructions to a Painter, for the drawing of the posture of his majesty's forces at sea . . . and victory obtained over the Dutch, June 3, 1665*, and yielding only to the three hundred quatrains of Dryden's *Annus Mirabilis* (December 1666), both of which celebrated the brief initial success of the English fleet. It was Waller's misfortune to have established the model for a series of satires that set a hostile interpretation on events and personalities of the naval war. Recent scholarship has reclaimed for Marvell the *Second Advice to a Painter* of April 1666 and the *Third Advice* that followed it in October, the two printed together in 1667 as *Directions to a painter* with an attribution, improbable even then, to Sir John Denham, who would have had little difficulty in repudiating it.[9] The conclusion of the war was greeted in an anonymous *Fourth* (August 1667) and *Fifth Advice* (Sept.-Oct. 1667), both duly included in an enlarged reprint of the *Directions*.[10] The overwhelming popularity of these satires is demonstrated by Peter Beal, who records no fewer than forty-seven loosely contemporary copies of the *Second*, twenty-eight of the *Third*, thirty-five of the *Fourth* and ten of the *Fifth Advice*, along with later manifestations of the genre represented by forty-two copies of *Advice to a painter to draw the Duke by* (August 1673) and twenty-four of the *Further Advice* (early 1671).[11]

Faced with such widely-circulated sedition and libel the government moved to silence, if not their authors, who remained—and still remain by and large—anonymous, then at least those involved in publishing them. Individual royalists too were scandalised. John Beale, D.D. and Fellow of the Royal Society, who from his Yeovil parish kept a critical eye on developments in contemporary poetry, recalled in an indignant letter to John Evelyn of 13 May 1671 that

> The *broadest Libell* that ever I heard of, was in the Dutch war, *the Malicious Painter*, about 300 verses; which I noted to be scatterd about the West by Sir J[oh]n Cop[lestone] O[liver] C[romwell']s K[nigh]t errant. Though it was swallowd down by the generall odium against Clar[endon], yet it wounded Royalty. And the same pencill is afresh busy, with a thousand other rank poysons, & white powder. Hath his Majesty lost the benefit of the *Revels*; or wants he true Antidotes, or true friends to detect dangerous enemyes. Is no Royal Act worthy to escape public reproach? Or are the lawes effete, or the Gangrene incurable? In other dayes a touch had been capital; &, though libels lookd abroad under the severest Tyranny of old; yet the calmest princes found their seasons to chastise this insolence.[12]

The reference here is evidently to *The Second Advice* which in 366 verses praises the conduct of former commonwealth men while, as Pepys wrote, 'abusing the Duke of York and my Lord Sandwich, Pen, and everybody, and the King himself, in all the matters of the Navy and Warr'.[13] Sir John Coplestone had been sheriff of Devon, where he commanded a regiment after the civil war, was knighted by Cromwell in June 1655 and helped to administer the new oath to MPs in the Protector's last parliament.[14] Little more than a year after the *Second Advice* appeared in print he showed his continuing interest in poetry and politics in two letters addressed to the Duke of Richmond from Westminster.[15] On 20 August 1667, he reported fears over the delay in receiving ratification of the Treaty of Breda, along with his judgement on Denham's recent elegy on Cowley, 'wch shewes hee is become a downe right flatt poett'. On the 31st he gave news of the return of the English delegates from Holland and the surrender of the seals by Clarendon who, he wrote, 'fear'd the mallice of his Enimies would not rest there'.

In circulating an anti-government satire Coplestone was taking a considerable risk, for the penalties for distribution were severe. In July of that year it had been ordered that the Stationers' Company be questioned concerning an attempt by the publisher Francis ('Elephant') Smith to find a printer for the *Second* and *Third Advice*.[16] Yet, as the sheer volume of extant manuscript copies shows, fear of prosecution did little to inhibit mass circulation, even among courtiers and those serving in civil service posts. Pepys himself had received the *Second Advice* in December 1666, 'sealed up', from Sir Hugh Cholmley, gentleman usher to the Queen, and the *Third Advice*, which he took home to copy, from John Brisbane, a fellow naval official, in the following January.[17] It may have been from the printed *Directions* that in July he and some colleagues inspecting the new battery at Gravesend were 'very merry, and fell to reading of the several *Advices to a Painter* which made us good sport; and endeed, are very witty'.[18] In September he met with the *Fourth Advice* at the house of James Pearse, surgeon-general to the fleet, which 'made my heart ake to read, it being too sharp and so true'.[19] Beale was therefore quite right that 'other rank poysons' were in circulation, if mistaken in thinking them to be from the same pen (while his allusion to 'white powder' is apt given that, in contemporary usage, it 'does Execution but makes no noise').[20] Two months previously news of another such libel had reached the ears of the authorities, for 'One Palmer a bookseller has been convicted of circulating a scandalous pamphlet in MS. called the 'Advice to a Painter," in which their Majesties and many of the nobility were maligned. He is fined, and is to stand in the pillory, besides the other punishments usual for such offences'.[21] This is thought to relate to *Further Advice to a Painter* ('Painter once more thy pencil reassume'), more outspoken than *The Second Advice* about Charles II's private life, which remained unprinted until *Poems on Affairs of State*, 1697.

Nevertheless Pepys, though at the very centre of naval administration, seems to have remained wholly unaware of *The Last Instructions*. But then, even as late as 1927 Marvell's Oxford editor, H. M. Margoliouth, had no knowledge of any manuscript, conjecturing that 'the satire is perhaps too long to have invited copying'. In the reprint of 1952 he was able to add a prefatory note concerning that in the copy of Marvell's *Miscellaneous Poems* (1681) supplemented with handwritten texts of his unpublished poems and satires that had been acquired seven years earlier by the Bodleian Library as MS Eng. poet. d. 49.[22] This had been identified by Hugh Macdonald with the second of two manuscript sources drawn on by Captain Edward Thompson for his collection of Marvell's *Works* (1776).[23] Since then, length notwithstanding, four further near-contemporary manuscript witnesses and a brief extract have come to light. The extract occurs in British Library Additional MS 18220, a verse-miscellany compiled by the reverend John Watson in July 1668, and first brought to general notice by Osborne in 1949, that was mentioned only in passing by Pierre Legouis in his 1971 revision of Margoliouth. So too was Osborn PB VII/15, a neatly-written copy in the Beinecke Library that had already been collated by George deF. Lord for the Yale edition of *Poems on Affairs of State* (1963).[24] A self-contained text in a pamphlet in the Portland Literary Collection Pw V 299 at the University of Nottingham and a careless copy in an anthology in the Library of the University of California, Los Angeles, 170/68 (pp. 67–89), were drawn to the attention of Marvell scholars by Peter Beal in 1993, though the former was identified in the typewritten catalogue of verse-manuscripts issued by the Department of Manuscripts at Nottingham in 1962.[25] Four years later another professional text was discovered in a Restoration verse-miscellany acquired by the British Library, where it is now Additional MS 73540, ff. 1r–26r.[26] Of these, only the last and the Osborn copy can compete with the Portland manuscript in offering a complete and sequential text, for one couplet (lines 463–464) is lacking from the Bodleian version and five verses (lines 402–405, 422) from that in the UCLA MS. As to printed editions, the earliest did not appear until eleven years after Marvell's death, in *The Third Part of the Collection of Poems on Affairs of State*, 1689. Later still the satire figured, along with other pieces whose wholesale attribution to him was seen as a selling-point, in the 1697 *Poems on Affairs of State* and in the various expanded editions to 1716. An undated pamphlet comprising *The Last Instructions* and the related satire *The Loyall Scot* survives in a sole recorded exemplar in the Library Company of Philadelphia.

Although individual editors of *The Last Instructions* made use of each of these witnesses in turn as they were recovered, only the most recent of them, Nigel Smith, was able to collate the full complement.[27] Their small number relative to those of the *Second* and *Third Advice* prompted him to suggest that it 'may be that a very limited circulation, or even none at all, was intended'.[28] Though ignorance of the poem's existence on the part of Pepys, who was both centrally placed and personally concerned, tends to support the notion of restricted access, it is surely inconceivable that Marvell, in this case above all, was writing solely for his own amusement. His authorship, had it been known, of the extended mock-heroic description of the excise debate (lines 105–396) and the three gross caricatures of royal and public figures with which the poem begins (lines 29–104) might have led to questions in the House. But apart from the loss of his considerable labour (and the approbation of, at least, friends and like-minded colleagues) had he kept it close, it had all-too-obvious propaganda value as a tool in the campaign to unseat Clarendon. The only early text that is clearly dated is the rather garbled version of the lines lampooning Henry Jermyn, Earl of St Albans (lines 29–49) that were passed on in July 1668 by Henry North of Mildenhall in Suffolk to the local vicar, John Watson, who shared a natural interest in a member of a prominent local family, the Jermyns of Rushbrook.) Only one other of the remaining manuscripts seems likely to be contemporary with the poem's composition, and this is Portland Literary Collection MS Pw V 299, which forms the main subject of the present investigation.

The Provenance of the Portland Manuscript

MS Pw V 299 belongs to that portion of the library formerly at Welbeck Abbey in Nottinghamshire, seat of the Cavendish-Bentincks, Dukes of Portland, which passed to Nottingham University Library in the middle of last century. The founder of the dynasty, Hans Willem Bentinck, had arrived from Holland with William III in 1689. His grandson, the second Duke, married Margaret Cavendish Harley, heiress not only to Edward Harley, second Earl of Oxford, but, through her mother the Countess of Oxford, to John Holles, Duke of Newcastle-upon-Tyne, and in turn to his predecessor in the same title, the cavalier and playwright William Cavendish (d.1676). In 1753 Countess and Duchess agreed the sale to the nation of the magnificent collection of manuscripts formed by Robert, first Earl of Oxford, and his successor Edward, which duly became one of the foundation collections of the British Museum. By contrast, the correspondence, private papers and archives of the Nottinghamshire dynasties of Cavendish, Holles and Bentinck, families prominent in English history, politics and literature, were transferred by the second Earl's widow from his town house in Dover Street and his country seat at Wimpole to Welbeck. There they remained until their gradual dispersal after 1949 by the seventh Duke, when a large body of material originating with his Harley ancestors was progressively transferred on loan to the Museum, to be incorporated in due course as British Library Additional MSS 70000–70523.[29] Most of the remaining items, extending to some hundred and forty volumes and fifteen hundred loose items, including a large and important collection of seventeenth- and eighteenth-century verse, were lodged with Nottingham University.

Several large miscellanies of late Restoration and Williamite satirical and topical verse that now form part of the great Harleian collection were acquired by the first Earl of Oxford in 1703, and three others were copied during the 1720s for his successor.[30] The second Earl has also been identified as the owner of a small cache of autograph poems by Rochester and his Countess, on the grounds that six of the pieces there were transcribed together for him into the miscellany that is now British Library Harley MS 7316 (fols 20r–23v).[31] A fourth such compilation that has only recently come to light includes copies of the Rochester letters now preserved in Harley MS 7003.[32] These items apart, out of a dozen Restoration and later miscellanies in the collection at Nottingham none so far can be proved to have been acquired even as early as the first half of the eighteenth century.[33] Three have an established provenance outside the family.[34] Two, moreover, are known to have been purchased by the sixth Duke of Portland, bibliophile, member of the Roxburghe Club and collector, who had long taken a keen interest in the arrangement and cataloguing of his family papers.[35] This raises the possibility that, although so far untraced in any bookseller's list or auction-house catalogue, *The Last Instructions* in fact arrived at Welbeck in the early years of the twentieth century.

In February 1930 the seventh Duke had appointed as his librarian Francis Needham (1900–1971) who had spent the previous seven years as Senior Assistant at the Bodleian Library, Oxford, where he founded the Friends of the Bodleian.[36] From his first arrival Needham busied himself with the manuscripts at Welbeck, freely forwarding items for inspection to former colleagues and to the staff of the British Museum. Between May and October his researches led him to seek advice from Edmund Craster in Oxford about a section of the Yorkist prose *Brut* he had found behind a bookshelf, H. W. Meikle in Edinburgh about the Scots chronicle of Andrew Wynton, and, along with an unspecified 'Welbeck morality', the bibliographer Strickland Gibson regarding the present manuscript.[37] Having spotted printers' cast-off markings in the margins of *The Last Instructions* he sent it for comparison with the printed text of 1689 to Gibson, who in a reply of 23 October, now preserved loose with the manuscript, rejected the notion:

> No, your MS. does *not* seem to be the copy used for printing the 'Third Part of the Collection of Poems on Affairs of State'. For one thing, in the printed version proper names are given in the form M——t &c. passim. The lines which your MS. directs to be deleted are there: and 'To the King' at the end follows without any extra four lines or space therfore.

This statement seems to have discouraged independent enquiry. The latest editor of the satire, while acknowledging the presence of 'instructions for, and notes by, the printer . . .', concludes that 'it is not clear that either [this or the Bodleian text] were used as copy text for 1689 or 1697', adding that 'no confident claim can be made for a complete version in MS that predates the printed version of 1689'.[38] In fact, close examination confirms that the Portland manuscript had served as copy for this very version. *The Last Instructions* thus joins *Paradise Lost*, published in August 1667, one month before Marvell completed his satire, and the anonymous *Further Advice to a Painter* of August 1673 as the third poem printed in the Wing period for which manuscript copy-text is now known to survive.[39]

Description of the Manuscript

Marvell's satire is the sole item in a small quarto manuscript that was the subject of a careful restoration undertaken probably in Oxford in 1930, for the sheet used as backing for the front cover is countermarked 'BODLEIAN'.[40] The twenty-two leaves of the pamphlet, each measuring approximately 190 mm by 152 mm, are attached to late seventeenth- or early eighteenth-century marbled covers of stiff paper decorated with a columnar pattern in red, yellow, blue and white double-comb and most probably imported from France or Germany.[41] Damage suffered at beginning and end of the text-leaves suggests that the covers were not in place before printing, though some inconsequential jottings or pen-trials found inside both may not be much later than the turn of the century. The leaves have been re-sewn to the covers at eleven stitching-points, but five further small puncture-holes are visible towards the foot from f.7 onwards. Reinforcement during conservation of the inner edges of some text-leaves—along with the outer ones of others—means that the original make-up is difficult to reconstruct with absolute certainty. If faithfully replicated it consisted of a single bifolium (fols 1r and 2r), comprising a blank fly- and title-leaf, followed by five gatherings of four leaves each (fols 3–22) for the text. Chain-lines run across the page, and the watermark, which is best seen on ff.10 and 18–20, is said to measure approximately 50mm by 35mm and to belong to the common type of a horn in an ornate shield, offering in the present state of our knowledge little clue as to date.[42]. Much of the front fly-leaf (fol.1) has been torn away, but a sliver remaining at the top bears an ink stroke like a bracket or the upstroke of a capital 'M'. The title, copied out at the head of the recto of the following leaf, to face the first page of text, reads 'The last Instructions to | A | PAINTER.', while at the foot is written 'London. | September the 4th 1667.' Nowhere does the poet's name appear.

Portland seems likely to be the earliest of all the major manuscripts in point of transcription, and, if not certainly contemporary with the poem's composition, belongs at least to the poet's lifetime. Script and presentation are perfectly consistent with a date during the late 1660s or the 1670s, and far remote from the looser type of hand favoured by professional copyists of verse, working individually or for entrepreneurs, in the two decades that followed. Though in the present state of our knowledge the watermark proves of little help, it would be strange if the hand were not at some point to be detected in similar work of the period. One potential pointer to identification is the idiosyncratic rendering of the nouns 'leavs' (line 71) and 'Theevs' (lines 333, 940) and the verbs 'Believs' (line 271), 'receivs' (line 306) and 'reprievs' (line 850; though cf. 'revolves' in line 925), spellings untraced in Marvell's autograph letters from this date. The copyist was an accomplished and practised professional whose main hand, a calligraphic and stylish italic, is complemented for proper names and for emphatic words by a thick roman script imitating print. There are no obvious signs of pricking or ruling as a guide to lineation, and there are no catchwords. The care taken over presentation was considerable; in the neat layout, the beauty and regularity of the script and the overall cleanness of the text the work makes it something of a *tour de force*. Yet, unusually handsome though it is, textual accuracy was the principal aim here. For clarity and ease of reading not a single abbreviation is used, and a measure of the general efficiency is the disposition of roman characters, which fail only, among a dozen occurrences of the word, in not differentiating '*King*' (line 498). However, besides a single couplet added later in the margin, three corrections do appear, all made in the copyist's own hand and seemingly in the same ink as the original text. In the line '*Grosse Bodyes, grosser Minds, but grossest Cheats*' (line 179) '*but*' was overwritten with '*and*', the reading found in all other witnesses. In the description of the merchant ships that were sunk below Woolwich in an attempt to forestall the further incursion of the Dutch, the initial transcription as '*From* South *Perfumes, and Spices from the* East' (line 718) was altered to read, as elsewhere, '*From the* South *Perfumes, Spices from the* East' by inserting '*the*' between the lines and crossing out '*and*'. Thirdly, where Aeson '*With bitter Herbs, rose from the Pot renew'd*' (line 338) the adjective was scrubbed out and '*magic*' substituted below. Elsewhere too there are lapses, though over close on one thousand lines of text these are trivial indeed, extending merely to 'Sent' (line 95)—half-corrected to 'Scnt'—for 'Scent', 'valiants Acts' (line 191), 'rises' for 'rise' (line 896)—though the final 's' may have been added later, in a darker ink—'Plenepotentiary' (line 452) changed to 'Plenipotentiary', and 'coy Vission' (line 901). The lighter brown ink in which the two last-mentioned errors were corrected was also used for pointing the hundred lines beginning with the paragraph '*Mean while the certain News of Peace arrives*' to the end of the main poem (lines 849–948), not including the envoy. The punctuation here was clearly added as a single operation.

Immediately after transcription the verses were numbered by tens in the left-hand margin. We can be sure that this was the case because, although the copyist later inserted, sideways along the outer margin of the text at f. 11v, the couplet (lines 455–6)

And that, by Law of Arms, in martiall strife,
Who yeilds his Sword has title to his Life.

no corresponding adjustment was made to the numbering. As a result the reckoning runs two lines short of true from that point as far as '980' (*i.e.* line 982) which is now barely visible under the smudges of printers' ink in the margin of f. 21v. Yet it is hard to see then how the final verse came to be labelled correctly as '990'. One, not very convincing, explanation might be that the original was also numbered and that the copyist, having ignored this in favour of an independent count, unthinkingly brought his work into conformity with his copy-text at this cardinal point. Line-numbering is also present in the apparently professional Osborn and the amateurish Los Angeles copies but not in any of the manuscript poems in the Bodleian compilation, nor yet, for reasons of space, in the octavo miscellany that is Additional MS 73540. Generally speaking, numbering is rare in contemporary verse, manuscript or printed, even for long non-stanzaic poems, though there are obvious advantages to the scribe in checking his work and to the printer both in this and in estimating press-work and costs, and it may well have led to detection of the omitted couplet. One notable exception is the fair-copy manuscript of *Paradise Lost*, where they were added by the copyist. While the printed version of Milton's epic, decked out as befitted its serious subject, sets the numbers in a double rule at the outer edge of each page, Marvell's topical satire in its ephemeral form does not—not least, perhaps, because of the labour and hence cost of justifying the lines of type.

Among the manuscript witnesses Portland stands out by virtue of the exemplary care lavished on its layout and its complete and wholly coherent text, and we may wonder who but its author would have gone to the trouble to commission such a sophisticated artefact. Though sufficiently clear and accurate to have acted as the master from which other copies could be made for circulation the manuscript is handsome enough—more than usually so, in fact—to have served for presentation to a patron or friend (such, for example, as Lord Wharton, to whom in his letter of April he had reported on the progress of the war.) Could it perhaps have been intended for publication? Despite their politically explosive character the *Second* and *Third Advice* reached the press in the year after their composition. Given his position as M.P. and the state of affairs at the time of writing, Marvell would have had reason enough for not sending out the text in his own extremely legible hand, since an autograph manuscript of an anti-government satire detected in the public domain would, to say the least, have embarrassed him. It would be entirely natural for him to have recourse to the subterfuge that he was later to adopt with his controversial prose. An investigation by the licenser Roger L'Estrange into *The Growth of Popery* (1677) was to trace the suspected publisher, Anne Brewster, to 'the house of a former officer under Cromwell, that writes three or four very good hands, . . . from which one may fairly presume that all those delicate copies, which Brewster carried to the press, were written by her landlord, and copied by him from the author. If she be questioned, probably she will cast the whole on Mr. Marvell, who is lately dead, and there the enquiry ends'.[43] Yet the manuscript is altogether too elaborate and expensive to have been commissioned as mere printers' copy, far exceeding anything that would have been required for the printing-house. That said, the manner of its presentation, including the separate title-page, lacking attribution but dated, and the frequent painstaking recourse to print-hand, proclaims its conscious kinship to printed verse-pamphlets of the time. Indeed, but for the press-markings it might well have been taken for a copy of *1689*, rather than the reverse: no doubt its variants would have been readily enough explained or discounted.

The Manuscript as Printers' Copy

The Glorious Revolution of 1688 that ended the rule of the male line of Stuarts also brought the whigs for a period to ascendancy in the Commons and the offices of state. A declaration of February 1689 listing grievances against the government of James II was followed shortly after by the proclamation of William and Mary as joint sovereign, in May by the Toleration Act, and in October by the Bill of Rights. One rapid result of the change of regime was that an accumulation of Restoration political and religious verse-satires which until then had circulated clandestinely in individual manuscript copies or in larger aggregations produced by professional scriptoria began to be released in print. Within the year there appeared three separate miscellanies, all of which proved so popular that each was soon supplemented by further parts bearing the same imprint date.[44] *A Collection of Poems on Affairs of*

State includes 'Spread a large canvas . . .' ('Further Advice'), 'Britannia and Raleigh' and 'Nostradamus' Prophecy', all falsely attributed to '*A. M.* Esq;', and the unattributed but genuine 'On the Statue at Stocks Market'. *The Second Part* opens with 'A Dialogue Between two horses. By A. M——l Esq.' and, without name of author, 'On the Lord Mayor and Court of Aldermen . . .', and *The Third Part* with *The Last Instructions*. In 1697 almost all of these pieces were reprinted, with six ascribed to Marvell, three of them wrongly so, and a further two unattributed but genuine poems, in the three editions of *Poems on Affairs of State: From the Time of Oliver Cromwell, to the Abdication of K. James the Second. Written by the Greatest Wits of the Age*, and, with the addition of 'The Statue in Stocks Market' previously omitted, in its successive re-incarnations to 1716, the second full year of the Hanoverian dynasty.[45]

We do not know how the Portland manuscript came to the hands of the publisher, though it is tempting to speculate that *The Last Instructions* derives from the personal papers of Marvell's close friend and colleague at Westminster, the presbyterian Sir Edward Harley, K.B. (1624–1700). Harley, a former parliamentary commander who had entered parliament at the Restoration, was grandfather and namesake of the second Earl of Oxford.[46] Both men were members of the country party in parliament and opponents of Clarendon. Harley's correspondence, now preserved among the Portland papers in the British Library, includes six intimate letters from Marvell, addressed from London between 1673 and 1677 to his house in Herefordshire.[47] Here politics, religion and literature mix. The first announces Marvell's intention of replying to Samuel Parker's attack on his anonymously-published *Rehearsal Transpros'd* (1672), while another, diplomatically unsigned, discusses the reception of *Mr Smirke* (1676), a defence of Harley's friend and diocesan Herbert Crofts, which is circumspectly described here by its author as 'a book said to be Marvels'.[48] As owner, and perhaps even recipient, of the Portland manuscript Harley would be a likely intermediary. Since in 1688 he took up arms with his sons for William of Orange he would have had every inducement to seize the opportunity offered by the change of regime to bring his friend's most considerable political satire to light. In Westminster, where he spent the greater part of 1689, he may well have come across *A Collection of Poems on Affairs of State* and decided to offer the manuscript to its publisher, specifying its return after printing. Late in the succeeding decade his son Robert, as leader of the country party in parliament, was to play his part in reviving the writings of former republicans, encouraging John Toland, a protégé of Shaftesbury, to edit the *Works* (1700) of Marvell's friend the Commonwealth political theorist James Harrington.[49]

The Last Instructions is very much the major item in what the title-page proclaims as 'THE | THIRD PART | OF THE | COLLECTION | OF | POEMS | ON | Affairs of State. | Containing, | Esquire Marvel's further Instructions to | a Painter. | AND | The late Lord Rochester's Farewel. | [rule] | *LONDON* | Printed in the Year M DC LXXXIX'.[50] Neither the publisher nor printer is, or has so far been, identified. Although the exact month of publication is unknown, the paper, watermarked with a fleur-de-lis and pendent 'EB', is of the same or closely similar stock to that already used for *The Second Part*, which opens with Marvell's 'A Dialogue between two Horses' and '*On the Lord Mayor and Court of Aldermen, presenting the l—— K—- and D— of Y— each with a Copy of their Freedoms*, Anno Dom. 1674'. No great interval seems to have elapsed between their being set up in print. Marvell's poem, which follows the title-leaf and its blank verso, occupies pp. 1–25, and the 'Farewel', pp. 26–30, of a quarto of sixteen leaves comprising four sheets signed A and C–E^4. The false title given to Marvell's satire on the general titlepage is corrected at the head of the first text-page to 'THE | LAST INSTRUCTIONS | TO A | PAINTER'. If Elizabeth Donno was right in supposing that the error followed on the inclusion under Marvell's initials of *Advice to a Painter to draw the Duke by* in the first part of the *Collection*, the general title-page was certainly printed off without reference to the text itself, and perhaps even before it.[51] (As a university-man and M.P. he was entitled to the courtesy of 'Esquire', but the format 'Esquire *Marvel*' and the lack of forename are unusual.[52]) The omission of the legend 'London. | September the 4th 1667.' that stands at the foot of the title-page of the manuscript may have been a casualty of the generous caption-heading on the first page of the printed text. As for the so-called 'Rochester's Farewel' of July 1680 ('Tir'd with the noysome Follies of the Age'), this has been rejected from the Rochester canon by modern editors, and on the authority of Alexander Pope tentatively attributed instead to Charles Sackville, Earl of Dorset.[53] Danielsson and Vieth who, besides listing twenty contemporary manuscript copies that carry the same title or its equivalent, characterised the text printed in the State Poems of 1697 as having been 'conflated from a manuscript and the miscellany of 1689'.[54]

The physical state of the manuscript that served as copy-text seems to have altered little from the date of its copying, beyond being subjected to processes necessary to preserve it and make it fit for readers. Evidence of handling at the press is at once apparent from the presence of printer's instructions, markings by the compositor or proof-corrector, and not least by frequent smudges of oily black ink and some remarkably clear fingerprints. On the surviving lower portion of the partially restored leaf (fol. 1) that carries the title on its verso is jotted the direction '46 Pica lines', but the measure adopted here for the 948 lines of the poem proper, page-numbers and catchwords not included, was as in 'THE SECOND PART' 40 verses per page. The subsequent reversion to the original 46-line measure for the 42 lines of the envoy was not signalled in the same way. Instead, to the left of the caption-heading 'To the King' the printer wrote 'allow 6 lines', then erased it (though still visible) and between heading and first verse substituted 'allow 4 lines'. Although Gibson read this as a call for a 4-line gap after the heading its true meaning is that was to be allocated space equivalent to four verses in the smaller type-face and increased lineation. The new measure that allowed the envoy to be fitted into a single page (E2 recto) was carried through for the 212 lines of the 'Farewel' that followed (E2^{v}–[E4]^{v}).

The mechanics of the setting are reflected in the margins. Various explanations have been offered for the signature-marks found in copy-texts of the early modern period: that they were added by compositor during setting; or by the corrector in reading proof; or by the printer in costing the work by estimating the paper and press-work required; or else to allow non-sequential composition in order to make best use of available type or setters.[55] (The verse-medium was, of course, a boon to a printer in the essential matter of estimating copy.) Here the markings appear to be of two types, the first representing work already completed. These begin with signature C, signalled in the right-hand margin of f. 7 by a crochet drawn around the first word of line 227 and reading, vertically, 'Q | C p | 7', signifying that quire C began at the head of page 7, with the 'p' standing for 'prima [pagina]' (see PLATES 1 and 2). The next mark, at line 547 (fol. 13 verso), is 'Q | D p | 15', though the relevant printed page is numbered 22, following the accidental reversal in ordering the pages of the outer forme, which now stand as pp. 22, 16, 17, 19, 18, 20, 21 and 15 respectively. Defective imposition is also found in the reset second issue of the first part of the *Collection*, where sheets C and D were affected.[56] In both cases the sheets were printed off and the type re-distributed before the error could be rectified. The absence of signature B from the register in *1689* is not necessarily significant, and was parallelled by the omission of sig. C from the first issue of the first part.[57] Taken with the changes of page-measure, occasionally uneven presswork, errors of imposition and rather less than immaculate press work, it merely underlines the haste incident to a serial publishing venture.

From this point the markings change to a series of lower case numbers, still keyed to the text by crochets, that occur at forty-line intervals in a hand and ink different from that of the previous ones. They repre-

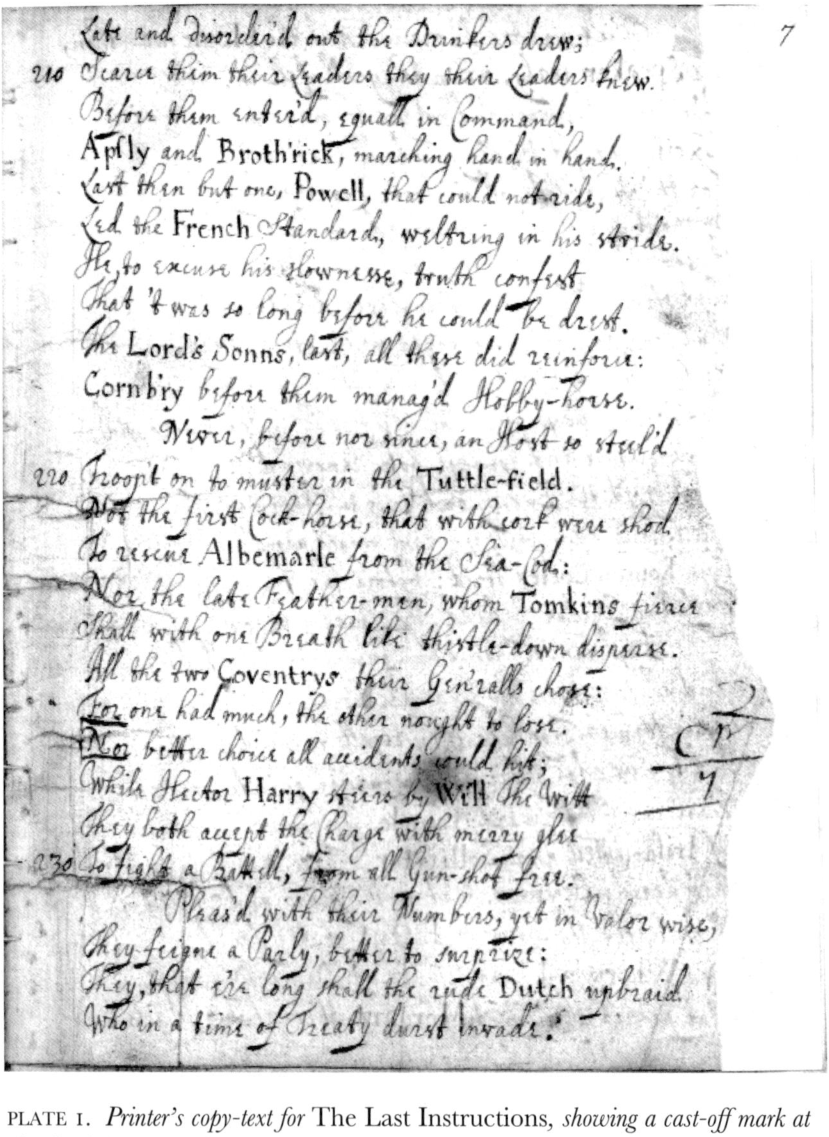
7

Late and disorder'd out the Drinkers drew;
Scarce them their Leaders they their Leaders knew.
Before them enter'd, equall in Command,
Apsly and Broth'rick, marching hand in hand.
Last then but one, Powell, that could not ride,
Led the French Standard, weltring in his stride.
He, to excuse his slownesse, truth confest
That 't was so long before he could be drest.
The Lord's Sonns, last, all these did reinforce:
Cornb'ry before them manag'd Hobby-horse.
Never, before nor since, an Host so steel'd
Troopt on to muster in the Tuttle-field.
Not the first Cock-horse, that with cork were shod
To rescue Albemarle from the Sea-Cod:
Nor the late Feather-men, whom Tomkins fierce
Shall with one Breath like thistle-down disperse.
All the two Coventrys their Gen'ralls chose:
For one had much, the other nought to lose.
Nor better choice all accidents could hit;
While Hector Harry steers by Will the Witt
They both accept the Charge with merry glee
To fight a Battell, from all Gun-shot free.
Pleas'd with their Numbers, yet in Valor wise,
They feigne a Parly, better to surprize:
They, that ere long shall the rude Dutch upbraid
Who in a time of Treaty durst invade.

PLATE I. *Printer's copy-text for* The Last Instructions, *showing a cast-off mark at sig. C of the 1689 edition: University of Nottingham, Portland Literary Collection,* MS *Pw V 299, fol. 7r (Original page size 190 × 152mm.) Reproduced by permission of the Keeper of Manuscripts and Special Collections, University of Nottingham.*

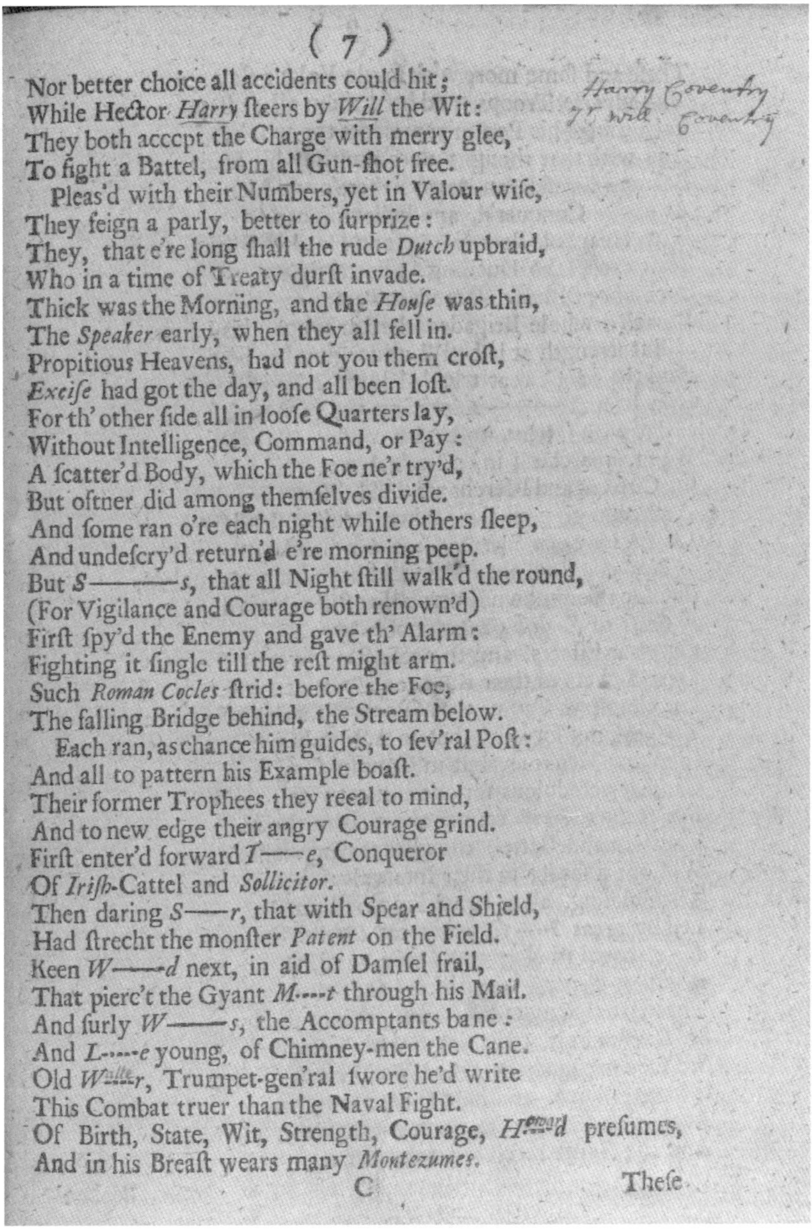

(7)

Nor better choice all accidents could hit;
While Hector *Harry* ſteers by *Will* the Wit:
They both accept the Charge with merry glee,
To fight a Battel, from all Gun-ſhot free.
Pleas'd with their Numbers, yet in Valour wiſe,
They feign a parly, better to ſurprize:
They, that e're long ſhall the rude *Dutch* upbraid,
Who in a time of Treaty durſt invade.
Thick was the Morning, and the *Houſe* was thin,
The *Speaker* early, when they all fell in.
Propitious Heavens, had not you them croſt,
Exciſe had got the day, and all been loſt.
For th' other ſide all in looſe Quarters lay,
Without Intelligence, Command, or Pay:
A ſcatter'd Body, which the Foe ne'r try'd,
But oftner did among themſelves divide.
And ſome ran o're each night while others ſleep,
And undeſcry'd return'd e're morning peep.
But *S———s*, that all Night ſtill walk'd the round,
(For Vigilance and Courage both renown'd)
Firſt ſpy'd the Enemy and gave th' Alarm:
Fighting it ſingle till the reſt might arm.
Such *Roman Cocles* ſtrid: before the Foe,
The falling Bridge behind, the Stream below.
Each ran, as chance him guides, to ſev'ral Poſt:
And all to pattern his Example boaſt.
Their former Trophees they recal to mind,
And to new edge their angry Courage grind.
Firſt enter'd forward *T——e*, Conqueror
Of *Iriſh*-Cattel and *Sollicitor*.
Then daring *S——r*, that with Spear and Shield,
Had ſtrecht the monſter *Patent* on the Field.
Keen *W——d* next, in aid of Damſel frail,
That pierc't the Gyant *M----t* through his Mail.
And ſurly *W———s*, the Accomptants bane:
And *L----e* young, of Chimney-men the Cane.
Old *W----r*, Trumpet-gen'ral ſwore he'd write
This Combat truer than the Naval Fight.
Of Birth, State, Wit, Strength, Courage, *H----d* preſumes,
And in his Breaſt wears many *Montezumes*.
C These

PLATE 2. The Last Instructions, *1689, page 7, showing the first page of sig. C: London, British Library, Printed Book 1077.h.32(7) (Original page size 212 × 162mm.) Reproduced by permission of the Board of the British Library.*

sent an estimate of the number of pages required for the final section. The first of them stands in the left-hand margin of f. 19v, beside line 869 (actual number), the first verse of sig. E (p. 23) of the printed copy. It consists of a crudely-written secretary 'E' followed by a superscript stroke. The number '2' is found at line 909, which in the printed text heads p. 24, and '3' before the heading of the envoy, which occupies the whole of p. 25. The '4' that appears to the right of line 983 (fol. 21v) comprises the sum of the six lines originally envisaged for the heading of the envoy and the first thirty-four lines of text, leaving a run-over of eight lines to completion. At this point it was realised that by changing to a smaller measure and reducing the caption-space the whole envoy could be contained in a single page. Consequently the final reckoning, calculated from line 869 to the end, is jotted after the 'Finis' as '3 Pags' (fol. 22). This left room for the 'Farewel' to stand as a self-contained entity in the remaining five pages of the sheet. Scribal problems with line-numbering did not affect the setting of the printed version which, as an essentially ephemeral production, need not extend itself to the added labour and cost of justifying the lines of type.

Transmission of the Text

Comparison of the manuscript text with *1689* allows us to follow the transmission of Marvell's satire into what was surely—notwithstanding the still unresolved uncertainty over the date of the Philadelphia pamphlet—its earliest known printed form. What should have been a relatively smooth compositional process was marred by physical accidents, problems of perception and inconsistencies. Tedious as the rehearsal of the details may be, it demonstrates the genesis of apparent 'variants' in a way that cannot be achieved by a conventional apparatus. The sole printed text consulted for this purpose survives in a composite volume in the British Library that is made up of all seven parts of the two 1689 miscellanies *A Collection of the Newest and Most Ingenious Poems, Songs, Catches, &c. against Popery* and *A Collection of Poems on Affairs of State.*[58] Its particular interest lies in the speculative identifications interpolated throughout in several different scripts: Grosart was the first editor to make use of them.[59] The common provenance and early association of the tracts are established by the recurrence throughout of one particular annotating script, and by the early pricing '7 p^{ts}–4^{s}. 6^{d}.' jotted on a preliminary leaf. A potential indicator of dating is the fact that while many of the persons mentioned in *The Last Instructions* are accurately identified and others either wrongly or not at all, almost all the names were easily accessible in *Poems on affairs of State* of 1697.

A single act of mutilation has marred the integrity of the copy-text at several points. A rectangular sliver of paper roughly torn away at the foot and towards the outer edge of ff. 19–21 obliterated the first words of four verses (lines 983–6) towards the very end of the poem. The final leaf (fol. 22) being now largely defective, the perceived source of the damage falls at the foot of the last-but-one (fol. 21v), with a gap about the size and shape of a middle finger's end, diminishing in size as it spreads inwards until it leaves a final trace in a large squarish ink blot on the verso of f. 18. Splashes of what appears to be printing ink surrounding it on f. 21v indicate that defacement took place at the press, but before setting. Words mutilated or obliterated were completed or supplied by conjectures added above or beside the affected lines, apparently in two distinct hands, one using a black ink (cp. lines 885–6, 936–8, 910–1 and 957) and the other (lines 958–60, 'Light', '[astr]ay' and 'way') a lighter shade. Even in the absence of any other witness, as was surely the case, some of the lacunae were easily enough rectified, but others only imperfectly. By far the worst lapse was the cobbling together of a heavily-blotted passage (fol. 21v, lines 983–986) towards the end of the envoy. A mysterious greyish smudge overlain by blots of printing ink in the margin now conceals any later attempts that may have been made on the page to supply the missing text (those still visible signalled below by square brackets):

> [*But*]
> <———> *they whom, born to virtue and to Wealth,*
> <———> *[F]latt'ry binds, nor Want to Stealth;*
> <———> *Conscience and whose Courage high*
> <———> *Counsells their large Soules supply;*

In the printed version this was rendered by guesswork, with loss of the paragraph indent and a disregard for both sense and metre in the second couplet, as

> But they whom born to Virtue and to Wealth,
> Whom neither flatt'ry binds, nor want to stealth;
> Whose Conscience and whose Courage high
> With Counsels their large Souls supply;

Comparison with the Bodleian text supplies the true reading:

> But they, whom born to Virtue and to Wealth,
> Nor Guilt to Flatt'ry binds, nor Want to Stealth;
> Whose gen'rous Conscience and whose Courage high
> Does with clear Counsells their Large Soules supply.

Substantially the same version is printed in *1697*, which clearly originates from a separate source. Mutilation also caused minor problems earlier on. The round brackets enclosing lines 959–60, of which the closing one was obscured, were dropped, along with the paragraph indent at line 885, owing to interpolation of the word 'paint' for the obliterated 'Paint'. The final legacy of the damage rests with the large ink-blot (fol.18v) in the verse '*And threaten* Hide *to raise a greater Dust*' (line 834), resulting in the 'threatens *H—e*' of the printed version, a singular verb for a plural subject, '*all*'.

Several other apparent variants resulted from simple misreading, from lapses of memory in turning from copy-text to composing stick, or from mere inadvertence. Some of the fault lies with the copyist's small italic, where 't' and 's', 'e' and 'i' and 'c' and 't' proved eminently confusable. In line 424 of the manuscript '*At* London's *Flame, nor so the* Court *complain'd*', '*nor so*' was, quite understandably, read by the compositor as 'nor to'. The copyists of British Library Additional MS 73540 and of Osborn PB VII/15 fell into the same trap, though the latter at least queried the reading, writing 'so' above his original. In the well-known crux at line 943, 'Painter adieu: *how well our Arts agree*', a similarly ambiguous letter-formation misled the compositor into '*Painter* adieu, how will our Arts agree', while to emphasize the point the copyist of Additional MS 73540 added a further variation with 'well o^{r} acts'. Word-endings could present problems. A blurred comma after '*Robber*' (line 624), possibly representing the scribe's correction of the mis-copied '*Robbers*' but further obscured by a smudge of printing ink, was misprinted as 'Robbers', a reading shared also by *1697* and Phila., though 'him' in line 628 proves it false. A crude attempt at rectification scrawled after the gap at line 911 caused the compositor to read 'led' instead of 'fled'. At line 40, '*That, disavowing Treaty, asks supply*', the verb was rendered, perhaps by mental elision, as 'ask'. But sheer carelessness was to blame for the rhyme-destroying substitution of 'Rope untwines' for 'Ropes untwine' (line 321) and for the addition of a final *e* to 'here' in the verse that elsewhere invariably runs '*And* Richmond *her commands, as* Ruyter *those*' (line 764).

The wholesale replacement in *1689* of proper names spelled out in their full form throughout the manuscript by first and last letters separated by dashes was one of the arguments advanced by Gibson against its having served as printers' copy. This pre-emptive form of censorship is widely encountered in printed verse-satire of the time as security against prosecution, even with works issued at some distance from the events treated. It was bound to be something of a fig-leaf, for the combination of letters and metre provided a strong clue as to the hidden identities—or, as the annotated British Library copy shows, at least some of them. Its application here was uneven and inconsistent. While the principal butts of the satire were carefully vetted, a handful of others slipped through the net (e.g. at lines 50, 188, 399, 406, 631). The late Duchess of York was diplomatically 'concealed' under the title of '*Her H——ss*' (line 49), though the same courtesy was denied to her love-rival '*Denham*', by then deceased, and to her still-living favourite '*Sidney*' in the same paragraph (lines 75–6). *Dray-man's* (line 31), printed without the hyphen, may have been mistaken for a proper name. The retention of names in non-satirical contexts, such as those of Hook and Bacon (lines 16, 36), De Witte and Ruyter (line 437) or Monk and Douglas (lines 649–676), argues a guiding intelligence, and one sufficiently educated to recognise allusions to classical mythology or later literature, though an odd lapse occurs in the case of Chaucer (lines 883–4):

> At night, than *Chanticleer* more brisk and hot,
> And Serjeants Wife serves him for *P——tt.*

The lack of any signs of expurgation in the manuscript itself raises an interesting question regarding the procedure that had been adopted here. The most economical course would have been for evisceration to have taken place during setting, but the degree of selection involved would presuppose a fairly considerable fund of general and literary knowledge on the compositor's part. Alternatively we must assume that a press-corrector made the necessary excisions in a separate operation after the full text had been set up, or else reinstated the non-contentious names in a wholly expurgated text. But here the frequent resetting and justification necessary would have been time-consuming and expensive, while the inconsistencies and oversights become even harder to account for.

Two passages in the manuscript are distinguished by crosses and strokes drawn in red crayon, though their provenance and purpose are unclear. The cruel caricature (lines 49–78) of the Duchess of York and the elegiac account (lines 649–696) of the death of Captain Douglas are each marked off by a cross in the indent of the first verse and a horizontal stroke in that of the succeeding paragraph. It is an odd pairing. The lines on Anne Hyde, though uncancelled in *1689* and later in *1697*, during the reign of her daughter Mary, were manifestly libellous, if for no other reason than that they revived the accusation of her having plotted the murder of Lady Denham (lines 65–68; and see also line 342). The publisher may well have hesitated over their inclusion. The Douglas elegy, on the other hand, is an unexceptionable celebration of heroism. Might there be anything in the coincidence that these lines, printed as part of *The Loyal Scot* in Gildon's *Chorus Poetarum* of 1694, were physically transferred from *The Last Instructions* when the two satires were printed together in the State Poems of 1697 and in the

Philadelphia pamphlet? Equally mysterious is the red cross drawn lightly above the proper name in the verse '*Black* Birch, *of all the earthborn race most hot*' (line 143), duly 'censored' in the printed text. The epithet applied here to John Birch, M.P. and auditor of the excise, who was still alive at the time of publication, seems to have been current at the time, and not of Marvell's own coining. It occurs in a letter written by his friend Lady Ranelagh on 15 June: 'here are preparations makeing of horse & foote The Earl of Manchester. S^r^ Wm Waller. Rocester, Ingoldsby. Norton, Black Birch haveing Comissions to rayse Regm^ts^'.[60] Its origin may lie in his irrascibility: one MP was reluctant to approach him for arrears, 'knowing the temper of Col. Birch, who he believed would have torn him in pieces'.[61]

Yet another red cross drawn through the couplet (lines 349–350)

> *Now M——t may, within his Castle, Tow'r;*
> *Imprison Parents, and the Child deflowre.*

coincides, whether by chance or design, with a clear intervention by the printer or press-corrector, who at the proof-stage marked off the lines in ink with square crochets and wrote the word '(Out)' in round brackets in the right-hand margin beside it (PLATES 3 and 4). (Whether, in fact, a press-corrector was employed by the printer may perhaps be doubted, given the confusion in page-numbering here and in the previous collection.) Gibson saw this as an injunction to omit the couplet, and took the compositor's apparent failure to respond as furnishing further evidence of the lack of any nexus between manuscript and printed text. The reverse is the case. The ink markings conform to those prescribed in Joseph Moxon's *Mechanick exercises on the whole art of printing* (1683) for an omission made during composition: 'If a whole Sentence be *Left out*, too long to be Writ in the *Margin*, [the printer] makes the mark of *Insertion* where it is *Left out*, and only Writes (Out) in the *Margin*.'.[62] Since the whole sheet had already been set, the oversight had to be remedied by increasing the measure at p.10, sig. C2^v^, to 42 lines (lines 347–388). But in doing so the compositor failed to remove the indent that he had at first setting inadvertently transferred to the next verse, which makes the couplet a self-contained paragraph, giving it a wholly unauthorised prominence and fracturing the integrity of the passage that is intimately linked by sense and syntax to the two couplets that immediately follow. (Interestingly, both indents are present also in *1697* and in the Philadelphia pamphlet, though modern editions correct the error.) The conjunction of the cross with the printer's instruction here offer the only strong, though far from conclusive, indication that all the red crayon markings originated at the press.

Moxon's famous handbook, published serially between 1678 and 1683, presents a detailed account of contemporary printing-practice. The compositor is recommended first of all to read his copy-text 'with consideration; that so he may get himself into the meaning of the *Author* . . . the better to sympathize with the *Authors* Genius, and also with the capacity of the Reader'.[63] But while the primary business is to follow copy, '*the carelessness of some good Authors, and the ignorance of other Authors, has forc'd* Printers *to introduce a Custom . . . to discern and amend the bad* Spelling *and* Pointing *of his* Copy'. Hence the compositor must '*know the present traditional* Spelling *of all English Words*', besides having '*so much Sence and Reason, as to* Point *his Sentences properly: when to begin a Word with a* Capital Letter, *when (to render the Sence of the Author more intelligent to the Reader) to Set some Words or Sentences in* Italick *or* English Letters'.[64] His strictures were amply fulfilled in the setting of *The Last Instructions*, where, alongside less obviously redundant features like apostrophes signalling possession or elision, the scribe's final *e*s and double consonants were throughout removed. (The apparent attempt at reform and modernisation had, in fact, much to do with economies of type in the printing-house.) Initial capitals in nouns were sometimes dropped, and sometimes added—by the provision, presumably, whereby 'Words of a smaller Emphasis may be *Set* in the running Character [here roman] . . . but begin with a *Capital*'. For all this, occasional inconsistencies occur in *1689*, such as the scribe's '*Lackye's*' (line 81) appearing as 'Lacquies' while his '*Reliques*' (line 691) and '*Poetique*' (line 944) were changed to 'Relicks' and 'Poetick'. This does not necessarily imply that more than one journeyman was at work here. In punctuation the compositor alternated between inserting marks where none had existed—in copy that is far from under-punctuated—and dispensing with them entirely. Overall he placed rather less reliance on colons and semi-colons and more on commas, especially at the end of lines, though this sometimes threatens the syntax: typical examples occur after 'meet' at line 289 and after 'array'd' in line 175.

The only historical, or old-spelling, text of *The Last Instructions* to have appeared in modern times is that in Margoliouth's original Oxford edition of 1927, and it remained almost wholly unchanged by Pierre Legouis in the third edition of 1971. As the basis for his edition, in the absence of any contemporary text other than the two posthumously-printed ones of 1689 and 1697, Margoliouth adopted the former, since the other 'exhibits numerous variations from the text of 1689, mostly slight, but nearly all for the worse . . . It may be conjectured, therefore, that the edition of 1697 was set up carelessly from 1689, with some alterations made intentionally'.[65] He followed his copy in almost all

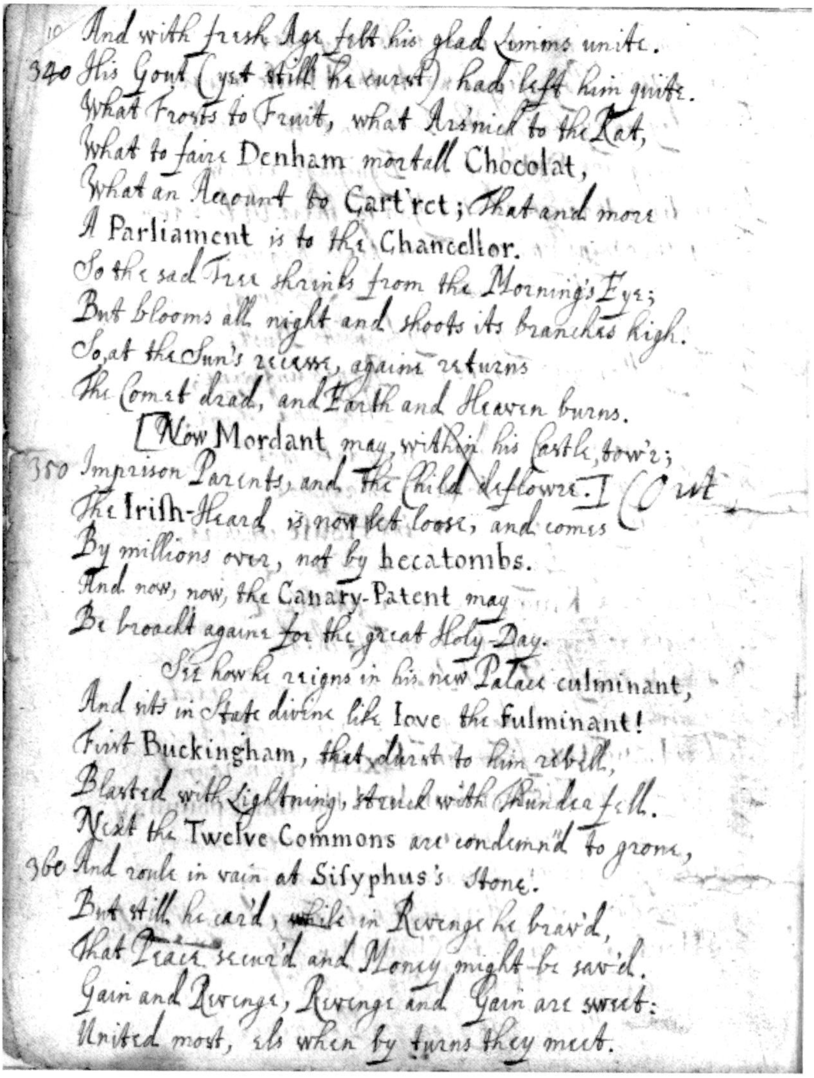
And with fresh Age felt his glad Limms unite.
His Gout (yet still he curst) had left him quite.
What Frosts to Fruit, what Arsnick to the Rat,
What to faire Denham mortall Chocolat,
What an Account to Cart'ret; That and more
A Parliament is to the Chancellor.
So the sad Tree shrinks from the Morning's Eye;
But blooms all night and shoots its branches high.
So, at the Sun's recess, againe returns
The Comet dread, and Earth and Heaven burns.
[Now Mordant may, within his Castle, tow'r;
Imprison Parents, and the Child deflowre.] Out
The Irish-Heard is now let loose, and comes
By millions over, not by hecatombs.
And now, now, the Canary-Patent may
Be broacht againe for the great Holy-Day.
See how he reigns in his new Palace culminant,
And sits in State divine like Iove the fulminant!
First Buckingham, that durst to him rebell,
Blasted with Lightning, struck with Thunder fell.
Next the Twelve Commons are condemn'd to grone,
And roule in vain at Sisyphus's Stone.
But still he car'd, while in Revenge he brav'd,
That Peace secur'd and Money might be sav'd.
Gain and Revenge, Revenge and Gain are sweet:
United most, else when by turns they meet.

PLATE 3. *Printer's copy-text for* The Last Instructions, *showing the press-corrector's mark of omission: University of Nottingham, Portland Literary Collection,* MS *Pw V 299, fol. 9v (Original page size 190mm × 152mm.) Reproduced by permission of the Keeper of Manuscripts and Special Collections, University of Nottingham.*

(10)

So, at the Suns receſs, again returns,
The Comet dread, and Earth and Heaven burns.
Now *M*——*t* may, within his Caſtle Tow'r,
Impriſon Parents, and the Child deflowre.
The *Iriſh*-Herd is now let looſe, and comes
By Millions over, not by *Hecatombs*.
And now, now, the *Canary-Patent* may
Be Broach'd again, for the great Holy-day.
See how he Reigns in his new Palace *culminant*,
And ſits in State Divine like *Jove* the *fulminant*!
Firſt *B*[uckingha]*m*, that durſt to him Rebel,
Blaſted with Lightning,ſtruck with Thunder fell.
Next the *Twelve Commons* are condemn'd to groan,
And roul in vain at *Siſyphus's* Stone.
But ſtill he car'd, while in Revenge he brav'd,
That Peace ſecur'd, and Money might be ſav'd.
Gain and Revenge,Revenge and Gain are ſweet:
United moſt, elſe when by turns they meet.
France had St. *A*[lban]*s* promis'd (ſo they ſing)
St. *A*[lban]*s* promis'd him, and he the *King*.
The *Count* forthwith is order'd all to cloſe,
To play for *Flanders*, and the ſtake to loſe.
While Chain'd together two *Ambaſſadors*
Like Slaves, ſhall beg for Peace at *Hollands* doors.
This done, among his *Cyclops* he retires,
To forge new Thunder, and inſpect their Fires.
The *Court*, as once of War, now fond of Peace,
All to new Sports their wanton fears releaſe.
From *Greenwich* (where Intelligence they hold)
Comes news of Paſtime, Martial and old:
A Puniſhment invented firſt to awe
Maſculine Wives, tranſgreſſing Natures Law.
Where when the brawny Female diſobeys,
And beats the Husband till for peace he prays:
No concern'd *Jury* for him Damage finds,
Nor partial *Juſtice* her Behaviour binds;
But the juſt Street does the next Houſe invade,
Mounting the neighbour Couple on lean Jade.
The Diſtaff knocks, the Grains from Kettle fly,
And Boys and Girls in Troops run houting by;
Prudent Antiquity, that knew by Shame,
Better than Law, Domeſtick Crimes to tame,
And

PLATE 4. The Last Instructions, *1689, page 10, showing the reset page of text: London, British Library, Printed Book 1077.h.32(7) (Original page size 212 × 162 mm.) Reproduced by permission of the Board of the British Library.*

accidentals, though borrowing a few readings from *1697* and later editions, and adding some conjectures of his own. Thus, he followed *1689* in lines 660 and 943, though for the latter a better reading was available in *1697*, and was misled by both *1689* and *1697* at lines 40, 398 and 624. The Portland manuscript supports his preference for *1697* at lines 187, 271, 321, 911, as also for 'so' against the 'to' of 'nor to the *Court* complain'd' (line 424; and cf. Additional MS 73540, *1697* and Phila.) and 'ras'd' for 'rais'd' in 'And a poor Warren once a City rais'd' (line 982), the two last borrowed by him respectively from Grosart and from Cooke's 1726 edition of Marvell's *Works*. His own interventions amounted merely to the addition of a comma after 'mild' (line 174), where *1689* has a full stop and Portland nothing at all, and the unincorporated conjecture 'her' in 'their Master's Name' (line 616).[66] As to names, he treated *1697* and the guesses of the annotated British Library copy with equal caution, recording but not incorporating the former's 'Duke' or, because it 'may be correct', the latter's hypermetrical '*Dildoes*' in the verse 'To make her glassen *D—s* once *malleable*' (line 60), while merely noting his own, as it happens accurate, conjecture of 'Dukes'. For some reason he also retained the evisceration also '*C———n*' (line 181), though citing the 'Charleton', since confirmed by Portland, of the Bodleian manuscript and *1697*.[67] From these last two he rightly adopted '*Thurland*' (line 186), while noting 'Trenchard' as the suggestion of the anonymous annotator.[68]

The present study of the transmission of the Portland text from manuscript to print has produced little more than a practical explanation for the handful of readings in which the two differ. Aside from corruption in one four-line passage (lines 983–6) mentioned above and the misrendering of '*fled*' as 'led' (line 911), both resulting from mutilation of copy, substantive 'variants' are confined to a few words and phrases, most of them insignificant and long ago emended by reference to other witnesses or by conjecture. They comprise (Portland reading first) lines 40 *asks*: ask; 42 *wear*: were; 137 *wheres'ere*: where e're; 187 *Rabble*] Rubble; 271 *theirs*] there's; 321 *untwine*] untwines; 348 *drad*] dread; 398 *Of*] Off; 424 *so*: to; 624 *Robber*] Robbers; 660 *Love's*] Love; 764 *her*] here; 817 Thames's] *Thames*; 834 *threaten*] threatens; 943 *well*] will; 982 *ras'd*] rais'd. There is no reason to suspect that the readings of *1689* derive from any independent source, written or oral, and therefore though the two versions represent essentially a single stage of the text, it is in the manuscript that sole authority resides. Even though Marvell's inferential archetype has been refracted, to a degree that is hard to assess, through the medium of scribal spelling and punctuation, the Portland manuscript cannot fail to bring us one step closer to the version that he, at least initially, put into circulation. Moreover, among witnesses that offer a wide range of (at least seeming) variants the specific state of the text represented here is not without close parallel elsewhere.

Textual Affinities

Bodleian MS *Eng. poet. d. 49*

By far the closest relative of the Portland text is that found in Oxford, Bodleian Library MS Eng. poet. d. 49, long regarded as the most important single witness to Marvell's poetry. This consists of an annotated copy of the *Miscellaneous Poems* of 1681 from which some of the printed pieces have been excised, others emended and the whole supplemented by a generous section of manuscript pieces. Whoever commissioned it was clearly aiming at a more definitive collection of Marvell's work, possibly with a new edition in mind. It has been credibly identified with the second of two sources passed on to Marvell's late eighteenth-century editor Edward Thompson, who had been 'politely complimented by Mr. Mathias with a manuscript volume of poems written by Mr. William Popple, being a collection of his uncle Andrew Marvell's compositions after his decease.'[69] Popple (1638–1708), the son of Marvell's sister Mary and husband of Mary Alured, great neice of Marvell's stepmother Lucy Alured, was the poet's favourite nephew. Though the bulk of the manuscript portion is in the hand of a copyist (see PLATE 5), the rumoured family connection cannot be lightly dismissed, since Vincent Mathias (d.1782) had married the daughter of William's son Alured Popple.[70]

Although the *Miscellaneous Poems* was published in 1681 and Popple no doubt acquired a copy as soon as possible afterwards, we can only guess at the date of compilation of this collective edition. Caroline Robbins has explained how, after some fourteen years spent in the wine trade in Bordeaux, Popple had found himself in a double bind.[71] A naturalised French citizen who felt obliged by the edict of Nantes to become a catholic convert, for three years after the departure of his family to England Popple was held back by French law from joining them. Early in 1688, through the influence of James II and via the good offices of his friend William Penn, he managed to secure exceptional leave to return to England, with the promise of assistance in 'conveighing his books', taking up residence in Essex Street, near the Middle Temple. Until his appointment in 1696 as secretary of the Board of Trade and Plantations he is said to have been 'largely occupied in intellectual pleasures'. While adhering to no particular religious sect, he surpassed even his late uncle in concern for freedom of conscience. While still in Bordeaux he

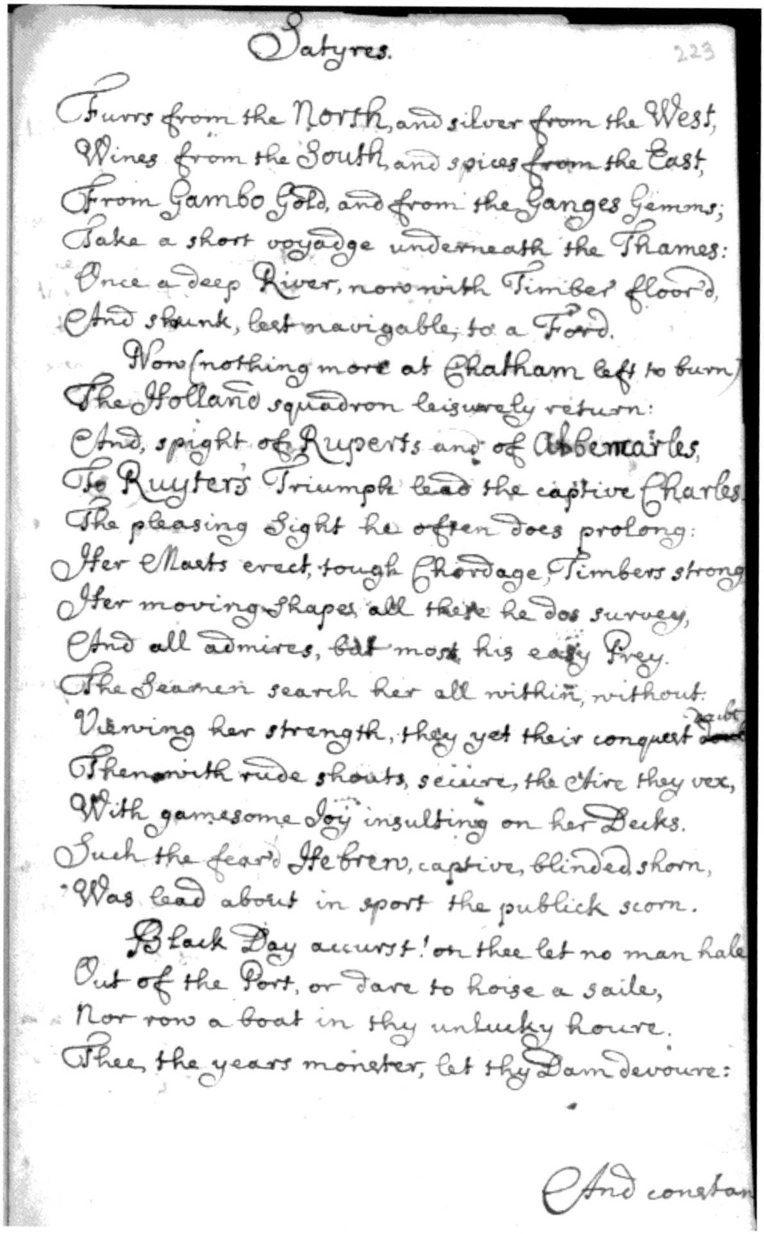
Satyres. 223

Furrs from the North, and silver from the West,
Wines from the South, and spices from the East,
From Gambo Gold, and from the Ganges Gemms;
Take a short voyadge underneath the Thames:
Once a deep River, now with Timber floor'd,
And shrunk, lest navigable, to a Ford.
Now (nothing more at Chatham left to burn)
The Holland squadron leisurely return:
And, spight of Ruperts and of Albemarles,
To Ruyters Triumph lead the captive Charles.
The pleasing Sight he often does prolong:
Her Masts erect, tough Chordage, Timbers strong
Her moving Shapes, all these he dos survey,
And all admires, but most his easy Prey.
The Seamen search her all within, without:
Viewing her strength, they yet their conquest doubt
Then with rude shouts, secure, the Aire they vex,
With gamesome Joy insulting on her Decks.
Such the fear'd Hebrew, captive, blinded, shorn,
Was lead about in sport the publick scorn.
Black Day accurst! on thee let no man hale
Out of the Port, or dare to hoise a saile,
Nor row a boat in thy unlucky houre.
Thee, the years monster, let thy Dam devoure:

And constan

PLATE 5. *A page of the Bodleian manuscript of* The Last Instructions, *lines 717–40: Oxford, Bodleian Library,* MS *Eng. poet. d. 49, page 223 (Original page size 273 × 163mm.) Reproduced by permission of the Curators of the Bodleian Library, Oxford.*

had published a dialogue entitled *A Rational Catechism* (1687), and now, as secretary of John Locke's Dry Club, translated from Latin his *Letter concerning toleration* (Nov. 1689).[72] Popple was apolitical, and despite *The Last Instructions* appearing in print within two years of his return, the debt that he owed to the deposed king makes him an unlikely conduit for the publication of anti-Stuart satires in 1689 or 1697. The date of compilation is unknown, and there is no reason to assume that it took place before texts of the satires began to appear in print. It may have been the increasing public exposure that his uncle's satirical verse was receiving that spurred him to collect all the texts that he could find in family papers or those of the poet's friends, with a view to establishing a proper canon. Not all the pieces here have been accepted as genuine, but the fact that they include full texts of the three Cromwell poems that had been cancelled from (all but two known copies of) *Miscellaneous Poems* after printing suggests privileged information.

In character and physical appearance—bold, simple layout, open and rounded script, enlarged letters for emphasis and lack of line-numbering—the manuscript portion very obviously belongs with the professionally-copied collections of the late seventeenth century. As such it contrasts markedly with Portland, a single entity presented in close facsimile of typographical format, evidently for some special purpose. Nevertheless there are clear signs that their copy-texts were closely, and indeed intimately, related. The affinity shows itself at the most basic level. In layout, the fifty-two paragraphs into which the Bodleian copy is divided, if we include the breaks signalled at lines 697 and 761 by crochets added after copying by scribe or corrector, are all matched in Portland, which, however, adds a further three at lines 585, 596 and 611. Shared instances of bracketing number twenty-three, including a couplet (lines 973–4) unmarked in all other texts but British Library Additional MS 73540, though the Bodleian text uniquely adds another set at line 892. The remaining witnesses show much wider variations: among manuscripts, Additional MS 73540 has twenty-six paragraph-divisions and fourteen brackets, Osborn thirty-eight and twenty-two respectively, and Los Angeles thirty-five and eighteen, while of the printed texts Philadelphia has a vastly increased seventy-six and thirty, with *1697* yielding seventy-seven and, depending on the particular issue, twenty-nine or thirty-three brackets. One might have expected some degree of variation in the work of copyists operating in different contexts, with their own distinctive habits and apparently at some interval of time. There are considerable differences between them in the handling of accidentals. The Bodleian text does not distinguish thirty proper names and emphatic words that are picked out in Portland, while omitting one hundred of its initial capitals and adding forty-seven. Punctuation varies equally, sixty of Portland's commas being unmatched here, though (coincidentally) forty-seven others are added. In spelling, like the compositor of *1689*, the Bodleian scribe opts for economy, avoiding redundant and final medial *e*s and double consonants, along with apostrophes indicating elision. But the absence of more than a very few corrections, and those generally current, testifies to the copyist's skill in his craft, and his only major slip was the omission of a couplet at lines 463–4.

Yet the detailed resemblances are, if anything, more striking than the differences. Firstly, and most important, agreement in substantives is markedly closer than subsists between these two texts and any of the others. Most notably, they share a dozen readings not found elsewhere (except, of course, in *1689*), all of them entirely credible: lines 109 Trick-track; 116 *goes*; 242 *oftner*; 244 *e're*; 471 *many a time*; 566 *Bullet showrs*; 616 *their*; 728 *Masts . . . Timbers*; 855 *come*; 909 *Canon*; 969 *on*; and 977 *Earthquake*. The disposition of colons and semi-colons in narrative passages—frequently altered in *1689* and generally rejected by modern editors—turns out to be much the same in both: for example, the important Douglas episode (lines 649–96) stands in the two texts with significantly less variation in accidentals than elsewhere. Admittedly, the pointing of the last hundred lines of the poem proper (lines 849–948), which in Portland was added as a separate operation, differs in the Bodleian copy, which has a single substantive variant only, in no fewer than forty lines. Parallels are found in the deliberative pointing of lines 749–50 (Portland text)

> *And Father* Neptune *promis'd to resigne*
> *His Empire, old, to their immortall Line!*

at lines 761–2

> *The* Court *in Farthing yet it self dos please,*
> *And female* Stuard, *there*, rules the foure Seas.

and even in such minute details as 'Thighs, (the Face . . .)' (line 85), and 'An *English* Pilot too, (O Shame, O Sin!)'. It may be mere coincidence that the spelling 'dos', adopted for the auxiliary verb in all forty of its appearances in Portland, is matched in the Bodleian text in all but six cases (which use 'doth' and 'does'). But this is far less likely to be the case with idiosyncratic spellings such as the nouns 'Sent' (line 95, for 'scent') and 'leavs' (line 71) and the verbs 'receivs' (line 306) and 'reprievs' (line 850), which appear in both, the Bodleian text adding 'themselvs' (line 558), the plurals 'Theev's' and 'Thiev's' (lines 333, 940) and the verbs 'cleav's' and 'heav's'. Even the emphatic capitals given in the envoy to 'There', 'Themselves' and 'They' (lines 956, 966, 967) seem to betray a common origin.

Extended textual discussion of *The Last Instructions* has largely been confined to a perceptive article of 1970 in which the late Michael Gearin-Tosh compared the version then recently published in the Yale *Poems on affairs of state* with Bodleian MS Eng. poet. d. 49 on which it claimed to be based.[73] In particular, he pointed to some spellings not reproduced in Yale's modernised version that, as it turns out, also occur in Portland. In the lament at lines 737–739

Black Day accurst! on thee let no man hale
Out of the Port, or dare to hoise a Saile,
Or row a Boat in thy unlucky houre

the nautical terms '*hale*' and '*hoise*', rendered in Yale as 'hail' (inappropriately) and 'hoist', occur thus in all the early witnesses. Precedents may be traced in Barnabe Googe's 'Therefore with ropes they hale and hoise' and Turberville's Ovid, with 'He both will hoyse, and hale the sayles . . .'.[74] Again, in the passage on the sunken merchant vessels (lines 715–6, *ibid.*)

Those Ships, that yearly from their teeming Howle
Unloaded here the Birth of either Pole;

where '*Howle*' signifies the hold of a ship, the same spelling is found in both manuscripts, and was evidently the original reading of Additional MS 73540 before the scribe or corrector changed it to 'hole'. Although Marvell himself was elsewhere to refer to 'The Hole of some Amsterdam Fly-boat', the spelling may be compositorial; while the O.E.D., which lists the term under 'holl', quotes from Captain John Smith's *A sea grammar* (1627) 'When you let anything downe into the Howle'.[75]

The recovery of authorial readings obscured by standardisation may be pursued further. A poem that works partly through a parodic mix of literary genres, from mock-heroic to pastoral elegy and narrative romance, may occasionally resort to conscious archaism. At lines 347–8 the Portland and Bodleian texts read

So, at the Sun's recesse, againe returns
The Comet drad, and Earth and Heaven burns.

while the rest—except for British Library Additional MS 73540 and Osborn PB VII/15, both of which misread as 'dead'—opt for 'dread', the form found in *1689* and adopted by most editors. But 'drad', which harks back to medieval poetry, is found in Spenser and frequent in Sylvester, two poets whose work Marvell knew well.[76] A similar effect seems to have been intended by his choice of 'strid', a verb rarely found in seventeenth-century poetry, in the couplet (lines 249–50)

> *Such* Roman Cocles *strid: before the Foe,*
> *The falling Bridge behind, the Stream below.*

This and the punctilious colon that follows it stand also in the Bodleian text and in Additional MS 73540 (where the copyist has inserted it at a later stage), and even survived into *1689*.[77] Elsewhere, the conjunction of pointing and spelling sometimes, as in lines 397–8, merits greater attention than has been given to it:

> *But a fresh News, the great designment nips,*
> *Of, at the Isle of* Candy, Dutch *and Ships.*

This is what stands in both texts, though the otherwise almost universal reading 'nips / Off' obscured the prose sense until corrected in Donno's edition. Convoluted syntax was compounded by contemporary ambivalence over 'Of/Off', the Portland copyist alone of the two observing the difference in '*Chop's off*' (line 137).[78] A further point may be made. Despite an allusion to a recent pamphlet by Castlemaine's cuckolded husband '*Pilgrim* Palmer' the passage that follows, in which complacent government officials are mocked for confusing Canvey Island with Candia (the old name for Crete), seems peculiarly far-fetched until we realise that locals like John Conny, a naval surgeon at Chatham, knew it as 'Candia Iland'.[79]

Although the Portland and Bodleian texts clearly represent very much the same state of the text, seventeen substantive readings wholly unique to the latter suggest that neither was likely to have been copied directly from the other. These are (with Portland cited second): lines 36 *Bacon* never] *never* Bacon; 158 know] *knew*; 205 these] *those*; 265 *How'rd* on's Birth, Wit, Strength, Courage, much presumes] *Of Birth, State, Witt, Strength, Courage* How'rd *presumes*; 299 ready] *equall*; 422 That] *But*; 462 grant] *give*; 482 indeed] *alas*; 643 And] *But*; 712 be burnt] *should burn*; 718 Wines from the *South*, and spices] *From the* South *Perfumes, Spices*; 729 shapes] *Shape*; 739 Nor] *Or*; 829 are in Stage-Coach *changed later to* in Stage-Coach are] *are in Stage-Coach*; 874 made] *make*; 948 *Painter . . . Poet*] Poet . . . Painter; 968 our . . . his] *the . . . his*. While several of these readings (e.g. lines 36, 158, 205, 299, 729, 739, 874, 948) could conceivably be dismissed as scribal error, others (lines 462, 482, 643) are not so easily explained away. But supposing that some, at least, of the substantive variants may be genuinely authorial, the problem for intending editors lies in estimating the direction of change. The provenance of the Bodleian copy in itself gives no greater warrant to prefer those found there than does the *de luxe* presentation of the Portland manuscript. One reading, for instance, suggests that the Bodleian version is the later of the two. Both, along with Additional MS 73540, originally agreed that Aeson '*With bitter Herbs, rose from the Pot renew'd*' (line 338), but the Portland copyist scrubbed out '*bitter*', writing '*magic*', with an underline, below it. (One might argue that while Ovid's account of the restorative brew in *Metamorphoses*, Book VII, lines 160–293 makes no mention of taste its magical properties scarcely needed emphasis.) On the other hand, two of the more radical variants in the Bodleian version seem to imply an earlier stage of composition. For '*How'rd* on's Birth, Wit, Strength, Courage, much presumes' (line 265)—now metrically defective but salvageable as it stands if we assume that the copyist omitted, possibly by eye-skip, 'State' before 'Strength'—all other texts reverse the sentence structure and make a wholly neutral change from 'presumes on' to 'presumes of'.[80] Again, the otherwise universal reading 'From the *South* Perfumes, and Spices from the *East*' may seem in the context of exotic wares to be preferable to 'Wines from the *South* . . .' (line 718). The Portland scribe's difficulty, noted above, with the structure of this verse may indicate a copy-text that was unclear at both these points. At all events, one change made in the Bodleian manuscript is evidently not in the hand of the main scribe. The deletion of 'are' and its re-copying above the line so as to read 'Plain *Gentlemen* in Stage-Coach are o'rethrown' (line 829), regularising ictus, is the sole instance of an interlinear alteration here. It seems to be the work of the so far unidentified contemporary who throughout has supplied the word-endings that were cut off in trimming the manuscript for binding uniformly with the printed text.

Given the huge area of agreement between these two witnesses over substantive readings, the evidence for distinct copy-texts relies largely on differences in accidentals in many, though far from all, areas. But we cannot easily gauge what latitude their respective copyists were free or disposed to exercise here. Since the variants are comparatively few and so strictly localised we ought also to consider the possibility that the two copies derived immediately from the same manuscript in different states, one of them before and the other after this had been subject to light revision. It is feasible, for example, that Marvell's own fair-copy—not necessarily autograph—served as the basis both of the *de luxe* Portland version and later, having with some revision survived among his papers, as that of the Popple compilation. As to the confusion apparent at several points in both, instances of ambiguity in revision are not far to seek. In reviewing the scribally-copied manuscripts of his poems and plays Fulke Greville frequently added an alternative reading, often signalled by an underline, above the original one, while in his verse-notebook John Oldham underlined words and jotted his second thoughts in the margin.[81]

British Library Additional MS 18220

Evidence of a now lost but contemporary copy of the satire survives in a twenty-line extract extending to a single episode only (lines 29–48), which besides being the earliest dated text, boasts the clearest provenance of all the manuscripts. It is preserved in a notebook of poems and extracts brought together by John Watson, a Suffolk clergyman, between 1667 and 1673, acquired long ago by the British Library[82]. Watson, vicar of Mildenhall, had received the volume, largely blank, from Barbara, widow of John Rhodes, rector (1662–1667) of the adjacent parish of Barton Mills, shortly after her husband's death. He set to work almost immediately, transcribing the first poem on 31 January 1667/8 (fol. 5) and continuing to 31 May 1673 (fol. 114v), two months before his own burial on 30 July. Special value attaches to his dated notes regarding contributors of material. The present lines (fol. 23) on the prominent courtier Henry Jermyn, Earl of St Albans are headed 'A Libell Taken out of the Painter', and the subscription reads 'Com*m*unicat*a* ab H. North Arm^ro^ Julii 10: 1668'. Henry North (*c*. 1635–95), elder son of Sir Henry North, first Baronet, was to succeed to the title on his father's death in August 1671, but his contributions to Watson's anthology had begun in April of 1668 (fol. 13). It is an easy matter to establish a connection between the anthologist, his informant and the subject of these scurrilous lines. The North family of Mildenhall had for some generations been neighbours of the Jermyns of Rushbrook Hall, occupied at this time by Thomas Jermyn (d.1703), a nephew of St Albans.

The brief extract, copied within a year of the poem's composition, incorporates some unique variants that inspire little confidence. From the bold summons of the opening 'Paint me', for Portland's '*Paint then*', through 'Sup' (line 29)—variously rendered as 'soop' in the Bodleian, 'Soap' in the Los Angeles and 'sauce' in the Osborn texts—to the hypermetrical 'having now allayed' (line 37), these may be dismissed as errors originating somewhere along the line of transmission.[83] Others, such as 'pleasures salt' (line 32) for the '*pleasure salt*' of Portland and the rest, and 'cheat' (line 38) for their '*treat*', are parallelled in the 'pleasure's Salt' of the 1697 and Philadelphia printings, while 'And disavowing treaties, ask supply' (line 40) differs from them only in the plural noun,

Portland reading '*That, disavowing treaty, asks supply*'. The most intriguing variant occurs with lines 41–42

> He needs no Seal, but to St James's lease
> Whose Breeches wear the instruments of peace;

where the verb in the second verse corresponds to that found in the Portland and Bodleian texts, and in Additional MS 73540 where the scribe immediately corrected his original 'were' by interlineation to 'we^a^re'. The earlier version receives support in the next couplet, in which, if challenged for his credentials, the priapic envoy

> . . . from thence
> Can streight p*ro*duce them a Plenipotence.

The blander reading made its first appearance in *1689*, without warrant of copy-text, and modern editors, led by Grosart, who delightfully glossed the passage as 'a vague hint of intrigue . . . not to be further explained', have followed suit.[84]

British Library Additional MS 73540

The most recent addition to contemporary witnesses to *The Last Instructions* is a neatly-written octavo miscellany of Restoration poems and verse-satires that was purchased by the British Library in 1997. It comprises forty-one satires and lyrics dating mostly from the 1670s, of which some twenty-six are of established or attributed authorship, the great majority being by Marvell and Rochester. Its early ownership is unknown, but it carries inside the front cover the book-label of Edward Vernon Utterson, F.S.A., whose library was sold in 1852.[85] The wheat-sheaf that is gilt-stamped on the covers and the armorial bookplate of Robert, Marquess of Crewe, pasted on the front flyleaf show that it later formed part of the rich collection of literary manuscripts assembled by his father Richard Monckton Milnes (1809–55), Lord Houghton[86]. Pride of place here goes to the text—happily complete—of 'The Last Instructions to a Painter' (fols 1r–26r), dated London, 4 Sept. 1667 and subscribed 'p*er* Andrew Marvel', followed immediately by a 315-line version of 'The Loyal Scot' (fols 26v–32v), with 'The Chequer Inn' (fols 50r–54v) and 'The Statue in Stocks Market' (fols 57r–58v) figuring later. The final section (fols 58v–89r) is largely devoted to work from the Rochester canon, including 'A Supplement to my Lord Rochesters Satyre against Man' (fols 88r–89r), described as 'not Printed', and thus apparently datable to some time before 1679 or 1680[87]. The latest datable piece is anonymous: 'The Caracter' (fols 33r–35v), beginning 'The Lords and Commons having had their doom', belongs apparently to July 1679[88].

Pencilled at the foot of a brief and imperfect title-index at the end (fol. 89v) is the apparently contemporary note that 'This Book is Written by Brown'. This so far unidentified copyist practises a stylish italic that, as with the Portland scribe, incorporates some unusual features that may help in recognising his hand elsewhere (see PLATE 6).[89] Unsounded final syllables in past participles are signalled by a diagonal bar drawn through the final *d*, in preference to the more conventional apostrophe, while a strange diaeresis appears in 'allaijng' (line 37) and 'displaijng' (line 301). Frequent abbreviations, apparently forced on the copyist by the constraints of the format, include besides more familiar forms 'y^{a}' for 'they', and result in verses like 'Scarce y^{m} y^{r} Leaders, y^{a} y^{r} Leaders knew' (line 210). His spelling throughout follows the older pattern, with final *e*s and double consonants abounding, along with forms like 'Anticke Masters' (line 9), 'Auntient race' (line 673) and 'descide' (line 112), though 'phlippant stile' (line 465) seems merely idiosyncratic. Pointing is often remarkable by its absence, particularly at the ends of verses, even where the period has come to a very definite close. Here too, enlarged script is employed for proper names and emphasis. Although the initial copying was far from faultless, successive attempts at checking, resulting in over fifty changes by the scribe, including the addition of initial capitals for emphasis, show that considerable trouble was taken to achieve accuracy. The recurrence here of the barred final 'd' shows them to be the work of the copyist himself, though made at different times, in black ink and in the reddish brown that was used for corrections and annotations in other poems, including 'The Chequer Inn' (fols 53v, 54r).

The later insertion of the colon after 'strid' (line 249) and the correction of his false readings 'Wife' (line 181) and 'that glorious thing & sweet' (line 290) to 'Coife' and 'think & sweet', might suggest that the copyist was either working from or had acquired for consultation a relative of the Portland and Bodleian texts. But 'Wife' and 'thing' stand also in Osborn, Los Angeles, *1697* and Philadelphia, and further investigation shows that the reality is rather more complex. To save space in the (selective) collations that follow simple sigla have been adopted: *N* for Portland, *T2* for the Bodleian copy, *BL18* and *BL73* for British Library Additional MSS 18220 and 73540, *O* for Osborn and *LA* for Los Angeles; and for the printed texts, *89* for *1689*, *97* for *1697* (first, second and third issues not being separately distinguished), and *P* for Philadelphia. In each case the 'control' reading is that of the Portland manuscript; minor variations in spelling, capitalisation, in the other texts are not recorded.

Although, as in all witnesses, the basic text of *BL73* is overwhelmingly consistent with that of *N/89* and *T2* it shares several variant readings

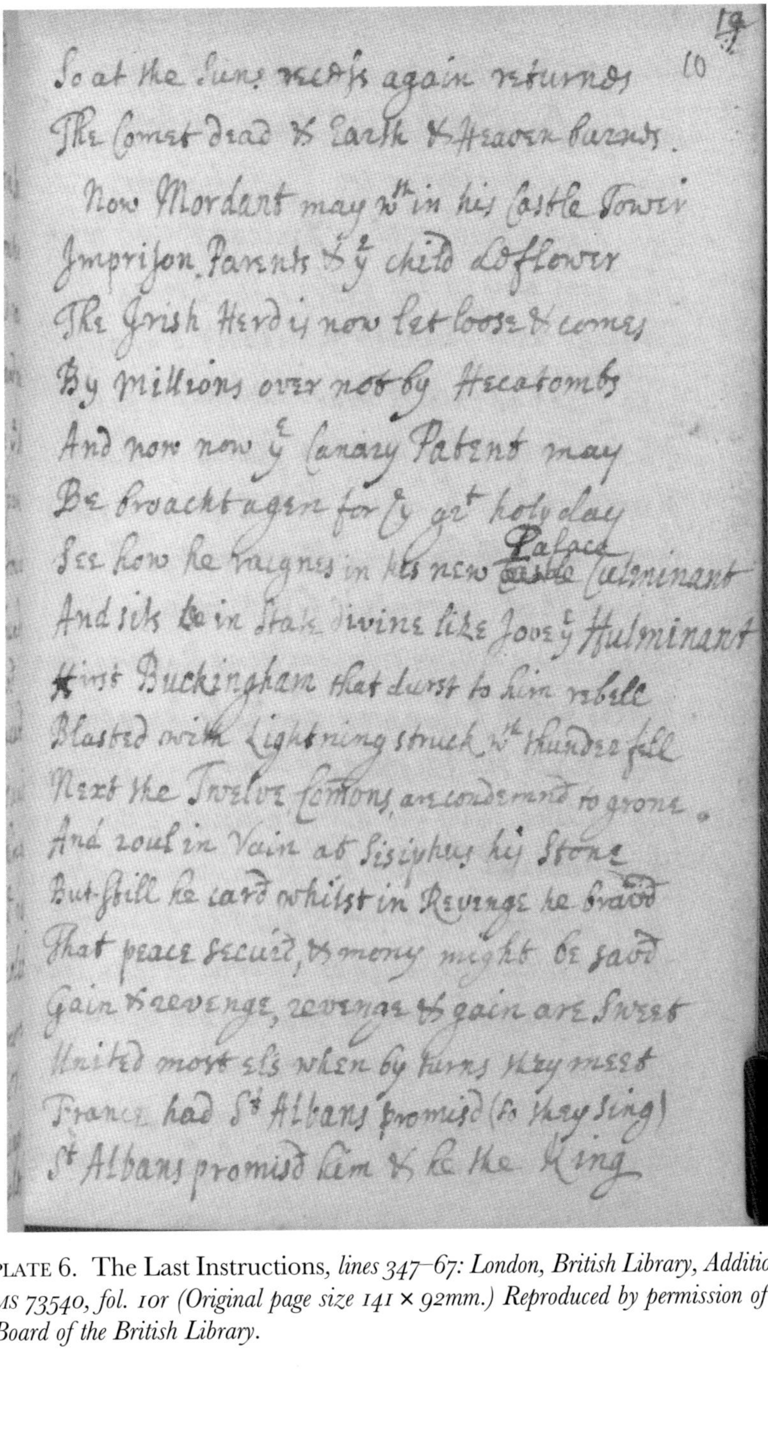

So at the Suns recess again returnes 10
The Comet dread & Earth & Heaven burnes.
Now Mordant may wth in his Castle Tower
Imprison Parents & ye child deflower
The Irish Herd is now let loose & comes
By millions over not by Hecatombs
And now now ye Canary Patent may
Be broacht agen for ye gt holy day
See how he raignes in his new ~~castle~~ Palace culminant
And sits in State divine like Jove ye fulminant
First Buckingham that durst to him rebell
Blasted with Lightning struck wth thunder fell
Next the Twelve Comons are condemnd to grone
And roul in Vain at Sisiphus his Stone
But still he card whilst in Revenge he braved
That peace secured & mony might be saved
Gain & revenge, revenge & gain are sweet
United most els when by turns they meet
France had St Albans promisd (so they sing)
St Albans promisd him & he the King

PLATE 6. The Last Instructions, *lines 347–67: London, British Library, Additional MS 73540, fol. 10r (Original page size 141 × 92mm.) Reproduced by permission of the Board of the British Library.*

with *O*, *LA*, *97* and *P*. These include (Portland reading first): lines 109 Trick-track] Tick Tack; 116 *goes*] go; 201 *quarrell*] quarrels; 242 *oftner*] often; 443 *the*] this; 471 *a time*] times; 559 *Such*] So; 855 *come*] came; 969 *on*] by; 977 *Earthquake*] Earthquakes. In three more cases it agrees with *O* and *LA* alone (lines 13 *if*] still; 94 *those*] her; 930 *inclose*] disclose)—the last instance a manifest error—in three with *O* alone (lines 468 *a*] &; 868 *with . . . edge*] of . . . edge; 887 *gleams*] beams), and in one with *LA* alone (line 662 *run*] ran). It also shares with *LA* three cases of inversion (lines 21 *so, long having*] haveing soe long; 322 *Mine and Thine*] thine & mine; 952 *are but*] but are) that individually could be dismissed as of little significance but collectively suggest a common intermediary, though it adds a further instance all of its own in line 972 (*to burn at last*] at last to burn).

In addition, *BL73* displays at least twenty unique readings, including: lines 4 *or*] &; 55 *how*] her; 70 *sicke*] thick; 124 *should*] dos; 188 *Care*] share; 321 *Hammer sleeps*] Hammers sleep; 326 *tire*] Fire; 393 *chose*] thought; 420 *mure*] barr; 427 *may*] might; 459 *from*] to; 503 *scrip*] Skipp; 569 *dwell*] live; 587 *so*] too; 646 *be*] are; 685 *Mind he*] soul had; 730 *his*] her; 741 *keep his course yet*] course yet ever; 742 *space*] course; 783 *in*] to; 901 *hand*] Heart. Although a few of the variants are not obviously the result of mere mechanical error it would be too risky to accept them as originating, at whatever stage of composition, with the author himself. This is true particularly where Douglas surrenders himself to the fire '*As one that's warm'd himself and gone to Bed*' (Portland, line 690), a verse that underwent some mysterious transformations. *O* and *LA* play with the tenses in 'y^{t} warmes himselfe, & goes to Bed' and *P* with 'that warm'd himself, and went to bed', while *BL73*, trumping them all in sheer homeliness, reads 'that huggs himself in a warme bed'.

Osborn MS *P.B. VII/15 and UCLA* MS *170/68*

Before considering the implications arising from collation of Additional MS 73540 it is necessary to examine the remaining witnesses. The relationship between the two texts now at New Haven, in the Beinecke Library at Yale, and in the Library of the University of California at Los Angeles, is close enough for them to be considered together. MS P.B. VII/15 in the Osborn collection is a disbound pamphlet of thirty-eight pages, date unknown, watermarked with a horn-in-shield device and countermarked 'IV'. Nothing closely comparable is recorded by Heawood, but the countermark may denote one or other of the Jean Villedarys who ran paper-mills in Perigueux and Angoulême from 1672[90]. The text of the poem is complete, and the verses were numbered down the inside margins in tens, though with a miscalculation that left two different reckonings still visible after line 900. Notable features of the rather loose and straggling Restoration hand are generous capitals and flourished ascenders and descenders (see PLATE 7). The execution of the work was averagely negligent, with false starts, crossings out, overwritings and insertions mostly added *currente calamo*. Eyeslip at lines 381, 382 resulted in the omission of line 381 and its subsequent insertion between the lines. Twice the scribe carelessly allowed one verse to overrun into the next, catching himself in the first instance (lines 127–8) but not in the second (lines 69–70). Efforts to remain faithful to the copy-text are seen in the occasional interlineation of omitted verses, the rectification of internally mis-ordered lines (e.g. lines 402, 566) by the device of writing numbers above the words, and in the capitals with which he frequently overscores his original lower case initials. Yet the blank space in line 104 shows that 'Campaspe' defeated him, and his 'Morelant' (line 260) for 'Mordant' suggests no great awareness of current politics. Otherwise a few unique variants of no real significance are found in lines 261 Williams] William; 589 Skipper] Shipper; 626 *by*] at; 903 *touch*] hand; 907 *startling*] startled.

University of California at Los Angeles MS 170/68 is a collection largely of Restoration satirical verse and some prose. Although it incorporates (fols 11r–19v) the well-known elegies on Cromwell's death by Sprat and Waller, with Sir William Godolphin's parody of the latter, the bulk of its contents date from the mid-1660s to mid-1680s, and work by Rochester predominates. The identity of the principal compiler, evidently a private individual, is not known: the only clue to provenance lies in the final section, added in another hand in the mid- to late-1720s, which comprises an epithalamion and a series of Latin epigrams subscribed with the initials 'E. W.'. *The Last Instructions* occurs towards the middle of the volume (fols 30r–41r), being followed immediately by an incomplete copy of the *Second Advice* (fols 41v–43r). Fortunately it is possible to establish an upper limit for the transcription of these satires, thanks to the fact that the copyist was himself an aspiring poet. The partially revised draft of an unfinished 'Essay on Heroick Poetry' (fols 50r–52r) in 120 lines of verse was inspired by his hearing the news that 'Roscommon's now no more' (d. 17 January 1685), and the dating is confirmed by unflattering allusions to Dryden's '*Threnodia Augustalis*' and the Northleigh poem that have been assigned respectively to *circa* 9 March and some time after 24 June of the same year[91]. His copy of *The Last Instructions* thus predates the earliest printed version by at least four years.

As apparently the only known copy of the satire to have been transcribed by a literary amateur rather than a professional scribe—a remarkable feat of perseverance—UCLA MS suffers from being the least

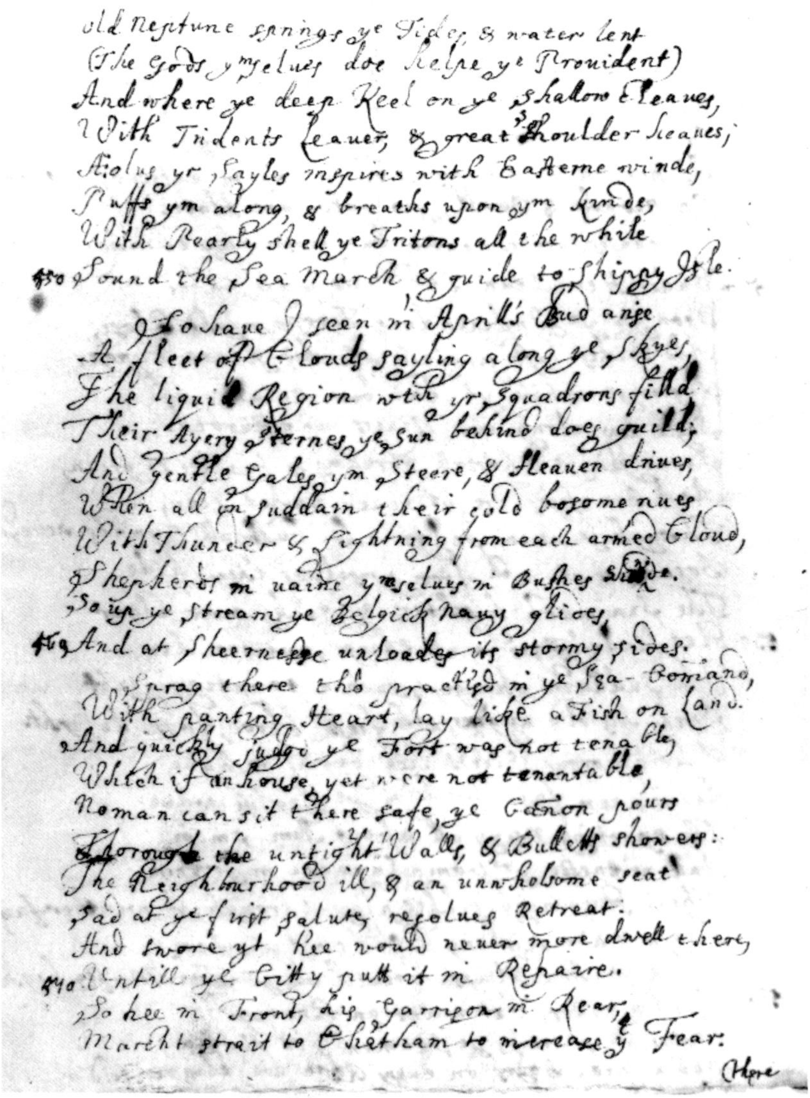
old Neptune springs ye Tides & water lent
(The Gods ymselues doe helpe ye Provident)
And where ye deep Keel on ye shallow cleaues,
With Tridents leauer, & great Shoulder heaues;
Aeolus yr Sayles inspires with Easterne winde,
Puffs ym along, & breaths upon ym kinde,
With Pearly shell ye Tritons all the while
Sound the Sea March & guide to Shippey Isle.
So haue I seen in Aprill's bud arise
A fleet of Clouds sayling along ye Skyes,
The liquid Region wth yr Squadrons filld,
Their Ayery Sternes ye Sun behind does guild;
And gentle Gales ym Steere, & Heauen driues,
When all on suddain their cold bosome riues
With Thunder & lightning from each armed Cloud,
Shepherds in vaine ymselues in Bushes shrowde.
So up ye stream ye Belgick Navy glides,
And at Sheernesse unloades its stormy sides.
Sprag there tho practisd in ye Sea-Command,
With panting Heart, lay like a Fish on Land.
And quickly judgd ye Fort was not tenable,
Which if an house, yet were not tenantable,
No man can sit there safe, ye Canon pours
Thorough the untight Walls, & Bulletts showers:
The Neighbourhood ill, & an unwholsome seat
Sad at ye first salute, resolues Retreat.
And swore yt hee would neuer more dwell there,
Untill ye Citty putt it in Repaire.
So hee in Front, his Garrison in Rear,
March't strait to Chetham to increase ye Fear.
Here

PLATE 7. The Last Instructions, *lines 543–72: New Haven, Connecticut, Yale University Library, Osborn Collection P.B. VII/15, fol. 11v (Original page size 195 × 155mm.) Reproduced by permission of the James Marshall and Marie-Louise Osborn Collection, Beinecke Library, Yale University.*

careful of all the surviving texts. The presentation itself is painstaking enough, the copyist taking an almost professional care in laying out the poem within margins—the outer one pricked to achieve consistently straight lines—and supplying a running head, 'Advice to | a Painter', spread across each opening, with catchwords at the foot of each page. The numbering proceeds by tens in the left-hand margin. Despite this, lines 402–405 of the text were overlooked, fol. 34v of the manuscript ending with lines 400 (duly numbered), 401 and 406–8. Further, as line 442 is wanting, the verse beginning 'ye first entrusts' is numbered as '450', though line 460 is correctly counted, while the copyist still contrives to reach the proper total for the poem. As with the Portland this shows that his text derives from a complete and accurately numbered exemplar. One particular feature is difficult to account for even in an amateurish production. A section in the Pett indictment (lines 773–785) is mis-ordered, so that, in comparison with the received text, it runs lines 773, 774, 779, 780, 775–778, 781, 782, 785, 783, 784. Only the three last verses, where the rhyme-scheme is obviously defective, were later righted by numbering them in the margin as 3, 1 and 2 respectively.

The extent of its agreement with the Osborn manuscript, sometimes in variants that are wholly inappropriate in the context, shows either that it was transcribed directly, but inefficiently, from the other or, more probably, that both were copied from a common source. Close kinship is established by the numerous shared substantives not found elsewhere. Most are plainly attributable to scribal misreading, but it is more than doubtful whether any even of the less obviously corrupt ones would ever have originated with Marvell: lines 158 *well could*] how to; 166 *Spice*] Spire; 203 Cart'ret] Cartwright; 383 *just*] first; 481 *our*] one; 576 *or*] &; 595 *open'd*] open; 607 *ill-deserted*] ill defended; 670 *its*] y^e^; 680 *of*] on; 802 *And*] Hee's; 803 *lesse*] least; 823 *jobb*] goe; 833 *And all with Sun and Choler come*] With Sun & Choler all come up; 897 *anguish*] Anger; 904 *th'airy*] ye angry; 938 *will*] would; 951 *obscure . . . while . . . please*] obscur'd . . . when . . . presse; 960 *of*] from; 988 *on . . . stare*] in . . . share. Strangely, at the beginning of lines 123 and 568 the adverb that stands as '*So*' in all other texts is rendered in both as 'Sad', while in Osborn the '*Such*' that elsewhere invariably introduces line 623 carries interlined above it 'so', and this alternative has been adopted in the UCLA text. Several trivial variants unique to the latter, but barely worth mention, may be set down to simple carelessness in copying: such are lines 140 *by*] at; 271 *theirs*] them; 318 *the Ships*] their Ships; 469 *came*] comes; 539 *the . . . on their*] their . . . in their; 579 *The*] like; 773 *Storms*] storm; 892 *her*] the.

Haste or carelessness in the UCLA copy is evident from the corruption that emerges when it is compared with Osborn. Notable instances occur at: lines 175 Bronkard *Love's Squire; through all the field array'd*] Bronkart . . . allaye'd O: Brokart . . . are layd LA; 309 *Where Force had*] Whersoe're that O: wherefore t'had LA; 346 *But blooms . . . its*] And blooms . . . its O: But blowes . . . his LA; 503 *with a scrip*] in a scrip O: in a ship LA; 840 *for three Dayes, thence*] from 3 dayes thence O: from thence 3 dayes LA. A broad hint that it derives not directly from Osborn but from a common source comes in the misreading of line 450. Here Portland, along with all other texts, reads '*In cipher one to Harry Excellent*'. The Osborn scribe at first wrote 'In Cypher; Haruey one to Haruey excellent', then corrected the names to 'Harry', but UCLA retains the original version.

'Poems on Affairs of State', 1697, and the undated Philadelphia pamphlet

The second earliest dated printing of *The Last Instructions* is in the octavo collection of 1697 entitled 'POEMS | ON | Affairs of State: | FROM | The time of *Oliver Cromwell,* to the | Abdication of K. *James* the Second. | *Written by the greatest Wits of the Age* . . .'. Case identifies three states, of which the first has addenda totalling eight pages and the second sixteen, while the third is a reprint of the second[92]. The arrangement of material is broadly chronological, beginning with the three poems written in praise of Cromwell by Dryden, Waller and Sprat, followed by Waller's *Storm* and by the three Advice poems that had been printed as Denham's in *Directions to a painter* (1667). After this comes a long section of satires by or attributed to Marvell, its 70 pages making up more than a quarter of the whole content. In reprinting the volume in a slightly enlarged second edition called for by its popularity few changes other than those commonly incident to resetting were introduced. The other, undated but near-contemporary, printing, is at present known only from a single exemplar. The small pamphlet in which it occurs is the sixth in a composite volume of twenty-one tracts mostly bearing imprints between 1659 and 1681 that has been in the Library Company of Philadelphia since 1801, where it is press-marked 935.Q.6. Consisting of two sheets, A-B^8, and totalling thirty-two pages, it lacks a general title-page, but the two satires that it contains bear individual caption-headings running 'THE LAST | INSTRUCTIONS | to a PAINTER, 1667' (pp.1–26) and 'The Loyall Scot. | *By* Cleaveland'*s Ghost upon the Death of Captain* | Douglas *burnt on his Ship at* Chatham.' (pp.27–32). Both pieces are subscribed at their conclusion 'By *A. M.*'. Despite the title of the second piece the text of the Douglas episode was incorporated in the longer one, with a simple cross-reference '*Vid. page* 17'. One physical feature has defied explanation. Though the standard measure throughout is forty lines to the page, sig. B2 verso (p.20) was changed to thirty by increasing the spaces between the lines, the passage affected including most (lines 751–780) of the Pett indictment. Unless owed to a miscalculation in casting-off copy the reason for resetting is not immediately apparent.

A note of provenance inserted loose in the volume points out that the Marvell item is 'sandwiched between two other pieces dated 1667 and 1674 respectively, and its position is so indicated in the old table of contents yet some pundits claim it is a piece of 18th-century printing.' Among Whigs of the early 18th century, it is true, Marvell's name still had sufficient propaganda value for Cooke to publish his own octavo edition of the *Works* in 1726. Pierre Legouis, whose attention was first drawn to the pamphlet by Caroline Robbins ventured that 'it may be as early as 1669'[93]. Elizabeth Donno believed that the pamphlet antedated *1697*.[94] Despite the different disposition of the Douglas episode, the two texts do exist in a very close relationship, sharing, most notably, some twenty-nine unique readings.[95] However, several others in which *P* differs from *1697* (and agrees with Portland) imply independent copy-texts or possibly that the editor consulted another authority—perhaps even *1689*—here.[96]

Conclusion

Texts of *The Last Instructions* are seen to fall into three groups: the first and evidently the earliest is made up of Portland, its immediate descendant *1689*, and the Bodleian copy, the second the Osborn and UCLA manuscripts, and the third and latest the State Poems of 1697 and the Phildelphia pamphlet. These groupings represent two major lines of transmission, in which collation shows the remaining witness, Additional MS 73540, to have occupied a pivotal position. The manuscript from which it was copied was clearly the ancestor both of *1697* and *P*, though by a separate line of descent, as well as of *O* and *LA*., which were apparently copied from a common original. *97* and *P* may be considered for practical purposes as identical, and the text from which ultimately they derive managed to introduce even more unique variants into the poem than did the scribe of *BL73*. The present investigation has failed to establish any inherent likelihood that any but the Portland and Bodleian texts has clear value as independent witnesses, their variant readings being explicable as scribal errors compounded by progressive corruption. Both are manifestly reliable witnesses in their own right, and but for some dozen substantive variants at the best, and something more than occasional disagreement over accidentals, there is little to choose between them. But the more obviously accomplished artefact is the one from which the earliest printed version was set up. The more than ordinary care lavished on Portland's production suggests—though we cannot be certain—an attempt at a definitive version of the satire, at least as it stood at the time of copying. A directly commissioned text is a supervised one; and since all variants found in *1689* can be laid at the printer's door means that the focus of editorial attention must inevitably shift to the manuscript, as bringing us one step closer to the author than the version that was set up from it eleven years after his death.

This is not to dispute that had Marvell lived to see his poem through the press he might well have accepted a fair degree of change in presentation so long as the sense was not threatened. Compositorial intervention in the area of spelling and punctuation had been taken for granted by Moxon: it continued to be welcomed explicitly by authors of all periods who either mistrusted their own abilities or were simply unconcerned by such minutiae.[97] As late as 1931, after studying the printer's manuscript of *Paradise Lost*, Helen Darbishire could pronounce that the 'printed page of the first edition is nearer than the manuscript to what he would have written if he could', basing her subsequent Oxford editions of his poems on this theory.[98] Yet the notion of a printed artefact as representing the 'ideal' format for the presentation of an author's work before the readers of the day has not won general acceptance among bibliographers and textual critics, not least because it ignores the testimony of other contemporary documents of potentially greater authority. As long ago as 1950, W. W. Greg in his famous essay on 'The Rationale of Copy-Text' advocated following the accidentals of the earliest authoritative witness for old-spelling editions. His recommendation that readings from other sources might nevertheless be incorporated wherever they were deemed superior had already been anticipated in practice by Margoliouth, with some profit. His remarks on scribes and compositors are relevant in the context of this discussion:

> as regards accidentals they will normally follow their own habits or inclination, though they may, for various reasons and to varying degrees, be influenced by their copy. Thus a contemporary manuscript will at least preserve the spelling of the period, and may even retain some of the author's own, while it may at the same time depart frequently from the wording of the original: on the other hand a later transcript of the same original may reproduce the wording with essential accuracy while completely modernising the spelling.[99]

His argument has been carried even further. By 1987 Thomas Tanselle could state baldly that 'a fair-copy manuscript, when it survives, becomes the copy-text, except when there is convincing evidence pointing toward the first (or some later) edition as the proper choice'.[100] He went on to conclude that an author's implicit endorsement of press changes did not mean that he actually preferred them; that what we may think of as 'bad' punctuation may have seemed perfectly appropriate to him; and that it is inconsistent to follow the substantives of a text while rejecting its other features. This would tend to counter any reservations that editors might have about the pointing of the Portland text—more particularly, its frequent resort to semi-colons and colons in discursive passages. At the same time, modernisers, who are faced with no such problems, may take heart from the ample evidence for the construction of a substantively reliable text that, despite the uncertain refractions of the scribal medium, is afforded by the two principal manuscript witnesses.

NOTES

1 *The Diary of John Evelyn*, ed. E. de Beer (Oxford, 1955), I, 486 (28 June 1667).
2 *The Diary of Samuel Pepys*, ed. Robert Latham and William Matthews (1974), VIII, 256–312 *passim.*
3 *The Poems and Letters of Andrew Marvell*, ed. H. M. Margoliouth, 3rd edn, rev. Pierre Legouis with the collaboration of E. E. Duncan-Jones, 2 vols (Oxford, 1971), II, 309–13.
4 Cf. with lines 849–50 here of *The First Anniversary of the Government under O.C.* (January 1655), lines 39–40, 'yet Reprives / From the deserved Fate their guilty lives'.
5 Pepys, *Diary*, edn cit., VIII, 410–11 and 415.
6 *The Diary of John Milward, Esq., Member of Parliament for Derbyshire, September 1666 to May 1668*, ed. Caroline Robbins (Cambridge, 1938), p.116.
7 *A Reproof to the Rehearsal Transprosed* (1673), p.227.
8 Letter of Hull Corporation to Marvell, 23 August 1675 (O.E.T., 3rd edn, II, 366–7).
9 Mary Tom Osborne, *Advice-to-a-Painter Poems, 1633–1856* ([Austin], Texas, 1949), pp.28–33, items 10–11.
10 *Ibid.*, pp.33–5, items 12–13.
11 Peter Beal, *Index of English Literary Manuscripts*, vol. II: 1625–1700, part 2 (London, 1993), MaA 314–499.
12 London, British Library, Additional MS 78313, fol. 53. Contractions, except in proper names, have been silently expanded in transcription.
13 Pepys, *Diary*, edn cit., VII (1972), p. 407. A copy possibly of local provenance survives among the papers of the Carew family of Crowcombe Court, Somerset: see Beal, *IELM*, II/2, MaA 353.
14 W. C. Abbott, *Writings and speeches of Oliver Cromwell* (Cambridge, Mass., 1937–47), III, 712–3, 734, and IV, 703–4, 952.
15 British Library, Additional MS 21947, fols 121, 141.
16 National Archives (Public Record Office), *CSPDom. 1667* (1866), p.330 (26 July 1667).
17 Pepys, *Diary*, edn cit., VIII, 21.
18 *Ibid.*, p.313.
19 Pepys, *Diary*, edn cit., VIII, p.439.
20 Nat Lee, *The Princess of Cleve* (1689), II, ii, cited in the *Oxford English Dictionary*, sub 'White', *a* (11).

21 Historical Manuscripts Commission, 12th Report (1890), 'The Manuscripts of S. H. Le Fleming, Esq., of Rydal Hall', Appendix, Part VII, p. 76 (newsletter dated 21 March 1670/1).

22 *The Poems and Letters of Andrew Marvell*, 1st edn (Oxford, 1927), I, 267; reprinted 2nd edn (1952).

23 *The Works of Andrew Marvell, Esq . . . with a New Life of the Author, By Capt. Edward Thompson* (1776), I, xxxviii–l; *Bodleian Library Record*, 2 (May 1945), 125; and Hugh Macdonald in *Times Literary Supplement*, 13 July 1951, p.444.

24 M. T. Osborne, *op. cit.*, p.36; *The Poems and Letters of Andrew Marvell*, 3rd edn, I, 346; and *Poems on Affairs of State: Augustan Satirical Verse, 1660–1714*, ed. G. deF. Lord (New Haven, 1963), pp.452–3.

25 *The Portland Collection: Literary Manuscripts* (Nottingham, [1962]), p.24. For the dating and other assistance I am indebted Dr. Dorothy Johnston, Keeper of Manuscripts and Special Collections at the University of Nottingham.

26 Beal, *IELM*, II/2, pp. 65–6.

27 *Andrew Marvell: The Complete English Poems*, ed. E. S. Donno (London, 1972); *Andrew Marvell*, ed. Frank Kermode and Keith Walker (Oxford, 1990); and *The Poems of Andrew Marvell*, ed. Nigel Smith (London, 2003).

28 Smith, p. 360.

29 A calendar of material covering the period from 1582 to 1714 was published in H.M.C., 13th–21st Reports, vols. I–IX, 1894–1931. The dispersal is described in R. J. Olney, 'The Portland Papers', *Archives*, 19 (1989), 78–87, and Clyve Jones, 'The Harley family and the Harley papers', *British Library Journal*, 15 (Autumn 1989), 123–33.

30 Respectively British Library, Harley MSS 7312, 7315 (a double volume), 7319; and Harley MSS 7316–7318.

31 The originals make up Portland Literary MS Pw V 31: see *Welbeck Miscellany No. 2. A Collection of Poems by Several Hands*, ed. Francis Needham (Bungay, 1924), p. 51, cited in David M. Vieth, *Attribution in Restoration Poetry* (New Haven, 1963), p. 205 (and see pp. 204–30 *passim*).

32 Bonham's sale catalogue of *Atlases, Maps and Manuscripts*, London, 27 June 2006, lot 383.

33 Portland Literary Collection, MSS Pw V 32 and 38–48.

34 *Ibid.*, MS Pw V 40 (ex libris Thomas Fermor (d.1753), first Earl of Pomfret); MS 46 (William Craven (d.1697), Earl Craven); and MS 47 (Sir John Hynde Cotton (d.1752)).

35 *Ibid.*, MS Pw V 48, a miscellany of the early 1700s, came from the library of Sir William Augustus Fraser (d.1898), while MS Pw V 30, a miscellany owned in 1671 by 'J. H.', figured in Bertram Dobell's sale catalogue of *Literature of the Restoration* (1918), item 1253.

36 *Bodleian Quarterly Record*, 4, No 37 (1923), p. 7, and 6, No. 65, p. 106; and see W. J. A. C. J. Cavendish-Bentinck, sixth Duke of Portland, *Men, Women and Things: Memories* (1938), pp. 83–6, 101, and A. S. Turberville, *A History of Welbeck Abbey and its Owners* (1938), I, xi.

37 See replies regarding the *Brut* in British Library, Additional MS 70516 (unfoliated), regarding Wyntoun's chronicle in Nottingham University, Portland Literary MS Pw V 152/2, and about *The Last Instructions* in MS Pw V 299. The 'morality' may have been William Cavendish, Duke of Newcastle's 'A Pleasant & Merrye Humor off a Rogue' (MS Pw V 24, pp. 36–58).

38 Smith, pp. 360–1.

39 Respectively New York, Pierpont Morgan Library, MS MA 307, discussed in *The Manuscript of Milton's Paradise Lost Book I*, ed. Helen Darbishire (Oxford, 1931), and

Bodleian Library, MS Rawlinson D 400, fols 76–7v, erroneously attributed to Denham in J. K. Moore, *Primary Materials relating to Copy and Print in English Books of the Sixteenth and Seventeenth Centuries* (Oxford Bibliographical Society, Occasional Publication No. 24, 1992), pp.25, 50.

40 In a letter of 8 May 1930 (British Library, Additional MS 70514, fol. iiv) Bodley's Librarian wrote to Needham: 'I have got Wilmot to re-unite your leaf of music'.

41 Similar types are reproduced in Richard J. Wolfe, *Marbled Paper: Its History, Techniques and Patterns* (Philadelphia, 1990), Plates XXIII(8) and XXV(32), and see pp. 179–82.

42 Information from the electronic database held in the Department of Special Collections at Nottingham.

43 National Archives, *Calendar of State Papers Domestic 1 March–31 December 1678, with Addenda 1674–1679* (1913), pp. 372–3 (23 August 1678), cited in Marvell's *The Rehearsal Transpros'd and The Rehearsal Transpros'd: The Second Part*, ed. D. I. B. Smith (Oxford, 1971), p.xxi.

44 Arthur E. Case, *A Bibliography of English Poetical Miscellanies 1521–1750* (Oxford, 1935), pp. 130–4, Nos 188–9, 191.

45 *Ibid.*, pp. 147–50, Nos 211(1)(a-h).

46 See the entries for him in the *Oxford Dictionary of National Biography* and *History of Parliament 1660–1690*, ed. Basil Duke Henning (1983), II, 494–7.

47 Harley's general correspondence is now British Library, Additional MSS 70002–71119 *passim* and 70112–70130; the Marvell letters are Additional MS 70012, fols 58, 247, 249, 254, with two (unbound and unfoliated) in Additional MS 70120.

48 *Poems and Letters*, 3rd edn, II, 328, 346.

49 See the entry for Toland in *ODNB*.

50 Case, pp. 130–1, No. 188(3).

51 *Andrew Marvell*, ed. Donno, pp. 279–80.

52 The earliest occurrence recorded in the *Oxford English Dictionary*, sub 'Esquire', n.1b. is from 1710.

53 Beal, *IELM*, II/1 (1987), p. 349 and DoC 336–61, includes it among Poems of Doubtful Authorship.

54 Bror Danielsson and David M. Vieth, *The Gyldenstolpe Manuscript* (Stockholm, 1967), pp. 361–5. Twenty-six texts are listed in Beal, *IELM*, DoC 336–61.

55 Joseph Moxon, *Mechanick Exercises on the Whole Art of Printing (1683)*, ed. Herbert Davis and Harry Carter, 2nd edn (Oxford, 1962), pp.239–44; Percy Simpson, *Proof-Reading in the Sixteenth Seventeenth and Eighteenth Centuries* (Oxford, 1935, reprinted 1970), pp. 49–51; and Philip Gaskell, *A New Introduction to Bibliography* (Oxford, 1972), p. 40 and n. 4a.

56 Case, p.130, No. 188(1)(b), *A Collection of Poems on Affairs of State.*

57 *Ibid.*, No. 188(1)(a).

58 British Library, Printed Book 1077.h.32(7), noted in *Notes and Queries*, 5th Ser. 6 (9 September 1876), p. 401, as being in the possession of Alexander Gardyne, whose library was offered for sale at Sotheby's, 7 July 1885.

59 *Complete Works, in Verse and Prose, of Andrew Marvell, M.P.*, ed. A. B. Grosart (Fuller's Worthies Library, privately printed, 1872–5), I, 286–8, has a long note citing and evaluating its readings.

60 British Library, Additional MS 75354, fol. 82. The appointments are mentioned in Pepys, *Diary*, VIII, 265.

61 Herbert Aubrey, cited in the *History of Parliament 1660–1690*, ed. Basil Duke Henning (1983), I, 569.

62 Moxon, p. 248 (the passage is reproduced in facsimile on p. 368). Actual instances from 1684 are illustrated in J. K. Moore, *Primary Materials.*, plate 36.

63 For this and the other quotations in this paragraph, see Moxon, pp. 212, 192–3 and 217 respectively.

64 By the mid-eighteenth century this practice was going out of fashion: James Smith, *The Printer's Grammar* (London, 1755), p. 201, described it as the 'old way'.

65 Marvell, *Poems and Letters*, ed. Margoliouth (1971), I, 346.

66 At line 174 the Bodleian text and Additional MS 73540 have no mark, *1697* and *Philadelphia* a semi-colon, while at line 616 Additional MS 73540 reads 'its' and *1697* and *Philadelphia* 'his'.

67 Cf. Margoliouth's notes in *Poems and Letters*, 1st edn (1927), I, 272, 276 (reprinted in 3rd edn, pp. 148, 353).

68 *Ibid.*, p. 276 (reprinted in 3rd edn, pp. 152, 356).

69 *The Works of Andrew Marvell, Esq . . . with a New Life of the Author*, 3 vols (1776), I, xxxviii. The arguments are rehearsed in Marvell, *Poems and Letters*, ed. Margoliouth, 3rd edn (1971), I, 233–5.

70 For the hand of the main copyist in lines 239–66 of 'A Poem upon the Death of His Late Highness the Lord Protector', see Hilton Kelliher, *Andrew Marvell: Poet & Politician 1621–78* (London, 1978), p. 65.

71 'Absolute Liberty: The Life and Thought of William Popple', *William and Mary Quarterly*, 3rd ser. 24 (1967), 190–223, reprinted in *Absolute Liberty: A Selection from the Articles and Papers of Caroline Robbins* (Hamden, Conn., 1982), pp. 3–30 (esp. pp. 12–4).

72 Annabel Patterson, 'Lady State's First Two Sittings: Marvell's Satiric Canon', *Studies in English Literature*, 40, No. 3 (Summer 2000), pp. 401–2.

73 'Marvell's "Last Instructions": Textual Errors and their Poetic Significance', *Studia Neophilologica*, 42 (1970), 309–18.

74 Barnabe Googe, *Popish Kingdom* (1570), I, line 978, and George Turberville's translation of Ovid's *Heroides* (1567), Epistle XVII, line 443, identified here from the Chadwyck-Healey English Poetry database.

75 Marvell, *Growth of Popery* (1677), p. 11, and *OED*, 'Holl' *n., sub. obs.* exc. *dial.* 2.

76 Adjectival usages (3 in Spenser and 44 in Sylvester) are noted in the Chadwyck-Healey English Poetry database.

77 Cf. Sir Arthur Gorges's translation of Lucan's *Pharsalia* (1614), IV, 216, 'floods hath all things ouer-strid', and William Lisle of Heliodorus's *The Faire Ethiopian* (1631), Book X, 697, 'then strid, and strongly pight His feet'.

78 Cf. 'we can not yet get of the difficultyes': letter to Hull Corporation, 23 November 1667 (Marvell, *Poems and Letters*, ed. Margoliouth, 3rd edn, II, 61).

79 See the entry for Palmer in *ODNB*, and the letter of John Conny to John Evelyn, 14 June 1667 (British Library, Additional MS 78321, fol. 75): 'on ye 10th in ye Morninge they putt some fewe Men on shoare at Candia Iland to steale Mutton'. The form is not recorded in P. H. Reaney, *The Place-Names of Essex* (English Place-Name Society vol. XII, Cambridge, 1969), p. 148.

80 For 'Presumes of' see *OED* sub. 'Presumes', v. 3.b. (intrans.).

81 British Library, Additional MSS 54566–54570 *passim*, the first illustrated in Kelliher, 'The Warwick Manuscripts of Fulke Greville', *British Museum Quarterly*, 34, Nos 3–4 (1970), plate XXIV; and Bodleian Library, MS Rawlinson poet. 123, illustrated in P. J. Croft, *Autograph Poetry in the English Language* (1973), I, plate facing p. 59.

82 Purchased by the British Museum from the bookseller Joseph Lilly, 13 July 1852.

83 Watson's text is illustrated in Kelliher, *Andrew Marvell*, p. 99.

84 Marvell, *Complete Works*, ed. Grosart (1872–5), I, 290.

85 Sotheby's sale catalogue, 19–28 April 1852, lot 1318, where it is described as 'Poems in Manuscript, of the XVII Century, by various Authors, written on 172 pages, with an Index of Contents on the last page. Russia, gilt edges. 1667, &c.'

86 Christie's, 26 November 1997, lot 75 (and see lots 74, 76–911 *passim*, along with others that had belonged to his descendant Sir John Colville (d.1987) in the sale of 28 November, lots 84–111.

87 'A Satyre against Reason and Mankind', lines 174–223: cf. *The Works of John Wilmot, Earl of Rochester*, ed. Harold Love (Oxford, 1999), pp. 561–3.

88 Printed in *Poems on Affairs of State* (1704), III, 79–82.

89 *The Scriveners' Company Common Paper 1357–1628 with a Continuation to 1678*, ed. Francis W. Steer (London Record Society, 4, 1968), pp. 119–26, lists various men of this name between 1649 and 1675.

90 Raymond Gaudriault, *Filigranes et autres caractéristiques des papiers fabriqués en France aux XVIIe et XVIIIe siècles* (Paris, 1995), p. 278.

91 *The Poems of John Dryden*, ed. Paul Hammond, II: 1682–1685 (1995), 389, 429.

92 Case, Nos 211 (1) (a–c); and see Wing 2719 (260 pp., with two settings at Yale) and 2719A.

93 Marvell, *Poems and Letters*, ed. Margoliouth, 3rd edn, rev. Legouis (1971), p. 385.

94 *Andrew Marvell*, ed. Donno, p. 280.

95 They occur at lines 38, 53, 88, 105, 154, 192, 200, 209, 294, 314, 319, 364, 429, 479, 492, 497, 500, 513, 579, 596, 613, 616, 624, 628, 804, 903, 913, 930, and 968.

96 Cf. lines 39, 105, 162, 179, 201, 214, 257, 337, 364, 950.

97 James Thorpe, *Principles of Textual Criticism* (San Marino, 1972), pp. 131–70.

98 Darbishire, p.xxiii. The position was later restated in Gaskell, pp. 338–43.

99 First printed as 'The Rationale of Copy-Text', *Studies in Bibliography*, 3 (1950–1), 19–36, and reissued in his *Collected papers*, ed. J. C. Maxwell (Oxford, 1966), pp. 374–91 (see esp. pp. 376–7).

100 G. Thomas Tanselle, *Textual Criticism since Greg: A Chronicle 1950–1985* (Charlottesville, Virginia, 1987), p. 58 (and see pp. 58–61).

Manuscripts at Auction: January 2004 to December 2005

A. S. G. Edwards

This list is intended to provide a summary of manuscript items produced in the British Isles between 1100 and 1700 and those which were either produced abroad for a market there or which were demonstrably in the British Isles from an early stage in their history that have appeared for sale at the major auction houses in London and New York, and in other auction house or booksellers' catalogues, where these have been available to the compiler. I would be pleased to receive notice of any auction or booksellers' catalogues containing relevant items for the period from January 2001, as well as any omitted from the period covered by the present record.

The list cannot claim to be exhaustive but is offered as a guide to these materials. Where known, the names of purchasers and/or prices paid have been given, and also the present locations of the manuscripts or their subsequent appearance in booksellers' or auction catalogues. Prices and buyers for mixed collections of leaves sold as a single lot and only partly comprising English manuscripts are given after the last relevant item in each lot. The price given for items at auction is normally the hammer price, exclusive of buyers' premium. For those in booksellers' catalogues it is the offered price.

Items which can be dated, in whole or in part, approximately to before 1500 are indicated by an asterisk (*) before the lot or item number. Significant provenances are noted.

Generally, manuscripts chiefly of literary, rather than historical interest, have been included. Royal letters and documents are usually omitted, as are single letters written by statesmen, ecclesiastics and other public figures. Charters, grants and other items judged to be mainly of archival interest have generally been excluded, as have maps and surveys, cookery books and collections of recipes. No attempt has been made to include any manuscripts offered for sale over the internet.

Thanks are offered to the various members of the book trade and other scholars who have provided information and other assistance in the preparation of this article. I am particularly indebted to Dr Peter Beal for corrections and information.

Abbreviations

ALs(s)	Autograph letter(s) signed
attrib.	attributed to
Ds(s)	Document(s) signed
ill.	illuminated
Ls(s)	Letter(s) signed

LONDON

Bonham's

28 September 2004 The Enys Collection of Autograph Manuscripts

363 KILLIGREW (THOMAS): ALs 8 January 1667/8 to Samuel Pepys. £3,200
392 SACKVILLE (THOMAS, EARL OF DORSET): Draft verses. £2,000. Now in the Bodleian Library.
403 TAYLOR (JEREMY): ALs 2 December 1665 to unidentified recipient. £520

16 November 2004

*197 STATHAM (NICHOLAS): *Abridgement of Statutes* (Pynson [1490]; STC 23238), with a Middle English poem (*NIMEV* 1488), and Latin verse and prose added on flyleaves in a fifteenth-century hand. £21,510 (see below, Quaritch, Spring 2005).

15 March 2005

596 HALL (JOSEPH): Autograph deposition, MS on paper, 26 April 1636. £1,500.
*608 BOOK OF HOURS (SARUM USE): 7 ill. leaves, MS on vellum, from Book of Hours with English prayers, added in sixteenth-century hand, *c.* 1475–1550. £700.
*611 LATIN BIBLE, BOOK OF HOURS (SARUM USE): Lot includes single leaf from Bible, MS on vellum, *c.*1375; Single leaf from East Anglian Book of Hours, MS on vellum, fourteenth-century; both ex Thomas Phillipps. £1,700.

Christie's

3 March 2004 (Halsted B. Vander Poel Sale)

28 DONNE (JOHN): ALs, 26 October 1624 to Bridget, Lady Kingsmill. £110,000 (including premium).

2 June 2004

29 GENEALOGICAL ROLL: MS on vellum; made for Richard Anthony by William Ryley (d.1677). £1,792 (including premium).

8 June 2005

*25 BOOK OF HOURS (SARUM USE): ill. MS on vellum, *c.*1430–1440; written in Bruges for English market and partly decorated in England (probably London). £4,500.
*26 BOOK OF HOURS (SARUM USE): ill. MS on vellum, third quarter of fifteenth century; probably London. £4,800 to Fogg.
82 RALEGH (SIR WALTER): Ls, 16 June 1618, to Sir Thomas Wilson (1560?–1629). £35,000 to Maggs.

16 November 2005

*15 LATIN BIBLE: ill. MS on vellum, first half of thirteenth century; from the Benedictine Priory of St Cuthbert, Durham. £40,000. Now in Durham Cathedral Library.
*18 AMBROSIUS AUTPERTUS ETC: Collection of patristic texts, MS on vellum, second half of fifteenth century. £6,000 to Quaritch.
*19 NOVA STATUTA: In Middle English, ill. MS on vellum, *c.*1445, probably London. £49,000. Now British Library Additional MS 81292.
*20 SARUM MISSAL: ill. MS on vellum, *c.*1455, probably London. Unsold.
*21 BOOK OF HOURS (SARUM USE): ill. MS on vellum, *c.*1465; written in Bruges for English market; with 18 historiated initials in the style of Willem Vrelant. Unsold.
28 LIVES OF THE SAINTS: In English, MS on paper, early seventeenth century. £2,400 to Christopher Edwards.
144 NEWTON (SIR ISAAC): Autograph MS fragment, on paper, mathematical calculations. £14,400
145 NEWTON (SIR ISAAC): Autograph MS fragment, on paper, on idolatry. Unsold.
146 NEWTON (SIR ISAAC): Autograph MS fragment, on paper, on the Christian Church. £7,200.

Sotheby's

27 May 2004 (John R. B. Brett-Smith sale)

226 ETHEREGE (SIR GEORGE): MS transcript of his letterbooks as British Resident at Ratisbon (Regensburg); [*c.*1687–8]. Unsold.
227 ETHEREGE (SIR GEORGE): Another MS transcript of his letterbooks as British Resident at Ratisbon (Regensburg); [*c.*1687–8]. Unsold.
492 ROCHESTER (JOHN WILMOT, second EARL OF): MS of his poem 'In imitation of ye 10th Satyr of ye 1st Book of Horace'; [*c.*1670s]. £400 to Nicholas Fisher.
608 WHARTON (ANNE): MS volume of 24 poems by her, on *c.*85 pages, 4to; [? early 18th-century]. £33,000 to Arthur Freeman. Now at Yale University, Beinecke Library, Osborn Shelves b 408.

22 June 2004 (Earl of Macclesfield Sale)

*582 HERMANN OF REICHENAU, *De compositione astrolabii* etc: MS, on vellum, first half of thirteenth century. £110,000.
*583 JOHANNES OF SACROBOSCO, *Opera*: MS on vellum, possibly Oxford, late thirteenth century. £58,000.
*587 MACCLESFIELD PSALTER: MS on vellum, East Anglia, possibly Gorleston *c.* 1320–30. £1,500,000. Now in Fitzwilliam Museum, Cambridge.
*589 NICHOLAS OF LYNN, *Kalendarium*, with Middle English mathematical treatise: MS on vellum, perhaps Cambridge, early fifteenth century. £46,000.

22 June 2004

*44 DOCUMENTS AND FRAGMENTS: MSS on vellum, various dates between thirteenth and seventeenth centuries. £750.
*55 STATUTES OF COLVILLE CHANTRY CHAPEL: Cambridgeshire, possibly Ely, mid-fifteenth century; MS on vellum. £97,000 to Fogg.
*56 BRUT CHRONICLE: MS on vellum; in Middle English; possibly Oxford, mid-fifteenth century; on vellum; *olim* Foyle, sold Christies, 11 July 2000, lot 75. Unsold.

8 July 2004

7 ESSEX (ROBERT DEVEREUX, second EARL OF): MS accounts of his execution, [*c.*1601]. £1,200 to Christopher Edwards.

16 SAMUEL PEPYS: ALs, 9 July 1688, to Edward Gregory, Clerk of the Cheque at Chatham. £1,200.
57 EGERTON FAMILY: Verses relating to Egerton family, Earls of Bridgewater; 17th century. £2,200 to Maggs.

5 July 2005

*50 FLORILEGIUM: MS on vellum, Oxford (?), mid-thirteenth century. £12,000 to Les Enlumineures.
*80 BOETHIUS, *Consolatio Philosophiae*: MS on vellum, late tenth or early eleventh century, probably Christ Church, Canterbury; *olim* Wodhull, Cockerell, Bodmer. £680,000 to Fogg.
*91 BREVIARY: Use of York; MS on vellum, late fourteenth century. £1,100 to Quaritch.
*96 BOOK OF HOURS (SARUM USE): ill. MS on vellum, *c.*1390 and *c.*1420. £46,000.

12 July 2005

64 DONNE (JOHN, the Younger): ALs, to Lord Conway, [1650?]. £1,500 to Quaritch.
76 SHAKESPEARE (WILLIAM): MS copy of lines 91–102 of *Venus and Adonis* on the verso of a draft legal document relating to Ticehurst, Sussex; 1630s. £5,000 to Christopher Edwards. Now in the Folger Shakespeare Library, MS X.d.562.

6 December 2005

*4 (2) LATIN BIBLE, INTERPRETATION OF HEBREW NAMES: Fragment of leaf: part of lot; MS on vellum, fourteenth century. £1,400.
*31 ZACHARIAS CHRYSOPOLITANUS: *In unum ex quattuor*; MS on vellum, third quarter of twelfth century. £32,000 to Quaritch.
*50 BOOK OF HOURS (SARUM USE): ill. MS on vellum, *c.*1440; made in Netherlands (? Bruges) for English market. Formerly owned by Jane Blenerhassett and Edward Banyster. £6,000.

15 December 2005

1. DETHICK (WILLIAM): ill. MS, with arms of the Garter created by Edward IV, presented probably as a New Year's Gift to Queen Elizabeth I, on vellum, 20 leaves, 4to; 1591. Unsold.

NEW YORK

Christie's

14 April 2004 (Mary, Viscountess Eccles sale)

34 ESSEX (ROBERT DEVEREUX, second EARL OF): MS account of his arraignment in 1601 (in the hand of the 'Feathery Scribe'); *c.*1620s–30s. $2,390 (including premium).

SAN FRANCISCO & LOS ANGELES (SIMULCAST)

Bonham's & Butterfield

14 November 2005

*1018 INGOLDISTHORPE PSALTER: ill. MS on vellum, made in Bruges for English market; *olim* Joan Tiptoft, Lady Goldisthorpe (1425–94); William Foyle (sold Christie's 11 July 2000, lot 34).
1078 NEWTON (SIR ISAAC): Autograph MS fragment, on paper, of work on Christianity.

BOOKSELLERS' CATALOGUES

Christopher Edwards

List 33: Recent Acquisitions [2005]

28 COTTON (CHARLES): Autograph (?) MS list of books 'borrowed of Wm Hardestee'. £250. Now in the Folger Shakespeare Library, MS Acc. 260943.

Simon Finch

Catalogue 60, 2004: English An exploration of Englishness in books, manuscripts and art from c. 1230 to 2004

*1 LATIN BIBLE: MS on vellum, *c.*1230.

Jorn Gunther

Brochure No. 8, 2004: Eight Centuries of Manuscript Illumination

*7 BOOK OF HOURS: Use of Sarum, from Bruges for the English market; MS on vellum; *c.*1430–40; twenty one miniatures.

Maggs

European Bulletin No. 23, 2004. Illuminated Miniatures, Manuscripts and Single Leaves

*1 ILLUMINATED PSALTER: *c*.1200, Northern England; ill. MS on vellum. £24,000.
*4 BOOK OF HOURS: Use of Sarum; from Flanders for the English market; ill. MS on vellum; nine miniatures; *c*.1450. £20,000.
*104 LATIN BIBLE: single leaf from index of Hebrew names; ill. MS on vellum; *c*.1250. £375.

Catalogue 1376, 2005. Continental Books and Manuscript Leaves from the Library of James Stevens Cox

*1 ST JEROME: Commentary on Ecclesiastes, single leaf, MS on vellum; *c*.950–1000. £7,500.
*15 PSALTER: two fragments, MS on vellum; *c*.1200–1250. £1,400.
*16 LATIN VERSE: bifolium, MS on vellum; *c*.1250. £350.
*17 LATIN BIBLE, single leaf, ill., MS on vellum; *c*.1250. £1,500.
*18 LATIN BIBLE, single leaf, ill., MS on vellum; *c*.1250. £250.
*29 BOETHIUS: bifolium, MS on vellum; *c*.1250–1300. £500.
*33 SCHOLARLY QUESTIONS ABOUT GENESIS: two leaves, MS on vellum; *c*.1300. £425.
*36 LATIN BIBLE: single leaf, ill. MS on vellum, East Anglia, *c*.1345. From a lectern Bible, the first part of which is BL Royal 1. E. IV, other leaves from which are widely dispersed. (See also below Maggs, European Bulletin 24, No. 18). £1,500.
*37 LATIN BIBLE: single leaf, ill. MS on vellum, East Anglia; *c*. 1345. (From same MS as 36). £2,000.
*38 LATIN BIBLE: single leaf, MS on vellum, East Anglia; *c*. 1345. (From same MS as 36). £300.
*42 EXEMPLA: single leaf, MS on vellum; *c*.1300–50. £275.
*43 PETER LOMBARD: single leaf, MS on vellum, *c*.1300–50. £240.
*44 VICES & VIRTUES: single leaf, MS on vellum, from a treatise on this subject; *c*.1300–50. £240.
*47 LATIN VERSE: bifolium, MS on vellum, discussing lexicography; *c*.1350–1400. £350.
*49 CANON LAW: bifolium, MS on vellum, from a treatise on this subject; *c*.1400. £300.

European Bulletin 24, Catalogue 1385 (2005)

*18 LATIN BIBLE: single leaf, ill. MS on vellum; East Anglia; *c*.1345. From a lectern Bible, the first part of which is BL Royal 1. E. IV, other leaves from which are widely dispersed. (See above Maggs, Catalogue 1376, Nos 36–8.) £1,500.

Quaritch

Early Books and Manuscripts (Spring 2005)

*59 NICHOLAS STATHAM: *Abridgement of Cases* (Pynson [1490]; STC 23238), with a Middle English poem (*NIMEV* 1488), and Latin verse and prose added on flyleaves in a fifteenth-century hand. (See above, Bonham's 16 November 2004, lot 197). Now in a private collection.
*60 JOHN WYCLIFFE: Treatises on Logic, fragment of ten leaves, MS on vellum, late fourteenth century. Now in the Bodleian Library.

From Carolingian to Gothic. Four Centuries of Medieval Manuscripts from an English Private Collection [June, 2005].

*[10] SERMONS: MS on vellum, late twelfth-thirteenth century; probably Yorkshire, from Fountains Abbey; previously Christie's, 9 July 2001, lot 9. £50,000 to Fogg.

Early Books and Manuscripts (Autumn 2005)

*15 CARTULARY: of Otterton Priory, Devon; MS on vellum, *c.*1360, with later additions. £48,000.

Robert H. Rubin, Brookline, Mass.

Catalogue 59

88 HERALDIC MANUSCRIPT: on paper; late seventeenth century. $1,500.

Bernard J. Shapero

English Books & Manuscripts to 1800 (ii), 2005

31 BIBLE TRANSLATION: Transcription of an English version of Luke 15:1–8 in a contemporary hand on end blank leaves of a copy of Nicholas Udall's translation of Erasmus's *Apophthegmata* (1564; STC 10444). £4,500.
32 SAMPSON ERDESWICK: *A view of Staffordshire*; MS on paper, *c.*1650. £2,500.
116 GEORGE VILLIERS, DUKE OF BUCKINGHAM: *A true jurnall or diarie of all the materialle passages and occurrences hapininge at and after our landinge at the isle of Ree* and *A journall of the Duke of Buckingham his voyage and taking of the Isle of Rey*; MSS on paper, *c.*1627. £1,750.

Andrew Stewart, Marazion, Cornwall

Catalogue 63, 2004

*15 PSALTER: single leaf, ill. MS on vellum; East Anglia; *c.*1330. £3,250

Notes on Contributors

JOHN BURROWS is Emeritus Professor of English at the University of Newcastle, Australia. He remains an active member of the University's Centre for Literary and Linguistic Computing, of which he was the Foundation Director. His numerous publications on computational stylistics include *Computation into Criticism: A Study of Jane Austin's Novels and an Experiment in Method* (Clarendon Press, 1987). He received the Roberto Busa Award for Humanities Computing in 2001 and an Australian Centenary Medal in 2003.

GUILLAUME COATALEN is Lecturer in Renaissance English Literature at the University of Cergy-Pontoise (France). He has a strong interest in unedited material or unknown extracts in manuscript and their implications on the history of reading and composition.

LARA M. CROWLEY received her B.S. and M.A. from North Carolina State University and is currently a doctoral candidate at the University of Maryland. With the assistance of a Mellon fellowship she is completing in London her dissertation 'Manuscript Context and Literary Interpretation: John Donne's Poetry and Prose in Seventeenth-Century England'.

A.S.G. EDWARDS is now Professor of Textual Studies, De Montfort University, Leicester. He has published various books and articles on late medieval and early Renaissance English literature. His *New Index of Middle English Verse* (with Julia Boffey) was published by the British Library in 2005.

NICHOLAS FISHER is Visiting Research Fellow at the Institute of English Studies in the School of Advanced Study, University of London, and a member of the senior common room at Merton College, Oxford. He has edited a collection of essays on the Earl of Rochester, *That Second Bottle* (2000), and is currently preparing a bibliography of the works of Rochester for the British Library/Oak Knoll Press.

PAUL E.J. HAMMER is Senior Lecturer in the School of History at the University of St Andrews. His numerous publications include *The*

Polarisation of Elizabethan Politics: The Political Career of Robert Devereux, 2nd Earl of Essex, 1585–1597 (1999) and *Elizabeth's Wars: War, Government and Society in Tudor England, 1544–1604* (2003). He is currently completing a book on the Earl of Essex and the late-Elizabethan crisis of 1598–1603.

GABRIEL HEATON completed his doctoral thesis at the University of Cambridge in 2003. He has published articles on early modern manuscripts and on court entertainments. He is an Associate General Editor on the John Nichols Project, for which he has edited a number of Elizabethan progress entertainments, including Woodstock. He now works as a manuscript expert at Sotheby's.

HILTON KELLIHER was formerly Curator of Manuscripts at the British Library. He has published extensively on English literary manuscripts from Malory to Wordsworth and Coleridge, including work on Robert Sidney, Shakespeare, Francis Beaumont, Crashaw, Herbert, Cowley, Katherine Philips, Cleveland, Dryden, and Marvell.

MARGARET JANE KIDNIE is Associate Professor of English at the University of Western Ontario. She is editor of Ben Jonson's *The Devil is an Ass and Other Plays* (2000) and of Philip Stubbes's *The Anatomie of Abuses* (2002). She is co-editor of *Textual Performances: The Modern Reproduction of Shakespeare's Drama* (2004), and has also published articles on textual studies and performance. Her most recent book is *The Taming of the Shrew: A Guide to the Text and its Theatrical Life* (2006). She is currently editing *A Woman Killed with Kindness* for the Arden Early Modern Drama series, and completing a book on late-twentieth century performance and adaptation.

TOM LOCKWOOD is Lecturer in English Literature in the Department of English, University of Birmingham. His book *Ben Jonson in the Romantic Age* was published by Oxford University Press in 2005. He is currently working on *Shakespeare and His Texts*, a volume in the Arden Critical Companions to Shakespeare series.

TIMOTHY RAYLOR is Professor of English at Carleton College, Minnesota. He is author of *Cavaliers, Clubs, and Literary Culture: Sir John Mennes, James Smith, and the Order of the Fancy* (1994) and of several articles on Edmund Waller. He is currently collaborating with Michael P. Parker on an edition of Waller's poems for the Oxford English Texts series.

JEANNE SHAMI is Professor of English at the University of Regina, Saskatchewan. A former president of the John Donne Society, she has published various books and articles on Donne and on early modern sermons, including her edition of *John Donne's 1622 Gunpowder Plot Sermon* (1996) and *John Donne and Conformity in Crisis in the Late Jacobean Pulpit* (2003). She is currently co-editing, with Tom Hester and Dennis Flynn, the *Oxford Handbook for John Donne Studies*.

P.G. STANWOOD is Professor Emeritus of English at the University of British Columbia, Vancouver. He has edited a number of works, including Richard Hooker's *Lawes of Ecclesiastical Polity* (Books VI, VII, and VIII) for the Folger Library Edition (1981) and the Clarendon Press edition of Jeremy Taylor's *Holy Living and Holy Dying* (1989). He was a contributing editor of the John Donne Variorum *Holy Sonnets* (2005).

Index of Manuscripts

General Index

This index consists largely of proper names appearing in the volume including the section on Manuscripts at Auction (except for the names of the buyers). It excludes the footnotes and some commonly cited place names (for example, London, Oxford, Cambridge), or those mentioned in passing. Titles of works are generally subsumed under the names of their authors.